'THE MOST ENGLISH MINISTER...'

By the same author

★

THE PASSING OF THE WHIGS

Lord Palmerston in his old age

'THE MOST ENGLISH MINISTER...'

THE POLICIES AND POLITICS OF PALMERSTON

By

DONALD SOUTHGATE

B.A., D.PHIL.

SENIOR LECTURER IN MODERN POLITICAL AND CONSTITUTIONAL HISTORY IN
THE UNIVERSITY OF ST ANDREWS (QUEEN'S COLLEGE, DUNDEE)

MACMILLAN

London · Melbourne · Toronto

ST MARTIN'S PRESS

New York

1966

MACMILLAN AND COMPANY LIMITED
Little Essex Street London WC 2
also Bombay Calcutta Madras Melbourne

THE MACMILLAN COMPANY OF CANADA LIMITED
70 Bond Street Toronto 2

ST MARTIN'S PRESS INC
175 Fifth Avenue New York 10010 NY

Library of Congress Catalogue Card No.: 65–22794

PRINTED IN GREAT BRITAIN

CONTENTS

Maps

LIST OF ILLUSTRATIONS

INTRODUCTION

PHILIP GUEDALLA placed us in his debt more by his publication of *The Palmerston Papers — Gladstone and Palmerston, 1851–65* (1928) than by his *Palmerston* (1926), described by Pemberton, a subsequent biographer (*Lord Palmerston*, 1954), as 'entertaining reading, but of little use as a contribution to historical biography'. Not the least virtue of the 1928 volume is the introduction in which Guedalla argued that a biography (as distinct from an official 'Life' or 'Life and Letters', the literary equivalent of a recumbent statue) should be a one-value work of 500 pages based on 'a rigorous exploration of all printed or unprinted sources of information', informed by the highest standards of accurate scholarship, and executed with a high standard of craftsmanship, so that it shows a man and not a mummy. 'A man's true memorial is a book in which the world will read about him rather than an impressive, but unread, biography', he said. But, if the memorial is not to be a libel, it must be based on an exhaustive study of the raw materials of biography.

Palmerston must long await his true memorial. Unless a man of private means and single-minded devotion gives the best part of his life to the study of the Palmerston Papers at Broadlands and the archives of half a dozen capitals, no definitive life can be written until many have slaved at the galleys over many years. We shall need a dozen or so works of the kind of Guedalla's *Gladstone and Palmerston* and Brian Connell's *Regina* v. *Palmerston* (1962), made possible by the continuing courtesy of the owner-custodians. The fate which was so kind to Palmerston in his lifetime has been against him in the twentieth century. The world has changed, so that men playing the game of statesmanship for stakes undreamed of by Palmerston, and their critics, informed or facile, either dismiss 'the Palmerston touch' as obsolete or, worse, regard it as to be damned in retrospect simply because it has, so they say, become inappropriate now — as though there were some ground, unknown to the present writer, for assuming that the Palmerston who was so careful to prevent a general war in 1830–1 and 1848–9 would have been less careful in a Berlin Crisis (when Aneurin

Bevan wanted to send the tanks through the Russian Zone) or a Cuba Crisis. And fate has frustrated the good intentions of those who have made Palmerston their study. Guedella 'proposed to publish the Palmerston Papers, inaugurated by the present volume'. The second volume never appeared. Sir Charles Webster, introduced to the Broadlands Papers by Guedalla, arranged 20,000 pieces for the years 1830–41 alone and intended to publish a volume of selected letters. He never did. We waited till 1962 for the next instalment from Mr Connell.

Equally formidable is the task of extending to the years 1846–51 (and, indeed, 1855–8 and 1859–65 when, though Palmerston was not at the Foreign Office, his strong will brooded over it) the full orchestral treatment of Webster's two-volume *Foreign Policy of Lord Palmerston 1830–1841* (1951). We have, for 1846–51, the tantalizing snatches of overture provided by Mr A. J. P. Taylor's *The Italian Problem in European Diplomacy 1847–9* (1934) and the late Mr Charles Sproxton's *Palmerston and the Hungarian Revolution* (1919). Admirable in themselves, they provide strong clues as to the theme of the whole, for reconstruction by a successor to Webster. Both show that Palmerston, despite the sincerity of his belief in the future of European Liberalism, was a realist devoted to the maintenance of European Order (at the expense of Nationalism and even of Liberalism), quite unconscious of any short-term or long-term incompatibility between 'the interests of England' and the interest of Europe, but clearly aware of the conflict between current expediency and long-term solutions. But even when Webster has found successors, the record will be too incomplete for a definitive 'life' until there has been full research into Palmerston and the Slave Trade, Palmerston and the Americas, Palmerston and the Far East, Palmerston and the Press, and, indeed, a systematic treatment of Palmerston and Defence.

The limited purpose of the work here offered is to present a study of Palmerston, with some attempt at assessment of his foreign policy, and, it is hoped, some degree of understanding — enough, perchance, to shake certain stubborn misapprehensions of the kind not held, in general, by scholars, but surviving after the manner of secondary folk-legend through the medium of the school text-book of former days. It is an attempt, within the limits of the published information, to make some sense of Palmerston's career, not only by considering his conduct of foreign affairs, but by explaining, or at least reiterating, his political pre-eminence in the '50s. The source of that pre-eminence has, indeed, been expounded brilliantly by Kingsley Martin in *The Triumph of Lord Palmerston* (1924), recently reissued and acclaimed, but it was not his purpose, primarily, to relate it to his career before 1848 or to trace its continuance after it won Palmerston the premiership.

This is not a biography. But it is biographical in the sense that it aims to let Palmerston live through the dispatches and speeches, and not to bury him under them. Its subject is not British foreign policy 1829–65, but Palmerston's effect upon it. Nothing could be more inappropriate than to make of that least intellectual of men a disembodied intellect arbitrating between conflicting advices; to represent 'Palmerston' as a signature on a document representing the view of an institution called 'the Foreign Office'; to reduce the pen dipped in gall to the status of an ordinary standard-issue Government department quill. It is biographical, too, in its frank intention to 'celebrate' the centenary of the death of that happy, and doughty, warrior who made the world talk of what 'England would do or dare' (or at least dare to say) and, by so doing, set himself apart from — and above — other public men in Britain, winning a personal prestige that survived even successive verdicts against major features of his own policy.

In Palmerston, policies and politics were almost uniquely related. Initially, he drew much of his political strength from the popularity of his foreign policy, and he retained it, at least partially, from the same cause. It is, however, a prime purpose of this present book to show that his foreign policy, as understood by contemporary opinion from the selective publicity accorded to it (partly under his inspiration), was not the whole of his foreign policy, as it should be understood by posterity. The popular image was a distorted image, partly because the public was so attracted to the icing that it overlooked the texture of the cake. The elements of traditionalism, of conservatism, and of high responsibility in the hour of greatest crisis, have often received less attention than they deserve, so that the statesman is submerged beneath the quarrelsome bully, the showman, the poseur.

That Palmerston was sometimes a bully and often a showman is conceded. That he was a poseur is not. That his policy was marred by 'excesses' which bedevilled Britain's international relations is undeniable. The suggestion that the only motive for these 'excesses' was to bask in popular favour seems to the present writer a gross libel of his political adversaries. The implication that they were, when they consisted, as they often did, of violent propaganda not intended to be made good by war, 'hypocritical', derived, and derives either from genuine misunderstanding or from acceptance of the proposition that one should not bless where one will not aid and should not curse where one will not crush *plus* the indefensible proposition that no one can sincerely believe otherwise. If Palmerston is to be condemned for the words that made him popular, it can only be because he refused to conceal deeply-held views simply because they could not currently prevail, and that he threatened where he did not mean to perform, on the off-chance that the threat would suffice.

'Least said, soonest mended', said his critics. 'Nothing said, nothing mended', Palmerston would have replied. Sometimes what he said was harsh and selfish. Often it was wise and prescient. At other times it was neither wise nor prescient, and yet had about it a quality of optimism and good intention of which the worst that can be said is that it was 'almost sentimental'. But it was liable to be popular whether it was harsh and selfish, wise and prescient or sentimental and futile. For Palmerston proved fortunate in that, in the last two decades of his life, his distinctive opinions proved representative. Yet he twice suffered defeat (in 1851 and 1858) because he *refused* to bow to the popular mood, being sure that to do so was contrary to the national interest.

Palmerston's long public career was bisected by the Reform Bill of 1832. When it became law, he had been in the House of Commons for nearly twenty-five years and in office for nearly twenty-three. After it, he was in the House of Commons for nearly thirty-three years, and in office for twenty-four and a half. In the nineteenth and twentieth centuries only four men — among them Gladstone and Churchill — have sat longer in the House than his fifty-eight years (1807–65) and no politician has approached his total of forty-eight years in office. This record was achieved with only one change of party, a change entirely honourable to Palmerston, and it was achieved although from 1831 onwards his name was indelibly linked with highly controversial policies. Yet if, *faute de mieux*, Palmerston lived by party, in the sense that the supremacy of his party kept him in power in the '30s and '40s, he never lived for party. By 1850 he had won a personal renown which gave him a choice of parties, and he found his most violent calumniators in his own. It is arguable that later his supremacy kept his party in power, instead of vice versa. For his appeal, which cut across classes, cut also across parties; their natural strife was blurred and distorted as long as he lived, since he had the choice of governing in uneasy alliance with the Radicals in his party or governing with the tolerance of the Conservatives under the attacks of the Radicals. A violent critic, Urquhart, who was convinced that Palmerston was a Tsarist agent, put, with customary emphasis, the point here made[1]—

Born as it were, for party, formed for party, devoted to party, employed by all parties for the last half century, because useful to all in the sense that Talleyrand was indispensable to countless consecutive governments, and faithful to each by the time being, he has been the destroyer of party: has risen to the utmost attainable altitude on the ruins of party: and now, alone of all men in our history, holds the first place in England, and the place of the first subject in Europe, not in virtue of party strength, but in right of that party feebleness which he himself has mainly wrought.

This extract undervalues the extent to which Palmerston was lucky in the mistakes of his competitors, Lord John Russell and Lord Derby, but is in substance true. When the accredited leaders failed, and the predestined leaders found themselves after 1846 without a party, Palmerston was available, favoured outside parliament in his own right, preferred inside parliament by the Whigs (because he would give them places, though not as many as they wanted) and by the Tories because, 'never having had a party of his own, he seemed more disinterested' than Russell (who 'gave too much importance to the influence of the great Whig families he represents'),[2] and was the only 'Whig' with the will and calibre to maintain the *Conservative Cause*.

The supremacy of Palmerston is an example of that alliance of power derived from popularity with power derived from property of which Burke wrote, not long before Palmerston was born, in connexion with the alliance of the elder Pitt with Newcastle. The point is worth making, because, in a very real sense, Palmerston like Pitt, was raised to the purple by opinion out-of-doors, to win a war. But the contrast between Chatham and Palmerston is great. Though the former had to wait long for even a share of supreme power, his whole previous life had been one of histrionic aspiration

to it, and his weapon was his tongue. Four years after Palmerston
became Foreign Secretary, it was still possible to dismiss him as
politically negligible, mainly because he was not gifted with
eloquence or even that natural gift of repartee which assists debate
though it does not constitute oratory.[3] His voice was an elocu-
tionist's nightmare. He could compose (when he had time)
workmanlike speeches full of matter, delivered, till he was past his
seventieth year, from memory, and he learned in time to do what
earlier he could not, and talk at length without saying anything,
often delighting the House with banter though sometimes mis-
taking its mood and offending by an inappropriate levity or undue
savagery towards honourable opponents. But probably in nearly
sixty years of parliamentary life not more than four of his speeches
could be called, in any sense, 'great'. The famous Don Pacifico
speech, when he was fighting for his political life, stands alone.
The speech on Kars in the summer of 1856 deserves mention as a
masterly statement of a poor case. The speech of 1st June 1829 was
Palmerston's successful bid for importance. Delivered in a thin
House, it was composed, and distributed, as a pamphlet. Also
delivered on a parliamentary 'off-day', twenty years later, the
speech on Britain's attitude to the Habsburg empire has been
applauded by later generations as a frank and comprehensive
statement of his views on the relationship between British interest,
the Balance of Power, and the patronage of Liberalism. If, then,
Palmerston owed so much to what Urquhart called 'the mis-
stating power', it was the power of the pen, not the tongue. It was
by dispatches from the Foreign Office, and by leakage of information from the Foreign Office, that he won public opinion, via the
press.

For thirty-seven years Palmerston was immersed in the study of
foreign affairs, and for nearly twenty-four of them in the conduct
of foreign affairs, as Foreign Secretary or prime minister. He was
intimately involved in them longer than any modern statesmen.
Lord Salisbury, the next man to reach the premiership through the
Foreign Office, had, unlike Palmerston, first made his mark in
politics as a vivid controversialist on domestic subjects. Palmerston
followed Canning consciously, in far less than he pretended, and
was sometimes not following him when he thought he was, but he
followed him in this, that 'far from shunning publicity, he gloried
in it'.[4] He published voluminously, and he primed the press. We

still await an authoritative study of Palmerston's relations with the newspapers, but we know enough to see that they were systematic, skilful and important in an age when the reading public was rapidly increasing. The Palmerston of the dispatches — 'powerful and imperious only with his pen in his hand'[5] — 'got across' to the public, and the public loved him.

That the Don Pacifico speech was more popular out of parliament than within told its tale. And when Russell, having resigned early in 1851, and failed to contrive a coalition which would have ousted Palmerston, was asked by the Queen nevertheless to remove him from the Foreign Office, he replied that he could not think of it, for he (Russell) 'was in fact the weakness and Lord Palmerston the strength of the Government *from his popularity with the Radicals*'.[6] Considering that Russell was both progressive and pliable and more aggressively Protestant than Palmerston, who was a landed aristocrat with views on home affairs indistinguishable from those of at least the less reactionary of the Tories, this was an extraordinary phenomenon. Indeed, there were observers then who saw, as many have done since, that part of Palmerston's appeal lay in the fact that the great domestic issues were settled, that politics had become prosaic, and that Palmerston's conduct of foreign relations, by imparting glamour to affairs, filled a vacuum.

G. M. Young remarked that there is nothing so bloody-minded as a Radical turned patriot.[7] Palmerston, a patriot concerned above all to serve 'the interest of England', neither ashamed to coerce a weak state nor afraid to rebuke a strong Power, could turn to political profit the hatred of the foreigner, by boasting that he had earned it, and that this was only to be expected when 'the minister of England' spoke his mind manfully, because foreign statesmen were jealous of the power and prosperity of Britain and trembled lest her example of liberty spread across Europe. Nothing annoyed his high-minded critics at home more than to find that the very test which seemed to them to prove he ought to be deposed from the management of affairs strengthened his anchor. But they do Palmerston and his public wrong who think he owed his popularity entirely to mere 'jingoism' of a brash and shallow kind. The man in the street was, no doubt, as indisposed to judge nicely the proportion of means to ends when he was told that British subjects or property abroad had been violated, as he was unqualified to examine the subtleties of the Balance of Power diplomacy and gauge how adeptly Palmerston often managed them. But, on the largest issue, he believed that now Russia, now France, sought a predominance harmful to British security and must be stopped sooner rather than, with more difficulty, later, and he could not see any conflict between the interest of Britain and the interests of Europe. He believed, with Palmerston, that Britain could stand simultaneously for her own interest and for 'justice and right'. The criticism that Palmerston ministered to the vanity at the expense of the interests of England,[8] because his 'missionary diplomacy' exacerbated international relations, kept up the taxes and imperilled peace, was not accepted because it was held to be manly, and spirited, and 'British' to denounce tyranny and preach freedom. A. J. P. Taylor bids us remember not only that Palmerston lectured, but also the theme of his lectures.[9] The *Illustrated London News* in December 1851 greeted his dismissal with the tribute: 'Wherever there is an absolute tyranny in Europe, his Lordship is looked upon with hatred or mistrust, and wherever there is a desire for constitutional liberty, repressed by bayonets or threatened by irresponsible autocrats, there has his Lordship admirers and friends'.[10] The ordinary Briton did not think the less of Palmerston for that, and he rose supreme because, as a historian of Radicalism regretfully concedes, 'the Radical passion against continental autocrats . . . (rose) . . . to a height from which . . . a "popular war" would have been easy to wage'.[11]

Palmerston did not wish to wage wars, though he despised diplomats who shrank from using every card in the pack, including the threat (or more often the hint) of war. In large crises he was grave and careful, if sanguine and intrepid, and it is likely that, if he had controlled policy in 1853, Britain would have avoided the one considerable war in which she was involved in his time. 'The name of Palmerston, long the terror of the Continent, will ever be connected in the minds of Englishmen with an epoch of unbroken peace and unparalleled prosperity', said *The Times* at his death. If it is true that time and again he was saved from war by luck rather than discretion,[12] as had often been held, one can only say 'some luck!' He saw, of course, that it was his fate to fight the bayonet with the pen, and that in the short run the bayonet would prevail. But he was sure that 'opinions were mightier than armies', and he believed while a careful diplomacy could, and should, be directed towards the avoidance of war across frontiers, Britain should take her place, fearlessly and vocally, on the side of the angels in the war of opinion which was an abiding and principal feature of the years 1830–65. It may be argued that this was *impolitic*. It cannot be held that it was *unworthy* unless it can be shown that Palmerston did not believe what he preached, and preached it only for some private or narrowly national gain. That this was so some of his critics at home believed, as Metternich believed, and Metternich's henchman Ficquelmont who wrote:[13] 'Lord Palmerston is not a statesman in the usual sense of the term; *he is an English party man* (which it is necessary to be in England), who uses foreign affairs to strengthen his position at home, in the country as well as in parliament; he does not write a note which is not designed to that end. In this respect he is the most dangerous Minister of Foreign Affairs England has ever had, because he is without conscience or principle. Formed in the Tory school during the Great War, he has taken from this epoch the principle of popular agitation, as a weapon to employ against those to whom he is hostile. . . . The English rejoice in glories that are not dangerous; the phrases please John Bull: they make Italy turbulent, which is bad for us, without making her powerful, which would harm England'. But this is to transpose effect and motive and to dodge the question of why Palmerston was hostile to Austria, the 'natural ally', and Palmerston would not have accepted that a powerful Italy was bad for England. Rightly did *The Times* obituary say: 'Above all, he was a steadfast and devoted partisan of constitutional liberty in every part of the Continent'. Most of those who (not counting the cost) regretted that he would not go to war for the freedom of Hungary, or Poland, or Italy understood that when he abused the foes of freemen he wrote what was in his heart as well as in theirs, and many who would have been horrified by the suggestion of going to war for such causes, shared his sentiments and doubted not his sincerity. Palmerston did not have to play the part of John Bull; he lived it. Except in the great crises of relations with France or Russia, he refused to be deterred from saying what he felt simply because he happened to be Foreign Secretary or prime minister. He dared to use the authority of great offices of state to add weight to his convictions. And those convictions were congenial to the Britain of the 1850s.

While some, in his own day, and since, have attacked Palmerston for pandering to the national instincts and prejudices (assuming, what is not true, that these were wholly bad and selfish and narrowly chauvinistic), others have sought to demote him to the level of a mere symbol, or even symptom, of a particular and transient phase in British political, economic and social development.^A His dominance coincided with Britannia ruling the waves and London ruling the exchanges, with Britain dominating world trade, enjoying economic growth at a rate unknown before or since, and finding in social peace, political equilibrium and deepening prosperity grounds for the optimism so often wrongly thought characteristic of the whole Victorian era. Palmerston's Britain was less critical of itself than it had been, or was to be, for decades; it was proportionately more critical, more arrogantly critical, more abandoned in its criticism, of others who lacked and spurned its own enlightenment. 'Priding itself on its economical and prosaic disposition', it looked abroad for its excitements and its heroes, and found that Palmerston 'had given to the Foreign Policy of England something of a heroic character'.[14] His great merit as a governing man, said Trollope, 'arose from his perfect sympathy with those whom he was called upon to govern; his demerit, such as it was, sprang from the same cause'.[15] But to say that Palmerston was a fit representative of the nation he governed, 'the proper ruler of a nation arrogant and intoxicated . . . they have the Government they most deserve' (to quote John Bright),[16] and that *therefore* 'he is not the fit object of the praise he has received, or of the vituperation with which he has been encountered', because every minister had to carry into foreign policy the wishes of the urban shopkeepers,[17] is to sin against reason. It is to say, either that everything would have been the same if Aberdeen, or Granville, or Clarendon had been in Palmerston's place — which is absurd — or that, failing Palmerston, another man of the same ilk as himself would have had his place. Other ministers might have been dragged screaming where Palmerston went willingly (as

---

^A This doctrine was stated in its most emphatic form by Gavin Henderson (*Crimean War Diplomacy and Other Essays*, 205–6): 'Palmerston's greatness lies not so much in himself, or in his policy, as in the age which he represented. Never was a foreign minister more fortunate; . . . his diplomatic currency had a sounder basis than that of any of his rivals. . . . It was not Palmerston who was great, but Britain; and Britain has never been greater, before or since. . . . Contemporaries and posterity, in praising Palmerston, have praised him not for himself but for his incarnation of Britain at her peak of glory.' Cf. Pemberton, 349: 'Of this England, expiring with him, Lord Palmerston had been a worthy and faithful representative.'

Aberdeen was dragged into a war probably avoidable if he had been less squeamish about entering it). Other ministers would have gone with relish whither Palmerston, towards the end of his days, was dragged unwillingly. But the willingness is of the essence. The other ministers would not have been Palmerston. And he was not pretending to be what he was not, and merely registering, like a dial, the blood pressure of the populace. He was what he had been before it was so fashionable to be it, and he had all the time to wrestle with colleagues who wished he were less uninhibited. His was a personality too strong to be depersonalized into a symptom, though proud to be a symbol. 'His readiness to swim with the stream is a great thing in a statesman',[17] wrote a biographer before he had died. But he chose his own direction. He swam in it when the tide had hardly turned; he continued, at the end, to battle against the flood. One does not quarrel with the verdict that he lacked the final dimension of greatness, that he was 'but a man of the time, while Pitt, Fox, Burke and Canning were men for all times. He even ranks below Sir Robert Peel'[18] (though one might quibble). But there is no profundity in Bright's picture: 'He knows the ignorance and the foibles of the people, and suits himself to them. That he is an impostor is evident enough, but to expose him does nothing: he exactly suits the frothy politicians that are so numerous among our countrymen. He is to the middle classes what Feargus O'Connor was to the working classes.'[16]

This judgement tells us more about Bright than Palmerston, just as Palmerston's attacks on Bright as 'the reverend gentleman', 'un-English', 'an Americanizer', a man who attacked classes, tell us more about Palmerston than Bright. If the public disagrees with Bright it is ignorant and has foibles. That a man of goodwill should disagree fundamentally with Bright is inconceivable, and therefore a man who so disagrees is an impostor. He succeeds because of 'frothy politicians', who are clearly to be distinguished from the high-souled agitators of the Anti-Corn Law League, the Peace Society and the Reform Association. And to John Bright, Feargus O'Connor's Chartism was the sin against the Holy Ghost, and Palmerston the Satan who led not only the sinful, working-class man astray, but part, indeed the majority, of the angelic, bourgeois host itself. Cobden, a countryman who led urban armies, said similar hard things about Palmerston, and, having said them, would not serve with him, because he meant them. But he often saw both Palmerston and the middle classes whom Palmerston led astray with more objectivity than did Bright. He granted Palmerston a certain sincerity and even nobility of aspiration, and he acknowledged in Palmerston that quality of magnanimity (so often commented on in tributes to Winston Churchill) which, if Bright had noticed, he would have attributed to lack of principle and serious purpose.

For nothing gave greater offence to Palmerston's more convinced opponents than his light-heartedness, an easy, genial, sanguine air which appeared immune to the batterings of criticism and the maxims of morality. Palmerston refused to be solemn when they felt that he had much to be serious about, and he met his attackers with a withering scorn which was intolerable because it was not, like the scorn of Disraeli, assumed, but the fruit of an utter inability to see the adversary's point of view. This was a major defect of character. It bedevilled his dealings with foreign envoys. It always seemed so clear to him what Vienna or Paris would propose if the true interests of Austria or France were duly weighed, that he revealed a most undiplomatic impatience of what was actually proposed if it differed sharply from what he thought right. And he had no conception of the effect of his harangues on his auditors. For there was no malice in him. He did not harbour grudges and nurse resentments, and those (including Queen Victoria)[19] who thought otherwise misunderstood his habit of 'labelling' people as prone to this or that misapprehension and being quite outspoken about them and their weaknesses. A patron of the boxing and wrestling rings (and cheerfully unconcerned when accused, as prime minister, of conniving at illegal contests)[20] Palmerston believed in giving knock for knock, the object of the exercise being to have the opponent counted out or at least to win on points. This sportsman's attitude to public life and to diplomacy was apt to grate on men who took themselves too seriously, and they thought it betokened not merely a lack of the higher statesmanship but of all sincerity. Yet in his own youth he took himself seriously enough to be called by a pleasure-loving young lady a prig (because he hung about at the Admiralty in the hope that there would be something for a junior lord to do). He had, obviously, a sense that public service was an obligation of aristocracy and that an occupation was essential to one's self-respect, and it is quite evident from his private correspondence that from the beginnings of his intensive interest in foreign affairs he had enthusiasms and convictions and even vision. And no man in public office ever worked harder or more conscientiously for so long, exacting of subordinates no more than he demanded of himself. One of the most striking features of Palmerston's career is, indeed, his stamina. Physical strength, husbanded by such exercise as he could make time for, though sometimes (in the view of his doctor) imperilled by his love of fresh air and insistence on exercise, was combined with the strongest of wills, as physical courage was combined with moral courage. It is typical of the man that he insisted on dying in office whether he was to die at eighty, eighty-one or eighty-two, and the crisp clarity of his letters up to the last month forbids us to say that he was 'past it'.

It was, it is true, a little difficult for the ordinary man to take Palmerston seriously as a statesman even when he was fifty, and had the Belgian Conference and the Quadruple Alliance to his credit and vigorous contention with Metternich to his name. This was because he was so evidently a man of fashion, a 'swell', a Regency beau who for twenty years had ranked far higher in the world of fashion than the world of public affairs. If he had worked hard, he had played hard too, and the dancing, the flirting, the seducing and being seduced (he was 'Lord Cupid') had brought him a recognition that the work had not. When he went to Tiverton to become its member in 1835, an obstinately youthful survival of that Society of which Miss Georgette Heyer writes with such understanding and such dauntless regularity, in white trousers, blue frock coat with gilt buttons, and a white hat, his black hair a triumph of the perruquier's art, tall, handsome, round-faced, merry-looking, his twinkling eyes and a touch of swarthiness perfecting his charms, 'the light and jaunty manner . . . perfectly natural and easy' could still deceive people — as it had deceived Lord Ashley — into seeing in him 'nothing . . . of the statesman, but a good deal of the dandy'.[21] To electioneering in the market-place of a country town he took like a duck to water, for the Town swell had, as a landlord, the countryman's interests, and in particular a passion for horses. Moreover, it was his natural way in public speeches outside parliament — and often in — to utter commonplaces. Tiverton, which knew him in the flesh where most of the people, and even of the electors, knew him only from newsprint and from cartoons, confirmed the national verdict that 'he was not a common man, but a common man might have been cut out of him'.

It was felt of Palmerston that he was 'the most English minister that ever governed England',[22] and this judgement gives the book its title.[A] The commonplaces which he uttered with such conviction were the commonplaces of an Englishman, boasting in the Napoleonic War that 'the masculine energies of the nation were never more conspicuous, and if we do not present the opposition to invaders of those numerous fortresses which are to be found on the Continent, we do present the more insuperable barrier of a high-spirited, patriotic and enthusiastic people'. He believed that 'the English nation' was the greatest on the earth — and even, though he had lived in Italy, that its climate was the best in the world. He believed that English institutions were a model for all Europe, and believing this, he said so, repeating it so often that to the foreigner it became monotonous, but never to the Englishman. That it was his country's high destiny, under Providence, to police the seas, to abolish the slave trade and so put an end to slavery, to assure that a subject of the Queen was safe however hostile or barbarous the region into which he ventured, to take the leading part in bringing commerce, and with it, Western civilization, to Asia and then to Africa; all this he assumed and, in assuming, represented, and articulated, the sentiments of the nation. Britain could not do all this unless the navy was stronger than that of any two European Powers (and the United States as well), for only the navy had earned her this role, and the island home itself must be proof against the invader. Hence it fell to this colonel of yeomanry to revive the militia, to give his imprimatur to the Volunteers (in 1859–60), to insist on the fortification of the ports, to probe the implications of the steamship and to demand — despite the current

[A] Gavin Henderson went so far as to say: 'Castlereagh was a good European: Gladstone was a good Christian: Palmerston was a good Englishman — working for national ends, and praiseworthy only from national standards.' If Palmerston had a theme, he wrote, 'it was a narrow and bigoted desire to enhance Britain's prestige', and he 'interpreted British interests narrowly' (*Crimean War Diplomacy, etc.*, 203–4). It looks as though W. Baring Pemberton was nettled by this dogmatism, for he writes that his theme, if any, was to answer the question whether Palmerston sought to use Britain's power, prestige and wealth for purely national, personal or selfish ends, 'or was there in his mind a nobler, wider, and more generous aim?'. He concludes that Palmerston never failed to put his country first but honestly convinced himself that there was no real conflict between the interests of his country and those of Europe. (*Lord Palmerston*, x, 350.)

trend to economy — a programme of shipbuilding in the 1860s. To awaken public opinion, and impress parliamentarians, he did not scruple to awaken public alarm, and even what Cobden called 'panic', but this was not to win popularity, but to win support for what he firmly believed the national interest required. He spurned the back-handed compliment offered by Gladstone, the tight-fisted Chancellor who preached a doctrine of defence by prosperity rather than by ships and rifles which Palmerston thought dangerous and deluded, and who said that it was only Palmerston's popularity 'and not the public conviction or desire' that kept up the Estimates. Palmerston's retort may serve as an epitaph: 'If I have in any Degree been fortunate enough to have obtained some share of the Good Will and Confidence of my Fellow-Countrymen, it has been because I have rightly understood the Feelings and Opinions of the Nation, and because they think that I have, as far as any Scope of Action of Mine was concerned, endeavoured to maintain the Dignity and to uphold the Interests of the Country abroad, and to provide for its security at home'.[23]

ACKNOWLEDGEMENTS

I wish to acknowledge, with much gratitude, the assistance of Professor Asa Briggs, Dr Christopher Bartlett and Mr Alan Cass, each of whom read part of the typescript and made helpful comments, and of Mr Philip Witting, G.M., who can advise one to be less long-winded more diplomatically than anyone else I know. All those connected with my publishers with whom I have had contact have been helpful beyond belief, and Mr John Barker's staff in the Queen's College Library of the University of St Andrews long-suffering beyond belief. My colleagues and my family* have borne nobly, if not always without badinage, my habit of chatting, sometimes repetitiously, about Palmerston, as someone I know more intimately than I know those whose private correspondence is entirely closed to me. I had, indeed, intended to dedicate the book to 'stimulating colleagues past and present', until the death of Sir Winston Churchill put into my mind an

* Christopher, aged 11, fetched, carried, and played happily at being a copy-editor.

alternative which I am sure would have pleased Palmerston. Thereby hangs a tale. It is customary to regard Palmerston, in home affairs, especially in his last years, as a crusted Conservative masquerading as a Liberal, and to assume, more or less consciously, that his deep sense of history, on which his conception of a Foreign Secretary's task was founded, will have led him to value the symbolic survival, as he valued classical architecture. But the man who delighted in the reconstruction of London and Westminster (providing, inter alia, the Thames Embankment) thought it a scandal that newly-created Knights of the Garter should have to pay heavy fees (they were not relieved until 1905) and intended to abolish the office of Lord Warden of the Cinque Ports as obsolete. He desisted when he was given to understand that, though an 'office of profit' requiring the new incumbent, if an M.P., to submit himself for re-election, it attracted virtually no perquisites (other than residence in Walmer Castle), while the vestigial functions still attached to the organization of which the Lord Warden was the ex officio head had some importance. One is glad that he reprieved, and occupied, an office so redolent of historical associations directly bearing on the defence of Britain, adding his name to those of Pitt and Wellington, like whom he played a part (if a lesser part) in beating Napoleon, an office later to be filled by the man who played so inimitable a part in beating Hitler.

D. G. S.

Henry Temple, 3rd Viscount Palmerston, aged twenty

CHAPTER I

THE EMERGENCE OF PALMERSTON

O N 1st June 1829 a middle-aged ex-minister with no reputation for oratory rose in wrath in the House of Commons to
declare that the foreign relations of England had in the
past twelve months been conducted in a spirit far different from
that of previous years, and to the discredit of the country and the
peril of its interests. 'The event of last week was Palmerston's
speech on the Portuguese question, which was delivered at a late
hour and in an empty House, but which they say was exceedingly
able and eloquent', Greville recorded in his diary. 'This is the
second he has made this year of great merit. It was very violent
against Government. . . . He has launched forth, and with
astonishing success.'[1]

The astonishment is understandable. Palmerston was well
known, and well liked, especially by the ladies, in aristocratic
society, to which, as an Irish peer and considerable landowner, he
had had ready access on leaving Cambridge in 1806. The three
most prominent hostesses of Almack's — Lady Jersey, the Princess
Lieven (wife of the Russian ambassador), and Lady Cowper —
each, at one time or another, thought he was in love with her, and
Lady Cowper was quite right. 'Lord Cupid' was probably the
father of her younger children, and her arrival at middle age did
not dampen his determination to marry her if her husband should
die (he had to wait till 1839). But as a minister — Secretary at
War from 1809 to 1828 under five premiers — Palmerston had
seemed an industrious plodder. And as a parliamentarian he had
been a dull dog. He had an unattractive voice and a halting manner,
and trusted himself to speak only after elaborate preparation. In
twenty-one years in the House of Commons he had hardly spoken
at all, except to move and defend the Army Estimates, showing an
occasional touch of fire when dealing with the Radical champion of
economy, Joseph Hume ('dull and blunder-headed', Palmerston
called him). There had been no sign that he was to be distinguished
from that valuable, but hardly inspiring tribe of only semi-political

ministers who supervised departmental work and conducted routine business in the House of Commons, making less impact on policy than leading civil servants. Peel, his junior, had leapt above him to be Home Secretary and now Leader of the House; Aberdeen, his contemporary at Harrow, occupied the Foreign Office and was the principal target of the speech of 1st June. It was something of a mystery that, as a young man, Palmerston had preferred to take a humdrum office without the cabinet, rather than the Chancellorship of the Exchequer, and had held on to it for nearly twenty years, resisting in the 1820s efforts to edge him out with the compensation of a peerage or to dispatch him to Jamaica or, less ingloriously, to Bengal. The explanation is that he wanted an occupation befitting his rank, had a strong sense of public duty and could do with the £2,280 a year, having been left by his father with notable properties and little ready money. But where were the signs of ambition, or of strong political interest? They were few, until in 1829 Palmerston made two carefully prepared speeches — one on 18th March on Ireland, the other on 1st June on foreign affairs — *and circulated copies of them*. This action showed, and the content of the latter speech confirmed, that this 'dark horse' had entered the running for high stakes.

It is easier for us, who know what followed, and can read private letters and journals, than it was for contemporaries in 1829 to understand Palmerston's emergence as a man who wanted to be Foreign Secretary and was sure he would be a better one than anybody else. He had not really lacked ambition when, at the age of twenty-four, he rejected apparently glittering prizes. The office of Chancellor of the Exchequer was important when the prime minister was in the Lords, but it was an innovation to separate it from a premier when he was in the Commons. Palmerston was only being asked to 'devil' for the uncongenially Evangelical Mr Spencer Perceval, to handle details very like those which went with the office of Secretary at War, and to do a lot of drudgery in the Commons, where he had made only a single speech. 'All persons not born with the talents of Pitt or Fox', he wrote, 'must make many bad speeches at first if they speak a good deal on many subjects, as they cannot be masters of all, and a bad speech . . . would make a Chancellor of the Exchequer exceedingly ridiculous, particularly if his friends could not set off against his bad oratory a great knowledge and capacity for business'.[2] And it occurred to him to wonder what were the prospects of a government so bereft of talent — partly because of the quarrel between Castlereagh and Canning — that, at a critical stage of the great war against Napoleon, such considerable responsibilities were offered to an untried stripling the moment the most gifted of back-benchers had turned them down.[3] His refusal was not simply a sign of modesty, due or undue. There was a vanity in it, or at least strong self-respect, and a caution and calculation which invalidate the picture, sometimes drawn, of one to whom ambition came late. With the instinct of a breeder of racehorses, he feared to prejudice his career by risking early, and probable, failure. He deliberately chose to have a formative phase. He did not choose that it should be so prolonged as it proved. During the fifteen years of Lord Liverpool's régime, 1812–27, there were times when ambition slept. But it seems that when he reached the age of forty, he took stock of himself and the worm of discontent began to gnaw. It was now that he made an energetic effort to improve his estates, it was now that the placeman became an expectant, or at least an aspirant. But the difficulties of getting out of the rut were formidable. He had no personal following, and no evident means of winning one. He sought not notoriety, but higher office and the cabinet.

The King disliked him, perhaps originally from jealousy, for when Harry Temple first appeared among the *ton*, handsome, debonair, the ladies' man, the First Gentleman in Europe, sadly gone to seed, a vain, irascible, jaded roué, was reminded of irrecoverable youth. It was difficult for a ministerial man to advance himself against George IV's opposition, and well-nigh impossible when he continued to be undervalued by his colleagues. Palmerston's admission to the cabinet formed by Canning in 1827, after Lord Liverpool's paralytic stroke, was an almost accidental by-product of the refusal of the ultra-Tories to serve under the new prime minister, because (like Palmerston) he believed that Roman Catholics should be admitted to full civil equality with other citizens.

Thirteen months in cabinet transformed Palmerston's own outlook. He became fascinated by foreign affairs. Of these he had known no more than an ordinary minister outside the cabinet might pick up from sitting on the Treasury Bench while Castlereagh (1812–22) and Canning (1822–7) explained them; from the newspapers; from social acquaintances including the foreign

B

envoys and the Princess Lieven, an accredited Russian agent in her own right. His views were those of a simple patriot, reared in the school of Pitt in the years of mortal combat with Napoleon. This, at bottom, he ever remained. Any minister defending the estimates against Brougham in that immediate post-war stage when there is always a cry for retrenchment would have said what Palmerston said in 1816 —

Would it . . . be a wise or expedient course . . . to abdicate the high rank we now maintained in Europe, to take our station amongst secondary powers and confine ourselves entirely to our own island . . . to abandon all our colonial possessions, the fertile sources of our commercial wealth, and descend from that high and elevated station which it had cost so much labour, so much blood, and so much treasure to attain . . . ?

Mere platitude? Not to Palmerston. It was rumoured that he, a minister outside the cabinet, introduced these Estimates in defiance of a cabinet instruction to cut them down. This is probably not true, but when in old age men told the story, all agreed that it would have been utterly in keeping with the Palmerston they knew, the Palmerston who in 1827–9 emerged from the chrysalis of mediocrity and revealed energy, ambition, and a passionate concern for the safety and reputation of his country. For nearly forty years he would cry out, whenever it was opportune, against military, and still more naval, weakness, being, as he told the House when defending the level of forces maintained in British North America in 1816, 'firmly convinced that amongst nations weakness would never be a foundation for security'. But he abhorred equally weakness of purpose — indecision, lack of realism, inability to recognise the good cause and the right course, lack of political courage. Impatience with these vices of statesmen, which are also the inherent vices of responsible government by a committee, was nothing new in Palmerston. In 1809 the youth who had just refused the cabinet wrote scornfully of those who were in it[4]—

It has at length been determined to abandon Walcheren. . . . It is only to be regretted that this decision was not sooner taken, as the Cabinet have for a month had all the documents before them on which it is founded, and in the meantime a great number of lives have been lost.

Important consequences were to follow, for Europe and Britain, from the view of Metternich which Palmerston developed during his first months in the cabinet. 'Metternich must be an idiot if he does not see that Russia is the windward quarter of the heavens, and that his dirty weather must come from thence, and that he should look for shelter to the westward.' He did not think that the chancellor of Austria was quite such an idiot as that, but, he declared: 'Metternich has acted a shabby and foolish part. From what I have seen of him since I came into the Cabinet, I am convinced he prefers the tortuous to the straight course, where the option is before him. . . . Cunning men are always foolish actors.'[5] Equally withering was his scorn of Wellington and Aberdeen after he had ceased to be their colleague. They had forfeited influence both with the slave and the free — 'the fate of those who are unable to pursue a straight course, because, their inclination leading one way and necessity driving the other, they are forced into the diagonal'.[6] This was his theme in the speech of 1st June 1829.

Palmerston never understood that circumstances demanded of a Habsburg diplomat sophisticated method, liable to look to outsiders shabby and foolish. He was quite sure that Britain's power and prestige — and the security of her island position — made it superfluous in Whitehall. Before he became Foreign Secretary he denied that there was anything occult about diplomacy which put it beyond the understanding of an ordinary man such as himself, who was no genius, and knew it. Later, he fell a victim to the professional hazard of believing that nobody but himself could hold a worth-while opinion on foreign policy because only he had read all the papers, and grumbled about colleagues' lack of judgement, directness and self-assurance. Characteristic strength and weaknesses flowed from his faith in his own judgement and scorn for the niceties of diplomatic intercourse. He offended foreigners by the manner of his speech and writings; he underrated their sincerity and clarity whenever their objectives appeared to him to be confused or misconceived. He was capable enough of guile, but — and this was a great strength — he was unwilling to compromise objectives once he had formulated them. He was clear-headed (even when he was wrong-headed) and he was very, very persistent.

Palmerston's preference for the straight course was seen in the cabinet discussions on Greece. Aspiring to restrain Russia by co-operating with her, Canning secured the Treaty of London, 6th July 1827, in which Britain, Russia and France envisaged an autonomous Greek state and concerted pressure on the Turk to recognize it. The destruction by the Allies of the Turco-Egyptian fleet at Navarino (20th October 1827), though not expected, was regarded by the Canningites, among whom Palmerston had very recently come to be counted, as a posthumous triumph for their master. In the cabinet of Goderich in 1827 and of Wellington in 1828 they sought virtual independence for Greece and opposed the narrowest suggested boundaries. The stronger and freer Greece was, and the more beholden to Britain, the less likely was she to be a satellite of Russia. This seemed crystal clear to Palmerston. But Wellington, who was suspicious of Russia, could not see it. He described Navarino as 'an untoward event', and in 1828 he, Ellenborough (anti-Russian), Aberdeen ('Austrian') and Bathurst tried to erode the Treaty and make Greece a narrowly delimited dependency of Turkey. Palmerston could not understand how any sensible, experienced person believed this offered prospects of stability in the Balkans. He wanted to drive straight towards what he believed to be Canning's objective. But he found himself alone in Goderich's cabinet in demanding the dispatch of an Anglo-French force to the Morea to 'prosecute the work of pacification' (as the Treaty put it). He it was who took the initiative over the return of enslaved Greeks carried off by the Sultan's Egyptian henchman, Ibrahim. He alone in Wellington's cabinet sought persistently to obtain for Greece, Livadia, or at least Attica, as well as the Morea, and urged acceptance of the French proposal to send a joint force to expel the Turks.[7] Only after the Russians declared war on Turkey and Metternich swung belatedly to support Greek independence did the Duke agree that a French force should go to clear the Morea, but he remonstrated successfully against their entering Attica. In the speech of the 1st June 1829 Palmerston rejoiced that the Morea was free, but wished the arms of England had had a more direct and prominent share in that honourable exploit, and regretted that she must bear the odium of having vainly attempted to check the progress of France. How absurd, he said, to think of Greece without Athens, Thebes, Marathon, Salamis, Plataea, Thermopylae, Missolonghi (where Byron had died). Why did the Allies not at once occupy Livadia and Attica, 'all that which must be assigned to Greece'?

These references to Greece on 1st June were an interlude in a speech mainly devoted to Portugal. To understand the significance of this speech it is necessary to understand both why Palmerston made it and the diplomatic background. He intended, he told his brother, to awaken public opinion (usually apathetic on foreign questions) and show ministers they were watched. He meant to influence policy, and had arranged to have the same matter raised in the French Chamber. But he meant also 'to put on record my opinion, *both now and when I was in the cabinet*'.[8] He would banish the idea that he was only half a politician, and show himself a fully armed combatant, in the arena from which he had formerly shrunk. It was the only arena that counted. The speech was like the innings which gets a man chosen for a test match. (Palmerston would have liked the simile, for he had played cricket against Eton and, when unable to find enough like-minded men in Edinburgh, mourned the inferiority of golf.) It was a bid for the Foreign Office. But since he believed what he said, it was also an indication of the sort of Foreign Secretary he would like to be. And although he always proclaimed himself a disciple, even a pupil of Canning (to whom in fact he had been no closer than to Castlereagh), and was painted with the master's bust behind him, it was evident that there were questions of foreign policy, and those of the highest importance, on which he diverged from Canning, perhaps without realizing it. He sought public approval of views too forthright and trenchant for the other Canningites. In proclaiming these views he belaboured a government which claimed, perhaps sincerely, to be following, in Portugal, Canning's policy.

*   *   *   *

The major European question of the day concerned the doctrine of *non-intervention* in the internal affairs of independent states. To this Britain was committed, as part of the politics of Balance of Power, for it is intervention by one state beyond its frontiers which upsets the balance, and induces other states to try to right it, thus producing war. Britain, it was known, would counter-intervene to protect the Netherlands or Portugal from attack; her interest demanded it. But what should she do if it were Spain, or Naples? Presumably circumstances would alter cases. One circumstance in particular was always coming to the fore, the intervention of a powerful state to suppress revolution in a weaker one, at the invitation of the ruler threatened by the revolution. It was the view of Russia and Austria that 'the order of things' which the Allies in the late war were bound to co-operate to maintain consisted not merely of the territorial settlement made at Vienna in 1814–15, but also the constitutional status quo in the various states. Britain, through

Castlereagh, decisively repudiated the interpretation. His State Paper of 5th May 1820 — a response to the Tsar's invitation to discuss what reply should be made to any request from the King of Spain — has been called the most famous one in British history 'and the one with the widest ultimate consequences'.* The Treaty of Vienna, he insisted, 'never was . . . intended as an Union for the Government of the World, or for the Superintendence of the Internal Affairs of other States'. There were moral as well as political objections to the principle of one state interfering by force in the internal affairs of another, and generalized and reduced to a system it was one upon which no country having a representative system of government could act. 'We shall be found in our place when actual danger menaces the System of Europe, but this country cannot, and will not, act upon abstract and speculative Principles of Precaution: the Alliance which exists had no such purpose in view in its original formation.' In other words, Britain would not accept the argument that there was, in a rising in Spain or Naples to recover a constitution revoked by a ruler, such a presumptive danger of unleashing throughout Europe those excesses of liberalism and republicanism associated with 'French Revolutionary Principles' and universal war that the Alliance (plus Bourbon France) should use force almost as a matter of course.

It went to Castlereagh's heart to snub the Powers. For he was himself the chief author of the system of periodic congresses at which they were to meet to maintain their 'unity' and hence the general peace. But what he privily stated in May 1820 he repeated in a circular of January 1821 and this he published. Canning, succeeding him in 1822, laid before Parliament in the spring of 1823, and endorsed, the effective parts of the State Paper. He instructed Wellington at the Congress of Verona 'frankly and peremptorily to declare, that to any such interference, *come what may*, His Majesty will not be a party'.[9] The Duke did so on 30th October 1823 and in effect killed the Congress System, because the other Powers insisted on putting on the agenda subjects regarded by Britain as out of order.

Canning, never enamoured of Congresses, was only too willing to make a virtue out of necessity, and proclaim in public what

* The asterisks indicate that the document, or the relevant part of it, can be found in H. W. V. Temperley and L. M. Penson, *Foundations of British Foreign Policy*, 1938.

Castlereagh wrote privately, transforming Castlereagh's negative — that Parliament and national sympathy would be against a war to suppress a revolution that did not menace Britain or the general peace — into a positive assertion of 'the right of any Nation to change, or to modify, its internal institutions'.[10] The use of public opinion as an instrument of foreign policy is Canning's chief innovation. It was one of which Palmerston vastly approved. But it resulted in the true springs of Canning's actions being misunderstood, just as Castlereagh's had been misunderstood because of his privacy. Palmerston was among the misinterpreters, who remembered that Canning said the object of England was 'to keep within reasonable bounds that predominating areopagitical spirit',[11] and forgot that his theme was one of aloofness. When they read the speech in which Canning said that a general war would be one 'not merely of conflicting armies, but of conflicting principles' and that, if Britain were involved, she would wield a power 'more tremendous than was perhaps ever yet brought into action in the history of mankind', because she would 'see under her banners, arrayed for the contest, all the discontented and restless spirits of the age, all those who — whether justly or unjustly — are dissatisfied with the present state of their own countries',[12] the misinterpreters dwelt upon the massive power of Britain, the power of opinion. They forgot that his theme was that from such an Armageddon all men of goodwill should shrink; that Britain should adopt a position of neutrality 'not only between contending nations but between contending principles';[11] that 'our business is not to seek opportunities of displaying [this strength], but to content ourselves with letting the professors of violent and exaggerated doctrines on both sides feel that it is not their interest to convert an umpire into their competitor'; that 'nothing short of a point of national faith or national honour ... would make desirable at the present moment, any voluntary approximation to the possibility of a dangerous war'.[12]

Palmerston had been reading this speech of 12th December 1826 before he spoke on 1st June 1829, and he sought to ground his allegation, that the Wellington government had departed from Canning's policy, on the claim that national faith and honour were involved in the fight against Dom Miguel in Portugal, that this was one of the *special* occasions' when, as Canning had told his nephew Stratford Canning, 'interference in the concerns of other states'

might be justified.[13] Canning had made his speech when that
Spanish régime which the French armies had restored in 1823 was,
as he said, waging a war of opinion 'commenced in hatred of the
new institutions in Portugal',[12] a war, which, he warned, might
escalate into the dreaded war of opinions, unless arbitrary governments realized that in the acknowledgement of the principle of
'non-intervention', in the co-existence of despotic and free
governments, lay the only hope of general peace.[13] Canning had
just planted the Union Jack on the heights of Lisbon. But this he
had done because a frontier was involved, and Portugal invoked the
treaty of alliance which bound Britain to defend her independence.
The Portuguese government was a constitutionalist one, and
Palmerston wrongly assumed that to Canning this was a virtue —
the Canning who had said publicly 'Freedom ceases to be a distinction, in proportion as other nations become free'[11] and told his
envoys that it was 'not a British Interest to have free States established on the Continent'.[13] Peel stressed in the debate of 1st June
1829, on the authority of Canning, that the expedition of 1826 was
not intervention in the internal affairs of Portugal; the troops did
not go to guarantee the success of any particular individual or the
existence of any political institution in Portugal. When therefore
the absolutist Dom Miguel deposed his niece and intended bride,
the child Queen Maria da Gloria, the Wellington government
claimed, not without colour, that it was pursuing *Canning's*
policy of 'strict and undeviating neutrality' in the internal dissensions of Portugal. Britain had guaranteed neither Miguel's
(admittedly broken) engagements to the Portuguese people and his
sovereign, nor the rights of Maria. Miguel had not been made king
by foreign intervention, but by the Cortes, and there was no
peculiarity in his usurpation to require British action against him.

To Palmerston this was mere pedantry. He asserted that in the
past twelve months (since he had left the cabinet) the foreign
relations of England had been conducted in a spirit far different
from that of previous years. This was as true of Portugal as of
Greece. Did ministers not appreciate that the special relationship
of Britain and Portugal consisted in this, that the ablest statesmen
of England held it important to the security of England that the
Tagus should be in friendly hands, while it was the opinion of the
wisest statesmen of Portugal that 'the best security for Portuguese
independence was to be found in the selfish interests of England'?

How could they talk of neutrality when 'the whole history of the connexion between England and Portugal [had been] almost one unbroken chain' of intermeddling by the former? In 1807 the Royal Navy had conveyed the Court of Portugal to Brazil as Napoleon's armies neared Lisbon. It was from the quarterdeck of a British man-of-war, the sole refuge of the lawful government of Portugal, that King John in 1824 proclaimed the banishment of his absolutist queen from the Court and his absolutist younger son Miguel from the country. Britain had actively and successfully interfered to secure the separation of the thrones of Portugal and Brazil — 'an interference founded upon a just regard to the interests of England'. When the elder son, Dom Pedro, sent a constitutional charter from Brazil to Portugal on his father's death, a British envoy conveyed it. (Canning explained that he did not do so ex officio and that Britain had inspired neither the document nor its dispatch, for 'it is not her duty, nor her practice, to offer suggestions for the internal regulation of foreign states'.) When Pedro opted to rule Brazil, and abdicated in favour of his daughter Maria, Miguel signed in Vienna protocols 'written under the eye, if not at the dictation of' the British ambassador there, by which he secured the regency in return for recognizing Maria as queen and swearing to maintain Pedro's laws and institutions. Miguel was escorted to Lisbon from England by the Royal Navy and the British minister, and to his palace by British troops. He had asked that part of the army sent by Canning stay, and under the shield of its standing orders to protect royal personages, had dismissed his constitutional ministers, officers and magistrates and dissolved the Chambers. Eventually he accepted from a compliant Chamber his niece's crown. During the process of the usurpation, the British envoy had ceased to release funds to Miguel and delivered remonstrances of increasing vigour against his misgovernment. His mission was suspended and, after warnings, his withdrawal provisionally ordered in May 1828, the month the Canningites left Wellington's government. After the defeat of loyalist troops at Oporto, many of them had taken refuge in Spain, where they were maltreated. Britain had intervened on their behalf, and allowed 3,000 to 4,000 to Plymouth, on condition that they ceased to exist as an embodied force and mounted no expedition to any part of Portugal.

Miguel's breaches of engagement were, Peel admitted, 'no doubt

an indignity to England'. 'Was it fitting', cried Palmerston, 'that
the king of England should be made the stalking-horse, under
whose cover this royal poacher should creep upon his unsuspecting
prey. I say that if the insulted honour of a sovereign is a legitimate
ground of national quarrel, we are entitled to demand, and to
extort, reparation from Dom Miguel.' The withdrawal of the
envoy, when Miguel seized the crown, was 'the last bolt of the
English cabinet . . . their quiver was exhausted'. This measure, 'in
the usual intercourse of nations big with fearful import', had
merely deprived British subjects of protection and relieved Miguel
of a nuisance. No action had been taken to aid Donna Maria, the
lawful sovereign, at Oporto, while civil war still raged, and Miguel
was not even king de facto, as Peel now said he was. And what of the
refugee army at Plymouth? It had been licensed to send its powder
and muskets to Brazil, and had sent them instead to Terceira in the
Azores, still holding out for Maria. Its leaders had then asked for
permission to take the men to Terceira 'unarmed'. When this was
refused, they sailed with false clearances, and the Royal Navy was
ordered to turn them back, as the Government recognize Miguel's
blockade of the island as effective and 'the duty of neutrality is as
strong in respect to a de facto [government] as to one de jure'
(Peel). This infuriated Palmerston. 'The navy of England . . . was
made the subservient tool of tyranny and usurpation.' To the
refugees 'their country was Terceira, where the authority of their
queen was still maintained and obeyed'.

It may be that Palmerston succeeded, by his speech, in one of
his aims. He feared that Britain would be the first major Power to
recognize Miguel (only the Pope and Spain had done so). Interro-
gated by Palmerston on the eve of the fall of the Tory government
at the end of 1830, Peel said that Britain had been doing all in her
power 'by advice and friendly interference' to secure an amnesty for
Portuguese political prisoners. It had been made clear to Miguel
that, although Britain did not require an amnesty as a condition of
granting recognition, she would not recognize him unless he
published an amnesty to the world.[14] Palmerston thought the whole
approach of Wellington and Aberdeen to Miguel a legalistic one
which either took no account of the fact that the man was an
absolutist and tyrant or deliberately bent the laws and conventions
in his favour. To Palmerston Miguel's despotic character was the
most relevant thing of all, next to the interest of England, with

which, however, it was intimately involved. He did not merely say that it was nauseating to see Her Majesty's ministers 'making a pet of Miguel, and that *if* their 'neutrality' was going to be biassed, it ought to be biassed *against* despotism. He clearly thought it ought to be biassed in favour of freedom, and all the benefits of the slightest doubt given to Maria as its champion. Why had she not been helped when she was at Oporto? Why now behave as though Miguel were undisputed king? Britain had taken Madeira in trust for Maria I in 1807; why not do as much for Maria II now? As for the doctrine of 'non-intervention', it was, of course, 'sound'. 'It ought to be sacred; and I trust that England will never be found to set the example of its violation.' But all it meant was that 'general principles and our own practice' forebade interference *by force of arms*. The implication was clearly that it might be right for Britain to interfere in every way, short of actual war, to influence the outcome of an internecine struggle in which the moral influence and some of the sinews of war were supplied to one side by the neo-Holy Alliance.

Palmerston could have found in Canning's papers a copy of a letter to Liverpool giving him some ground for the belief that Canning might, *in the case of Portugal*, have adopted a line different from that of Aberdeen. 'Portugal appears to be the chosen ground on which the Continental Alliance have resolved to fight England hand to hand, and we must be prepared to meet and defeat them, under every imaginable form of intrigue and intimidation, or be driven from the field.' Canning was resolved, as any Balance of Power statesman ought to be, that Portugal 'always must be English'.[15] Palmerston was sure he would never have allowed himself to be driven from the field, or worse, have gone over, or half-gone over, to the enemy, like his successors. Canning might indeed have intervened to restore the status quo. More probably he would have worked to restore Maria *without* the charter, which he did not think suitable for Portugal, and which, in the debate of 1st June, Huskisson, speaking for the Canningites, called an unwise and injudicious grant. In doing this, Canning would have betrayed none of his own principles and gone against none of his own sentiments. For he thought it no part of Britain's duty to export her constitution, even to Portugal, by high-pressure salesmanship. A note in his hand, dated 4th December 1824, reads: 'Not . . . a British Interest to have free States established on the Continent. Much better and more convenient for us to have neighbours, whose Institutions cannot be compared with ours in point of freedom.'[13] And at Liverpool he said on 30th August 1822 that in contests between monarchy and democracy Britain ought to stand on the defensive, 'a spectatress interested in the contest only by her sympathies . . . for the sake of both a model, and ultimately perhaps an umpire'.[16] If she participated in the struggle she would commit, and therefore impair, her authority, lose the chance of mediating, and bring the danger of foreign struggle to her own hearths and institutions. Palmerston would perhaps have said the same, but he would not have meant the same. He would never have said (and probably forgot that Canning had said) that it was not a British interest to have free states in Europe. He did not inquire, as Canning did, whether the Portuguese wanted Maria or Miguel, charter or no charter, charter or some other charter. He took it for granted that the Portuguese wanted Maria and the charter, which was almost certainly untrue. When Peel said the real issue was whether to go to war for Maria or not, and that the principles of 'non-intervention' bequeathed by Canning, as well as the country's desire for peace, gave the clear answer, Palmerston insisted that 'to war against Miguel would not be to war against the Portuguese nation; it would be to war in their aid'. Intervention by all means short of open war was perfectly compatible with the principle of 'non-intervention'.

'His name was the terror of tyrants', it was said when Canning died. But, except when the Portuguese frontier was violated, all he had done was chide them (and warn them off the New World). Palmerston used, already in 1829, not the language of rebuke, but of *participation* on the other side in Europe's ideological war. His complaint was not that ministers were taking sides, but that they were taking the wrong side in a battle in which no one had the right to be neutral or aloof or smug. They were taking it not only in Portugal but in Greece and everywhere else. He had predicted that they would. Explaining in March 1828 why if Huskisson, the leader of the Canningites, left Wellington's cabinet he must go too, Palmerston said that, with Huskisson removed, the arbitrary party in the cabinet would predominate, break with Russia and probably France and back out of the Greek Treaty. 'We should unite ourselves again with Metternich, and adopt the apostolical party in Spain and Portugal', he said (showing that he misunderstood

Castlereagh's policy).[17] Now, in 1829, he showed that he misunderstood Canning's principles and sentiments, for he said:
'Time was, and that but lately, when England was regarded by
Europe, as the friend of liberty and civilization, and therefore of
happiness and prosperity in every land; because it was thought that
her rulers had the wisdom to discover that *the selfish interests and
political influence of England were best promoted by the extension of
liberty and civilization.* Now, on the contrary, the prevailing
opinion is that England thinks her advantage to lie in withholding
from other countries that constitutional liberty which she herself
enjoys.' It was wrong, humiliating, intolerable to have Britain as
'the keystone of that arch, of which Miguel and Spain, Austria and
Mahmoud, are the component members'.

The proposition here stressed marks Palmerston off clearly from
Castlereagh and Canning as well as Aberdeen and Wellington. It
cannot be explained away as the extravagant verbiage of opposition
politics. Portugal, one might indeed say, was a special case, as it
had been for Canning, because Portugal 'always must be English'.
But then what of Greece? Palmerston hoped that for Greece the
Three Powers would propose a form of government giving 'free
political development to the intellectual faculties of the people'.
Britain should 'take care to secure to a liberated Greece the permanent enjoyment of popular institutions. I hope the constitution
will be of London and Paris manufacture, and not the production
of any artist in a capital nearer to Greece.' 'Ah', says the critic, 'but
then Greece too was a special case, for her future was at the disposition of the Three Powers.' This is true. But where is the
geographic limitation in the purple passage that followed, in which
were depicted the two great parties in Europe, one endeavouring
to bear sway by the force of public opinion, the other by the force
of physical control? Where is the detachment, the neutrality, the
Canningite reserve, in the famous declamation: 'There is in nature
no moving power but mind. . . . In human affairs this power is
opinion; in political affairs it is public opinion; and he who can
grasp this power, with it will subdue the fleshly arm of physical
strength and impel it to work out his purpose.' Austria, by the
narrowness of her views and the prejudices of her policy, had
almost reduced herself to a second-rate Power. Men who 'know
how to avail themselves of the passions, and the interests, and the
opinions of mankind' may win influence far beyond the power and

resources of their state. 'Those . . . who seek to check improvement, to cherish abuses, to crush opinions, and to prohibit the
human race from thinking . . . will find their weapon snap short in
their hand, when most they need its protection.' This is not only an
inspired forecast of the fate of Charles X of France in 1830 and
Louis Philippe and almost all the German and Italian princes in
1848. It is taking up Canning's exploitation of public opinion for a
purpose which Canning had specifically disapproved.

Palmerston did not, of course, mean to incite men to revolution,
and he hoped, like Canning, that Britain, standing between the
extremes of despotism and democracy would serve as a model, and
perhaps an umpire. But he did wish to export the British constitution, and he did proclaim, and wish Britain officially to proclaim,
that freedom is the natural state of society, and that rulers and
diplomats working against it were working against the grain and
could not in the end prevail. Lest there be any doubt of it, he took
occasion on 10th March 1830 to declare that Britain must assume a
moral leadership on the side of freedom. 'By leaguing with the
oppressors and trampling upon the oppressed . . . we gradually
break down and confound all those moral distinctions in which our
strength ought to lie.' By allowing the Spaniards to attack Mexico,
after refusing to let the Mexicans forestall the attack by assailing
Cuba, the government was guilty of 'a gross act of partiality between two contending parties and a direct violation of the system of
neutrality on which our Government professed to act'.[18] A fair
character and a good name in the eyes of the world was as necessary
to nations as to individuals, and plain dealing, sincerity and a
regard to justice was the most successful policy in the intercourse
of cabinets as well as of individuals.

At this time Palmerston believed that among the examples of
Wellington's 'leaguing with the oppressors' was connivance in the
plans of the French Ultras to curb the constitutional liberties
provided by the Charter of 1814. When news came of the imprisonment of the Ultra minister, Polignac, and the flight of Charles X,
Palmerston wrote, privately 'We shall drink the cause of Liberalism
all over the world. . . . This event is decisive of the ascendancy of
Liberal Principles throughout Europe. . . . The reign of Metternich is over and the days of the Duke's policy might be measured
by algebra, if not by arithmetic.'[19] This was not a Canning-like
reaction. Only four years earlier Canning had written to the Prin-

cess Lieven: 'I don't know why M. de Metternich imagines that I like constitutional governments. Unquestionably, as an English Minister, it is not my place to oppose them; but as a matter of taste, I should much prefer to do without them.'[20] Full allowance must be made for the fact that this letter is written *ad hoc*. But full allowance must also be made for the fact that those statements of Canning which read most like those of Palmerston, and seem to make of Canning a patron of Liberalism in Europe, were made to appeal to public and/or parliamentary opinion in Britain. They won him the applause of many Opposition Whigs, who had misread Castlereagh's attachment to the Concert of Europe as approval of the Holy and neo-Holy Alliances. Palmerston, it seems, was deceived by Canning's propaganda into believing that Canning had been a Palmerstonian. The orthodox Canningites knew better.

If Palmerston's attachment to the Liberal cause had been less genuine, one would have been tempted to write off the speeches of 1829 and 1830 as a mere courting of the Whigs. They were much more acceptable to his Whig constituents of Cambridge University than to the Tories. They came out of the stable of Charles James Fox rather than of Pitt. They won the respect of Grey, Fox's successor at the Foreign Office and now the paramount chief of Whiggery. They made him think of Palmerston as a potential Foreign Secretary. Indeed, it is probably true that but for the speech of 1st June 1829 Palmerston would not have received the Foreign Office from Grey in November 1830. But, although Palmerston, whenever he was approached by Wellington with offers of office in 1830 made the (unacceptable) condition that the Whig chiefs be brought in too, it would be stretching probability to ascribe this attitude to a single-minded pursuit of the Foreign Office. The other leading Canningites made the same condition, and on the same ground, that only a predominance in the cabinet of liberal-minded men could guarantee the pursuit of Canningite policies in the fiscal, commercial and diplomatic fields. Grey himself was thought to be willing to consider seriously an offer of the Foreign Office from the Duke, for, unlike most of the Whig parliamentarians, this starchy patrician had extended his dislike of Canning as a flashy upstart to dislike of his policy, and preferred the Duke's as more pacific and economical. One can say no more than that Palmerston's speech of 1st June 1829, and subsequent interventions in debate in 1830, all of them genuine expressions of his views, made him *a* candidate for the Foreign Office in any coalition constructed on the ruins of the Duke's administration.

He was far from being the principal candidate. Lansdowne and Holland stood clearly ahead of him. Palmerston and Lansdowne had come to respect one another when they served together, albeit briefly, in 1827 in cabinets not liberal enough for Palmerston, the second of which fell (partly) on the issue of whether Holland should (against the king's wishes) take over the Foreign Office. It must have been Lansdowne in particular of whom Palmerston was thinking when he said that he regretted the Duke's decision, when forming his cabinet in 1828, to include the Canningites but not the Whigs 'as I like them much better than the Tories and agree with them much more'.[21] In 1829 Palmerston seized the initiative in the House of Commons when the Whigs were in disarray. He qualified himself to be the colleague of Holland, who as Fox's nephew was regarded as the keeper of the conscience of Whiggery. When Aberdeen claimed that Britain under the Duke had the respect of foreign governments more than ever before, and was therefore 'probably looked upon with dislike by the disturbed spirits of Europe, who longed to be let slip to recommence the work of destruction' he showed that inhibiting horror of the French Revolution which Palmerston, though reared in it, had quite thrown off. Holland rebuked this Metternichian pronouncement by the British Foreign Secretary as 'a vulgar insinuation'.[22] Palmerston had made it very clear that he, like Holland, thought the respect of arbitrary rulers, earned by leaning towards their cause, was no proper objective for His Majesty's Government and certainly no subject for boasting. When Lansdowne and Holland preferred lighter tasks than the Foreign Office, both recommended Palmerston to Grey as the man to conduct the foreign policy of Britain (November 1830).

THE MAN OF CONFERENCE

THE Greek state had not, as Palmerston feared, been throttled at birth by Wellington and Aberdeen. By February 1830 he could rejoice that Greece, under the protection of the English wing, was not to be doomed to the fetters and shackles of despotism. But, if his predecessor (though personally philhellene) had stayed in office another week or two, Greece would have been so constricted as to leave its survival in doubt and its prosperity impossible. At Poros in December 1828 the representatives of the Three Protecting Powers, Britain (represented by Stratford Canning), Russia and France, had recommended that Greece receive a frontier on the Arta–Volo line, Euboea, Samos and perhaps Crete. Wellington would nevertheless, if he could, have denied them all three of these large islands and this land frontier. He was chiefly responsible for the Protocol of 22nd March 1829 and its modification in February 1830 which provided that Greece should be fully independent, but whittled at frontiers which even in 1829 had fallen well short of the Poros proposals. The Greeks were not to have most of Aetolia, and they were to evacuate those parts of Acarnania which they had occupied despite all attempts by Wellington to restrain them. This plan was nonsensical even on the assumption that an independent Greece would be hostile to Britain, the plaything of Russia. Palmerston utterly rejected this assumption. He held that, if Greece was to be independent, with its own foreign policy, and not merely autonomous, she must have a militarily realistic frontier on a line from the Gulf of Volo to the Gulf of Arta, and Euboea and the Cyclades as well. It was important to Britain that Greece should be decidedly able to maintain herself in an independent situation. He therefore came into office knowing exactly what he intended to do about Greece. On 28th December 1830 the British representative, Dawkins, was ordered to delay the Greek evacuation of Acarnania 'on any fair pretence'. Metternich was told that Britain intended to reconvene the London Conference to reconsider the frontiers.[1]

Palmerston carried his point. Another protocol issued in London on 26th September 1831 dismissed the frontier line of February 1830 as drawn on the wrong map, and Stratford Canning was sent to Constantinople to secure the Turk's acceptance of the Arta–Volo line, which gave the Greeks Aetolia and Acarnania. With an Egyptian army under Ibrahim approaching his capital, the Sultan gave way (21st July 1832) in expectation of British aid. In eighteen months the affairs of Greece had been, Palmerston could claim, well disposed. War, and its concomitants of piracy, blockade and interruption of trade, had become a memory. Instead of the autonomous principalities originally proposed, which were expected to be Russian puppets, there was an independent kingdom which, Palmerston assured the House of Commons on 8th August 1832, would not be a Russian province. 'The interests of civilisation, the interests of commerce, and the interests of political independence are all the interests of England, and all have been signally promoted by the emancipation of Greece', he claimed triumphantly.

'The interests of England.' The phrase must be noted, for there has been a tendency simultaneously to assume that Palmerston believed, or professed to believe, in a sort of Wilsonian national self-determination and to abuse him for often betraying the principle. It is surely much simpler to assume that he did not believe in it, and *could not believe in it*, because it was incompatible with the Balance of Power. On this he was at one with Canning. Their concern for Greece was not sentimental. It was due largely to Russia's interest in the Balkans and Constantinople. Having the wit to see that Greek independence would be better secured by the interests of the Powers than the enthusiasm of the people, Mavrocordato, when pressing on Canning the role of supreme arbiter, used the argument that a viable Greek state was a European necessity and a British interest.[2] It was because Russia could not be allowed to fish alone in Ottoman waters that Canning sent Wellington to St Petersburg to set in train the diplomacy which led to the Treaty of London.[3] The Powers acted, whether Canning, Dudley, Aberdeen or Palmerston represented Britain, on the assumption which they brazenly and unashamedly proclaimed in the Protocol of 3rd February 1830. The Greeks were told that their country 'owed its life to the assistance lavished upon it by the three powers', which, consequently, were entitled to 'positive rights and complete deference'. The London Conference did not invite, nor attach much importance to, Greek ratification of its dictates. So positive did it deem its rights, so literally did it interpret the term 'act of submission' used to describe the Greek appeal (to Britain alone) in 1825, that a Greek historian reminds us, in a chapter entitled 'The Forfeiture of Sovereignty', that independence of Turkey was succeeded by 'a Bavarian protectorate under the suzerain control implicit in the "guarantee" of the three Powers'.[2] In Wellington's time the Conference had decreed, first that Greece should be tributary, then that it should be independent; had fixed one Frontier and then substituted a meaner one; had determined that Greece should be a hereditary, constitutional monarchy and then (1st July 1830) that it would refrain from anticipating the nature of the institutions and laws to be derived from the monarchy. This last decision was made after the king designated for Greece by the Conference, Leopold of Saxe-Coburg, withdrew his acceptance of the crown because of the erosion of the frontier. Palmerston was largely responsible for the offer of the throne to Otho of Bavaria (February 1832). This youth's father accepted it in the Convention of London (7th May 1832). With his assent, the Powers provided for the succession to the throne and a regency till Otho came of age. They made the interest and amortization of the Three-Power Loan a first charge on the public revenue of Greece and decreed the defence of the country and the maintenance of order by Bavarian troops at Greek expense.

This outcome was entirely consistent with the maintenance of the Ottoman Empire in Europe, to which Palmerston had become an enthusiastic convert by mid-1832. It had been the Greek revolt and the Russian interest in it which led Britain towards the independence of Greece as the best solution in Balance of Power terms. There was no more suggestion under Palmerston than Aberdeen that Greece would be allowed to try to wrest from Turkey the 'unredeemed lands' (which in Greek eyes embraced Constantinople itself and much of Asia Minor), nor that any other nationalist revolts in European Turkey would be welcomed or in any way succoured, let alone invited. 'English ministers noted with a grudging eye each gain of national privileges as a new field for the extension of Russian influence; it did not occur to them or to anyone else to go one step further and actually promote independence.'[4]

* * * *

The same hard realism motivated British policy with regard to Belgium. The settlement of the critical question raised by the revolt of the Belgians against the Dutch took the form of Great Power recognition and *guarantee* of an independent state raised by revolution in defiance of the Treaty of Vienna. Belgium under Leopold of Saxe-Coburg became what Greece under Otho of Bavaria did not become, a stable constitutional monarchy, and was highly esteemed by Palmerston as an all too rare vindication of his belief in liberal institutions. But it is misguided to attribute the recognition of the separation of Belgium from Holland to any theoretical belief in national self-determination or to Palmerston's Liberalism. Frenchmen, Poles, Belgians and a few Italians wished to undo the Treaty of Vienna; Palmerston did not. He uttered no criticism of Castlereagh and the other statesmen who made the postwar settlement on realistic lines taking small account of nationality. Belgium had never been a nation; it had never been, as a unit, independent. The King of the Netherlands, against whose regimen the Belgians successfully revolted in August 1830 (originally not for independence but for administrative separation from Holland), was more of a constitutional monarch than most in Europe. He played a role in the state very like that which Leopold was to play. The Powers had accepted the inevitability of Belgian independence (declared by the provisional government in Brussels on 4th October after the Dutch army had retaken and then evacuated the city) before Palmerston became Foreign Secretary. He would have liked, if possible, to maintain at least a dynastic link between the sundered Netherlands, but on the very day (22nd November) that he became Secretary of State the Belgian National Congress voted the exclusion of the House of Orange from the throne. It was not the case with regard to Belgium, as it was with regard to Greece, that Palmerston came into office determined to change the policy of his predecessor. It is true that Aberdeen (as we shall see) had been driven reluctantly to a policy which he disliked, and that Palmerston was free from this disability; this was important. But the policy was set. British national interest had determined it, an interest sincerely believed to coincide with the interest of Europe. What Palmerston did for Belgium — and he did much — he did only incidentally for the Belgians. He did it for Britain, and for Europe. He did it, not for nationalism, but for the Balance of Power.

He did it, not for Liberalism, but for the containment of France.

The Belgian settlement did not become definitive till 1839, but, in essentials, it was worked out by November 1831. For a strenuous eleven months Palmerston, without any training in diplomacy, trod as Castlereagh had done the difficult paths of multilateral negotiation between Great Powers. That he relished the chance to prove his capacity to handle great matters is evident. But it was no delight to him that the great matter which now pressed involved the partial demolition of the system of bulwarks erected in 1814–15 against a renewal of French aggression, the system of which Castlereagh was the chief architect. To France's east, Switzerland had been *guaranteed*. To the south-east, Piedmont (officially called the Kingdom of Sardinia) had been enlarged, and all Lombardy and Venetia awarded to Austria. To the north-east, the Prussians were placed athwart the Rhine, and their troops in the fortress of Luxemburg. And to the north had been erected the Kingdom of the United Netherlands, under the House of Orange, which held also the grand-duchy of Luxemburg. The famous 'barrier for-tresses' of the Belgic Netherlands were made the joint responsibility of the powers of the Quadruple Alliance (Britain, Russia, Austria and Prussia) and the British taxpayer contributed seven million pounds to their improvement and maintenance after Waterloo. The Four Powers also bound themselves to exclude a Buonaparte from the governance of France; to join together to repel any renewal of French aggression; to consult together and with His Most Christian Majesty of France if 'the same Revolutionary Principles, which upheld the last criminal usurpation, [should] again, under other forms, convulse France and thereby endanger the repose of other States'.

This last provision became highly relevant in 1830. We have already seen that Britain's Great Power allies in the war against France, and France herself after she was admitted to the comity of Great Powers in 1818, acted as though there was a further clause in the Treaties of Vienna and Paris 1814–15 binding them to consult, and permitting them to act, if 'Revolutionary Principles' convulsed *any* European state. Against this view Britain, both through Castlereagh and Canning, protested. When her protests were ignored, she withdrew from the Congress System. The issue between her and the other Powers was not a new one. Pitt had professed and practised, for more than three years after the storming of the Bastille, non-intervention in the internal affairs of France, while Austria and Prussia went to war for the preservation of monarchical order, doomed the monarch they hoped to rescue, saved the Revolution they aimed to destroy, and provoked from the Convention in Paris encroachments upon Belgium and Savoy and 'the formal declaration of a design to extend universally the new principles of government adopted in France' (November 1792). Only because of these *external* manifestations of the Revolution had Britain been drawn to war.[5] Her essential aims, promulgated by Pitt in his State Paper of 19th January 1805, were the reduction of France to her former limits and the establishment of more effective barriers, military and diplomatic, against renewed encroachment. The best hope of the restoration of the monarchy, and of the Bourbons, lay in making it clear to the French people that there was no desire 'either to dictate to them by Force any Particular Form of Government, or to attempt to dismember the antient Territories of France'.* Castlereagh took this as his text in 1814–15. He was quite clear what engagements he then made, in common with the other members of the Quadruple Alliance, and what he, and they, had not made. More important, he left a clear record for his successors, in the form of his Memorandum to the Cabinet from the Congress at Aix in October 1818* and the State Paper of 5th May 1820,* of an authoritative view as to what the Powers might properly do in various contingencies not precisely covered by the Treaties of Vienna and Paris. Reference to the latter would guide the statesman as to his attitude should revolution break out in a country other than France. The former declared that no Power had the right, still less the duty, to intervene in France on the sole ground of internal changes 'whether legally effectuated or brought about by indirect means'. Only if internal proceedings in France endangered her neighbours would the Powers have a right to intervene, and they should 'exercise a sound discretion'.

If Palmerston had been in office when in July 1830 His Most Christian Majesty King Charles X fled (before he could be consulted); when Louis Philippe, of the Orleanist line of the Bourbons, was hailed by the republican Lafayette king, not of France, but of the French; when the new ruler took for his emblem not the Bourbon lilies but the tricolour, Palmerston would have recognized the *fait accompli* and declared that the Quadruple Allies 'must act in perfect union and concert founded on their determination to preserve the state of territorial possession as settled in the Treaties of Vienna and Paris'.[6] That is what Wellington did; the quotation is not from Palmerston, but from Aberdeen. But prompt recognition by Palmerston must have been read by the Eastern Powers in the light of his speech of 1st June 1829 and that of 10th March 1830 in which he endorsed the Whig view that Napoleon had been beaten by the peoples of Europe responding to 'the name of Freedom and National Independence . . . roused by the magic sound of Constitutional Rights' and grievously betrayed, after victory, by their sovereigns. It was much more impressive in Berlin, Vienna and St. Petersburg to see the régime erected on Polignac's political grave receive acknowledgement from a British government supposedly privy to those reactionary designs of Polignac which precipitated the revolution.

All British public men breathed relief that the product of the revolution was not a republic but a monarchy resting on the upper bourgeoisie, which reputable moderates like Casimir Périer and the French Whig de Broglie (and, of course, the inevitable Talleyrand) could serve. But they were not, by and large, immune from the apprehension which was strong in the Eastern capitals, where the British distinction between the Revolution in its internal and external aspects was regarded with suspicion. To Metternich and the Tsar it was *the Revolution* itself which was the enemy and the danger, and its soul was in Paris. As it happened, in 1830 only the Tsar talked of 'action', and he could not act without Austria or Prussia. The Powers therefore, for the moment, answered in the negative, like Wellington (whose influence with them on such a matter as this was of course very great), the question Castlereagh had taught his colleagues to ask — 'whether revolutionary principles have appeared in such a form as to endanger the repose of other States'.[6] They, as well as Britain, adopted the non-interventionist posture of Pitt (1789–92), dimly understanding what was clear even to Aberdeen, that this gave the best hope of defeating the designs of 'those who would throw France into confusion and render foreign war inevitable'.[6] But everyone knew that revolution in Paris would have repercussions far and wide through Europe. It was not without effect in England, and helped to bring the Whigs and Canningites to power and Palmerston to the Foreign Office.

'That it must operate some movement . . . in Spain, Portugal and Italy sooner or later one can hardly permit oneself to doubt', wrote Palmerston with a satisfaction as yet untempered by responsibility. Years later he argued that the July Revolution had divided the states of Europe into two ideological camps, and that the division could not 'really cease till all the questions to which it applies are settled'.[7]

There was cause for great anxiety for the peace of Europe when the Belgians revolted against the Dutch. Reactions in Britain varied in detail according to the political cast of men's minds. Palmerston was unlikely to assume, as Aberdeen did, that the Belgians had not grievances enough to explain demands for genuine autonomy if not for separation. He could not go all the way with Aberdeen in holding that 'it is no cause, real or pretended, of Belgium which has triumphed at Brussels. If it is not the cause of the French Government, it is the cause of a French faction which is superior to the Government and the result must be the same for the rest of Europe'.[8] But the rising was clearly inspired by the Parisian example, and partly incited by French and pro-French agitators. The temptation for an unstable French régime, too moderate for many of those who had helped at the barricades, to risk the liberal crusade for which enthusiasts cried, was very great, when to refuse it was to risk another and more radical revolution. That 'war of opinions' which Canning had feared seemed imminent.[9] If Britain fought with the despotic Powers against a constitutional France, she would find all the forces of European Liberalism against her, and be subject to savage divisions of opinion at home. If she did not, what would become of the restraints erected against French chauvinism, and how could she justify the breach of clear treaty obligation to repel any renewed French aggression? It was vital to prevent war, even if one had to recognize the independence of Belgium to do it. Slow-minded and conservative, no man for a crisis, Aberdeen grumbled. He had been so foolish as to say that British public opinion would never allow Belgian separation. He thought, quite wrongly, and quite inexcusably (he had been on Castlereagh's staff in 1813–14) that 'we have *guaranteed* the union of Holland and Belgium'.[8] Deeply suspicious of France, both before and after the recent revolution, he sharply rebuffed the French proposal for Anglo-French mediation between the Dutch and the Belgians and/or a conference in Paris. He thought it an impertinence. If the policy of Britain had depended on him, he would have drifted. But the Duke, either very good or disastrously bad in a crisis, got him to see that the question was not *how* to return the revolting subjects of the House of Orange to their allegiance, but whether it was safe to try any such thing. And to this question, such was the state of feeling in France, there could be but one answer.

The King of the Netherlands helped the Belgian cause, and the cause of international peace, by failing to strike at the Belgians with all his force, and condescending to negotiate with them, in fact, if not in form. Finding them, as he thought, unreasonable, he appealed to the Quadruple Powers for aid, to maintain the Vienna Settlement which had created the United Netherlands. He forgot that the United Netherlands had not been created on account of the merits of the Dutch (who had helped Napoleon) or of the House of Orange, but to serve Europe's interest by being a bulwark against France. He did not understand that his actions were an admission that, unless there was at the very least a radical revision of the position of Belgium, his kingdom, even if it survived, could not serve the purpose for which it had been invented. The Powers would have had to act anyway, but he deceived himself if he thought that, by invoking them, he would get them to serve his interest, rather than Europe's interest in avoiding a general war. 'The *short* of the matter is this', wrote Wellington; 'the affairs of the Netherlands can never be permanently settled without the concurrence of France.' Nothing could be more desirable than 'to get France into a negotiation with us, where her separate interest must be pressed at a great disadvantage, in case she is disposed to pursue it'.[10] When the Dutch asked for British assistance in the defence of Antwerp which, with Maastricht, was all of Belgium that they held, the Duke remarked testily that 'it was surely necessary that, before we provoke a fresh revolution at Paris, or a war, either with the existing French Government or with another which may displace the present Government, of which war the first movement would be to place all the Netherlands fortresses in the hands of France, we should try at least the effect of showing to the world, and to the Netherlands, France engaged in concert with England and all Europe in an endeavour to pacify Belgium, and the effect of further negotiation'.[10] The conference of the Great Powers met, not as the Dutch asked, in or near Holland, to discuss how to maintain the Treaty of Vienna, but in London, to discuss how to maintain the peace of Europe by revising the Treaty of Vienna. When the Belgian delegation arrived, the Dutch found themselves relegated, like the rebels, to an ante-room.

The first Protocol of the London Conference, on 4th November, urged, authoritatively, a three months' armistice. Three weeks later Palmerston succeeded Aberdeen as chairman of the Conference. Four weeks after that (on 20th December 1830) the Conference imposed an armistice, declared the dissolution of the United Netherlands, and invited the Belgian provisional government to send representatives to London. Palmerston inherited from Wellington both a policy and an instrument — the Conference. The policy was, basically, that which Canning had applied to Russia over Greece — restraint by co-operation. The instrument was one, prima facie, more suited to a pupil of Castlereagh, the champion of Congresses, than to a self-proclaimed disciple of Canning. But Aberdeen was a very bad pupil of Castlereagh, and Palmerston showed in the next twelve months skill in the formulation of detailed objectives of which either Castlereagh or Canning might have been proud and ability as a negotiator hardly surpassed by Castlereagh himself. He was entitled to boast that he had proved himself 'a good European'.

*   *   *   *

As the novice addressed himself, the moment he took office, to this weighty matter, he took comfort in the strength of Britain's moral position, strikingly contrasting with her run-down military and even naval power. Britain had the very strongest interest in the fate of the Netherlands, and everyone recognized it. It was a cardinal principle of British foreign policy that Antwerp, 'the pistol pointed at the heart of Britain' must never be allowed to remain in hostile or likely-to-be-hostile hands. It had been so for centuries. Peel had solemnly reminded the world on 3rd November 1830 that when Pitt in the State Paper of 1805 distinguished between those countries where 'owing to their situation the interference of this country would be just and proper' and those remote, where it was 'seldom or never justified', he put the Netherlands chief among the former. 'The Importance of preventing the Low Countries, the Military Barrier of Europe, from being melted down into the general Mass of French Power, whether by Insurrection, or by Conquest, might enable the British Govt to act more promptly upon this, than perhaps upon any other Case of an Internal Character that can be stated', wrote Castlereagh in the State Paper of 1820.* Distrustful though they were of Palmerston's penchant for the constitutionalism of Louis Philippe, and his desire for co-operation with France, the Eastern Powers could never suspect him of wanting to put Belgium in pawn to France. Assuming, as they did, that it was French power and French ideas which menaced the European order, they could not fail to recognize the basic coincidence of Britain's interest and their own, and Palmerston never ceased to point it out. 'Europe never will consent, unless forced to it by a disastrous war, that Belgium should be united, directly or indirectly, to France', became his theme.[11]

Here, then, was an opportunity to make brokership between Belgium and Holland, between France and the other Powers, as honest as that of an interested party can ever be. If Palmerston became the only consistent champion of the interests of the Belgian nation, this was not because of any partiality, but from the nature of the case. For the French, as he said of Talleyrand, 'never wished to make Belgium really independent'.[12] The Dutch, the Prussians and the Russians (their reigning dynasties interrelated) all toyed, more or less seriously, with ideas of partition of the Belgic Netherlands. Palmerston's ability to say, with truth, that Britain alone had no designs for the partition, enslavement or debilitation of their country, gave him a lever with which to loosen the obduracy of the Belgians, which the French encouraged for their own purposes. The chauvinism of France was his lever for use on the Dutch and their Great Power patrons. British resolution and the ill-will of the Eastern Powers towards Louis Philippe (whom the Tsar never recognized as a bona fide monarch) was his lever on the French. His difficulties, apart from those caused by the obduracy of the weak (the Dutch and the Belgians) lay in a deficiency of *Realpolitik* on the part of the Eastern chancelleries. They were ready to say they would not tolerate a Belgium that was French. They were, on the whole, though not uniformly, willing to resist the dismemberment of Belgium, because it could hardly fail to give prestigious and military, as well as territorial, gain to France. But they were prejudiced against a people impudent enough to raise the claim of nationality against the Treaty of Vienna (what an example to the Italians and the Poles!). And though they saw, with Wellington and Palmerston, that the United Netherlands was doomed, they did not seem to see that the spirit of the Vienna Settlement required its replacement by two kingdoms *each as strong and prosperous as was feasible*. This would be but a poor second best — so poor that Palmerston suggested and secured an international *guarantee* for Belgium — but it was worth working for. The promulgation and persistent advocacy of this theme is Palmerston's distinctive contribution to policy on the Belgian question. It is also the thread that leads us through the tangled maze of negotiations at London, Brussels and the Hague.

The Eastern Powers, prejudiced in favour of Holland, were convinced that Palmerston was prejudiced in favour of the Belgians, if only from the perversity to be expected of a Liberal. They suspected, and alleged, that his support for Belgian claims with regard to the transit of persons and goods on the major riparian and land routes into Germany, much of which must be left in Holland, was dictated by British economic interest. Palmerston replied with characteristic crispness: 'Our interest in the navigation of the Scheldt, though positive and direct and not to be sacrificed, was relatively to other English commercial interests of very minor importance but to Belgium it . . . involved the decision of whether she is or is not to have any commerce at all.'[12] Could they not see that what was at issue was the viability of the Belgian state? Britain could have no interest in seeing *either* Belgium *or* Holland weak and poor. It was bad economics and worse diplomacy to accept the Dutch argument that if Antwerp were allowed to flourish as an entrepôt in Belgium, Rotterdam and Amsterdam must languish. The aim must be 'to make Belgium independent and Holland prosperous and strong'; 'to constitute Belgium substantially and really an independent state; and at the same time, to take care that the interests of Holland were not sacrificed'.[14]

The Protocol of 20th December 1830, the first important public document on which appeared Palmerston's handsome signature, bold and clear like the mind of its author, approved an independent Belgian monarchical state and implied, as did the existence of the Conference, mutual abstention by the Powers from separate intervention during the current dispute. The Protocol of 20th January 1831 enunciated the principle of mutual self-denial as a feature of the settlement. Each of the five Powers pledged itself not to seek 'any augmentation of territory, exclusive influence or isolated advantage in Belgium'. This became Palmerston's basic text. France was not to get even 'a cabbage garden or a vineyard' in Belgium or the Rhineland.[15] Nor should she get a French prince on the Belgian throne. On 3rd February 1831 the Belgian assembly was to choose between Leuchtenberg, whose Russian and Buona-partist connexions made him unacceptable to the French, and Louis Philippe's second son, le duc de Nemours, who was unacceptable to everyone else — except the Belgians. On 1st February the Conference produced a Protocol extending the principle of self-denial to exclude from the throne a prince of any of the ruling houses of the Powers. Talleyrand refused to sign, and, the same day, the Foreign Minister, Sébastiani, who had been actively canvassing the cause of Nemours in Brussels while dis-counting it in London and Paris, made the election certain by repudiating Talleyrand's signature on the Protocol of 27th January. This Protocol, together with that of 20th, constituted the *Bases de Séparation*, and prescribed the frontiers and economic relationships which were to obtain between Belgium and Holland. They fell far short of Belgian aspirations. Palmerston did not waver. He ordered ostentatious naval movements, and sent a sharp warn-ing to Paris. 'We are reluctant even to think of war', he wrote, 'but this is a legitimate occasion, and we find that we could not submit to the placing of the Duc de Nemours on the throne of Belgium without danger to the safety and a sacrifice of the honour of the country. . . . We require that Belgium should be really and not nominally independent.'[15]

In the House of Commons, on 18th February, his old assailant Hume, untiring apostle of retrenchment, complained that in interfering in the affairs of Holland and Belgium Palmerston was following the doctrines of the Holy Alliance. It was the first time that Palmerston, as Secretary of State, was challenged by that school of extreme non-interventionists of which Cobden and Bright were to be, from the next decade, more notorious spokes-men. Never was it easier for Palmerston to answer with an almost unanimous House behind him. There was no parallel, he said, between interference in the internal affairs of an established state aimed at the subjection of a people or dictating its form of government, and this exercise in determining boundaries and the conditions of co-existence of the two parts of the Netherlands; Holland was 'a state whose independence concerns the security of the other countries of Europe' and the Powers had a right to tell the Belgians that they might not despoil her of ancient and historical boundaries or commit aggression against Holland or Luxemburg. (Ten days earlier the Conference ordered the Belgians to evacuate Maastricht and Luxemburg, threatening blockade in the event of non-compliance.) And the Powers had a right to say that such and such a king would be dangerous to them, 'and such a person, therefore, we will not have'.

This the Powers had said, with effect. On 5th February Louis Philippe declined the throne for his son. The magnitude of Palmerston's work for European peace in 1831 is apt to be underrated because it seems self-evident that so long as Britain took her part with her Allies of 1813–15, France must give way. But the Eastern Powers were distracted, first by the threat, and then by the reality, of revolution in Poland, in Italy, in southern Germany, and Britain's land power was very weak and her social condition disturbed. *Realpolitik* in the end prevailed in Paris, but there was no guarantee that it would. Any French government must take account of the number of Frenchmen who thirsted for Napoleonic vigour, prestige, recovery of territory and who longed to turn into protégés of France states erected or enlarged to confine her, the number (if rather smaller) who wished to unfurl the banners of revolutionary Liberalism and Nationality must also be considered. Their appetites were not sated by the considerable diplomatic triumph accorded them by Wellington, the admission of France as an equal partner in a conference to revise part of the treaty imposed upon her in defeat in 1814 and 1815. The French government must therefore go through the motions of truculence, or yield to one more genuinely truculent. And 'going through the motions' is apt to drift into becoming the real thing. It was, moreover, far from certain that out of the divisions and distractions, actual and potential, of the other Powers, and the cupidity of Prussia and even of Austria, France would not be able to snatch advantage. There was much to be said for being obstructive, and for encouraging the Belgians to be obstructive, in the hope that 'something would turn up'. General de Gaulle is not the first man

Emily Lamb in her youth, when she was Lady Cowper

to understand that being obstructive inflates the importance of France. But Palmerston, the sole Foreign Minister well disposed towards the French régime, never wavered in his insistence that out of the Belgian question France must win no advantage. In April 1831 the cautious realist, Casimir Périer, came to power in Paris. On 17th he accepted the *Bases de Séparation* and the Protocol of 19th February calling on the Dutch and Belgians to accept them. It only remained, apparently, to secure Belgian acceptance.

Palmerston had so far been as careful as possible to minister to the self-respect of the Belgians. 'We are not conquerors disposing of subjugated kingdoms', he informed the British representative in Brussels, Lord Ponsonby, a relative of Lady Grey: 'We are Powers looking after our security and mediating between contending parties.'[17] But he had used the Protocol of 19th February to remind both the Powers and the Belgians that the crucial question was the maintenance of peace. He was now winking at the strenuous efforts of Ponsonby to secure the election of Leopold of Coburg, whom Grey had favoured from the first, approving the proposal that he should marry a daughter of Louis Philippe. But Leopold was no cipher. He had withdrawn his acceptance of the Greek throne because the frontier arrangements were unpopular in Greece and even if he could secure election in Belgium with the *Bases de Séparation* unmodified, he did not intend to start with such a handicap. Notwithstanding Palmerston's threat on 29th May to withdraw Ponsonby if the Belgians did not accept the *Bases*, Leopold (elected 4th June) made his acceptance conditional upon their amendment, and the Belgian acceptance contained reservations. The Powers then agreed certain modifications, contained in the *Eighteen Articles* of 26th June. Belgium accepted these terms and Leopold assumed the throne (21st July).

It was now the turn of the Dutch to defy the Powers. Their armies marched into Belgium and would have overrun it if the French had not moved. Nothing could prevent them moving. But Palmerston contrived that they should be made to work for Europe, not France. He prevailed upon the other Powers to accept the French army and the British fleet (which played an observer's role) as the mandatories of the Conference, on the strict understanding that the French would withdraw when the armistice lines had been restored (6th August). The Dutch withdrew. The French tried to bargain from their position of strength. In particular, they

c

resented the fact that France was excluded from discussions on the future of the Barrier Fortresses, and submitted proposals of their own. Such pretensions, Palmerston asserted on 17th, were utterly inadmissible. One did not consult the housebreaker as to the bolts and bars on one's doors and windows. These fortresses were part of Europe's protection against France, and Europe was not to be dictated to at bayonet point. 'The French must go out of Belgium, or we have a general war, and war in a given number of days' (17th August).[18] Once again the solidarity of Britain and the Eastern Powers was decisive. The French withdrew. But there was a price to be paid. The Eastern Powers remarked that the events of the month of August had shown the Belgians they could not stand on their own, and insisted on a revision of the *Eighteen Articles*. The *Twenty Four Articles* of 14th October 1831 were therefore a retreat towards, though not to the *Bases de Séparation*. The Belgians rejected them. Palmerston took the gloves off. He could not have these foolish people for ever playing into the hands of the French. And so he wrote, 18th October. 'The patience of the Five Powers is exhausted. We have interests of our own to consult, which prescribe the preservation of peace, and a general war can be prevented only by putting an end to the local contest between Holland and Belgium. If the Belgians should refuse consent to these Articles we should immediately take steps to compel their acquiescence.' Leopold, referring to the conditions of his election, hinted at abdication. Palmerston replied: 'With Your Majesty's retirement would vanish the independence of Belgium.' The Belgians yielded.[19]

Now came Palmerston's coup — 'an immense thing done', he called it. Back in January he had taken up, but pruned out of all recognition, a proposal of Sébastiani and Talleyrand for a Belgium both federal and neutral, a Switzerland without Switzerland's natural defences. If there must be a Belgium, the French wanted it loosely constructed, feeble, doomed to dependence, in no sense an impediment to future French designs. Palmerston seized on the idea of neutralization to make Belgium the ward of Europe, a country needing no alliances because each Power was pledged to defend it against any other. After Palmerston's death, ministers would try to explain away this collective *guarantee* as not obliging any to act unless all did. But it was not for such a worthless agreement that Palmerston struggled from January, when the principle was approved by the Conference (France equivocating), to 15th November, when he 'got Austria, Russia and Prussia to sign a formal treaty of friendship and guarantee with Leopold',[20] thus, obliquely, recognizing a state raised by national revolution in breach of the Vienna Treaty. France signed too. If, strictly speaking, 'the scrap of paper' which the Germans ignored in 1914 (and thereby brought Britain to war to redress the Balance of Power and uphold the sanctity of treaties) was the Treaty of London, 19th April 1839, the essential point was contained in the Treaty of 15th November 1831.

* * * *

Palmerston's diplomacy between November 1830 and November 1831 won from that slippery veteran Talleyrand the tribute that he was perhaps the ablest man of affairs he had ever encountered. Palmerston, of course, started with certain advantages. Britain's stake in the fate of the Netherlands was direct and acknowledged. She was the natural mediator between France and the Eastern Powers. Palmerston was the only Foreign Minister at the Conference; he was its convener and its chairman. But he was an untried amateur confronted with diplomats of the calibre and experience of Talleyrand, Esterhazy, Lieven and Bülow, behind whom lay the expertise of the professionals specially accredited to the Conference. Yet fixity of purpose, the steady pursuit of practicable and sensible aims, cogently enunciated, pungently explained, unceasingly reiterated, combined with much finesse and sheer hard work, enabled him to achieve dominance. He saw the wood, but he also studied the trees. He had behind him no chancellery such as those of Vienna and Paris, compared with which the Foreign Office was a crude machine, but he extracted from the departmental officials, high and intermediate, labours of which they had not thought themselves capable, and from clerks and copyists an excellence never demanded before. He himself set a formidable standard of efficiency, although his unpunctuality soon became the despair of subordinates and almost an insult to the principal foreign envoys, which the vastness of his business explains but does not altogether excuse. His diary and private correspondence show the pace at which he lived[21]—

[31st December 1831] — My day was not an idle one, for, having left the office only at three in the morning the night before, I had, before the

Cabinet at one, to write an important despatch to Vienna, to hear Czartoryski's account of the whole Polish War, and to discuss with Cluptede all the squabbles of the German Diet. After the Cabinet I had to see Van de Weyer, Lieven, Bülow, Esterhazy and Wessemberg upon various different subjects, and afterwards to send off messengers with dispatches and private letters to Vienna, Berlin, Paris and Brussels. However, I contrived to get it all done by about two this morning — and now, for my consolation, I have staring me in the face thirteen boxes full of papers, which ought all to be read forthwith, and which have come to me since yesterday morning. . . .

They also show how it was that, living at this sort of pace for the greater part of the time, he enabled an evidently tough physique to survive the ravages of gout for thirty-four more years, to the eve of his eighty-first birthday. He professed a proper respect for English doctors (Paris, he said, was healthier than London but the French medicos killed more of their patients), but no more than that. He had his own golden rules for health, which he tirelessly expounded to all and sundry. The principal one was that it was no good abstaining from this or that, if one abstained from exercise. Time must always be found, or almost always, for a ride in the Park, or, failing that, to the office. Fresh air was a thing to be courted. So[21]—

[31st October 1831] — After dinner yesterday I went and slept at the 'Star and Garter' to have a cool night and fresh ride in today, besides getting four hours' work at a paper I had to draw up, free from one single interruption. . . .

It should be added that he was not one to stint himself of sexual relief. He was very much a man of the world, moving on easy terms with the aristocracy of Europe, deploying, in the Belgian negotiation, social graces and a persuasive tongue, though often longing to speak as bluntly and woundingly as he thought and was in the future often to talk and write. Yet there was ruthlessness behind the mask of gaiety and savoir faire. When powerful advocacy, adroit drafting, and patient cajolery (in fluent French) failed, he deliberately exploited his superior physical and mental stamina to see if the sheer attrition of time, fatigue and hunger would carry the day. He was equally ruthless with himself. He taxed to the full a wonderful memory and chronically weak eyesight by the sheer drudgery of mastering his subject-matter. This he achieved, not, indeed, completely — he was no prodigy, only a man of intelligence and capacity — but beyond most of the professionals. And when he addressed himself to the minutiae, as in his *Theme* of September 1832 (a detailed scheme for the regulation of the economic and financial relations between Holland and Belgium), his War Office experience of drafting close arguments in small causes proved its worth. Draughtsmanship was one of his strongest points.

At the heart of his achievement in 1831 lay strength of will. It is too easy to say that the Conference succeeded because the price of failure was a general war. High stakes do not guarantee success. Palmerston provided the will to succeed, many of the vital initiatives, many of the formulae for breaking deadlocks. Largely through his sense of direction, his persistence, his finesse, the negotiators frequently found themselves behaving as though they were a European cabinet. It was a coalition cabinet, to be sure, in which each had in mind the special interests which he was accredited to represent, and there were jealousies and even treacheries between colleagues. But the Conference acquired, as it were, a collective personality, well suited to its mandate. Its members spoke for the general interest, as in their Protocol of 19th February 1831, when they said: 'Each Nation has its particular rights: but Europe also has its right: it is the Social Order which has given it this.' A camaraderie developed. They allowed themselves to act on the maxim proclaimed by Palmerston to the Belgian envoy: 'The only use of a Plenipotentiary is to disobey his instructions. A clerk or messenger would do, if it is only necessary strictly to follow them.'[22]

Palmerston's very success had its own peculiar perils. By November 1831 he thought everything would be plain sailing. (He was an incurable optimist.) 'The Dutch King may sulk if he will, but he can no longer endanger the peace of Europe, since all the five would be equally bound to resist him, and his only hopes were placed on the possibility of a division among them', he said.[23] But with the Treaty of 15th November came a relaxation, not only of tension, but of resolve. The Eastern Powers were unwilling to coerce the Dutch. They were even reluctant to ratify the Treaty. And they severally, but with instructive unanimity, decided (in effect) to call a halt to the pretensions of the Conference. It had become too much the organ of its president, 'a sort of European power of itself . . . a despotic assembly . . . promulgat[ing] its decrees in protocols and treaties' complained Ancillon, the

Prussian.[24] The chancelleries of Europe had never known what to expect from the next protocol, except that it was more likely to represent the view of Palmerston than of any other participant. This was a very unpalatable experience for Metternich and the Tsar. The former thought that all the threads of diplomacy ought to meet at Vienna. Both disliked accepting, and to boot 'guaranteeing', the fruits of a successful, and national, revolution. Their ratifications were not effective until May 1832. Palmerston had declined to summon the Conference again until they were to hand. Only then could he tell Parliament that assuredly Belgium was safe, and Holland preserved as 'a second Line of Defence should the Neutrality of Belgium at any time be violated by France', and 'venture to predict' that the arrangement would be more stable and effectual for its purpose than that of 1815.[25]

The Eastern Powers had been ready enough to join in telling the Belgians that the Powers would 'cause their decisions to be respected and executed' (8th February 1831). There was annexed to the Protocol of 14th October the pledge, drafted by the Russians, that if Belgium accepted the *Twenty-Four Articles* of that date, the Powers would secure the execution of these terms. According to Palmerston's later account (to Metternich, 7th October 1837*) the Eastern Powers expected Belgium to reject the terms, and, when they found they were wrong, treated the annex as a dead letter. Palmerston, who stigmatized the Dutch rejection as 'the most impudent communication in the annals of diplomacy', gave the Eastern Powers the choice between sulking while the two Western Powers executed the Five-Power agreement or endorsing the Anglo-French operations as they had in August 1831. He dismissed the marshalling of Prussian armies in the Rhineland as mere bluff (was it not prudent precaution?). The British and French impounded Dutch ships and merchandise. A French army showed the Dutch troops out of the citadel of Antwerp (which they had never lost) under the guns of the British fleet (23rd December 1832). Still the Dutch would not accept the Articles, though they opened the Scheldt. And so Palmerston continued the blockade. Peel contended that, since Belgium was now de facto free, the embargo was 'in favour of third parties' and contrary to international law. Palmerston's retort was crushing: 'I should like to know what honourable member will undertake to tell me, that the faithful performance of an engagement entered into by the

King of England, by a treaty signed and ratified by him, is not a duty connected with British interests, which he is morally and legally bound to fulfil by every means in his power.'[25]

On 21st May 1833 the King of the Netherlands entered into a convention with Britain and France recognizing, on a temporary and de facto basis, the status quo. This meant that the Belgians retained Limburg and much of Luxemburg which, by the Treaty, were to go to Holland, and made no contribution to the public-debt charges of the former United Netherlands. Not until 1838 were the Dutch willing to recognize the de jure existence of Belgium. The Treaty of London, 19th April 1839, declared Belgium independent and perpetually neutral under 'guarantee' of the Five Powers.

CHAPTER III

THE PATRON OF LIBERALISM

THERE had been a spirit in Palmerston's speech of 1st June 1829, and other speeches in 1830, to give the neo-Holy Allies cause to fear that where Canning had scourged them with Whips, Palmerston would scourge them with scorpions. But until 1832 there was precious little sign of it. His attitude as between Belgium and Holland was arbitral. The Powers, he told the Commons on 18th February 1831, had a right to say to the Belgians: 'You have never been an independent state, never had a national King; you have been the servants of one master after another. . . . You are a legislature of yesterday, your independence has hardly been established, and you have no right to claim as yours that which by right belongs to another.' There was a nation in Europe in very different case, an ancient Catholic monarchy that at times had mastered one province after another of European Russia, whose legislature had been swept away by foreign intervention, and its territory divided between Russia, Prussia and Austria. While the Belgians rose for what they had never had, and had never been suspected of desiring, national independence, the Poles rose with, at least as their minimum demand, no greater ambition than the security of constitutional rights granted by the Russian Tsar (as King of Poland) in accordance with promises contained in a treaty annexed to that of Vienna. So, at least, argued those Radicals who tried to make a case for manly protest by Britain which could stand the strain of International Law. Others, and a far more numerous faction at Paris, wanted a crusade to win full independence for the Poles, whose leaders were in fact so unrealistic as to demand of Nicholas I the attachment to Poland of vast and vital areas of Russia and whose Diet on 25th January 1831 declared the deposition of the Tsar, thus (it must be thought) putting themselves in sharp conflict with the Vienna Treaty.

Palmerston gave neither aid nor comfort to the Polish nationalists. Even his suggestion that it would be wise to be clement

43

and to maintain the constitution — sweetened by the addendum 'We do not intrude our advice nor offer our mediation much as we have been pressed by several to do so'[1]—was delayed until the Poles (who under the constitution had maintained a considerable army) seemed to be winning. But Warsaw fell in September. It was against his judgement that Palmerston was compelled by the cabinet to insist that the Tsar's obligation to maintain the constitution was unimpaired by the revolt, and that if he did not do so, Britain might not recognize his title to Poland. He feared the protest would embarrass the Belgian negotiation, and cited Canning's precept that one should not threaten where one did not mean to act.

Palmerston's concern for peace and the maintenance of the Balance of Power — which meant, in effect, the containment of France — was seen in his attitude to Italian affairs. Italy was distinguished from the Rhineland and Switzerland, other possible directions of French aggression, in two respects. Firstly, the scene of Napoleon's first triumphs was to most Frenchmen, including those with grandiose designs of making the Mediterranean a French lake, the most attractive field of all for adventure. If revolution came to Italy, as in 1821, but this time by direct contagion from Paris, and Austria, as in 1821, intervened to suppress it, the impulse to French intervention was likely to be irresistible, or at least not resisted. Flahaut, the former general of Napoleon, a friend of many of the new British ministers, told Palmerston in February 1831 that 'the interference of Austria in Italy would produce a more popular war than the reunion of Belgium or the Rhenish provinces'.[2] Secondly, Italy had a place in British memories too. The navy had several times loosened, and even disturbed, Napoleon's hold on the peninsula. Sicily he had never obtained; Sardinia and Corsica for a time he lost; Malta was snatched from under his nose. Here, then, the navy could act. If the French attacked the Austrians, they were very liable to find British marines at Genoa to threaten their communications and ensure their withdrawal. The Austrians had been pressed by Castlereagh to take Lombardy (in exchange for the Belgic Netherlands) to be a bulwark against France, sustaining Piedmont. And who could doubt that a revolutionary government anywhere in Italy would be under French influence and infect all neighbouring states?

Ideally, therefore, revolution should be averted by reform, on the model being attempted by the British government at home. Piedmont was told this when she asked for a British 'guarantee' against France. But the Italian rulers in general lacked the intelligence to see that this was true in the long run, and in the short run knew that Austrian intervention to save them would be almost automatic. When the Austrians entered Modena, Parma and Bologna, were they to be condemned? Palmerston thought not. To condemn would be to imperil the Belgian negotiation and incite the French to counter-intervene. He therefore, in a cautionary note, refused 'to enter into the abstract and not easily definable principles upon which interference and non-interference should depend', and concentrated on trying to prevent a Franco-Austrian war.

The most likely arena of conflict between France and Austria was Piedmont. Britain, like Austria, was bound to aid Piedmont against French aggression, but not bound to aid her against Austria. An Austrian attack was, however, bound to produce a French response. Both could probably be prevented by a British 'guarantee', but British prejudice was against definite commitment. When the government in Turin expressed the hope that the British government's declared policy of peace and non-interference did not preclude assistance against a French attack, Palmerston replied that its best security lay in making clear that it would not permit either French or Austrian intervention in the internal affairs or on the territory of Piedmont. But there was French interference *against* the Piedmontese government by propaganda, inflaming Liberals who were especially strong in Genoa (awarded against its will to Piedmont in 1815), and there were small raids across the Alps. Instead of open attack there was subversion. The more formidable it became, the more it would drive the government at Turin into the arms of Metternich, ever ready to embrace it, for Austria dare not have a pro-French republican government on the borders of Lombardy. Palmerston pointed this out to the French, but even Casimir Périer, so far from suppressing subversive activities against Piedmont, warned Turin that they would be intensified if Piedmont were to reject a French request for the passage of troops across the country. Turin naturally turned to Vienna. But, before doing so, she turned to London, asking for formal assurances. Even though they would have implied 'guaranteeing' a regime no more liberal than the Austrian and less competent, Palmerston was prepared, in the circumstances, to give them. His colleagues, however, demurred.[3] Piedmont, in July 1831, signed a secret defence agreement with Austria. The Dutch invasion of Belgium (see above, p. 35) came at a fortunate time, distracting the French from Italy. They merely indicated that if Austrian troops again intervened beyond the frontiers of Lombardy and Venetia, they would have to do so too.

*   *   *   *

Palmerston had made it clear that his approval of the French régime implied no weakening of Britain's resolve to maintain the territorial status quo in Europe, subject only to Belgian independence; that it was conditional upon Louis Philippe agreeing with Palmerston that the interests of France, and of the Orleans dynasty, were better served by internal improvement than foreign adventure. Britain's 'desire for "terms of the most intimate friendship" depended on France not meaning "to open a new chapter of encroachment and conquest" '. There were to be no 'nibblings', for 'if once these great Powers begin to taste blood, they will . . . speedily devour their victim'. Appeasement (as the twentieth century would call it) was ruled out. If the French were 'bent on encroachment and war, no concession will keep the peace, and the surrender of rights will only be . . . a temptation to a speedy repetition of such profitable attempts'. Should Talleyrand repeat his complaint that 'our confidence in him seems abated', he was to be told that 'this was the natural consequence of our finding that he was aiming at obtaining for France territorial acquisitions, at the same time that France was crying out for non-intervention and peace'.[4] When Louis Philippe had to disclaim the Belgian throne for Nemours Flahaut, to soften the blow, suggested an offensive and defensive alliance (involving the repudiation of Castlereagh's Quadruple Alliance against France). Palmerston told him that 'if danger exists, it is more likely to come *from* than against France'.[5] 'The greater part of our difficulties with the Belgians have arisen from the double diplomacy, double-dealing, infirmity of purpose and want of principle of the French government,' he wrote, in characteristic terms, to Paris.[6]

Soon this ceased to be true. After the French evacuation of Belgium, consequent on Palmerston's ultimatum of 17th August

1831, relations improved. The thorny problem of the Barrier Fortresses was settled by a convention on 14th December. Like the British, the French ratified the Treaty of 15th November, and they disbanded large bodies of men. On 9th February 1832 Palmerston made in parliament a significant speech. 'We are fully sensible of the value of the friendship of so liberal and intelligent a power as France,' he said. 'We trust that the days are now gone by when petty feuds and paltry jealousies, and selfish notions of mistaken interests, will have any influence on either Government. The two countries have too many interests, and, I trust, too many feelings, in common, to allow themselves to be separated by those who are the enemies of free institutions in both.' The Prime Minister spoke similarly in the Lords. These speeches outraged the common British feeling that France was the 'natural enemy', and the Opposition tried to exploit this prejudice by misrepresenting Palmerston's relations with the French, saying that he had really given them Belgium. But the French had found Palmerston a tough and unyielding obstacle to their designs. Now, however, it was the Eastern Powers who were giving him most trouble. February 1832 was the month that Dom Pedro sailed from France with an army of Napoleonic veterans and Palmerston's blessing (which was about all he had to give) to Terceira to prepare an attack on Oporto. Palmerston had been willing to give up the charter (perhaps he had read Canning's comments on it) if the Powers and Spain would co-operate in getting rid of Dom Miguel.[7] The Eastern Powers' reply was to threaten Spanish action if Pedro attacked. This touched Palmerston's most exposed nerve. If he was committed to anything by what he had said before he went to the Foreign Office, it was to the expulsion of this usurper. If Britain by all her traditions was committed to anything it was, next to the safety of the Netherlands, the preservation of Portugal as a client state. Even the fact that the Treaty of 15th November had not yet been ratified did not prevent very blunt communications to the British envoys in the three Eastern capitals. These people must learn that 'the days of the Holy Alliance are gone by never to return and that such propositions do not belong to the present time'. Britain would see 'fair play' in Portugal, and if anyone else broke into the ring, 'there may be more bloody noses than those of the original combatants'.[8] (Palmerston was an enthusiastic devotee of wrestling and boxing as well as horse-racing.)

'The estate of Portugal' was in the hands of a robber belonging to that syndicate of arbitrary powers of which Tsar Nicholas was the patron. In March 1831 Palmerston had predicted that when the Russians had reconquered Poland their tone over Belgium would change, and sway that of Austria and Prussia.[9] In June 1832 he told Matuszewic that for a twelvemonth all the difficulties had come from Russia[10] — a poor return for his restraint over Poland and the unpopular 'Dutch Loan' agreement of 16th November 1831.[A] But if of the neo-Holy Alliance the Tsar was the patron, Metternich was the brain. Sooner or later he and a Palmerston with the prejudices revealed in that speech of 1829 were bound to collide. There were already fierce skirmishes over the awful misgovernment of the Papal States. At the time of the Austrian intervention, Palmerston warned Metternich that the temporary application of external force was no recipe for permanent tranquillity and he, recognizing the need for some reform, agreed to a Five-Power conference to advise on the matter. This was a modest triumph both for Palmerston and for France; it was Europe acting not in neo-Holy Alliance style to restore order by suppressing revolt (Austria had just done that), but in Castle-reagh's sense of concert to deal with a threat to peace (caused by domestic tyranny and incompetence). But at the conference only the British representative was in earnest about a thorough-going reform, and so Palmerston ordered him to withdraw. In 1832 another revolt in the Papal Legations, perhaps deliberately pro-voked by Austrian and papal agents, brought the Austrians back. The French, understanding that Britain would react badly to an advance through Piedmont, but bound by their warning of 1831 to do something, sent an expedition by sea to the Ancona. Palmer-ston refused to get excited about 'this lark in the Adriatic' and (in effect) declined Metternich's anxious request to press for the simultaneous withdrawal of the Austrians and the French. He knew only too well that Metternich wished to get the French out of

[A] Castlereagh had committed Britain to share with the United Netherlands the sums due as interest and payments into the sinking fund on account of a Russian loan during the war, conditional upon the maintenance of the United Netherlands. By the Palmerston–Lieven Convention of 16th Nov. 1831 Britain agreed to bear the greater part of this obligation, as Holland openly and Russia covertly objected to the separation of Belgium, which Britain promoted. The Convention was sharply attacked in parliament, and was perhaps responsible for awakening dark suspicions in David Urquhart's mind. The sums due continued to be paid to the enemy during the Crimean War.

Ancona in order to get the Pope out of his promises to reform his administration. Shortly afterwards there came news of the long-awaited Austrian ratification of the Belgian Treaty of November. This, however, was found to be dependent on the Prussian, which was itself dependent on the Russian. Palmerston could not easily forgive Metternich for 'making an April fool of him'.[11] He was in no mood to receive, in June 1832, hard on the Russian ratification of the Belgian Treaty, a démarche from the Eastern Powers on the affairs of Portugal, intended to prevent the Pedroist landing. He determined to retaliate in kind.

★   ★   ★   ★

So far Palmerston had conducted the foreign affairs of Britain in a masterly manner, but on traditional lines. He had formulated no 'system' of Balance of Power diplomacy, no intellectual system of foreign policy. He had inherited the former from Castlereagh, the latter from Canning. His activity, shrewd, empirical, confident, had been conformable with both, though accident decreed that he should seem rather a Castlereagh than a Canning, and the resemblance had been increased by his lack of eloquence, his aristocratic manner, his failure to exploit public opinion in support of his policies. Certainly his conduct had seemed hardly at all tinged by his declared liberal sentiments and not at all by sentimentality or ideology. Its keynote was a hard realism, for which, however, he was not given due credit at home because of the intense concentration upon Parliamentary Reform and the fact that virtually all the speaking talent in the House of Commons was Tory or Radical.

Anyone who imagined, however, that the Palmerston of 1831 was not at heart the Palmerston of 1829–30 was due, in 1832, for a rude shock. The truth is, that in 1831 he was under restraint — the restraint of colleagues; the restraint of home politics (the battle for Reform was no time for a government which claimed to be conservative to frighten waverers by an outburst of Liberalism in its foreign policy); the self-restraint imposed because Palmerston rightly gave priority to the Belgian negotiations and saw that a time when there was a real danger of revolutionary France breaking her bounds was no time to preach a Liberal crusade. But such restraint went against the grain; for Palmerston's natural method of expressing his views on foreign questions was vehement and

exaggerated. Even if one dismisses the speech of 1st June 1829 as
an Opposition speech intended to make him the alternative Foreign
Secretary, one cannot get over the ringing declaration of faith in
the mysterious alchemy of constitutionalism contained in a private
letter on the July Revolution in France[12]—

> Well what a glorious event this is in France! How admirably the French
> have done it! What energy and courage in the day of trial, and what
> wisdom and moderation in the hour of victory. . . . And what has wrought
> this mysterious change [from 'the excesses and outrages and horrors and
> insanity of 1792 and 93']? . . . Nothing but a short and imperfect enjoy-
> ment of a free Press and a free constitution. Let the Metternichs and
> Wellingtons, who would chain down the mind of man to the scale of their
> police regulations and military codes, and would have the human race
> think, speak and write by ordinance and general order . . . say whether
> any men are so interested in the diffusion of knowledge and the extension
> of political civilisation as arbitrary ministers and tyrannical monarchs.

Palmerston kept himself on a tight rein throughout 1831, but felt
that he could allow himself an unwonted freedom just when his
patience, which had been great, and was not a natural gift, was
exhausted. Eighteen months' experience at the Foreign Office had
confirmed, rather than modified, the picture of the neo-Holy
Alliance he had formed in cabinet in 1827–8 and published in
1829–30. He had become thoroughly tired of seeing at every corner
the shadow of Metternich 'sally[ing] forth like another Mahomet
with the Koran of Vienna in one hand and martial law in the other,
to dragoon all Europe into passive submission to what he thinks,
and they not, the perfection of human society'.[13]

   The factors which dictated restraint, and tactful dealing with the
Eastern Powers, had, by mid-1832, melted away. The Reform Bill
was law. Everyone knew that in the elections to be held, under the
new arrangements, at the end of the year the Tories would be
scattered like chaff, and the only question was whether the new
members would not be too radical for a ministry of moderates.
There are indications that the sense of relief inspired the whole
cabinet with a new courage in matters of foreign policy. The
Convention of London (7th May 1832) had settled the future of
Greece; the Treaty of London regarding Belgium had been ratified
by all the Powers. Ministers were not to be intimidated by the
impertinence of the Eastern Powers over Portugal. Palmerston
thought that it was bad enough having to mount the operation
against Miguel by indirect means, because of the constricting

inheritance of 'non-intervention' which was rejected by the Eastern Powers and by French hearts if not official lips. He and Grey, both deeply committed to the expulsion of Miguel, had been tempted to abandon 'non-intervention', but concluded, regretfully, that the thing must be done 'decently', with formal regard for Portuguese independence.[15] For, as Grey said, 'what pretence have we for assisting openly an invasion of Portugal of which he is sovereign de facto, without much appearance on the part of the people to shake off his dominion?'.[14] Miguel's leading opponents were in exile or in gaol, and the priests, peasantry and many of the nobility believed that Pedro, branded a Liberal and Freemason, was an enemy of God and the Church. Palmerston accepted Grey's verdict, but wished they had 'boldly and openly espoused the cause of Donna Maria'.[16]

Sir Charles Webster held that Palmerston's failure, in June 1832, to answer in Parliament Radical attacks on the Russian proceedings in Poland was an 'eloquent silence' and marked 'the beginning of Palmerston's public defence of the Liberal Movement'.[17] Palmerston could not condone the proceedings, and therefore said nothing. But he took occasion on 7th August to remind the House that it was the Poles who, justifiably or otherwise, began the war; to defend the Russians against charges of aggression in Persia and Turkey; to refer to Russia as 'one of those Powers with whom we are in alliance, who profess to be, and whom I believe to be, desirous to be upon the best terms with this country'. He had marked down Metternich as his antagonist — Metternich, who was trying to sabotage the Belgian settlement, to preserve papalist iniquity in central Italy, to secure the dominion of Miguel in Portugal, to contrive the succession of his Spanish equivalent Don Carlos, and to erode such constitutionalism as existed in Germany. On 2nd August 1832 Palmerston made in the House of Commons an electrifying pronouncement upon Britain's relationship to Europe's ideological war. He assumed the moral leadership of the Liberal cause for which he had called in 1829–30. It was said that 200,000 copies of the speech were printed by the German Liberals.

The key words in this dramatic departure from the norms of British diplomacy were these:

I, for one, am prepared to admit that the independence of constitutional states, whether they are powerful, like France and the United States, or of less relative importance, such as the minor States of Germany, never can be a matter of indifference to the British Parliament, or, I should hope, to the British public. *I consider the constitutional states to be the natural allies of this country*; and, whoever may be in office. . . . I am persuaded that no English ministry will be performing its duty if it is inattentive to their interests.

British Foreign Secretaries had talked and written much of a common interest in preventing foreign intervention in domestic quarrels; a common interest in settling in conference disputes threatening the general peace; a common interest with all the other Powers in preventing aggression by France; a special British interest in the fate of the Netherlands and Portugal. Canning had sometimes, for applause at home, seemed to imply some special identity of interest between constitutional states. But to ascribe to Britain a special role in regard to any state, irrespective of other circumstances, *because* it was constitutional, was an unheard of thing for a British minister to do. The Tories were horrified. They had been wont to profess in public (what Canning confessed in private) neutrality in Europe's ideological war, while in fact leaning, as far as the British political system allowed, to the 'Party of Order'. Any other course, they believed, branded its author a friend of the 'Party of Movement', the European equivalent of those 'Destructives' whose advent to a reformed House of Commons they awaited with almost hysterical apprehension.

*   *   *   *

Lord Durham, the Radical, in his self-vaunted effort to improve relations with Russia, explained Palmerston's speech away as an effort to prevent France monopolizing the field as the champion of Liberalism in Germany. Any idea that it was the mere aberration of one man disappeared with public knowledge of the dispatch to the German courts, dated 7th September 1832, for that had been revised by the Prime Minister and approved by the cabinet. In its letter, indeed, the dispatch does not depend on the doctrine of 2nd August, for it professes to be, like dispatches on Poland, an expression of opinion by one of the contracting parties on the construction of the Treaty of Vienna. The Constitution of the German Diet was one of the documents annexed to the Treaty. Palmerston held that the Six Resolutions recently passed (unanimously) by the Diet (which consisted of the representatives of the unmediatized German states, including Austria, Holstein and

Luxemburg) against the freedom of the press and any extension of the suffrage in any of those member-states which had representative institutions were a breach of the Constitution and hence of the Treaty. Metternich replied that Palmerston did not understand the German Constitution and called to the German states to repulse 'arbitrary interference in the affairs of Germany'. Perhaps he enjoyed being able to use this 'tu quoque' argument, but Palmerston, too, was pleased to see the chancellor of Austria fleeing to the unaccustomed refuge of 'non-intervention'. Palmerston had answered him in advance:

... As long as our commerce is of importance to us — as long as continental armies are in existence — as long as it is possible that an overgrown power in one quarter may become dangerous to a power in another — so long must England look with interest on the transactions of the continent; and so long is it proper for this country, in the maintenance of its own independence, not to shut its eyes to anything that threatens the independence of Germany. ...

Here was a species of diplomatic revolution. Britain had often shown such interest in the past, but what seemed presaged now was a spate of lectures from Britain on the internal affairs of other countries. The 'interference by friendly counsel and advice' which Palmerston on 2nd August contrasted with armed interference, was surely a case of threatening where one did not mean to perform. It was likely to waste Britain's moral influence in what Palmerston's American biographer, Professor Bell, calls, apropos of Germany, 'a series of barren episodes' and impart unnecessary heat to diplomatic intercourse. It is fair criticism of Palmerston that he rather relished the latter. With regard to the former he was converted to the view that 'ineffective protest is better than tacit acquiescence in wrong'.[18] And there is this to be said for him, that in a war of opinion protest is never utterly ineffective. The battle goes on, and things can never be quite what they would have been if the protest had never been made. Palmerston, by implication, convicted his predecessors of failing to see the battle whole, a mistake never made by the arbitrary Powers. Castlereagh and Canning had been concerned with the maintenance of the *territorial* settlement of Vienna. Palmerston was in no sense disloyal to that. But in the contest between arbitrary government and freedom the neo-Holy Allies did not recognize the importance of frontiers. Was Britain to go on washing her hands in pious abstention while they poured troops in here, money and supplies there, propaganda somewhere else? Why not drive them on to the defensive by appealing to the opinion of free men and would-be free men? Why not tease and torment them, if only to undermine the self-confidence of all but the most unimaginative and bone-headed of their rulers, generals, ministers, policemen and bureaucrats? Why not make life difficult for Metternich? For Metternich lived in fear that he had set his hand to a life's work which was bound to fail. Before he came into office Palmerston had recalled to the House of Commons 'that gloomy discontent — that reckless disquiet — that murmuring sullenness which pervaded Europe after the overthrow of Buona-parte . . . so unlike the joyful gladness that might have been looked for among men just released from the galling yoke of a foreign military tyrant'.[19] That spirit was still abroad. The chancellor of Austria himself did not see 'how with such a France and such an England it is to be withstood'.[20] But he deemed it his duty to go on trying.

The Austrian representative, Neumann, was instructed to protest against the speech of 2nd August. Palmerston told him 'what I had refrained from saying in the House of Commons'[21]—

. . . It was impossible not to fancy one saw a settled design on the part of the Austrian government to put down constitutional freedom wherever it exists and to cherish bad government wherever it is to be found; that the symptoms of this were to be traced from the Vistula to the Tagus; that Austria, as we *know*, counselled Russia to destroy the Polish constitution; that she has mainly contributed to prevent any tolerable system of government from being established in the Roman States; that in Germany she is the author of measures which if pushed to their full application would overthrow all the constitutions; that in Switzerland she wished to persuade us to interfere and to strip the country of its neutrality; and that as to the Peninsula she wanted to establish the position that Spain had an exclusive right to uphold by her arms the monstrous misgovernment and tyranny of Miguel . . . that the only time when Austria had shown the slightest disposition to real friendship for France was when Paris was declared in a state of siege and it was thought that Louis Philippe was going to govern against law and by military force. . . .

This analysis of neo-Holy Alliance policy might have been made, mutatis mutandis, by Castlereagh or Canning, though it would not have been expounded in those terms, certainly not by the former, to an envoy calling on official business. But Palmerston proposed to take the very argument on which Metternich rested his policy — that every emanation of Liberalism endangered the peace of

Europe and must be repressed before it engulfed Europe in the dreaded war of opinion — and stand it on its head. Every emanation of reaction was to be regarded as potentially endangering the peace of Europe, and made the subject of remonstrance, possibly even if it was strictly internal, certainly if it was not. The despatch of 7th September 1832 was justified to a reluctant monarch on the plea 'it is better that the British Cabinet should be taxed with entertaining groundless or premature apprehensions than that it should be accused of blind indifference to events which might place the peace of Europe in jeopardy'.[22] 'Whatever affects the general condition of Europe or of any important part of it, is a legitimate object of solicitude to England, and a proper subject for the exercise of her moral influence in the first place, or even of her armed interference if she should think the occasion required it', he wrote to Lamb, the ambassador in Vienna: 'An English ambassador has a better right to be listened to at Vienna when he speaks of such topics in Vienna, than an Austrian Chargé d'Affaires at London, when he takes upon himself to give us his opinions as to the course we ought to pursue about Portugal, or a Russian Minister everywhere, when he meddles with everything'.[23] When the Diet threatened the free city of Frankfort, Palmerston avowed that nothing could be more dangerous to settled institutions than 'a war of political opinions commenced upon the Rhine, by the aggression of power against legal rights'.

The letter to Lamb, quoted above, was sent by the ordinary post, so that Metternich's censors should convey a copy to him, it being Palmerston's aim to 'play the good genius at his ear to whisper to him sounder and saner principles'.[23] Lamb much disliked this new method of diplomacy. He wanted quiet relations with the Court to which he was accredited, regarded Austria as the natural ally of Britain against either France or Russia, and held to the Canningite principle of non-involvement in the ideological war. His reluctance to pass on in unsoftened terms what Palmerston instructed him to say only confirmed Palmerston in his determination to use this unorthodox method of reaching Metternich. Of course, the letters could not convince the chancellor that he was 'unconsciously provoking those events which he fancies he is preventing'.[24] He thought Palmerston was merely what the Tories and the non-interventionist Radicals said he was, a restless interventionist whose unquiet spirit exacerbated international relations and doomed his own country to an unnecessary level of armaments, a man who made mischief almost for the sake of making something. The point has never been better made than by A. J. P. Taylor, in his earliest book: 'He [Metternich] never realized that Palmerston opposed to the Metternich system a political system as deeply thought out and more consonant with the needs of the time. In short, he thought that Whiggism meant, as it often had, factious opposition; he never comprehended that it was Whiggism . . . which rebuilt the British empire and saved England, alone among modern European countries, from a revolution. Palmerston's impudence and jaunty air have blinded later historians as well as Metternich to the real merits and the real significance of his political philosophy. . . . As a European statesman, his objects, though he would have hated to confess it, were the same as Metternich's — the preservation of Peace and Order; but he did not confuse peace with petrification or order with death. . . . He differed fundamentally as to the means by which Peace and Order were to be preserved.'[25]

★   ★   ★   ★

Because, said Mr Taylor, although Palmerston 'regarded revolutionaries as conspirators, he did not regard revolutions as merely conspiracies; discontent seemed to him to show that something was wrong', Metternich labelled him an irresponsible either willing to incite to revolution or too foolish to understand the consequences of his words and actions. Palmerston had his answer to that:[23]

Not that we want all other countries to adopt our Constitution of King, Lords and Commons, or fancy that because such institutions are good here, they must necessarily answer *at once* everywhere else, and least of all do we want, as the Absolutists *affect* to think we do, to see *revolutions* spread everywhere. But we do think that the maintenance of good order, no less than the happiness of mankind, is promoted by redressing admitted grievances and remedying acknowledged evils, and we think that the policy which consists in prescribing the bayonet as the sole cure for all political disorders to be founded in ignorance of human nature, and to be pregnant with the most disastrous consequences. But this is Metternich's creed.

Palmerston from 1832 preached and practised involvement in the European ideological war, rejecting Castlereagh's distressed 'non possumus' and Canning's vigorous withdrawal. But if he became a participant, instead of standing aside as an observer with thoughts of becoming an umpire if the war of opinions assumed a violent form, he did not simply join one side against the other. He preached to both peace by compromise; he advocated the adoption of the British way of doing things, so recently (and so narrowly) vindicated at home as a result of the Whigs' standing between the oligarchy to which they belonged and an infuriated multitude. Britain was in the ring, interested in all that passed, making it more difficult for Metternich to keep watch and ward for the pleasure of princes and the pain of peoples. But her mission was mediatorial. It was to save the aristocracies and the bureaucrats in spite of themselves. It was to explain that there were not two sides in the conflict, but three; to declare that while reaction breeds revolution, concession may avert disaster; to deny Metternich's assumption that the inevitable victory of Liberalism could not be gradual and peaceful; to proclaim the faith that the European peoples were sufficiently mature to work, within measurable time, a constitutional system (which, if meant as a universal truth — and it was — Metternich did right to doubt).

The classic exposition of Palmerston's attitude to revolutionaries and reactionaries comes from the Civis Romanus speech of 1850 (see below, pp. 272, 275–6):

It has always been the fate of advocates of temperate reform and of constitutional improvement to be run at as the fomenters of revolution. It is the easiest mode of putting them down; it is the received formula. . . . Now there are revolutionists of two kinds in the world. In the first place there are those violent, hot-headed and unthinking men who fly to arms, who overthrow established Government, and who recklessly, without regard to consequences, and without measuring difficulties or comparing strength, deluge their country with blood and draw down the greatest calamities on their fellow-countrymen. . . . But there are revolutionists of another kind; blind-minded men, who, animated by antiquated prejudices, and daunted by ignorant apprehensions, dam up the current of human improvement until the irresistible pressure of accumulated discontent breaks down the opposing barriers, and overthrows and levels to the earth those very institutions which a timely application of renovating means would have rendered strong and lasting. Such revolutionists as these are the men who call us revolutionists. . . .

But the theme was cogently expressed in 1832 when Metternich was canvassing the Six Resolutions — [13]

I am afraid that Metternich is going to play the Devil in Germany . . . *Divide et impera* should be the aim of Government in these times.

Separate by reasonable concessions the moderate from the exaggerated, content the former by fair concessions and get them to assist in resisting the insatiable demands of the latter. This is the only way. . . . If Metternich would only leave people a little alone he would find his crop of revolutions which he is nursing up with so much care soon die away upon the stalk.

As a pure expression of opinion, this was mere common sense. But as a prime ingredient in foreign policy it approached 'sentimental idealism'. Here was an innovation in British foreign policy, Palmerston's most characteristic contribution to it. How great a gulf it opened up between him and his recent predecessors and former colleagues is shown by a letter from Aberdeen to the Princess Lieven on 26th September 1832. Referring to the attempt to impose on the Dutch Europe's award, to which all the Eastern Powers had put their hand, but which they were now trying to frustrate, the former Foreign Secretary wrote, 'France and England are to be the joint executioners of the iniquitous decree. How this can be surpasses my comprehension, but when the object is to make our Ministers the dupes of French intrigue, or the instruments of revolutionary injustice, all things are easy.'[26]

CHAPTER IV

EASTERN QUESTION AND
WESTERN ALLIANCE

IT was a standing assumption of British diplomacy for most of the
nineteenth century that there were two likely peace-breakers,
two encroaching Powers, France and Russia, whom Britain
might have to fight. To keep them from trying to divide the world
between them, as they had seemed to do when Napoleon met
Alexander I on the raft at Tilsit in 1807, was basic to Britain's
security. There was, however, little prospect of this danger while
Louis Philippe ruled in France. In mid-1833 Russian batteries on
the shores of the Sea of Marmora were trained on the French fleet,
to ensure that Russia should settle the fate of Turkey on her own.
What is astonishing, and discreditable, and requires explanation,
is that the British fleet was not there — and this although relations
between London and St Petersburg were bad.

In the fifty years before Palmerston became Foreign Secretary
the stature of Russia in world affairs had grown beyond all recognition. Under Peter the Great she achieved the status of a European
Power, but hardly the stature to match it. When Palmerston was
six, the far-sighted Pitt had wanted to fight over Ochakov, where
fifty years later reared the formidable naval base and arsenal of
Odessa. He did not prevail, and the Treaty of Jassy, ending Russia's
second war with Turkey, gave her control of the whole northern
littoral of the Black Sea. When the successive partitions of Poland
between Russia, Austria and Prussia were completed in 1795, the
Muscovite power stretched to Brest Litovsk, a hundred miles short
of Warsaw. The Treaty of Vienna, 1815, gave Russia control of
'the Congress Kingdom', with a frontier less than fifty miles from
the Oder. Here the Russian hold was riveted when the Polish army
which revolted in 1830 was disbanded and the constitution replaced
(despite British protests) by an Organic Statute (26th February
1832) which proved mere window-dressing; Russian Poland was
governed as if it were a province. The third Russo-Turkish War
ended in 1812 with the Treaty of Bucharest (a young Stratford

Canning negotiating for the Turks). It gave Russia the most northerly of the Danube mouths. The Treaty of Adrianople, 1829, which enforced Turkish acceptance of the London Conference decisions on Greece, left the Russians in control of the Danube delta and the principalities of Moldavia and Wallachia became virtually Russian protectorates.[A]

This was a staggering record of aggrandizement. In his most sober moments Palmerston grasped the danger to the Russian state and economy of too rapid over-extension.[1] But Constantinople was a tempting prize for a Tsar. It had been for a thousand years the seat of Orthodox empire, till it fell to the infidel. Its adjacent water joined the Black Sea to the Mediterranean. To keep foreign fleets beyond it was important to Russian security; to have access through it for commerce and war was a natural Russian objective. To have it as a Russian base would transform and distort the Balance of Power in Europe, and vitally affect Europe's communications with the East. The Treaty of Adrianople had rounded off Russian possession of the eastern coast of the Black Sea. Persia seemed a Russian puppet, and the hand whose shadow lengthened towards the Golden Horn also pointed towards Diarbekir and the Great Valley of Mesopotamia. 'Constantinople was the first strategic position in the world, and no Great Power could allow another to possess it.'[2] Britain, in particular, with her interest in the routes to the East and her need to dominate the Mediterranean in time of war, could not allow Russia to have it. Therefore the Sultan must never be left to depend on Russia or France alone. Therefore Britain must shrink from the partition of the Ottoman Empire, rotten though it seemed. Therefore, also, she must hesitate long before she approved of the predominance over the Ottoman Empire, or large parts of it, strategically placed, and certainly over Constantinople itself, of that contender for the Sultan's inheritance, Mehemet Ali, the Pasha of Egypt. For nothing could be worse — except a Franco-Russian alliance directed against Britain — than the alliance with either Russia or France with such an active, ambitious ruler, so placed.

Ever since in 1807 he had made Egypt too hot for the British, closely engaged elsewhere, this former Albanian tobacco-dealer turned soldier had been laying the material basis for a forward policy which at some time or another threatened every part of that

A See map p. 561.

sprawling agglomeration of territories formally constituting the Turkish Empire. They stretched from the Pillars of Hercules to the Persian Gulf, from the Danube to the Upper Nile and the Gulf of Aden. In most of them the power of the Sultan, whose ancestor had in the late seventeenth century beaten at the gates of Vienna, was a shadow. Among those who thought that the Greek rebellion marked the beginning of the dissolution of the empire was Mehemet himself. He might have attacked his nominal overlord while he was engaged with the Greeks. He chose to send his son, Ibrahim, to be the Sultan's saviour, that he, Mehemet, might be the Sultan's successor. His price for aid against the Greeks was to be a position in Hellenic, island and Anatolian bases where he could stand poised to take over Constantinople, perhaps with a coup d'état. Even after he was baulked by Navarino, he kept his agents incessantly busy in the capital, which remained his ultimate goal. But one eye roved to Syria and Arabia and beyond to the Great Valley and the Persian Gulf. He aimed at least to 'establish an Arabian kingdom, including all the countries in which Arabic is the language', Palmerston thought in 1833.[3] Many of the Europeans who worked in Mehemet Ali's service were French, and officials in Paris thought intermittently of using the Pasha to bring the beginnings of modernity to the southern littoral of the Mediterranean. The prospect was obnoxious to the British Admiralty and Board of Trade. The French bowed to the representations of Wellington (and Metternich). They themselves occupied Algiers, but the larger prospect lapsed. Mehemet was busy enough. He had long ago made the Arabian ports on the Red Sea, and the Holy Cities, tributary, and now (after conquering the Soudan in the early '20s) strengthened his hold in Arabia (to the disadvantage of British commerce).[4] But his main project was an assault through Syria on Constantinople. It was halted only by the sight of Russian camp fires on the Marmora shore (1833). For all the British knew, or could do about it, a most dangerous alliance between Russia and Mehemet Ali might have come about at this moment. For Palmerston had failed to give the Eastern Question adequate attention, and by the time he had (more or less) decided between Sultan Mahmoud and Pasha Mehemet as the 'keeper of the gate' to the East, he could not make his choice effective in action.

The choice had not been easy. To say that the Ottoman Empire was capable of revitalization under anyone other than Mehemet

Ali, if it could be revitalized at all, was to make a large assumption, especially as anyone else would be under constant threat from Mehemet and Ibrahim. True, there was much facade about Mehemet's modernization of Egypt. Cobden, who had no good word for the Turk, and was not frightened by the prospect of the Russianization of Turkey-in-Europe, thought the Pasha 'puffed up by his creatures in Europe as a regenerator and reformer' was 'only a rapacious tyrant . . . pursuing a course of avaricious misrule which would have torn the vitals from a country less prolific than this, long since'.[5] But it was not until November 1832 that Palmerston first suggested that the Turk might be a better reformer than the Albanian.[6] This was not an absurd conclusion. Mahmoud was aware of Western ideas, and knew that his régime must change or perish. The ultra-faithful called him the 'infidel sultan' because of his benevolence to his Christian subjects. On the line of the Balkans, in Asia Minor, in Armenia, in the Great Valley, he made the authority of Constantinople more secure than it had been for two centuries. There was more to his reforms than putting soldiers into Western uniforms and civil servants into frock coats, fezzes and black boots. If he had not 'made a modern unified state for the first time possible in Turkey',[7] it is extremely doubtful whether Britain, or, for that matter Russia, would have backed him. But Britain did not opt for Mahmoud because he was a better reformer than Mehemet, but because Mehemet's designs implied the dismemberment of Turkey.[8] Only when the choice was firmly made did Palmerston and Ponsonby, the ambassador at Constantinople, consistently write off Mehemet Ali as a shyster and, latterly, a mere instrument of the French, while they expressed, especially in public, optimism as to the Turk's capacity to make himself by the reform of administration and justice, and the recreation of an army and navy, a respectable ally for a Christian Power. Partly this was self-deception; partly a case of whistling to keep one's courage up.[9] But until Mahmoud's death in 1839 there was no question of justly condemning Palmerston as the champion of Turkish oppression of the Christian nationalities of the Balkans. ·

★   ★   ★   ★

Acre fell to Ibrahim on 27th May 1832. That month an order was sent from the British embassy in Constantinople to Campbell in Alexandria to keep on good terms with Mehemet Ali. This order was repeated in October by the *Under*-Secretary at the Foreign Office. All these months Palmerston had given little attention to the Eastern Question and shown no urgency. Yet from Constantinople Stratford Canning offered Palmerston a policy. He did more than any other man to prevent Mahmoud's power crumbling and, after the fall of Acre, 'to obtain a new Greek frontier . . . virtually pledged the British Government to support the Sultan against his vassal'.[10] He had not been authorized to do so, but when he had been to such trouble to insert into Mahmoud's ear (by the devious channels appropriate to the Turkish court) the notion that Britain would be his shield, the Sultan was certainly entitled to think that if Ibrahim approached the capital he would be confronted with massed British sail-of-the-line. But Stratford's dispatches, and Turkish delegations, supported though they were by Metternich, could draw from Whitehall no commitment. There are circumstances which palliate Palmerston's negligence. The Egyptian attack on Acre coincided with the supreme crisis of the Reform Bill, when the Whigs were momentarily out of office and violent revolution threatened Britain. After they returned, Althorp, the parsimonious Chancellor of the Exchequer (who was very pro-French) and Brougham opposed taking action against Mehemet, the progressive ruler whom the French admired. To them, Palmerston later asserted, Grey weakly gave way. 'Would either the Parliament or the people support us in a war which would be generally felt to arise for the sake of a remote and problematical interest?' asked the premier (in ominous anticipation of Neville Chamberlain's remark in 1938 over Czechoslovakia) of a colleague, Holland, a francophil, who was certain to answer 'No'.[11] Palmerston would have had to fight hard for the adoption of a policy for which there was little positive public support and to which there was much public opposition. But the cabinet was, after its victory on Reform, in notably high fettle, resolute on Holland, willing to challenge Metternich on Germany and to go with Grey and Palmerston over Portugal. Palmerston did not fight, because, to quote the careful words of Webster, his *convictions* and influence in the cabinet were not strong enough to carry Stratford's policy. A strong legacy of dislike inherited during the Greek War held him back. He was not sure whether the Ottoman Empire should be, or could be, maintained; whether it should be preserved to

Mahmoud or permitted to Mehemet; whether it should be shared between them, and if so on what basis. As he said himself, afterwards, 'postponed decision became practically a negative'.

In November Palmerston at last came to the (still tentative) conclusion that 'it was in the general interest of all Europe except Russia to uphold the Sultan's power against the Pasha'.[12] He was swinging over to Stratford's policy. But it was too late. Engrossed in Western affairs, he had committed his resources. Of the Sultan's call for assistance he would tell Parliament, in August 1833 and on 1st March 1850, that 'the British Government was not at that time in a condition to render that assistance. We had not a naval force at our disposal sufficient for that purpose'. As a fact, it was true. The fleet, steadily run down since 1815, could meet simultaneously two large commitments, but not three. And at the latest date at which a decision to rescue Mahmoud from Mehemet could have resulted in the dispatch of adequate ships to the Middle East, they were fully committed in Netherlands and Portuguese waters.[13] By the time the Turkish appeal for naval aid at last received a firm (and negative) answer, the Russian fleet was in the Bosphorus. By the time a fleet with contingent orders to blockade Alexandria arrived in the Levant, those orders had been rendered out of date by an accommodation made between the Pasha and the Sultan. It could only join the French outside the Dardanelles, dominated by Russian guns.

Palmerston had given an excessive attention to Western Europe at the expense of the East. He had not bothered to grasp the elements of the Eastern Question, to consider what was involved in his own opinion, expressed as long ago as 1828, that 'Europe has a clear right . . . upon general principles, and independently of any engagements by Russia, to see that a war between her and Turkey shall not derange the balance of power, and alter the state of possession as fixed by the last general peace' — an opinion delivered when, in despair of Wellington and Aberdeen, he looked to the Russian army to force the Sultan to let the Greeks go in peace.[14] He had not considered the possibility, fraught with menace to British interests, that Nicholas and Mehemet might become joint partitioners of Turkey. There may be some ground for Halévy's belief that there was an unspoken agreement to yield the initiative in the eastern Mediterranean to France as a compensation for the failure to get anything out of the Belgian crisis and Britain's refusal to cut her in as a partner in dealing with Portugal. Certainly, after Ibrahim crushed the Sultan's army at Konieh (21st December 1832) and began his advance across Asia Minor, it was the French representative in Constantinople who took the lead in an attempt to secure terms for the Sultan. In March 1833 Palmerston thought that Roussin had 'settled capitally the Turkish dispute with the Egyptian and has done well in sending back the Russian admiral with a flea in his ear'.[15] But Mehemet refused the terms, and the Sultan, despairing of Britain, appealed again to the Russians.

The Wellington cabinet itself could hardly have been more inert and inept. Lord Ponsonby arrived as ambassador to find British prestige, and hence influence, at Constantinople at its nadir only a year after Stratford had raised it to its zenith. There was little for him to do but try, unsuccessfully, to ferret out details of Orlov's negotiations with the Turks which resulted in the Treaty of Unkiar Skelessi (8th July 1833). There was little for Palmerston to do but make it clear that in another crisis Britain would be in her place to prevent the dismemberment of the Turkish Empire. This he did in the House of Commons on 11th July 1833 in one of those statements that stand apart from others because they fix the policy of a country for a generation or more. He said:

It is of the utmost importance for the interest of England, and for the maintenance of the peace of Europe, that the territories and provinces forming the Ottoman Empire should be an independent State . . . If Russian conquest should lead to the christianizing and civilising of the inhabitants of that country, these advantages . . . would be counter-balanced by the consequences that would result to Europe from the dismemberment of the Turkish Empire. I say, then, that undoubtedly Government would feel it to be their duty to resist to the utmost any attempt on the part of Russia to partition the Turkish Empire; and, if it had been necessary, we should equally have felt it our duty to interfere and prevent the Pacha of Egypt from dismembering any portion of the dominions of the Sultan. *The integrity and independence of the Ottoman Empire are necessary to the maintenance of the tranquillity, the liberty and the balance of power in the rest of Europe.*

This is a very strong and important statement, and the circumstances in which it was made must be recapitulated. It was not made to prevent the Russians interfering in the Sultan's dominions. Russian ships were at that moment parading the narrows by Constantinople. Russian batteries on the Asiatic shore were turned, some eastwards in case of a landward advance by Ibrahim, some seawards to counter any French move. Three days earlier, though Palmerston did not yet know it, the Sultan had signed at Unkiar Skelessi a treaty of eternal peace and alliance with Russia, containing a secret provision which bound the Sultan to close the Straits to all warships but his own while Turkey was at peace. The declaration was not made to prevent the Pasha of Egypt from possessing himself of 'territories and provinces of the Ottoman Empire'. The Sultan had just recognized his control of the pashaliks of Syria and Ibrahim's 'presence' at Adana, the gateway to Asia Minor (Convention of 5th May). But it was a notification that Britain had, after all, opted for Mahmoud as keeper of the gate between the Mediterranean and the Black Sea and custodian of the northern route to Persia. It was a warning that Britain, who had allowed Russia on her own to save the Sultan in his extremity, would not repeat the error. It was a bid for influence where influence had been wantonly cast away.

In the years to come, Palmerston did not minimize his error. He used it as a terrible example of negligence to be avoided in the future. 'We might with the greatest of ease have accomplished a good result', he wrote to Lamb in 1838. 'There is nothing that has happened since I have been in this office which I regret so much as that tremendous blunder of the English Government.' At the height of the next Eastern crisis, in 1840, he argued to a colleague, admittedly *ad hominem* (to Holland) that 'no British cabinet at any period . . . ever made so great a mistake in regard to foreign affairs'. It had been, he said, 'the cause of more danger to the peace of Europe, to the balance of power, and to the interest of England than perhaps any one determination ever before produced'.[16]

Posterity has been inclined to accept this verdict, regardless of whether it is thought that in backing Turkey for most of the nineteenth century Britain backed the wrong horse. For these were the years of decision after which for two or three generations Englishmen were pro-Turk because, and only because, they were anti-Russian. Unkiar Skelessi, wrote Temperley, was 'a true turning point in the attitude of English statesmen towards Russia. It bred in Palmerston a fatal hostility to Russia and converted even Whigs to the Tory policy of bolstering up Turkey'. And he adds that the anti-Russian feeling of Stratford and Palmerston 'was one profound cause of the Crimean War'.[17] Palmerston, so conciliatory over Poland, and as long as there was any prospect of Russian

Viscount Palmerston K.G.

co-operation over Belgium, after Unkiar Skelessi deliberately stirred up anti-Russian feeling in Britain, encouraging, inter alia, the publication by the turcomaniac Urquhart in the *Portfolio* of damaging documents brought from Warsaw by Polish exiles. It is right to add that he did this mainly to secure the augmentation of the fleet, and that, when the seed was sown, he ceased to water it, and adopted in public a responsible attitude both towards the growth of the Russian fleet in the Baltic and Russian behaviour in the Near East. But the memory of 1833 loomed large, for him and for the country.

The tragedy is that, although no one knew it, a vital decision had been taken at St Petersburg in June 1829. The rulers of Russia knew the danger of over-taxing resources (their recent victory over the Turks had been hard-won and less conclusive than it looked). They had seen as far back as 1812 that it would pay them to be moderate in victory, to advance their power slowly and tentatively, avoiding unnecessary complications with the Powers. They had before going to war in 1828 assured Europe that they would take no territorial aggrandizement in Europe, and, though Aberdeen protested vigorously against the terms of the Treaty of Adrianople (the Duke being very anti-Russian), they had literally kept their word. Now they decided that, though the dissolution of the Ottoman Empire was something that would have to be faced sooner or later, it had better be later rather than sooner. Turkey was to be regarded as a neighbour to be lived with, rather than a corpse to be dismembered. Of course, there was no guarantee that this policy would not be changed. But it seems likely that if Palmerston had acted on the text that the state of Turkey was the business of Europe, and not of any one Power, the Russians would have been reasonable in a Five-Power Conference in 1832 or 1833. Even after Unkiar Skelessi, Britain's predicament was less acute than it seemed. Palmerston assumed that the treaty made the Sultan the Tsar's vassal, as a preliminary to making him his victim. He (and the French) protested against it as irritably and as impotently as Aberdeen in 1829. But the Russians were not immoderate, and the terms, despite the secrecy, were less sinister than Palmerston had feared. It proved possible for Ponsonby to take advantage of the Turkish instinct to play off one foreigner against another and become, gradually, the chief foreign confidante of Mahmoud.

* * * *

It is right, at this point, to pay some attention to the theory, pursued with implacable irrationality by David Urquhart, that Palmerston was a Russian agent. Urquhart 'discovered' this after Palmerston relieved him of the secretaryship of the embassy at Constantinople (to which he had appointed him) and repudiated the *Portfolio*. The enraged turcophil — who introduced the Turkish bath into England, and lived with a harem, though marrying the Evangelical sister of Chichester Fortescue[18] — spent the rest of his life looking for Russian spies under beds and between sheets. The fuel from which for thirty years he continued to extract the smoke of calumny was basically the connexion of Palmerston — and also of Grey — with that born intriguer, the Princess Lieven. Both Palmerston and his future wife were brought up in the very lax sexual morality of the late-eighteenth-century aristocracy, and it is almost certain that the relationship between Palmerston, Emily Cowper and Dorothea Lieven was only not a *ménage à trois* because (Earl Cowper being alive) it was not a *ménage*. The princess was certainly not merely the wife of the Russian ambassador but herself an agent of the Russian Foreign Ministry. In 1826 Palmerston was in financial difficulties, in common with many other people (including the young Disraeli) as a result of the stringency brought on by over-speculation.[A] The details are obscure,[19] but he had certainly just begun to lay out capital on his Irish estates, and found

[A] P. J. V. Rolo (*George Canning*, p. 149, n. 2) repeats Pemberton's account (*Lord Palmerston*, p. 26) of the reason why Canning's offer to Palmerston of the Exchequer was 'rudely withdrawn' (Pemberton) on account of 'speculations . . . on the Stock Exchange and some carelessness [the shareholders called it swindling] in the affairs of a company of which he was a director'. Rolo says the offer was 'promptly' withdrawn when (this) became known to Canning. The authority is Guedalla, citing a hint by Canning to Princess Lieven. No word of this had reached Mrs Arbuthnot, furiously anti-Palmerstonian (*Journal*, ii. 129) and it was Herries — the King's candidates for the Exchequer, who got it — whom she, with many others, regarded as 'a mere stock jobber' (ibid., p. 159).

Palmerston wrote to his brother, 19th April and 4th May 1827, that he was to be Chancellor at the end of the session (B. i. 188–9, 191), Croker having contrived the delay (ibid., Autobiographical fragment, pp. 374–8). He left for posterity the allegation that it was the King who prevented his appointment, then as later after Canning's death, because 'there were questions coming on about palaces and crown lands which the King was very anxious about'. He leaves it to be inferred that the 'something behind, which [Canning] did not choose to tell' was royal interference (pp. 375–6). It is difficult to reconcile with his account of this interview W. B. Pemberton's statement: 'His excuses and explanations were accepted; but it was a chastened and a penitent Palmerston who emerged from a painful interview with his Prime Minister, having learnt a lesson in boardroom ethics which he never forgot.'

himself being pressed by creditors. The tale peddled by Urquhart was that the Lievens paid out twenty thousand pounds of the Tsar's money to save Palmerston from ruin. The intermediary was said to be a seedy Jew who ran a gambling salon in St James's and was later made by Palmerston British consul in Leipzig. The story is most improbable. Why was an intermediary needed? It is surely not suggested that Palmerston lost all this money gambling, for, though he backed horses to supplement his prize money and make his stables pay, he was not a heavy gambler. And was he worth the money? He was not even a cabinet minister, and did not seem likely to be. Liverpool had tried to prize him from his office, Canning said of him that he almost reached the top of mediocrity, and the Duke was to say that he did not fire great guns at sparrows. As for services rendered 'in return for the bribe', it is certainly true that in Wellington's cabinet in 1828 he fought against a pro-Turk, anti-Russian policy, and Princess Lieven called him 'our minister'. Out of office, he joined with the Lievens and Leopold of Saxe-Coburg to make difficulties for Wellington and Aberdeen. That the material on which he based an anonymous newspaper attack on Wellington's policy consisted of diplomatic documents shown him by the Lievens is almost certain.[20] But these activities were in furtherance of reputable public aims — the continuance of Canning's entente with Russia over Greece (to restrain Russia); the prevention, and then the termination, of the Russo-Turkish war; the creation of a viable Greek state *which would not be a Russian satellite*.[21] It is neither necessary nor realistic to think that Dorothea Lieven either bought or deceived Palmerston. She amused him; he flattered her. According to Mrs Arbuthnot (who hated Palmerston), Wellington (who despised and resented him) told her that the King had told him that Princess Lieven in February 1830 advised him to substitute Palmerston for the Duke.[20] It was useful to allow her vanity to convince the lady that she called the tune for leading British politicians, captivated by her outstanding charm and personality, to follow. Grey seems to have allowed her to think she was responsible for getting Palmerston the Foreign Office in 1830. An editor (of the *Courier*) who was kept waiting for an hour and a half while the princess was with Grey during cabinet-making said that when he was handed the list, containing Palmerston's name for the Foreign Office, there was an earlier list on the back, containing it not. According to Urquhart, Palmerston repaid Grey by securing his 'dismissal' from the premiership in 1834 by showing the King a private letter from Grey to the Lieven copied by the Post Office! The whole sinister story became clear to Urquhart when he was dismissed. And, of course, it explained everything; why Palmerston would not help the Poles; why he continued to pay the Russians on account of the Dutch Loan; why he did not send ships to the Dardanelles in 1832; why, after 'bowing to patriotic fervour', he desisted from anti-Russian propaganda, and much that was to follow.[22] An alternative theory that Palmerston was in the pay of the Jesuits has even less to commend it.[23] A fascinating party-game for an academic week-end school is to accumulate the 'proofs' that Palmerston was the key figure in the sinister operations of the Grand Orient Freemasonry (Pedro, Mazzini & Co. Ltd).

The Princess Lieven became a woman doubly scorned, disillusioned first by Palmerston and then by Grey. 'The inconvenience of his (Palmerston's) Liberal principles and obstinate character are very great, and we should see him go without regret', she wrote to Nesselrode on 1st October 1832. But it was she who 'went'. She had become vindictive, and therefore an embarrassment rather than an asset to Russian policy. That was why the Lievens were recalled from London, though she believed that Palmerston had driven them away. She carried her animosity over to the French camp, reappeared in London as Guizot's mistress and accompanied him back to France when he became Louis Philippe's chief minister.

One of the reasons that 'our minister' had become by October 1832 'a mule' was his insistence upon the appointment of Stratford Canning as ambassador in St Petersburg although he was known to be persona non grata to the Tsar. It is difficult to explain or exculpate this unnecessary quarrel with Russia. The Tsar was adamant, and Stratford was available to go on a special mission to Madrid at the end of 1832.

*   *   *   *

In the House of Commons of 15th February 1833 Palmerston 'ventured to say . . . that as long as France and England remain united, they can command the peace of Europe; and for this reason, because France and England, united, never can, and never will make an unjust war against other countries . . . and I should like to know, where is the confederacy of States which would venture to attack two such powers united?'. The speech was a defence of Anglo-French co-operation against Holland, which had been encouraged by the Eastern Powers to defy the decisions of the Conference. It was made at a time when Palmerston thought the French were on the point of securing a settlement in the Levant satisfactory to Britain because it would confine Mehemet's conquests to southern Syria, and avoid peril to Constantinople. An entente with France seemed on all counts the best way of both of preventing disputes between the two countries; of preventing a rapprochement between France and any other Power, such as Austria; of preventing the French from taking lone initiatives which might lead to war, for instance in Italy, and of preventing the Eastern Powers from achieving anywhere in Western Europe a victory in the ideological war. But it was repugnant to those British politicians and diplomats who hankered after Castlereaghan concert and those who were principally francophobe, and thought in terms of the old Quadruple Alliance to curb France. The former had grounds for complaint against Palmerston; the latter simply did not understand that as long as the entente lasted, Palmerston intended that it should be another example of restraint by co-operation. They imagined that Palmerston was allowing the French to run away with him, either from simplicity or because he wished to spread revolution through Europe. Devotion to the cause of 'Order' made strange bedfellows: 'An enemy of revolution is almost compelled to look favourably to the cause of Don Carlos, in spite of his bigotry and his Jesuitism', wrote Aberdeen, a Scottish Presbyterian.[24]

Don Carlos was the brother of the abominable Ferdinand, the dying king of Spain. The priestly party, backed by Dom Miguel and the Eastern ambassadors, strove, against the Queen, Maria Cristina, to secure him the succession at the expense of Isabella, the infant daughter of Ferdinand and Cristina. Stratford Canning's mission in the winter of 1832–3 was to try to cover with a single cloak of red, white and blue the cause of Maria da Gloria and Isabella against their wicked uncles. What Palmerston feared was that a victory for Don Carlos would be decisive in Portugal, and the whole Iberian peninsula would join Italy and Germany as an adjunct of the arbitrary Powers. Nothing seemed more likely to happen, for since he had achieved his foothold at Oporto Dom

Pedro had been besieged there by the Miguelites. No wonder Palmerston was prepared to let the Portuguese charter sleep if the Powers, or at least Spain, would denounce Miguel.[25] For the victory of 'the wicked uncles' would be a major setback for the patron of European Liberalism. His initiative would be reduced to the unprofitable task of trying to persuade Prussia (basically under the influence of Russia) to do battle in the Diet against Metternich as the champion of constitutionalism and of the smaller states of Germany. The prestigious importance of the outcome in the Iberian peninsula helps to explain why Palmerston would not spare ships for the East, and why the Franco-British entente blossomed in 1834 into formal alliance.

Ferdinand died in September 1833, the month the rulers and chief ministers of the Eastern Three met at Münchengratz. There Metternich reached an accommodation with the Tsar on the Eastern Question which was the more disturbing because its terms were not revealed. There, also, was made a demonstration of solidarity against the cause of revolution. The orthodox doctrine that any monarch threatened by revolution could look confidently to a Big Brother for aid was strengthened by an understanding between the Big Brothers that if one of them were attacked while responding to such an appeal, the others would go to his assistance. It is a measure of the gulf which now yawned between Aberdeen and his successor that the former Foreign Secretary could write: 'The meeting of the Emperors gave me more satisfaction than any publick event which has recently taken place, because it held out the prospect of arresting the progress of revolution in Europe. . . . The present Government of England is revolutionary by choice; that of France by necessity. I lament that a new field of action is opened to their destructive intrigues in the Peninsula.'[24] He regarded the Münchengratz agreement, as far as it concerned western and central Europe, as defensive; so, indeed, did Metternich. But it could not seem so to Palmerston, for the Tsar and Metternich were dominant in Germany and Italy and it was not unlikely that a subordinate member of their syndicate would emerge the victor in Spain. Even Portugal was not yet safe, though there the prospect had been transformed in the summer by that intrepid seaman, Captain Charles Napier, R.N., who, as Admiral Carlo Ponza, destroyed the Miguelite fleet and enabled the Pedroists to capture Lisbon (July). Palmerston certainly regarded München gratz as a challenge rather than a response. Grey and he decided that, if the Eastern governments communicated their agreement, they would reply that it seemed either a lesson or a menace. If the former, they did not need it; if the latter, they did not care for it.[26] This was spirited enough, but Palmerston had moments of despondency over Portugal, and reason enough for them. Even urban Portuguese hardly preferred Pedro's vengeful predators to Miguel's. Napier said he had not come 'to fight for these blackguards' and Lord William Russell reported that they were unprincipled democrats with no more love of liberty and justice than Miguel himself, and most hostile to England, so that their victory was dreaded and deprecated by moderate Portuguese and English merchants.[27] The majority of the House of Lords, which on 3rd June 1833 voted an address to the King to maintain neutrality between the contending factions in Portugal, would have liked to know that Palmerston told Pedro's envoy that if there was to be but a system of plunder, it was a matter of indifference whether Pedro or Miguel presided over it or whether they divided the country between them. Metternich would have chuckled to read Palmerston's confession: 'I do not know that it is part of the duty of England to rescue all other nations from the consequences of their own folly. We are neither the tutors nor the police officers of Europe.'[28] But he was not one who sets his hand to the plough and then turns back. When in January 1834 Pedro asked the British to take control of Lisbon and Oporto to free his troops to clear the interior, Palmerston felt that 'the time for action is come'. This opinion was confirmed by the fact that Don Carlos and his retinue had, months before, crossed into Miguelite territory.

Palmerston's desire for positive action in the Peninsula raised serious questions — how far could interference go, and to what extent was France to be invited to co-operate. We have quoted Palmerston's striking statement on 1st June 1829 that 'non-intervention' did not proscribe interference by all means short of 'force of arms'. With regard to the Belgian crown, he had said: 'There is nothing in the principle of non-interference, fairly and reasonably laid down, which prescribed to a State the absence of all interference in what passed in a neighbouring country when that which was passing concerned the interests of the other party.'[29] With regard to the affairs of Germany he had distinguished between 'interference by friendly counsel and advice' and armed intervention (2nd August 1832) and to Lamb he had written of answering the encroachments of armed bands with dispatches.[30] Now he felt (like Canning) that 'to defeat the Holy Alliance in the arena which they themselves have chosen (Portugal) would be no common victory'. But it could not be done by 'friendly counsel and advice', and all dispatches could do was complain that Metternich was passing round the hat for Miguel and Carlos. It was not even enough to wink at half-pay officers serving with Pedro in defiance of British law (striking them off the Navy List if, like Napier, they became too prominent). Aid must be given by all means short of 'force of arms'. But the cabinet, especially Althorp who held the purse, thought that the use of British troops for garrison duty in Portugal too strong an action, and although for a moment it looked as though Grey might resign in protest at this veto, Palmerston was baulked. He turned his mind to the fact that the absolutists had themselves brought a frontier into the issue; Carlist 'armed bands' avowedly disloyal to the child queen Isabella, recognized de jure by Britain and France, were on Portuguese soil. They should be flushed out by Spanish troops, necessarily co-operating for the purpose with the Pedroist army fighting Miguel. The Portuguese usurper and the Spanish pretender would be disposed of in the same operation. The fact that Portuguese did not trust Spaniards any more than Piedmontese trusted Frenchmen made it desirable that Britain should not only sponsor an agreement on these lines between Pedro and the Regent Maria Cristina, but be a party to it, thereby guaranteeing to Portugal Spanish evacuation after the completion of the operation. And to make the operation decisive, the Royal Navy, under treaty obligation to the sovereigns of Spain and Portugal, would prevent the escape of Miguelite and Carlist leaders and partisans.

This project raised, inevitably, the problem of France, with whom Palmerston had lately and triumphantly co-operated to coerce the Dutch and whose co-operation was required in the East. They had responded appropriately to Münchengratz. The gist of the Münchengratz agreement had been conveyed by the Eastern Powers not to London but to Paris. The French replied that they would not tolerate intervention in Belgium, Switzerland or Piedmont. 'I am glad that de Broglie had given a set down to that consequential political coxcomb, Metternich', was Palmerston's comment.[31] It seemed to the French logical that there should now be a general treaty of alliance between Britain and France, and Talleyrand desired passionately to crown his long career by washing away Castlereagh's Quadruple Alliance, which the Belgian affair had shown to be still alive. But general treaties to meet hypothetical cases always encounter strong opposition in Britain, and Palmerston had no use for them. On the other hand, France had a frontier with Spain, and it would be dangerous to carry through the proposed Anglo-Spanish-Portuguese treaty in such a way as to alienate France. Frenchmen had not forgotten their long tradition of alliance with, or hegemony over, Spain; they were sensitive on the subject of the Spanish War of Liberation against Napoleon; they did not see, indeed, why they should not, now that Spain was distinctly an inferior power, enjoy the same sort of 'special position' at Madrid that the British insisted on at Lisbon. Many of Cristina's supporters — especially the less liberal ones — were pro-French. Some were in French pay. The Regent must be careful to cultivate French goodwill, because the most reputable and serious support for Don Carlos came from the northern provinces nearest to France, always hostile to Madrid as the enemy of provincial privileges and diversities, and especially hostile to Liberalism as a centralizing creed.

It needed no genius to see the solution. Palmerston had always proposed that, when the Iberian treaty had been signed, the contracting parties should invite France to 'accede' to it. Such a place in the scheme France could hardly tolerate. So, as early as February, Palmerston wrote to George Villiers in Madrid: 'The great object of our policy ought to be now to form a Western confederacy of free states as a counterpoise to the Eastern league of the arbitrary governments.'[32] There is nothing like making a virtue of necessity. The Quadruple Alliance of Britain, France, Spain and Portugal was essentially a device for the settlement of the affairs of the Peninsula according to British prescriptions. It was puffed up by Palmerston as not only incidentally, but as *essentially*, something more. 'I reckon this to be a great stroke. In the first place it will settle Portugal, and go some way to settle Spain also. But what is *of more permanent and extensive importance*, it establishes a quadruple alliance among the constitutional states of the west, which will serve as a powerful counterpoise to the Holy Alliance of the east'[33] (present author's italics). It was represented as the natural and beneficent development of the new departure in British foreign policy propounded in the speech of 2nd August 1832. 'We shall be on the advance, they (the arbitrary governments) on the decline, and all the smaller planets of Europe will have a natural tendency to gravitate towards our system.'[32]

Whatever the verdict on the Quadruple Alliance of 1834, 'a capital hit and all my own doing', Palmerston boasted[34] — there can be no doubt that it is a notable example of his technical competence. But for his skill as a draughtsman and his facility as a linguist, the treaty could never have been ready for signature on 22nd April 1834, only twelve days after he carried it through the cabinet by what, with some exaggeration, he claimed was 'a coup de main'. And but for the full deployment of the negotiating gifts shown at the Belgian Conference he could never have got the draft agreed.

The immediate results of the Treaty were all that Palmerston could have desired. Portugal at last appeared to be 'settled'. On 26th May Dom Miguel capitulated at Evora, retired to Rome (the Pope alone of all the rulers continuing to recognize him as king of Portugal although he had renounced his pretensions) and never reappeared in Portugal. The death of Pedro on 24th September seemed gain rather than loss. 'The Western Confederacy may now be looked upon as firmly established; Spain and Portugal are irrevocably constitutional Powers, and necessarily allied, therefore, to England and France', Palmerston wrote to Minto in Berlin on 23rd September, adding that the sympathies of the German people were with western constitutionalism.[35] But when the resignation of the government deprived Palmerston of the Foreign Office in November 1834, such optimism seemed a little strained. Don Carlos had been conveyed to England. But there was no means of keeping him there, and he slipped away to raise his standard in Navarre.

CHAPTER V

WILL HE RETURN?

FROM 1832 until his death in 1865 Palmerston was repeatedly attacked with the jibe that he was a liberal abroad and a conservative at home. Literally true, this failed as an indictment, for he wished for other countries the civil liberties and representative government which Britain had already won. He wanted them to have their 1688 and their 1832. Radical revolution and republicanism he desired neither for Britain nor for any part of Europe, and he begged arbitrary governments on the Continent to avoid both by behaving like sensible Whigs and Canningites.

It is true, indeed, that until 1830 Palmerston did not see the need for any considerable parliamentary reform at home. After he joined Canning's cabinet, which Wellington and the Ultra Tories decided to boycott, in 1827, the Duke's confidante, Mrs Arbuthnot, wrote that she would be delighted to see Palmerston suffer any indignity because 'he had behaved the most shabby of any'; having been so long a 'High Tory' minister, he now 'professed himself a Whig'.[1] But Palmerston had never been a 'High Tory', for that would have involved opposition to Catholic Emancipation, which Palmerston always supported, finding it 'strange that in this enlightened age and enlightened country people should still be debating whether it is wise to convert four or five millions of men from enemies to friends and whether it is *safe* to give peace to Ireland'.[2] On the other hand, he had not ranked as a Canningite, as did most of those Tory ministers — such as Huskisson and Charles Grant — who combined approval of the Catholic claims with a more liberal outlook than that of the Ultras, and none knew that his views on domestic questions were those of Liberal Toryism. He had certainly not become a Whig. But for the Ultra ministers — 'old women like the Chancellor [Eldon], ignoramuses like Westmorland, old stumped up Tories like Bathust' he felt an increasing contempt,[3] and this turned to anger when, long a minister, and nearly as long the sitting member, he found himself, at the general election of 1826, opposed for Cambridge University by two other

'Protestant' ministers, who were abetted by the Ultra members of the cabinet (other than Wellington) and by H.R.H. the Duke of York. He told Lord Liverpool, the prime minister, that if he were beaten he would resign. In retrospect he said that this was the first decided step towards a breach with the Tories 'and they were the aggressors'.[4]

What Palmerston had lacked was fire in his belly. Only occasionally had there been signs of it, mostly long ago. There is no ground for ascribing to mere pique or to the Whig support which carried him to victory at Cambridge the new tartness which creeps into his private correspondence, but the Cambridge election certainly stimulated thought on political matters. Who was it who thwarted and impeded the progress of the government in every improvement they attempted? — 'The stupid old Tory party, who bawl out the memory and praises of Pitt while they are opposing all the measures and principles which he held most important.' 'On the Catholic Question; on the principles of commerce; on the Corn Laws; on the settlement of the currency; on the laws regulating the trade in money; on colonial slavery; on the game laws . . . the Government finds support from the Whigs and resistance from their self-denominated friends.'[5] He showed his convictions, and not his ambition, when he joined Canning's cabinet; when, as a member of Wellington's, in the first speech that attracted more than polite applause from his friends, he stated forcefully the view that ministers deserved confidence only in so far as they followed Canning's principles; when, over dinner at the Travellers Club, late in 1829, he told an envoy of the extreme Ultras that, though his opinions on economic questions had not been declared, they were 'formed, and formed upon some reflection . . . and not likely to be altered' — they were the views of Huskisson.[6]

Palmerston had the Canningite capacity to sniff the wind of change; to see that there was a more genuine conflict in existence than the mere strife of Whig and Tory and that the Liberal Tories had more in common with the moderate Whigs than with the Ultras, apart from the more mundane consideration that without Whig support the ministries of Canning and Robinson (by now Viscount Goderich) could not stand. He rejoiced that 'the Whigs join us in a body and with zeal . . . manfully and in earnest', found in Lord Lansdowne a natural colleague, and regretted that in January 1828 Wellington excluded the Whigs 'as I like them much better than the Tories and agree with them much more'.[7] But he had not become a Whig, and if he had not taken office under the Duke, would not have sat with them on the Opposition benches. He who had not been a Canningite while Canning lived, now acted with the Canningites — Huskisson, Goderich, Charles Grant, William Lamb (soon to become Viscount Melbourne) — who joined the Duke 'as a party' in January 1828 and left as a party in May 1828 because Huskisson was turned out. (They tried vainly to procure his return.)[8] They had accepted office because they were given the key offices of Foreign Secretary, Colonial Secretary and President of the Board of Trade. After they had left, they took the line that this was not enough to secure a liberal policy, and Melbourne and Palmerston severally met overtures from the Duke with insistence that leading Whigs must come in too.

Cabinet experience, as we have seen, transformed Palmerston's interests and ambition. The office of Secretary at War was primarily a financial one (and must not be confused with that of the Secretary of State for War and Colonies). It was the Exchequer Palmerston had been offered in 1809. It was the Exchequer he wanted in 1827, and was promised, only to be 'tricked', as he later alleged, into postponing the move, which the King then contrived to prevent altogether.[9] Palmerston's mother, grandmother and great-grandmother had all been daughters of City businessmen, but his commonsense must have told him that he was less fitted for the Treasury than Huskisson or Peel, if as fitted as the humdrum Goulburn and more fitted (if only by long official experience) than Althorp, an inept Chancellor (though effective Leader of the House) under Grey. Palmerston's grasp of fiscal, currency and economic problems was superficial. If he had gone to the Treasury it would have ceased to be so; he always 'did his homework' thoroughly and became adept in the recondite study of International Law. But one cannot imagine him bringing to the preparation of a budget the zest he brought to framing dispatches and haranguing diplomats. By 1829 he wanted the Foreign Office. He had had enough of indenting supplies, manipulating estimates, auditing accounts. He now aspired not to juggle taxes but to instruct ambassadors and ordain the movement of fleets. And he had developed prejudices and preferences (not all of them new) which were to be writ large on British foreign policy. They were not, like his views on home questions, mainly derivative, though he thought they were Canningite. The other Canningites did not endorse them, and because of this, partly, he stood, in 1829 and 1830, a little aloof from them, with them but not quite of them.[10] This isolation was remarked, and misinterpreted as meaning that he was open to offers. When the more unyielding Ultras determined to try to turn out Wellington for his temerity in emancipating the Catholics (1829) they cast Palmerston, despite his record on the Catholic question and his striking speech on foreign affairs, for Leader of the House.[6] It was a position he did not covet; he would find the 'perpetual state of canvass' irksome, apart from his deficiencies as a speaker. But in any case he would have nothing to do with what he described as an attempt to 'mix, with a predominance of old fellows saturated with the brine of Toryism, a few young men of the Liberal parties'. (He was 45, but a man is as young as he feels.) 'As to going to the Tory party . . . to belong to people you do not think with, cannot answer', he wrote. No wonder Peel thought him 'unsafe'.[11] But he could no longer be written off as a second-rate hack. He was a politician to be reckoned with, and showed it by taking on the role of principal interrogator of the government on foreign affairs, with three speeches in less than five weeks at the opening of the session of 1830. 'The best of that party and certainly a good speaker' (!) Mrs Arbuthnot called him.[12]

Being self-reliant, interested in administration rather than politics, and not in the Commons, the Duke of Wellington was slow to understand that his government, even though its policy of peace, retrenchment and economical reform recommended it to many Whigs, required more House of Commons talent. But after the death of George IV in June 1830 he was induced to make approaches to Melbourne and Palmerston (separately) with the idea of taking in three Canningites. Both said he must have Whigs as well. On the death of Huskisson in September Palmerston was approached, with a view to his taking War and Colonies.[13] He went to Paris to escape this opportuning, which was renewed on his return, when he had an icy six-minute interview with the Duke.[14] Early in November, Croker came with a last offer. Repulsed, he asked 'Are you to vote for Parliamentary Reform?'. Palmerston replied: 'I am.'[15]

The last barrier to co-operation with Whiggery was down. But it was far from certain that Wellington would cease to be prime minister, and as long as he was Palmerston could never be Foreign

Secretary, even though the King's death removed one impediment. The election necessitated by the demise of the sovereign showed a considerable demand for parliamentary reform. It was generally expected that the Duke, on the same grounds that he had emancipated the Catholics (with Canningite and Whig support) would reform the electoral system, for after the news of the July revolution in Paris, someone had to, if revolution was to be avoided. His opportunity would come on Brougham's motion for Parliamentary Reform. Palmerston was at the meeting of Canningite chiefs to determine their attitude to this. They decided to support it, thus shifting from Canning's ground to that of the youthful Pitt of the 1780s and of Fox and Grey in the 1790s, ground hastily reoccupied now by the (till lately despondent) Grey. To the surprise of all, and the dismay of many, the Duke took the earliest opportunity, when the new parliament met, to refuse to consider any reform of the electoral basis of the Commons at all. He was swept away — by Whigs, Canningites and Ultras, aided by ministerialist abstentions — before Brougham's motion even came on. Instead of the Duke heading a concessionary administration excluding perhaps only the extremes of Right and Left, Lord Grey became premier, with a government excluding only the Wellingtonian loyalists (led in the Commons by a reluctant Peel) and dedicated to peace, retrenchment, and, most particularly, Parliamentary Reform. And Palmerston was Foreign Secretary.

* * * *

In 1829–30 there was a notable congruence between Palmerston's view of Europe and his view of Britain. The import of the speech of 1st June 1829 was that the outstanding phenomenon in the Europe of the day was the contest between arbitrary and constitutional government, as illustrated in Portugal. At home he saw that the real issue was not between Whig and Tory but between the Ultras and the rest of the politicians; between intransigents and 'the liberal parties'; between obscurantists and impressionables; between those who feared to do anything and those who feared to do nothing; between those who viewed public opinion as a thing to be resisted and if possible repressed and those who by noting and following (and even guiding) 'respectable' opinion qualified themselves to carry out reforms without seriously endangering aristocratic predominance. At home and abroad, radical revolution threatened if the Ultras prevailed, 'the stupid old Tory party' of Britain, of Austria, of France. Visiting Paris in January and December 1829 (he had been there ex officio in 1815 and 1818) he predicted what would happen, and rejoiced when, in July 1830, it did. He was impressed but not frightened by the accentuation of the movement for Parliamentary Reform at home which resulted from the events in Paris. He could echo with complete sincerity the warning of Grey, in the Lords on 2nd November 1830, that with the spirit of liberty breaking out all around, it was wise, and even necessary, to safeguard institutions by 'the temperate, gradual and judicious' correction of the defects produced by time.

It is certain, however, that Palmerston, when he joined Grey's government, did not expect so considerable a Reform Bill as the measure of which Grey, Althorp, Russell and Durham were the principal authors. He duly made his contribution to the great debate, on the third night (3rd March 1831). This 'large and more comprehensive change' would not be necessary, he said, if three years ago (when the Canningites left the Duke) the policy of gradual transfer of seats from corrupt boroughs to manufacturing towns and large counties had been initiated. Ministers would not be in office if there had not been a rash neglect of public opinion by those whose unbending notions had set all Europe aflame and covered these islands with disorder. Why had they not heeded the maxim of Canning (the anti-Reformer) that those who resisted improvement because it was innovation might find themselves compelled to accept innovation when it had ceased to be improvement. Since the people of England were remarkable for tenacious adherence to old institutions, 'the calm and steady insistence (on Reform) of those whose property and station put them in a position to judge wisely' proved that behind 'the veil of sanctity with which hereditary respect had invested even the imperfections of our constitution' lurked gross abuses. To these the Bill applied a sound and safe remedy, well adapted to preserve and consolidate institutions. It would confine the franchise to 'the great body of respectable householders, who had an interest in preserving the institutions of the country' (the public of whom, by the 1850s, Palmerston was to be the hero). It would unite with the aristocracy 'the respectable and intelligent classes of society', binding the latter to the constitution.

This was the speech of a man of the centre driven by events to support something he does not really like, aptly addressed to a House persuaded by extra-parliamentary pressure to give the Bill a majority of one vote. It exactly represented the point of view of the country gentry who could see that reform was necessary, but thought Russell's Bill too radical, though pleased that it was to give more seats to the counties than to large manufacturing towns. The latter, Palmerston said, had a special need for members who understood their interests, but the landed interest was the basis on which the best interests of society and the sacred institutions of the country rested. Even after a new House of Commons, with a large majority elected on the cry 'The Bill, the Whole Bill, and Nothing but the Bill', had done its work, Palmerston, who had warned Grey that he could not regard himself as bound to all the details, tried to modify it and thus both overcome his own doubts and secure the necessary support for the Bill in the Lords by negotiation with the 'Waverers', led by the Canningites Harrowby and Wharncliffe. But the talks he had initiated after the Lords defeated the Bill were broken off by the cabinet's decision to introduce a third Bill before Christmas. Greville (Clerk to the Privy Council) named the moderate party in the cabinet as Richmond, Lansdowne, Stanley, Melbourne and Palmerston. His source was Lady Cowper — 'between Palmerston, F. Lamb and Melbourne she knows everything and is a furious anti-Reformer'.[16] The most radical minister, the irascible Durham (who would have liked the Foreign Office) wrote: 'I see what Palmerston is driving at. He does not mind the disfranchisement of rotten boroughs, or the enfranchisement of great towns, provided he can get such an elective qualification as will make the large towns as little representative of the people as the boroughs he has destroyed. And as a thorough anti-Reformer, which he is, he is right.'[17] Palmerston in mid-February 1832 arranged discussions with the Waverers which resulted in the second reading of the Bill in the Lords, but it was obstructed in committee. Believing that this was due to the Waverers 'ratting', Palmerston himself moved the adoption of the cabinet's minute to the King giving him the choice between creating fifty peers or accepting the government's resignation.[18]

Though wishing for amendments, Palmerston held from the first that 'whatever the Tories may say, the Bill will not be Revolution, but the reverse'.[19] He displayed towards Reform the commonsense concessionary conservatism which has been the chief stumbling-block to British Radicals in every age, and this he would preach, in and out of season, to the monarchs and statesmen of Europe. But, like all the cabinet except Durham, he looked on the Reform of 1832 as final, and he never departed from this view. He was 'quite satisfied with the constitution of the country under which I have been born, under which I have lived, and under which I hope to die', he told the Tiverton electors in 1852, and he believed that any considerable further reform would make a different and inferior constitution. Dearly as he loved the Foreign Office, he nearly left the cabinet rather than sponsor a new Reform Bill in 1850-1, the only case for which was that Russell had precipitately and without consultation abandoned the role of 'Finality Jack' which he assumed in the '30s. But it is quite unjust to write off the Palmerston of the '30s as a crusted old Tory who, from accident or ambition, had strayed among the Whigs. He had seen the *need* for Reform when the Tory party denied it; he had helped to pass it where Peel only said that, having been passed, it must be acknowledged to have inaugurated an era in which all champions of the Conservative Cause must be concessionary if they were not to be irrelevant. Palmerston's position, however, necessarily involved him in saying 'thus far' to the public men of Europe while saying 'no farther' to the public at home. Those who objected to either maxim, or to both, naturally made what they could of the apparent inconsistency which was really no inconsistency at all.

Foreign Powers had watched with interest the long battle for the Reform Bill. If the cabinet's preoccupation with this battle gave Palmerston an unusually free hand to conduct diplomacy without much interference from his colleagues or scrutiny from parliament, it also had its drawbacks. For the Eastern Powers and the Dutch believed (as did indeed many of the British ministers themselves) that Grey's government would not survive. Grey complained to Princess Lieven that old Pozzo di Borgo, in the Russian service, was telling the German courts that Britain's 'jacobinical' ministry could not last because the most powerful classes in the community were against it, and when he reached London Palmerston told him roundly that the Lievens were encouraging the Tories.[20] The arbitrary courts expected a counter-revolution, perhaps by a Wellington coup d'état, and they were elated when William IV accepted Grey's resignation and called upon the Duke to form a government to carry a more moderate Reform Bill (May 1832). But a few days of teetering on the brink of revolution were enough. The Whigs returned to office, the Reform Bill became law. The famous speech of 2nd August 1832 was made, and the dispatch to the German courts was sent.

Keen supporters of the Reform Bill had commented rather acidly on the failure of the Canningite Foreign and Colonial Secretaries to share with Althorp and Russell the grievous burden of the Bill.[21] Now that the Bill was law, the Eastern statesmen saw in the Palmerston of 2nd August 1832 the very symptom of the catastrophe which, in their view, had overtaken Britain. Even now they did not give up the effort to influence British politics. During the elections to the first reformed House of Commons the Russian and Dutch consuls helped the Tories organize a meeting in the City, where business interests suffered from the blockade of the Dutch and the strife at Oporto. The Commons, however, gave Palmerston a majority of 361 to 98 as a riposte to the Lords' censure on his Portuguese policy, and the Foreign Secretary wrote in triumph to his brother (25th June 1833): 'I condole with the Holy Alliance, but they must bear with us still, for they cannot get rid of us.'[22]

The hopes of the Eastern courts rose again when in the spring of 1834 a controversy over Irish policy between Lord Stanley and Lord John Russell led to the secession of four members of the cabinet, three of whom (Stanley, Graham and the Canningite Ripon, formerly Robinson and then Goderich) were among Palmerston's most intimate friends. It is true that the ministers who went were from the conservative wing of the party, but the Eastern courts hoped that the quarrel indicated that the government was disintegrating. They seemed to be right when, a few weeks later, Grey and Althorp found themselves (also with regard to Ireland) in a position where one or other had to go. And again it was the more conservative minister who went. Palmerston was disappointed and even disturbed at this weakening of the conservative elements in the government; the importance attached to the retention of Althorp and the entry into the cabinet of the garrulous intriguer Ellice seemed to confirm a trend which Russell's victory over Stanley had revealed. The new premier, Melbourne, was, indeed, conservative, but he was less influential than Grey. Moreover, he was less apt to agree with Palmerston over foreign policy.

The net effect of these disputes was therefore to weaken Palmerston's position in the cabinet and to emphasize his isolation in the party. He remained confident. Granville, a close friend of Canning and an old acquaintance of Palmerston, sent a warning from Paris, remarking 'Metternich seems to have the same jealousy of you that he had of Canning. He does not like those whom he cannot bamboozle, and he besides knows how much you have done towards cementing the alliance between England and France which has nullified his ascendancy in the direction of European affairs.'[23] Palmerston replied: 'The Holy Alliance have entered into a solemn league and covenant to demolish the Scy of State for foreign affairs; but I will back him against them all and wager odds that he makes his stand good against the whole gang.'[24]

It would indeed have been impossible for Palmerston's colleagues to offer him up as a sacrifice to the neo-Holy Alliance. However little the public liked France — described by William IV at a regimental dinner as 'the natural enemy' — they did not approve of the arbitrary Powers (as Canning had known and shown). And it did not occur to Palmerston that the whole government might fall, for there were less than two hundred Tories in a House of Commons of 658. He was of far too sanguine a temperament to be a good judge of political events he did not control. He had overestimated the chances of carrying the first Reform Bill in the Commons[25] and the second in the Lords.[26] When Melbourne succeeded Grey, he said that Metternich really must get over his delusion, which he had harboured since 1830, that in six months' time he would have his dear Tories back again.[27] That was on 15th July 1834. On 1st November he wrote: 'Melbourne goes on very well, and the Government is, I think, likely to stand.'[28] On 11th November, as we have seen, he breathed defiance, in the letter to Granville. But on 16th November he had to write 'We are all turned out neck and crop.'[29]

William IV was a vulgar nonentity, but he was a king, and he did not understand that the Reform Bill had reduced the scope for the sort of initiatives which his father George III had been able (and sometimes forced) to take, often with success. He did not realize that the king's government could never be again, in quite the old sense, the King's. Taking advantage of the succession of Althorp to the peerage as Earl Spencer, he said that there was nobody else on the Whig side fit to lead the Commons, and sent for the Duke who took all the responsibility for government upon himself until Peel arrived from Italy to be prime minister. It required the failure of Peel to win a majority of seats at the general election which was immediately called to show that it had ceased to be true, as it had been since 1714, that the King never lost a general election. What neither Palmerston nor the public realized was that the constituencies were, in effect, determining not only whether the Whigs should return to office, but whether, if they did, Palmerston should return to the Foreign Office. It seems likely that if their majority had been bigger, he would not have returned.

★　　★　　★　　★

Palmerston welcomed a few weeks' partial rest before resuming the Foreign Office — it could only be partial, for he had 'to commence itinerant spouter at inn meetings of freeholders, and to ride about the country canvassing' in his own southern division of Hampshire.[30] He needed relaxation from the strain of 'more intense and uninterrupted labour than almost any man ever went through before'. This was no idle boast, for the man who once measured the industry of the War department by the number of subordinates who had died in their prime 'of pulmonary and other complaints arising from sedentary habits'[31] drove himself hard. That the Foreign Office clerks would have liked to celebrate by illuminations his defeat in Hampshire, as Greville recorded with glee,[32] was a tribute to his virtues — a perfectionism with regard to the use of copperplate and of the English language hardly inferior to Sir Winston Churchill's; high standards of proficiency and long hours of work, even at inconvenient hours — which bore hard on underlings not brought up in such high traditions. In the spring of 1833, a time of Eastern crisis and abortive attempts at concert with Vienna, he had been disabled for a month by influenza and biliousness, treated by blistering, calomel, quinine and a diet of sago and gruel, and when he resumed work a hacking cough detracted from the delights of lamb and sherry.[33] He had managed a couple of weeks at Broadlands at Christmas, and a week at the end of March 1834, 'working all day, and almost every day' on Foreign Office boxes and three years' neglected estate accounts, though finding time to inspect his racehorses, admire his young plantations, and get rid of a keeper who spent every night at the ale-house (at the poachers' expense?).[34] A short interlude over

Christmas and the new year (1835) would therefore be pleasant. If the unexpected happened, and the Tories stayed in for a while, it would be no bad thing 'in a political point of view' to have a year's regular work in the Commons on the Opposition Front Bench.[35] It would make up ground lost by speeches in 1834 which Palmerston was vaguely aware were judged harshly by the connoisseurs.[36] There had been no time to prepare them properly and the majority of members, elected for the first time in 1833, thought the Foreign Secretary a very poor parliamentary hand. There might be a chance to show them the style of 1st June 1829. But Palmerston did not anticipate the great increase in Tory representation, re-christened 'Conservative' by the sagacity of Peel, which delayed the return of the Whigs till April, nor expect to lose his seat and thus be unable to take any part in the struggle to turn Peel out. Least of all did he apprehend the possibility that there would never again be any Foreign Office papers to take to Broadlands. When, with Melbourne, Lansdowne, Holland and Spring-Rice, he signed on 11th April 1835 a letter to Grey urging the old man to take either the premiership or the Foreign Office, it was with little expectation that Grey would abandon the retirement for which he had craved, and in full expectation that he would return to the Foreign Office under Melbourne. He had no inkling that Melbourne would next day write as he did to the prospective Leader of the House, Russell, who was on his honeymoon. The question of two men, said Melbourne, was as important as any point of principle. One was Brougham, who had given ostentatious and unforgiveable offence to the King and his colleagues. The other was — Palmerston.[37] The latter would have been astonished to know that Grey also felt that he should not resume his old office.

Grey had been a good prime minister for Palmerston to work with. Even Palmerston, 'deficient in the organ of veneration'[38] (as Pozzo and Talleyrand knew) must defer to one who had lived with Fox and fought Pitt, had been himself Foreign Secretary (though briefly and a quarter of a century before), and had given Palmerston his chance. If the two men agreed, Grey's prestige, sometimes exploited by hints of impending retirement, was usually (though not on Portugal as 1833 turned into 1834) sufficient to guarantee cabinet endorsement. And, by and large, they did agree, on Belgium, Greece and Portugal, though Grey was rather more pro-Pole than Palmerston and even slower to overcome his anti-

Turkish prejudices. There were occasional rumours of friction. Palmerston was thought to dislike the direct relations of Grey with his brother-in-law, Ponsonby, in Brussels, more overtly and actively for Leopold's candidature than Palmerston thought wise. Grey was over-considerate to his son-in-law, the moody and arrogant Durham, a thorn in Palmerston's flesh, and to his brother-in-law, Ellice, often touting for Durham in clubs and salons. Palmerston absolutely vetoed the appointment of Durham to the Paris embassy, but sent him on a special mission to Russia 'as a diversion' after a bereavement. Durham returned convinced that he was a consummate diplomat, holding the only key to good relations with Russia, and the Eastern Powers tried to use his ambitions and his resentment that Palmerston attached no weight to his counsel as a lever to separate Grey from Palmerston, 'the mule'.[39] But Grey seconded Palmerston's persistence over the nomination of Stratford Canning to St Petersburg which, not without doubt, he had endorsed, and he could hardly complain of weak representation at Constantinople in critical months of 1833, for it was because of the dilatory progress of Lord Ponsonby to his new embassy.

On the whole there is no reason to criticize Palmerston's assertion, as to his relations with Grey, that 'no two men, I believe, ever went on better together in office, and very few half as well'.[40] There had been no quarrel. But on Grey's side there was little cordiality, and there was perhaps some coolness over the mishandling by Grey of the dispute between Russell and Stanley. Palmerston and Lansdowne had tried to avert the departure of the four ministers, while Holland and Ellice worked the other way. Palmerston believed that the split could have been avoided and that it was due to the intrigues of Durham and Ellice, whom he knew for foes of himself. Grey, on his side, seems to have resented the failure of the more conservative ministers, when the premier quarrelled with the Leader of the House and one of them had to go, to fight for their champion, so that it was Althorp who stayed. But it was very near to Grey's heart in 1835 to ensure that, without participating himself, the new Whig government should be conservative. Since Palmerston was one of the more conservative ministers, Grey's concurrence in Melbourne's view that he should not return to the Foreign Office is striking evidence of how little Palmerston counted politically. And that he should have given as the reason that the objection to Palmerston was 'general' showed that a formidable case could be made against his reappointment.

Melbourne was, in all but name, Palmerston's brother-in-law. But Palmerston had not understood how unhappy Melbourne (then Home Secretary) had been from mid-1832 at the departure from Canning's negative style of 'non-intervention' and his neutrality in the ideological war. His instinct and his reason led him to try to lower the temperature, both in politics and diplomacy. A sceptic, sometimes a cynic, he was suspicious of the 'almost sentimental idealism' which Palmerston brought to the ideological war and his feeling for political quietude was bruised by Palmerston's restlessness. It is characteristic of the two men that Melbourne, an agnostic, read the lives of the Fathers of the Church for relaxation (it being before the days of detective fiction) while Palmerston hardly read anything except Foreign Office archives, consciously or unconsciously looking for points to score. Melbourne mistrusted devotees. He had sympathized in his heart with the Lords when they censured interference in Portugal. His few months as prime minister had given him new evidence of how bad were Palmerston's relations with the Eastern Powers, and, with the Carlist war in Spain, they were hardly likely, if Palmerston was at the Foreign Office, to improve. Moreover Melbourne had a feeling for Concert. Originally a Foxite Whig, he had drifted to the Canningite outworks of Toryism partly because he could not share the Opposition's passionate misrepresentation of Castlereagh. He disapproved the personal animus which Palmerston brought to his contest with Metternich, the contentious spirit which had led him to write: 'I should like to have seen Metternich's face when he reads our treaty; I dare say he is in a state of considerable wrath, the turn which affairs have taken both in Spain and Portugal must be enough to drive him almost mad.'[41]

Melbourne's brother, Frederick Lamb, who was often teased by their sister, Emily Cowper, for his 'little Austrian twist',[42] hardened all these doubts into adverse decision when he came home to make sure, if he could, that Palmerston did not become again his master. From Palmerston's point of view, Lamb was not the man to represent Britain at Vienna once the Belgian treaty had been ratified. But Greville, though malicious, probably has the right explanation of why he kept at the Habsburg court an ambassador described by Greville as completely be-Metterniched — 'The

Chief [Palmerston] is devoted to the Sister [Lady Cowper], and the Sister to the Brother [Frederick Lamb]. The Sister would not hesitate between the Lover and the Brother, and any injury to the latter would recoil upon the head of the former. [And so] in this pleasant circle the convenience of Government and the interests of their policy are passed over or compromised as they may.'[43] From Lamb's point of view, Palmerston was not the right man to send instructions to ambassadors, and he found those private letters for the censor's eye unforgiveable. He came home to argue that Palmerston's enthusiastic Liberalism was an aberration from which flowed most undesirable consequences. Had it not been the reason that there was no international conference on the Eastern Question, no concert between Britain and Austria ('natural allies' against Russia) in the early months of 1833? Had it not therefore been the reason for Russia's triumph and for the Münchengratz agreement on Turkey?

If the matter had come to open debate, Palmerston could have made some partially effective replies. He and Metternich had both wanted concert on Turkey, but Palmerston was not prepared to accept Vienna as the *centre* and Metternich would not hear of a Western *centre*. Was there not adequate explanation of this in his attitude to the Belgian conference, which, Palmerston suggested, could have been reconvened to deal with the Eastern Question? Palmerston had no intention of going to war 'for abstract principles'[44] and his engagement in propaganda betokened no weakening of his desire to co-operate with all or any Powers to maintain the peace of Europe and the Balance of Power. To the complaint that the Quadruple Alliance of 1834 obscured this, divided the states of Europe into rival camps, and appeared to quash the old Castlereaghan Quadruple Alliance to check France, Palmerston could reply that the alliance was both defensive and provoked; that it need not affect the co-operation of the other Powers against France if required, but that until and unless the alliance proved a sham it would not be required, for the new Quadruple Alliance was the best way of restraining the French. He could point out that Wellington 'made no arbitrary changes in our system of policy' and if this was partly because he felt that the existence of Peel's government was precarious, was it not also true that 'English interests continue the same let who will be in office, and that upon leading principles and great measures men of both sides, when they come to act dispassionately and with responsibility upon them, will be found acting very much alike.'[45]

But this last was a very dangerous argument, for the charge was that Palmerston was not dispassionate and was irresponsible. So it seemed to all Tories (and that would be important now that the Whig–Liberal–Radical–Irish majority was small), to that school of Radicals who preached peace and retrenchment as a dogma and the many Whigs who by tradition and instinct thought similarly. The credit gained by the Quadruple Alliance among those many Whigs who were primarily pro-French was partly offset by the fact that many of them were, like Althorp, devotees of economy and often of 'non-intervention' in its pre-Palmerston sense. Moreover, some of them were so pro-French (or so realistic) as to think that Palmerston's boast 'I have satisfied their vanity by giving them a proper place among us'[46] was as wrong-headed as Talleyrand's boast (accepted at its face value by the Tories) that British policy was now subject to French control. The francophils thought Palmerston ungenerous in his attitude to French aspirations. But even men broadly sympathetic with Palmerston's policies, and appreciative of his successes could feel that the opposition of so many British envoys and of almost all the diplomatic corps in London to Palmerston's return to duty constituted a strong prima facie case against it.

Some of the criticisms of Palmerston's habits and diplomatic manners were captious and unjustified, partly a hangover from his past reputation as a man-about-town and his casual air. By putting together George Villiers's complaint of lack of instructions in Madrid and Palmerston's pursuit of the twenty-two-year-old Mrs Laura Petre the Princess Lieven (a woman scorned) could concoct, and Greville repeat (and Halévy accept!) a charge of idleness and negligence.[47] Palmerston, indeed, was rarely abreast of his work, and the cost of special messengers and conveyances to the ports to catch the mails was considerable, but that was because he took too much on himself. He read everything and wrote prodigiously. Greville was genuinely surprised when his higher officials praised his abilities, saying that he wrote admirably, was perfect in French, sufficient in Italian, could get the hang of German, and that his diligence and attention were unwearied.[48] He was astounded when Lady Granville said his capacity was first-rate and that he approached greatness because of his 'enlarged views, disdain of trivialities, his resolution, decision, confidence and above all his contempt of clamour and abuse'.[49] Talleyrand himself said that among the ministers there was but one statesman — Palmerston. Greville was driven to conclude, fairly enough, that there was a contrast he had not divined between the minister conducting business and the man whose 'ordinary conversation exhibits no such superiority'. (Palmerston refused to 'talk shop' on social occasions and as he was not a man of cultivated mind his talk was pretty small.) 'When he takes his pen in his hand his intellect seems to have full play.' But were not his writings, as Queen Victoria was to complain, 'bitter as gall'? Did he not show contempt, not only of clamour and abuse, but of *persons*, if he disliked the policy or ideology they represented? Not a man to abide fools gladly, his diatribes to ambassadors, which he thought mere honest plain speaking about the folly or knavery of their masters, had an abrasive effect on international relations. He thought himself 'a good European', but was never viewed as such on the Continent, because he set no value on goodwill in diplomacy. His 'disdain of trivialities' extended to the normal niceties of diplomatic intercourse and even of social commerce with the diplomats. Social slights helped to drive the Duchesse de Dino, Talleyrand's niece and hostess, into intrigue with the Lieven to get Palmerston turned out. Palmerston's unpunctuality and refusal to give important foreign envoys priority of admission to him caused much rancour. So far as 'old Tally' was concerned, Palmerston explained that he was too busy to have his afternoons taken up by random chatter, but was it necessary to show Pozzo and Talleyrand quite so clearly that he thought them 'over the hill'?

Palmerston was supremely unconscious of having given just offence in any of these ways. His own account of the harangue to Neumann (quoted above, p. 54) reads: 'The Baron grew pale with emotion as I went through my catalogue and his upper lip curled about like Brougham's nose. . . . He left me indifferently pleased with the conversation, but promising to make a faithful report of it to his Court. . . . However we parted remarkably good friends and mutually much pleased at having had an opportunity of explaining our views to each other.' Such a tone could not be explained away as the fruit of over-work or the passion of a moment, for sometimes it was clearly calculated. It was significant that, according to Melbourne, Palmerston kept his temper well in cabinet.[50] One could contend that Palmerston's faults of tone and manner were luxuries that Britain could afford. But was she wise to do so, bearing in mind the inevitable jealousy of foreigners of her wealth and power? That, in a great crisis, he could take himself in hand and negotiate brilliantly, the Belgian crisis had shown. But that had come in the beginning, and it was possible to argue that there had been a deterioration into mere bullying since. Confronted with the certainty that, if Harry resumed the Foreign Office, Harry would resume, impenitently, his old ways, continue to conduct diplomacy in language more suited to the hustings, condemning his colleagues to unease and to avoidable expense and to parliamentary contention and diplomatic rancour, Melbourne and Grey (Spencer concurring) decided that Palmerston should be offered another office. It was apparently intended that Lord John Russell, though physically delicate, should combine the Foreign Office with the leadership of the House. He was a Whig to the core, broadly in agreement with Palmerston's policy, and far from dispassionate. Yet his brother was probably justified in writing to Russell: 'On the Continent the Conservatives look upon you as a most dangerous and detestable democrat. But they would have preferred you to Palmerston, who gives them all the stomach-ache.'[51]

★　★　★　★

Besides the virtue of not being Palmerston, Russell had two advantages. Despite his old-world affectations, he was a far more proficient parliamentary speaker than Palmerston had proved himself in office. When Melbourne suggested Russell, Spring Rice or Abercromby for the succession to Althorp, the King said that Russell would make a wretched figure and the others would be worse. Palmerston was not mentioned as a possible Leader of the House (November 1834), nor was this honourable position offered him as an inducement to forego the Foreign Office in April 1835. Palmerston was no worse a speaker than Althorp, but he had not, as Althorp had, won the general respect of the House. Nor had he Russell's other asset, a strong political connexion. It is therefore highly probable that Palmerston owed his reappointment to the Foreign Office simply to the fact that the Whigs had only an exiguous majority. When he declined any other office, saying that the objections to his return made it impossible, since they amounted to a censure and an indication that policy was to be changed,[53] it was borne upon Melbourne, firstly that this was true and would be hard on Palmerston and inconvenient for his successor, and, secondly, that it would never do to have Palmerston going the way of Stanley and Graham, now more than half-way towards the Tory camp. And it might be even worse if he recovered his tongue, to have him analysing the policy of Russell or Howick from below the gangway in the guise of a 'candid friend'. So Melbourne, not without misgivings, sanctioned the reappointment as His Majesty's Principal Secretary of State (for the Foreign Department) of his friend, his sister's more-than-friend, his diplomat brother's bête noire.

CHAPTER VI

PLOUGHING THE SANDS

AT the same time that Palmerston began to show signs of rekindled political ambition, he undertook seriously for the first time the development of his properties and investments. He spent time and trouble on the Cornwall and Devon Mining Company, showed a faith superior to that of other investors in a North Welsh slate quarry, instituted a (vain) search for coal on his small estate in the West Riding. But above all, he visited annually from 1825 to 1828 what his father on his only visit in 1761 called 'the most dreary waste I ever yet beheld', in County Sligo, which Palmerston on *his* first visit in 1808 found still 'wholly unimproved'. He set in hand pilot works for the reclamation of blowing sand at Mullaghmore by the planting of bent and for the reclamation of bog by sanding and then planting roots, to be followed by rape and oats. Characteristically, he started with the worst stretch of bog.

There is a parallel in all this with his diplomacy. He persevered in investment in a dubious enterprise in Spain; he searched unceasingly for the solid mineral of political stability in Greece; he sought to plant a British-type constitutionalism in the unrewarding soil of Portugal. It was such a sad mistake, Queen Victoria was to say, to try constitutions 'in these Southern countries', and many without her monarchical prejudices held that the belief that these peoples could work a free constitution was a sentimental illusion and the idea that a constitutional government would want, or dare, to be more pro-British than an arbitrary one both an illusion and a non sequitur. But despite recurrent disappointments, and intervals of despair, Palmerston strove unremittingly to establish and maintain constitutional government and British influence. His optimism was congenital and impervious to argument.

In Portugal, all was supposed to come right with Maria, the Cortes and the Charter of 1826. But in violation of the Charter the queen assumed the monarchical power at the age of fifteen. She married, also in violation of the Charter, two foreign princes in succession. The second of them was Ferdinand of Saxe-Coburg (1836). Her ministers pillaged the national property. The politicians were divided into the more conservative Chartists and the Septembrists, who stood for the democratic constitution of 1822, were more nationalist, and also, if only because Britain had backed the Chartists, susceptible to French influence. Under either constitution, a victory for the Opposition meant the substitution of the other; under either, a victory for the government would be held by the Opposition, usually with justice, to have been improperly gained and there would be revolt. In September 1836, when the Chartist government won, an army revolt forced the queen to restore the constitution of September 1822. An abortive counter-revolution staged by Maria (to which the British envoy was privy) drove the queen and her retinue to the protection of British ships and marines. Palmerston could only tell Howard de Walden to rest on his oars and try to win influence with the victorious ministers.[1] In March 1838 there were bloody battles in the streets of Lisbon, followed by a compromise constitution and an amnesty (excluding Miguelites).

Was the surreptitious, but widely known, involvement of the British envoy in Portuguese politics to keep the favour of the queen, to hold French influence at bay, to tip the scale for the Chartists against the Septembrists as being more conservative and monarchical if equally corrupt and incompetent, worth while? There was much to be said for the view that the only valid British influence in Portugal rested on the knowledge that the navy would go to the Tagus to protect the independence of the country or chastise it for insult or injury to British interests. Palmerston himself understood that one of the aspirations of the Portuguese was independence from Britain, and that any government, of whatever label, which wished to rest upon consent must go as far in resisting British domination as it could without risking penal action. Was Aberdeen so foolish after all to base his refusal to interfere on the ground that there was no half-way house between abstention and 'a constant and minute interference in the affairs of Portugal . . . for His Majesty could never consent to hold his fleets and armies at the disposal of a King of Portugal without any of those due precautions and that superintendence, which would assure him that his forces would not be liable to be employed in averting the effects of misgovernment, folly or caprice'?[2] Palmerston, in opposition, had condemned this as craven: 'Why, sir, do what we will, there is a fatality which draws us, like the moth into the candle, to entangle ourselves in the internal affairs of Portugal; and so it must be, for no man can deny that England is deeply interested in the tranquillity of Portugal.'[3] But the candle often singed the moth!

Portugal at least in 1835 had a constitution (with an alternative one in the wings) and a monarch who had been associated in her absence with constitutionalism. Spain had no constitution and a greedy and immoral Neapolitan queen-regent was under pressure on the one hand from the Carlists and on the other from a Left standing like the Septembrists for a former constitution based on popular sovereignty. The first prerequisite for a constitution was the defeat of Don Carlos, who slipped away from England to join the Biscayans and the Navarrese in the fastnesses from which these defenders of provincial privileges forayed far and wide every summer against the Cristinos who held Madrid and, if they did not control, denied to the Carlists most of Spain. The civil war was a squalid affair. There was not very much to choose, as to atrocities in the heat of battle and its cold aftermath, the lust of advancing and the vengeance of retreating armies, between the two sides. Carlos was bigoted; Cristina was worthless. Each was in the end shouldered aside by generals, Maroto and Espartero who, by the mediation of British agents, brought the war to an official end by the Convention of Bergara in 1839. There was no pretence of neutrality or non-intervention on Palmerston's part in this war. 'It was in principle an interference', he told the House on 24th June 1835, and 'other countries had a right, if they chose to exercise it, to take part with either of the two belligerents'. The Quadruple treaty was amended to provide for a French blockade to prevent assistance organized by Metternich reaching the Carlists, for supplies from Britain to the Spanish government forces (including, in all, half a million muskets), for the 'observation' of Carlist coasts by British warships. Within a few months of the return of the Whigs to office the Foreign Enlistment Act was suspended to allow the formation of a British Legion which numbered 10,000 (many of them foreign, especially Belgian, mercenaries). Its commander, de Lacy Evans, a Radical politician deeply distrusted by the Horse Guards, was handpicked by Palmerston on the principle that only ardent minds were fit for dangerous enterprises. Frigates sailed as morale-boosters off beleaguered coasts, especially off

Bilbao, the capture of which by the Carlists might have made a Cristino victory impossible. Naval patrols blockaded Carlist harbours. Sardinian frigates were shadowed by British. Naval steamers transported Spanish troops to the relief of Santander. British shells fell on San Sebastian and the besiegers of Barcelona. British marines acted as artillerymen to Spanish detachments. The Tories and the pacific school of Radicals thought it scandalous. Palmerston was unapologetic — 'I only pray Heaven, that so long as I have the honour of retaining office . . . I may never be exposed to any more serious charge than this — that, in the execution of our engagements with foreign powers, we have gone not only to their full extent . . . but that, out of a sense of delicacy towards our ally, we have, if possible, gone beyond it.'[4] Fresh articles would have been required if Britain and France had decided to respond to the Regent's appeal for armies to be sent, but 'they would not have been beyond the spirit of the Quadruple Treaty'.[3]

How was this policy justified? On the theory that the genuine independence of Spain, and its membership of the Western confederacy of constitutional states, was both a British and a European interest. 'It is an English interest that the cause of the Queen of Spain shall be successful. It is of great importance to this country that the alliance which has been fortunately cemented between the four Powers of the West — England, France, Constitutional Spain and Constitutional Portugal . . . should continue; and it can only continue by the success of the Queen of Spain.'[5] 'I say that it is to the interest of England that Spain should be rich, that she should be powerful, that she should be independent.' Under a government such as Ferdinand's had been, and Carlos's would be, she could be none of these. But 'we could extricate her — we could retrieve her from that abasement into which she has fallen, and so regenerate her as to make her a power worthy once more to take her place among the dominions of Europe, and as an ally of Great Britain'. That would be 'a noble result'. And 'I tell the noble Lord, that if Spain shall establish herself as a free and constitutional Government — if she shall be, as she must be in that case, a free and substantive power — beyond all doubt we shall find her useful in the general system of Europe in maintaining the balance of power, and useful as an available friend of England, with respect even to our commercial interests.'[6] The struggle in Spain was 'not between Persons but between Principles'.[7] 'We know that

Europe, since the French Revolution of July, has been divided, I will not say into hostile, but into different parties, acting each according to their respective principles.'⁵ A sceptical House of Commons was invited to applaud a crusading enterprise, and warned (when attacks were made on the activities of de Lacy Evans, who was not in the British service, and Lord John Hay and his marines, who were) that the vote it was to take would be read as 'an opinion as between those opposite principles that, more or less, divide the suffrages of every country in Europe, and that more or less influence the policy of every country'.⁴ Palmerston's part was taken:⁶

We have been accused of favouring innovations, and encouraging revolution. But that accusation is unfounded and unjust. We have, indeed, given our moral support — we have given our good wishes — to this great Spanish nation, who have been endeavouring, of their own accord, to improve their institutions, and to imitate, though at a distance, the proud example of this country, by acquiring the inestimable privileges of representative government. It has been the part of His Majesty's Ministers to give their acquiescence in, and support to these objects, as we are bound to do. We may say, that during the period in which we have had the honour to administer the affairs of this country, the principles of national liberty have made greater progress in Europe than they have ever before made, within the same time, at any period of our history. To the diffusion of these principles we have given every support, and it is our boast that we have done so . . . The people in Belgium have been free, happy, powerful and tranquil. . . . Portugal has established free institutions, is prepared to profit by them, and is on the high road to that prosperity which, in my opinion, free institutions alone can open to a country. Spain . . . I may be allowed to hope . . . may yet follow the example which has been set to her by Belgium and Portugal. . . . And if she shall do this, I humbly beg to say for myself, that notwithstanding all the taunts, and all the reproaches — . . . if I may claim however humble a share in the triumph of bringing about such a state of things — I shall feel a high degree of pride, and most lasting satisfaction.

There was to be decided in Biscay, 'upon that contracted scene . . . by the issue of battle that great contest between the opposing and conflicting principles of government — arbitrary government on the one hand, and constitutional government on the other — that contest which is going on all over Europe only, fortunately, for mankind, in other countries it is waged by arguments instead of by arms, and the peace of nations is not disturbed by it'.⁴

The idealism was genuine, the over-optimism characteristic. At its base was an utter inability to understand the point of view of those who said Britain had no business in the ideological war. Europe must have the benefit of Britain's experience and counsel. 'Palmerston's impudence and jaunty air have blinded later historians as well as Metternich to the real merits of and real significance of his political philosophy', wrote A. J. P. Taylor: 'We have grown so used to talking of Pam's lectures that we have forgotten what he lectured about; his pride in England was so aggressive that it concealed the cause of his pride.'[8] What was his philosophy? 'It is the just pride and boast of England, that wealth accumulates rapidly here, owing to the Constitution we enjoy, and the enterprise of her people.'[9] So also in Spain, the real question was 'whether Spain shall fall back *under the arbitrary System of Govt which has so long paralysed the Natural Energies of the Spanish Nation*, or whether a Constitutional System similar to that which exists in England and in France or in Portugal shall be established also in Spain'.[7] Of course, Palmerston saw the point that the British constitution was a product of indigenous evolution, and acknowledged that 'all changes in national institutions to be useful and permanent should be made to grow out of what is and should be in harmony with the antient institutions and habits of the people'.[10] But it was fatal to dwell on necessary local variations on the British model, for that opened the way to an all too familiar argument, which Palmerston never ceased to controvert:[11]

You say that a constitution is but a means to an end and the end is good government; but the experience of mankind shews that this is the only road by which a goal can be reached and that it is impossible without a constitution fully to develop the natural resources of a country, and to ensure for the nation security for life, liberty and property. I hold that there is no instance in past or present times under a despotic government where these objects have been achieved. (To Frederick Lamb, Lord Beauvale, 31st Jan 1841).

. . . It is always easy to say, with regard to any Country in which men do not wish to see Constitutional Government established, that such a Country is not fit for it, and that it would not work there; but Her Majesty's Government do not happen to recollect any Country in which Constitutional system of Government has been established that has not on the whole been better off in consequence of that system than it had been before. (To Granville, 19th March 1841, official dispatch).

. . . For my part, I believe that if any nation should be found not fit for constitutional government, the best way to fit such a nation for it would be to give it to them. (House of Commons, 14th March 1844, hailing the revolution in Greece).

Palmerston firmly believed that the British system of representative and responsible government was destined to be, and
fitted to be, the European norm. This is implied by the italicized
portions of the letter to Lamb in July 1833:

... Not that we want all other countries to adopt our Constitution ... or
fancy that because such institutions are good here, they must *necessarily*
answer *at once everywhere else.* ...

It is explicit in the dispatch to Granville for the eye of Guizot,
quoted above —

Her Majesty's Govern is not pedantically attached to any particular Form
of political Constitution, and although they may be of opinion that the
Form which ... has been established in England and France is, on the
whole, the best, they by no means wish to press the *immediate* adoption of
that Form upon the King of Greece.

This pride in the superiority of British institutions has often been
regarded as arrogant, and so it must seem to a foreigner who does
not happen to believe that this sort of constitution is suited to his
country. But what Palmerston was in fact asserting was that the
Greeks, the Spaniards and the Portuguese, given a chance, could
do after a fashion what his colleague, the third Earl Grey, when he
was Colonial Secretary from 1846 to 1852, took the risk of believing that British and French Canadians could do — govern themselves under free institutions. It was those who, while genuinely
approving British freedom, thought it inapposite for most
European peoples, at least in their existing state of development,
who were arrogant, unconsciously (sometimes consciously) writing
them off as 'lesser breeds without the law'. As to the naïveté of the
conception, was it more naïve to hypothecate the capacity of the
nations of southern Europe to work a constitutional system with
profit to themselves, after centuries of authoritarianism and recent
interludes of anarchy, than to hypothecate the same of Indians or
Nigerians in the 1950s? It is true that the progress of comparative
studies and sociological and economic research is reconciling the
Western world to the notion that the public interest may sometimes
in under-developed countries be better served by a political system
very different from the Western prescription. But those who, in a
superior kind of way, predicted that Africans and Asians would
turn to dictatorship, more or less disguised, and those who, when
they have done so, justify or excuse them, share, unless they are

Communists, a twinge of regret that this should happen. Palmerston erred, if he erred, not in the worst, but in the best company. But did he err? All non-Communist progressives felt in the 1930s that the failure of many European states to work a democratic system represented regression from a constitutionalist norm established (as Palmerston prophesied it would be) by the first decade of the twentieth century, when even Russia and Turkey conformed, at least nominally, to it. And it has yet to be proved how life, liberty and property can be protected without representative institutions of the Western sort. To Whigs the safeguarding of these was the chief end of government. Palmerston (to Lamb, 31st January 1841) links them with the development of natural resources. The justification given in the twentieth century for dispensing with fully free elections, freedom of speech, freedom from arbitrary imprisonment, etc., is that priority must be given to the development of resources, and that this requires an imposed unity and a protected leadership. But in the nineteenth century that was, so far as Europe was concerned, a Metternichian, not a Palmerstonian, proposition.

*   *   *   *

Where arrogance intruded, and a high ideal was tarnished, honesty compromised and clarity of purpose lost, was not in the effort to secure for Portugal, and for Spain, a chance of constitutional government, but in incessant interference by British agents on behalf of this party or that. When Palmerston told the House of Commons he was happy to acknowledge that Britain did not possess in Spain 'that influence which consists in the power of procuring the dismissal of one ministry . . . by underhand intrigue, and the substitution of another, by means equally objectionable',[6] he was less than candid, and everybody knew it. When he added that he trusted no English government would ever seek to exercise that species of influence, and that it would deserve signally to fail if it did, he invited Nemesis. Of course, there were extenuating circumstances — there always are. The British were more eager to get the war over, not only than the French, but than many of the Spanish politicos. Was it not therefore right to try to uphold ministers of some determination and ability? After Cristina granted a Cortes in 1836 and a (compromise) constitution in 1837, there was extreme political instability. If the British envoy worked against an incumbent, he could always feel the man was not likely to last long anyway, and when he worked for one, he was assisting both the war effort and stability. Who better qualified than Britain, by 'friendly counsel and advice', a push here, a lure there, to help constitutional Spain over its initial difficulties? Palmerston sometimes had to rebuke George Villiers in Madrid, like Howard de Walden in Lisbon and Lyons in Athens, for excessive zeal, when interference proved to have been obviously impolitic. But he defended him warmly in the House of Commons and approved his prolific exhortation of the regent and his systematic liaison with Spanish politicians, usually of the *Progressista* faction. What Palmerston would never admit, in the complex hurly-burly of conflict between *Progressista* and *Moderado* was that, in the words of a historian of Spain and Portugal, 'no constitution could command the respect of both sides in a nation profoundly divided against itself. A constitution that enshrined the principles of one was of necessity directed against the other and became in effect an incitement to civil war; a constitution that kept to the middle position was respected by neither and inevitably succumbed to attacks from both'.[12] Nor would he admit the existence of a third, unconsidered, interest, the mass of the Spanish nation. Canning, with his superior realism, had seen that 'a vast majority still entertained a decided . . . predilection for arbitrary government'. Villiers, the man on the spot, came to the same conclusion, which, when he was a cabinet minister and Earl of Clarendon, coloured his whole future policy. The Spanish masses, he said, were honest, Carlist and absolutist. The Liberals were 'hated by the whole nation, which has no desire for or fitness for liberal institutions'. The younger generation, wanting improvement, wanted an enlightened dictator.[13] Palmerston was proof against such scepticism. 'We did not interfere . . . for the purpose of imposing upon the Spanish people a government to which they themselves were averse, or which they themselves had not adopted', he said,[6] and likened the change of régime to that of 1688 and July 1830.[4]

Any reservations that Palmerston might have felt about the propriety or wisdom of systematic interference in the internal affairs of Spain melted away when it became crystal clear that a contest was going on for predominant influence between the British and the French. The British Opposition, many Radicals, and, indeed, some, perhaps most, of Palmerston's own colleagues, could follow his proposition that an absolutist Spain must be anti-British and that therefore a constitutional Spain was a British interest, without being able to follow, let alone share, his assertion that an independent, constitutional, Spain would be pro-British. Might it not be pro-French? Ought it not to be simply pro-Spanish? But French intrigue enabled Palmerston to square a circle. If one assumed, as it is quite clear from the coincidence of Palmerston's private correspondence with his official pronouncement that he did, the extravagant equation

$$\text{Liberal state} = \text{independent state} = \text{pro-British state}$$

a highly convenient conclusion followed. Palmerston believed, as we know, that the natural condition to which any European country tended was one of freedom, and that only the artificial contrivances of power prevented it embarking, however stumblingly, upon a course of constitutionalism. Therefore the operations of the Eastern Powers, and, intermittently but increasingly, of the French, constituted a conspiracy to prevent Spain from assuming its normal condition. Therefore a Spanish patriot could look only to Britain for support against reaction and subversion. Pro-French leanings on the part of a Spanish faction or government were therefore either signs of French intrigue or of the insecurity of illiberal Spaniards who, liberalism being the natural destiny of their country, required external support. Since 'England can have no interest but in the prosperity of Spain'[14] it was quite proper for British agents to press men and measures on the regent. Their efforts to substitute British for French influence in court or Cortes were to be regarded simply as a defensive reflex restoring the natural order of things.

As early as November 1835 Palmerston wrote that Louis Philippe and Talleyrand 'both look on the change from despotism to free institutions as unfavourable to French ascendancy at Madrid. They both see that if Spain becomes a free and constitutional state, it will also become . . . instead of a satellite of France an independent ally of England'.[15] In 1840 he avowed that the policy of making Spain a dependency of France (as Portugal was of Britain?) 'would be pursued by every French government, Carlist, Philippist, Buonapartist or Republican. But our business is to endeavour to thwart and counteract such policy, and our means of doing so lie in the activity and exertions of our Minister

at Madrid . . . [who] as a general rule . . . should always be as
forward to give good counsel as the French representative to give
bad'. The minister is told to show the regent that 'it is for the
interest of the Spanish sovereign and nation to pursue an independent course, to have Ministers who sympathize with the people
and to prefer an alliance with England, who can have no interest
but in the prosperity of Spain, to an alliance with France who must
wish to make Spain what she was during the last century, a
satellite of France'.[14] French policy, inveterate, because 'natural'
to France, was 'bad' for Spain. British policy, though dictated by
British interest, was 'good' for Spain. French policy was essentially
encroaching and British policy essentially defensive, directed to
producing a result that was 'natural' and 'good' for Spain (and
'good' for Britain).

It was, of course, difficult for foreigners to understand self-
deception on so massive a scale. They attributed to British
hypocrisy the claim for the *moral* superiority of British meddling
over Austrian, or Russian, or French meddling, which was really a
symptom of British insularity and arrogance. They were confirmed
in their diagnosis by Tory and Radical attacks and Whig scepticism,
which were informed by insularity of another kind. But although
it is not claimed that in the '30s the majority of the British political
classes adopted Palmerston as their hero — as they were later to
do — his combination of unabashed insularity and patronizing
philanthropy towards Europeans gave articulation to prejudices and
sentiments strongly felt by Britons. Morley, the biographer of
Palmerston's ablest fundamentalist critic, Cobden, an Englishman
who to his political disadvantage was praised by foreigners for his
freedom from many of these prejudices, understood this. What
made Palmerston formidable was that, although 'in all this untiring
restlessness' there was no sense, his conception 'had about it a
generous and taking air. It was magnificent', for Palmerston 'was
moved by an honest interest in good government, or by a vigorous
resolution that his country should play a prominent and worthy
part in settling the difficulties of Europe'.[16] Cobden wrote:[17]

My visit to Spain has strengthened, if possible, a hundredfold my conviction that all attempts of England to control or influence the destinies,
political and social of that country are worse than useless. . . . I have
always had an instinctive monomania against this system of foreign interference, protocolling, diplomatising etc. . . . the Palmerston system. . . .

But . . . the evil has its roots in the pugnacious, energetic, self-sufficient, foreigner-despising and pitying character of that noble insular creature, John Bull. Read Washington Irving's description of him fumbling for his cudgel the moment he hears of any row taking place anywhere on the face of the earth, and bristling up with anger at the very idea that any other people dare have a quarrel without first asking his consent or inviting him to take part in it.

This was no caricature. In one and the same speech Palmerston quoted with emphatic approval Canning's maxim that 'with every British minister the interests of England ought to be the Shibboleth of his policy' and declared 'the real policy of England is to be the champion of justice and right . . . giving the weight of her moral sanction and support wherever she thinks that justice is, and wherever she thinks that wrong has been done'.[18] And, again, 'The only party which it was the interest of the British Government to support in Spain was the Spanish nation. . . . We had no party interest to maintain in Spain. The interest of England was to maintain whatever party was best capable of supporting and maintaining the real independence of the Spanish nation.'[19]

Foreigners were, of course, unconvinced, even though Palmerston took credit for resisting the temptation proffered by Villiers — to bribe a Spanish government, by parliamentary guarantee of a loan, to subject the textiles of Barcelona (and of France) to a withering blast of competition from Lancashire. They could not see this moral superiority of British to other interference. Had not Villiers, on whose nationwide intelligence service the Cristino government relied for prompt and accurate news from distant parts of Spain, boasted that he 'governed Spain'? Was this Spain for the Spaniards? — or only for the pro-British Spaniards, that British commerce might prosper, and Downing Street rest from the fear of finding the whole North Sea–Channel–Biscayan–Atlantic coast of Europe again in unfriendly hands and naval supremacy in the Mediterranean imperilled? Many British politicians held that the incessant meddling was wrong; others that, right or wrong, it was unprofitable. But Palmerston was quite unconscious of muddled thinking or hypocrisy and unwilling to admit failure. 'The Spaniards and Portuguese . . . with the consent of their legitimate sovereigns, and with the protecting aid of England, have obtained for themselves the inestimable blessing of representative government', he claimed after leaving office.[20] He had left it at a fortunate time (1841). Cristina, now openly pro-French, had been displaced (October 1840) by a strong man, Espartero, who was pro-British, and, further proof of virtue, denounced by the Vatican. The extent to which his régime was military dictatorship under a thin constitutional facade was as yet hidden, as it was hidden that from 1842 Portugal's strong man would be Costa Cabral, *not* a British choice. It could be said that Portugal, now recognized by the Eastern Powers and Rome as rightly belonging to Maria, was at last achieving a consensus, even though it was a Chartist consensus which foreshadowed another change of constitution. But when Palmerston returned to office in 1846, it was to face the necessity of saving the queen from the fruits of her own folly while shielding her opponents, rebels in arms, from her vengeance. And in Spain there ruled in Espartero's place another dictator, Narvaez, not pro-British and even less patient of constitutional forms. Without hesitation, Palmerston set about once more rolling stones uphill, ascribing all the trouble to the fact that Aberdeen, trying in office to practice what he had preached in opposition, 'gave up Spain to France'. 'The fight between Narvaez and *the interests of Spain and England* is still going on, but *I hope we shall win*, though no doubt Narvaez is well furnished by Louis Philippe and Cristina with the sinews of war'[21] (present writer's italics). When the revolution of 1848 expelled Louis Philippe from France, Palmerston turned aside briefly and brusquely from weightier matters than Spain's internal affairs to address to Isabella peremptory advice to change her ministers. When they protested, he reminded them that but for Britain she and they would be exiles in a foreign land. The British minister, Bulwer, was ordered out of Spain. Now at last Spain was 'genuinely independent' in Spanish if not in British eyes. Bulwer's self-defence is highly revealing. 'Dispatches of a much more offensive character had frequently been addressed to Spanish Governments', he says. The humiliation was solely due to the 'extreme caution' of ministers after his expulsion. Why was the fleet not sent to Cadiz?[22]

Palmerston's Iberian policy has had an almost uniformly bad press. 'It would probably have been better in the end to have adhered to Canning's doctrine of non-intervention with more strictness, and to have left Portugal and Spain to their own futile and sordid disputes. . . . There is perhaps no episode in Palmerston's career more to his credit than his Belgian achievement, and none less to it than his building of castles in Spain and his adventures in the country of Don Quixote' (Temperley and Penson). 'A phase in Palmerston's diplomacy which can be written off as very nearly without value. Of all the measures associated with his name, those which he took in connexion with Spain were the most lacking in lustre and significance' (Pemberton).[23] But they are an integral part of the Palmerston story, highly illustrative of his aspirations, his illusions, his combination of confused reasoning with a sense of mission and a clear objective. Unfortunately, as Pemberton says, 'it was not that Palmerston was here backing the wrong horse so much as putting money on one incapable of running'. Atkinson makes the same point: 'The long, unhappy reign of Isabella II (1833–68) . . . provided from first to last eloquent commentary on the impossibility of governing through representative institutions a country where the area of political agreement was so much smaller than that of disagreement. . . . In the end Spain was a country rotting from constitutional disease and crying out for the strong hand that could save it from itself.'[24]

*   *   *   *

Portugal was a special case, for there the primacy of British interest was more or less generally acknowledged, and the reign of Pedro V (1853–61) even suggested that Palmerston might have been right after all, and that constitutional government could work after a fashion under the guidance of a ruler more intelligent than Maria and more reputable than Isabella. Greece was a special case, in a different sense, because it was under the *guarantee* of three Powers none of which ever admitted that their rights were limited to the maintenance of the country's territorial integrity. There was thus no great dispute between Palmerston and Aberdeen on the *principle* of exercising a surveillance over the Greek constitution. 'I think it will be desirable that we should take our ground at once in support of the Greek Revolution. . . . I have never known a change more imperatively called for, more fully justified, or more wisely carried into effect.' The Foreign Secretary who wrote this in 1843 was not Palmerston but Aberdeen. Nor was he simply reacting as he had done to the July Revolution in Paris in 1830. For he insisted that the Protecting Powers must reserve the right to 'moderate the projects of the Greek patriots' while at the same time impressing on King Otho the wisdom and necessity of strict

adherence to the promises he had been forced to make. He entered
into details of the constitution which he wanted for Greece, and the
resultant document of 1844 'had as its ultimate source of inspiration . . . the conservative constitutionalism of the British Foreign
Secretary'.[25]

Palmerston would have claimed that the influence of his successor on the Greek patriots was the result of his own willingness to
be the 'odd man out', the only minister of the Great Powers and
the Protecting Powers who ever pressed on Otho, in and out of
season, the grant of constitutional freedom. He deeply regretted
that he had saddled Greece with the wrong king and neglected to
provide it with a constitution before or when he came. The Three
Powers (in Wellington's time) 'abstained from anticipating the
nature of the institutions and laws to be derived from an independent monarchy' (Protocol of 1st July 1830) and actually prohibited
the Greeks (Palmerston concurring) from settling their own
constitution before Otho arrived. But the lad's father, the King of
Bavaria, had acknowledged on his behalf 'the duty of providing the
political institutions which the needs of the country and its state of
civilization may render expedient' and the Protecting Powers on
30th August 1832 called on the Greeks from London to 'rally round
the throne' and 'assist their King in the task of giving the State a
definitive constitution'. Palmerston always insisted that 'a real and
bona fide Constitution . . . is the end which the Three Powers
ought to resolve to reach'.[26] But the other Powers had other ideas,
and Otho, chosen by Palmerston from the most liberal of the
German dynasties, ruled after he came of age as his Bavarian
regents had ruled, through a German court and bureaucracy much
influenced by Metternich's representative Prokesch Osten and
with French financial advisers. 'I am obliged to own that one of the
worst things I ever did was to consent to Otto's election', Palmerston confessed.[27] It became a moral duty to 'recommend such
measures of Improved Administration as may tend to secure to the
Greek Nation that civil and political Freedom which the Treaty of
1827 was destined to secure for them'.[26]

Greece thus fell a prey to that very fate which Palmerston, when
claiming for her defensible frontiers, had deprecated: 'It is not for
the interest of England, as bearing upon transactions in the
Mediterranean, that the new state should be made the arena in
which different foreign influences may contend and struggle for

mastery.'[28] A Greek historian has remarked that his country 'provided a peculiarly propitious stage for that ideological sham battle of liberalism and constitutionalism against absolutism, which anticipated by exactly one hundred years the analogous international conflict between democracy and fascism, as a convenient disguise for the struggle for power among the major European states'.[29] The bitterness is understandable, but, so far as Palmerston was concerned, there was no sham about the ideological war. Palmerston, of course, found, in Greece as elsewhere, that Austria was 'one of our most determined opponents in this struggle', and mourned in 1837 that 'Greece is virtually handed over to Austria and Russia'.[30] He found France more anxious to acquire influence than to spread constitutionalism. Each Power had a 'party', at court or in the country, each a recipe for the management of Greece. But of them all, Britain was least likely, in the short run, to prevail, for the two aims, of seeking a 'bona fide' constitution and influence with King Otho, were incompatible. The bifurcated enterprise was self-defeating; the instrument, Lyons, peculiarly ill-chosen. It was perhaps inevitable that he should 'get himself into the situation of head of the opposition to Otho's government', but he was tactless and irresponsible.[31] As for Palmerston himself, even Sir Charles Webster, who defends his interventionism in Iberia and Greece, and claims a qualified success for it in the Peninsula (as at 1841), admits that 'he gave too free expression to the frustration and anger caused by the refusal of the incompetent and obstinate Otto to carry out the terms on which Palmerston had consented to his succession'.[32]

The rationale of it all, apart from the special moral and, as Palmerston claimed, legal duty to get Greece a constitution, was what we should expect from the quotations on interference in Spain. 'The party in Greece whose cause England espouses is certain of ultimate triumph.'[30] Why? Because it was the party of justice and right, frustrated only by the intrigues of foreigners, and destined to prevail in the end because despotism will not endure. For Metternich on 18th February 1841* Palmerston despatched what might be described as a backward child's introduction to the case for constitutions. Metternich had opined that the proper solution for admitted misgovernment in Greece was to strengthen the king's position by securing him able ministers. But, Palmerston retorted, the evils complained of were 'occasioned by the obstinate

pertinacity with which a King devoid of all capacity for governing'
retained in his hands all the powers of the state, and departmental
detail as well. What was the use of finding him able ministers?
Would he take their advice? Probably he would not, and they would
resign, and bad ministers return. What was required was machinery
for controlling the royal will and 'the only real controul which can
be established upon the obstinate but wrong-headed opinions of
King Otho' would be an institution requiring the concurrence of
other persons. But the real interests of the Greek nation would not
be safeguarded unless those persons 'were themselves liable to be
controuled by the opinion of their fellow subjects. Therefore, in
order that the measures of the Government should be calculated to
promote the general welfare, it seems indispensable that the Power
of the Executive should be limited' as to legislation, taxation and
expenditure 'by bodies of men answerable to the Country at large.
But this is what in common parlance is called a Constitution'
(Q.E.D.). No doubt, as Metternich said, 'there may be in assemblies of this kind . . . much idle and unprofitable talk'. But,
Palmerston insisted, indomitably, 'in such assemblies the true
interests of a Nation are sure to be brought into publick discussion;
abuses and Evils of all kinds are made publicly known, remedies
are publicly proposed and examined, the general intelligence of the
nation is brought to bear practically on the general welfare, and the
Country is sure to advance in the Career of improvement'.

Aberdeen, as we have noted, welcomed, with Palmerston, the
coup d'état of the constitutionalists in 1843, though he had prided
himself on abstention from intermeddling for purely prestigious
reasons, and made a point of rejoicing that the revolution was a
Greek one against the Germans (ignoring the incitement given to
the revolutionaries by the Russians). Palmerston had spent much
time in his last months in office in 1841 trying to secure Three
Power agreement on strong representations to Otho, but in vain. If
he concentrated on trying to curb 'abuses of Power . . . repugnant
to the practice of civilized Nations in the present times' —
torture of suspects, poisoning of brigands, quartering soldiers to
live off the property of the families of persons who offended
authority, connivance at the African slave trade — Guizot replied
in tones of righteousness for France that these were small things in
which the Protecting Powers had no mandate to interfere, as they
had in the constitutional field. Palmerston, his humanitarian

passion roused, retorted that they were 'great crying enormities involving important and fundamental Principles of Government'. When he urged Guizot to propose steps, however gradual, for Greek advance towards a bona fide constitution, with the removal of the Bavarians as an essential preliminary, Guizot was not to be moved.[26] France was on the worst of terms with Britain. If the Western alliance was the culmination of Palmerston's first spell as Foreign Secretary, the disintegration of the alliance was complete by the end of the second.

CHAPTER VII

EASTERN ANSWER AND WESTERN QUARREL

PALMERSTON had failed until the very end of 1832 to formulate a policy on the Eastern Question and had to admit in mid-1833 the bankruptcy of his diplomacy. All he could say was that this would not be allowed to happen again. The policy was formulated. At the next crisis in the Levant Britain would be in her place to prevent the dismemberment of the Ottoman Empire. But by whose side would she stand?

In countering Russian embitions, Austria was the 'natural ally', a defensive Power interested in the Balkans and central Europe and with no material ambitions which clashed with Britain's. It was because Palmerston and Metternich could not decide *how* to negotiate with another in 1833 that the Russians stood alone on the Dardanelles. Webster talks of Metternich's 'illusion' that he could act as the intermediary between Russia and the Maritime Courts. It was Palmerston, as Lamb never ceased to point out, who made it an illusion by ignoring, damning with faint praise, even snubbing successive overtures from Vienna. The chancellor, however unwavering his attitude to Liberalism, was realist enough over Austria's territorial and commercial interests and the Balance of Power. He told Lamb in January 1833 that Austria would regard any Russian annexations in Europe as a *casus belli* and Neumann repeated this to Palmerston in April. In 1834 he even went so far as to mention in the same context the Roumanian principalities (important to Austria because of her Danube trade) and the approaches to India. But all Palmerston could see was that Austria would not break with Russia. He did not ask how, if she thus imperilled herself, she would advance the cause of international agreement on Constantinople. Münchengratz filled him with suspicion — 'An eventual partition of Turkey between Austria and Russia is thought to be one of the topics.'[1] He misread a (secret) arrangement for co-operation between Vienna and St Petersburg to maintain the dynasty of Mahmoud (inter alia against Mehemet) and for concert if, nevertheless, the Turkish empire in

117

Europe should fall into dissolution. He thought it a conspiracy to carve up the Balkans, and give Russia Constantinople. He ought to have understood that this was the reinsurance Russia extracted in return for reinsuring Austria in her fight against Liberalism. But he was, of course, deeply involved in the construction of the Quadruple Alliance, after which Metternich was more than ever resolved not to allow the London Conference (on Belgium) to 'rise bit by bit to the stature of a political institution . . . an areopagus, in which the representatives of the 3 continental Powers would be reduced to the role of accomplices of the reforming policy of the 2 Maritime Courts'.

When Palmerston returned to office in 1835 he treated renewed overtures from Metternich as though they were simply intended to separate Britain from France.[2] The chancellor's language sometimes justified this suspicion. Fearful above all of a Franco-Russian détente, Palmerston treated the French alliance and the ideological war as more important than securing European concert on Turkey, yet apparently resented Metternich's refusal to subordinate all other considerations to solidarity with Britain on the Eastern Question. He evidently regarded Anglo-French co-operation against Russia in the East as the complement of Anglo-French alliance against the neo-Holy Alliance and its Carlist allies in the West. He envisaged the Sultan, threatened by Russia, asking for British and French squadrons in the Bosphorus, and thought they ought to go.[1] By early 1836 he was writing: 'What we ought to do is to sign our treaty [with the French], offer it to Turkey, and send our two fleets to the entrance of the Dardanelles, with orders to go up to Constantinople the moment they are invited to do so by the Sultan. We ought then to tell Mehemet Ali to evacuate Syria and retire into his proper shell of Egypt.'[3] Feeling that 'Austria will join us, if she sees we are in earnest and determined to show fight',[4] his preferred method of securing a Four-Power treaty with Turkey — the supreme objective being to substitute a general treaty for Unkiar Skelessi — was for Britain and France to draw one up and invite the Austrians to join them in presenting it to the Russians. Neither Melbourne nor Louis Philippe (anxious for better relations with the Eastern Powers as his own reinsurance) thought this a promising approach. With less trust than his brother Frederick in Metternich's sincerity, reliability and goodwill, the prime minister was anxious for a rapprochement with Austria, which would 'put us in a better condition'; he was more worried than Palmerston at the possibility of an attack by the Russian fleet.[5] By August 1836, after a negative response to further overtures, Metternich had more or less given up hope of doing business with Palmerston. He told Lamb he would be happy to see Britain give Turkey a 'guarantee' and that any attack on Turkey by a Great Power would bring Austria into the conflict.

Palmerston's coldness to Metternich's advances was the more marked because these were the years when relations with Russia were worse than they had been since the Peace. Palmerston described them as of 'cold civility', then of 'snarling at each other, hating each other' (March–April 1834) though, he said, neither country wished for war, and the Russians were not ready for it. They had, perhaps, decided to proceed rather by sap than by storm.[6] But they must be watched — 'Russia has advanced specially because nobody observed, watched and understood what she was doing. Expose her plans, and you half defeat them. Raise public opinion against her and you double her difficulties. I am all for making a clatter against her. Depend upon it, that is the best way to save yourself from the necessity of making war against her.'[7] Unkiar Skelessi and Münchengratz had bred suspicion and hatred of Russia and the Tsar's savage anti-Polish speech in Warsaw in October 1835 confirmed these sentiments. Temperley considered that in 1833–5 Palmerston showed a depth of feeling against Russia which excluded calm calculation. Powerful indeed was the Tory argument that Palmerston had not merely recognized the existence of an ideological conflict and plunged into it, but that his doing so had had the inevitable, and highly dangerous, effect that Europe was split in twain and relations between the two groups deteriorating. This was strongly felt in the cabinet. Palmerston recognized its force, and recovered his balance with regard to Russia. He played down the anti-Russian passions he had helped to arouse, and seemed to go out of his way to be more conciliatory to Russia than to Austria. This made good sense, for he was far more likely to have to go to war with Russia than Austria. It involved restraining Ponsonby's desire for some ostentatious challenge to Russia. It also made Palmerston the target of Urquhart's hymn of hate.

The affairs of the *Lord Charles Spencer* and the *Vixen* were handled by both Britain and Russia with a discretion that angered

Ponsonby and infuriated Urquhart who, at his post in Constantinople, had encouraged the merchant, Bell, to send the *Vixen* with a cargo (salt), which the Tsar had forbidden foreigners to import, to a roadstead in Circassia which the Tsar had forbidden to all foreign trade. The port was in Russian hands, but in the Caucasian mountains, within sight of the Black Sea, the proud and brave Circassians continued for thirty years to resist Russian imperialism. Palmerston wished to avoid either admitting or challenging Russia's rights, which raised difficult problems of international law,[8] and, when Bell and Urquhart alleged (with some colour) that they had been encouraged by the Foreign Office, stated that they had tried and failed to trap him into a project designed by them to produce war.[9] He had earlier said that the Russian Baltic fleet was larger than required, and England had a right to view it with jealousy, but that since representations had been made in 1835, there had been nothing to indicate hostile intentions on the part of Russia to any other Power. She was 'not in a situation to give reasonable alarm'. England was secure from aggression, and Londoners need not fear that they would wake up to find the Tsar's fleet anchored in the Pool and the crews parading the streets.[10]

Palmerston remained conscious of Russian threats, or potential threats, in Central Asia — they were almost an obsession. But he had contrived to end 1836 on better terms with St Petersburg than Vienna, channelling his wrath against Metternich. For Austria reversed her former attitude and recognized the Tsar's blockade in Circassia, and Palmerston assumed, quite wrongly, that Metternich, and not the Tsar, had instigated the occupation by the Eastern Powers of the *neutral* state of Cracow, a violation of the letter of the Treaty of Vienna but not, as Palmerston admitted, of its spirit, since Cracow had provoked the action. It was a pro-Polish speech and an anti-Austrian, anti-neo Holy Alliance speech, but not an anti-Russian speech.[11] And it was with Metternich that Palmerston fought a diplomatic duel over his threat to send a British consul to Cracow.

★   ★   ★   ★

Crisis threatened in the East before the Powers had come together on the Eastern Question, as they might have done if Palmerston had shown more flexibility and calculation. And the crisis was to some extent provoked by Palmerston's hostility to Mehemet Ali.

In view of his pledge to 'interfere and prevent the Pasha of Egypt from dismembering any portion of the dominions of the Sultan' Palmerston would look ridiculous if the territories in the hands of Mehemet and Ibrahim became formally, as well as effectively, independent. By negotiating a commercial treaty with the Sultan which would bind Mehemet as his vassal, Britain could re-emphasize the subordination of the Pasha and (incidentally) liberate a vast area from Adana to the Yemen from Mehemet's monopolies and obstructions to foreign commerce. To get it, Palmerston dangled before the Sultan, with whom Ponsonby was now a great favourite, the prospect of a formal, unequivocal, commitment against Mehemet. The treaty was important to British commerce with the whole of the Ottoman Empire and with Persia, and also a great diplomatic triumph. Lyons at Athens even said there had been nothing like it for British prestige since Canning had planted the flag on the heights of Lisbon. Ponsonby's influence reached its zenith, for the Sultan was delighted. He now had British reinsurance as well as Russian insurance; he said that he would not ask for Russian aid if Britain would 'guarantee' him against a Russian attack. Better still, it was a challenge to Mehemet, who must either operate the treaty and thus weaken his resources as well as swallow his pride, or reveal himself a rebel. Best of all, the provocation, and the joint cruise of the British and Turkish fleets, might induce the Pasha to take the offensive, and thus release the Sultan from the technical difficulty that the British kept on dissuading him from attacking Mehemet.

Palmerston was, of course, quite right to say 'We can give the Sultan no encouragement in his warlike propensities against Mehemet; you may extinguish all hope he may entertain of that.'[12] But it was not very effective, in view of the declarations that 'the integrity and independence of the Ottoman Empire are necessary to the maintenance of the tranquillity, the liberty and the balance of power of Europe' and that Britain would be ready 'in case hostilities should arise, to extend to Turkey such assistance as circumstances may render necessary'.[13] With Russian assurances, underpinned by Austria, to fall back on, should Britain nevertheless default, the Sultan felt he could not be deserted even if he attacked Mehemet and lost.

The Pasha reacted to the commercial treaty by announcing his intention of declaring his independence. He was met by remonstrances from all the Powers, and from Palmerston the emphatic statement: 'Her Majesty's Govt at once and decidedly pronounce the successful execution of the attempt to be impossible; and its inevitable Consequence to be Ruin to the Pasha . . . The Pasha must expect to find Great Britain taking Part with the Sultan in order to obtain Redress for so flagrant a Wrong done to the Sultan, and for the Purpose of preventing the Dismemberment of the Turkish Empire.'[14] Mehemet gradually withdrew his pretension. But war was brought appreciably nearer, for there was no restraining Mahmoud. In March 1839, seven months after the commercial treaty, Reschid Pasha replied to Palmerston's final refusal of an offensive alliance against Mehemet that a defensive alliance was useless. The Sultan was going to attack Syria. He did so, and his forces were destroyed at Nezib on 24th June 1839. His fleet deserted to the Egyptians. Mahmoud himself died, and in the court of his juvenile and unimpressive successor there were many, some suborned, some from policy, prepared to sell out to Mehemet. Nothing but foreign ships and troops could save Constantinople from Ibrahim. And Palmerston had not set the scene in such a way to give ground for confidence that out of this crisis he could pluck the objective he had set in 1833 — the confinement of Mehemet to Egypt and the merging of the Treaty of Unkiar Skelessi 'in some more general compact of the same nature'.[15] Palmerston had, indeed, at the time of the commercial treaty, deferred to the cabinet's desire for a joint or collective démarche at Alexandria and the dispatch of British, French, Russian and Austrian forces if Mehemet declared his independence.[16] On 13th August 1838, with the approval of Sébastiani, the ambassador of France (from the position of prestige acquired by the commercial treaty, so strikingly contrasted with the impotence of 1833), he proposed that the matter be dealt with by an ambassadorial conference in London, on the same lines as the Belgian. This Metternich could not tolerate. He repulsed Palmerston, and he made his own overtures to Paris, where feeling for the Western alliance was wearing thin. And so as Ibrahim marched towards the Straits, the diplomatic initiative was in the hands of Austria and France, and seemed likely to result in a triumph for Metternich. For when he suggested a Vienna *centre*, having in mind the dispatch of the ships of the Four Powers to the Sea of Marmora, time was short. Every day's march brought Ibrahim nearer Constantinople, where the situation was deteriorating rapidly. Vienna was suitable for rapid communication with Constantinople.

Palmerston choked down his suspicion of Austria, and agreed to co-operate, provided that the aim was to send joint instructions to the ambassadors at Constantinople and to the admirals. Metternich, he said, could 'do more to consolidate the peace of Europe than any man has done since the 18th June 1815' — provided Lamb kept him up to concert pitch.[17] This is an example of Palmerston overcoming, in time of dire crisis, the prejudices and pettiness which often marred his dealings when the stakes were not so high. It was proof of the sincerity of his assertion that the ideological war need not prevent the operation of the Powers as representing the European community when there was a major threat to the Balance of Power. The fruit of Metternich's initiative was the Collective Note of 27th July 1839, concocted and presented to the Porte by the ambassadors of the Powers after urgent instructions from the clearing-house at Vienna. This is the key document on which Palmerston through many critical months took his stand. By bidding the Turk to trust the Powers to maintain the integrity of the empire, it committed all the Powers to that objective. When the French government reversed its direction and recalled its ambassador in disgrace Palmerston brushed aside the setback with the comment that the refusal of one Power to honour the Collective Note need not deter the rest.

But now came near-catastrophe. The Tsar, who thought Metternich a bit of an old woman, was angry that Metternich had ventured to say that Austria could answer for Russia. He repudiated the Vienna *centre* and so prostrated Metternich that even Lamb (Lord Beauvale) advised Palmerston to look to the Tsar rather than the chancellor for a determined ally against the Pasha. Palmerston's note to Vienna, of 25th August, showed that he accepted this advice.[18] Clanricarde (the son-in-law of Canning) showed it to Nicholas at the pageant at Borodino. The Tsar at once responded. By the end of September Brunnow was telling Palmerston that the Tsar would entirely agree with his views and join in whatever measures might be necessary, and unite with Britain either with or without France. He would sign a convention laying down the objectives and the means, assigning to each Power its appropriate part. Brunnow added, in confidence, that the treaty of Unkiar Skelessi would not be renewed.[19] In fact, the

Realpolitik of the Tsar had already made it virtually a dead letter. He knew his country was not strong enough for a major war, respected both the firmness and restraint of British policy (especially the restraint of Ponsonby by Palmerston), and had done nothing in the Middle East to provoke a conflict with Britain. He was impressed by the warm welcome given to his heir in London. He understood Palmerston's feelings about Unkiar Skelessi and had taken in good part his note of 10th October 1838 insisting that there could be no repetition of lone Russian action or of her gaining advantage to the detriment of other Powers. 'Europe never would endure that the matter should be settled by the independent and self-regulated interference of any one Power . . . Therefore, the only way in which Turkey could be assisted without risking a disturbance of the peace would be by the establishment of that concert between the Five Powers which Her Majesty's Government have proposed', wrote Palmerston.[20]

But Palmerston was to have to make do with Four. As he stated to Paris on 22nd November 1839: 'in proportion as the course of events have rendered the active assistance of the Powers of Europe necessary for maintaining the Integrity and Independence of the Turkish Empire, exactly in that proportion, and precisely for that reason, the French Government has become unwilling to afford to the Sultan any assistance at all'.

⋆   ⋆   ⋆   ⋆

A cabinet which would have been willing enough to endorse Five-Power concert shrank from action without France, as it had previously shrunk from formal commitment with France alone.[21] Metternich confirmed Palmerston's opinion that, in matters not ideological, he was a wobbler. Even Russia's co-operation could not be relied on if her terms were not met, and none could foretell whether, in the absence of international engagements, she would exercise her right (or duty) under the Treaty of Unkiar Skelessi or at first leave Ibrahim free to work his will. Certainly, unless Palmerston could secure agreement with Russia he could not achieve the objectives which had now become realistic — the abdication by the Tsar of the special position *vis-à-vis* Constantinople which he had obtained in 1833, and the confinement of Mehemet to Egypt (which Brunnow said Britain could take and keep for all the Tsar cared). Palmerston therefore pressed on his colleagues an immediate closing with the Russian offer. The Tsar had asked for entire trust, and, said Palmerston, there was no satisfactory mean between that and distrust.[22] It was understandable that Russia, alone of the Powers, should object to the French proposal to put the Sultan under collective 'guarantee', since this would impair, if not cancel, Russia's rights under treaties prior to Unkiar Skelessi. The Straits convention offered by Brunnow should be accepted. Palmerston was even willing to agree that, in the coming emergency, the operations of the West should be confined to the Mediterranean and the coasts of Syria and Egypt, leaving the Russians to act in the Bosphorus and Asia Minor. For Russia would be acting as the mandatory of Europe, and her interference would not be 'independent and self-regulated' action under Unkiar Skelessi (now described by the Tsar as 'a burden'). But the whole cabinet felt that Russia was trying to split Britain from France, with whom it had hoped (now that the war in Spain was ending) for improved relations. Palmerston was bidden to inform the French that Russia's proposals had been rejected out of deference to them. This decision greatly encouraged French intransigence.

Britain and Russia had the chance to discard their posture of mutual animosity — which both had prudently kept within bounds — and take the lead in the settlement of a principal European problem. Was Palmerston to be cheated of this diplomatic revolution, and the results that would flow from it, because 'people who do not follow up questions in a way that the head of the department is obliged to do are generally for the doubting line'?[23] If so, it would not be from lack of determination on his part. He did what he could to sway the French, but without result, and retired to Broadlands to marshal facts and arguments in an impressive paper dated 29th October. Addressed to Granville, this scathing indictment of French policy (it would 'touch Louis Philippe in the raw' he admitted, and agreed to soften the tone) was really for cabinet consumption. Palmerston was resolved to have his way, for on the same day he sent Ponsonby (already instructed to reverse his accustomed role of competition with the Russian envoy in the secret haunts of Turkish power) a dispatch showing that his approach had not been altered by the setback. 'It is not necessary to enquire what the reasons are which have led Russia to adopt her present course', he wrote, 'nor yet to examine whether among them may be a hope that she may thus at least retain some portion of her influence at Constantinople. It is our business to take advantage of her present temper, and to encourage her to work with us for her own objects, as long as she is willing to do so. . . . Russia cannot appear less friendly to Turkey than England.'[24] Slowly the restraining hand of his colleagues relaxed. On 2nd December Palmerston, reminding the Turk that 'it has been the British Government which has mainly prevented the Porte from being pressed by the Five Powers to submit unconditionally to all the demands of Mehemet Ali', adjured him to be true to his own interests, relying on the fact that 'The British Government has taken its line. . . . England has stood firm to the Principles which she laid down in the outset of the negotiation, and her steadiness has encouraged Austria to adhere to the same line, while it has made it impossible for Russia to adopt the views of France, even if she had been disposed to do so.'*

On 16th December 1839 Palmerston acquired a wife. Despite the opposition of her family, and the doubts of her brother, the prime minister (who was worried about Palmerston's shortage of ready money), Emily Cowper, after two years of widowhood, succumbed to the importunities of 'Dear Harry' (to whom from her deathbed Emily's rakish mother had adjured her to be true). 'It will make you smile', wrote the twenty-year-old Queen Victoria to her Uncle Leopold in Brussels;[25] the lovers were both over fifty. Though Palmerston's name continued to be linked with a succession of young ladies, his viscountess idolized him, and was delighted to find he could be jealous. She gave Palmerston the matchless gift of a happy private basis for public activity, not excelled by Disraeli's Mary-Ann, and the asset of a notable political salon. She was a great hostess (though the cooking, especially at Broadlands, was bad). She was a fierce and energetic propagandist. Rarely had he needed one more than in his first year of married life. For he was prepared to stake his reputation and his political future on a course of proceedings which he deemed essential to British interests, while all around doubted its wisdom and/or its chances of success and branded his courage restlessness, his optimism irresponsibility.

Viscountess Palmerston became aware at once of the claims of office on her husband's time, energy and resource (and the strained eyes, stabbed with pain after a few hours' reading). For the centre of negotiations had shifted from Vienna and Constantinople to Broadlands. Two days after the wedding, Brunnow and Neumann,

Metternich's special envoy, landed at Dover. Palmerston and they spent Christmas Day considering whether Brunnow's instructions could be fashioned into a practical agreement to make effective the promise of the Collective Note of 27th July. If agreement was reached by the Five, or the Four, the Tsar would permit the token appearance of warships of the other Powers in the Dardanelles.[26] And when the crisis was over, he would join his coadjutors in inviting the Sultan to declare the Straits closed to all non-Turkish warships, and the Powers jointly would then pledge themselves to respect the Sultan's announcement. The Black Sea would become, for the West, a *mare clausum*. On the other hand, Russia would be bound not to send her ships of war into the Mediterranean. The awkward question of Russia's earlier treaties with Turkey (before 1833) would be evaded.

The principal difficulty remaining was the reluctance of the cabinet to accept that, during the coming operations, the number of British and French ships in the vicinity of Constantinople was to be limited. Ministers still distrusted Russia, and felt that this proposal would make definitive the breach with France. But, with the removal of Sébastiani from the London embassy, because he had been talking to Palmerston and other diplomats as though French co-operation against Mehemet Ali was still possible, the Tsar agreed to British parity in any naval demonstration required in the Straits. Yet it was more than six months after those Christmas negotiations at Broadlands before a definitive agreement between the Four Powers and Turkey was signed. It was to require all the talents, the infinite patience, clear objectives, intensity of purpose which Palmerston had brought to the Belgian negotiation, with steadfast courage, no little cunning and a gambler's optimism, to win the day. For 'no British Foreign Minister, save perhaps Canning, won such a diplomatic victory with a Cabinet so divided on the main issue'.[52]

★ ★ ★ ★

Great importance now attached to Palmerston's relations with his brother-in-law, Melbourne, whose doubts as to whether Palmerston ought to have the Foreign Office had been increased by nearly five years' experience. He was less interested in, and knowledgeable about, foreign affairs than Grey, and more negligent of business. This meant that, normally, Palmerston could make decisions and dispatch missives with some freedom. Russell, Leader of the House of Commons, complained that as Paymaster-General under Grey he had had on foreign affairs 'more information and power of advising'. On the other hand, where Grey had usually agreed with Palmerston and had been able to prevail with the cabinet, Melbourne was less apt to agree and less apt to try to prevail, and less likely to succeed if he did, though the newer ministers were on the whole inferior men. Melbourne himself had a congenital liking for non-commitment and procrastination. Unfortunately it is not always true in diplomacy that a problem left is a problem solved. By nature sceptical, Melbourne wrote habitually to Palmerston in terms of doubt. This was often valuable. 'I own myself to be much afraid of moving, lest it should hasten the catastrophe which we dread and wish to avert' (the disintegration of Turkey), he had written in 1836 — and doubted whether without Austrian aid the Russians could be kept out of Constantinople. But it was serious, when, as in 1839–40, inaction meant victory for Mehemet Ali, that Melbourne doubted whether Turkey could be propped up; doubted whether external force could restore to the Sultan Syria and Egypt; doubted whether the Commons or the country would support a war for the Balance of Power; doubted above all whether the majority of the cabinet would 'concur in measures which may lead to long and difficult operations'. Some, he said, were entirely for Mehemet Ali; others would be apprehensive of the Commons and the country.[27]

Palmerston told Clarendon (the former George Villiers, who had recently joined the cabinet) that he and the veteran Holland had 'a weakness in favour of that aged afrancescado freebooter, Mehemet Ali'. Clarendon denied it, but put forward, in a cogent memorandum of March 1840, the view that Mehemet should be 'guaranteed' by the Powers in Egypt and his Syrian conquests hereditarily, the Sultan being 'guaranteed' European Turkey and Asia Minor; that to restore Syria and Arabia by force to the Sultan so that he could resist Russia was hazardous as to the operation itself and uncertain as to the result; that, in any case, 'England's first and most indispensable necessity was peace.'[28] Holland had always believed in co-operation with France, and passionately so since the revolution of July 1830. He was too old to change, and seemed to Palmerston to think that the maintenance of the entente with France, and of the régime of Louis Philippe, ought to be not only an objective, but the principal objective, of British diplomacy. He was too old also to change his vexatious habit of blabbing confidential information to all and sundry. Consequently, Ellice passed to and fro between Holland House and Paris, armed with reports of cabinet meetings, in a way hardly compatible with his Privy Councillor's oath, while the Clerk to the Privy Council, Greville, carried everything to Guizot, the ambassador of the Thiers government in Paris, which took over in March. Ellice thought it was madness to cast off the French and rejoin the Holy Alliance, playing into the hands of Russia, and all for a crusade to destroy what he (like Clarendon) regarded as the effective and progressive part of the Mussulman power.[29] Earl Spencer, who as Althorp had often checked Palmerston's policies in the name of economy, passivity and caution, insisted that the French were 'by situation, institutions and civilisation' the nation most fitted to be our friends and that a war to drive the Egyptians out of Syria would be criminal.[30]

Well might Palmerston recall later 'the greatest difficulties which I had to encounter in the whole transaction arose from the unprincipled intrigues in our own camp'.[31] In a letter of resignation on 5th July he told Melbourne that while he had been negotiating with the knowledge and sanction of the cabinet in furtherance of the view that the independence and integrity of the Turkish empire must be maintained[32]—

other members of the Cabinet have, in their conversations with those very foreign ministers with whom I was thus negotiating, held language and opinions founded upon a different view of the matter; and I have been told from various quarters, that persons not belonging to the Government, but known to be in habits of intimacy with members of the Government, have studiously, both at home and abroad, inculcated the belief that my views were not those of the majority of my colleagues, and that consequently I was not in this matter to be considered as the organ of the British government.

It was a clear allusion to Ellice and Greville, and their relations with Holland and Clarendon. Palmerston had always been able to rely on Melbourne's straight dealing. The premier had in 1836 repulsed Metternich's attempt to use him, rather than the Foreign Secretary, as a channel of communication via Lamb, and warned Vienna that an imperious tone would only irritate William IV without weakening Palmerston. He passed on to Palmerston letters criticizing him and had a suitable contempt for 'busybodies and tattlers' like Ellice.[33] But that was not the point. That Palmerston was adamant and Melbourne honest the pro-French party knew, but they thought their view might prevail in cabinet, and encouraged French intransigence as helpful to that end. Palmerston alleged that Thiers had ignored the strong note he was allowed to send in April about the mobilization of the French fleet, because Ellice and Guizot misled him into thinking that 'if France would only hold out firmly the rest of Europe would yield to her will'.[34]

Palmerston would not have it. 'We can never allow that (Mehemet), acting through a fictitious public opinion in France, shall dictate to us; neither indeed can France herself, even if it be the real and deliberate opinion of France, give law to Europe.'[35] But it would not have done to stage a showdown prematurely. Fortunately for him, the French overplayed their hand. Every time Neumann made an overture to them more generous than the last, they raised their price. Thus France isolated herself. Austria abandoned the view that Mehemet could not be coerced without French assistance. Her offer to participate in sanctions against the Pasha was, as Holland bitterly commented, Palmerston's trump card. 'There is more meaning than two frigates and three corvettes in that piece of bunting', said a joyous Foreign Secretary, referring to the Austrian flag.[36] Only his colleagues now stood in the way of a formal agreement on the lines adumbrated at Broadlands at Christmas. To bring the matter to issue, Palmerston on 5th July 1840 submitted his resignation, to relieve Melbourne, he said, of the embarrassment caused by the opposition of a minority to proposals which Palmerston said he believed the majority of the cabinet would accept.[37]

Nobody could complain that he did not make the issue clear:[32]

... The question which the British Government now has to decide is whether the four Powers, having failed in persuading France to join them, will or will not proceed to accomplish their purpose without the assistance of France....

My opinion upon this question is distinct and unqualified. I think that the object to be obtained is of the utmost importance for the interests of England, for the preservation of the balance of power, and for the maintenance of peace in Europe. I find the three Powers entirely prepared to concur in the views which I entertain on this matter, if those views should be the views of the British Government. I can feel no doubt that the four Powers, acting in union with and in support of the Sultan, are perfectly able to carry those views into effect; and I think that the commercial and political interests of Great Britain, the honour and dignity of the country, good faith towards the Sultan, and sound views of European policy, all require that we should adopt such a course.

I think, on the other hand, that if we draw back, and shrink from co-operation with Austria, Russia and Prussia in this matter, because France holds aloof and will not join, we shall place this country in the degraded position of being held in leading-strings by France, and shall virtually acknowledge that, even when supported by the other three Powers of the Continent, we dare embark in no system of policy in opposition to the will of France, and consider her positive concurrence as a necessary condition for our action. Now this appears to me to be a principle of policy which is not suitable to the power and station of England. . . .

The immediate result of our declining to go on with the three Powers because France does not join us will be, that Russia . . . will again resume her separate and isolated position with respect to those affairs; and you will have the treaty of Unkiar Skelessi renewed under some still more objectionable form. We shall thus lose the advantages on this point which it had required long-continued and complicated efforts on our part to gain, and England will, by her own voluntary and deliberate act, re-establish that separate protectorship of Russia over Turkey, the existence of which has long been the object of well-founded jealousy and apprehension to the other Powers of Europe.

The ultimate results of such a decision will be the practical division of the Turkish empire into two separate and independent states, whereof one will be the dependency of France, and the other a satellite of Russia; and in both of which our political influence will be annulled, and our commercial interests will be sacrificed; and this dismemberment will inevitably give rise to local conflicts and struggles and conflicts which will involve the Powers of Europe in most serious disputes.

I have given to these matters for some years past my best and unremitting attention. I do not know that I ever had a stronger conviction on any matter of equal importance; and I am very sure that, if my judgement is wrong on this matter, it can be of little value upon any other.

Palmerston did not expect his resignation to be accepted, for it is no discredit to Melbourne to say that, like Walpole, he esteemed peace and especially the peace of his administration. When, at the cabinet, Holland offered his resignation as an alternative to Palmerston's, he received the classic reply: 'We must have no resignations. We cannot stand them, and, what is more, the country cannot stand them . . . Either policy would do, if firmly and summarily adopted; otherwise — neither.' Palmerston's policy was upheld, in one of the last formal cabinet minutes to the monarch, dated 8th July 1840, a device adopted because it enabled Holland and Clarendon to append, in the eighteenth century way, their dissents, with argument. But Melbourne's statement gave

F

Palmerston his cue, whenever there were signs of his colleagues faltering. The policy accepted by the cabinet must be carried through.

On 15th July 1840 there were signed in London between the Four Powers and Turkey two conventions.[38] The first of these instruments provided for assistance to the Sultan if he was attacked by Mehemet, and to the Syrians whose rebellion was partly inspired by British agency after Palmerston had been convinced of the unpopularity of Ibrahim's rule. The second laid down the terms to be offered to Mehemet. He must restore the Turkish fleet, and could have Egypt hereditarily and the pashalik of Acre for life. This meant withdrawal from Adana, North Syria, Crete and Arabia. If he did not accept this offer within ten days of receiving it, he would be confined to Egypt. These were the terms offered by Neumann (in concert with Palmerston) through the Sultan's representative, Nourri Pasha ('a perfect cypher but he can hold a pen and write his name'), to Thiers and a retreat from a later offer (through Chekib Pasha) the rejection of which by Thiers had overcome Austrian hesitations. Until the dispute with Mehemet was settled, the navies of the Powers might go up to Constantinople as requested by the Sultan, who, however, restated for the future 'the ancient rule' closing the Bosphorus and the Dardanelles to foreign ships of war. The signatory Powers bound themselves to recognize this rule.

★   ★   ★   ★

From Palmerston's point of view the matter was now to be 'decided in the Levant'. There the French ambassador failed by a threat of war to prevent the Sultan ratifying the instruments of 15th July and the consuls in Alexandria notified a defiant Pasha of his deposition (23rd September) — defiant in the hope that France would fight or that her threats to fight would weaken resolution in Downing Street. Palmerston thought the French were bluffing — 'Let the French say what they like, they cannot go to war with the Four Powers in support of Mehemet Ali' (11th March); Louis Philippe was 'not a man to run amuck' (21st July).[39] For once the Opposition leaders — Wellington, Peel and Aberdeen — approved his policy, agreed that the French had no case, felt it impossible that Louis Philippe 'should permit the personal feelings of M. Thiers, or the national vanity of his people to precipitate him into a position so dangerous to the existence of his dynasty as a war with the Great Powers of Europe, and for no real French objects or essential interests. . . . If the four Powers are united they have nothing to fear from the ill-humour of France in a question of this kind, nor is there any danger of the French people undertaking a crusade against all Europe in support of such a barbarian as the Pasha of Egypt'.[40]

But would the Four stay united? Would the cabinet's resolution hold? Would the French behave sensibly? 'People do not act as they ought. You calculate a little too much upon nations and individuals following reason, right and a just view of their own interest. . . . There are other motives which exercise at least equal power and influence', wrote Melbourne to Palmerston on 17th September in answer to a sharp protest against Lord John Russell's proposal for a cease-fire, backed by a threat of resignation by the Leader of the House.[41] The new recruit to Palmerston's critics was on weaker ground than Holland and Clarendon, for he had strongly supported the Foreign Secretary at the critical cabinet meeting of 8th July. But he had been 'got at' in Scotland through his brother, the Duke of Bedford, by Ellice;[42] was coached and flattered at Holland House by its master and mistress, Clarendon, Guizot and the Lieven;[43] filled with fear of war and with a personal animus against Palmerston ('conducting matters simply as he pleases without concert or control'; 'peace should not be thrown away as a child throws away a toy which it has had too long');[44] enticed by the lure of the Foreign Office. The line now peddled was that the French were really very reasonable, conceived they had been ill-treated, and should not be irritated by notes like 'the capital paper' (Melbourne's description) in which Palmerston on 29th August had warned Thiers that if he imagined that menaces and revilings dealt out 'through his irresponsible organs' had affected British intentions, he had much to learn of the character and habits of the English nation. Thiers, said the francophils and passivists, was at worst the prisoner of a policy he had inherited,[45] at best the head of the first administration in Paris honest to the British alliance! (Ellice). The trouble was all Palmerston's fault. He was accused of inflaming the Sultan through the 'criminal' Ponsonby,[46] while the so reasonable M. Thiers was restraining Mehemet. King Leopold, the son-in-law of Louis Philippe, wrote to explain that the French were warlike only because of incivilities, because the King of the French believed that Palmerston 'likes to put his foot on their necks' and wished to reduce France to a second-class Power.[47]

There is evidence of close articulation between the campaign against Palmerston at home and the Tuileries; a leakage in Paris enabled the chargé d'affaires, Bulwer, to warn Palmerston that an attack was to be made on him at the next cabinet meeting.[48] For his part, Palmerston breathed confidence, optimism and defiance. On 17th September Thiers made to Bulwer, though unofficially at his private estate, his clearest threat of war unless new terms being conveyed from Egypt by Walewski (the French special envoy) were accepted. These terms, Palmerston declared, were absurd (they would give Syria to *Ibrahim* for life). 'I still hold to my belief that the French Government will be too wise and prudent to make war', he wrote to Bulwer on 22nd. '. . . If France throws down the gauntlet we shall not refuse to pick it up; . . . if she begins a war, she will to a certainty lose her ships, colonies, and commerce before she sees the end of it; . . . her army of Algiers will cease to give her anxiety, and Mehemet Ali will just be chucked into the Nile.' He found, he said, that if he hinted at this when Guizot or Bourqueney began to swagger, it acted as a sedative, and now, when Thiers was blustering, Guizot 'is getting conveyed to me through all sorts of out-of-the-way channels, that if we would but make the most trifling concession . . . the French Government would jump at our proposals, and the whole thing might be settled satisfactorily (to France he means, of course)'.[49] Only, of course, the concession turned out not to be trifling.

Behind the gay assurance (denounced by his critics as levity), Palmerston fretted for good news from the Levant. But September passed without tidings of any action by Admiral Stopford, but with indications that Ibrahim was suppressing the new Lebanese revolt, and to hearten the appeasers, stories of Kolowrat challenging Metternich's policy at Vienna and of Nesselrode being at odds with the Tsar. Russell demanded a cabinet on the Walewski proposals. With luck, he might turn Palmerston out and replace him; if he failed, he was to resign and speak out in Parliament. He might have considered that, on his own view of Palmerston and Ponsonby, the Sultan would already have denounced the proposals and, trusting to the Convention of July, formally deposed Mehemet. Melbourne pleaded the Queen's first pregnancy to give Russell pause, and sat silent (Greville, who was not there, alleges asleep) as Lord John fretted. Palmerston thundered, in a controlled rage against France, and talked of 200,000 Prussians on the Rhine as a guarantee of peace. But it was wise to give a little ground. Cabinets on 1st and 2nd October agreed that Thiers should be sounded on a proposal which Palmerston knew would, if Thiers accepted it, be vetoed by Russia. In between the two meetings appeared an article in the *Courier*, obviously inspired by Palmerston, bitterly attacking his critics. This was fair enough in view of the facilities given by *The Times* to Greville and Guizot through Henry Reeve, a subordinate of Greville in the Privy Council Office, though it did not improve Russell's temper. Lord John secured a cabinet for 10th October to make proposals of which Melbourne, crippled by lumbago and (unusually for him) out of sorts from anxiety, remarked that 'he much doubted whether, after all that had passed, it would be right to submit the whole matter, as it were, to the decision and arbitration of France'.[50] For a fortnight longer Palmerston was willing to make, under suitable pressure, conciliatory gestures to France, and for a month conciliatory gestures to Russell.[51] One had to think of the fate of the government as well as the chastisement of Mehemet. But Palmerston was now riding to a triumph 'perhaps the greatest which he ever won in his long connection with foreign policy'.[52] There was not merely a Stopford in the Mediterranean, responsible but cautious; there was a Napier, dashing and willing, like Palmerston, to take a risk. On 5th October preliminary reports enabled Palmerston to write to Granville: 'Napier for ever! I thought Carlos da Ponza would do all that man could do; and among other things, that he would drive the Egyptians out of Syria; and this he seems likely to accomplish. Pray try to persuade the King and Thiers that they have lost the game, and that it would be unwise now to make a brawl about it.'[53] If the French did not make war now, victory in the East and peace in Europe were both secure. It was up to the French, for, as ministers dispersed, Greville confessed sadly: 'The Peace Party in the Cabinet are silenced; their efforts paralysed' (though Russell still twitched). On 3rd October Stopford took Beirut. Acre was next on his list. Ibrahim would have to take the desert route home to his father. On 21st October Thiers fell. On 22nd Lord Holland died — the colleague of whom Palmerston complained that he daily spoke 'to all who came near' of the policy and members of the cabinet 'just as a member of Opposition would speak of the policy of an administration which he was labouring to turn out'.[54] The continued and rapid success in Syria and the fall of Thiers would lead 'to the full execution of our treaty without any interruption of peace', wrote Palmerston on 23rd: 'Mehemet is a beaten man.'[55] After the (deceptively easy) capture of Acre on 3rd November, Napier sailed off to Alexandria to make the Pasha admit it.

⋆   ⋆   ⋆   ⋆

On 8th November Palmerston was able to report to the Queen not only the fall of Acre and the dispersion of Ibrahim's forces but the victory of the new Guizot government in the French Chamber after a debate in which Guizot made public his relations with Palmerston's critics and Thiers eulogized Holland. If the fallen minister spoke the truth when he said that he would have been ready, when his preparations were complete, to fight Europe, he only vindicated Palmerston's insistence that the faster the operation against Mehemet was mounted, the less chance there was of war with France. Colleagues teased Palmerston by asking how long he had had Thiers on his payroll. Greville complained of his 'wonderful luck' but admitted that half the secret of his success lay in the sanguine temperament that expected the luck. Former critics congratulated Palmerston on his success. Even Greville compared him with Chatham. And if Thiers' testimony that Palmerston was 'the first statesman of his age and perhaps of any other' resembled Talleyrand's, and came from the same stable as the allegedly frequent remark of Bradman that the ball that got him was unplayable, it was nevertheless sweet.[56] 'It is a great pleasure to see all our enemies floundering in the Mud, and not knowing how to get on their legs again,' wrote Emily, who, like the Queen, had been astonished at her lord's sang-froid. She confessed that while she had defended him so vigorously over the dinner-tables her heart had quaked.[57] Now she, reputedly less magnanimous than he, could afford to be magnanimous. The Russells went to stay at Broadlands in the new year, still wondering how to take Palmerston's letter to Lord John of 4th December[58]—

It is quite true that our policy in the Levant has been more completely and more rapidly successful than the most sanguine of us could have ventured to hope; and I think you must feel gratified that it was your support of the Treaty of July which chiefly induced the Cabinet to adopt it.

CHAPTER VIII

ENCIRCLING THE GLOBE

'THE sun never sets upon the interests of this country,' retorted Palmerston on 1st March 1843, when the Radical Roebuck (later his strong supporter) complained that his mischievous and restless activity had encircled the globe. 'If France . . . begins a war, she will to a certainty lose her ships, colonies and commerce before she sees the end of it', he had warned during the Eastern crisis.[1] There was nothing Palmerston liked better than 'sending the fleet'. 'Diplomats and protocols are very good things, but there are no better peace-keepers than well-appointed three-deckers.'[2] It is not possible to understand Palmerston, or the conduct of British foreign policy, without having in mind all the time that trade and seamanship had made Britain (as earlier and more fleetingly it had made Holland) a World, not a European, Power; that Palmerston's lifetime coincided with what is called with dramatic, if not exact, truth the Industrial *Revolution* and with that phase of economic history when foreign industrializing Powers could challenge Britain commercially only in their own markets, with the aid of tariffs. At the same time the vast expansion of Britain's productive power required an unceasing search for new markets. Palmerston, without any originality of mind on economic questions, understood this in principle and very often made a practical contribution to the process of opening and keeping open markets outside Europe, while also doing what he could (it was not very much) to reduce impediments to trade with Europe by the Huskissonian technique of reciprocal commercial treaties. He appears to the twentieth century as the very personification of that phase in history when Britain was able, and was impelled by national interest, to be the guardian of the Pax Britannica, the mistress of the seas, the protector of ocean commerce, the scourge of slavers and pirates, the cartographer of waters, the builder of lighthouses and lightships, the home of Lloyd's Shipping Register and the money market of the world, incidentally, but nevertheless really, and proudly, bringing advantage to the traders of all Europe and America while serving those of Britain first of all.

This was an extension of responsibility which Palmerston delighted to bear. It involved no essential conflict with the basic, inherited principles of the Balance of Power. For while it remained true as it had always been that Britain could not conduct *in Europe*, single-handed, a war against a major Power, it had long been the case that every war in which Britain was involved was in some sense a world war. The main causes of three of her five eighteenth century wars with European Powers had been American, and to a smaller extent Indian. One fought Spain in American and Pacific waters as well as European; one fought France in the Caribbean and the Indian Ocean as well as the Channel, the North Sea, the Atlantic and the Mediterranean, and often when one fought in home waters it was to protect colonies. The experiences of Palmerston's physical youth and of his political youth showed that everything depended on the Navy, because Britain's military manpower was never proportioned to her wealth, and, though mercenaries could be employed and European states subsidized, these were unreliable instruments. The conception of Palmerston, the aristocrat, as the champion of the external interests of nineteenth century industrial Capitalism, is a tremendous tribute to Palmerston's gifts of salesmanship in the public opinion mart of the '40s and '50s, but it tends to obscure the deep impression made upon him by the coincidence of his youth with the great war that lasted almost without intermission from the ninth to the thirtieth year of his life. His first political speech was a defence of Canning's seizure of the Danish fleet in order to deny it to Napoleon; as Secretary at War he was much concerned with the supply of Wellington's army in the Peninsula. It is perverse not to see as a partial explanation of his passionate interest in all the margins of Europe from the Baltic to the Aegean, and his apparently excessive alarm at the intrusion of Russia and Egypt into the land mass of the Middle East, the vividness of personal recollection. When he was nine 'the Glorious First of June caused France to revert to her by now traditional acceptance of naval inferiority';[3] a septuagenarian Palmerston would have it ever thus. When he was twelve Jervis at St Vincent crippled the Spanish fleet and Duncan at Camperdown the Dutch — and saved England; the only French invaders who landed tramped over Palmerston estates in Sligo. He was thirteen when Nelson at

Aboukir made the Mediterranean 'almost a British sea', and then Smith's handling of ships and naval guns made Acre, in Napoleon's words, 'the mudhole which spoiled my destiny'; Nelson and Smith together rendered India immune from Napoleonic imperialism. When Palmerston was at Cambridge Trafalgar assured Britain's command of all the seas and put the French and Dutch and Spanish empires in her gift.

From these lessons much followed. There must be preparedness to meet invasion; hence Palmerston's alarm when he thought that the steamboat might provide Louis Philippe with the bridge across the Channel Napoleon had lacked. There must be an unremitting devotion to a diplomatic strategy which the military history of the long war seemed to Palmerston to make self-evident. What dangers had flowed from enemy control of the Scheldt, Biscay and Cadiz! What setbacks had been averted by taking the Danish fleet in 1801 and 1807! How difficult had been the task of re-entering Northern Europe with Antwerp in hostile hands, how providential the seizure of Lisbon, the stand on the lines of Torres Vedras! How then could a statesman guard the interests of Britain without a fleet in or within call of the Tagus, without seeing that Spanish policy was not geared to that of France; that the Netherlands was independent; that the Sound stayed Danish and in time of peril Sweden or Denmark should be at least an ally or a benevolent neutral? Those who think that Palmerston's concern with Schleswig-Holstein, when technological change had rendered the Navy independent of Baltic supplies and Russia's economic centre had moved to the Ukraine was simply a case of an old man fighting the ghosts of his youth, and meddling because to meddle had become a habit, should ponder, as he did, what use a united Germany might make of the isthmus of Kiel.[4] At the same time, Britain should be careful to avoid any war in the heart of Europe where her navy could make little impact. Much that seems strange in Palmerston's diplomacy, especially the perennial apprehension that some part of Western Europe or North Africa was about to fall under hostile influences, slips into place if one senses the deep impression made upon him by the great war.

Balance of Power diplomacy required, above all, that the two encroaching Powers, France and Russia, should never contrive another Tilsit. British commitments must never be so rigid as to prevent necessary adjustments to meet new threats. If possible, as in Greece in 1827, one would have an alliance with France and Russia to restrain both; otherwise, one had an alliance with limited objectives to restrain France by co-operation with her (as in Belgium and the Quadruple Alliance of 1834) or with Russia to restrain Russia and thwart France (as in 1840). One must see that estrangement from Russia was accompanied by détente with France (as in 1832–5), that estrangement from France was accompanied by détente with Russia (as in 1839). Aware of the need for this freedom of manoeuvre, Palmerston declined proposals from Metternich and the Tsar, approved by Prussia, to freeze the Powers in the diplomatic posture of 1840, so reminiscent of 1813–15; 'the Cabinet of St Petersburgh should be satisfied to trust to the general tendency of the policy of Great Britain, which leads her to watch attentively, and to guard with care the maintenance of the Balance of Power'.[5]

★   ★   ★   ★

The articulate orthodoxy of the second quarter of the nineteenth century held that colonies were unprofitable, but Palmerston assumed as a matter of course the duty of protecting Britain's dependencies overseas, despite Cobdenite attacks on the expense of governing and guarding them. He was, however, not in favour of taking other people's colonies, and in his long connexion with foreign affairs Britain was never involved in a war about colonies with any Power.

The string of strategic bases (and, as sail gave way to steam, coaling stations) which held the colonial beads together was also vital to the protection of trade with distant lands which were not the colonies of any European Power. The need for markets outside Europe, the United States and the British Empire had been felt acutely when Napoleon partially closed Europe and Madison the United States to British trade, and the rising productivity of British industry confirmed it. Many said, with Political Economy on their side, that all commerce required was peace. Palmerston repeatedly declared, of the period 1830–41, that no government had ever done more to extend British commerce by treaties and by peace, and that the best means of promoting the commercial interests of the country was peace.[6] But a policy of peace, he insisted, must be distinguished from one of isolation, or passivism, or pacifism. All of these were dangerous, and a false economy.

When Roebuck on 17th March 1837, anticipating the arguments of
Cobden and Bright, said he cared not for the Balance of Power but
only for the commerce of England, Palmerston replied that 'the
only mode of continuing a free commerce is to keep a watchful eye
upon that balance of power'. When it was said that the patronage
of European Liberalism was irrelevant to commercial expansion,
he had an answer: it was a British interest that Spain, for example,
should adopt Martinez de la Rosa's constitution 'even from the
narrow view of our relation with Spain as a trading and commercial
country'.[7] There were those on the Continent who believed, or
pretended to believe, that commercial interest was the only reason
for Palmerston's interest in the constitutions of Portugal, Spain,
Greece and Frankfort, and the spring of his Belgian *Theme*.
British critics of Palmerston however complained of Belgium's
commercial treaty with France and constitutionalist Portugal's
attack on British trading privileges. As to the argument about
Frankfort, it is true that she had a commercial treaty with Britain,
which her occupation in 1834 jeopardized; it is true that Palmerston (probably from insular prejudice) anticipated the conclusions
of modern scholarship by seeing in the Zollverein not a spontaneous movement towards German unity but an instrument of
Prussian power. But it was Metternich whom he challenged for
imposing upon the constituent states of the Diet a unity of
despotism, and Prussia whom he tried to get to rise against Vienna.

But when he spoke of treaties and of peace Palmerston was thinking in terms of Europe and of the United States, with whom
Britain's relations ought to be intimate especially because of the
trade connexion.[8] This had nothing to do with the 'police' functions of the Royal Navy for the protection of British commerce —
and lives and property — in unsettled seas and uncivilized or
politically unstable lands, the vigorous execution of which was a
source of complaint from Cobdenite Radicals. It seemed to
Palmerston quite natural that there should be 'policemen' patrol-
ling off Canton and the fog-bound fishing banks of Newfoundland;
suppressing piracy in the Caribbean; showing the flag in the Pacific
islands; looking in at the North African ports; limiting the impact
on trade of Central and Southern American revolutions, coups and
internecine wars; and, anywhere, punishing or exacting retribution
for crime. The use of blockade or seizure of merchant ships or
goods for the last purpose outside Europe was not a matter of party

dispute between Whig and Tory; Palmerston differed from Aberdeen only in vigour. These methods became party-controversial chiefly when they were employed against European states. It was in very special circumstances that the Navy in Canning's time had illustrated in Levantine waters the whole gamut of uses for ships of war — trade protection, suppression of piracy, privateering and slaving, prestige missions, assertion of Britain's right to trade with all contending parties, the blockade against Turkish supplies and reinforcements, finally Navarino. In 1840, knowing that Stopford would be bringing his fleet back from Syria to Malta, Palmerston warned his brother, the minister in Naples, that, as it was clear that the Bourbon king did not intend to keep his promise to cancel a sulphur monopoly granted to a French company in contravention of Britain's commercial treaty of 1816, the admiral would be looking in to obtain satisfaction, by seizing merchant ships if necessary.[9] The Neapolitans duly surrendered (via a French mediator) before the fleet arrived. In 1850 Palmerston's decision that the fleet which had been showing the flag to protect the Hungarian refugees in Turkey should do some debt-collecting at Athens led to the Don Pacifico affair.

Both in the case of Naples and of Greece, Palmerston's hatred of despotic government combined with commercial and prestigious motives for action. It irked him that cruel misgovernment should be conducted from maritime capitals at the mercy of the Navy's guns, which respect for independence prevented him from using. In South America, when the Spanish blockade of the revolted colonies threatened equally their survival and British commerce, Britain broke it; Bolivar the Liberator testified that the Royal Navy (not the empty words of President Monroe) constituted his only protection 'against the united forces of European reaction'. In Europe, too, in Canning's time, the sight of British topsails had heartened Liberals. It was Metternich who asked for them in 1820–1, but it was the revolutionary ministers who said 'We are all lost' when they sailed away from the Bay of Naples. Palmerston was determined not to have this happen at Lisbon where, also, in 1825 the British envoy had written on the arrival of the fleet 'No one is afraid to be a Constitutionalist now.'[10] In 1860, by Palmerston's command, the Navy shielded Garibaldi the Liberator on his passage from Sicily to the Neapolitan mainland.

★   ★   ★   ★

Opposed to seizing colonies, Palmerston was determined not to allow portions of the world unoccupied by European Powers from being pre-empted by any of them, whether for strategic, prestigious or economic reasons, or all three. France was warned off New Zealand, Tahiti, Morocco, and (in the 1860s) Russia off a Korean island. The study of the conduct of Palmerston and Aberdeen in Morocco and in China shows that this too was not an issue of principle between the parties; both would prevent pre-emption by another European Power (or the United States) and both insist that these economically backward lands open their doors to the trade of all the Powers.

In Morocco their theme — 'Her Majesty's Government wish that the Empire of Morocco should exist according to its present limits, and they would see with very great concern . . . any [conferment] upon a Foreign Power [of] a right of occupancy' prevented the French from extending their power from Algeria or seizing ports. This insistence involved Britain in onerous responsibilities in Morocco without any exclusive privileges, for she could not without scandal maintain it unless she saw to it that the interests of other European countries and their subjects were protected along with her own. So the British agents, the Drummond-Hays, father and son, were often unpopular at the Moroccan court. In purely local terms the advantage to Britain of their skilful diplomacy was slight. Other Powers were stopped from obtaining exclusive commercial rights and the economic facilities for British, and other European, interests were improved. But the only point of it all was that 'if British commerce and intercourse are destroyed, in a few years we shall be forgotten'. The aim was simply to maintain the strategic status quo.[11]

This 'imperialism' was not merely informal but negative, and the complaint made in the twentieth century against Britain's 'thou shalt not' principles in Morocco and the region of the Horn of Africa and Arabia, which offered no great commercial opportunities but had strategic importance, is that by Britain's edict they were doomed to remain backwaters, excluded from Western progress. But Palmerston's Britain was not ready for the positive, formal imperialism of the later nineteenth century. By 1850 it had abandoned the old concepts of colonial monopoly held by Mercantilists, and asked only that less enlightened (and less industrial) Powers should be prevented from expanding their empires and thereby exclude British commerce, and that the government, without assuming further burdens of empire, should compel native rulers to admit British traders on 'most favoured nation' terms. Even where 'informal' imperialism was most active, not to say aggressive, in China and parts of West Africa, it was a thing not of soldiers but of sailors; not of administrators, but of consuls; not of legislators, but of diplomats. Sovereignty was not an objective. Power was not for routine imposition by garrison or ordinance, but something held in reserve. Palmerston refused to indulge in the partition of Asia or Africa[12]—

. . . It is very possible that many parts of the world would be better governed by France, England and Sardinia than they are now; and we need not go beyond Italy, Sicily and Spain for examples. But the alliance of England and France has derived its strength not merely from the military and naval power of the two states, but from the force of the moral principle upon which that union has been founded. Our union has for its foundation resistance to unjust aggression, the defence of the weak against the strong, and the maintenance of the existing balance of power. How, then, could we combine to become unprovoked aggressors, to imitate, in Africa, the partition of Poland by the conquest of Morocco for France, of Tunis and some other state for Sardinia, and of Egypt for England? and, more especially, how could England and France, who have guaranteed the integrity of the Turkish Empire, turn round and wrest Egypt from the Sultan? A coalition for such a purpose would revolt the moral feelings of mankind, and would certainly be fatal to any English Government that was a party to it. . . . What we wish about Egypt is that it should continue attached to the Turkish empire, which is a security against its belonging to any European Power. We want to trade with Egypt, and to travel through Egypt, but we do not want the burthen of governing Egypt, and its possession would not, as a political, military and naval question, be considered, in this country, as a set-off against the possession of Morocco by France. *Let us try to improve all these countries by the general influence of our commerce, but let us all abstain from a crusade of conquest* which would call down upon us the condemnation of all the other civilised nations. . . .

One may well smile, recalling that it was Gladstone, of all people, so opposed on moral grounds to Palmerston's treatment of weak and coloured peoples, who was responsible for the occupation of Egypt, after the bombardment of Alexandria, in 1882, allegedly on a temporary basis, but in the interest of British bondholders, a class whom, in general, Palmerston tried to avoid having to uphold by force, feeling that they had invested their money in dubious public authorities at their own risk.[13] It may well be that, had he lived a generation more, into the age of full-blooded, formal imperialism, the time of the scramble for Africa, the exuberant Palmerston would have planned landfalls which Gladstone only made when blown off course. The passages marked by vertical lines show that Palmerston would have weighed, like Salisbury, the reluctant imperialist, the Balance of Power issues against the 'burthen of governing', and our knowledge of Palmerston gives warrant for believing that he would more readily than Salisbury have expatiated upon the advantages of European government. Sentimental attachment to these as an incentive to empire would then have replaced the conventional sentiments of deterrence in the quotation (and would have been equally representative of the time). These conventional sentiments may, indeed, be too easily dismissed as tacking to the public mood, as mere hypocrisy, for Cobdenite principles (opposed even to informal empire) were by 1860 coming to the height of their fashion. But let us note that Palmerston talks of improving these countries by the general influence of commerce. The reconciliation of his public attitude to the acquisition of Egypt with his public defence of aggression in China is simply this — *he did not admit the right of any 'backward' country to exclude European influences*. In this sense he was a true imperialist, but not at all unique, for Aberdeen proposed to treat Japan (the one Asiatic maritime country which had in the seventeenth century repelled Western penetration) as Palmerston and he had treated China; though it was left to the Americans to 'open' Japan, on the 'treaty port' system, the British gained the principal commerce.

The China War of 1839–42 was a product of the abolition in 1833 of the East India Company's monopoly of the British trade at Canton (where alone it was permitted) and the Manchu emperor's decision (largely prompted by the drain of silver) to crush the large imports of opium from India. This trade had long been illegal, but the local officials had connived at and profited from it. Sir James Graham's narrowly defeated censure motion in the spring of 1840 was literally true — 'the hostilities in China were mainly to be attributed to the want of foresight and precaution on the part of Her Majesty's present advisers'.[14] Palmerston's colleague, Sir John Hobhouse, President of the Board of Control for India, had neglected to give Her Majesty's Superintendent at Canton instructions not to protect those who violated Imperial Chinese law. By the time such orders arrived, this official had begun operations, and, since the British government did not wish to 'lose face' and the prospects of lush profits for British merchants (if trade could be freed from the narrow regulations heretofore imposed and the unpredictable vagaries of the corrupt officials) the war received official endorsement. The government knew the sort of treaty it wanted, and disavowed Elliot, its negotiator, for pusillanimity; it was left to the Conservative government of Sir Robert Peel to renew the war and secure the treaty desired by its predecessor. The Treaty of Nanking, 29th August 1842, ceded Hong Kong to Great Britain; opened the trade at five ports, where consuls would be appointed; provided for a 'fair and regular tariff'; freed Europeans from the onerous Chinese criminal law, and was silent on opium.[15] Not only was opium important to the Indian revenue; it paid for tea and for silver which financed Indian purchases from Lancashire. Palmerston spoke in grandiose terms of the economic advantages to Britain of 'a satisfactory arrangement of commerce with a nation of two hundred millions of people' — 'a greater benefit to British manufactures could hardly be conceived'. 'The manufacturing districts ate in great work, thanks to India and China, and in spite of all hostile tariffs in Europe', he wrote in 1845.[16]

Opium or no opium, the confrontation of the West with the Celestial Empire was bound to be violent, for the Chinese attitude to the Western barbarians was not one that European Powers were likely to tolerate or even understand. This is perfectly evident from the italicized phrases in Palmerston's letter of 9th January 1847 to the British plenipotentiary insisting that the Treaty of 1842 and the supplementary treaty fixing the tariff and regulating extra-territorial rights 'must be respected, unless (the Chinese) choose to have their seaports knocked about their ears'[17]—

... We have given the Chinese a most exemplary drubbing, and taught them to ... leave off the system of *pretended contempt under which they have so long concealed their fear*. ... If we permit the Chinese ... to resume, as they will, no doubt, be always endeavouring to do, their former *tone of affected superiority*, we shall very soon be compelled to come to blows with them again. ... Of course ... all the English in China [ought] to abstain from giving the Chinese any ground of complaint, and much more from anything like provocation or affront; but we must stop on the very threshold any attempt on their part to treat us otherwise than as their equals.

Where was the equality when, in Chinese eyes, the very existence
of these new privileges for barbarian traders, extorted by force
from the Son of Heaven, was a provocation and affront? That
Chinese officials, their outlook moulded by a splendid heritage of
civilization whose value Westerners had hardly begun to explore,
did genuinely despise the European as inferior (and had no conception of the equality of states, regarding an ambassador as someone
who brought tribute) did not occur to Palmerston, the heir to centuries of Western hegemony, the minister of the Power which, as
Aberdeen said, must control the Eastern seas, and, as Palmerston
said, would command the navigation of the Indies.

★ ★ ★ ★

It is pleasant to turn from Palmerston forcing opium on China
that Lancashire might prosper and the Indian budget balance, to
Palmerston as the scourge of slave-traders. Although the Marxist
will be convinced that his motivation in this crusade was a desire
to enable the plantations of the British West Indies and Mauritius
to compete with the slave-grown sugar of Cuba and the coffee of
Brazil, there is no warrant for this in his writings. Palmerston
inherited from Castlereagh and Canning the policy of trying to
secure general international agreement on and enforcement of, the
suppression of the trade from Africa to the Americas. But he
brought to it, before and after the abolition of slavery itself in the
King's dominions in 1834, a personal passion. This was the 'world-
bettering' for which he wished to be remembered, and which is all
too often forgotten. On this subject he waxed lyrical, and was
entitled to do so:

... And if England should have the glory of succeeding in her efforts and
exertions completely to extinguish this guilty traffic among the nations,
and finally to close this long account of misery and crime, I think that that
good deed alone will be sufficient to hand down her memory in undying
brightness to all posterity, through the lapse of countless ages. (House of
Commons, 8th August 1839).
... If ever, by the assault of overpowering armies, or by the errors of her
misguided sons, England should fall, and her star should lose its lustre, —
with her fall, for a long period of time, would the hopes of the African,
whether in his own continent, or in the vast regions of America, be buried
in the darkness of despair. I know well that, in such a case, Providence
would, in due course of time, raise up some other nation to inherit our
principles, and to imitate our practice. But, taking the world as it is, and
States as they are constituted, I do not know — and I say it with regret

and with pain — I do not know any nation that is now ready, in this respect, to supply our place. (House of Commons, 18th May 1841).

Palmerston was conscious of Britain's special responsibility in the matter, because her subjects and ships had held the lion's share of the infamous traffic until they were forbidden it in 1807 and because of her naval command of the Atlantic.[18] His ardour was sharpened by the knowledge that, once his arrangements for intercepting the slave-ships began to bite, the voyages became more speculative and furtive, their cruelty and horror much greater. Captains often ditched their human cargo on sight of a pursuing vessel, sometimes in casks on the off-chance of being able to return and pick them up. Every step forward made the next more urgent.[19]

By treaties of 1831 and 1833, although France insisted that all her subjects and property must be adjudicated on in her own courts, she agreed, on a reciprocal basis, to allow the Royal Navy to search and seize ships flying her flag. 'The ships of both countries became mutually special constables, as it were, to one another.'[18] In 1835 Spain, like Sweden and the Netherlands before her, agreed to the right of search and seizure and adjudication by mixed commissions. This left Portugal the chief European offender, under whose flag 'the refuse and scum of the earth — pirates of all nations and of no nation' as Palmerston said, carried on the traffic 'upon the pure spirit of criminal adventure',[19] protected by powerful politicians in Lisbon in liaison with interests in Brazil. Palmerston had borne much from constitutional governments in Portugal striving to show that they were 'genuinely independent' of the protecting Power, including the abolition of the British commercial privileges of the treaty of 1810 (high-water mark of Portugal's dependence) and the revocation of a long-standing right of British subjects in Portugal to process before a special tribunal. But he would not tolerate the failure of Portugal to give reality to its formal abolition of the slave trade in 1817, secured by a British bribe of one million pounds. On 10th May 1838 he told the Commons that 'no predilection in favour of the system of government now fortunately established [in Portugal] . . . will I allow to interfere, by mitigating, in the slightest degree, the indignation which I feel on this subject'. He warned the Portuguese that if they did not co-operate, he would appeal to Parliament for power 'to do ourselves and on our own authority that which Portugal herself refuses to permit us to do by Treaty'.

These were not idle words. In 1839 the power was sought and obtained. Palmerston was not mealy-mouthed in defence of what they called in Lisbon Britain's 'infamous policy'. Portugal, he said, had violated her engagements 'in a greater degree, I will venture to say, than any country in the history of the civilised world could be found ever to have violated the solemn obligations of treaties . . . For, instead of suppressing the slave trade, and abolishing it, she encourages it . . . She has substituted her slave-trading flag in the place of all the slave-trading flags of the world . . . There is now not a slave-trader that crosses the ocean who does not carry his protection under the prostituted flag of Portugal . . . The Governments of Portugal — upon pretexts the most frivolous, upon objections the most unfounded, upon allegations totally destitute of truth — have rejected the pro-posals . . . The conduct of the Portuguese has, in this respect, disentitled them to the esteem of all mankind'. Certainly the ships of the Royal Navy which searched, and seized, and liberated slaves to Sierra Leone, and the captain who was rewarded by Palmerston for initiating (without authority) the policy of landing on the West African coast to destroy slave depots, either by agreement with chiefs or on the ground (or pretext) that there might be British negroes among those waiting for shipment, performed a clearer service to mankind than the ships which cruised off the Tagus when they were not in it. The Slave Trade (Portugal) Act also contained a provision that slave ships seized and carrying no flag or papers by which their nationality could be established should be treated in the Admiralty Courts as British.

When he left office in 1841 Palmerston was very near to enlisting 'in this league against the slave-trade every state in Christendom which has a flag that sails on the ocean, with the single exception of the United States of North America'. In the debate of 10th May 1838 he had regretted that they had not found in the Government of the United States the same willingness as in the French 'to waive national jealousy and national etiquette'; he feared that when they had succeeded with every other flag the slavers would attempt to carry on under the protection of the Stars and Stripes. The Americans refused to give British officers the right to search, or even to visit, suspected slavers flying their flag, so Palmerston assumed the right of visit to ascertain whether the ship was bona fide American or not. If not, the slaves were liberated. Aberdeen agreed that this procedure was 'indispensable', and Palmerston never forgave him for retreating from that position after American protests at 'officious interference',[20] or for his pedantic disapproval of a special Palmerstonian device for liberating slaves from bona fide American ships. Such vessels were apt to find themselves escorted to a British colonial port (on arrival at which the slaves became free), upon some pretext such as saving them from foundering in bad weather. Compensation would then be paid to the United States provided the American subjects responsible were proceeded against under U.S. law, at which slave-trading was piracy. Not until 1862 did Palmerston obtain, from Lincoln, a satisfactory treaty with the United States. He must often have wished that he had yielded to pressure to take a mortgage on the revenues of Cuba as a condition of his loan to the Cristinos, for it would have given his agents a *locus standi* in that Spanish possession which was the last refuge of the Atlantic slave-trade.

When in 1845 the Anglo-Brazilian treaty against the slave trade expired, and Brazil refused to renew it, Aberdeen had, to his credit, passed an act akin to Palmerston's with regard to Portugal. Palmerston took great pleasure, on his return in 1846, in enforcing this, even to the extent of seizing suspected slavers as they came into Brazilian ports. By 1850 Brazilian resistance was over more, perhaps, as a result of local political circumstance than Palmerston's 'bullying'; within two or three years import had been reduced to an illicit trickle. Palmerston near the end of his life called this 'the Miraculous Conversion from Slave Trade of a Nation which up to that Time had committed that Crime to the greatest extent of any Nation, and in Spite of the Strongest Remonstrances which the English Language could convey'. He absolutely declined to consider Brazilian demands for the repeal of the Aberdeen Act, and its replacement by a treaty, because the treaty with Spain did not prevent 15–20,000 negroes a year being imported into Cuba, the treaty with Portugal did not prevent a considerable trade, and even France was not yet without offence in the matter — 'if we were to repeal the Aberdeen act the Slave Deluge would again inundate Brazil'.[21] Righteous, and deeply felt, indignation against the duplicity of all the southern Atlantic states (France, Spain, Portugal, Brazil) in the matter of enforcement coloured Palmerston's attitude to their governments, who made it a 'nationalist' grievance against him in their turn. His

support of the independence of Uruguay against Argentina may
have been dictated by distrust of the latter, and British commercial
interests; his support of it against Brazil was certainly guaranteed
by Uruguay's abolition of slavery.[22] And Palmerston's overbearing
attitude to Brazil, involving a blockade of Rio in January 1863 and
a breach of diplomatic relations which lasted until the Tories came
in after his death, was certainly motivated in part by his memories
of Brazilian perfidy over the Trade and the refusal of the Brazilians
to answer British requests for information on the fate of the slaves
released by the mixed courts in Rio 'still held in Slavery after the
Lapse of many years'.[23]

In terms of man-hours, the suppression of the slave trade was
the principal occupation of the Foreign Office under Palmerston.
It was not only foreigners who made the going hard. Thus
Palmerston writes to Russell (when they were respectively prime
minister and Foreign Secretary), 13th August 1862: 'No First Lord
and no Board of Admiralty have ever felt any interest in the suppression of the slave trade ... If there was a particularly old,
slow-going tub in the navy, she was sure to be sent to the coast of
Africa to try to catch the fast-sailing American clippers; and if
there was an officer notoriously addicted to drinking, he was sent
to a station where rum is a deadly poison.'[24] The maintenance of
the West African squadron was repeatedly attacked by the
Cobdenites in the name of economy, with many jibes at meddling
philanthropy and allegations of over-tenderness to the West
Indian planters, who, in fact, blamed all their troubles on the
abolition first of slavery and then of imperial preference (now a
preference on free as against slave sugar) by the Whig governments.
At a time when they might have pleaded an anxious international
situation in excuse, Russell, as premier, and Palmerston, were
prepared to stake the existence of their government on the issue of
continuing the Squadron.[25] It was no more than the truth that
Palmerston wrote to the minister in Madrid, 17th February 1864,
'... there are no two men in England more determined enemies of
the slave trade than Lord Russell and myself, and certainly we are
neither of us bigoted enthusiasts nor West Indian proprietors. ...
During the many years that I was at the Foreign Office, there was
no subject that more constantly or more intensely occupied my
thoughts, or constituted the aim of my labours; and though I may
boast of having succeeded in accomplishing many good works ...

yet the achievement which I look back to with the greatest and the purest pleasure was the forcing the Brazilians to give up their slave trade. . .'.[26]

Before, at about the time of Palmerston's death, the Atlantic trade virtually ceased, the pressure against the upkeep of the Squadron would probably have succeeded but for the increasing importance of legitimate commerce with West Africa, requiring protection, and the lure of hardwood for the navy. Apart from needing support from some of the commercial classes for the Squadron, Palmerston welcomed this development because he 'wish[ed] most earnestly that civilization may be extended in Africa, being convinced that commerce is the best pioneer for civilization'.[27] But the Cobdenites said that, though Macgregor Laird's 'faith in the ultimate of triumph of commerce allied with Christianity' was justified, traders and missionaries ought to work at their own risk. Laird's first explorations had been sponsored by Russell as Colonial Secretary; the Palmerston government in 1857 offered him a considerable subsidy if he would undertake an annual commercial mission up the Niger. The Cobdenites witnessed with suspicion the acquisition of a new colony (Lagos), and, when this merely diverted the trade to more northerly lagoons, found their suspicions justified. Palmerston received with approval — as an example of 'a little real vigour' — the bombardment of Porto Novo, the slavers' principal escape hatch (1861). In 1862 a war with Ashanti showed that, further north too, a colony and protectorate (the Gold Coast) which, even at the best of times required subsidy from home, was likely to be a source of military expenditure and probably, if retained, a growth point of empire. From Lagos the governor reported that the alternatives were total evacuation or gradual absorption of surrounding territories. In the last months of Palmerston's life Parliament's desire to 'lay down the burden' was manifest and the Colonial Office itself leaned to the view that the best thing to do with Africa was to leave it alone, because the introduction of a market economy of the 'legitimate' type would only substitute large-scale slave cultivation in Africa for large-scale export of slaves. But Palmerston and Russell held to their text that 'it is only by the establishment of legitimate trade that we may hope totally to eradicate the slave trade' and held the Colonial Office to its theme that existing colonies must be retained for 'a solely and entirely . . . disinterested' motive, to end the slave trade and 'extend the advantages of religion, civilization and commerce to the miserable inhabitants of Africa'.[28]

* * * *

The miserable inhabitants of India, where the bones of the weavers whitened the plains that Lancashire might thrive, were not conscious of having benefited by the British Raj, but Palmerston, insulated by the nature of the offices he held from seeing any but the most important dispatches from India (those that bore on foreign policy), yet constantly receiving from Foreign Office agents news of the turpitude of other Powers, was probably quite sincere in comparing the success of the British in India with the slow progress made by the French in Algeria, ascribing the latter to the atrocities committed by the invaders.[29]

During Palmerston's lifetime the British Empire changed its character in the eyes of the public at home. By 1850 what was left of the original Atlantic-Caribbean empire of the eighteenth century was held to consist of troublesome relics, in the south the depressed West Indian islands, in the north the Canadas, expected by almost every public man (except perhaps Palmerston) to drop away into independence and probably union with the United States.[30] The centre of gravity had shifted to the East. The empire meant India; guarding the empire meant guarding the approaches to India, and this involved the Foreign Office and the Board of Control, with the Admiralty, in responsibilities from Morocco and the Cape to Ceylon and Rangoon, and for all the routes to India (Atlantic, Mediterranean, even Euxine) and, in Palmerston's interpretation, the land mass of Central Asia to boot. Interest in Singapore and China and Japan was a logical consequence of the possession of India as well as of Britain's search for new markets. When Palmerston weighed up the pros and cons to try to answer the question whether Sultan Mahmoud and Pasha Mehemet would be the better keeper of the gate at Constantinople, he meant the gate to India. In determining the attitude to Mehemet, it was irrelevant whether one thought with the Liberal-Evangelicals, who included colleagues like Charles Grant (Lord Glenelg) and Macaulay, of the duty to communicate to India 'the blessings of the European condition' so that in the course of time a Westernized India would become self-governing, or went a long way (as Palmerston did) with that unfashionably ostentatious Tory imperialist,

Ellenborough, who wished to strengthen the Raj and thought of it as permanent.[31] Whatever India's destiny, empire in India was a current fact. Palmerston's attitude to Egypt was always that 'we do not want Egypt any more than any rational man with an estate in the north of England and a residence in the south, would have wished to possess the inns on the north road. All he could want would have been that the inns should be well kept, always accessible, and furnishing him, when he came, with mutton chops and post horses'.[32] But Mehemet must not have a monopoly of all the inns in mid-journey. Between 1833 and 1840 Mehemet gave cause for fear that, from his Syrian and Arabian territories, he was grasping at the Great Valley of Mesopotamia and the Persian Gulf. It was thought that, while the Russian ambassador at Constantinople worked against Ponsonby's plans for the military, naval, administrative, judicial, fiscal and commercial reform of the Sultan's dominions (to keep the Sultan dependent on Russia), St Petersburg might connive at Mehemet's securing Diarbekir on the Upper Tigris, athwart the gap between the Caucasus and Syria, whose importance as 'the central key of the whole of Asia Minor' was stressed in the reports to Palmerston of the explorer, Colonel Chesney.[33] These reports set Palmerston studying the military geography of the area under the tuition of the Polish general Chrzanorski. This seemed to foreshadow a carve-up of the Ottoman Empire between Tsar and Pasha and a serious threat to British prestige and commerce.

The British and British-Indian response was swift and resolute. On 8th December 1837 Palmerston wrote to the Consul-General at Alexandria that Mehemet's troop movements in Syria and Arabia 'seem to indicate intentions on his part to extend his authority towards the Persian Gulf and the Pashalik of Baghdad. . . . You will state frankly to the Pasha that the British Govt could not see with indifference the execution of such intentions'.[34] A Canningite friend, Robert Grant, as Governor of Bombay, proposed the acquisition of Aden as a coaling-station for the new regular steam service from Britain to India via the isthmus of Suez, and a bar to Mehemet Ali. When Mehemet tried to make the best bargain open to him by securing British recognition of his recent conquests in Arabia he was told that 'Her Majesty's Govt is not aware that any interest of Great Britain is promoted by the continuance' of the Egyptian occupation of the Yemen; 'the British Govt have no

desire that such occupation should continue ... on the contrary. ...
Great Britain could not see with indifference any attempt ... to
invade the country lying at and beyond the mouth of the Red Sea'
(May 1838).[34] Orders were sent by Hobhouse from London for the
occupation of Aden, and it was taken on 16th January 1839 as a
dependency of Bombay. The Egyptians had meanwhile been
thrusting through Nejd towards Bahrein, a Persian Gulf island
adjoining the British protected sultanate of Muscat. On 29th
November 1838 Palmerston sent to Alexandria a warning that the
occupation of Bahrein could not be viewed with indifference by the
British Government,[34] and the authorities in India indicated that
they would defend Bahrein by force if necessary. By January 1840
Anglo-Russian firmness on the Eastern Question provoked the
withdrawal of Egyptian troops from Arabia to assist in the defence
of Egypt, and as part of the settlement imposed on the Pasha, the
status of the Egyptians in Arabia became simply that of tradesmen
serving Turkish authority. By now the spectre of a partition of the
Sultan's dominions between Russia and Egypt — which did not
entirely vanish until the Convention of July 1840 — had been
replaced by the conception of Mehemet as a tool of France. In his
impressive memorandum of March 1840 Clarendon argued that
Palmerston's attitude to Mehemet was perverse. The important
route to India was the Suez one, and Britain's interests lay more in
the progress of Egypt than the stagnation of Turkey. Why label
Mehemet (formerly regarded as the tool of Russia) the minion of
France, when Britain could offer him much more than France?
Britain ought to ask the Powers to *guarantee* him and his dynasty in
Egypt and most of Syria, and the Sultan elsewhere.[35] But that
would have meant accepting France's terms, and seemed to Palmerston to reveal naïveté as to the political virtue of the Pasha and to
be just another ingenious argument of his passivist francophil critics.

The détente with Russia came too late to avert the British invasion of Afghanistan. One hundred and ten years later Western
strategists surveying the Middle East talked of a 'northern tier'
stretching from Turkey-in-Europe through Asia Minor, Iraq and
Persia to northern India (West Pakistan) which must somehow be
kept out of Russian hands. Only the detail of their maps and the
scale of their weapons would have surprised Palmerston. Visions of
Russian expansion set him poring over sketchy maps of the little-
known khanates of Turkestan, stretching east from the Caspian to

the innermost limits of the Chinese empire; he gathered that the Oxus might be navigable to a point not far from where the upper waters of the Indus complex (not yet in British hands) were (wrongly) thought to be navigable, with only the outworks of the Hindu Kush between. Well might Melbourne say 'The Black Sea and the Caucasus and these great Asiatic Empires inflame imaginations wonderfully'[36] and Salisbury later talk of the peril of small maps. But by 1783 the Russians had perfected control of the Sea of Azov and by 1829 of the eastern shores of the Black Sea. The re-routing of British trade to Persia was forced by wars between Russia and Persia which gave the former the country between Georgia and the Caspian in 1813 and parts of Armenia in 1828.[37] Having made a lodgement on the Eastern shores of the Caspian, the Russians had every reason required by an imperialist Power to go to Khiva, where their traders and emissaries had been ill-treated by the khan. It lay on the Oxus, half-way between Astrakhan, at the head of the Caspian, and Kabul, capital of the principal Afghan principality, south of the Hindu Kush. Palmerston required that Khiva 'should be a non-conducting body interposed between Russia and British India' and warned the Russians that if they went there he did not know how far north of the Hindoo Koosh [sic] Lord Auckland, the Indian governor-general, might have to go.[38] Both London and St Petersburg underestimated the resilience of the peoples of Turkestan. The Russians did not get within two hundred and fifty miles of Khiva and it was thirty years before they occupied it. The ruler of Bokhara, east from Khiva, executed British envoys, while other British emissaries escorted the Khan of Khiva's Russian captives back to their own people.

But the danger via Persia and Afghanistan seemed immediate. Despite a defence treaty of 1814 (a product of Canning's outbidding of Napoleon) the failure of Persian attacks on Russia and Russian encouragement of Persian designs against the Afghans made Persia seem in the 1830s a client state of Russia. Palmerston induced Persia to abandon its attack on the Afghan city of Herat and accept a military mission (1834), but even the russophil Durham admitted that the renewed attack on Herat in 1837 was Russian aggression by proxy. The not very competent and unpopular British envoy and the Russian envoy, in whose favour the dice were loaded, both accompanied the expedition, the one arguing against, the other for it. British diplomacy failed, but the resolution of Lieutenant

Eldred Pottinger on the walls of Herat and a landing from India in
the Persian Gulf carried the day. The independence of Persia,
Palmerston said, was 'a great object to us' both 'as connected with
the Independence of Turkey' and 'with reference to India'.[39]
Persia must not be allowed to serve Russian purposes. It is important to grasp that the whole history of India has been one of
successive invasions from the north-west. It did not seem absurd
that an Alexander or Nicholas of Russia should tread in the steps
of Alexander of Macedon, the Parthians, the Arabs, successive
armies of Turks, Persians and Afghans. We think of Afghanistan
as a backwater, slowly being modernized in the 1950s by competing
Russian and American aid programmes. But it was from Afghanistan that the Moghul empire had been established in the sixteenth
century, and it was sundered from its allegiance by the Shah of
Persia who in 1739 carried off the Peacock Throne from Delhi.
Only twenty-two years later an Afghan who had thrown off the
Persian yoke was back in Delhi and defeated the great Mahratta
confederacy at Panipat. In the 1830s Afghanistan was in chaos and
when the British sent Captain Burnes from India to enlist the
help of Dost Mohammed at Kabul against the Persians at Herat, he
found that Dost's prime objective was to recover Peshawar from
the Sikh Napoleon, Ranjit Singh. Britain could not have friendship
both with Dost and Ranjit, and both prudence and honour
prevented her from encouraging or risking the descent on Delhi of
the formidable European-trained and equipped Sikh army. The
one-eyed Sikh leader was a stabilizing factor on the north-west
frontier; he was impressive; he was admired, and he was, indeed,
admirable. Therefore the conclusion was drawn that if, while there
was no wish to make Afghanistan a British province, 'we must
have it an ally upon whom we can depend',[40] Dost must be
replaced. Therefore, at Windsor Castle in October 1838, the
decision was taken (by Melbourne, Palmerston, Hobhouse, Russell,
Glenelg, Lansdowne and the Lord Chancellor) to adopt a forward
policy in Afghanistan, and the hesitations of Lord Auckland at
Simla were overborne.

Not until after the Whigs fell from Office was the result of the
occupation of Afghanistan, and the subsequent weakening of the
victorious army as a prelude to withdrawal, seen to be tragedy. The
hope was that Afghan objections to the restoration by the British
of Dost's predecessor, Shah Suja (alliance with whom had been

part of Canning's diplomatic complex for the frustration of
Napoleon's designs in the East) would be overcome by securing for
him the whole principality of Herat. Burnes's warnings that the
Afghans would not accept a discredited ruler imposed by British
arms and intolerable to them because he was acceptable to the
Sikhs were edited away when the Afghan Papers were laid before
Parliament. For this Palmerston was bitterly attacked after the
terrible denouement[41] — the murder of Burnes and then, at a
parley, of Sir William Macnaghten; the decision to withdraw the
garrison and its vast number of camp-followers from Kabul, under
safe-conduct, to the Khyber; its fearful fate in the defiles at the
hands of merciless tribesmen, only three white men getting
through with the tale; the return of the British to rescue prisoners
and wreak revenge; evacuation and treaty with Dost. In truth if
Palmerston and Hobhouse are to be censured for concealing
Burnes's warnings, the Tory President of the Board of Control,
Ellenborough, is more to be censured than they for ignoring them.
Enabled by the Anglo-Russian entente (Palmerston's achievement)
to take a different view, and eager for party and personal glory to
take a different view, he abandoned the expedition to Herat 'because of the deep interest taken by Russia' in that place.[42] Having
thus removed the only hope (ill-founded though it was) of making
Shah Suja palatable to the Afghans, the Tories held to the Whig
policy of evacuation 'as soon as Shah Sooja should be firmly
established upon the throne he owes to your Majesty's aid',[43]
which was 'thumbs down' for Burnes and Macnaghten and the
army of occupation. The sensible decision to recognize and try to
influence Dost was now possible because Ranjit Singh was dead
and his successors were less well-disposed to the British and rent
by internecine conflicts. Dost's help would now be useful against
the Sikhs, who attacked British India in 1845. Defeated, they broke
out again, and Russell as prime minister endorsed the governor-
general's conclusion that 'the Dynastys of the Sings' must be
subverted for ever by the annexation of the Punjab (1849), though
the driving force behind this decision was Hobhouse.[44]

It is easy enough to sit in an armchair and mock as strategic folly
Palmerston's statement that as, one day, the British and the
Russians would meet in Asia 'it should be our business to take care
that the meeting should be as far off from our Indian possessions as
may be convenient and advantageous to us. But the meeting will

not be avoided by our staying at home to receive the visit'.[45] Surely, it would be foolish to drive forward, precipitating a clash that was better postponed (and in fact never happened), and condemning the British in India to an inexpedient extension of lines of supply through hostile country. But, as a later governor-general, Dalhousie, warned at the time of the Crimean War — when there were Persian pressure on Herat, Russian intrigues against Dost at Kandahar and an emissary from the Khan of Kokand brought news that the Russians, by-passing Khiva, Bokhara and Samarkand, had come (prematurely as it proved) within striking distance of the Hindu Kush — one had to think of the disturbing talk in the bazaars. British rule in India depended on the belief of Indians that it would be maintained, and, Dalhousie reported, 'the notions entertained of Russia, and the estimates formed of her powers, by the nations of India, are exaggerated in the extreme. Although our pride must wince on hearing it, it is an unquestionable fact that the general belief at this moment is that Russia gravely menaces the power of England, and will be more than a match for her in the end'.[46] Moreover, on behalf of the Palmerston of the '30s it should be stressed that not until 1849 did the British achieve, on the ruins of the Sikh military power, a mountain frontier running from west of Karachi by the Bolan Pass to and beyond the Khyber, a frontier on which it made military sense to stand and wait for an enemy.

CHAPTER IX

PALMERSTON THE INTEMPERATE

THE Anglo-French entente, which foundered in 1839–40 on the Eastern Question, had been holed on the Spanish rocks. Palmerston's attitude towards it is clearly expounded in a letter to Howard de Walden in May 1836, explaining that Britain must bear with 'little ebullitions of national conceit' on the part of France. 'Remember that it is of great importance to us, not only to be well with the French Govt, but to appear to all Europe to be so. England alone cannot carry her points on the Continent; she must have allies as instruments to work with. We cannot have the co-operation of our old allies, the 3 Powers, because their views and opinions are nowadays the reverse of ours. France thinks with us, and from her peculiar position is compelled to work with us, and by her assistance, whether willingly given, or extorted by the force of circumstances, we are enabled to controul the 3 Powers, or to give what direction we wish, to many of the great events of the day.'[1] Palmerston, even while rebuffing Metternich and thus throwing himself more than ever upon the French alliance, which he wished to use to solve the Eastern Question as well, made it all too clear to all and sundry that his conception of the French as allies was that they were 'instruments to work with', an attitude which positively invited 'little ebullitions of national conceit'. He became ill-tempered and tactless when he found that the French were not living up to the spirit of the Quadruple Alliance; so far as Spain was concerned, they did so only for three short periods, and at times they actually facilitated aid to the Carlists. It seemed that they preferred disorder in Spain to stable constitutional government, except briefly and intermittently when the Moderados were in office. As early as September 1836 he wrote, privately, that the Quadruple Alliance was really at an end, and in January 1837 the omission of all mention of France in the King's Speech eloquently expressed the Foreign Secretary's disgust with the Molé government. In March, indeed, he repudiated the suggestion that the alliance was dissolved; it was a stable alliance between nations who would long continue to have the same friends and the same enemies and 'in all important questions of European policy the governments will have the same interests'. No alliance 'founded on a right perception of the mutual interests of two great nations, was ever destined to a longer existence'.[2] But the French king, anxious to receive the accolade of respectability from the Eastern Powers, was less intractable with Vienna than Palmerston. The French did not feel that in Spain their interests were the same as Palmerston's and Spanish facts belied his brave words.

Palmerston's colleagues felt less distressed than he at developments in Spain, for many of them felt with Melbourne that it was idle to expect to establish permanent 'influence' in a country like Spain, especially by the road of constitutionalism — Portugal seemed to confirm the premier's dictum that Chambers and free presses did not abate hostility towards England.[3] They welcomed the end of the Carlist war as an opportunity to improve relations with France, and at the same time with Austria; they were not mentally prepared for the Anglo-Russian détente, and, throughout the events which followed, often seemed more concerned to prevent a breach with France than to settle the Eastern Question according to Palmerston's prescription, or even to settle it at all. Hence the efforts of Paris were shrewdly directed towards isolating Palmerston from his colleagues, and inculcating the belief that, if relations were so bad, it was all his fault.

Lacking Palmerston's confidence that France was bluffing, if only because she was not ready, financially and militarily, to make war,[4] the cabinet, at the beginning of October 1840, adopted the view of Russell that, although the July Conventions were sound policy and the anger of the French government and people was unreasonable, no chance of peace should be lost, and that, if the French would subscribe to them in principle, they should not be expected to participate in enforcing them.[5] In view of Russell's intention to suggest at a cabinet on 10th that the Four Powers should consult with France on the terms to be offered to the Pasha by the Sultan, Palmerston appended to a stiff message to Granville on 8th, telling him to indicate to the French the disastrous results of any 'Anconade' or some declaration of what France would or would not permit, the addendum 'if France makes us a friendly communication tending to lead to an amicable discussion of the present state of affairs, we shall receive it and deal with it in the spirit in which it is made'.[6] But this was not enough for the cabinet, which agreed that the Four Powers ought to tell France they would use their good offices to get the Sultan to withdraw his official deposition of Mehemet Ali from Egypt, and, as Melbourne confessed to the Queen, watched with great impatience and not a little suspicion to see how the Foreign Secretary would carry out his instruction, for Guizot had said that this was the last effort of the peace party in France.[7] Pressed by the Queen, Palmerston agreed that Granville should say how much Britain regretted France leaving the concert, and how pleased she would be if she returned, and sent a note to Ponsonby instructing him to urge on the Sultan the revocation of the firman.[8] Any hint of weakness was, however, removed by warnings from both Victoria and Melbourne to King Leopold that if France's warlike preparations (directed, it was later found, to the seizure of the Balearics) continued, Britain would have to emulate them. These were passed on to Paris and contributed to the fall of Thiers.[9]

We see Palmerston at the end of 1840 wearing the laurels of a major diplomatic triumph, and when parliament met in 1841 Melbourne and Russell defended his proceedings as warmly as if they had never questioned them. Part of the cabinet's caution in foreign affairs had been due to its parliamentary weakness and to a serious domestic situation. The government had actually fallen in April 1839 and returned to office, ingloriously hanging onto the skirts of a stubborn young lady whose refusal to dismiss the principal Whigs from her Bedchamber caused Peel to decline office. Trade was bad, and the threat of social disturbance from Chartist exploitation of a deep inherent hostility to the New Poor Law in the manufacturing districts was severe. In 1840, if the situation in the country eased, the Whig government sank even lower in political credit and, during the session, found in Palmerston's outstanding speech on China its only compensation. Now, although Clarendon said that Palmerston had been able to win his way because of apathy in parliament, country and cabinet, that was hardly true as regards the cabinet, and Palmerston might well not have triumphed there had not the applause of the Opposition leaders and the growing anti-French tone of the press indicated that he had become, to an extent he had never been before, the champion of a national feeling. A hostile Gladstone, writing in the mid-fifties, recalled that Palmerston's triumph on the Eastern

G

Question, culminating in the Straits Convention of 13th July 1841, was the one brilliant achievement of a dying administration.[10] To this treaty France was a party, as well as the other Powers and Turkey; it established the 'ancient rule' as agreed 363 days earlier.

No sooner had Thiers fallen than ministers and the Queen (bombarded from Brussels with complaints of Palmerston's recklessness)[11] sought by all means in their power to move a Foreign Secretary, who said that nothing should be given to the Guizot government which would not have been given to Thiers,[12] into the paths of conciliation. However much, and however sincerely, they praised the qualities which had enabled Palmerston, consistently supported only by Hobhouse among the five ministers with the full circulation of dispatches, and, among other cabinet ministers, only by Minto (First Lord of the Admiralty) and Macaulay, to win his great success, they could not forget the anxiety he had caused them, and seemed not to feel; the risks he took, and appeared not to weigh; the vehemence of his language. Greville was an extremely prejudiced witness, but the sting in the tail of his tribute to Palmerston represented general apprehension, if not general conviction. In parliament, he wrote, Palmerston had shown consummate impudence, skill and resolution. The tone of his writings was dashing, bold and confident. If war came it would have been wholly his doing, and yet he was off-hand about the clamour in Paris, convinced that Mehemet would yield and that the French would not be such fools as to fight. How very dangerous that a man of such flippant tone, such undoubting self-sufficiency, such levity, should wield so absolute a despotism over foreign policy![13]

Palmerston, therefore, was pressed as hard as was possible when parliament was not sitting and most cabinet ministers were out of London, to moderate panache by tact towards the French. When Russell heard (31st October) of the dusty answer that Palmerston, *before* the fall of Thiers, had returned to Metternich's proposal of a Congress, he wrote a resignation letter and refused to attend a cabinet unless Ponsonby was recalled or temporarily superseded by a special envoy.[14] No doubt, Lord John, a vain man, wanted to score a point, but there was some ground for his fear that concessions promised in cabinet would be eroded at Constantinople with Palmerston's connivance. Palmerston agreed to apologize about the note to Vienna (sent without reference to the cabinet) but stood firmly by Ponsonby. He did, however, agree that French pride should be salved by the revocation of the firman, that coup of Ponsonby's which 'has given us something to go to market with to the French, and has created something for the French to insist upon, and for us to acquiesce in without touching the stipulations of the treaty'.[15] But as in substance this was only what everyone had expected, it would hardly count as a triumph for French diplomacy unless it were made to seem so. And Palmerston would not play that game. France was to be *informed* that the Powers had advised the Sultan to leave Mehemet hereditary pasha of Egypt, Nubia, etc., if he submitted within a time-limit; there was to be no engagement with France on this. The French, he wrote, wished 'that the final settlement of the Eastern question shall not appear to have been concluded without their concurrence ... this is exactly what I now wish should appear'. And, determined that Mehemet should be 'really and *bona fide* a subject of the Sultan, and not a protected dependent and tool of France', Palmerston used Ponsonby to stiffen the terms of the Sultan's new firman.[16] Issued on 13th February 1841, this prescribed the tribute Mehemet was to pay for Egypt and the Soudan, and limited the number of his army. Palmerston allowed Russia to call the tune with regard to negotiations between the Powers and Turkey over other matters, to veto both Metternich's proposed communal treaty of mutual self-denial and the international 'guarantee' of the independence and integrity of the Turkish Empire proposed by France in 1839 and now again by Guizot. And France was not allowed to sign the *draft* Straits Convention initialled by the Powers on 15th March.[17]

The impression began to grow that, if 1840 showed a diplomatic triumph for Palmerston, 1841 was a triumph principally for the Tsar, the most anti-French of sovereigns, whose ambition had long been to split Britain from France, and that Palmerston knowingly granted it to him. It is true that when the Tsar proposed (Metternich concurring) a Four Power agreement 'providing for the contingency of an attack by France upon the liberties of Europe', Palmerston demurred[18] (the cabinet would not have considered it). But his attitude to France seemed as overdrawn in one sense as in 1834 it had been in the other. Thus[19]—

My opinion is that we shall not have war now with France, but that we ought to make our minds up to have it any time.

All Frenchmen want to encroach and extend their territorial possessions at the expense of other Nations, and they feel what the *National* has often said, that an alliance with England is a bar to such projects. . . . I do not blame the French for disliking us. Their vanity prompts them to be the first nation in the world; and yet at every turn they find that we are their equals. It is a misfortune to Europe that the national character of a great and powerful people, placed in the centre of Europe, should be such as it is; but it is the business of other nations not to shut their eyes to the truth, and to shape their conduct by prudent precautions.

For one line of propaganda which arrived in England from Paris via Brussels Palmerston had only contempt, and the following letter deserves quotation *in extenso* as an example of his direct and crisp manner of thought and argument;[20] it also introduces a tribute to the Germans calculated to appeal to the House of Coburg —

Viscount Palmerston to Queen Victoria.

WINDSOR CASTLE, 11*th November* 1840.

Viscount Palmerston presents his humble duty to your Majesty, and with reference to your Majesty's memorandum of the 9th inst., he entreats your Majesty not to believe that there exists at present in France that danger of internal revolution and of external war which the French Government, to serve its own diplomatic purposes, endeavours to represent.

There is no doubt a large Party among the leading politicians in France, who have long contemplated the establishment of a virtually, if not actually, independent State in Egypt and Syria, under the direct protection and influence of France, and that Party feel great disappointment and resentment at finding their schemes in this respect baffled. But that Party will not revenge themselves on the Four Powers by making a revolution in France, and they are enlightened enough to see that France cannot revenge herself by making war against the Four Powers, who are much stronger than she is.

. . . But your Majesty may be assured that there is in France an immense mass of persons, possessed of property, and engaged in pursuits of industry, who are decidedly adverse to unnecessary war, and determined to oppose revolution. And although those persons have not hitherto come prominently forward, yet their voice would have made itself heard, when the question of peace or unprovoked war came practically to be discussed.

With regard to internal revolution, there is undoubtedly in France a large floating mass of Republicans and Anarchists, ready at any moment to make a disturbance if there was no strong power to resist them; but the persons who would lose by convulsion are infinitely more numerous, and the National Guard of Paris, consisting of nearly 60,000 men, are chiefly persons of this description, and are understood to be decidedly for internal order, and for external peace.

It is very natural that the French Government after having failed to extort concessions upon the Turkish Question, by menaces of foreign war, should now endeavour to obtain those concessions, by appealing to fears of another kind, and should say that such concessions are necessary in order to prevent revolution in France; but Viscount Palmerston would submit to your Majesty his deep conviction that this appeal is not better founded than the other, and that a firm and resolute perseverance on the part of the Four Powers, in the measures which they have taken in hand, will effect a settlement of the affairs of Turkey, which will afford great additional security for the future peace of Europe, without producing in the meantime either war *with* France, or revolution *in* France.

France and the rest of Europe are entirely different now from what they were in 1792. The French nation is as much interested now to avoid further revolution, as it was interested then in ridding itself, by any means, of the enormous and intolerable abuses which then existed. France then imagined she had much to gain by foreign war; France now knows she has everything to lose by foreign war.

Europe then (at least the Continental States) had also a strong desire to get rid of innumerable abuses which pressed heavily upon the people of all countries. Those abuses have now in general been removed; the people in many parts of Germany have been admitted, more or less, to a share in the management of their own affairs. A German feeling and a spirit of nationality has sprung up among all the German people, and the Germans, instead of receiving the French as Liberators, as many of them did in 1792–93, would now rise as one man to repel a hateful invasion. Upon all these grounds Viscount Palmerston deems it his duty to your Majesty to express his strong conviction that the appeals made to your Majesty's good feelings by the King of the French, upon the score of the danger of revolution in France, unless concessions are made to the French Government, have no foundation in truth, and are only exertions of skilful diplomacy. . . .

Victoria and Albert, prompted by Uncle Leopold, were urging that Britain should do everything possible to uphold the Orleans régime, lest a red, and chauvinistic, republic under Odillon Barrot — or Thiers! — arise. Palmerston's letter was the reverse of encouraging, and, having read it, Leopold wrote with Coburg emphasis, in terms calculated to inspire his nephew to action (26th November 1840) — 'Palmerston, *rex* and autocrat, is, for a Minister finding himself such fortunate circumstances, far *too irritable and violent.* . . . One does not understand the use of showing so much hatred and anger.'[21]

When Palmerston, during the general election of 1841, went out of his way at an unopposed election at Tiverton to make a gratuitous attack on the French army in Algeria, he confirmed the uneasiness of the Court and of his cabinet colleagues. His response to Guizot's official protest was that he had purposely chosen an opportunity to say what he could not say in a diplomatic communication or a speech in parliament, to endeavour to promote the interests of humanity by drawing attention to 'proceedings which I think it would be for the honour of France to put an end to'. It had not occurred to him, he said, 'to consider whether what I said might or might not be agreeable . . . and if the public discussion which my speech produced shall have the effect of putting an end to a thousandth part of the human misery which I dwelt upon, I am sure M. Guizot will forgive me for saying that I should not think that result too dearly purchased by giving offence to the oldest and dearest friend I may have in the world'.[22] Louis Philippe and Guizot struck back by postponing until after the defeat of the Whigs when parliament met the French signature of the Five-Power Treaty against the slave trade with which Palmerston had hoped to crown his second tenure of the Foreign Office. Palmerston 'did what neither man, woman or nation ever forgive; he deeply wounded their vanity and their pride', complained Greville.[23] His colleagues shook their heads at the escapades of one whose 'notion (was) that everything was to be done by violence' (Melbourne), who 'intrigued against France in every part of the world, and with a tenacity of purpose that was like insanity' (Sir Francis Baring, Chancellor of the Exchequer). Already one could foresee — though Palmerston did not — the powerful case, supplementary to that of 1835, which would be made against his ever getting the Foreign Office again.

*   *   *   *

Palmerston had not taken a prominent part in cabinet proceedings except on those occasions when foreign affairs were the main concern, and these he tried to keep to the minimum. But he was a loyal party minister, ready, for instance, to spring to the defence of that other ex-Canningite, Glenelg, against charges reflecting the anger of the white settlers in South Africa against Whitehall's regard for the interests of non-whites,[24] and adept at giving the most liberal colour (i.e., that most acceptable to the Free Trade School) to the government's commercial policy. He had long spoken as a free — or at least freer — trader in the abstract, declaring that Britain had prospered not because of protective duties, but despite them, and that if Britain removed impediments on her side, other nations would be forced, against their will, to act on sound commercial principles, and describing the difficulties encountered in commercial negotiations from the existence of high duties on the staple products of, for instance, Germany.[25] It must therefore have been a relief when the cabinet at last decided in 1841 to risk an attack on the great home and colonial interests which upheld the sugar, timber and corn duties. The budgetary proposals were withdrawn one by one, after defeat, and when Peel carried a vote of no confidence by a majority of one, the cabinet had to decide whether to resign or dissolve. Palmerston, with his usual over-optimism, was one of the minority which, because of the strong partisan wishes of the Queen, urged an election.[26] He urged the men of Tiverton to join with him in condemning commercial monopoly as they had condemned political monopoly.[27] But in the country at large either Protection or 'disgust at Whig rule', or both, carried the day, few Liberals giving enthusiastic support to ministers who were felt to have embraced anti-monopoly policies from desperation rather than conviction. Ministers met the new parliament only to be turned out.

Palmerston now took his seat, for the first time in nearly thirty-four years, on the Opposition benches, and with a political status very different from 1835, on account of his recent triumphs in foreign affairs. For the first time in his experience, he had been borne along on a wide current of popular approval, and the taste was sweet. If Russell's sponsorship of a mitigated Corn Law made him acceptable as member for the City of London, Palmerston, it was thought, could have had Liverpool, the constituency of Canning and Huskisson, in tribute to his endeavours to open markets.[28] He refused the prospect, as he had refused Southwark in 1832 and would refuse the City in 1857, clinging to Tiverton for the rest of his life. He had won a new respect from the Tories; Aberdeen told a foreign diplomat that his conduct of the Eastern Question 'made him forgive Palmerston many things of former years, which he had thought he never should have forgiven'.[29] The Whig aristocrats perhaps felt more than ever before that he was not one of them. Melbourne, according to Greville, thought he would go back to the Tories, and the insatiable gossip opined that in the event of a dislocation of parties Palmerston was 'free to adopt any course, and to join with any party, and with a reputation as a bold, able and successful statesman'.[30]

Lady Palmerston had wondered anxiously whether her energetic husband would not find time hanging on his hands now that there were no Foreign Office boxes. He threw himself, however, with some gusto into estate management at Broadlands, and the study of it, for, he said, agriculture and horticulture had now become sciences. By 1843 he had got all his farms into the hands of tenants with proficiency and means, though he was a trifle rueful to find that his head gardener was a Methodist lay preacher.[31] There were long visits to the Cowper mansion at Panshanger in Hertfordshire and nearby Brocket, seat of the ailing Melbourne, and to the country houses of friends and colleagues, with hunting, shooting, riding and, of course, the races. He revisited the Irish estates (in 1842 and 1845) and at last, in 1844, contrived a long foreign holiday, seeing Germany for the first time. But in 1841 it would have horrified him to learn that he was to be out of office for five years, for he chafed at the absence of power. Clarendon's remark on the last day of 1841 that Palmerston believed he could rout the Tories foot and horse and re-establish himself at the Foreign Office before six months had passed was an exaggeration, but it bore witness to the essential belligerence of the only opposition leader in whom all energy and intention did not seem dead.[32] Of course, Palmerston had every incentive to activity, for it could make him — especially if foreign affairs could be kept to the fore — indubitably the second man among the Whigs in the House of Commons, and who knew what might not happen to Russell, younger but far less robust? During the session of 1842 Palmerston was indefatigible in the House of Commons. He made a big speech on the Address at the outset ('a good slashing speech on Corn' — Greville) and was there on the last night of the session for a 'brilliant single combat' with Peel in an empty House in August. Russell had gone away before the end of the session, leaving Palmerston with one Front Bench colleague, Vernon Smith, and a few Radical back-benchers, to maintain 'incessant fire' against ministers.[33]

Palmerston did not confine himself to foreign affairs, though they remained his only study, apart from the books on husbandry. He intervened largely in economic debates, never ceasing to remind the country of his record of fifteen commercial treaties, two of them (with Austria and Turkey) important, and the Fisheries Convention with France in 1839.[34] No respecter of persons, he hoped 'that the Duke of Wellington would add another wreath to the laurels that grace his brow, and attain commercial emancipation for his country'. He teased the Tory Protectionists for their rapid transition from exultation to lamentation when they found their leaders, presumably from long meditation while in opposition, had 'come into office fully imbued with those sound principles the enunciation of which has excited so much admiration on this side of the House'.[35] There was much mere knock-about, with Palmerston laying into Conservative ministers as though they were Metternichs and Guizots, and as though the system the Protectionists behind the ministers upheld was not the same one the Whigs had refrained from assailing until their recent 'death-bed vow'. But Palmerston was showing once again, as in 1828–30, that he sniffed a wind of change, which, as he said, could not be avoided simply by changing the men in power, because it was the natural result of 1832. He doubted whether it would be possible to maintain a high protective tariff on corn much longer, thought Peel's Corn Law of 1842 a 'trifling mitigation' and wondered whether the fixed duty of eight shillings proposed by Russell would be low enough.[36]

Whatever the subject of debate, Palmerston's vehemence was such that it looked as though the strong wine of Opposition, to which he was unaccustomed, had gone to his head. But it was in his chosen field, of course, that his indignation against his successors found the freest vent. The mere sight of them sitting in his place was an insult, the idea of them staying there long intolerable. For, like Chatham, he believed that he could save his country, and that no other man could, and a few months of Aberdeen at the Foreign Office convinced him that it needed saving. Of temperate appraisal of Aberdeen's proceedings he was no more capable than he was of writing a colourless dispatch. Out came the sword which he had used in 1829 and 1830, in that same arena, to hack his way to fame, against the same adversaries. Palmerston would speak for England from the Opposition bench, as he had from the Treasury bench, only better (for now he could choose his occasion). The conflict was so personal that he must deeply have regretted the fact that Aberdeen was in the Lords, so that he faced Peel, whose calm, analytical manner was the perfect foil for Palmerston's exuberant invective. Palmerston was singularly free from that inhibition which is apt to afflict a sensitive former Foreign Secretary, the knowledge that in office he would have done very much the same as the incumbent. Each of the ex-Harrovians thought the other peculiarly wrong-headed and almost the worst person ever to be entrusted with the conduct of foreign affairs. Aberdeen, obsessed by concern for the maintenance of the social order in Europe, bore the taint of pro-Austrianism. He attached importance to goodwill in diplomacy, which Palmerston was prone to ignore. He was by nature passivist, where Palmerston was activist; he was anxious to be a good European, which was not the most common description of Palmerston. He took office determined to avoid Palmerstonian exuberances, and make the conduct of affairs by the Conservatives a reproach to their predecessors. Though by prejudice anti-French, he saw it as his mission to repair the entente which Guizot had publicly repudiated as a result of Palmerston's 'famous diplomacy'.[37] Palmerston was furious that, having signed the Anti-Slave Treaty after Aberdeen came into office, Guizot, could not, or would not, get it ratified, and even angrier when Aberdeen tolerated, in response to pressure from the French and the Americans, retreats on the matter of enforcement. Within a year the Palmerstons were chuckling at a story that Aberdeen was complaining privately that his attempts to 'plaster and conciliate' met only with insolence and arrogant pretensions from France, so that, having honestly believed bad relations were due to Palmerston personally, the Tories could now only hide from the public the way France bullied them and tried to impose upon their weakness.[38] But Aberdeen persisted, and, with Queen Victoria and Prince Albert, trod the road to Eu to meet Guizot and Louis Philippe *en famille* in September 1843.

When Greville went to Broadlands in September 1842 he found his host complaining that universal concession was now the rule of policy.[39] He had been 'virulent, bitter and contemptuous' about Spain, the Hanover tolls, Afghanistan, but now he raged about the treaty signed in Washington on 9th August 1842 by that notable American, Daniel Webster, and Alexander Baring, Lord Ashburton.[40] Aberdeen can have had no natural sympathy with American democracy, but his love of peace led him to a settlement of the Maine boundary which conceded to America territory adjudged British by a commission appointed in Palmerston's time. Palmerston had no particular love for the United States, having been at the Admiralty when she was trying to annul the economic effects of Britain's command of the seas by her doctrine 'free ships make free goods'; and at the Foreign Office when she

denied the right of search of slavers and defaulted on her obligation
to help the Royal Navy keep watch on the West African coasts; at
the War Office when the nationalism and imperialism of the
Warhawks threw itself in vain against Canada in 1812. His knowledge of establishments and fortifications in British North America
shielded him from that myth of the historians, 'the undefended
frontier'. The anti-British overtones of President Jackson's attack
on the Bank of the United States were specimens of the kind of
nationalism Palmerston emphatically did not relish.

On the other hand, Palmerston knew how great and — as the
crash of 1836 showed — how perilous was the stake of British
capital and commerce in the development of the United States. He
was not altogether insensitive to the bonds of race and tongue.
The U.S. minister Van Buren (Jackson's successor as president)
and his stylish son ('Prince John') were his friends, and he had
succeeded, in 1836, in mediating a dispute between the United
States and France.[41] When British relations with America were
threatened because arms, ammunition and agents passed across the
border to rebels in Canada, Palmerston behaved with restraint,
informing the American minister that 'Her Majesty's Government,
well knowing the constitutional difficulties of the United States,
and convinced that the President has employed to the utmost the
very limited means within his power to check and discountenance
the proceedings . . . , have not pressed the Government of the
United States with representations against a state of things which
under other circumstances would scarcely have been compatible
with the continuance of friendly relations between the two
Governments.'[42] But naturally he was unhelpful when the Americans protested at the loss of an American life when Canadian
loyalists sent an American vessel, the *Caroline*, blazing over the
Niagara Falls, after relieving it of its cargo of arms. Fortified by the
opinion of the Law Officers, Palmerston took the line that this was
a natural hazard of taking advantage of the weakness of the American executive. But when, early in 1841, a British subject, Alexander
McLeod, was arraigned in the courts of the State of New York for
the murder of the Niagara victim, Palmerston was not to be put off
with the State Department's declaration that the matter was no
concern of the Federal authorities. The House of Commons
cheered when Palmerston affirmed that the execution of McLeod
would bring on the United States a war of retaliation and revenge.

He told his wife he thought it would all be settled quietly; the American government, 'pushed on unwillingly by its tail' had no wish for war.[43] But it would never do to be soft to the Americans, who still had their eyes on Canada, and he thought the Ashburton Treaty a 'disgraceful surrender'. At first he imagined that the envoy had been outwitted, but then concluded that the terms were the natural result of sending a 'half-Yankee' to negotiate for Britain.

Palmerston's campaign against the Ashburton Treaty illustrates alike his use of the press to further his views; his self-reliance and refusal to give to a shadow-cabinet even the reluctant deference he showed to a responsible cabinet; what his American biographer calls his 'degrading intemperance'. The session was over when news of the Treaty came, but Palmerston had a medium of expression other than the House (Melbourne said he could never have won through on the Eastern Question without the *Morning Chronicle*). In 1842 the anonymous attacks in Sir John Easthope's journal on Guizot, Webster, Ashburton and, of course, Aberdeen, reproduced phrases used at the Broadlands breakfast-table. Since Palmerston had not consulted any colleagues before launching the attack, they were alarmed. Melbourne and Clarendon especially shuddered at the idea of a war with America of which the French would be sure to take advantage. Ellice, Bedford and Spencer were, of course, active in their several characteristic ways, and Russell, the Leader of the Opposition in the House of Commons, after seeing Lansdowne and Clarendon at Bowood, addressed to Palmerston a strong remonstrance. The Opposition ought not to irritate France or America. Palmerston, who always denied — or rather, never admitted — his connection with the *Chronicle*, replied that it did not do to try to exercise too much control over the newspapers! And were not the French papers violently anti-British? The Opposition ought not to truckle to foreigners, even if ministers did. Of course he would be happy to consult and co-operate with his party colleagues, but he must claim the same right of private judgement as the Radicals and Old Whigs who took their line from Ellice — 'I happen to think I understand our foreign relations better than he does.'[44] He made a slashing attack on the Ashburton Treaty in parliament on 2nd February 1843, though on 20th March he agreed that the United States, because of the commercial link, was above all countries the one with which it ought to be the object to maintain not merely peace, but the most intimate relations.[A]

Palmerston was not to be deterred from protest against 'the low submissive tone taken on all foreign questions' and the set of dotards and fools (other than Stratford Canning) whom Aberdeen was sending to replace his envoys abroad. This year (1843) brought a new rock of offence. Despite protest from the Queen, Aberdeen had abdicated interference in the internal affairs of Spain. The pro-British regent, Espartero, fell to the intrigues of France and Cristina. 'British interests, in my opinion, were sacrificed in his downfall', avowed Palmerston.[45] His attitude to the meeting at Eu could not have been more suspicious if he had *known* that Bulwer at Madrid was to be ordered to work with his French opposite number, Bresson, and that Aberdeen approved Metternich's idea to marry Isabella to the son of Don Carlos (on the principle that anybody was better than a French prince).[46] In January 1844 France was mentioned, for the first time since 1836, in a Speech. And with what result? A French admiral in the South Seas deposed a Tahitian queen who had twice sought, in vain, a British protectorate and then succumbed to a French. Pritchard, the former consul (personally known to Palmerston), who had stayed on as a missionary and the Queen's principal adviser, was expelled, and other Protestant missionaries harassed. Here, when even Peel spoke like Palmerston, was an opportunity to appeal simultaneously to national pride, the commercial interests and the churches. Palmerston denounced 'the system of purchasing temporary security by lasting sacrifices, and of placing the interests of foreign ministers above those of this country'.[47]

The Queen noted that 'poor Aberdeen stood almost alone in trying to keep matters peaceable'.[48] He succeeded, and Louis Philippe was over in October to collect his K.G. But it was not self-evident that appeasement was more conducive to national

---

[A] Alexander Baring (1774–1848), created Lord Ashburton in 1835, was the head of the finance house which played so notable a part in providing investment and credit facilities for Anglo-American trade and for development in the United States. He had married in 1798 the eldest daughter of the American merchant-banker (Senator) William Bingham of Philadelphia.

In assailing him so personally, Palmerston embarrassed his political colleagues, for Sir Francis Baring (lately Chancellor of the Exchequer, and married to the sister of Sir George Grey) was Ashburton's nephew, and so was Labouchere (recently at the Board of Trade), while Labouchere's wife (his cousin) was Ashburton's niece and sister of Sir Francis.

security than Palmerston's more forthright methods. When French truculence drove even Ellice to demand an increase in Britain's naval effectives and Clarendon to urge Palmerston's return to the Foreign Office,[49] was it not clear that England needed an 'English Minister' rather than a 'good European'? The good intentions of Aberdeen had produced only an invasion panic. This was what came of 'almost licking the dust before their French ally' who became 'every day more encroaching, more overbearing more insulting and more hostile' so that 'even the quietest and most peaceful among us are beginning to look forward to a war with France as an event which no prudence on our part can long prevent, and for which we ought to lose no time in making ourselves fully prepared'.[50] Concerned at evidence of slow capacity to mobilize the fleet, Palmerston complained to Russell that the country existed 'only by the sufferance and by the forbearance of other Powers' and told the House of Commons that 30,000 men might cross the 'steam bridge' and take London in three days.[51] This, and the fear that French troops landed by steamers might seize the ports and dockyards (undefended from the landward) and burn at their moorings the ships of the battle fleet which took a minimum of six weeks to get to sea, appears so alarmist as to cast doubt on its sincerity. But the danger was new, and it was some time before Admiralty opinion settled down to the view that there would be considerable warning of any invasion by steamer, and that the danger would not be acute if Britain had small steamers able to fire shells and a 'squadron of evolution' (of which Palmerston was a champion).[52] The Duke of Wellington braved the gales to inspect fortification sites on the south-east coast (as Palmerston was to do at an even greater age twenty years later). The Conservative government drafted a Militia Bill. In September 1845 Aberdeen submitted his resignation, protesting that 'the note of preparation' would stultify his policy of friendship with France.[53] It was not accepted, but when Peel himself in December submitted (abortively) the resignation of his government (on account of the Corn Laws) he told the Queen he would support a new ministry increasing the service estimates.

The pacific policy did not appear to pay. 'We yield to every foreign state and power all they ask, and then make it our boast that they are all in good humour with us,' Palmerston wrote privately. But where — despite the friendliness of the Tsar on his visit of 1844 and another British pilgrimage to the Chateau d'Eu in September 1845 — was the good humour, when everyone except Aberdeen thought war imminent? This was poor reward for removing almost all British ships of war from the Mediterranean lest the sight of them offend Frenchmen. Influence abroad, Palmerston said, must be based on hope or fear. Weaker states ought to be taught to hope for support in time of danger, and more powerful ones to fear the consequences of affronting Britain; had Spain cause for hope, the United States for fear? There had been 'a great diminution of British influence and consideration in every foreign country'. Britain had dropped quietly astern, taking up her berth in the wake of all the great foreign Powers.[54]

★   ★   ★   ★

A man was at hand, of course, to remedy this — a most English minister. But how could he get into power? Peel was an able prime minister, responsive to the needs of the times. The Opposition was at sixes and sevens. The Government majority had actually risen in the four years since the general election. What use was it for Palmerston to harangue on the Right of Search, Texas, Greece, Spain, national defence, not seeming to care that 'nobody takes the slightest interest in his orations, though they are prepared with indefatigable industry and delivered with extraordinary skill'?[55] Of course he cared, and chafed. And then the potato blight and the rains came, not only to 'wash away the Corn Laws' but to change the foreign policy of England — or so it seemed when Russell, being in opposition, was able, more swiftly than Peel, who had a cabinet to convert, to respond the cue offered by these natural phenomena. Palmerston did not approve what he called the 'temerity' of Russell's letter from Edinburgh to the electors of the City of London, published in the *Chronicle*, denouncing the Corn Laws. But Palmerston wanted to get back to the Foreign Office, and voted in the majority of nine against five in the shadow-cabinet (which had not been consulted on the Edinburgh Letter) for the acceptance of the premiership by Russell (18th December 1845).[56]

It did not surprise Palmerston that Russell spoke to him as Melbourne had done ten and a half years before, inquiring whether he would take War and Colonies. He replied, as he had done to Melbourne, that he had no wish to be an embarrassment, and

would support the ministry out of office, but that 'his taking
another department than his former one would be a public
recognition of the most unjust accusations that had been brought
against him'.[57] This tedious formality over, he was offered, and
accepted, the Foreign Office. Ellice and the Old Whigs had failed
again. But one terrier dug in his teeth. To Russell's astonishment
the ex-cabinet minister who, constitutional questions apart, was
the most radical of them all, and who wished to stipulate for the
abolition of all tariffs except those for revenue, and complete
religious equality in Ireland, the third Earl Grey (till lately Lord
Howick, M.P.) claimed that Palmerston's appointment was 'an
infringement of their compact'. This was a reference to Russell's
acceptance, in general terms, of the proposition that his administration should not be formed so as to seem to the public 'a mere
revival . . . of the last Whig Government' (from which Grey had
excluded himself in 1839) and that he should 'allow no deference
for the personal objects of others to interfere with (his) making the
arrangement best calculated to secure . . . the largest possible
measure of public confidence and support'.[58] Because, or on the
ground that, Lord Grey would not join his cabinet if Palmerston
went to the Foreign Office, Russell gave up his attempt to form a
government, and Peel returned to office. But Russell, replying to
Grey's long letter of explanation afterwards, was tart: 'I gave way
to no personal preference in proposing that office (to Palmerston).
I think he is the person in the United Kingdom best fitted for that
department. No doubt impressions, the result of unjust aspersions,
deserve some consideration, but not to the extent of excluding
such a person against his will from the office for which he is fitted,
and which alone he is willing to accept.'[59] It was a warning to Grey
that he had been heeded only because the Whigs were divided
among themselves and within their own minds as to whether to
take office. By March Lady Palmerston reported that Grey was
flying the white flag, and blaming the influence of Ellice for his
aberration. 'Palmerston might well afford to forgive them', she
said, 'for he only stands higher for the attack on him.'[60] When on
30th June 1846 Russell, after consulting four colleagues of whom
Palmerston alone was a member of the Commons, accepted the
Queen's commission, it was understood that Palmerston was to be
Foreign Secretary. Grey accepted the Colonial Office — 'and was
lucky to get it'.[61]

SECTION C

The Third Term, July 1846 - December 1851

CHAPTER X

PALMERSTON ENCOUNTERS THE PRINCE

W E had occasion to notice, in connexion with the attempts to get Palmerston to work for rapprochement with France, once his victory in the Eastern Question was assured, the appearance of Queen Victoria's consort, Albert of Saxe-Coburg, as an influence on policy-making. During Palmerston's third term at the Foreign Office, beginning in 1846, the Prince became one of Palmerston's foremost critics. After Palmerston was dismissed by Lord John Russell in December 1851 the prime minister, as part of his explanation to the House of Commons, cited a Royal Minute and charged Palmerston with constitutional impropriety and breaking his pledged word to the Queen. She and the Prince hailed Palmerston's removal as making possible at least a marginal modification of the cabinet's foreign policy.

The royal persons, taking too literally Aberdeen's parting injunction 'You must try to keep him straight', were determined to exercise over the Foreign Office a vigilance of which Palmerston had no experience under William IV (who, though not liking the French alliance, liked Palmerston better than any of the other ministers) or in the early years of Victoria, when she was closely under the influence of Melbourne. Victoria herself had grown in knowledge and assertiveness, and since her first pregnancy in 1840 there had been at her side as amanuensis, minute-taker, file-keeper and political partner Albert, who was sometimes her representative in dealings with ministers and prospective ministers. Albert wrote letters summarizing the Queen's views; Victoria copied out (usually with some amendment and often with correction of his English) drafts prepared by Albert, or wrote at his dictation. Therefore we shall often refer to the royal couple as *They*.

On the participation of the Prince in disputes over foreign policy and the handling of political crises the lips of privy councillors were, as far as the public was concerned, sealed. But the privy pen of the Privy Council's clerk, Greville, flowed on. He tells us that by 1845 Albert was 'King to all intents and purposes' (a typical exaggeration) and that, when the question of Palmerston's return-ing to the Foreign Office arose, the Duke of Bedford said, apropos of controlling Palmerston, that the Prince had grown more prominent, important and authoritative as a result of the adminis-tration of Peel and Aberdeen.[1] It would be quite wrong to think of Aberdeen as a mere cipher, under the royal thumb. But, until the youthful and courtly Granville came into view, Aberdeen was the Prince's ideal Foreign Minister, as Peel was his ideal premier, and Louis Philippe was (always excepting Uncle Leopold) his ideal ruler, who blended representative institutions with royal direction of policy and some attention to the material progress of his country. There was a natural reluctance to have back Palmerston, whom Louis Philippe called 'the enemy of my house'. Palmerston had become disenchanted with the French in the late '30s over Spain and Greece and Mehemet Ali, and his suspicions were confirmed by the naval threat implied in a publication by Louis Philippe's son Joinville; by Tahiti; by the French bombardment of Tangier (all in 1844). Guizot remembered (the Lieven would not let him forget) Palmerston's remark that 'the Government of this country has not the right to sacrifice either the honour or the Interests of England in order to continue M. Guizot in power'. During the political crisis of December 1845 Louis Philippe sent to Victoria an encomium of Peel and Aberdeen, and the Queen expressed to Russell her apprehensions at the effect of Palmerston's return on Anglo-French relations. Later she wondered whether this was a wise thing for her to have done. Albert therefore got his secretary, Anson, to write to Melbourne, for the eye of Palmerston, an explanation that *They* had merely been conveying 'the way in which other persons' might view his return.[2]

This gave Palmerston an opportunity to answer, in a letter to Melbourne for the eye of the Queen, the case made by Earl Grey in his letter to Russell. He pointed out that in ten years there had only three times been any real danger of war, and that in two of them (1830 and 1833) he had been the friend of France, and that in the third Wellington, Peel and Aberdeen had approved his course. Palmerston continued:[3]

I am well aware, however, that some persons both at home and abroad have imbibed the notion that I am more indifferent than I ought to be as to running the risk of war. . . . These parties wanted to attack me, and were obliged to accuse me of something. They could not charge me with failure, because we had succeeded in all our undertakings, whether in Portugal, Spain, Belgium, Syria, China, or elsewhere; they could not charge me with having involved the country in war . . .: and the only thing that was left for them to say was that my policy had a *tendency* to produce war, and I suppose they would argue that it was quite wrong and against all rule that it did not do so.

He might have added that Aberdeen's policy of entente with France, so far from making the prospect of war with France more remote than in 1841 (though not 1840), had failed to avoid a panic about the national defences in 1844–5, so that Peel, while determined to do all he could 'to prevent it from being considered as indicative of hostile or altered feeling towards France' recommended an increase in the Estimates.[4] In the spring of 1846 the Palmerstons visited Paris. They made valuable contacts with the Opposition, but they did not contrive to induce cordiality in the Court or ministers. In May 1846 Louis Philippe wrote again to Victoria of his active desire that Peel and Aberdeen would hold fast and still be ministers when he came to 'make his court' to Her Majesty.[5] But on 7th July the Queen had to write to Leopold of the parting with Peel and Aberdeen, two devoted friends 'who are irreparable losses to us and to the Country. . . . We felt so safe with them'.[6]

Palmerston had assured Russell in December that nobody had a stronger conviction of the necessity of keeping in amity with France than he, and in his letter to Melbourne repeated his profession that the tension of 1840–1 had been a 'temporary inconvenience'.[7] Against that was the view propagated by the Whigs who agreed with Earl Grey that the feelings he had excited in France were made 'doubly alarming from the manner in which he picked and stirred that wound, the strange perseverance and curious skill with which he compounded and dropped his acids into the sore'.[8] When, to the vast indignation of British public opinion, and of the Queen and Albert, Louis Philippe, in breach of faith, contrived the betrothal of his son Montpensier to the heiress-presumptive to the throne of Spain, Louis Philippe (so Albert's mentor Stockmar reported) said that the matter was principally 'a private affair between myself and the English Secretary, Lord Palmerston'.[9] The Queen held that Palmerston had 'behaved most openly and fairly towards France, I must say, in this affair', but had already decided that 'if our dear Aberdeen was still at his post, the whole thing would not have happened', partly because Guizot would not have wished to triumph over him as he did over Palmerston, and so 'say what one will, it is *he again* who *indirectly* gets us into a squabble with France'.[10]

Trouble, then, if it was not Palmerston's fault, was his fate — because of his past faults. But even now it was partly his fault, and it is difficult to dissent from the Queen's verdict 'Certainly at Madrid he mismanaged it — as Stockmar says — by forcing Don Enrique, in spite of all Bulwer could say'. Bulwer has given his side of the story. He tells how Aberdeen so literally expected him to obey the instruction of October 1843 (after the visit to Eu) to work in full harmony with the French envoy Bresson, that when the two queens Cristina and Isabella and the (normally pro-French) Moderado ministry surreptitiously offered, if Britain would support them, to promote the marriage of Isabella to Leopold of Saxe-Coburg (cousin of Victoria and Albert and brother of the King-Consort Ferdinand of Portugal), Aberdeen reprimanded Bulwer for not telling Bresson, and himself informed Guizot, who let the Spanish government know that he knew it — and how he came to know it. Palmerston was not flexible enough to draw from this incident the lesson Bulwer tried to teach him, that French plans and influence could be defeated only by working through the Spanish queens and ministers.[11] He desired to defeat them, as in the late 30s, 'for the two Governments have... different objects in view in these matters, England wishing Spain to be independent, and France desiring to establish a predominant influence in Spain'.[12] But his way of trying to achieve the object was one derived from the past rather than related to the present. He had 'labelled' the parties in Spain and Portugal. In Spain only the Progressistas, on whose leaders in exile he too much leaned for advice, were even off-white; Cristina and the Moderados were at best a dirty grey. Therefore he tried to secure a large injection of the Progressistas into the ministry, and to promote the marriage of Isabella to her cousin Don Enrique, the patron of the Progressistas, although both prospects were repugnant to Cristina and (of course) the Spanish government. When he showed Jarnac, the French envoy, a dispatch to Bulwer abusing the Spanish government (although it was still prepared to be anti-French), Guizot naturally transmitted its gist to Bresson for conveyance to the Spanish government. In the end Cristina and Isabella, their overtures rebuffed by Palmerston as by Aberdeen, and unpalatable advice given them instead, preferred the personally repugnant Don Francisco to his politically repugnant young brother Enrique and agreed that Isabella's younger sister should marry Montpensier on the same day as Isabella married Francisco.

This triumph of French diplomacy was thus the fruit of Palmerston's ineptitude. That, however, did not prevent even Greville (whose pages are full of complaints of delay on Palmerston's part in answering French proposals for common action in Spain) from declaring that 'we have been *jockeyed* by France in a very shabby, uncandid underhanded way', and the Queen from complaining 'This is *too* bad ... this conduct is *not* the way to keep up the *entente* which *he* [Louis Philippe] wishes. It is done, moreover, in such a *dishonest* way' and 'Have confidence in him I fear I never can again.'[13] For once the Princess Lieven could find no single sympathizer in the upper political circle in London. For Palmerston had been continuing, with regard to the Spanish Marriages, Aberdeen's policy of declining to sponsor the Coburg candidature, accepting Louis Philippe's condition that the king-consort of Spain must be a Bourbon descended from Philip V (about whose title the War of the Spanish Succession had been fought 1701-13), and opining that he should be a Spanish prince. It seemed to Palmerston that this meant Don Enrique, since Don Francisco was objectionable to the Spanish queens and reputedly impotent. He therefore showed Jarnac his dispatch to Bulwer dated 18th July 1846 recommending Enrique, and repeated the advice a month later. The Queen objected that Don Enrique was not palatable to the queens, would be a symbol of political division, and that his promotion as the 'English candidate' was associated with an attempt to secure 'more democratic' government in Spain 'for the avowed purpose of counteracting the influence of France', which could only mean that England would have to 'keep up a particular party in Spain to support her views', that France must take up the opposite party, and Spain would be doomed to eternal convulsions and reactions. 'This had been the state of things before; theory and experience therefore warn against the renewal of a similar policy.'[14]

This was fair enough, but neither Palmerston nor the Queen dreamed that the French would 'barefacedly' (as the Queen put it) violate their assurance to Aberdeen that Montpensier would not marry the Infanta until Isabella (whoever she married) had issue.

Guizot had given this assurance at Eu in September 1845 and it was never at any time suggested that this was not an official commitment as binding after Aberdeen left office as before. It was, indeed, alleged by the French after the announcement of the Spanish Marriages that Aberdeen was told verbally on 27th February 1846 that this promise was binding only as long as Britain accepted that the Spanish king-consort should be a Bourbon and did not promote the Coburg match. Of this Palmerston knew nothing and Aberdeen rebutted the suggestion that anything new had been said in February, or that any such interpretation had been accepted by him. Even so, how had Britain offended? She had actually *opposed* the Coburg marriage and spurned the invitation of the Spanish queens and government to promote it. Not at the time, but after the triumph at Madrid, the French alleged that in the dispatch shown by Palmerston to Jarnac on 19th July Britain sponsored the Coburg candidature and thus released Paris from the Eu pledge as allegedly reconstrued in February. The Queen declared that this was 'an absurd ground', and Palmerston's remonstrance to Paris was, Greville wrote 'very able and conclusive . . . express[ing] with great force the shuffling, tricking and unfair conduct of the French cabinet', though very proper and kind in tone (the Queen said).[15] The dispatch of 18th July had indeed named Leopold of Coburg as a possible husband for Isabella. But it had made clear that he was not the British candidate, that Palmerston thought a Spanish prince would be best. The dispatch also named Don Francisco, to whom Britain positively objected. It indicated a preference for Don Enrique, and him the French pretended to support until their mine was ready for detonation. At the time of the announcement in Madrid of the simultaneous marriages, Jarnac was telling Greville that he was well satisfied with Palmerston and that things might go on amicably though not, of course, exactly as with Aberdeen.[16]

★   ★   ★   ★

It was the general opinion in Britain that Palmerston, though perhaps sinning, was much more sinned against by Louis Philippe and Guizot. The Queen said that even if suspicion of Palmerston was the cause of the French action, that action was unjustifiable. 'Our *entente wantonly* thrown away!' she complained to Brussels. And though she 'felt more than ever the loss of our valuable Peel' she had to 'do Palmerston the credit to say that he takes it very quietly, and will act very temperately about it' and avowed 'Lord Palmerston is quite ready to be guided by us.' She even said that if the French did suspect Palmerston, 'they should have been more cautious to do anything which could bring on a quarrel', on that very account.[17] But further experience of Palmerston, and above all the fall of Louis Philippe in February 1848, bringing in its train, as King Leopold had predicted, revolutions everywhere, changed the attitude of the Queen and the Prince. Palmerston became the villain who, helped by Louis Philippe's own folly and avarice (the Infanta was rich!) had contributed to his fall.

Any sympathy Palmerston may ever have felt with the theory that the predominant consideration governing British relations with France should be the desire to maintain Louis Philippe on the throne evaporated with the Spanish Marriages, achieved by means 'odious and offensive to the last degree' even in the eyes of Greville.[18] Palmerston watched without pity or regret the grinding of the mills of God — how Guizot lurched into entente with Metternich and was set to do some of his dirty work in Italy, so that Thiers' opposition in the French Chamber abused his foreign policy and became pro-British; how the arbitrary flavour of his diplomatic associates rubbed off on to the conservative constitutionalist until, when faced by the growth of opposition, he behaved like a caricature of Polignac; how, when only a speedy change of men and measures could save him, Louis Philippe told German diplomats not to be afraid of constitutions, because they could be 'managed' and refused Reform because it was 'another word for the advent of the Opposition'; how, nevertheless, he had to call the Opposition to power (23rd February 1848) and then, the following day, to scurry away, in less dignity and comfort than Charles X in 1830, to exchange 'the champagne and claret of the Tuileries for the unwholesome water and small beer of Claremont', Leopold's English property.[19]

Palmerston had not wanted the republic that followed. He would rather have cried 'Vive Thiers' than 'Vive Lamartine' and would have preferred a reformed monarchy. That is what he had worked for, when he approved the ambassador, Normanby, becoming very intimate with the French Opposition, and winked at the embassy supplying diplomatic documents to Thiers's newspaper. Improper though this was, Palmerston felt he owed Guizot nothing, for the minister had published (contrary to usage) extracts from Palmerston's dispatches to Bulwer in Spain (the *Chronicle* countered with attacks based on Spanish documents procured by Bulwer).[20] And he could argue that he was not so much working for Guizot's fall, still less the disappearance of the Orleans monarchy, as ingratiating himself with those to whom Louis Philippe must turn to avert his ruin, which Normanby predicted. This, once the monarchy had fallen, the Queen, as a monarch, could not accept. She was convinced that Palmerston had, with malice aforethought, helped bring down a monarchy in favour of a republic, and a monarchy which, according to Uncle Leopold, had a virtue Britain could not claim — that in 1830 'they changed nothing but the dynasty' while in England 1832 had abolished the very spirit of the old monarchy.[21]

Palmerston's French policy has been vigorously condemned by one of the ablest of modern historians, the late Dr Gavin Henderson. He conceded that 'French policy may again and again be proved responsible for its own failures'; he conceded Palmerston's claim, in the letter to Melbourne, that 'if now and then it unavoidably happened . . . that in pursuing the course of policy which seemed the best for British interests, we thwarted the view of this or that Foreign Power, and rendered them for the moment less friendly, I think I could prove that in every case the object which we were pursuing was of sufficient importance to make it worth our while to submit to such temporary inconvenience'. But he claimed that 'Palmerston's policy towards the Orleans monarchy was dangerous and unsound.' He had not, he judged, the strength of mind to avoid scoring diplomatic successes at France's expense. 'Britain, and the whole of Europe, should have been very grateful to Louis Philippe for his efforts to cure his subjects of their revolutionary tendencies', but Louis Philippe was given no help. The Anglo-French alliance always worked for British interests, and was regarded by Palmerston as a convenience, and not necessarily a permanent alignment. France was not allowed to get enough out of it, and so Louis Philippe was driven to repeated attempts to 'free himself from this thraldom'.[22] There is, indeed, a case for arguing that the French should have been allowed the ascendancy in Spain which Britain enjoyed in Portugal; their pride (more galled than Palmerston allowed for, Dr Henderson thought) would have been salved, and they would have found the luxury as onerous as Britain did her position as 'trustee for the estate of Portugal'.

But it is strange that so proficient a diplomatic historian should have suggested, by implication, that France should have been allowed paramountcy in North Africa as well. Louis Philippe found that he could not cure his subjects of their revolutionary tendencies unless they had prestige victories as well as full bellies. But the scope Britain could allow for such victories was necessarily limited. France was regarded, and inevitably regarded, as an encroaching Power, whose encroachments were not necessarily connected with revolutionary tendencies, but were always supported by revolutionary nationalists. To suggest that the tendency to demand encroachment could be cured by permitting some encroachment, as though it would act as an inoculation rather than an aperitif, seems perverse. It is, of course, true that the Orleanist régime fell when it could fill neither Parisian bellies nor purses and could produce no diplomatic triumph to counteract the effect of revelations of moral and financial corruption in high places and attacks in the Chamber on the bankruptcy of its foreign and domestic policies. But all that is valid in Dr Henderson's point seems to be this — that it takes two to maintain an alliance and to make a quarrel. There was a lack of proportion in Palmerston's dialogue with Louis Philippe over Spain in the 30s (if not in 1846) and a lack of magnanimity after the British triumph in 1841 which conspired with a certain pettiness of mind at the Tuileries to involve Anglo-French relations in a vicious circle of misunderstanding and recrimination and (on the French side) treachery.

But it was, after all, more the business of Louis Philippe and Guizot to save the July régime than of Palmerston, and to bite Britain over Spain and bark with wagging tail at Metternich's heels, hoping for a bone, was not the way to do it. That, in Palmerston's view, was what they were doing in 1847 in Switzerland and Italy. Feeling itself threatened by seditious movements at home and in adjoining states, especially Switzerland, the July monarchy gave a friendly ear to the suggestion of the Eastern Powers that if the Swiss Confederation did not comply with their demands, the 'guarantee' of Swiss neutrality should be withdrawn (a 'guarantee' repugnant to Frenchmen as part of the Treaty of Vienna). Palmerston stood in their way, with blistering rejoinders. On the morrow of the Spanish Marriages, Metternich had taken opportunity to break *his* pledges; in November 1846 the Three Powers proclaimed the annexation of Cracow to Austria. Palmerston had pointed out, in 'an answer as strong as it is advisable to make any document which there is not intention of following up by any action'[23] that this precedent (the first formal violation of the Treaty of Vienna not submitted for the endorsement of the old Quadruple Alliance) might be exploited in a way the Powers did not relish. Now he pointed out that the 'guarantee' had not been given for the sake of Switzerland, but for the sake of Europe, and inquired how, after Cracow, Britain could be expected to join them in 'quoting the Treaty of Vienna as requiring the maintenance of Cantonal authority in Switzerland'. In that country both the contending factions were in breach of a constitution which needed amendment, but could not be amended because its revision required the assent of all the twenty-two cantons which were 'sovereign within their powers'. The Eastern Powers, and France, looked only to the complaints of the Sonderbund, a defensive alliance of Catholic cantons; Palmerston alone considered the case of the Liberal majority, though not holding it blameless. He viewed with deep suspicion the proposals of Guizot — whom the *Chronicle* alleged had been privy to the occupation of Cracow — for joint mediation by the Powers, and would not hear of it taking the form of a *diktat* to be obeyed on pain of intervention by the Powers. As the Treaty of Vienna was involved, he insisted on a Conference of the Powers, to prevent any separate intervention, but he would not send a representative to it unless satisfied that its function would be genuinely mediatorial. While the basis of the Conference was still undecided, the despatch of arms to the Sonderbund from the French government arsenal at Besançon confirmed Palmerston's worst opinions of Guizot. But the Liberal armies prevailed, and Palmerston then opposed a Conference on the ground that there was nothing for it to do.[24] Meanwhile, evidence accumulated that Guizot had agreed with Metternich to intervene, if necessary, at Rome, where the advent of a liberal pope, Pius IX, in 1846, raised the morale of Italian Liberals and filled Metternich with consternation.[25] The Pope therefore sought 'a public manifestation of the goodwill of Great Britain' and Palmerston sent, to provide it, an old collaborator and member of the cabinet, the premier's father-in-law, the Earl of Minto.

By a nice twist, the Austrian ambassador Dietrichstein explained the Minto mission by saying that Palmerston hated Austria as an associate of Louis Philippe and Guizot.[26] Certainly, in a sense, the mission was a riposte to the entente between Paris and Vienna; it was extended to include Turin and Florence as well as Rome and its object was to deter either the Austrians or the French, or both in concert, from intervention in Italy. But most of all it was intended to increase the chance of Italian rulers granting moderate constitutions to their subjects before revolution broke out. Prince Albert, although his cataloguing German mind included Italy with Switzerland and Germany as areas where, in contrast to Spain, Portugal and Greece, constitutionalism might work, was hostile to the Minto mission. He said it would strengthen the continental view that the British, for selfish purposes, were trying, like Jacobins, to disseminate disorder and anarchy in all other states[27] — a curious description of a visit bespoken by a pontiff, and a significant indication of the gulf which now yawned between the attitude of the Foreign Secretary and of the Palace.

★   ★   ★   ★

The Queen and the Prince were convinced that they were not illiberal, but they were very conscious of their membership of the European union of princes. This had adverse effects, of some of which they were unconscious. It meant that they constantly received reports in private letters reflecting adversely upon the policy of the government or the activity of one or other of its diplomats. The Queen was justified in her opinion that Palmerston did not sufficiently acknowledge the difficulties in the way of his particular Spanish objective (Progressista ministers and Enrique for consort) 'which all those who are on the spot and in the confidence of the Court represent as almost insurmountable',[28] but that did not make the international royal intelligence service harmless. In reply to a letter from Palmerston attacking Maria da Gloria, Victoria cited one from Cousin Ferdinand, Maria's husband.[29] The royal anger against Louis Philippe could not long survive the constant attrition of letters from Uncle Leopold and Aunt Louise (who was Louis Philippe's daughter). In addition to normal correspondence between royalties, the activities of their special agents were important. Stockmar was in Madrid in 1846; he had a letter stating the British case in moderate terms laid before Louis Philippe, but sent Albert criticisms of Palmerston. In the crisis in Portugal Albert's equerry, Colonel Wylde, played a curious schizophrenic role as the Court's Jekyll and the cabinet's Hyde (or

vice versa, according to the point of view). And Cousin Mensdorff
visited Lisbon to advise both British and Portuguese royalty. The
Queen and the Prince did not realize the extent to which they were
imbued with a conception of the loyalty of subjects as a part of the
natural law which gave kings their title to rule, and of revolution as
not only aberration but impiety. They almost fell into the Metternichian error of regarding Palmerston as an apostle of revolution
because he thought a revolution proof of the deficiencies of a
threatened régime while they tended to the view that the disaffec-
tion of subjects justified repression (their foreign correspondents so
often wrote to them of Ireland!). They displayed a monarchical
bias and prejudice which was sometimes almost indistinguishable
from Legitimism. When, for instance, the Queen spoke of the
importance of possessing 'the confidence of Europe' ('that is the
reason why the Queen is uneasy about our dealings in Greece, and
anxious that we should not be misunderstood with regard to
Italy'[30]) it was perfectly evident that it was in dynastic eyes that
she wished the policy to be 'beyond reproach'. And the 'public
opinion' which she was wont to invoke was an ideal public opinion
which reflected the views of European royalty.

Regarding their own opinions as the norm, the Queen and
Prince regarded Palmerston as biassed and prejudiced. When
Russell claimed that it was his policy to be neutral in the battle
between despotism and democracy (shades of Canning!) he meant
exactly what he said — the Whigs approved of neither. But
Victoria complained that Palmerston had gone a long way in taking
up the side of democracy.[31] She meant that his constitutionalism,
and missionary diplomacy, was subversive of European order and
did not give an absolute priority to maintaining thrones. An even
more insidious effect of the letters from foreign royalty was to
inflate the Queen's ideas of what she ought to be able to do in the
field of foreign policy. She was scrupulous in submitting to ministers letters from occasional correspondents who were kings and
queens (except for those in the family), if the purport was clearly
political, and in taking advice on the reply. But letters to Albert
were not always so treated, and the assumption of foreign royalties
that the Queen was really a maker of foreign policy encouraged her
(without being conscious of it) to play the part. This could be done
in two ways. On the one hand, letters to Cousin Ferdinand, for
instance, could blunt the effect of one of Palmerston's missives to

the British minister in Lisbon at the point of impact; on the other, a rigid insistence on the royal right to approve diplomatic documents, and see incoming dispatches, could be a means of reducing the explosive charge before take-off. Palmerston suffered much on both counts. It made him more than usually evasive. Equally provocative of royal intervention in foreign policy were letters from abroad commiserating the Queen on her impotence. Of this genre Leopold's letter to Albert, written from the Tuileries on 15th January 1847 is a prime specimen — 'When one looks to the changes brought about in England in consequence of the Revolution of July one is quite astounded. Here they changed nothing but the dynasty, in England *the very spirit of the old Monarchy has been abolished. . . .*'21

On the whole, the royal effort in foreign policy was confined to trying to alter the 'slant'. But in foreign affairs 'slant' is, if not everything, nearly everything, and the tendency of the Palace to try to substitute, in a draft, its own 'slant' resulted in a tendency for Palmerston to withhold from the Queen, until after it had gone, the very dispatch *They* were most likely to wish to censor, to claim the right to insert his own 'personal' opinions by way of argument into public dispatches[32] and even to contest the right of the Palace to amend documents not written for presentation to foreign powers — what the twentieth century might call 'background briefings' to British envoys.[33]

There were plenty of opportunities for friction between the Foreign Office and the Palace when so much of the subject-matter of diplomacy directly concerned royalties — succession disputes (as in Portugal, Spain and Schleswig-Holstein); king-making (in Belgium and Greece); royal marriages (as in Spain); gross personal misconduct (like that of Cristina and later the lecherous Isabella) which discredited monarchy; the public acts of sovereigns. If Greece had no constitution, it was Otho's fault; if constitutional government gave way to dictatorship, it was Isabella's; the Portuguese civil war of 1846 was provoked by Maria. Palmerston was not accustomed to mince words about royal personages; Victoria found Palmerston's manner, as had her uncle the Regent, 'si fier'. Thus, he wrote, 'Viscount Palmerston . . . will be most happy to find that he is mistaken [in the "painful convictions expressed in the above-mentioned drafts"] and will most truly and heartily rejoice if events should prove that the confidence which your Majesty reposes in the sincerity and good faith of the Queen of Portugal is well founded.'[32] His attitude to monarchy and monarchs was like the attitude of the Oxford Movement to episcopacy and bishops — the institution was admirable, the incumbents often a sore trial to the faithful. It was so difficult to get emperors and kings, reigning grand dukes and princes, to behave like sensible Whigs or Canningites, even when they were advised by peripatetic missionaries like Minto and Stratford Canning. The Palace always tended, per contra, to believe the best of foreign monarchs, and to prevent the worst being said by ministers. Constitutions were such a sad mistake 'in these Southern countries'.[34] Doubtless the 'poor queen' in Lisbon was in an impossible position by being saddled with one, and Palmerston ought to be more considerate of her difficulties. They regretted, with some sincerity, instances of patent inhumanity, glaring illiberality, obvious folly by sovereigns. Perhaps, however, they regretted them most when the effect was to imperil thrones. They regretted duplicity by monarchs in dealings with Britain or in breach of international treaties or constitutional engagements, for these tarnished the image of monarchy and furnished grist for Jacobin mills. They reprobated all revolutions, but gave retrospective approval to those which proved conservative in tendency, and were willing to greet successively Louis Philippe and Napoleon III as 'frère'. But mere expediency could not reconcile the Queen to accrediting an ambassador to a French republic when responsible ministers urged it, or to receiving, other than as a friend introduced by Palmerston, the republican envoy with whom the Foreign Office was dealing (1848).[35] To Palmerston all revolutions were worrying, and especially to be deprecated if republican, but they were usually the fruit of monarchical stupidity and their leaders (when triumphant) were to be guided, not abused. To him revolutionaries might be heroes — provided they were not Reds — and were to be positively applauded if provoked to action by reaction, as distinct from mere conservatism.

The difference in outlook between Palmerston and the Palace emerged clearly during the troubles in Portugal. While the Palace would have liked to confine intervention to the protection of royal persons, Palmerston thought that this standing commitment of the Royal Navy conferred on the Portuguese monarch an unfair advantage which, if he thought her wholly or partly in the wrong, he was determined to counter-weigh.[36] The Queen did not deny

that Maria's dismissal of the Palmella government before the end
of 1846 was unconstitutional and unsafe (and unnecessary); she did
not deny that it was proper for the British representative to recommend to Maria reforms to ensure (what had been lacking) the basic
practice of representative government and the rule of law, and, if
possible, an accommodation with the rebels at Oporto.[37] But she
objected to 'these peremptory and dictatory notes, these constant
complaints', not only on the valid ground that they only irritated
their royal recipients and prejudiced them against taking advice,
but because to her it seemed that they were not impartial and fair.
The question of right and wrong required 'a most minute, impartial
and anxious scrutiny', which could certainly not be left to the
chargé d'affaires, Southern, whose 'tone and bearing are more
those of a Portuguese Demagogue than of an English Representative'. She was horrified to find that not only Palmerston's drafts
(habitually submitted to Her Majesty after the dispatch had gone)
but Russell's memoranda merely echoed Southern's views, which
did not (of course) tally with what she heard from Cousin Ferdinand. Her conception of a settlement was that the rebels — who
must expect to be punished for violating their oath of allegiance
and, in any case, belonged to the party that had been the greatest
enemies of England — should capitulate in reliance upon a 'grace
and favour' promise from an oath-breaking queen to preserve the
constitution and punish only their leaders. Palmerston, she protested, treated the queen and the rebels as equals. Worse (via
Southern) he gave the impression that 'we entirely espouse the
cause of the rebels, whose conduct is, to say the least, illegal and
very reprehensible'. 'Lord Palmerston . . . takes the nation and the
opposition to be one and the same thing.'[38] Palmerston was unre-
pentant, and told the electors of Tiverton that the rebels at Oporto
'acted in accordance with principles which have been consecrated
in the history of our own country by the blood of some of our most
distinguished ancestors, and upon which our institutions repose'.
He was determined that Maria should enter into firm engagements,
and only when she had done so did he allow the navy to co-operate
with the Spanish army in reducing the rebels, who had rejected the
terms carried to them by Colonel Wylde (June 1847). When the
rebellion was over, Palmerston and the Palace continued to dispute
as to whether Maria was keeping her engagement. Her throne had
been saved for her, Palmerston said, by the influence of the

H

maligned Southern with her opponents. 'Another revolt founded upon a palpable breach of engagement on the part of the Queen of Portugal would be fatal to her possession of the Throne. . . . No assistance could be given her in such a case by England.'³⁹ She should remember that England was the final arbiter in Portugal.

At the Palace, *They* seized on the admission that Southern had influence with a political party opposed to the Queen of Portugal. Their theme was: 'let us not throw away this lesson, and, if it is still possible, not also lose Portugal'. The lesson was this, that in Spain a strong position based on integrity, morality and honour, as compared with French infamy, had been cast away by the intrigues and counter-intrigues of the British envoy, Bulwer. If this was a rather idealized picture, it was true enough that 'we have no longer the slightest influence. . . . France has it all her own way'.⁴⁰ It was true also that Bulwer was not able to remedy this situation when Isabella had her first quarrel with her husband, because of Palmerston's Progressista-fixation and because the Foreign Office did not gauge the determination of and ability of Narvaez, who, having returned to Spain with the goodwill of Louis Philippe, let Bulwer know that he would spurn French patronage. Bulwer was perhaps quite right to reject in 1848 the proffered alliance of so illiberal a man, about to emerge as the champion of order amid manifold and diverse conspiracies and rebellions, to some of which Bulwer was privy. But it is almost incredible that he should have handed to a brash and arrogant Spanish dictator (allied with Serrano, the first of the Spanish queen's innumerable paramours), at the very moment of his victory, yet when his consciousness of insecurity made him cast about for some appeal to Spanish nationalism, Palmerston's standard letter calling upon European governments to heed the warning of Louis Philippe's fall, with the routine Spanish addendum that the Progressistas should be admitted to political power. When the note was returned, Greville dubbed it 'a choice specimen of Palmerston's insolence and domination'. Bulwer says 'Any blame . . . given to me, fell necessarily on my chief', and this was constitutionally sound. But the dispatch, which Russell had somewhat doubtfully passed, was sent before Narvaez was installed by the Cortes as dictator, and Palmerston's colleagues, especially Lansdowne, defending him weakly in the Lords, privately blamed 'that fool Bulwer'.

Bulwer was thoroughly Palmerstonian in principle. Of the

recent tripartite action in Portugal (by Britain, France and Spain) he wrote, and justly, 'A more glaring violation of the Whig principle of non-intervention could hardly be cited, but it was a useful one and served to add to the many proofs . . . of the absurdity of establishing general theoretic rules to be practically applicable to every variety of case.' His defence of his action is as follows:

. . . Under ordinary circumstances such advice to a foreign Government is better left alone. But we had aided that Government in its struggles against a despotism less violent than the one it was exercising. We had an interest in maintaining constitutional monarchy against despotism or republicanism. We had for years been in the habit of giving advice to the Spanish Government in moments of difficulty.

And he adds: 'dispatches of a much more offensive character had frequently been addressed to Spanish governments'. 'We had supported Queen Christina's party against that of Don Carlos, because the former represented the constitutional cause; we had a sort of right, therefore, to speak in favour of constitutional principles; and under any other circumstances, and with any other ministry, our counsel would have been more likely to produce a good effect than a bad one.' But it was not to 'any other minister' and 'in any other circumstances' that Bulwer delivered the actual dispatch, instead of conveying its gist in a tentative way or waiting for new instructions. Palmerston, unaccustomed to having his dispatches returned, upheld Bulwer and sent a violent note to Madrid, which led to the peremptory expulsion of Bulwer from Spain, an insult which muted criticism in parliament and was answered, of course, in kind. But the British cabinet was unmoved by Bulwer's argument that if they held up a little finger, Narvaez and his seconds would topple like a pack of cards. No fleet appeared off Cadiz.[11]

The Palace scored a palpable hit. 'When the Queen considers the position we had in Spain, and what it ought to have been after the constitution of the French Republic when we had no rival to fight and ought to have enjoyed the entire confidence and friendship of Spain, and compares this to the state into which our relations with that country have been brought, she cannot help being struck how much matters must have been mismanaged.'[41] 'If our diplomatists are not kept in better order, the Queen may at any moment be exposed to similar insults as she has received now in the person of Sir H. Bulwer' dictated Albert on 23rd May 1848. How could one be surprised at the event when Bulwer 'has for the last three years almost been sporting with political intrigues. He invariably boasted of at least being in the confidence of every conspiracy, "though he was taking care not to be personally mixed up in them" and after their various failures generally harboured the chief actors in his house under the plea of humanity'.[42]

Very soon afterwards, the Prince found in a batch of incoming dispatches evidence that Sir Hamilton Seymour in Lisbon was privy to a plan for a coalition to overthrow the government of Portugal, in favour of men 'personally suspected by the Queen of Portugal of conspiring against her throne' (this information must have come from Cousin Ferdinand). The queen requested Russell, as prime minister, to see that Seymour was instructed to refrain from interfering in such matters. Palmerston did not answer Russell's letter, and when Lord John took the matter up on a train to Portsmouth 'struggled very hard against it . . . [but] at last promised to write'. There was in due course submitted to the Palace what Victoria called an 'ill-tempered note' which was 'almost a mockery of Lord John, the Cabinet, the country and herself'. It said, inter alia,

As it is quite evident that the Queen and the Government of Portugal will listen to no advice except such that agrees with their own wishes, I have to instruct you to abstain in future from giving any longer any advice to them on political matters, taking care to explain both to the Queen and Government your reasons for doing so. You will however at the same time positively declare to the Portuguese Government that if, by the course of policy they are pursuing, they should run into any difficulty they must clearly understand that they will not have to expect any assistance from England.

The country was suffering, the Queen complained, especially in regard to Spain, 'under the evil consequences of that system of diplomacy, which makes the taking up of party politics in foreign countries its principal object. This system is condemned alike by the Queen, Lord John, the Cabinet, and, the Queen fully believes, public opinion in and out of Parliament. . . . The Queen thinks it of the utmost importance that in these perilous times this question with regard to the basis of our policy should be *settled*.' Was 'that erroneous policy . . . to be maintained to the detriment of the real interests of the country, or a wiser course to be followed in future?' Russell agreed, with surely unconscious humour, which will not have amused the Queen, to 'insist on an instruction to Sir Hamilton Seymour *similar to that which was given to Sir Henry Bulwer* to take no part in the struggles of parties, and to refrain from any interference with regard to which he has not specific directions'. The instructions, when sent, were nearer Palmerston's views than the Prince's, and recapitulated the iniquities of the Portuguese government.[43]

The Queen's comment, 'Lord Palmerston has behaved about this note really like a spoiled child; because he was to do what he did not like, he insisted upon doing it in a manner which he knew must be displeasing to Lord John and (the Queen cannot help suspecting) particularly to herself and without the slightest pretext for it', seems justified. There is a sterility about Palmerston's policy in Iberia in his third period at the Foreign Office, a meddling almost for the sake of it, sometimes without purpose, often without profit. Yet he could make something of a defence. When the Palace, on 1st July 1848, remarked, justifiably, that 'in the countries where the greatest stress has been laid on . . . influence, and the greatest exertions made for it, *the least good* has been done — the Queen means in Spain, Portugal and Greece . . .' Palmerston struck back. He argued that Aberdeen 'advisedly, though, as Viscount Palmerston has always ventured to think, most injudiciously . . . gave up Spain to France' as part of the price of that entente cordiale which had been 'chiefly designed to deceive your Majesty and to cajole your Majesty's ministers, while the King of the French was pursuing his own schemes of family interest and political ambition'.[44] The blow was shrewdly struck, for the Spanish Marriages were a breach of faith by Louis Philippe with the Queen as well as by Guizot with Aberdeen. The entente cordiale had sometimes seemed only an aspect of a dynastic alliance between the Houses of Brunswick–Saxe–Coburg and Bourbon–Orleans, and the Queen herself did not doubt that the Montpensier marriage meant that the King of the French was seeking 'the government of Spain'.[45] But this riposte does not excuse the subsequent mismanagement by Palmerston and Bulwer. As to Portugal, Palmerston claimed that Britain, acting with France and Spain, had saved Maria and Ferdinand from probable dethronement in 1847, and 'if the influence of your Majesty's Government has not since that time been able to counteract those influences which have led the Queen of Portugal away from a strict and faithful performance of the spirit of her engagements, that influence has at least been among the causes which have prevented a renewal of disturbance in Portugal'. It was a modest claim, and, in fact, from now on, Palmerston largely abandoned the unfruitful effort to secure a dominant day-to-day influence at Madrid and Lisbon. But it may be said that Palmerston had denied despotism a free hand in Portugal, while, if the Queen and the Prince had had their way, reactionaries would have taken heart.

This broadside from the Palace on 1st July was, however, not really about Spain and Portugal at all. *They* were trying to get the cabinet to renounce the policy of 'seeking influence', because they disapproved of the line Palmerston was taking in Italy —

The Queen . . . cannot conceal . . . that she is ashamed of the policy which we are pursuing in this Italian controversy in abetting wrong, and this for the object of gaining *influence* in Italy. The Queen does not consider influence so gained as an advantage, and though this influence is to be acquired in order to do good, she is afraid that the fear of losing it will always stand in the way of this . . . .

But the attitude of the Queen and Prince to Palmerston's Italian policy in 1847–8 was a jaundiced one. To turn from Palmerston's direction of Bulwer in Madrid and of Southern and Seymour in Portugal to his handling of the Italian Question is to turn from the ridiculous to the sublime.

CHAPTER XI

THE PEACE-KEEPER

'I AM afraid that your Majesty has not a full appreciation of the people and the partisans who fill Switzerland with murders and the miseries of the most abominable Civil War', wrote the strange, unbalanced king of Prussia to Victoria (25th November 1847). If the godless and rightless Radicals were victorious in Switzerland, 'in Germany likewise torrents of blood will flow. . . . Thousands of emigrated malefactors wait only for a sign . . . to pour forth beyond the German frontier. . . . Governments are weakened by the modern Liberalism (the precursor of Radicalism, as the dying of chickens precedes the Cholera) . . .'. The suppression of Swiss Liberalism would have been a great triumph for the neo-Holy Alliance, for the country did serve as a centre for sedition in France, Germany, Piedmont and Austrian Italy. But the Four Powers were restrained from open intervention by Palmerston, and the Liberal forces in Switzerland won a military victory. The Austrian diplomat, Beust, judged that 'the bankruptcy of the Metternich system took place in Switzerland'. Here, he said, Palmerston made a game of everyone. We may indeed be sure that Palmerston achieved a triumph, when Prince Albert, at his most disparaging, admitted it, though he tried to give the credit to Stratford Canning, respected, as Palmerston was not, by the Powers.[1]

The nature of the triumph should, however, not be misunderstood. Helping Switzerland resist the menaces of the Powers meant helping the Liberal majority in the Diet, the Liberal majority of the cantons. It was an example of being attentive to the interests of constitutional states, the 'natural allies' of England, as promised in the great speech of 1832. But though Britain was the power most devoted to Swiss independence, and Palmerston the minister most friendly to Liberals as Liberals, his main aim was to preserve the peace of Europe. He did not take up the cause of the Diet blindly and uncritically as he often did the cause of the Progressistas in Spain. He saw that the activities of conspirators were a legitimate cause of complaint by neighbouring countries, that some of the acts of the Diet were unconstitutional, that some of the proposed constitutional amendments (which could never be passed by the prescribed constitutional processes) were unwise. He played the role of 'the candid friend', concerned to prevent the Swiss from provoking intervention by the Powers, and to settle by international diplomacy the thorniest question of all, the position of the Jesuits. Stratford's mission was intended to be one of mediation between the Liberals and the Sonderbund, and, when the Liberal victory made that superfluous, it became one of securing moderation on the part of the victors and of mediation between them and the Powers.

Palmerston's aim was thus to be, not merely the champion of Liberalism, but the good European, preventing or bringing to a speedy end a local war which was apt to escalate into a universal war of opinions.[2] He did not think the collaboration between Guizot and Metternich made this much less likely, for he doubted whether, in Switzerland or Italy, this friendly posture would survive joint or separate intervention. 'If [Metternich] takes upon himself the task of regulating by force of arms the internal affairs of the Italian States there will infallibly be War', he said, 'and it will be a war of principles which, beginning in Italy, will spread over all Europe.' Whatever the government in Paris promised the government in Vienna, 'in defence of constitutional liberty in Italy the French nation would rush to arms, and a French army would again water their horses in the Danube'.[3]

It followed that Britain's main aim must be to prevent intervention, and there seemed only one feasible way of doing this — by persuading rulers to grant moderate constitutions to avert violent revolution. For it was not Frederick William IV of Prussia alone who foresaw a cataclysm. Metternich knew it was coming; he received ominous reports from the Austrian provinces of Lombardy and Venetia. These, from 1815 till about 1840, had been the best-governed parts of Italy (except, perhaps, for Tuscany). But there had been deterioration, just when prosperity impelled the middle classes to demand more progressive administration, and revolutionary principles (French, not British) therefore made greater way than they had ever been able to do by the mere denunciation of alien and autocratic rule. Metternich sent Ficquelmont to report. He advised that without reforms revolution could not be combated. Metternich also, having completed his détente with Guizot, asked Palmerston to reaffirm Austria's right to be in Lombardy and Venetia and to defend all her territories. Of course, by reform Metternich meant administrative reform, and he armed himself against Palmerston's likely reply by the warning that 'the Emperor will not have laws made for him either by a foreign Government or by the leaders of a revolution'.[4] He could feel fairly safe that, however reformist Papa Pio Nono proved, his reforms in the Papal States and Legations would stop short of responsible government, though he envisaged the appearance of French troops at Rome in certain circumstances even if the Pope did not call for them. He would, as a matter of course, move into the duchies ruled by client princes of the Habsburgs if there were a rising against their incompetent obscurantism. But what of Piedmont? There the king, Charles Albert, meditated constitutional concessions (in a conscience-stricken way, for he had sworn never to grant them) and held out a hand to the Liberal pope. 'It was an essential part of Palmerston's policy not to make definite threats or promises for fear of having to carry them out',[5] and he only hinted that if the Austrians were to move into the Legations and the French go again to Ancona, the British might appear at Civita Vecchia. But he came nearer than ever to a definite promise to Piedmont, menaced by Austrian troop concentrations in Lombardy intended to deter Charles Albert from constitutionalism. 'Her Majesty's Government would deem it their duty to afford the Sardinian Government support in case of need.'[5] Minto's first port of call after Berne was to be Turin, where his son-in-law, Abercromby, was British minister; he would then call at Florence on the way to Rome.

Metternich addressed to Wellington, before Minto arrived in Italy, a complaint that there was not an English agent in the peninsula who did not join in the cry 'Death to Austria' and that Palmerston did not disavow them.[6] After Metternich's fall, Palmerston admitted that 'he had been openly hostile to the policy of Prince Metternich, because it was reactionary and would therefore lead to an explosion such as had occurred'.[7] Minto's mission was to stiffen the morale of rulers inclined to grant constitutions and to sway the decision of those who had not made up their minds. This was missionary diplomacy pure and undisguised. Even the Queen, once it was understood that Paris and Vienna would be informed of the purpose of the mission, agreed that 'the sending of Sir William Parker with his fleet to the West Coast of Italy . . . [was] a very proper measure to give countenance to the Sovereigns engaged in Liberal Reform, and exposed alike to the inroads of their absolutist neighbour, and to the outbreaks of popular movements directed by a republican party, and perhaps fostered by the Austrian Government'. Minto's aim was to avoid revolution.[8] He made it his business to meet not only rulers and ministers but those who would become ministers under a constitutional régime, and to urge upon the latter moderation, as he urged on the former concession. The message to Metternich explaining the mission, astutely based on the draft of a note proposed by Albert *as an alternative* to the mission, underlined Palmerston's resolution. It said that Britain could not view with indifference any attempt to convert reforming measures which might be taken by independent governments such as those of Turin and Rome 'into an occasion for any aggression whatever upon their respective Territories or Rights'.[9] This was stronger and more positive than Castlereagh's repudiation of, and Canning's defiance of, the areopagitic pretensions of the neo-Holy Alliance.

Metternich was pessimistic and resentful. Surely, he wrote in December 1847, the British Government could 'only want what we want' (stability and peace); yet 'we see the English Cabinet everywhere allied to the parties which desire revolution'. 'It is the policy of England which is the cause of the unrest in the Italian provinces [of Austria]'[10] — that was his constant theme in his last weeks of power. Of course, discontent in Italy needed no external encouragement. The Minto mission was not a gratuitous, unasked-for, interference. It was not dictated by hatred of Austria, nor, as Palmerston told the Austrian envoy, 'by absorb[ing] you in our hostility to France'.[11] It was not even dictated chiefly by love of constitutional government. It was dictated by a belief that Austrian policy was driving Italy, and Europe, to revolution and to war, and that both could be avoided only by the grant of constitutions. Of course, Metternich could not accept, or even see, this. To him, as A. J. P. Taylor has said, 'Revolution had remained in itself a Power; on the one side there was the Concert of Europe, on the other side the Revolution' and what made this timorous man so dangerous was that 'he rated the perils of constitutional concession much higher than those of a European war'.[12] The spectacle of constitutionalism being preached on Italian soil by a British cabinet minister saddened and horrified, and, indeed, puzzled him. How could he take seriously assurances that it was not Minto's business or Palmerston's wish to excite anger against Austria, but only to 'head him off from breaking cover towards Italy' (in which he succeeded)? For Minto, if he did not cry 'Death to Austria' did many times, basking in the unwonted fervour of excited Latin crowds, cry, in Italian spoken with a strong Scottich accent, 'Long Live Italian Independence.' Could that cry fail to carry across international frontiers into Lombardy and Venetia? Metternich and Dietrichstein said, and almost believed, that 'all [Palmerston's] policy [was] directed against the very existence of our Empire'.[13] This was quite untrue. Palmerston did not then even want the Austrians to leave Lombardy and Venetia. He was not in the least attracted to Italian Nationalism as a force militating against the frontiers settled by the Treaty of Vienna; he relished it only as a sentiment that encouraged the ministers and peoples of the particular states to defy Austrian attempts to deny them constitutional government.

'What does Lord Palmerston think of the disturbance he has created?', Ficquelmont asked of Metternich when news came of the revolution at Naples. What Lord Palmerston thought was that it was easy to see that the rest of Italy must have constitutions too, and urgent advice in that sense was sent to all the Italian courts. The changes could 'be affected with as little disturbance as is consistent with the nature of things' *if Metternich permitted.* 'The real fact is, that upon Metternich's decision in regard to the affairs of Italy depends the question of peace or war in Europe.' It would be a war of principles, with the Austrian government and the French nation as the principal protagonists on either side. Metternich should ponder how much help he would get from Bohemians and Hungarians who had their own grievances against his régime, and how many German states, what section of the German nation, would be thrown into the arms of the French as champions of liberty.[14] This danger was real, so long as Charles Albert hesitated. Would he grant a constitution, as the Grand Duke of Tuscany had done on 11th February? — and if so, would Austria move in against him, and France against Austria? Would he, reversing his recent tendencies, refuse a constitution and invite the Austrians in? — if so, the French were almost certain to move. Or would he abdicate, and leave his kingdom to republican anarchy, the theatre of confrontation between Austria and France? Charles Albert's choice became simple when Louis Philippe fled and a republic was proclaimed in France (24th February). 'It is necessary to fight Radicalism, and its chief, Charles Albert', reported Buol from Turin. 'It is not Charles Albert who is its chief, it is Palmerston, supported by liberal fanaticism',[15] Metternich replied. Yet it must have crossed his mind that Palmerston was seeking first the maintenance of the peace of Europe and the Balance of Power when Palmerston's response to the French Revolution was to suggest to Austria 'a prompt and intimate alliance with the Government of Sardinia with the object of repelling a possible attack by the French republic'.[16] To Palmerston's way of thinking, all Italy, except Lombardy and Venetia, would now be constitutional, and concerned with negotiations to secure some sort of federal tie, in which the Austrian provinces might be included. The vital thing was to make sure Republican France did not interfere, and that the Italians outside the Austrian provinces did not attack them. Metternich should therefore abandon all thoughts of securing an anti-constitutional reaction, 'guarantee' Piedmont (even if she became constitutional) against France, as he had in 1831, and protect Lombardy and Venetia by a grant of autonomy.

*   *   *   *

In the great tempest of 1848, which raged from the English Channel to the Carpathians, sweeping away absolutists and reactionaries, Metternich included, Palmerston and Nesselrode in St Petersburg exchanged salutes from the twin rocks which, with tiny Belgium, alone stood firm amid the swirling waves of revolution, of strife between Liberal and Radical, bourgeois reformer and social revolutionary, the wind of ebullient nationalism. Even Britain was splashed by the spray. Her 'Waterloo of peace and order' occurred on 10th April, when the Chartist demonstrators were stopped at the Thames bridges and contented themselves with a deputation to the Home Secretary.[17] Palmerston was tremendously impressed by this fiasco. It was the glory of Britain, he would say in the Don Pacifico speech, that —

. . . every class of society accepts with cheerfulness the lot which Providence has assigned to it, while at the same time every individual of each class is constantly striving to raise himself in the social scale — not by injustice and wrong, not by violence and illegality, but by persevering good conduct, and by the steady and energetic exertion of the moral and intellectual faculties with which his Creator has endowed him. To govern such a people as this is indeed an object worthy of the noblest man.

This sounds like the worst sort of Victorian cant, and invites remorseless Marxist analysis. But the Chartist fiasco of 1848 showed, as he claimed in the general election of 1852, the popular feeling that 'the course of legislation had been directed towards the general good'. It was a tribute to the repeal of the Corn Laws and the passing of the Ten Hours' Bill; it was the vindication of concessionary conservatism, Peelite and Whig. Palmerston's overdrawn picture of social peace, and of peaceful competition in self-betterment, material and moral, had enough substance to explain Britain's avoidance of revolution in 1848 — and was to have more, enough, indeed, to justify those who in the last decade of Palmerston's life pressed vainly, against his opposition, for a further instalment of electoral reform on the ground of the existence of an educated and responsible upper working class. To Palmerston 1848 was proof that 1832 had done its work, and he could say with genuine sincerity and pride —

It is a noble thing to be allowed to guide the policy and to influence the destiny of such a country; and if ever it was an object of honourable ambition, more than ever must it be so at the moment at which I am speaking. For while we have seen . . . the political earthquake rocking Europe from side to side . . . while in almost every country of Europe the conflict of civil war has deluged the land with blood, . . . this country has presented a spectacle honourable to the people of England, and worthy of the admiration of mankind.
We have shown that liberty is compatible with order; that individual freedom is reconcilable with obedience to the law. . . .

Frederick William IV had been right to predict general revolution, wrong to talk of 'rivers of blood'. They came only with the reaction. All over Italy and Germany, and in Vienna itself, constitutions came with little violence, except, momentarily, in Berlin. Britain's position was that, out of it all, she sought no exclusive influence anywhere; 'We are entirely guided by the desire to maintain political peace, the guarantee of which we find in the introduction of necessary reforms.'[18] When the Queen inquired why she had heard nothing lately on foreign affairs, Palmerston pleaded pressure of business and the need to safeguard the records and plan a scratch defence of the Foreign Office against the Chartists. He added that 'the position of your Majesty's Government has been one rather of observation than of action'.[19] And to Normanby: 'As to your not always getting letters from me by every messenger who passes through Paris, never wonder at that or think it extraordinary. Wonder rather when I am able to find time to write at all; I am sure you would if you saw the avalanche of dispatches from every part of the world which come down upon me daily, and which must be read, and if you witnessed the number of interviews which I cannot avoid giving every day of the week. Every post sends me a lamenting minister, throwing himself and his country upon England for help, which I am obliged to tell him we cannot afford him.'[20] The lack of 'action' implies no dereliction of duty. Britain and Russia did not require to 'act', but only to hold fast to the basic tenets of their foreign policies, each dictated by national interest, each, therefore, primarily concerned with the Balance of Power.

The Tsar and Palmerston had diametrically opposed ideological leanings. Nicholas was the incarnation of absolutism, Harry the patron of constitutionalism. The sovereign rebuked Frederick William and Charles Albert, strange, neurotic characters taken prisoner by the Liberalism, and still more the Nationalism, of Germany and Italy respectively; Palmerston blessed all liberal governments that were likely to stand. But both regarded as a nuisance that sense of common nationalism which straddled frontiers. In the search for a solution which would preserve peace, the Autocrat proposed self-determination for the inhabitants of Schleswig, while Palmerston was glad the proposal was not accepted. Palmerston threatened Liberal Germany with a Russian attack; the Tsar had no intention of making it. Both were pragmatists. Unlike Russia, Britain had no moral commitment to any régime that fell and had a moral commitment to the constitutional régimes which emerged. But both, in 1848, stood for Balance of Power, for non-intervention, for the containment of revolutionary France. Once again it fell to Palmerston to employ the technique of restraint by co-operation. Leopold of the Belgians (very much an interested party) put Palmerston's achievement of 1848 in a nutshell when he said that 'the acting together of England and France has been most useful, as it has facilitated to the French Government a system of moderation which it could but with great difficulty have maintained if it had not been acting in concert

with England'.[21] Palmerston's central theme was reported home to
Paris by de Tallenay on 2nd June — 'The cabinet is still ruled by
the treaties of 1815. As long as the internal arrangements of the
various States are alone in question, it supports or resists them
more or less openly according to its particular . . . views. But when
it is a matter of changing the territorial limits of the respective
European States, as the peace of 1815 established them, a serious
opposition on its part must be expected.'[22]

The Whig government, of course, had the advantage, in dealing
with the new government in Paris, though it was not the one
Palmerston would have wished, that it had been on the worst of
terms with Louis Philippe and Guizot. The King of Prussia
'blessed Providence for having placed Lord Palmerston at the head
of your Foreign Office . . . for a more active, more vivid, more
energetic Minister of foreign affairs, a man that would more in-
defatigably pursue great aims, your Majesty could probably never
have. If at this grave hour he sets himself to proclaim that our
forces are united; if he himself utters his message as befits St
George, he will earn the blessing of millions. . . .' What Frederick
William wanted was that the Great Powers should use 'the power
of united speech' ('criminally neglected' in 1830) to tell France
they did not mean to encroach upon her, but that the first breach
of the peace, in Italy, Belgium or Germany, would be a breach
with 'all of us' and revive 1813–15.[23] Before this was written,
Palmerston had already acted. 'We desire friendship and extended
commercial intercourse with France and peace between France and
the rest of Europe. We will engage to prevent the rest of Europe
from meddling with France, which indeed we are quite sure they
have no intention of doing. The French rulers must engage to
prevent France from assailing any part of the rest of Europe', he
had written on 26th February.[24] He knew that any provocative
statement from the Powers might cause the French to burst from
their borders, and, in view of the current instability of monarchical
régimes, which the Parisian revolution inevitably threatened, not
necessarily to the disadvantage of France. Evelyn Ashley, in his
volumes on his step-grandfather, suggests that a Tory government
might have joined in a coalition against France, for, although
Wellington had led the way to recognition of the revolutionary
régime in 1830, that had been monarchical and *haut-bourgeois*; a
republic with mass suffrage, dominated by men who professed to

believe in France's crusading mission in Europe, was a different proposition. Even Palmerston was 'grieved at the prospect of a republic in France', for 'large republics seem to be essentially and inherently aggressive, and the aggressions of the French will be resisted by the rest of Europe, and that is war; while, on the other hand, the example of universal suffrage in France will set our non-voting population agog, and will create a demand for an inconvenient extension of the suffrage, ballot and other mischievous things'.[25]

Imagine then the sentiments of Metternich! — though the Tsar, anxious to prevent an attack on Poland from the West, professed to find it easier to get on with a republic than a constitutional monarchy. Palmerston insisted from the first that the Three Powers must stand aloof, and recognize that Lamartine's government was 'the only security at present against anarchy, conflagration and massacre' and that in supporting him lay the only chance of 'tranquillity and order in France and for peace in Europe'. If the republic were decidedly established, they would have to give credentials to its government or billets to its troops.[26] Metternich, inflamed by Lamartine's Manifesto of 4th March ('the first official announcement by the government of a great Power that the Vienna settlement had no moral validity' — A. J. P. Taylor), drafted an ultimatum to be addressed by the old Quadruple Alliance to France calling on her to recognize the validity of all existing treaties.[27] To Palmerston this was mere foolishness, for the circular to the French diplomats was, in Labour Party parlance, 'a composite', blending chauvinism with peace and a formal repudiation of Vienna with a de facto acceptance of it, and Lamartine had sent assurances to the Duke of Wellington that the sound and fury signified nothing. Palmerston thought it would be wise for the Four Powers to assure France that they would not attack her as long as she attacked no one.[28]

Both proposals were overtaken by events, for Metternich fell on 13th March and was soon joined among exiles in England by the Prince of Prussia, whose brother the king stood in mourning by the graveside of the Marzgefallen — the popular martyrs mown down by his troops before he lost his nerve. There was briefly a danger of alliance between the new liberal government in Prussia, with Arnim as its foreign minister, and republican France to give expression to the 'blind hatred . . . against Russia' which burned in

Germany and France. But Frederick William would not draw the sword against the Tsar, least of all for the Poles; Lamartine's circular did not mention Poland, despite violently pro-Polish feeling among French radicals; Stratford Canning (sent, too late, to be a Minto to the courts of Germany) preached peace to everyone; Palmerston assured Nesselrode with regard to Poland that 'we, the Government, will never do anything underhand or ungentlemanlike in these matters';[29] Lamartine sent the only anti-Polish diplomat he could find to Berlin, and by mid-April the Prussians were fighting not the Russians but the Poles and crossing not the Vistula but the Eider (against the Danes).

This war between Germany (represented mainly by Prussian troops) and Denmark was the second local war to break out as a consequence of the constitutionalist successes of February–March 1848, for by now Piedmont, with a certain amount of help from other Italian states, was fighting the Austrians in Lombardy. Palmerston's one thought was to extinguish these fires before they spread. On the face of the record, he was more successful in dealing with the conflict which arose from the desire of the Germans of Schleswig–Holstein to have Schleswig, as well as Holstein, attached to Germany and detached, when the present king of Denmark died, from all ties with Denmark, for he was accepted as mediator. But appearances are deceptive. Britain, Russia and France all deprecated the Prussian action against Denmark, and if the Prussians (to the fury of the German Constituent Assembly at Frankfort) agreed to an armistice (July–August), it was mainly because Frederick William blushed whenever Nicholas frowned and did not like doing the work of the German Liberals.[30]

Yet Palmerston was entitled to pride when he told the Commons on 2nd February 1849:

. . . We stand here charged with the grave offence of having preserved a good understanding with the Republic of France and of having thereby essentially contributed to the maintenance of peace in Europe, . . . We stand here as men who have laboured assiduously to prevent war if possible; and where it had broken out, to put an end to it as soon as was practicable.

For, if Poland was far away from France, Belgium and Italy were not. A. J. P. Taylor thought that Palmerston, relying on the advice of Normanby, placed *undue* reliance on the pacific assurances of Lamartine.[31] But Palmerston certainly saw the danger of 1830 repeating itself, of republicans in Brussels calling in the French, and the danger that, even if the French government did not respond, the army might, and if the army did not, volunteers and arms might pour north. In the first days after Louis Philippe's abdication, reports were 'fearfully ominous for the peace of Europe'. The queen of the Belgians (Louis Philippe's daughter) hastily sent confidential documents to Leopold's English home for safety. Palmerston made it crystal clear that Belgium, the one country where Britain was bound by treaty to intervene against invasion (France being bound by the same treaty) was 'a case by itself'. 'We cannot sit quiet and see Belgium overrun and Antwerp become a French port; and even war in other directions will sooner or later draw us into its vortex.'[32] The 'other direction' where French intervention was very likely was Italy. We may accept Mr Taylor's conclusion that without Palmerston a European war would probably not have been averted in August, and perhaps again in September, 1848, and that, if his colleagues had not let him down, he would have secured a better practical solution in Northern Italy than was in fact achieved.[33]

★   ★   ★   ★

On the day that Lamartine issued his circular, Charles Albert granted a constitution. Nine days later the Emperor dismissed Metternich — as Greville put it, 'the Crétin settled it all; and the great Minister, who was in his own person considered as *the* Empire, and had governed despotically for forty years, slunk away'[34] (this was a common misconception of Metternich's role). Immediately they heard the news the Milanese rose and with, surprising ease, expelled the Austrian troops; the Venetians followed suit, provisional governments were proclaimed and appeals sent to the other governments of Italy, all now constitutional. On 25th March Charles Albert threw his army over the Ticino.

Palmerston did not welcome this war, and had advised Turin against it. Even Ficquelmont, when complaining to Metternich that Palmerston did not use his influence to prevent the Italians from making 'moral war' on Austria, had admitted that 'he regards England as bound and obliged by treaties not to allow the Italian princes to threaten Austria aggressively in her Italian possessions'.[35] To check republican France, Palmerston had proposed an

Austro–Sardinian alliance, and had warned Metternich that a policy of conciliation in Lombardy was urgent, as a rising there would bring in the French and their republicanism. The Balance of Power was at hazard. But when Ficquelmont, as Metternich's successor, said that 'he should attribute to the British Government the continuation of the attacks upon Austria in Italy' because, by ordering his diplomats no longer to excite hostility to Austria, Palmerston could prevent armed attack on Lombardy and Venetia,[36] he overlooked the salient fact that Charles Albert, who had granted a constitution to save his throne, had to declare war to keep it. 'The fate of Italy is in the hands of England; you are today the only power with influence there; this influence is greater, because it is the only one; the support of France is as much feared as her enmity', wrote Ficquelmont appealingly when in April Palmerston was going through the motions of proposing an armistice.[37] It was a mixture of the true and the false. The choice was between Piedmont making war under a monarchy suspicious of France, and Piedmont making war as a republic wedded to France. Palmerston had to frame his policy knowing that this was a fact, and knowing also that the choice might soon be different — between an Austria admitting defeat and a Piedmont, defeated, throwing herself, or thrown against her will, into the arms of France. It was obvious to him that he must not only seek to localize the war, by keeping the French out, but to end it as soon as possible, because the longer it went on, the more likely were the French to intervene. He drew the correct conclusion that this meant British mediation between Piedmont and Austria to secure freedom for Lombardy and Venetia, the question at issue being simply whether in either any sort of Austrian connection should remain.

It must be emphasized that in these heady weeks when the victory of constitutionalism all over Europe seemed assured, when the whole continent outside the Tsarist orbit appeared to be achieving what Palmerston had preached as its norm and its destiny, the issue was not seen as between constitutional and arbitrary government in North and Central Italy. Austria herself had 'gone Liberal'. When Baron Hummelauer came to London, his instructions, dated 14th May, included the statement that 'the internal policy of Austria has undergone a modification in line with the advice often given by the English Government',[38] and he was authorized to say that the offer of a constitution and autonomy for

Lombardy (made on 20th March by Ficquelmont rather as a result of the revolution in Vienna than of the rising in Milan) was extended to Venetia as well. Northern Italy, then, would be constitutional, whether it was linked with Austria or not, and it would be leagued in a confederacy with other Italian states, all monarchical (one of them, Naples and Sicily, a dual monarchy). As far as the question at issue was constitutional at all, it was whether all Italy should consist of constitutional monarchies, or whether, as the Lombards and Venetians would no doubt have preferred, there should be republics interspersed among them. In Louis Philippe's time, the Austrians had reproved Palmerston for serving French interests by encouraging 'revolutionary wishes and tendencies towards a political system similar to the French'.[39] Now that France was republican it seemed to Palmerston evident that it was Austria's interest, as well as Britain's interest and Whiggery's ardent desire, to see that the Palmerston prescription of limited monarchy prevailed everywhere in Italy and the French prescription of a republic and universal suffrage nowhere. There could be no prospect of stability in Italy if Austria's old prescription of arbitrary (though sometimes benevolent) government survived or if France's new prescription took root. It was taken for granted that republics in Italy would be client states of France, which Austria could hardly tolerate on her doorstep. Obviously they would be proselytizers, seeking to subvert monarchy in Piedmont, central Italy, at Rome itself. And instead of being an element in the European Balance of Power Piedmont, sandwiched between republican France and republican Lombardy, would be a prey to subversion and a problem-child for Europe's statesmen.

The issue of monarchy versus republic therefore bore directly on the Balance of Power, and it was Balance of Power that was uppermost in Palmerston's mind. On 15th April he remarked to Dietrichstein that a great Lombardo–Venetian kingdom would contain more guarantees for peace than the creation of one or more republics.[40] And, impressed by the vigour of the risings against the Austrians, he concluded that 'implacable national hatred had proclaimed against' Austria, so that 'Italy could never now be a useful possession for Austria'.[41] The Austrians had been put into Northern Italy, just as the House of Orange had been put into Belgium, by British contrivance to serve as a bulwark against French aggression. The question of the consent of the North

Italians and Belgic Netherlanders had not, in 1814–15, arisen in any critical way to affect the issue. Now the question of consent obtruded in Northern Italy as it had done in the Southern Netherlands in 1830, and the conclusion should be the same. Like the Dutch, the Austrians could no longer fill the role for which they had been cast in 1815. Therefore the Treaty of Vienna could no longer serve as the authoritative text for the future; it might have to be altered in the letter to preserve its spirit. Only, whereas in the case of the Netherlands the ill-feeling between the Belgians and the Dutch made it necessary to substitute two small kingdoms for one larger one, a distinctly inferior arrangement in Balance of Power terms (hence the 'guarantee' to Belgium), a solution was possible in Northern Italy which would actually be better than the 1815 arrangement. The whole could be made 'a good state' under Charles Albert.[20] 'The King of Northern Italy . . . [would become] a sovereign of some importance.' He might be expected to play off his two powerful neighbours, France and Austria, against one another, and to look to Britain, with her naval power, rather than to republican France. And so Palmerston explained to King Leopold[42] —

. . . I should wish to see the whole of Northern Italy united into one kingdom, comprehending Piedmont, Genoa, Lombardy, Venice, Parma and Modena. . . . Such an arrangement of Northern Italy would be most conducive to the peace of Europe, by interposing between France and Austria a neutral state strong enough to make itself respected, and sympathising in its habits and character neither with France nor with Austria; while with reference to the progress of civilisation, such a state would have great advantages, political, commercial and intellectual. Such an arrangement is now, in my opinion, Sire, inevitable; and the sooner the Austrian Government makes up its mind to the necessity, the better conditions it will be able to obtain.

The cabinet agreed that the objective should be to 'produce a frank abandonment of Lombardy and Venice on the part of Austria'. But public opinion 'had little interest in the things for which Palmerston cared — the European system and the preservation of the Balance of Power'.[43] It was purely and simply pro-Italian. And the prime minister, Russell, much influenced by his father-in-law, Minto, who was convinced that the Austrians were already beaten before the battle, that Italy could 'do it herself' but that it was very important to secure French acceptance of the approaching *fait accompli*, urged communication, if not direct concert, with France.[44] To do them justice, it did look, early in May, as though the French Army of the Alps would march, with or without its government, but these ministers had none of Palmerston's suspicion of involving the French, which had caused him to hold Lamartine at arm's length. He strongly pressed the Austrians to leave Italy gracefully rather than retire before a French army, with or without battle.[45] In the current defeatist atmosphere of Austrian diplomacy — the aged General Radetzky, nursing the Habsburg army in the natural redoubt of the Quadrilateral, was almost alone in thinking that army could recover the Lombard plain — this was telling enough for Hummelauer to withdraw his first suggestion, which was an autonomous, constitutional Northern Italy under the Habsburgs. There was substituted a proposal for an independent Lombardy, while Venetia should be autonomous and constitutional under the Habsburgs.

This may fairly be christened the Hummelauer–Palmerston Plan. It had disadvantages as compared with the complete withdrawal of the Austrians. But it was something Austria would accept. It could be recommended to the Italians with the argument that the formidable army of Radetzky was still undefeated on the Italian side of the Alps, and to Piedmont with the argument that she might not be able to beat Radetzky without calling in the Trojan horse of France. It was not even the worst result for France, because, if she could not have republics, at least she would not see created a Greater Piedmont extending from Nice to the Adriatic. Before many weeks Bastide proposed it himself, and was then told (for the first time) that it was the Hummelauer–Palmerston Plan. But Palmerston's colleagues rejected it. In their minds was much sentimentality and confusion, but they did point out the fatal flaw — that at the moment all Italians, whether Venetians, or Lombards, or Piedmonters, or Tuscans, would unhesitatingly reject it. Palmerston was compelled to report to the Queen[46] —

... The Cabinet, however, upon a full consideration of all the circumstances of the case, were of opinion that, although if it depended upon the decision of the British Government to determine the matter, it would in many respects be most desirable that the arrangement proposed by M. de Hummelauer should be carried into execution, yet in the present state of things, viewing the weakness and embarrassments of Austria, the strong and prevalent animosity against her all over Italy, the military means at the command of the King of Sardinia, and the almost certainty that if those means should fail in compelling the Austrians to retire from the Venetian State, the French would somehow or other be brought into Italy, this arrangement now proposed by M. de Hummelauer is not one which your Majesty's Government could undertake to suggest to the Italians with any prospect of its being accepted, and with any likelihood that it would put an end to the war.

Hummelauer went away with a formula to fall back on if Austria were defeated, which he and Palmerston understood to mean that she would keep at least part of Venetia but which Palmerston, to get it on the record, led his colleagues to believe meant that she would keep none.[47] The Hummelauer–Palmerston Plan itself Palmerston put into cold storage. If the Italians suffered a reverse, they might accept it. If the French decided not to intervene, *they* might accept it as well.

* * * *

It was now Palmerston's aim to keep the French out of Italy if possible, and to ensure, if possible, that if they went in, they went (as they had gone into Belgium in 1831) hampered by self-denying obligations.

The Italian self-confidence which rendered the Hummelauer–Palmerston Plan impracticable until Charles Albert had tested his army against Radetzky's at least had the advantage of making French intervention unwelcome. The French special envoy in March had reported that, in his view, Charles Albert would be defeated, and France would then have her chance, but that for the French to enter Italy uninvited would be to destroy French influence there for a long while.[48] By July the French government, its strong man Cavaignac having overcome the Radical revolutionaries, was non-interventionist in spirit, though it dared not be in profession. It desired neither an Italian victory, which would aggrandize Piedmont, nor an Italian defeat, which would lead to appeals to France which might be irresistible. As to the British attitude, Paris was under no illusions. 'The Cabinet of London has everywhere shown itself preoccupied with the desire to make the entrance of our army of the Alps into Italy impossible', wrote the foreign minister, Bastide on 31st May. 'England is as yet neither for us nor against us, but she already anticipates a situation where she would be rather against us than for us', wrote his envoy de Tallenay five days later.[49] If for 'the Cabinet' and 'England' one reads 'Palmerston' they were quite right. He was keeping aloof, but ready, if events in Italy and/or French public opinion made intervention by France highly likely, to practice the well-tried technique of restraint by co-operation. Normanby in Paris was on 26th July clearly given his cue — 'their object in co-operating with France in negotiations . . . would be thereby to dissuade the French Govt from armed intervention'.[50] In the crisis consequent on Charles Albert's defeat at Custozza, which had occurred the day before, Normanby was therefore able to take a vital initiative in assurance of Palmerston's support.

Abercromby at Turin was equally well briefed. If it was purely from pride, from the 'Italy will do it for herself' motif, that the Lombards and Venetians had not at the outset called in the French, to Charles Albert keeping them out was a matter not of self-esteem but of self-preservation. Therefore, after Custozza, Abercromby urged Piedmont to desert the Lombards; he refused to join the French in mediating until the last Piedmonter left Lombardy (the Lombards had asked the king to cover Milan until the French arrived). But the cabinet in Turin felt that, the Lombards having called in the French, Piedmont must ask at least for diplomatic aid from Paris. The envoy sent for that purpose, Ricci, however, was horrified by the Parisian talk of republics in Italy and was turned by Normanby into a card for Britain to play. He claimed that the French should take no notice of the provisional government in Milan, because the Lombards had voluntarily attached themselves to the monarchy of Charles Albert, and Ricci alone therefore represented Lombardy at Paris. On 5th August Normanby proposed joint Anglo-French mediation on the basis of the Hummelauer–Palmerston Plan.[51]

After a struggle with his colleagues, Palmerston obtained their endorsement of what Normanby had done. The triumph of Palmerston and Normanby is apt to be underrated because, as Mr Taylor had said, despite their 'unbroken series of declarations in favour of Italian independence' the French politicians throughout 1848 were mainly concerned to find excuses for not intervening in Italy. But the record shows that Normanby — who was, after all, manoeuvring the French into accepting the aggrandizement of Piedmont — had to struggle with Cavaignac before he prevailed, Taylor stresses the element of triumph: 'Palmerston, by agreeing to a common mediation, took the only step which could keep a French army out of Italy and so avert a general war. . . . By his action of August 1848, Palmerston undoubtedly provided the French Government . . . with the only possible excuse for not going to war. What is more . . . he prevented the French — until a time when their advocacy was purely academic — from supporting a system of Italian republics, which would have inevitably become French dependencies.'[52] Yet within a few days everything was again in the melting pot. When the Austrians had re-entered Milan and Charles Albert had concluded a military armistice with the Austrians (9th August) the Venetians retracted their accession to Piedmont and appealed to France. When the French sent to Vienna a peremptory demand for acceptance of mediation, and the Austrians seemed not to be intimidated by it, Normanby thought war inevitable. Palmerston's response to this crisis would have been to offer France an alliance — 'If we associate ourselves morally and politically with the move, Austria will not venture to treat it as war. . . . If France is to act anywhere in Italy, she ought to be tied up by a previous engagement with us as to the extent and object of her action.' But the cabinet, the same cabinet which had not seemed to mind French involvement in Italy when Palmerston was intent on avoiding it, now shied at committing Britain to France even for the purpose of holding France to objectives Britain approved. It was therefore not because of any initiative of Palmerston, paralysed by his colleagues, that the French retracted on 2nd September their decision of the previous day to go to Venice.[53]

Palmerston had tried to get the Austrians to accept the mediation by informing Ponsonby at Vienna 'Time presses. The French are growing impatient . . . We are holding them back . . . but they cannot be withheld much longer.' And he added words which, wrenched out of context, have given a false impression — 'As to the interference of France, it will be given if Austria is stubborn. . . . *I do not wish to see the French in Italy*; there are a great many strong and weighty reasons why I should dislike it; but *I would rather that they should go in than that the Austrians should retain Lombardy*; and the people at Vienna may depend upon it that if, owing to their obstinacy, our mediation should fail, *the French will enter Italy, and with the consent of England*, and we shall not then be content with Hummelauer's memorandum. . . .'[54] It is altogether wrong to stress the second phrase italicized by the present author without equal stress on the first and third. Palmerston's view was always what he explained to an angry and uncomprehending queen who was very hostile to the French republic: '. . . it seems to Viscount Palmerston that it is better that the French Government should look at a possible advance of its army into Italy as an operation that is to be subjected to the consent of Great Britain, rather than that it should view it as a measure to be determined upon according to the single will of France, and with a view to its own interests and convenience'.[55]

Palmerston sought peace. The French ambassador understood this — 'All that Lord Palmerston wants is peace; if larger concessions in favour of Italy are of a nature to be obtained without war, Lord Palmerston will be disposed to support them — by notes. . . . Peace, peace, always peace, on no account war, not even to help Italy, not even to accomplish the object of the mediation; war with nobody, negotiations with everybody.'[56] Peace — on principle; peace — because a renewal of war would be likely to bring in the French — was Palmerston's aim. But, of course, he wanted a settlement that would last, and continued to press the Hummelauer–Palmerston Plan upon the Austrians. Their attitude, however, hardened progressively as policy came more and more under the control of Schwarzenberg, who, like Radetzky, deprecated 'softness'. Schwarzenberg was, moreover, prepared to take towards the revolutionary republican régime in Paris the same attitude that Metternich had taken in 1847 towards the monarchical reactionary régime of Louis Philippe; by hailing it as the champion of Order against Socialism he gave it the accolade of respectability in the eyes of Europe which it craved (and which the Tsar had consistently denied to the Orleans monarchy). Grasping that Bastide, as a patriotic Frenchman, had opposed the unification of Germany, he induced him to agree to Lombardy being under an Austrian archduke instead of Charles Albert. This was a reversion to the original Hummelauer offer. It condemned the mediation to failure, but it made a war between France and Austria unlikely. When Piedmont invoked French aid, Cavaignac snapped that the French were not to be treated as though they were Swiss mercenaries.[57]

Palmerston's relations with the Austrians were now very bad indeed, and his relations with France not cordial. There is a letter to Abercromby of 28th December 1848 which is liable to misconstruction. Palmerston wrote: 'I do not wish to see Italy emancipated from the Austrian yoke by the help of French arms, but perhaps it would be better that it should be so done than not done at all; and if it were so done at a time when England and France were well together, we might be able to prevent any permanently bad consequences from resulting from it.'[58] But the circumstances were these: the Piedmonters had continued to make chauvinistic noises, and Palmerston, still seeking a settlement on the basis of the Hummelauer–Palmerston Plan, had encouraged them to do so, and warned Austria that if she broke the armistice 'it will not be with Sardinia alone that you will have to do'.[59] Now that the Austrians were frankly seeking a return to the status quo ante bellum, and it looked as though the Piedmonters would act, instead of merely talking big, Palmerston, to avoid war, tried to dissuade them with the argument that now they would fight alone, but that in some hypothetical future circumstances they might secure French aid with British approval. His objective is clearly stated: 'the great object is to keep things quiet; to re-establish peace in Northern Italy, and to trust to future events for greater improvements'.

CHAPTER XII

PALMERSTON AND THE NATIONS, 1848-9

O N 16th August 1848 Disraeli, in what Greville describes as 'a brilliant duel' with Palmerston — the first of many major encounters — accused the Foreign Secretary of being a convert to 'the sentimental principle of nationality'. He thus gave voice to a misapprehension common in his own day and persisting ever since. Liberalism and Nationalism in nineteenth century Europe were so intimately connected that it is impossible to define the former except, in part, in terms of the latter. The idea, therefore, that because Palmerston was a prophet and patron of constitutionalism he must have been also a patron of nationalities struggling to be free — a precursor of Woodrow Wilson — is superficially plausible, especially in view of his part in the establishment of Greece and of Belgium, the tone of some of his public speeches years afterwards taking credit for this, and his attitude to Lombardy and Venetia in and after 1848. But it is quite unjustified.

German historians have always known that Palmerston was a British nationalist rather than a sympathizer with the nationalism of others, though they have usually underrated or denied the existence of his sympathy with German nationalism in 1848-9. They have, characteristically, tended to the view that the Great Powers did at that time prevent the unification of Germany or that they would have done so had the Germans not saved them the bother by failing to agree among themselves when circumstances were propitious. In general understanding that it was France and Russia who had a direct interest in the failure of the Germans in 1848-9, while Austria was largely out of the German picture, they have not failed to condemn Palmerston too. One of them, Scharff, puts him first among the culprits and complains bitterly of 'the collaboration between the liberal western powers and the autocratic empire of the tsars'.[1] It is of some importance to understand Palmerston's attitude to the movement for German unification, the one expression of nationalism on the continent in 1848-9 which could have been satisfied without any change in the *territorial* settlement of Europe. Italy could not be united without the surrender of provinces by Austria; Hungary could not be free without turning the Habsburg empire into a dual monarchy; Roumania could not be independent without depriving the Sultan of sovereignty over two provinces of his empire. But Germany could have been united by the *partial* surrender of sovereignty by the independent German states to a federal centre. Britain, at first sight, had every interest in seeing this happen. Palmerston was, of course, bitterly hostile to the co-ordinated activity of the German states when the moving power was Metternich, and the purpose the suppression of the Liberal movement. He also regarded the Zollverein as 'a League founded in hostility to England', so that for the protection of her trade and manufactures England was bound to use her influence against the adherence of further North German states to this customs union, with its protectionist bias. But he had based his right to rebuke Metternich on Britain's interest in the fate of Germany (1832-4) and, in a memorandum to Prince Albert in 1847 he reiterated that the two countries had a mutual direct interest in assisting each other to become 'rich, united and strong'. For it was France and Russia who threatened Germany, and under the dispensation of 1815-48 Germany was a weak opponent for France, yet an effective shield for Russia.[2]

Britain had therefore no interest in preserving the status quo and, one would have thought, every interest in promoting the emergence of a constitutional, Western-orientated, mainly Protestant state in central Europe, anti-Russian, suspicious of Austria, determined to protect its national independence against France. Not without reason for hope did Heinrich von Gagern, the leading statesman of the Constituent Assembly at Frankfort, appeal to Britain to be the first Power to recognize the Provisional Federal Executive under the Archduke John and make the new Confederation 'the chief continental ally of England in place of Austria'. Such a 'countenance and encouragement for Germany in her progress towards Constitutional Government' would, he said, be 'most highly prized by the German nation'.[3] As Dr Mosse says in his admirable study *The European Powers and the German Question*, 'the consolidation of a *liberal* Germany . . . would serve the purpose of British diplomatic strategy'. It would virtually expel Russia from Europe. 'The new power might tip the scales between England and Russia . . . ; the future of Turkey and Central Asia, even of India herself, might be decided on the 'battlefields' of Germany'; an Austria cold-shouldered out of Germany might be expected to give far greater attention to the Balkans. So 'for England as well as Russia the stakes in the German question were high'.[4] Why then did Palmerston rest on his oars; fail to give authoritative moral support and patronage to the movement for German unification on a Liberal basis; fail, apparently, to give the German question any close and continuing attention at all, and adopt, in international questions, a hostile attitude towards the German nation? The answer is, that in the circumstances of 1848, the Powers — and Britain especially, intent upon keeping international peace — must distinguish between those 'Reforms and Improvements which the spirit of this age, and the wants and wishes of a Nation require' which Stratford (before the blizzard struck) had been sent to urge on the German courts,[5] and action over international boundaries, which Britain consistently opposed. There could be no question of Britain approving a German crusade against Russia, conducted in alliance with France on behalf of Polish nationalism, which was on the agenda of the Liberal, Arnim, who became foreign minister of Prussia in March, but which the Prussian king deprecated and a rising in Prussian Poland finally scotched. Nor was Britain ready to endorse the notion that, in the name of nationalism, Schleswig, like the other duchy of Holstein with which it was associated (both of them having the King of Denmark as their duke) should enter into Germany. The same principle could be invoked to detach Alsace from France! But the Prussians moved into the Elbic duchies in April and crossed into Denmark proper in May, and when they evacuated Denmark in June and concluded (after some hitches) an armistice in August, with the future of Schleswig unsettled, German public opinion was indignant and the assembly and executive at Frankfort reflected that opinion.

If the Danes and the Prussians had been able to agree on the division of Schleswig on ethnic lines, the Danish part being incorporated into the Danish kingdom, the German part attached to Holstein and in the Confederation, British coldness towards the Germans at Frankfort might have disappeared. It was Russia who proposed this solution, which Britain and Austria supported. Palmerston, however, thinking about the Baltic, and also about the possible repercussions of the ethnic principle upon the territorial arrangements of the Treaty of Vienna, was rather glad that the proposal failed. By mid-April he had come to favour the status quo in the duchies. When he offered his good offices to Denmark and Prussia, he had in mind the constitutional separation of Schleswig from Holstein as well as from Denmark, and at the end of June he told the Prussians that it was 'manifest and indisputable that no territory or state, which is not now according to the Treaty of 1815 included in the German Confederation, can be added to that territory without the consent of the Sovereign of that territory or state'.[6] The refusal of Frankfort to accept this combined with Palmerston's growing feeling that the constitution-makers there were (as Britain's representative Cowley reported, like Fox Strangways before him) 'a parcel of children who want whipping and caressing alternately' to produce in Palmerston an unfriendly attitude.[7] There is no reason to doubt the sincerity of his instruction to Strangways on 23rd March to support 'as far as you properly can without any direct or unfitting interference any plan which has for its object to consolidate Germany and give it more unity or political vigour'.[8] That remained his attitude, though it was never Russia's and after June definitely ceased to be France's. His reply to Gagern's appeal was not, however, the formal recognition requested, but the dispatch of Cowley in an informal capacity to Frankfort to express Britain's good wishes to the constitution-mongers, to press (when the time should come) for a German policy of low tariffs, and to urge the authorities to do anything necessary to expedite the armistice between Denmark and Sweden and Prussia.[9] Cowley's reports were discouraging. Of the ministers of the provisional executive he said that 'a more useless inefficient body of men were never brought together', and his lowest opinion was reserved for the foreign minister, Queen Victoria's half-brother Lieningen, who thought that war might be 'the best thing for us. It must at all events settle the question of Unity at once'.[7]

Palmerston now felt, like the Russians, that Frankfort must be made to understand that Schleswig was not merely a German, but a European, question, involving the Treaty of 1815 and (for Britain) the treaty of 1720. When Frankfort refused to recognize the armistice, even Queen Victoria complained that Frankfort seemed to show 'a lamentable want of *all* practical sense, foresight, or even *common* prudence' and Palmerston asked Cowley to inquire 'in civil terms' of his friends there 'whether they are mad . . . and deliberately determined to rush into Conflict with all Europe, including, as it seems, Prussia'.[10] The assembly did approve the armistice (and had to put down a Radical revolution in Frankfort as a result). But it was too late. Frankfort had lost all its importance internationally, and was fast losing it nationally; in 1849 the future organization of Germany depended on relations between Prussia and Austria. The German historian Stadelmann writes 'if the Germans had shown moderation and restraint in the Schleswig–Holstein controversy of 1848, Britain would have been willing to help create a German nation-State in conformity with the prevailing liberal attitude of the nineteenth century'.[1] It was obvious that Palmerston would wish to see the Diet liberalized once Metternich, 'the Old Man of the Mountain', had been lifted off the back of the German nation, especially if the result was an all-German customs union less protectionist than the Zollverein. But it was for the Germans to achieve this, to earn the goodwill of Britain and to moderate, if possible, the natural hostility of Russia and France. The Germans, in practice, contrived to stiffen Russian antipathy to constitutionalism in Germany; to play into the hands of the French, who desired a weak Germany; to alienate Britain, unwilling to accept the ethnic principle and tending, like Russia, to take her stand on 1815. No doubt as A. J. P. Taylor says, 'British policy . . . served the turn of France and Russia without these powers lifting a finger'.[11] But Palmerston, although his patronage of Liberalism was genuine, was not prepared to assist in a general subversion of the Treaty of Vienna, and was mainly concerned to prevent a war between Prussia and Russia. His role of peace-keeper took precedence over the role of constitutionalist. Patron of a nationalism which threatened existing sovereignties he did not aspire to be.

This outlook of Palmerston's was, however, obscured, and from the superficial or the prejudiced concealed, by the fact that he *did* come to advocate, publicly and strongly, the separation of Lombardy at least, and preferably of Venetia as well, from Austria. But it must be understood that he did so from no tenderness for the ethnic principle in general or nationalism in the abstract, but on an opinion formed — and correctly formed — from a study of the actual situation in Northern Italy. If it is open to critics to complain that Palmerston in 1848 failed to give the affairs of Germany the attention they merited, one of the principal reasons was his

I

concentration on the affairs of Italy, where the French were very likely to act.

★   ★   ★   ★

When Palmerston sent Minto to Italy to preach constitutionalism, he had no thought of trying to expel the Austrians from their Italian provinces, only to head them off from interference in Piedmont or central Italy. What he desired for Lombardy and Venetia were 'institutions of the most liberal and national character'. These, after the revolt of the provinces and the fall of Metternich, the Austrians were ready to offer. But by then the situation was transformed, and Palmerston no longer thought the participation of Lombardy and Venetia, as Austrian provinces, in some federal arrangement under the aegis of the Pope the best practicable solution. The risings — so furious as to achieve unexpected success — and the anti-Austrian feeling in Piedmont and, to a lesser extent, elsewhere in Italy, much impressed him. 'Northern Italy will henceforward be Italian, and the Austrian frontier will be at the Tyrol', he wrote to Minto on 28th March.[12]

This was meant simply as a prediction, made at a time when, of all the people closely concerned, only Radetzky, the veteran general of the Habsburgs, and the French special envoy Bixio, believed that Radetzky's army could recover Milan and Venice. But even if it could, would the French let it? Twice only did Palmerston write that he would prefer to see the Austrians expelled by the French than not expelled at all, and he did so in hope of persuading the Austrians to withdraw before the French intervened. The first time, he feared war within days;[13] the second time, he was trying, without much hope, to get Lombardy for Charles Albert without a renewal of war.[14] For, though he sought peace as a short-term aim, he also sought a stability without which, in the long run, there could be no peace. He did not see how, if the Austrians stayed in Lombardy, they could ever pacify it, now that 'implacable national hatred' had proclaimed against them.[15] Italy had become to Austria 'the heel of Achilles, and not the shield of Ajax'. She should see that the Alps were her natural barrier and her best defence.[16] She could hold Northern Italy, if at all, only by the sword, a tenure insecure and more expensive than useful. Austria could no longer play the part she had been put into Italy in 1815 to play. As long as she stayed there, her ability to play effectively her more general role in Europe, and her special role in the Balkans (both invaluable to British interests) would be impaired.

One of these two letters to Ponsonby is, indeed, couched in terms which invite misinterpretation.[13] In it, Palmerston stated that the Austrians had no business in Italy at all, since their failure to fulfil their treaty obligations to the Poles of Galicia and their annexation of Cracow had fatally weakened their claim of right based on the Treaty of Vienna. (This dangerous argument, subversive of the whole territorial settlement, was surely the fruit of haste and anger.) 'Providence', Palmerston went on, 'meant mankind to be divided into separate nations, and for this purpose countries have been founded by natural barriers, and races of men have been distinguished by separate languages, habits, manners, dispositions and characters' (what a gift to the French exponents of 'natural frontiers'!). Palmerston paused, as befitted an Anglo-Irish landlord, to guard from the impact of this argument the Union with Ireland, which he held justified by an intermixture of races and a common language, and the fact that 'the land, the wealth and intelligence' of Ireland were for the connexion (the wishes of the peasantry seemed irrelevant both in Ireland and in Northern Italy). Austrian rule in Italy had none of these justifications. There was no case on the globe in which the intention of Providence was more marked than that of the Italians and Germans 'kept apart by the Alps, and as unlike in everything as two races can be'. (This was hardly justified by the mediaeval history of Italy.) Austria's rule, Palmerston said, had always been hateful. This was not true, though it was valid to say (of Lombardy) 'it is impossible to expect that a Province in which there exists throughout the whole population . . . such deeply rooted hatred of Austrian domination can ever become either a secure or a useful possession of the Imperial Crown'.[14]

This letter is untypical, both in its sentiments, and in its wild disregard of the repercussions which would have followed from the general application of its doctrine. It was written in haste at possibly the most desperate moment of the whole Italian Question in 1848, when French intervention was hourly expected; its sole aim was to prevent war by securing Austrian concessions, though this its tone was hardly calculated to do. But even this letter does not, essentially, rest the case for Austrian concession on the abstract claim of nationality, which would have demanded the withdrawal or expulsion of the Austrians from Venetia as well as Lombardy. It must be insisted that 'the policy of Palmerston was not based upon sentimental considerations of nationalism, but upon the enduring principles of the Balance of Power'.[17] In Italy it was based on present facts and future probability; it was the policy of a statesman not a doctrinaire. Palmerston was compromising no principles when at the time of the Hummelauer mission he was willing to settle for a continued Habsburg presence in Venetia; the great thing was to get the war over quickly. And he was animated by no abstract doctrine when he continued to try to get Lombardy for Charles Albert after he had been defeated at Custozza. He wished to prevent French intervention, and avert the continuance of the war between the Austrians and Italians. He would have liked to provide for the stability of Northern Italy in the coming years; to get for Charles Albert a greater kingdom as a greater bulwark against republican France.

It was hardly to be expected that Austrian governments would appreciate being told by Palmerston that they should surrender Italy, although the caretaker successor of Ficquelmont accepted Stratford's assurance that Palmerston understood Austria's importance to Europe, and sent Hummelauer to London. When Palmerston continued to press the Hummelauer Plan, to warn Austria against attacking Piedmont, and in November sent to Ponsonby 'the most vigorous outburst' of the whole Italian negotiation, Schwarzenberg, the new master of Habsburg policy, believed, or pretended to believe, like Metternich before him, that Palmerston was hostile to Austria as a Great Power, that 'all his policy [was] directed against the very existence of our Empire'.[18] Palmerston's outburst was provoked, partly perhaps by frustration at his inability to persuade the Austrians that their true interest lay in abandoning Italy, partly, beyond doubt, by sheer indignation at Radetzky's repression in Lombardy — '. . . the moral feeling of mankind and every feeling of Generosity and Justice would have revolted against a proceeding conceived in the spirit of the most odious oppression and enunciated by Doctrines which belong only to the Disciples of Communism and which are subversive of the very foundations of social order . . . an announcement so utterly at variance with the Principles upon which the acts of a Government of a great European country ought to be founded'.[19] This gave Schwarzenberg an excuse to render abortive the European conference at Brussels to which he had assented in order to escape from the Anglo-French mediation. On 14th December he circulated to his diplomats a denunciation of Palmerston, not as an erring or mistaken member of the European comity of diplomatists, but as an enemy of Austria: 'Lord Palmerston regards himself too much as the arbiter of Europe. For our part we are not disposed to accord him the role of Providence. We never impose our advice on him in relation to Ireland; let him spare himself the trouble of advising us on the subject of Lombardy. . . . We are tired of his eternal insinuations, his protestive and demagogic tone, both offensive and unwelcome. We are resolved to tolerate it no longer. . . . I say, if he wants war, he *shall* have it.'[20]

Schwarzenberg could speak from a position of strength. Windischgratz had overthrown the revolution in Vienna on 30th October, and Radetzky was 'restoring order' in Lombardy. General Wrangel took control of Berlin on 8th November. On 10th December the candidate of the forces of Order, one Louis Napoleon Buonaparte (a few months earlier serving as a special constable on the Thames Embankment) was elected president of the French Republic (with the applause of Schwarzenberg, Queen Victoria and Louis Philippe!). Reaction had triumphed at Naples, whose king was reconquering Sicily by means which earned him the soubriquet 'Bomba'. Constitutions there would still be in most of the German states, and even in Austria, but the reality was counter-revolution, except where, as in Tuscany and Rome, extreme radicalism temporarily reigned. A bona fide constitution survived in Piedmont, but it committed Charles Albert to chauvinism. He broke out against the Austrians (March 1849), was decisively defeated at Novara, and abdicated, retiring to a monastery to expiate his sins, still wondering which to expiate — the sins of illiberalism and Piedmontese particularism, the sins of Liberalism and Nationalism, or the broken pledge to be illiberal. It was left to Britain and France to try to save his country from a vengeful peace.

* * * *

The Austrians failed to grasp that Palmerston was not motivated by abstract nationalism or Italian-nationalism or ill-will towards Austria as a Power; that he was concerned only with British interest, Balance of Power and, indeed, the interests of the Habsburgs as he saw them. He had been utterly sincere when he wrote: 'The Austrian Empire is a thing worth saving'; when he wrote: 'As to poor Austria, every person who attaches value to the maintenance of the balance of power in Europe must lament her present helpless condition', and advocated the removal of the imbecile emperor Ferdinand (which was accomplished in December); when he declared that 'the maintenance of the Austrian Empire is an object of general interest to all Europe, and to no country more than to England; north of the Alps we wish her all the prosperity and success in the world'.[21] Schwarzenberg did not give Palmerston credit for a realism as calculating and more long-sighted than his own, or for his strong conviction that for Austria to leave Italy would not diminish her security and influence as a European Power.

Soon Palmerston had an opportunity to prove the sincerity of these sentiments and, one would have thought, to kill for ever the legend that he was a sympathizer with European nationalism. On hard Balance of Power analysis, charity and diplomacy, compatible in Italy, were incompatible in Hungary. Palmerston saw the illiberality of the German Austrians who in October 1848 began to move in arms against a virtually independent Magyar nation more clearly than he saw the illiberality of the Magyars themselves towards their Slav subjects, who helped the Habsburg armies. In his heart he must have admired the valour with which the Hungarians, after the fall of Budapest in January 1849, rallied to recover most of the country, so that by May Austria was reduced to calling on Russia for aid. The Hungarian declaration of independence and deposition of the Habsburgs on 14th April was the natural retort of a spirited people to the formal abolition of their ancient constitution in March. But Palmerston hardened his heart. The Magyar publicist Pulszky reports sadly that Palmerston 'counselled us to reconcile ourselves with Austria, because in the frame of the European state-system it would be impossible to replace Austria by small States'. Palmerston told him that if Austria (i.e. the Habsburg empire) did not exist it would have to be invented.[22] It was a European necessity and England's natural ally in the East. He could only hope that, as the Austrians in their folly were adamant against reasonable concessions to Hungarian nationalism, they and the Russians would get the business of subduing the Magyars over quickly, and that Austria would not show too much gratitude to the Russians for their aid.

When the envoy commissioned by the Hungarian leader Kossuth sent his credentials to the Foreign Office, the Under-Secretary of State wrote that Palmerston could not receive him because 'the British Government has no knowledge of Hungary except as one of the component parts of the Austrian Empire'.[23] The Hungarian leaders and generals, going down before over-whelming odds (they surrendered at Villagos on 13th August) lost any illusion that strong British public sympathy for their cause would alter Palmerston's resolution when they heard of his speech of 21st July 1849,* which must be quoted at some length:

. . . Austria has been our ally. We have been allied with Austria in most important European transactions; and the remembrance of the alliance ought undoubtedly to create in the breast of every Englishman, who has a recollection of the history of his country, feelings of respect towards a Power with whom we have been in such alliance. It is perfectly true, that in the course of those repeated alliances, Austria, not from any fault of hers, but from the pressure of irresistible necessity, was repeatedly compelled to depart from the alliance, and to break the engagements by which she had bound herself to us. We did not reproach her with yielding to the necessity of the moment; and no generous mind would think that those circumstances ought in any degree to diminish or weaken the tie which former transactions must create between the Governments of the two countries. But there are higher and larger considerations, which ought to render the maintenance of the Austrian empire an object of solicitude to every English statesman. Austria is a most important element in the balance of European power. Austria stands in the centre of Europe, a barrier against encroachment on the one side, and against invasion on the other. The political independence and liberties of Europe are bound up, in my opinion, with the maintenance and integrity of Austria as a great European Power; and therefore anything which tends by direct, or even remote, contingency, to weaken and to cripple Austria, but still more to reduce her from the position of a first-rate Power to that of a secondary State, must be a great calamity to Europe, and one which every English-man ought to deprecate, and to try to prevent. . . . I firmly believe that in this war between Austria and Hungary, there is enlisted on the side of Hungary the hearts and the souls of the whole people of that country. It is true, as my honourable and gallant friend has stated, that Hungary has for centuries been a State which, though united with Austria by the link of the Crown, has nevertheless been separate and distinct from Austria by its own complete constitution. That constitution has many defects; but some of those defects were, I believe, remedied not long ago, and it is not the only ancient constitution on the continent that was susceptible of great improvement. There were means, probably, within the force and resources of the constitution itself to reform it; and it might have been hoped that those improvements would have been carried into effect. But, so far as I understand the matter, I take the present state of the case to be this: without going into the details of mutual complaints as to circumstances which have taken place within the last year, or year and a half, I take the question that is now to be fought for on the plains of Hungary to be this — whether Hungary shall continue to maintain its separate nationality as a distinct kingdom, and with a constitution of its own; or whether it is to be incorporated more or less in the aggregate constitution that is to be given to the Austrian empire? It is a most painful sight to see such forces as are now arrayed against Hungary proceeding to a war fraught with such tremendous consequences on a question that it might have been hoped would be settled peacefully. It is of the utmost importance to Europe, that Austria should remain great and powerful; but it is impossible to disguise from ourselves that, if the war is to be fought out, Austria must thereby be weakened, because, on the one hand, if the Hungarians should be successful, and their success should end in the entire separation of Hungary from Austria, it will be impossible not to see that this will be such a dismemberment of the Austrian empire as will prevent Austria from continuing to occupy the great position she has hitherto held among European Powers. If, on the other hand, the war being fought out to the uttermost, Hungary should by superior forces be entirely crushed, Austria in that battle will have crushed her own right arm. Every field that is laid waste is an Austrian resource destroyed — every man that perishes upon the field among the Hungarian ranks, is an Austrian soldier deducted from the defensive forces of the empire. Laying aside those other most obvious considerations that have been touched upon as to the result of a successful war, the success of which is brought about by foreign aid — laying that wholly aside, it is obvious that even the success of Austria, if it is simply a success of force, will inflict a deep wound on the fabric and frame of the Austrian empire. It is therefore much to be desired, not simply on the principle of general humanity, but on the principle of sound European policy, and from the most friendly regard to the Austrian empire itself — it is, I say, devoutly to be wished that this great contest may be brought to a termination by some amicable arrangement between the contending parties, which shall on the one hand satisfy the national feelings of the Hungarians, and on the other hand, not leave to Austria another and a larger Poland within her empire. . . . Sir, I do not think that the preservation of peace is in any degree endangered by the expression of opinion with regard to the transactions in Hungary or other countries. I agree with those who think — and I know there are many in this country who entertain the opinion — that there are two objects which England ought peculiarly to aim at. One is to maintain peace; the other is to count for something in the transactions of the world — that it is not fitting that a country occupying such a proud position as England — that a country having such various and extensive interests, should lock herself up in a simple regard to her own internal affairs, and should be a passive and mute spectator of everything that is going on around. It is quite true that it may be said, 'Your opinions are but opinions, and you express them against our opinions, who have at our command large armies to back them — what are opinions against armies?' Sir, my answer is, opinions are stronger than armies. Opinions, if they are founded in truth and justice, will in the end prevail against the bayonets of infantry, the fire of artillery, and the charges of cavalry. Therefore I say, that armed by opinion, if that opinion is pronounced with truth and justice, we are indeed strong, and in the end likely to make our opinions prevail; and I think that what is happening on the whole surface of the continent of Europe, is a proof that this expression of mine is a truth. Why, for a great many years the Governments of Europe imagined they could keep down opinion by force of arms, and that by obstructing progressive improvement they would prevent that extremity of revolution which was the object of their constant dread. We gave an opinion to the contrary effect, and we have been blamed for it. We have been accused of meddling with matters that did not concern us, and of affronting nations and Governments by giving our opinion as to what was likely to happen; but the result has proved, that if our opinions had been acted upon, great calamities would have been avoided. These very Governments that used to say, 'The man we hate, the man we have to fear, is the moderate Reformer; we care not for your violent Radical, who proposes such violent extremes that nobody is likely to join him — the enemy we are most afraid of is the moderate Reformer, because he is such a plausible man that it is difficult to persuade people that his counsels would lead to extreme consequences — therefore let us keep off, of all men, the moderate Reformer, and let us prevent the first step of improvement, because that improvement might lead to extremities and innovation,' — those Governments, those Powers of Europe, have at last learned the truth of the opinions expressed by Mr. Canning, 'That those who have checked improvement, because it is innovation, will one day or other be compelled to accept innovation, when it has ceased to be improvement.' I say, then, that it is our duty not to remain passive spectators of events that in their immediate consequences affect other countries, but which in their remote and certain consequences are sure to come back with disastrous effect upon us; that, so far as the courtesies of international intercourse may permit us to do, it is our duty, especially when our opinion is asked, as it has been on many occasions on which we have been blamed for giving it, to state our opinions, founded on the experience of this country — an experience that might have been, and ought to have been, an example to less fortunate countries. At the same time, I am quite ready to admit that interference ought not to be carried to the extent of endangering our relations with other countries. There are cases like that which is now the subject of our discussion, of one Power having in the exercise of its own sovereign rights invited the assistance of another Power; and, however we may lament that circumstance, however we may be apprehensive that therefrom consequences of great danger and evil may flow, still we are not entitled to interpose in any manner that will commit this country to embark in those hostilities. All we can justly do is to take advantage of any opportunities that may present themselves in which the counsels of friendship and peace may be offered to the contending parties. . . . Sir, to suppose that any Government of England can wish to excite revolutionary movements in any part of the world — to suppose that any Government of England can have any other wish or desire than to confirm and maintain peace between nations, and tranquillity and harmony between Governments and subjects, shows really a degree of ignorance and folly which I never supposed any public man could have been guilty of, which may do very well for a newspaper article, but which it astonishes me to find is made the subject of a speech in Parliament.

It is quite evident that Palmerston aspired to be the surgeon, not the murderer, of the Habsburg Empire.[24] A study of the symptoms convinced him that its Italian limb should be amputated for the general health of the rest, and he was as sure as ever that without liberal institutions there would be no stability in Hungary, in Austria proper or in Austrian Poland. But the criticism which should be directed against him is not that he wanted changes in the Vienna Treaty arrangements and in the accustomed Balance of Power, but that, in his desire to maintain peace and to retain the familiar landmarks of the European system, he was too cautious, too fearful, too wedded to the Treaty. He did not try very hard to substitute a strong Germany for Austria as Britain's ally in central Europe, although he would not thereby have sacrificed Austria as an ally in the Balkans. He did not deviate from what he thought the path of safety and of duty, even though constitutionalism was often a co-victim with the nationalisms which Palmerston failed to support. To Palmerston, says Mr Taylor, 'Poland meant nothing and Germany very little . . . [and] despite his liberal principles he welcomed Russia's action in restoring Austria as a great Power.'[25]

Although the sort of Germany they wanted was entirely different, Nesselrode and Palmerston did their utmost, throughout the Schleswig–Holstein crisis, to keep the policies of their countries in step, and, after the initial wavering due to Russian apprehensions over Poland, both stood by 1815. Palmerston was certainly very careful to do nothing to provoke or annoy the Tsar. He sent only the gentlest hint that some concession to Polish national feeling might be prudent.[26] He repeatedly assured Brunnow and Nesselrode that no revolutionary movement in Eastern Europe could count on any British support. He rebuked the consul-general in Bucharest for the sympathy he showed to the conservative revolutionaries, telling him that its 'actual status was the best the Principality [of Wallachia] could expect'. Its status was that of a Turkish dependency in which Russia had defined treaty rights.

Like Stratford at Constantinople, Palmerston would have been glad to see Russian influence reduced in Roumania (i.e. Wallachia and Moldavia) and Turkish prestige enhanced. Stratford and the consul Colquhoun did what they could to achieve a modus vivendi between the Sultan and the new provisional government of Wallachia. But when the Russians, having moved troops into Moldavia to counter revolution there, brought strong pressure on the Turk, Palmerston publicly and privately accepted Russia's assurances that she did not intend permanent encroachment. He was deaf to Stratford's appeal for a fleet, or at least a ship or two, at Constantinople. If the ambassador was ready to risk war, confident that 'in spite of Cobden the public will be with you against despotic reaction', the Foreign Secretary was not.[27] As the hearts of the Magyar patriots had sunk at the speech of 21st July 1849, so those of the Roumanian forty-eighters, driven into exile by Russian pressure, sank at the speech of 20th March 1849, in which Palmerston even (falsely) defended Russian troop movements as in accord with treaty rights. He made no protest at the use of Russian occupation forces to bring pressure on the Hungarians in Transylvania and, on Russian representations, withdrew the British vice-consul accredited to the Austrian commander in Transylvania, because he was working with the Hungarians. He made no protest at the massive Russian intervention in Hungary itself, through Roumania. The time for protests came later, when the issue was already decided.

★   ★   ★   ★

In view of the facts adduced above, it is hard to credit the belief at the Palace, and among the Tory Opposition, that Palmerston was fundamentally disloyal to the work of Castlereagh. He always guarded himself carefully from any undertaking to maintain by force any part of the Vienna Settlement not entrenched by a 'guarantee',[28] but there was no part that he wished to see amended except that relating to Lombardy and Venetia. This he regarded as a special case because, at the first quarrel between Paris and Vienna, the French would drive the Austrians out. But the Queen and the Prince were unable to see that he regarded Lombardy and Venetia in this light, because they had convinced themselves in advance that he would always do the wrong thing everywhere. Their letters are full of gibes contrasting Palmerston's desire for the aggrandizement of Charles Albert's kingdom with his grudging attitude towards Prussia; his willingness to see the rights of Italian dukes as 'disposed of by events'[29] with his refusal to treat similarly the rights of Fredrik VII of Denmark in his other guise of Duke of Schleswig-Holstein; his approval of the doctrine of the transfer of power in Italy by popular sovereignty with the denial of it in Holstein (where the law of succession differed from Denmark and the diet and the Prussians and the German people wished a different heir-apparent to be recognized). They were, indeed, themselves confused, for they protested at attempts to tear away Austrian territories without the emperor's consent, yet approved the attempt to tear away Schleswig (at least to the extent of including it in the German Confederation) without the consent of its duke.

Palmerston, as we have seen, came to support the aggrandizement of Piedmont for practical, Balance of Power reasons, and to support its annexation of small duchies from which the rulers had been expelled, as well as Lombardy and Venetia. He did not uphold the doctrine of popular sovereignty, for though he applauded the decision of Lombardy and Venetia to adhere to Piedmont, he ignored their cancellation of this decision after Charles Albert signed an armistice. If there is any dogma at all apparent in Palmerston's Italian policy in 1848-9, it is a preference for one constitutional monarchy over one or more republics. Even this was only another way of saying that he preferred a pro-British state to French puppets. But this the Queen and the Prince, pro-Austrian in Italy though not in Germany, could not, or would not see. To them, all was Palmerstonian perversity. 'The principle upon which Lord Palmerston goes is *Italian Nationality and Independence from a foreign Yoke and Tyranny*', They said.[30] Therefore, when Palmerston, *faute de mieux*, tried to induce the Austrians to surrender Lombardy while keeping Venetia, they complained that there was in him now no principle but only 'personal *passion*'. They alleged, of the Minto Mission (a mistake, because it had proved very prejudicial to Austria), that Palmerston had seized upon the earl's desire to pay with public money for a visit to his daughter in Turin to compromise Minto and bind the cabinet (through the premier, Minto's father-in-law) to 'support his whole later foreign policy towards Italy, even to its most extreme extravagances and immoralities'.[31]

This was grotesque, for Minto, with his cry of 'Italian independence' (which was no part of his mandate) compromised Palmerston rather than the reverse. If there was a cabinet minister bitten by the bug of Italian nationalism it was Minto not Palmerston, and if there was another, it was Russell not Palmerston. The cabinet, against Palmerston's advice, rejected the Hummelauer–Palmerston Plan because it did not include the surrender of Venetia, when Palmerston would have settled for the surrender of Lombardy. Yet it was against Palmerston that, a month later, the Prince fired a thunderbolt, because he would not now recommend this Plan to Charles Albert. Palmerston had pointed out that, if, as was probable, such advice was rejected, British influence would suffer for having tendered it, and if it was accepted, it would be undesirable for it to be known that Britain was behind it, since it would be very unpopular in Northern Italy.[32] The Queen replied (but the words were Albert's) that she was 'ashamed of the policy we are pursuing in the Italian controversy, in abetting wrong, and this for the object of gaining influence'.[33] The Palace was unable to see beyond Austria's treaty rights, could think of the Italians only as rebels, and of Charles Albert (though his dynasty was about the oldest in the Almanack de Gotha) only as a traitor to the brotherhood of princes. *They* could not understand 'why Charles Albert ought to get any additional territory', why Palmerston clung so stubbornly to his 'scheme of establishing a Kingdom of Upper Italy stretching from one sea to the other . . . [for which] scheme all considerations of ancient alliance with Austria, of the peace of Europe, the regard for treaties etc etc are to be sacrificed'.[34] Was Palmerston mediating between belligerents or trying to obtain advantage for a client? they asked later. Why did England not adhere to 'strict right and justice', to 'principles of justice and international faith'?[35] *They* altogether disapproved Palmerston's willingness to co-operate with the French in Italy, not seeing that he was willing to bring them in only when they could not be kept out. The monarchical prejudice which caused them to distrust General Cavaignac because the mother of that champion of Order was the widow of a regicide prevented them initially from seeing why relations with Paris should be cordial, and not merely correct, and why some courtesy should be shown to the envoy of the republic.[36] *They* were hostile to the suggestion that Normanby should be restored to ambassadorial status, and furious when Palmerston contrived this by a stratagem.[37] *They* could not forgive Normanby his 'uncalled for' approach to the French, asking why Britain should introduce the French into Italy and enter into an entente cordiale with the French republic against Austria.[38] They alleged that Palmerston was motivated by vindictiveness towards Louis Philippe, Guizot and Aberdeen, and the desire to recover from the 'almost personal' setback of Custozza. The French, of course, wanted the entente 'as a means of propping up their republic', but 'this can be no consideration for us'.[39]

Could anything be more transparent, more innocent of understanding of Palmerston's technique of restraint by co-operation than the sharp reproof composed on the yacht *Victoria and Albert* en route from London to Aberdeen early in September? Palmerston, *They* said, had agreed prospectively to 'a war against Austria to take from her a province which she holds by the Treaty of Vienna, to which we are a party. This is a line of policy to which the Queen cannot give her consent. It is quite immaterial, whether French troops alone are employed for such an unjust purpose, if this is done on previous concert with England'.[40] Could anything confirm more strongly Palmerston's contempt for the royal effort to alter the slant of British policy, and the motive which informed it? In a withering reply he said that of course he might have declared that England would join the Austrians against the French — only the government, the parliament and the country would not stand for it. Or he could have said that if the French entered Italy they might do as they liked, go as far as they liked, and settle matters as they liked. But he did not think this would have been effective in restraining them![41] The Palace persuaded Russell to assent to a conference on Italy to be held at Brussels, though Palmerston disliked the idea of a gathering at which the French would be bound to raise the whole question of territorial revisions. The Palace hoped that the conference would secure a reaffirmation of Austria's title to Lombardy and Venetia. Palmerston was anxious that the British representative should be Normanby. The Palace would not hear of it. 'If the object of our mediation were only to drive the Austrians out of their lawful dominions in Italy by means of threatening with French invasion, Lord Normanby would be the best instrument for the purpose, as he has throughout taken a most violent Italian line from his present connection with Italy and the Italians, holding even the doctrine that Lombardy belongs to the King of Sardinia as annexed . . . by universal suffrage under the sovereignty of the people, but this is a policy to which the Queen cannot assent.' Britain ought to be represented by the ambassador at Vienna, Lord Ponsonby — '. . . the Queen is always much pleased with the frankness with which he states his opinions to Lord Palmerston'.[42]

There is no sign that the Queen and the Prince realized that Palmerston was, in general, less of a revisionist than the cabinet, and certainly than Minto and Lord John Russell. At the time of the Lamartine circular the premier told Wellington that the annexation of Cracow had given the French ground for saying they were bound by the Treaty of Vienna only as long as they chose to be so. In a memorandum of 1st May 1848 he accepted that it would not be becoming or expedient for Britain to proclaim the invalidity of the 1815 treaties. But he held that current developments 'formed as good a ground for new transactions as the events of 1813–15 did for the Treaties of Vienna. Nor are these changes to be less justified in reason. . . . It is impossible to deny that France has as good a right to assist the movement of 1848 as Prussia and Austria had to assist the movement of 1813' against France and against 'treaties as sacred as that of 1815'. One ought not to go on clinging to the wreck if a safe spar was within reach. Although his actual proposals involved only the extrusion of Austria from Italy by Anglo-French mediation, the transfer from Britain to Austria of the protectorate over the Ionian Isles, and compensation for France in Savoy, Russell was obviously more of a revisionist in principle than Palmerston.[43] The Foreign Secretary never wrote in such terms. He had done his best for a policy which rested on no abstraction, unless the Balance of Power be regarded as such, and it had been a very good best. Because Radetzky succeeded beyond expectation in restoring the morale and fighting efficiency of Austria's long-service troops, singularly unaffected by the news of revolution and civil war in their varied homelands, he had not managed to secure the one revision of the Treaty of Vienna which he favoured. He had not, therefore, succeeded in providing for the future stability of Italy, a stability in which constitutionalism could flourish. But he had helped materially to prevent a war between two great Powers, and to keep the French out of Italy.[A]

[A] The French moved to Rome April 1849, but even when they showed themselves disposed to restore the Pope, Palmerston could hardly believe they would adopt 'the system of Metternich and Petersburg' (i.e. restore the Pope without the constitution he had granted in 1848). But they did!

Well might Russell tell the Queen in January 1849 that he entirely agreed with Palmerston in all the main features of his foreign policy, and meant to defend the course taken which preserved peace in Europe during one of the most trying years ever known.[44] But at the Palace they never understood Palmerston's policy aright. The Queen and the Prince, Greville reports, 'had seen with great satisfaction the downfall of the Hungarian cause, and chuckled not a little at the idea of its being a mortification to Palmerston'.[45] It was nothing of the kind. It had not occurred to him to champion a Hungarian republic, because from that only Russia could gain. 'If I might be allowed to express in one sentence the principle which I think ought to guide an English minister', he told the Commons early in 1848, 'I would adopt the expression of Canning, and say that with every British minister the interests of England ought to be the shibboleth of his policy.' The Poles, the Hungarians, the Roumanians, the Sicilians, the Venetians, the Germans — especially the Germans of Schleswig — knew that he was as good as his word.

CHAPTER XIII

A SOURCE OF CONTENTION

IT is possible that Palmerston would not long have survived at the Foreign Office after 1848 if the Palace had tried less hard to get him out. Ever since his return in 1846 Greville had noted, quarter by quarter, sometimes month by month, examples of rashness and independence which made a mockery of Russell's assurance to doubters in December 1845 that under him the Foreign Office would be 'a Department of the Government', its affairs 'considered in common, and not dealt with according to [Palmerston's] will and pleasure'.[1] Palmerston seemed to regard the conduct of foreign policy as a sort of game of hide-and-seek with the Palace and his colleagues. Sometimes one got caught, but hoped for better luck next time. 'On matters where he fully believed that he was master of the subject his conclusions were very decided and positively unchangeable,' writes a relative.[2] He did not take kindly to cabinet supervision, for there were 'very few public men in England who follow up foreign affairs sufficiently to foresee the consequences of events which have not happened' and those who did not were 'generally for the doubting line'.[3] He knew that while no colleague shared the Palace's illiberality many shared the Palace's distaste for his over-vehement language, his hectoring tone, and that some (especially Earl Grey) were passivists who wished for a quiet and peaceful policy of non-intervention, permitting retrenchment, and thought it no business of Britain's to trumpet her opinions in cases where she did not mean to act. He was impatient and evasive of restraint by 'the Broadbrims of the cabinet', as he called them, and often violated the spirit, if not the letter, of cabinet directives. This was what his critics had feared. Their attitude is well explained in a gloss on Earl Grey's attitude of December 1845:[4]

'. . . You may think to control tendencies — but not intentions . . . You may expect new things from caprice, but not from determined will. . . . You may check what you know, but you may be fatally committed by acts concealed and purposes unavowed. Such *has* been before, the case between us and this colleague — between him and Parliament. . . . [He] is not to be trusted. Be it from arrogance — be it from inveterate, unacknowledged, yet not deliberately culpable predilections if you will:— still, the fact remains, he has undershafts and galleries in which he labours at his solitary tasks . . . which are only disclosed to us when some mine is to be sprung, when the match is already lighted, and we have nothing to do but retire behind the screen he provides. . . . [He] *cannot* be controlled, and . . . we have oft-times been puppets in his hands. . . . Lord Palmerston cannot act secretly, and at the same time enjoy the benefits of frankness and candour. . . .'

Greville himself is a hostile witness, almost counsel for the prosecution, but his sources of information and rumour included the premier's brother, Bedford, and Clarendon, and there were certainly occasions when he was entitled to write that Palmerston's colleagues were 'full of resentment and mortification', because they found themselves 'completely implicated' without having been 'really consulted'.[5] Colleagues felt that Palmerston did not try very hard before the Spanish Marriages to rebuild the entente, and that Normanby, with Palmerston's approval, sabotaged a cabinet decision to seek a rapprochement after the Marriages. Greville says that Palmerston actually threatened to break off diplomatic relations unless Guizot made reparation to Normanby, but did not bother to tell the premier when he came to dinner. Russell happened to hear of this because he was with Wood (Chancellor of the Exchequer) when Clarendon called, the latter having heard it from Beauvale to whom the French ambassador, St Aulaire, had repaired after Palmerston saw him. 'Oh, no, he won't do that', said Russell. 'But he has done it', replied Clarendon. Russell was able to prevent St Aulaire reporting officially to Paris.[6] Even though the bellows were at work, there was fire beneath this smoke. Palmerston, as ever, was 'gay and dégagé', where, according to Greville, 'an honourable, straightforward man would not have acted as he did; a high-spirited one would not have endured such a rebuff and mortification'. It is, of course, absurd to deny Palmerston's high spirits; he regarded such rebuffs as a natural part of 'the game'. He could never see anything sinister in his attitude to cabinet control, for, of course, he was sure that the honour and interests of the country were safe in his hands, and would be safe in no other.

When the Bulwer affair was breaking, Greville thought that 'this must be the crisis' concerning the independent administration of the Foreign Office. But he soon changed his mind — 'I expect that Palmerston's audacity and good fortune, his rare dexterity, and total absence of sensitiveness will carry him through. They will probably . . . content themselves with some mild remonstrance in private, which he will receive with perfect good humour and treat with sovereign contempt.'[7] This was prescient. Important colleagues were angry. Lansdowne told Russell 'it must never happen again'; he must see the dispatches before they went. Wood wrote to the same effect after Bulwer's expulsion. Earl Grey complained that the events in Madrid were only the climax of 'the general system of intermeddling' and gave formal notice that he could take no part in defending Palmerston in the Lords, and that if taxed with disapproving his policy 'would be compelled by silence at least to admit it'.[8] It was notorious, said Greville, that most ministers would have disapproved the use of such a tone, and that they first read the dispatch in the newspapers. Russell himself was irritated (though he had apparently had an opportunity to see one of the two controversial dispatches to Bulwer). Palmerston's effort to avoid giving effect to Russell's wishes (really the Queen's) over the dispatch to Seymour in Lisbon shortly followed. A few weeks later Russell wrote to him: 'It is surely right that a person speaking in the name of her Majesty's Government should in important affairs submit his dispatches to the Queen and obtain the opinion of her Prime Minister before he commits the Queen and her Government. This necessary preliminary you too often forget.'[9] Russell was no better pleased than the Queen to learn that an important communication from Russia had been concealed by Palmerston until the fugitive Prince of Prussia mentioned it to Victoria and Albert.

On the other hand, Russell could not easily be brought to sacrifice Palmerston at the prompting of the Palace or one or two colleagues. It might be very unsafe to do so, for neither before nor after the general election of 1847 did the Whigs (even counting all Liberals, Radicals and Irish as of their following) command a majority of the House of Commons, though it is true that the Peelites (in general critical of Palmerston) held the balance. But Russell was himself no strict non-interventionist. He was a partisan in Europe's ideological war, and even showed some signs of being a partisan of Nationalism as well as constitutionalism. Palmerston certainly spoke for the premier as well as himself when he said in parliament on 5th June 1848 'although the British Government has

been in ancient alliance with and on friendly terms with the
Emperor of Austria, yet it cannot but feel a lively sympathy with
in the endeavours — and I hope successful endeavours — which
have lately been made in Italy and by the people of Italy to obtain
for themselves free and constitutional government'. When Russell
was eventually driven to propose (abortively) a successor to
Palmerston, his choice was — *Minto*.[10] Russell was not to be
tricked by the Palace into implicit acceptance of the proposition
that Palmerston, from false principles and improper partisanship,
was repeating in Italy the undesirable features of his intervention
in the internal affairs of Spain, Portugal and Greece, or into a
retrospective condemnation of the Minto Mission. While the royal
letters are full of complaints of injustice to 'poor Austria', so unreasonably expected to give up territory to suit Palmerston's whim
or his penchant for the French republic, Russell applauded, as a
precedent for the amendment of the 'forced arrangements of 1815'
the separation of Belgium from Holland. His programme was that
'Lombardy must have a civil Government virtually if not nominally
independent of Vienna; Sicily must have a Legislature and
Administration virtually independent of Naples'. Unfortunately
Vienna and Naples opposed compromise, but, if there was a short
reaction, it could, Russell said, only increase the strength of the
republicans in Italy as in Germany.[11] While the Queen wrote to
Uncle Leopold: '*What* a very bad figure we cut in this mediation!
Really it is quite immoral, with Ireland quivering in our grasp and
ready to throw off her allegiance at any moment, for us to force
Austria to give up her lawful possessions. What shall we say if
Canada, Malta etc begin to trouble us!' Russell wrote to Palmerston: 'We have now exhausted argument to induce Austria to give
up Lombardy. Your despatches on this subject cannot be surpassed,
and can only be repeated.'[12]

Russell would have been a nincompoop not to realize that,
although the Queen had just grounds for complaint at the non-
submission of dispatches before they were sent off, the real object
of the Palace was to change policy, and at least to change its slant.
When the Queen declared that the 'system of diplomacy which
makes the taking up of party politics in foreign countries its
principal object' was condemned by the Queen, Lord John, the
Cabinet and public opinion in and out of parliament,[13] she cannot
really (or can she?) have expected the Whig premier to assent to

the proposition that but for the Howard de Waldens, Bulwers, Lyonses and Seymours working their master's wicked will, all would be smooth in Madrid, Lisbon and Athens. Russell replied that he was unwilling to raise a question with Palmerston 'in the present critical state of Europe which might induce a belief that he had not conducted foreign affairs to the satisfaction of his colleagues or of his Sovereign'. And he added that it was 'just to Lord Palmerston to say that his general course of policy has met with the warm approval of the Cabinet, and that the cases of difference of judgement have been rare exceptions'.[14] Three months later, in September 1848, the Queen, whose dissatisfaction with Palmerston's conduct of foreign affairs was profound, summoned Russell to Balmoral to tell him that she felt really she could hardly go on with Palmerston, 'that I had no confidence in him, and that it made me seriously anxious and uneasy for the welfare of the country and for the peace of Europe in general', and that she often felt quite ill from anxiety. Palmerston, she said, was very vindictive, and that Spanish Marriage question, 'which had been the original cause of so many present misfortunes, would never have become so embrouillé had it not been for Lord Palmerston'; and that 'all that had been done in Italy last winter had also done harm, as it was done by Lord Palmerston'. So she was afraid that some day she should have to tell Russell that she could not put up with Palmerston any longer. By her own account, 'it ended by Lord John's promising to bear the subject in mind, and I must say that he took it all just as I could wish'. But all Russell had said was that his brother (after a talk with the Queen and the Prince) had already made him aware how strongly Her Majesty felt about it, and that he thought her anxiety 'a little overrated'; that he regretted if Palmerston was distrusted everywhere abroad (i.e. in royal palaces) and that, as the Queen put it, 'his writings were always as bitter as gall and did great harm'. His colleague, he said, 'was a very able man, entirely master of his office and of affairs, and a very good colleague, never making any difficulties about other questions, but (certainly unreasonably) complaining of other people mixing with and interfering in the affairs of his office'. He did not join the Queen in blaming Palmerston, via the Spanish Marriages and the Minto Mission, for all the troubles of 1848, nor in the judgement that 'he often endangered the honour of England by taking a very prejudiced and one-sided view of a question' (to which the Queen added the complaint that 'he was not always straightforward in his conduct and kept back things which he did not like should be known').[15] Russell shared some of the Queen's uneasiness, but he did not share her prejudices; they smacked too much of all that Whiggery abominated.

The Palace's current candidate for the Foreign Office was Clarendon, but Russell would not have considered him, because he seemed at that time 'pro-Austrian', and Clarendon did not long remain the royal candidate. His remark when the Palace in due course denied him the succession to Palmerston — 'The Queen and the Prince are wrong in wishing that courtiers, rather than ministers, should conduct the affairs of the country. . . . They labour under the curious mistake that the Foreign Office is their peculiar department and that they have a right to control, if not to direct, the foreign policy of England', was not mere sour grapes. More than four years earlier Clarendon had complained to Greville that *They* had developed in Aberdeen's time a habit of inconvenient meddling, and Greville apparently then concurred in the conclusion that Palmerston's defects were rather useful in dealing with the Court — 'To their wishes or remonstrances he expresses the greatest deference, and then he goes on in his own course without paying the least attention to what they have been saying to him.'[16] Russell often had to pass on to Palmerston royal reprimands, and sometimes add his own, when the Foreign Secretary neglected the normal courtesies. Palmerston regarded the Queen's right to see and approve documents as a mere formality which was being improperly used for the purpose not merely of subjecting them to the opinion of the premier and sometimes the cabinet, but of trying to amend or even veto them. After the interview at Balmoral, Russell wrote to Palmerston, who replied airily that the Queen was 'constantly suffering under groundless uneasiness'. Russell retorted that it was not always groundless, and that important dispatches ought to be submitted. But he hastened to add: 'as I agree with you very constantly in opinion, my only wish is that in future you will save the Queen anxiety, and me some trouble, by giving your reasons before, and not after, an important despatch is sent'. Russell felt that Palmerston too often by-passed the cabinet. He could not, ex officio, condone those many 'inadvertences' or 'mistakes in the hurry of business' — contrary, Palmerston assured him, to the standing orders he had given —

which were, as the Prince would justly allege, conducted 'upon principle, and with astonishing pertinacity'.[17] But he had more than a sneaking sympathy with Palmerston. Both ministers understood that more was at stake than mere formality. They were faced with an attempt on the part of the Palace not only to influence foreign policy but, in doing so, to extend the power of the monarch, or, at the very least, to maintain it against the tide which inexorably eroded it.

Only a few years were to pass before Bagehot formulated his famous thesis that the sovereign had but three rights — to be consulted, to encourage, and to warn; that she belonged to the dignified, as distinct from the efficient part of the constitution. It is not so well known that, while Bagehot accepted that the monarch's *power* had virtually gone, he held that the monarch's *influence* could be great, and that, if he had lived longer, Prince Albert's influence would have been very great indeed. The Queen never overtly claimed for herself the power to withhold assent from a decision of the cabinet deliberately arrived at, and Albert rarely admitted, even privately, pretensions on her behalf incompatible with Bagehot's maxims. Bagehot quotes as exemplary the royal memorandum to the prime minister (later revealed by him to the House of Commons) anticipated in the Prince's private letter of 2nd April 1850 to Russell — 'the sovereign has a right to demand from him that she be made thoroughly acquainted with the whole object and tendency of the policy to which her consent is required, and, having given that consent, that the policy is not arbitrarily altered from the original line, that important steps are not concealed from her and her name used without her sanction'.[18] Albert told Palmerston himself, that August, that the Queen quite understood that, if she was overruled by the cabinet, she must support ministers in executing a policy of which she disapproved.[19] The Prince, while consciously endeavouring to maintain and even increase the royal influence, was hardly conscious that, as an admiring biographer puts it, he was straining the constitutional authority of the Queen to the limit.[20] But the memorandum, in claiming the right of dismissal of a foreign secretary for *lèse-majesté* was, for the middle of the nineteenth century, anomalous. Foreigners do not readily understand the British distinction between the laws of the constitution, enforceable by the courts, and its *conventions*, which depend on general acceptance. Albert, like Victoria's mother,

Uncle Leopold and Cousin Ferdinand, came from the house of Saxe-Coburg, too many members of which had a sense of mission to bring light and leading to countries into which they had not been born. He shared Uncle Leopold's regret at the degradation of monarchical power which followed from the Reform Bill, the most evident example of which was that William IV in 1835 and Victoria in 1841 had to accept governments at the bidding of the electorate. His mentor was Baron Stockmar, and it was Stockmar who reported that 'the Queen had an undoubted constitutional right to visit with the dismissal of that minister' an act of 'dishonesty' towards the Crown such as the arbitrary modification of a measure which had received the royal sanction.[21] Both the Prince's letter of 2nd April and the Queen's formal memorandum were based on this *Uitlander* adviser's opinion. Moreover, Albert himself once let the mask of constitutional propriety slip, and told a Whig prime minister that he 'held the sovereign to have immense moral responsibility upon his shoulders with regard to his government and the duty to *whatch* [sic] *and control* it'.[22]

This was a pretension which no Whig prime minister, least of all Russell, the arch-Whig of the day, could admit. When he agreed with the Queen that Palmerston, even at the risk of provoking him to resignation, must be required to sign the dispatch to Seymour which, in its altered form, he so disliked, Russell insisted that 'it would not be conducive to your Majesty's service, nor agreeable to the wholesome maxims of the Constitution, to mix your Majesty's name with a proceeding which may lead to the most serious consequences'.[23] The persistence of the Palace in attempts both to increase or maintain the power of the Crown and to change, in an illiberal direction, the foreign policy of the country was self-defeating if, as seems probable, it deterred the premier from taking his own initiatives to restrain Palmerston. Lord John was often a poor judge of men and of affairs, but his Whig antennae were sensitive enough when it came to detecting monarchical encroachment. He was proud of an ancestry which was, in theory, republican, while the Queen and her consort were proud to belong to a 'union of princes'. It must be remembered also that Palmerston was older than Uncle Leopold, and Russell barely younger than Leopold. Palmerston had been head of a government department for ten years when Victoria and Albert were born. When he entered on his third term as Foreign Secretary in 1846 he was nearly sixty-two, and *They* were twenty-seven. He had held that office longer than Victoria had reigned and longer than Albert had been in the country. He had forty years' experience of British politics to Victoria's nine and Albert's seven. He had accumulated a vast knowledge of foreign affairs and experience of diplomacy. Though in personal dealings at Court he was (on the high authority of Prince Albert, who despised the British aristocracy) exceedingly well mannered, he was a masterful and self-confident man, and no respecter of rank — George IV had complained of his manner 'si fier'. He loved the spice of danger, and in his duel with the Palace he found it. He relished it the more because he did not rate very high the risk of being turned out. Russell, on the other hand, for ever being called upon to arbitrate between the Foreign Office and the Palace, was sorely harassed.

*   *   *   *

It was always easy to make a plausible case for removing Palmerston from the conduct of foreign affairs. The end of 1848 was no exception. Those who, like Greville, thought it 'a great thing to see reaction everywhere, and the revolutionary and democratick tide rolled back which has been deluging all Europe',[24] complained of unnecessarily bad relations with Austria at a time when a great question mark overhung British relations with the new ruler of France. But even those who regretted the victory of reaction must wonder whether Palmerston was the most appropriate representative of a Liberal Britain which had to co-exist with triumphant and vengeful reactionaries.

The Queen and the Prince were, of course, among the former. According to Greville, they poured out to Clarendon (a minister) their extreme dissatisfaction with the policy of the last six or eight months, their abhorrence of Charles Albert and their entire sympathy with the reactions now going on. Palmerston had complained to Russell that 'the Queen gives ear too readily to persons who are hostile to her Government, and who wish to poison her mind with distrust of her Ministers', and now he wrote to Ponsonby: 'Pray make the Camarilla understand that, in a constitutional country like England, those things cannot answer; and that a foreign Government which places its reliance upon working upon the Court against the Government of this country is sure to be disappointed'.[25] When Schwarzenberg branded Palmerston as the public enemy of European order, and told Koller to hold no unnecessary, and no social, intercourse with him, the Austrian chargé d'affaires was instructed to explain to the Queen that it was 'impossible to be on friendly terms with England so long as the present foreign secretary has control of affairs'.[26] Further to mark the disapproval of the Ballplatz, no archduke was sent to announce to the Court of St James the accession of the new emperor, Franz Josef. The Queen and Prince, who had encouraged Peel and Aberdeen — likely beneficiaries of Palmerston's fall — to attack his Portuguese policy in Parliament, now sent *Aberdeen* to tell the chargé d'affaires that they quite understood that this insult was directed against Palmerston and not the Queen.[27] Palmerston's prime offence was his denunciation of Austrian repression in Northern Italy. He described Radetzky's proclamation of the death sentence on Italians found in possession of arms as 'a savage proclamation, which savours more of the barbarous usage of centuries long gone by than of the spirit of present times', and the sequestration of property as 'imitat[ing] the most universally condemned excesses of the most desperate and unprincipled Revolutionists'.[28] And, of course, he continued to say that the Austrians ought to give up Lombardy.

In January 1849 it seemed to the Palace that delivery was at hand. Russell wrote to say that, if Lansdowne, the elder statesman of the cabinet, agreed, he would propose to Palmerston that he became Lord Lieutenant of Ireland, with an earldom or the Garter and a United Kingdom barony. He imagined that Palmerston would resign rather than put his signature to a note which the premier was prepared to insist should be sent to the Government of Naples.[29]

The question arose out of the revolt of the Sicilians against the Neapolitans, the first of the outbreaks of 1848. Minto had failed to get the Bourbons to agree to a purely personal union of the two kingdoms, on the lines of that between England and Scotland from 1603 to 1707. By the time that other revolutions, including the French, had shaken the Bourbons, the Sicilians had stiffened, and all Minto could do was dissuade them from becoming republican. It is to be noted that Palmerston, true to the basic British prejudice against permanent commitments, declined to 'guarantee' a personal union, though he thought it the best solution. But he vastly approved of Admiral Parker saluting the flag of independent Sicily (before orders from Palmerston to do so arrived), welcomed Minto's threat to resign unless the Sicilians were aided against a counter-assault from the mainland and, with the aid of this threat, induced the cabinet to join with republican France to impose an armistice and mediate on the basis of personal union. Meanwhile, the provisional government of Sicily placed a large order with a British contractor for munitions. The contractor could not immediately supply these guns, because he had just made a large delivery to Her Majesty's Ordnance. Hearing of this difficulty, Palmerston told the Ordnance there would be no objection to releasing the guns so that the Sicilians could have them.

Palmerston's colleagues — and the Palace — knew nothing of this until an article in *The Times* of 19th January 1849 set Lansdowne and Wood inquiring of Reeve and Delane (the editor of *The Times*). Russell declared that 'we ought as a strong power to do voluntarily what we should enforce upon a weaker State'. An apology must be sent to the Neapolitan government. Palmerston could not understand why, since Bomba had made no representations on the subject, but at the cabinet of 23rd January, to the general surprise, he agreed to send such an apology. The Queen and the Prince were furious, and demanded that Palmerston 'pay the penalty . . . for . . . want of ingenuousness' and for the humiliation of Britain in having to apologize to a government 'which stands so very low in public estimation'. But Russell said that he and Lansdowne 'felt very strongly that, after the many most unjust attacks made from all sides upon Lord Palmerston' (did his royal auditors blush?) it would look cowardly to throw him over. For 'the Government had approved of the whole foreign policy and considered it to be right in the main features'.

The royal regret that Palmerston had not resigned or been dismissed was all the greater when the signs mounted that Charles Albert was planning a desperate throw, and the Queen naturally found in Palmerston's drafts to Normanby the old 'partial' spirit. Wearily she warned Russell to watch for 'any other gradual deviation from the line of justice and impartiality'. But Palmerston, insisting, predictably, that he was 'an impartial mediator' between Austria and Piedmont, 'refused to go on his knees before Prince Schwarzenberg'.[30] After Novara, he could not bring himself to offer the Austrian diplomat Colloredo the customary congratulations on victory offered by everyone else at Court (a breach of etiquette which shocked Lansdowne). Soon the Palace was raging at the latest example of one of Palmerston's favourite techniques. Addressing himself to the question of the heavy indemnity Austria demanded of Piedmont, he repeated the French ambassador's argument that the demand was not only 'cruel and oppressive' but impolitic, as it would tend to drive the new king Victor Emmanuel into the arms of France. Even Russell objected to this dispatch, because of its 'dry and disparaging tone' towards Austria.[31] They must, he said, support France or court Austria. Palmerston had striven mightily to keep the French out of Italy, and he was not pleased when in April 1849 Louis Napoleon sent troops to Rome, with no very clear idea why, except to show the flag of France in an Austrian preserve (temporarily seized by Mazzini's republican poachers) at a time when (because the Austrians were engaged in Hungary) there was no prospect of a general war resulting. Palmerston's answer, however, to the alternative posed by Russell, was a refusal to go 'beyond civility . . . to the extent of any sacrifice of truth, principle or justice'. To do so would be to lose France without gaining Austria — 'We cannot outbid Russia in these matters; no fair words of ours can outweigh the fine divisions of the Autocrat' (which on 8th May intervened in Hungary).[32] Palmerston, when Austria in April increased her demands on Piedmont, was in favour of the French entering Savoy and the British entering Genoa, as a warning to Austria. From this the cabinet flinched; all he could secure was moral support for French action 'in case of necessity'. The Prince pounced on this, and an explanation was demanded. Palmerston replied, in a fine parody of the Queen's letters in support of Austria, that he had told the French ambassador he was convinced that the British Government would willingly join in 'assisting to rescue from such oppressive terms an ancient ally whose political independence is an important element in the balance of power in Europe'. The Palace believed Colloredo in July, as it had believed Metternich in December 1847, when he said that English support (for Piedmont) was the only obstacle to peace in Italy. The cabinet did not, but Russell felt it proper to remind Palmerston that 'Austria was our ally as well as Piedmont.'[33]

At this time, Palmerston was not unfavourable to the Erfurt scheme for the closer unity of Germany under Prussian leadership. But the effect of this approximation of view between Palmerston and the Palace (which had been suspicious of the effect of the abortive Frankfort constitution on the status of the ruling princes, and preferred the current scheme) was obscured by fresh differences of opinion on the question of Schleswig. There had been a renewal of war between the Danes and the Germans (in effect, the Prussians), from which King Frederick William desisted only because of the Tsar's disapproval, combined with Anglo-French diplomatic pressure. The Queen criticized Palmerston for pressing Prussia too strongly; he replied that British trade was being adversely affected. The Queen continued to complain that Palmerston's mediation was not sufficiently directed to securing what was right and fair. The Germans had the right and duty to see that the independence of Schleswig was secured before they abandoned the duchy; there must be sufficient securities against its incorporation into Denmark. The armistice and peace preliminaries of 10th July provided for the separation of Schleswig from Denmark (a defeat for Danish nationalism); for the policing of the north by the Swedes and the south by the Prussians, pending a treaty; for the administration of the duchy by a commission consisting of a Dane and a Prussian and an Englishman, who would in fact have to decide all disputed questions. The Queen acquiesced only under violent protest in the appointment by Palmerston of Colonel Hodges (a diplomat whose record in Serbia had been, to say the least, unpromising). He was, she declared, strongly prejudiced in favour of the Danes.[34]

It cannot be pretended that Palmerston's colleagues were pleased with him. Some felt as Greville did that on the matter of the Sicilian arms Russell had allowed both the dignity of the Crown and the proper authority of his office to be degraded and insulted.[35] Certainly Lansdowne, as Leader of the House of Lords, was much embarrassed. Even the premier said that he did not know how the sale of arms could be defended. Palmerston, however, replied that, if challenged in parliament, he would lay the papers, and put the incident in the context of far greater 'interferences', such as the saluting of the flag. The note to Naples said that the arms had been released 'inadvertently' (which was untrue) and on that adverb Lansdowne had to rely when challenged by the leader of the Opposition, Stanley (6th March 1849). Two months later Lansdowne again found himself in a false position. After inquiries at the Foreign Office, he told the peers that it was not true that Colloredo had explained to Palmerston the Austrian attitude on the Piedmont indemnity. The Austrians insisted that he had, and Palmerston then remarked that he had quite forgotten the interview.[36] Russell, as we have noted, was worried at the bitterness of Palmerston's tone towards the Austrians. He was prepared, therefore, to be accommodating when the Prince insisted on a proper oversight of official messages sent abroad. It was arranged that all dispatches (Palmerston pointed out that there were 28,000 per annum both ways) for transmission abroad should go to the Palace via the premier, and that the Queen (more often than not in effect the Prince) would make any 'remarks' to Russell, not Palmerston. Palmerston grumbled that this procedure would 'reduce my flint-gun to a match-lock', but said he would give instructions accordingly, and induced Russell to insert into a letter to the Prince a caution against any delay on the Queen's part in returning the drafts.[37]

In connexion with this arrangement three points should be noted. It was not really any gain on the part of the Palace to bring the prime minister so consistently into the picture; it might help restrain Palmerston but it would not enhance the royal authority, because Russell was congenitally suspicious of it. Secondly, while it reduced to a minimum the need for direct contact and controversy between the Palace and Palmerston (the Prince having decided that Palmerston's wrong-headedness was chronic and irremediable, so that the less contact there was, the better) it could not, as Russell's biographer suggests, deprive Palmerston of his constitutional right of direct access to the sovereign.[38] Palmerston used the arrangement as an excuse for not explaining himself to the Palace. And, thirdly, Russell continued to insist that, although, obviously, there were difficulties due to Palmerston's vehemence and want of frankness, there could be no question of any major change of policy. There could be no question of Clarendon succeeding Palmerston, because of his intimate connexion with *The Times* 'and the violent Austrian line of that paper'. There could be no change of persons 'which implied that we preferred the intimate alliance of Austria and Russia to those we had hitherto maintained'. The Palace was never left in any doubt that it was confronted by a prime minister resolutely opposed to any encroachment by royal power and by a cabinet of Liberal leanings. The best the Queen and the Prince could ever hope for was a change of persons and hence of 'slant', and their chief hope of securing that lay in the likelihood that sooner or later Russell would get tired of playing umpire between the Palace and the Foreign Office.

But Aberdeen, when he went to Balmoral in September 1849, was forced to indicate that he could see no prospect of Palmerston's deposition. For it was becoming evident that the man was popular.

* * * *

The long passage in the speech of July 1849, quoted in the previous chapter, on the importance of illiberal Austria (like illiberal Turkey) to 'the liberties of Europe', sincere though it was, could not banish from the Ballplatz or from Buckingham Palace the misconception of Palmerston, about which he joked to the electors of Tiverton — the idea that he was 'the great instigator of revolution — the friend and champion of all popular insurrections, the enemy of all constituted authorities . . . charged with disturbing the peace of Europe by giving encouragement to every revolutionary and anarchical set of men'.[39] In that speech he appealed to the national self-esteem of the British, by his insistence on their right to express an opinion on any subject of European concern, though doing so involved (as in the 1830s) a perpetual propaganda war against the purveyors of 'injustice and wrong'. Temperley and Penson describe this speech as 'politically . . . a masterpiece, for its sentiments brought the liberals to his side, while its realism won over the conservatives'.[40] The comments of Greville confirm at least the earlier part of this verdict. Already he had noticed that when the Tory Bankes returned to the charge about the Sicilian arms, Palmerston, far from being apologetic, made a sarcastic and joking reply and 'expressed ultra-liberal sentiments to please the Radicals, and he gathered shouts of laughter and applause as he dashed and rattled along'.[41] Of the great speech of 21st July he writes that it was a Saturday morning speech full of 'divers plausible claptraps for his Radical friends', delivered to an audience of about fifty M.P.s. Greville should have remembered that few had heard Palmerston on 1st June 1829. And, to do him justice, Greville did not underrate its effect. 'This exhibition was trumpeted forth as a great Palmerstonian triumph; and the close of the Session has left him and his spouse immoderately jubilant. It admits of no doubt that in spite of the enormous case there is against him, Palmerston has not only escaped undamaged, but seems to be invested with all the insignia of triumph. He is now evidently endeavouring to make for himself a great Radical interest in the H. of Commons, and this to increase his power, and render himself more indispensable to the Government by making them feel how dangerous he would be out of office.'

In this speech, on Hungary, Palmerston was justifying a policy of non-intervention and peace, but distinguishing, yet again, between non-intervention and disinterest, between peace and passivism. Peace is an object of policy, yes; but Britain must 'count for something in the transactions of the world'. Non-intervention is dictated by Britain's interest in the maintenance of the Habsburg element in the Balance of Power, but that does not mean one should abstain from 'friendly advice' (of the odious 'I think you ought to know' variety) or stay neutral between the contending factions of despotism and constitutionalism, or indifferent to evidences of gross inhumanity by allegedly civilized governments. Palmerston upbraided those who urged friendship with Austria for reasons which he regarded as wrong, contemptible, un-British.

. . . There are some persons who see in the relations of countries nothing but the intercourse of Cabinets. It is not as the ancient ally of England during the war; it is not as the means of resistance in the centre of Europe to any general disturbance of the balance of power; it is as the former symbol of resistance to improvement, political and social, that Austria has won the affections of some men in the conduct of public affairs. Sir, there are men who, having passed their whole lives in adoring the Government of Austria, because they deemed it the great symbol of the opinions which they entertained, at last became fickle in their attachment, and transferred their allegiance to the Government of France, because they thought they saw in that Government an almost equal degree of leaning to the arbitrary principle, and because they, forsooth, suspected that Government of designs hostile to the interests of freedom. . . .

Avowedly directed against Aberdeen, this was quite as wounding to the Queen and the Prince, and if it misrepresents Aberdeen, it does so rather less than people misrepresented Palmerston when they described him as a purveyor of anarchy who, to quote Metternich 'sets the house on fire, disables the fireman and then presents himself as the moderator of the fire'.[42] When one considers that the Hungarian cause attracted unusual sympathy in Britain (much more, for instance, than that of the Poles), and perhaps caused even Cobden a rare doubt as to the virtue of non-'intervention' in its strictest sense, it is not surprising that another breed of Radicals roared approval of Palmerstonian strictures on Habsburg policy. These, as we have seen, were not confined to occasional speeches in the House of Commons; they became the commonplace of dispatches. Not only did the Austrians fail to grant the vanquished Hungarians an amnesty and a modernized form of their ancient constitution. Their inhumanity shocked the Tsar. Their atrocities in Hungary and Transylvania, as earlier in Italy and Galicia, were, wrote Palmerston 'only to be equalled by the proceedings of the negro race in Africa and Haiti. Their late exploit of flogging forty odd people, including two women, at Milan, some of the victims being gentlemen, is really too blackguard and disgusting a proceeding'. The Austrians were 'really the greatest brutes that ever called themselves by the undeserved name of civilised men'. Ponsonby was bidden to 'maintain the dignity and honour of England by expressing *openly* and *decidedly* the disgust which such proceedings excite in the public mind in this country'. Schwarzenberg had lived in England, and must know something of English feelings and ideas; surely he must see that the good opinion of England was of some value to Austria 'at least to act as a check to the ill-will towards Austria, which he supposes, or affects to suppose, is the great accentuating motive of the revolutionary firebrand who now presides at the Foreign Office in Downing Street'.[43]

Schwarzenberg lived by the sword. He did not believe that opinions were mightier than armies, and he scorned Palmerston's abuse. But punishment was at hand. Balance of Power considerations had restrained Palmerston from giving even moral support to the Hungarians while the Russians helped the Austrians crush them, but Balance of Power considerations made it desirable that Britain should back the Sultan in refusing the demands of the victors to yield up eight hundred Poles (three of them important generals) who had fought in Hungary against the Russians and 4,000 Hungarians, including the nationalist hero Kossuth. In approving Stratford's encouragement of Turkish resistance to this demand, Palmerston proposed to tell the ambassador to inform the Sultan that he might say he refused 'in consequence of our remonstrance'. This remark was struck out as a result of Prince Albert's intervention via Earl Grey, currently minister in attendance

K

at Balmoral. But, to Palmerston's delight (and somewhat to his surprise) his colleagues agreed to 'hold a bottle of salts to the nose of a lady who had been frightened'. Remonstrances would be made at Vienna and St Petersburg, and the British (and, it was hoped, French) ships would go to Besika Bay.[44]

Once again, one is struck by the delicacy and realism with which Palmerston and the Tsar conducted their relations in times of stress. The Tsar did not wish to provoke an international crisis unless insulted honour forced him; Palmerston, though resolved that Russia should be resisted, was careful to see that she was not provoked. 'In this affair', he said, 'we are trying to catch two great fish, and we must wind the reel very gently and dexterously, not to break the line . . . We must be able to show to Parliament that we have used all civility and forbearance, and that if hostilities ensue, they have not been brought on by any fault or mistake of ours.' So, on 2nd October 1849, the Turkish ambassador was asked for a formal written request to Britain for moral and material support, and Brunnow was told that, because a formal request had been made, Britain could not stand aside. When he remarked that it would be unfortunate if Britain and France were found acting together, Palmerston replied that the Turks had appealed to both and that 'this system of duality did not begin with us'. But Palmerston and Brunnow laid the foundation for a graceful Russian withdrawal. They agreed that doubtless the Russian and Austrian envoys at Constantinople had been over-zealous; they agreed that, though by the Treaty of Kainardji the Turks were bound to see that exiles did not conspire on Turkish soil against Russia, the Sultan was not bound to yield them up to the Tsar. Palmerston fully took Brunnow's point that it would be dangerous to adopt towards the Tsar any note of menace, and assured him that the remonstrance would be civil and friendly. Both Normanby in Paris and Stratford in Constantinople were enjoined most strictly to see that nothing was said in public about naval demonstrations.[46] The fleet would go up to the Bosphorus if the Sultan asked for it, but the Sultan was to be told not to ask for it unless it was absolutely necessary. One did not wish to threaten Russia — or to set her a bad example. The Russians reached agreement with a shrewdly chosen Turkish envoy on Russian soil on 16th October, and could claim not to have yielded to threats, for none had been made. Palmerston's apology for Admiral Parker having taken his ships, in a gale, within the castles of the Dardanelles (contrary to the Straits Convention of 1841) enabled Nesselrode to claim a triumph. The Tsar was rather cold towards the British ambassador when he returned from leave, but the trouble between Britain and Russia was over, and Britain had re-asserted her interest in Turkish independence.[47]

Palmerston was delighted to find the Austrians more stubborn than the Russians. By the end of November he was describing their requirements as to the internment of the refugees as 'preposterous'. It was 'unreasonable and incompatible with the dignity and independence of the Sultan that he should be made the gaoler of the Emperor of Austria'.[48] The refugees were not kept in durance, under the inspection of Austrian officers, as the Ballplatz demanded. But it was two years before Palmerston could procure their freedom to leave Turkey. In February 1851 he told Stratford to explain to the Sultan and 'his white-livered ministers' (who were, after all, 'our protégés') that 'the enthusiasm of last year is rapidly turning into contemptuous disgust at their servile consent to perform the most degrading office of turnkey for Prince Schwarzenberg'.[49] It was the Sultan's refusal to yield up the Poles and Hungarians that first produced in the British public anything like enthusiasm for Turkey. This was sheer gain to a Balance of Power statesman. To Ponsonby in Vienna, indeed, it did not seem so, and the Queen and the Prince, unable to understand why Britain should jeopardize relations with imperial powers to rescue a few rebels, took over-seriously Vienna's refusal to accredit an ambassador to the Court of St James while Palmerston was Foreign Secretary. Palmerston sent Ponsonby a stinging rebuke: 'I desire you to do your best, though I hear from many quarters that you oppose instead of furthering the policy of your Government, and that you openly declare that you disapprove of our course. No diplomatist ought to hold such language as long as he holds his appointment. . . . It is idle trash to say we are hostile to Austria because we may disapprove of the policy of a Metternich or the cruelties of the Manning administration which now governs Austria.'[48]

We here see Palmerston behaving towards Austria as he had in the '30s, but with a new dimension of indignation added to his disapproval of illiberalism. For 'he bounded like a boy at any cruelty or oppression'.[50] He complained to Vienna not only of

Austrian brutality but of the monstrous treatment of political prisoners in the courts and gaols of the Bourbon king of the Two Sicilies. Aberdeen attacked him for this, but the Tory earl's private approaches to Vienna, at the behest of Gladstone, his devoted political follower, were ineffective. Gladstone, his Christianity submerging his politics, affronted Aberdeen by addressing to him two open letters which constituted a bitter indictment of the Neapolitan régime. Palmerston, so unlike Gladstone in moral and political character, congratulated him on this good work, boasted in parliament of having sent a copy of Gladstone's pamphlet to every Court in Europe, and told the Neapolitan envoy that it presented 'an afflicting picture of a system of illiberality, injustice and cruelty . . . such as might have been hoped would not have existed in any European country at the present day'.[51] In denouncing Austrian or Neapolitan inhumanity, and the impolicy of the humanity as well, Palmerston was entirely sincere. This is not denied by Sproxton, the author of *Palmerston and the Hungarian Revolution*, when contrasting Palmerston's caution before the fate of the Hungarians was sealed and his subsequent outspokenness. He concluded that the protests were a question 'partly — perhaps chiefly — of public opinion. For Palmerston . . . is the British statesman, par excellence, of public opinion. . . . *If it was possible to walk in the sunshine of popular favour without ignoring the path of duty, then Palmerston would do so*. Thus it comes about that as democratic passions mount at Tooting, and vituperation waxes more riotous at Notting Hill, the dispatches from the Foreign Office become more and more outspoken, and the advice less and less palatable. The Austrians deserved it, and *Hungary had been preserved to them, which was Palmerston's chief concern*'.[52] This is true, provided as much weight is given to the phrases italicized by the present author as to the rest of the quotation. Palmerston achieved popularity by 'being himself' — when the path of duty permitted. In 'being himself' he gave expression to, and represented, generous impulses in the national character. But soon he was to show that he also represented impulses commonly judged less admirable.

CHAPTER XIV

'THE MINISTER OF ENGLAND', 1850

I N one conjunction of circumstances only was Russell likely to consent to remove Palmerston from the Foreign Office. In the spring of 1850 this conjunction occurred. Palmerston's lack of straightforwardness in his relations with the monarch was matched by wanton disregard for the wishes of the cabinet, and with consequences which caused Russell to accept the royal verdict that Palmerston's diplomacy was a failure *judged by its results.* Palace and premier positively agreed that Palmerston was to go at the end of the session, and this Palmerston was told. The Greek affair, for ever associated with the name of Don Pacifico, had been decisive. Or so it seemed — until after the 'Don Pacifico debate' it proved impossible to dismiss Palmerston. He emerged, in 1850 as in 1840, as the one minister in a rather discredited government who had enjoyed a triumph and basked in popular favour.

In 1840 Palmerston had proposed to use Stopford's fleet, its mission in Syria accomplished, to extract reparations from Naples for injury to British economic interests. In 1850 he did use Parker's fleet, Malta-bound from Besika Bay, to exact from the Greek government apologies and compensations for wrongs done and rights denied to British subjects and British protected persons in Greece. Parker entered the harbour of the Piraeus, saluted the Greek flag, paid a courtesy call on King Otho, embarked the British minister, Wyse, and seized merchant ships and cargoes as 'security' against the payment of the claims.[1]

It must be understood that the issue between Palmerston and his colleagues, which now arose, was not principally the lack of proportion between the amount of the claims and the means used to secure their satisfaction. It was not the fact that a Portuguese Jew (who happened to be a British subject because he was born in Gibraltar) with a suspect story of vouchers allegedly proving a claim of £27,000 against the government of Portugal destroyed when an Athens mob pillaged his house, was hardly the most honourable personification of the British subject ill-treated in a foreign land. It was the way in which Palmerston had enraged major foreign Powers and the way in which he had treated his colleagues. The Greek government appealed to Russia and France and they, the co-guarantors with Britain of Greece, denied that British operations in the port of Athens could be dismissed as a private quarrel between Britain and Greece. Palmerston was indignant at the French attitude, for, in Morocco, the British consul-general Hay had just supported France in her extravagant demands for satisfaction for injuries and insults. The cabinet, however, wishing to avoid diplomatic isolation, agreed that, to assuage French pride, Baron Gros should be sent to Athens. Palmerston consented to alter his dispatch to Wyse to meet the insistence of Russell and the Queen that coercive measures should be suspended for three weeks and should not be resumed if a settlement seemed likely. This dispatch he sent off at once. But it was his view that the mission of Baron Gros had only one purpose — to secure Greek acceptance of the British demands. He did not share the cabinet's opinion that the claims, especially with regard to the Portuguese vouchers, might be compromised, at Wyse's discretion, and only after another cabinet meeting did he send off, by slow mail, and in grudging terms not in accord with the spirit of the cabinet's wishes, a permission to compromise. This communication he did not show Russell (because of the urgency!).[2]

The Palace could be relied upon to exploit the considerable annoyance of Palmerston's colleagues at such behaviour. Early in March 1850 Russell told Palmerston that the Queen's distrust was a serious impediment to the conduct of policy and suggested that, at the end of the session, he might leave the Foreign Office to become Leader of the House (Russell himself going to the Lords). Palmerston's reply was shrewd. He could not help having become aware, he said, that he had forfeited the Queen's confidence, 'but he thought this had not been on *personal* grounds but merely on account of his line of policy with which the Queen disagreed'.[3] He thus emphasized Russell's predicament. But he also warned the Prince that if Russell was to be induced to move Palmerston, it would be wise not to stress policy differences. The argument must be about results and methods, not aims and bias. So, when composing a considered indictment of the Foreign Secretary for the eye of the premier, dated 2nd April, Albert gave, as his main complaint, the fact that 'England was universally detested, mistrusted and treated with insult even by the smaller powers . . . not a sovereign or a government who do not consider Lord Palmerston as a personal enemy and would not rather prejudice their own interests than forego an opportunity to vent their spite against him.'[4] And he added the following character-sketch:

. . . Lord Palmerston is an able politician with large views and an energetic mind, an indefatigable man of business, a good speaker; but a man of expediency, of easy temper, no very high standard of honour and not a grain of moral feeling. He is consequently quite unscrupulous as to any line of policy that he is to follow, or any means he is to use as long as they lead to his ends. Whilst he is a most easy colleague and minister with regard to other departments, never making any difficulty, he is self-willed and impatient of any control in his own. His obstinacy arises from personal conceit, which makes him almost pity those who differ from him in opinion. He carries his own points with great boldness, by what is commonly called bullying, but if this fails he is equally ready to resort to any trick which may serve his purpose and is perfectly at ease if it has succeeded.

Both counts of the indictment — the alienation of foreign powers and a lack of straightforwardness — seemed truer than ever within a week or two. Palmerston was incorrigible. With the Gros mission grinding to a halt (because, Palmerston said, the Baron acted as 'the avowed advocate of Greece'), Palmerston's colleagues induced him to sign, with Drouyn de Lhuys, the French ambassador in London, a convention providing for the settlement of the whole affair. If this had been communicated to Wyse by the quickest means, he would have known of it before Gros threw in his hand. But Russell had to press before Palmerston drafted a note, and it went by the overland mail. Before it reached Athens, Wyse had instructed Parker to resume his activities, and the Greek government yielded.

Palmerston could see only the victory. Greece had accepted terms more onerous than those provided for in the convention, including a deposit against the Portuguese vouchers, pending further examination of Pacifico's claims. But the Palace and the premier counted the cost. The French recalled their ambassador, and when it was known that the French foreign minister had been reading out in the Chamber the dispatch recalling him on the very day that Palmerston and Lansdowne were telling Parliament that Drouyn had gone home 'to be a medium of communication' between the two governments, Palmerston looked a liar and poor

Lansdowne a dupe. On the night that Drouyn went away Brunnow absented himself from Palmerston's 'Queen's birthday' dinner and indicated that he too would be recalled in consequence of attacks on Russia in the *Globe* (the principal organ of Palmerston's views since the *Chronicle* passed into the hands of the Peelites). Palmerston was undismayed. He thought he could come to an understanding with France, and get back to the April convention without loss of honour, and he chuckled at the mortification of the Princess Lieven (representing both an Orleanist clique which 'wanted to knock me over' and the Tsarist conspirators in Paris trying to separate France from Britain) when she found that Normanby was not to be recalled. But Greville felt that at last there was a tolerable chance of Palmerston coming to grief. For when the Prince wrote that 'the queen may feel that her duty demands her not to be content with mere warning without any effect, and that for the sake of one man the welfare of the country must not be exposed', Russell replied that 'the Queen ought not to be exposed to the enmity of Austria, France and Russia on account of her Minister' and added that after the end of the session 'Lord John Russell will no longer remain in office with Lord Palmerston as Foreign Secretary'.[5] The prime minister accordingly wrote to Palmerston, 22nd May 1850, as follows:[6]

My dear Palmerston — I saw the Queen on Monday, by her desire, and it is right that I should inform you of the course which I stated to her I should pursue, which she has been pleased to sanction.

I first stated that all your colleagues were prepared to assume the responsibility of your conduct on the Greek question, and that if any change took place on that question it must be a change of the entire Ministry . . . But, supposing the Ministry to arrive at the end of the session, it was my duty to tell Her Majesty that I thought the interests of the country required that a change should take place in the Foreign Department; that, without imputing blame to you, I thought it must be confessed that . . . England . . . was encountered by more hostile feelings in her course than was natural or necessary; that I thought, if you were to take some other department, we might continue the same line of foreign policy without giving the same offence . . .

If this was a strong letter for a premier to write to a colleague whom he thought it important should remain a colleague, Lord John, for the repute of his office, could hardly do less. But Palmerston, by one mighty oratorical marathon, stretching from dusk almost to dawn (9.45–2.20) on the night of 8th–9th July 1850

turned the letter of 22nd May into a cruel mockery. Not even the
famous 'Civis Romanus' peroration drew more 'tremendous and
prolonged' cheering than there came at the spot marked (*X*) in the
following extract. Palmerston professed to be meeting the charge
that it was his hostility which had overthrown Guizot and Louis
Philippe, a charge, incidentally, found more frequently in royal
letters than anywhere else —

. . . Why, sir, what will the French nation say when they hear this? They
are a high-minded and high-spirited nation, full of a sense of their own
dignity and honour — what will they say when they hear it stated that it is
in the power of a British minister to overthrow their Government and
their monarchy? Why, sir, it is a calumny on the French nation to suppose
that the personal hatred of any foreigner to their minister could have this
effect. They are a brave, a generous, and a noble-minded people; and if
they had thought that a foreign conspiracy had been formed against one
of their ministers (*X*) — I say that if the French people had thought that a
knot of foreign conspirators were caballing against one of their ministers,
and caballing for no other reason than that he had upheld, as he conceived,
the dignity and interests of his own country, and if they had thought that
such a knot of foreign conspirators had coadjutors in their own land, why,
I say that the French people, that brave, noble and spirited nation, would
have scorned the intrigues of such a cabal, and would have clung closer to,
and have supported the more, the man against whom such a plot had been
made. . . .

A member of parliament would have had to be very out of touch
with the great world not to understand the allusion, and among the
many cheers in the course of the speech it was this one which told
his colleagues that Palmerston was more necessary to them than
they to him.

Vainly, after the debate, did the Palace argue that nothing was
changed; that the case for removing him was as strong as before;
that he was not only the same man, but more dangerous now.
Vainly did Russell repeat his former view that 'the *policy* pursued
with regard to the Foreign Affairs had been right and such as had
the approval of Lord John himself, the Cabinet generally, and he
believed the greater part of the country. But the manner in which
it had been executed had been unfortunate, led to irritation and
hostility; although peace had actually been preserved, and
England stood in a position requiring no territorial aggrandizement or advantage of any kind, yet all Governments and Powers,
not only Russia and Austria, but also France and the liberal states,
had become decidedly hostile to us, and our intercourse was not

such as was desirable. Lord John could instance many cases in which they had been unnecessarily slighted and provoked by Lord Palmerston, like M. Drouyn de Lhuys in the Greek affair'. Vainly did he go through the motions of proposing the exchange of offices of which notice had been given on 22nd May. Palmerston told him 'all was changed now'. To the premier he stated bluntly what to the House he had hinted so broadly, and what, since he repeated it in letters to his relatives he apparently believed, that there had been 'an attack on our foreign policy . . . by a foreign conspiracy, aided and abetted by a domestic intrigue', the principal villains being the same people as in 1840 — Clarendon, Greville, Reeve, Delane, Guizot and the Lieven. 'There had been a great conspiracy against him', he said. 'He had been accused in Parliament, put on his trial, and acquitted.' As for Britain's diplomatic isolation, and the ill-will of foreign states, Russell was not to trouble his head about it — 'that he should incur the momentary enmity of those states whose interests and plans he might have to cross was quite natural'.[7] Russell, had got himself on to very weak ground *vis-a-vis* Palmerston. On the last night of the debate he had saluted Palmerston as 'the Minister of England'; not the minister of France, or of Russia, but the Minister of England. How could one sack the Minister of England in deference to foreign diplomats and intriguants and *The Times*, even if they had the unpublicized patronage of the Palace?

*   *   *   *

Those who made a fetish of strict 'non-intervention' and did not like naval action to protect the interests of British subjects even outside Europe of course deplored the events at the Piraeus. The Manchester School, with Cobden and Bright as its most famous names, desired that Britain's immense wealth and power be held in reserve against the clear challenge of a rival, which was unlikely to come if Britain abstained from intermeddling in Europe and basked in the moral grandeur of an isolation defended as a principle, though it seemed to the critics of the School to be the fruit of calculated commercial choice. To the Mancunians the Balance of Power and a colonial empire were both expensive delusions; the diplomatic and colonial establishments a burden, an unwholesome field of patronage for the aristocracy, a source of international discords. The coercion of weaker states was immoral and superfluous.

The only 'influence' Britain ought to seek was the immense moral influence which would flow from minding one's own business and minding it well, treating all foreign countries with absolute respect.

Such was not the view of Palmerston, and it was not the view (as far as we can tell) of the majority of any class or great interest in the middle of the nineteenth century. Prince Albert's pseudo-Marxist explanation of the British outlook — a product of his zeal for German unity — is unjust as regards Palmerston's main objectives in Europe in general and Germany in particular. 'There is not a people', he wrote, 'who is not convinced that their internal dissensions and sufferings are fomented by England, in order to keep them weak and unable in consequence to compete with the English manufacturers.' But there is pith in his explanation of Palmerston's new popularity — 'this bullying tone to the weaker foreign powers is grateful to the taste of our manufacturers and small traders, who look upon other countries only as upon markets which the Governments, for selfish reasons, want to contract'.[4] Baring, the First Lord of the Admiralty 1849–52, was not happy at 'the constant employment of our ships to support our diplomatic agents'. One of those agents complained that he wished his interference (backed actually or prospectively by ships of war) was not ordered for every debt of twenty pounds.[8] But those who traded in distant parts were less likely to echo Cobden's complaint that sometimes British ships cost more than the trade they were stationed to protect than Palmerston's sharp riposte that this was like denouncing the police for standing about in the streets staring honest citizens out of countenance. When Russell said that the complaint against Greece was hardly worth the interposition of the British Lion, Palmerston begged to be told what was to be done 'when all diplomatic persuasion has been exhausted in vain to obtain from one of these small States just redress for a wrong done to a British subject'. Were they to sit contented and tell the complainant that he must bear the injury as well as he could? If so, 'what is the purpose for which in time of peace we keep ships of war in foreign stations, and why should [we] not agree to Cobden's motions for reducing a useless force, and thus save an unnecessary expense?' These cases, he said, had multiplied lately 'in consequence of the prevalence of the notion that British subjects may be wronged with impunity, and that the British Government will not stir hand or foot to help them. It is not so with French or North American citizens, and no State ventures to ill-use a Russian'.[9]

Palmerston, at least, had never given any ground for the suspicion that he was reluctant to stir hand or foot in such cases. He had made his view abundantly clear in the great speech of July 1849 —

... It is most desirable that foreign nations should know that, on the one hand, England is sincerely desirous to preserve and maintain peace — that we entertain no feelings of hostility towards any nation in the world — that we wish to be on the most friendly footing with all — that we have a deep interest in the preservation of peace, because we are desirous to carry on with advantage those innocent and peaceful relations of commerce that we know must be injured by the interruption of our friendly relations with other countries; but, on the other hand, it is also essential for the attainment of that object, and even essential for the preservation of that commerce to which we attach so much importance, that it should be known and well understood by every nation on the face of the earth, that we are not disposed to submit to wrong, and that the maintenance of peace on our part is subject to the indispensable condition that all countries shall respect our honour and dignity, and shall not inflict any injury upon our interests.

Against this attitude Cobden and Bright, and other passivists, to say nothing of the out-and-out pacifists, could make little headway. By the time of Palmerston's death in 1865 they had exploited new phenomena in Europe (especially the rise of Prussia) to advance the cause of isolation with regard to Europe, but Trollope, writing on Palmerston in the *English Political Leaders* series in 1882, wrote:[10] 'Let the people change their principles; let the Cobdens and the Brights teach them that war is altogether a bad thing, and that commerce will suffice to procure for us the respect of other nations. ... But ... until Cobden and Bright have taught their countrymen, the country requires such a Minister as was Lord Palmerston. They liked his honesty; they liked his self-assertion, and they did not like it the less, because he expressed himself with a hectoring tongue.' Britain was inclined at this juncture in her history, when her economic leadership of the world was becoming more decisive than ever before or since, when her naval predominance was unchallenged, when her internal reform had gone almost as far as the mass of the middle class insisted, to turn her thoughts abroad, to throw her weight about, to pass from the age of Peel to the age of Palmerston. Because Cobden and Bright did not prevail, and Palmerston rose to be 'the representative man', there has been a tendency to downgrade this strong-willed individualist into a mere symptom or symbol of John Bull flexing his muscles and eager to practice chauvinism on the cheap.[11] Palmerston was indeed very fortunate to live on into these times, which he so exactly suited. He was not the man produced by the hour; Nature had produced the man, and his hour was at hand. It is immensely significant that his triumph in the Don Pacifico debate was more popular outside parliament than within. The Tory historian, Sir Archibald Alison, shrewdly said that 'the Reform Bill having vested the government of England in the class of urban shopkeepers, the majority of whom are imbued with Liberal principles, the carrying out of their wishes into our foreign policy became a matter of necessity, to which every Minister, however otherwise inclined, must bend'.[12] Large sections of the nation took Palmerston to their hearts because he was not 'otherwise inclined'. Greville may well be right to attribute to Palmerston from as early as the spring of 1849 a design to play consistently to the Radical gallery, or at least that part of it not rendered obdurate by the faith of the Manchester School. But it was his good fortune to be able to evoke a remarkable response simply by 'being himself', by articulating those sentiments and prejudices which he shared with 'the common man'. The nation was learning, what the electors of Tiverton had long known, that though he was not a common man, a common man might have been cut out of him.[13]

In 1850, an inept Opposition played straight into Palmerston's hands, by choosing to fight in the wrong arena (the Lords) with the wrong weapons, leaving the conditions for the decisive battle in the Commons to the choice of the Government. Lord Stanley's motion, carried in the Lords, deplored the enforcement of 'claims . . . doubtful in point of justice or exaggerated in amount' by 'coercive measures directed against the commerce and people of Greece, and calculated to endanger the continuance of our friendly relations with other Powers'. This was fair enough, and the real issue. But the preamble stated 'the right and duty of the Government to secure to Her Majesty's subjects residing in foreign states *the full protection of the laws of those states*'. The clause italicized is the peg on which Palmerston hung the 'Civis Romanus' argument. This Tory principle, he said, was 'totally incompatible with the interests, with the rights, with the honour, and with the dignity of the country, and at variance with the practice, not only of this, but of all other civilised countries in the world'. One just could not leave British subjects to 'trust to that indifferent justice which they may happen to receive at the hands of the Government and tribunals of the country in which they may be'. They were bound, of course, to have recourse to such means as the local law afforded, but the matter could not end with a denial of justice or a decision manifestly unjust. After a passing reference to the judicial system of Russia (whose autocracy was repugnant to British Radicals, especially pro-Poles), Palmerston cited the case of an innkeeper of Catania executed under the laws of Bomba for possessing a weapon, on evidence wholly inconclusive, as the sort of thing that could not be allowed to happen to a British subject in Sicily. In many cases where a British subject sought redress from courts which could not or would not grant it 'to confine a British subject to that remedy only would be to deprive him of the protection which he is entitled to receive' —

. . . I therefore fearlessly challenge the verdict which this House, as representing a political, a commercial, a constitutional country, is to give on the question . . . whether the principles on which the foreign policy of Her Majesty's Government has been conducted, and the sense of duty which has led us to think ourselves bound to afford protection to our fellow-subjects abroad are proper and fitting guides for those who are charged with the government of England; and whether, as the Roman in days of old held himself free from indignity when he could say 'Civis Romanus sum', so also a British subject, in whatever land he may be, shall feel confident that the watchful eye and strong arm of England will protect him against injustice and wrong.

Upright and patriotic men laboured in vain to strip away the rhetoric and convict Palmerston of unworthily and recklessly trespassing against the mutual self-respect which ought to be the foundation of international relations. The man in the street had his first Latin lesson, and gathered that 'Palmerston would move the whole force of the British Empire in order that this Brown or Jones — Civis Romanus — might not be defrauded of his Worcester sauce amid the ice of Siberia, or of his pale ale in the Mountains of the Moon.'[14] Palmerston relished the 'image'. It was now predictable that his obituaries would call him 'the most English minister that ever governed England' and that his admirers would say that 'the Palmerston policy in the eyes of the world represented English policy, and we love the man who makes the world talk of what England will do and dare'.[15]

Palmerston had to meet the pointed argument that he used at the port of Athens a sledgehammer to crack a very small nut. His answer was more powerful than has sometimes been recognized. He always held that 'Mr Pacifico's' ill-repute was irrelevant. He was a British subject. His house had certainly been wrecked, and his chattels destroyed, by a mob headed by the son of a member of the Greek government, and the police had not interfered. Nor did his case stand alone. There was that eminent Scotsman, the historian of Greece, Finlay, whose property had been taken without compensation to extend the palace garden. (Were British subjects to receive less protection because they were Jews or Scotsmen? Palmerston asked; it is not recorded whether he glanced at the Scottish Liberal M.P.s.) A boat crew from a British warship had been set upon by a Greek gang while collecting water. Greek nationalists — and all Greeks were nationalists until some of them became Communists — wanted to annex the Ionian Islands, made by the Treaty of Vienna a British protectorate. Aid to rebels in the islands passed from the mainland, and Ionian Greeks on the mainland suffered, like other Greeks, from the depredations of brigands in the countryside and from police tyranny in the towns, regardless of their status as 'British protected persons'. Again and again apologies and compensation had been demanded, and never obtained, from a government which, furthermore, did not meet its obligations under the Three Power Loan. As long ago as August 1847 Palmerston had warned Nesselrode that if the Greeks did not give satisfaction, those orders would be given to the admiral in the Mediterranean which were in 1850 given to Parker.[16]

Some of Palmerston's critics implied, rather than stated, that while one standard would do for 'lesser breeds without the law' — for Asians, Africans, even Latin Americans — another was called for in dealing with Europeans. Palmerston had no patience with the view that what was appropriate or at least excusable at Canton, Bushire, the Barbary Coast or Vera Cruz was less so at the Portuguese colony of Macao near Hong Kong and inappropriate and inexcusable at Athens (or Naples or Lisbon). This was not a matter of colour or continents. No doubt, having, for all his easy ways with cosmopolitan aristocrats, a certain insular contempt for

274 THE MOST ENGLISH MINISTER

all foreigners, Palmerston had rather more for 'dagos' (though less than the Queen, who assumed that the inferiority of Mediterranean peoples to British and Germans was such that the former could never work a constitution). But this was more likely to operate against the Brazilians and the Portuguese, because of their slave-trading and their Popery, than against the Greeks as a people. The Tahiti affair, in Aberdeen's time, had aroused indignation on religious (as well as commercial and prestigious) grounds. Though Palmerston had always stood for the civil equality of Roman Catholics in the British dominions, he was deeply anti-papist. So was public opinion in England and Scotland, as would be evident later in 1850 when Russell, with his 'Durham Letter', tapped it. Palmerston made his own attitude clear when an old acquaintance, Lord Spencer's brother — they had been men-about-town to-gether — came to him as Father Ignatius, in the habit of a Passionist monk. 'As a politician', Palmerston told him, 'when we consider the way in which the Pope's government is opposed to the progress of liberty and liberal institutions, I cannot say that I wish to see England again under such influence.'[17] He evidently heard with relish of an incident at Macao. A visiting clergyman, failing to remove his hat at the passing of the Sacred Host during a procession, was clapped into gaol. There was a frigate off the town, commanded by Capt. Harry Keppel, a Whig whose ancestor had come from Holland with William of Orange, and who had no respect for the maxim 'when in Macao do as Lisbon does'. Capt. Keppel demanded the presence on board of the Portuguese governor. That dignitary came, and said that the law must take its course. Keppel replied: 'Now, sir, you will go ashore, and if in twenty minutes after you land the man is not liberated, I land and liberate him myself.' He did so, unopposed, in story-book style, the daughter of the quivering gaoler throwing out the keys. The Marquess of Lorne writes, no doubt representing the attitude of Clubland, that 'some of our friends in the House of Commons, who cannot see a good joke, made the cause of the Governor their own'. The Admiralty reprimanded Keppel. By the same mail he received the congratulations of the Foreign Secretary.[18] There will have been middle-class Nonconformists approving the action, as well as middle-class Nonconformists deprecating it on Mancunian principles, who could not see it as a joke. It is likely that the former exceeded the latter.

If no such animus against what he regarded as superstition and intolerance entered into Palmerston's attitude to Greece, a deep loathing of King Otho and his rotten régime quite evidently did. Even Buckingham Palace could hardly deny the king's 'total incapacity to govern with or without a constitution' and in Palmerston's eyes the death of Colletti (who, returning from Paris to Greece to be chief minister under the 1843 constitution, was described by St Aulaire as 'the chief and leader of all the robbers and scamps of Greece') left Otho clearly exposed as the chief author and instigator of evil. Palmerston had refused to apologize to the Palace for sending to Normanby (without sanction) a dispatch abusing Otho; he told the Queen he feared that Otho's defects lay quite as much in his moral as his intellectual qualities. Blamed by the Palace for the extinction of British influence in Greece, he cited Otho's unpopularity, the state of insurrection and anarchy and near-bankruptcy of the Greek state as proof of the evils which flowed from ignoring British advice. Naturally, British counsels were not heeded when all the other Powers encouraged Otho to follow his own inclinations.[19] Palmerston, however, seems to have assumed — it shows poor judgement — that Parker's action would lead to the expulsion of Otho. He was not at all surprised at the reaction of the other envoys in Athens. 'The bottle-holders of Greece', he said, 'are furious at seeing the spoilt child of Absolutism, whom they have been encouraging for many years past to insult and defy England, should at last have received a punishment from which they are unable to protect him.'[20] This comment is strong evidence that a prime motive in sending the order to Parker was to punish Otho for rejecting the path of constitutionalism and the rule of law.

When the great debate came, Palmerston, predictably, exploited — and with great skill — all the veins of British nationalism. There was a foreign conspiracy against him. The rights of British subjects were being violated. The offending government was a living proof of the evils of absolutism and neglect of 'the friendly counsel and advice' of England's minister. Even if the motion for debate in the Commons had been confined, as was that in the Lords, to the affairs of Greece, we may be sure that Palmerston would have allowed his indignation against the arbitrary, incompetent and contumacious Greek régime to spill over into a general and highly popular attack upon the denial of constitutional liberty to so much of Europe. But the motion tabled (on a hint from the Treasury bench) by the Radical Roebuck — who had changed his tune in the past decade — covered a broad field. It would be easier to get a vote of confidence in the general policy of the government than on anything specific, and many of Palmerston's colleagues would have been very unhappy about defending him on the late affair at Athens in particular. So the motion read 'that the principles on which the Foreign Policy of Her Majesty's Government has been regulated have been such as were calculated to maintain the honour and dignity of this country, and in time of unexampled difficulty to preserve peace between England and the various nations of the world'. The hand of Russell is discernible in the very wording. This was most disconcerting to the Queen and the Prince, for, as Russell said, the defeat of this motion would 'imply in the eyes of Europe a preference for the cause of despotism, and a willingness to interfere with Russia and Austria on behalf of absolute government'. The Palace thought nothing could be worse than a discussion 'placing despotic and democratic principles in array against each other in this country'.[21] It was very hard on the Opposition, and especially on the Peelites, too, but it is what happened. In his report to the Palace of Palmerston's speech Russell noted that 'he appealed from time to time to great principles of justice and freedom' and was received with cheering 'frequent and enthusiastic'.[22] Palmerston knew what he was about when he appealed to the country both as a commercial country and a constitutional country.

★   ★   ★   ★

No one has ever doubted that the speech and the vote constituted a tremendous personal success for Palmerston. Greville rightly said that the speech was not a sufficient answer and defence to all the charges brought, but admitted that it 'was admirably arranged and got up, entirely free from the flippancy and impertinence in which he usually indulges, full of moderation and good taste, and adorned with a profusion of magnificent and successful claptraps. The success of this speech has been complete, and his position is now unassailable. John Russell may save himself the trouble of considering, when this is all over, how he may effect some change involving the withdrawal of the F.O. from Palmerston's hands, for they are now all tied and bound to him in respect to the future as completely as to the present and the past. These discussions and attacks, which were to have shaken him in his seat, have only made *him* more powerful than he was before'. Earl Grey agreed that Palmerston was now the most popular man in the country.[23] Peel, the last vote of whose life was against Palmerston in the Don Pacifico division (it was his first vote against Russell's government) said of the speech 'it has made us all proud of him'. One hundred and twenty M.P.s presented to Lady Palmerston the Partridge portrait, in tribute to 'the independent policy by which he maintained the honour and interests of his country'. He was offered a dinner to be attended by a thousand at Covent Garden; he agreed to be feasted by two hundred and fifty at the Reform Club.

It was all more than a little unfair. By August Greville was carping as usual — 'His great speech immensely exalted his capacity, and placed him in the highest rank as an orator, and the division in the House of Commons gave him the semblance at least of great political power. His triumph was so loudly trumpeted forth, and there were such clouds of jubilation and flattery raised by the breaths of his admirers and parasites that the world was made to regard the success as far more considerable than it really was. It was convenient as much as possible to lose sight of the fact that all the most considerable men (outside of the Government pale) in both Houses of Parliament had pronounced a condemnation of his conduct. Such is the importance of a vote in the House of Commons that the moral effect of these concurrent opinions was sunk in the political effect of a majority of 46. . . .'[24] There is truth in this. More than 24 ministerialist members supported Roebuck's motion against their judgement. Only constitutional decorum induced Palmerston's colleagues to stand with him, and to have the motion framed so that they were more likely to stand (albeit, it was expected, by a frail majority) than fall. Notice had already been given him that he was, in effect, to be dismissed because the premier and cabinet had lost confidence in him. Palmerston gaily accepted the truth of Russell's reminder that he owed the majority to the support of his colleagues. But if without the efforts of the whips there might have been no majority, certainly without that powerful speech there could not have been so big a majority. And the whip was on among the Tories too. How many of them would have preferred to vote with him than against him? The majority

of 46 must be measured in the light of the fact that the
government had no reliable majority at all in the House elected
in 1847, and often survived important divisions by less than
twenty.

But all this was academic. Palmerston in parliament had won an
acquittal; in the country he had won a vindication. It was no idle
boast when he said that 'the degree of public feeling which has been
excited out of doors upon the matters on which the debate and
division turned is most remarkable, and would have led to very
strong manifestations if the result of the division had been to throw
the Government into the hands of our opponents'. It was hardly
an exaggeration to tell his brother that the conspirators had
'rendered me for the present the most popular minister that for a
very long course of time has held my office'.[25] According to Earl
Grey, Bright said that his vote had given great offence at Manchester and that Cobden's speech and vote would probably cost him the
West Riding at the next election. 'Amongst all the middle classes
Palmerston was immensely popular. . . .'[26] He was 'the minister of
England'.

CHAPTER XV

THE DEMAGOGUE DISMISSED, 1851

PALMERSTON had long ago lost the Palace. He had recently lost the premier. But he had won the public In circumstances of political instability accentuated by the death of Peel and Russell's personal commitment to further parliamentary reform (the former convinced Russell that he dare not leave the Commons for the Lords and the latter confirmed the conviction), Palmerston was a man of weight and importance. Russell confessed that he could not stay in office if Palmerston left, 'unless some new disagreement arose'. Palmerston was, as Greville even more gloomily admitted, irremoveable except in the event of 'some fresh acts of violence and folly, of insolent interference, of arrogant dictation or underhand intrigue, which may be so flagrant that his colleagues or some of them will not stand it'. But perhaps he would turn over a new leaf, and, having made his very unpopularity with foreign Powers the instrument of survival and popular triumph, 'renounce his offensive manners and change his mode of proceeding abroad'. It was 'almost impossible to make out what his objects and desires really are, or whether he has any fixed idea and acts upon any system. Hitherto he has appeared to be continually influenced and stimulated by caprice, passion and personal animosities, and all his astuteness has been employed in worrying and injuring those he disliked, and extricating himself from embarrassments of his own making. We shall now see if he has had enough of this sport. . . .' Greville thought there was evidence that Palmerston 'and his invaluable confederate his wife' had wisely set about conciliating their enemies, beginning with *The Times*.[1]

The Queen and the Prince were very angry indeed at the turn of events. It was now that the Prince let the mask slip and talked of 'whatch and control'; now too that he dredged up the allegation that Palmerston 'as her Secretary of State and while a guest under her roof at Windsor Castle, had committed a brutal attack upon one of her ladies'. He had introduced himself by stealth into her apartment at night and barricaded the door, and been prevented from 'consummat[ing] his fiendish scheme by violence' only by 'the miraculous efforts of his victim and assistance attracted by her screams'.[2] Palmerston was none too scrupulous in his pursuit of young ladies, but it appears that this incident (which had happened more than ten years earlier) was grossly misrepresented, the truth being that he absent-mindedly went to a room recently vacated by one of his girl friends and that its new occupant, the recently married Mrs Brand, born a Cavendish, lost her head when she saw him. The Prince stooped without chance of conquering. All the Palace salvaged from the ruins of the attempt to oust Palmerston in 1850 was what Greville described as 'a transaction . . . which will to a certain degree mitigate [the Queen's] resentment, or if it does not do that, will at least induce her to desist from the sort of war which she and Albert have been waging against their obnoxious Minister, for they appear to be fully conscious that they cannot get rid of him'.[1] This 'transaction', which will shortly loom large in our story, may here be described as a promise of good behaviour by Palmerston in regard to the Palace.

By November Greville was noting that the Queen's aversion to Palmerston was greater than ever, 'for to his former misdeeds is now added the part he takes about German affairs, on which Albert is insane'. Poor Albert! — the one nationalism with which he was in sympathy, the German, was the one which attracted no enthusiasm in Britain. 'They hated him before for all he did that was wrong, and they hate him now for doing what is right', wrote Greville severely. 'However, their love or their hate makes no difference to him.'[3] In the middle of 1849 Palmerston and the Prince had not been far apart in their attitude to the future of Germany. 'We should have had no objection to see Prussia take the first place; on the contrary a German Union embracing all the minor states, with Prussia at its head, and in alliance with Austria as a separate Power, would have been a very good European arrangement', noted Palmerston.[4] The Prussian scheme, combining unity with 'local nationality', was, however, stalled by some of the smaller kingdoms until Austria was again free to interfere in Germany. While able to reach some common ground on the organization of Germany, Palmerston and the Prince could never agree on Schleswig-Holstein. On the day that Palmerston was to speak in the Don Pacifico debate, the Queen demanded a cabinet on the ground that the agreement of Britain, France and Sweden to

Russia's suggestion of a guarantee of the integrity of the Danish monarchy (cutting out the Augustenburg succession in the duchies which Prussia and the House of Coburg favoured) was 'a direct attack upon Germany'.[5] The protocol was signed on 2nd August 1850. It had been submitted neither to Prussia nor Austria and was never submitted to the German Diet. But Austria adhered on 23rd August. The Queen alleged that Palmerston was secretly planning Russian intervention in the duchies. The Prince, in an hour-long interview with the Foreign Secretary at the latter's request, failed to extract from a tearful Palmerston (he must have been playacting!) any direct answer to the question what Britain would do if Russia did intervene.[6] In fact, though Palmerston often from 1848–51 threatened Germany with intervention by either France or Russia, both Britain and Russia were non-committal when in October 1850 France proposed common action over the duchies.

It began to look as though war between Austria and Prussia, because neither would agree to the other's plan for the reorganization of Germany, was inevitable. Austria was ready to fight rather than yield Prussia pre-eminence or even equality; she was sustained by the support of some of the German kings, by the appeal of the King of Denmark (in his capacity as duke) for a federal execution to restore his authority in Holstein, and another appeal from the ruler of Hesse-Cassel which, if complied with, would introduce the troops of Austria and/or her confederates athwart the military road which joined Berlin and Rhenish Prussia. Prussia too seemed likely to fight, and Radowitz came to London to seek a British alliance, offering lower tariffs as a bribe. This development produced an interesting reversal of roles in the dialogue between the Palace and Palmerston. The Queen, citing the Minto Mission, wrote, 18th November: 'Having *invariably encouraged Constitutional* development in other countries ... *consistency* would require that we should *now*, when ... *despotism* is to be *re-imposed* by Austrian arms upon Germany, throw *our weight* into the scale of *Constitutional* Prussia and Germany.' What a pity all the envoys of Britain in Germany except Lord Cowley at Frankfort were 'warm partisans of the *despotic* league against Prussia and a German Constitution, and *for* the maintenance of the old Diet under Austrian and Russian influence', which would condemn Germany 'to a further life of stagnation or new revolution'. Palmerston will have enjoyed replying that he quite agreed that 'a regard for consistency, as well as a sense of right and justice, ought to lead your Majesty's Government to give to the Constitutional principle in Germany the same moral support which they endeavoured to afford it in Italy, Spain, Portugal, and elsewhere'. But he did not believe, he said, that the Austrians could think it possible to 're-establish despotic government in a nation so enlightened and so attached to free institutions as the German people now is'. The danger surely lay in the opposite direction, from an excess of democracy arising from the rash and weak precipitation with which German governments which had refused every concession yielded all. No doubt very properly, the Prussians were currently engaged in restoring order by force in Berlin, Dresden and Baden and preserving their military interests in Electoral Hesse.[7]

This parody of so many of the royal letters made very vexatious reading. Palmerston would take no action, though he said that if war came, he believed British sympathy would be with Prussia, and it would be a British interest if she came out of the conflict unscathed and if possible enlarged and strengthened. But who after the last three years could trust Prussia? War between two Powers was to be avoided if possible. Britain must not back Prussia when Russia was backing Austria. Prussia's partisans tried 'to make out that the contest between her and Austria is a struggle between constitutional and arbitrary government, but it is no such thing; it is only a conflict between the two leading Powers in Germany as to which should be politically preponderant'.[8] This was true. It was also true that, as Palmerston told Drouyn frankly, it was a British interest to have a solid barrier between France and Russia. The dispensation of 1815 could not provide that and when Prussia, under pressure from Russia, surrendered her pretensions (at Olmutz, 29th November) Britain suffered a major diplomatic defeat.[9] It was one Palmerston had not tried very hard to avoid. But the British cabinet firmly abjured responsibility. 'It is not for forty millions of people to complain that they could not obtain good government because England has looked coldly upon them', wrote Russell to Stockmar. 'Their own mistaken wishes and blundering action must bear the blame. They . . . set their wits to work and their courage to fight for a bit of conquest — to deprive the King of Denmark of Sleswig, which neither justice nor England could tolerate.'[10]

The Queen was once again 'speaking plainly' to Russell about the unfortunate effects of Palmerston's diplomacy. '*Our* influence on the Continent is *null* . . . the *whole* movement on the Continent is *anti-Constitutional, anti-Protestant, and anti-English*; and this is so complicated, and we have (thanks to Lord Palmerston) contrived to quarrel *so happily*, separately with each, that I do not know *how* we are to stand against it all. . . . *Lord Palmerston* has contrived to make us *so hated* by all parties abroad, that we have lost our position and our influence, which, considering the flourishing and satisfactory state of this country during all the European convulsions, *ought* to have been *immense*. . . . What a noble position we *might* have had, and how wantonly has it been thrown away.'[11] It was, however, not true that Britain had no influence. Her objections, as well as those of France, and their insistence that Schwarzenberg's plan to incorporate the whole Habsburg monarchy in the Confederation would require the assent of the Powers, moved the Tsar away from that plan. It was only too true that, as Palmerston said, 'the course hitherto pursued by the Prussian Government has not been marked by so much prudence, steadiness and consistency as to justify us in promising to follow her future steps blindfold'. Russell was 'as sorry as an Englishman can be for these costly, perhaps fatal, errors' on the part of Prussia and Germany,[12] but he and Palmerston were agreed in their attitude.

*   *   *   *

With regard to the future of Germany, the Queen and the Prince were anti-Austrian, and Victoria, distressed at 'a furious Protestant feeling (in Britain) and enraged Catholic feeling in Ireland', believed that Austria was fanning the flame at Rome.[13] Russell was certainly fanning it in England, in a way that Palmerston could not think wise, and forcing Stanley, as leader of the political party closely associated with the Established Church, to do likewise. Early in 1851 Russell's Ecclesiastical Titles Bill proved the insuperable obstacle (perhaps, from the Peelite view, a convenient pretext) in the way of a Whig–Peelite coalition earnestly desired by the Palace, and desired not less because in it Palmerston could not have retained the Foreign Office.

The royal view that Palmerston was strange and wayward in his views, consistent only in that he was always wrong, was reinforced by the contrast between his 'pro-Austrian' attitude in Germany and his conduct in the Haynau affair. The Austrian General Haynau had been 'a war criminal' in Italy and Hungary, and was guyed as 'General Hyena' in the Radical press. Richly moustachioed and hence easily identifiable, he was so unwise to visit England in September 1850. To the Queen he was 'one of the Emperor's distinguished generals and subjects'. Palmerston described him to the Austrian minister as 'a great moral criminal'.[14] At Barclay's brewery — where one of the clerks was a refugee Viennese journalist — the draymen indicated, in an unceremonious way, that their opinion of the guest of the management was Palmerston's, not the Palace's. In correspondence with the Home Secretary, Sir George Grey — whom the Austrians expected to see that proceedings were taken against the draymen — Palmerston said that the visit to England was 'a wanton insult to the people of this country'. The draymen ought not, of course, to have struck Haynau ('which, however, . . . they did not do much'). They should have 'tossed him in a blanket, rolled him in the kennel, and then sent him home in a cab' (fare paid). When the envoy lodged an official protest, Palmerston told him there would be no prosecution, since the defence 'would necessarily be a minute recapitulation of all the barbarities committed by Haynau in Italy and Hungary'. He took his time over a formal reply to the note, and was then pressed for it, so that there was (alas!) no time to send the Queen the draft. When she eventually saw it, she was aghast, for to the expression of the Government's regret for the incident Palmerston had appended his 'personal' view that Haynau had only got what he deserved and had been warned by Metternich and Koller to expect. He argued thus, at length, when the Queen desired the substitution of another note without this paragraph, which she said was 'derogatory to the honour of the nation, as if no one could be safe in this country who was obnoxious to the public feeling'. Palmerston clearly felt that the public would have been lacking in spirit if there had not been some demonstration against Haynau, whose visit wore the appearance of 'bravado, . . . a challenge to an expression of public opinion'. When Russell endorsed the Queen's demand that a substitute note be handed to Koller, Palmerston replied that this 'must be done by another Secretary of State for Foreign Affairs'. But he complied. The Queen remarked to Russell that 'Lord Palmerston, in this transaction, as in every other, remained true to his principles of action' but that Russell had shown he could control him![15] One may feel rather that Palmerston had made his point.

A year later, a different visitor arrived in England — Kossuth.
Before he came, Russell urged Palmerston not to see him. On 30th
October 1851 he wrote, a third time, to say that while it might have
been thought not unnatural for Palmerston to receive Kossuth
immediately on his arrival, for thanks to be rendered to the
Government for its efforts for his safety and liberation, the case
was different now. For the refugee leader of Magyar nationalism,
in the course of a popular progress from Southampton, was
conducting a vituperative agitation 'against sovereigns in alliance
with her Majesty', and his reception by the Secretary of State
would impliedly sanction this agitation. Russell therefore dispatched a messenger to Panshanger, the Cowper mansion in
Hertfordshire, 'to positively request that you will not receive
Kossuth'. Palmerston did not detain the messenger. He replied:
'. . . there are limits to all things . . . I do not choose to be dictated
to as to who I may or may not receive in my own house. . . . I shall
use my own discretion on this matter. You will, of course, use
yours as to the composition of your Government.' Russell replied
that if his letter had been too peremptory Palmerston's was quite
unjustifiable, for this was a matter of public affairs, which might
lead to the withdrawal of the Austrian envoy. Finding his colleagues
unanimous on the matter, Palmerston gave way.[16] But, though he
could not receive Kossuth, he did receive a deputation of Radicals
from Finsbury and Islington. Their address referred to the
emperors of Russia and Austria as 'odious and detestable assassins',
a Kossuthian phrase.

Palmerston declared that he had not read the address before the
deputation arrived, and that he had repudiated 'those expressions
. . . which were offensive to the Austrian Government'. He had not
known that there was, with the delegation, a reporter, paid no doubt
so much per word, who concocted a report from memory and
'swelled it out into proportions incommensurate with reality' and
'put words into my mouth about the nationality of countries which
were nonsense'. Once again Palmerston had made his point, and
played with effect to the Radical gallery. The Queen demanded
that the matter be brought before the cabinet, but (4th December)
it declined to come to any formal resolution. The Palace's hope
that he might be censured or even driven to resign had never been
more vain. His resignation, Russell explained, would mean the
downfall of the government. Without it, 'somewhat of the good

opinion of the Emperor of Russia and other foreign sovereigns may be lost, but the good will and affection of the people of England are retained, a great security in these times'.[17] Yet on 17th December Russell wrote to Palmerston as follows[18] —

... I must now come to the painful conclusion — while I concur in the foreign policy of which you have been the adviser, and much as I admire the energy and ability with which it has been carried into effect, I cannot but observe that misunderstanding perpetually renewed, violations of decorum too frequently repeated, have marred the effects which ought to have followed from a sound policy and able administration.

I am therefore most reluctantly compelled to come to the conclusion that the conduct of foreign affairs can no longer be left in your hands with advantage to the country. ...

It was widely believed that the Kossuth affair had been the straw which broke the camel's back. Palmerston, though he could offend with impunity as long as the offence was popular, had finally forfeited the trust without which he could not safely do something unpopular, even if it was for the public benefit. His approval of the coup d'état of Louis Napoleon Buonaparte in Paris on 2nd December fell into that category.

*   *   *   *

The French republican constitution of 1848 imposed a rigid separation of powers which enabled the legislators to harass the president of the republic. It also prohibited the president from standing for re-election. It became evident that Louis Napoleon Buonaparte chafed at his inability to control the legislature and had no intention of standing aside at the end of his term; equally evident that the legislators had no intention of assisting an amendment of the constitution which would curb their power. As early as January 1851 Palmerston indicated to Normanby that his sympathies were with the President — France needed government.[19] Normanby's sympathies were otherwise and he predicted that the President would be worsted. A vain man, who did not like being proved wrong, he looked, after the coup d'état of 2nd December, for some sign from the patron of Liberalism of a Whiggish horror of locking up legislators, and of bloodshed. But Palmerston told him that respect could be due only to just and equitable laws and a constitution founded on reason and conse-

crated by antiquity and by happiness experienced under it, not to
'the day-before-yesterday tomfoolery which the scatter-brained
heads of Marrast and Tocqueville invented for the torment and
perplexity of the French nation. . . . It was high time to get rid of
such childish nonsense'. He warned Normanby, in harsh, humiliating, style, not to go on parading his social intimacy with the
'Orleanists' and took it for granted that Louis Napoleon had acted
to forestall an attempt to depose him. While Normanby was
unwilling to believe there had been serious plots against the
President, Palmerston was positively eager to discover signs of
them in the exiled Orleanist court at Claremont.[20] But Normanby
received his greatest humiliation when he called on the foreign
minister Turgot to communicate the instructions (dated 5th
December) sent in reply to his inquiry whether he was to consider
his mission suspended. They read — 'I am commanded by Her
Majesty to instruct Your Excellency to make no change in your
relations with the French Government. It is Her Majesty's desire
that nothing should be done by her ambassador at Paris which
could wear the appearance of an interference of any kind in the
internal affairs of France.' As the Austrian and Russian envoys had
hastened to offer congratulations on the coup d'état, Normanby
apologized for the delay. Turgot told him that it was of no
consequence, as Walewski had already conveyed Palmerston's
entire approval of the coup d'état. Normanby found that other
envoys in Paris had been told of this.[21]

Normanby poured out his sense of grievance to his wife, and she
wrote (on 7th) to his brother, Colonel Phipps, who was Prince
Albert's treasurer. Palmerston, she complained, 'who quarrels
with all Europe about a political adventurer like Kossuth, because
he was defending the liberties and constitution of his country,
now tries to quarrel with Normanby, and really writes in the most
impertinent manner, because Normanby's despatches are not
sufficiently in praise of Louis Napoleon and his coup d'état'.[22] A
feeble attempt by Normanby to argue the case with Palmerston
brought a stinging rebuke — '. . . Your despatches since the event
of Tuesday have been all hostile to Louis Napoleon, with very
little information as to events. One of them consisted chiefly of a
dissertation about Kossuth, which would have made a good article
in *The Times* a fortnight ago; and another dwells chiefly upon a
looking-glass broken in a club-house, and a piece of plaster

brought down from a ceiling by musket shots during the street fights'. Lady Normanby wrote again to Colonel Phipps on 9th — 'He . . . laughs and jokes at the Club being fired into, though the English people in it were within an ace of being murdered by the soldiers; says that Normanby is pathetic over a broken looking-glass, forgetting that the same bullet grazed the hand of an English-man, "a Roman citizen".' To make sure that her brother-in-law would pass this letter on to his royal master, the Marchioness indicated that she had written a long letter to the Queen, but had burned it, 'because events have now become so serious between Normanby and Palmerston that I do not think that I should be the person to inform Her Majesty of it, in case anything was to be said upon the subject in Parliament'. She went on to state what Turgot had said about Walewski's interview with Palmerston, and to say that Normanby had taken 'the grave step' of writing to Russell about it.[23]

Soon the Queen was also writing to Russell about it, and Lord John asked for an explanation to the Queen and himself.[24] Much was later made of Palmerston's failure immediately to reply. His plea of pressure of business was thin, and Russell was to complain in the House of 'a disdainful silence'. Probably Palmerston imagined that, with a little delay, the storm would blow over. When he did complete his answer, in the middle of the night, and sent it off to Russell at Woburn, he was not apologetic. No doubt what he was supposed to have said to Walewski on 3rd December had become highly coloured in its passage from Walewski to Turgot, Turgot to Normanby, and Normanby to England. But he *had* indicated to the French envoy, as his own views, opinions he sincerely held.[25]

There is no reason to doubt that Palmerston's dominant motive when speaking to Walewski was a desire to stand well with the master of France, who must view approval by constitutional Britain as more valuable than that of Russia or Austria. So to stand was all the more important if, as Normanby believed, Louis Napoleon was a danger to the general peace of Europe and dis-trusted Palmerston on account of Buenos Aires, the Greek affair and the Kossuthian address.[26] The Queen and Russell both held that Palmerston's offence was worse than it would otherwise have been, because it followed so hard upon the controversy over Kossuth and Russell's warning of 29th November[27] —

. . . Seeing the persevering enmity which the foreign policy of the Government excites, and the displeasure with which it is viewed in high quarters, I think it behoves you to guard most carefully against misapprehensions as well as misrepresentation. I think you owe this to me and to your other colleagues . . . I think you owe it to the country, which in these difficult times ought not to be exposed, in case of a rupture, to encounter unnecessary odium from the Governments that be. I trust therefore without swerving an inch from our policy, you will avoid as much as possible giving cause for irritation and hostility.

But what could be more illogical? On this occasion Palmerston's indiscretion was neither intended nor likely to cause irritation and hostility in France; the intention and the effect were to conciliate the new French government. It was, in truth, an act of statesmanship. We must seriously doubt whether Russell would have dismissed Palmerston if the latter had not included in his reply a dispatch (of 16th December) which he had sent to Normanby without showing it either to the premier or the queen. It was a riposte to Normanby's complaint that a week had passed without any explanation from Palmerston of the conversation with Walewski; that he must assume that Walewski's report was substantially correct; that he was necessarily subject to misrepresentation and suspicion in doing his duty according to 'the official orders received through your lordship from Her Majesty' if 'the language held in Downing Street is more favourable to the existing order of things in France than the instructions. . . .' Palmerston answered that he had never said anything inconsistent with the instructions of 5th December, sent in reply to Normanby's request for orders. It was not for the Secretary of State, nor a British ambassador, but for the French nation (at the plebiscite under mass suffrage which was to make Louis Napoleon president for ten years and endorse his new constitution) to express an opinion on the coup d'état. If, however, Normanby wished to know Palmerston's own opinion, it was that the co-existence of the President and the Assembly had become impossible, and that it was better for France and the rest of Europe that the President should prevail.[28]

This reply was disingenuous, for Palmerston *had* indicated to Walewski on 3rd the view he now gave to Normanby. It was also most injudicious, for it was a departure, in a diplomatic document liable to be presented to parliament, from the posture of neutrality towards the opposing factions in France. Russell wrote on 17th that the question was not whether the President had been justified in what he did, but whether Palmerston was justified 'as the Queen's Secretary of State, in expressing an opinion on the subject'. Palmerston must leave the Foreign Office.[18] Palmerston replied that he had the satisfaction of thinking that the interests, the honour, the character and the dignity of the country had not suffered while he had the seals. He declared that there was 'a well-known and perfectly understood distinction in diplomatic intercourse between official conversations in which the opinions of Governments are expressed, and by which Governments are bound, and unofficial conversations which have not that character and effect'. The very impropriety of a British government expressing a verdict on a French coup d'état was, he would argue, proof that he was not speaking to Walewski on behalf of the Government. Russell's doctrine was 'new and not practical'; if it were acted on, 'there would be an end to that easy and familiar personal intercourse which tends so usefully to the maintenance of friendly relations with foreign Governments'.[29] But Russell reiterated that no other course was left to him than to submit the correspondence to the Queen and 'to ask Her Majesty to appoint a successor to you in the Foreign Office'.[30] This was on 19th December. The other ministers, when assembling for a cabinet on 22nd, did not know that Palmerston was out, and Granville did not know that he had been asked to stay away from the cabinet because his fitness for the Foreign Office was to be discussed at it.

The public reaction to the news of Palmerston's departure from the Foreign Office was naturally one of surprise and bewilderment. 'The secret was as well kept as Louis Napoleon's, and the coup d'état nearly as important and extraordinary', commented Greville. 'Palmerston is out! — actually, really and irretrievably out. I nearly dropt off my chair yesterday afternoon, when . . . Granville rushed into my room.' No one believed that the Russellite version of the affair, given by *The Times* on the basis of inside information, told the whole truth. 'The case is cumulative', wrote Greville, 'and the Islington deputation is the causa causans.' The Leader of the Opposition inquired whether Palmerston taking up the cause of the President had 'anything to do with his sudden ostracism', and Malmesbury, his colleague, was sure 'there has been some intrigue besides'.[31]

There is, indeed, no simple answer to the question why Russell dismissed Palmerston. When in extreme old age he admitted that he acted hastily and ought to have seen Palmerston, instead of staying on at Woburn,[32] he was being wise after the event — and many other events. Palmerston probably banked on such a meeting, and on his ability to sway Lord John as he so often had before. A conscious or half-conscious awareness that this was so would account for Russell conducting the affair by correspondence. Russell was personally wearied at the incessant rows with Palmerston, and between Palmerston and the Palace, with himself in the middle. He was ex officio indignant at the flouting of the will of the cabinet, though here he was on weak ground so far as the Walewski interview was concerned, as it had taken place *before* the cabinet determined the instructions to be sent to Normanby, and Palmerston's real offence, if any, was to conceal from the cabinet the gist of the conversation which Turgot revealed. Russell knew, moreover, that the days of Whig government were numbered. He was concerned that it should be replaced not by a Tory government but by a Whig–Peelite coalition (which the Palace had already tried to contrive ten months earlier), and that this coalition should be headed by Lord John himself and not a Peelite chosen by the Prince. The presence of Palmerston at the Foreign Office was a major obstacle to coalition. When refusing the Board of Control in September the leading colleague of the late Sir Robert Peel in the House of Commons, the former Whig Sir James Graham, had stressed his objections to Palmerston — 'his crooked policy, his headstrong waywardness, and his dangerous artifices'.[33] Aberdeen viewed the House of Buonaparte with great hostility and was thought to be inspiring *The Times*'s attacks on the President after the coup d'état. The dismissal of Palmerston would conciliate the Peelites. Russell was also probably conscious of a certain poetic justice in the situation. In 1850 Palmerston, after being given notice of dismissal, had made himself indispensable by an appeal to public opinion at once skilful and blatant. In both the Haynau and Kossuth affairs he had shamelessly exploited (and at the same time increased) his popularity with the Radicals, in utter disregard for the cautions of the premier and the cabinet. But now he had done something unpopular, and most unpopular with those very Radicals who had so recently applauded him. He had approved the establishment of a dictatorship by military force. For the first time it seemed safe to dismiss him.

L

The Palmerston family account of the incident alleged, as one might expect, 'conspiracy'. Lady Palmerston wrote boldly to Russell on these lines. Palmerston himself wrote to his brother: 'It is obvious that the reason assigned for my dismissal was a mere pretext, eagerly caught at for want of a good reason. The real ground was a weak truckling to the hostile intrigues of the Orleans family, Austria, Russia, Saxony and Bavaria, and in some degree also of the present Prussian Government. All these parties found their respective views and systems of policy thwarted by the course pursued by the British Government, and they thought if they could remove the minister they would change the policy. They had for a long time past effectually poisoned the mind of the Queen and the Prince against me. . . .' Evelyn Ashley writes (as the heir to the family estates and the family explanation) 'There can be no doubt that the true reason could not be publicly assigned. The long-cherished hostility of certain foreign courts and governments acting upon our own was the motive power, and this occasion was seized upon merely as a pretext . . .'.[34] Urquhart himself, at a moment when he was more concerned to belabour the Prince than Palmerston, would publicize the charge that the dismissal was known in Vienna before news of it could have arrived from London. And from the embassy in Vienna there came a letter recording that 'these arrogant fools here actually think that *they* have overthrown Lord Palmerston; and the vulgar triumph of Schwarzenberg knows no bounds'.[35] Lord Howden resigned the Madrid embassy 'as the retirement of Lord Palmerston either is, or most certainly will be believed to be, a direct concession to the reactionary spirit which is riding rough shod over the world'.[36]

It is, of course, true that nearly every foreign Court joined with Victoria and Albert in wishing Palmerston gone and in hoping that his successor would alter the slant as well as the tone of British diplomacy. It is therefore necessary to stress as a fact that in the dismissal of Palmerston and the appointment of Granville it was the premier and not the Palace that took the initiative. Palmerston and his friends encountered criticism of the Foreign Secretary's disdainful silence by pointing out that Russell did not pass his reply of 16th December on to the Queen. He informed him that he would be replaced, and returned the letter (as requested) for copying by Palmerston, on 17th. On 18th Russell informed the Queen, at Osborne, that Palmerston's explanation was unsatisfactory and that he had written to him in 'most decisive terms'. But it was not until the Queen and the Prince arrived at Windsor on 20th that they found awaiting them the correspondence between Russell and Palmerston and 'the great and *unexpected* news' of the dismissal. 'It is a great and unexpected mercy', minuted the Queen, 'for I really was on the point of declaring on my part that I could no longer retain Lord Palmerston, which would have been a most disagreeable task, and not unattended with a small amount of danger, inasmuch as it would have brought me too prominently forward.' Informed by Albert that the Queen had contemplated removing Palmerston herself, Russell said that 'he had thought it his duty to put a stop to what was unnecessarily injuring me [i.e. the Queen] and the Cabinet; that he was par-ticularly anxious to prevent my being brought prominently forward, as, were I to be attacked by Lord Palmerston's admirers, I was not in a position to defend myself'.[37]

*   *   *   *

By taking the initiative himself, in haste, Russell avoided seeming to do what he did under royal pressure, or not being able to do it, because of royal pressure unwisely applied. He had avoided a constitutional crisis on the subject of the dismissal of ministers. He evaded another one on the subject of the appointment of ministers, because his candidate was the candidate of the Court as well. Granville was thus appointed without Russell acknowledging the Queen's insistence on her unfettered right to approve or disapprove the premier's nominee or taking note of her protest 'against the Cabinet's taking upon itself the appointment of its own Members, which rested entirely with the Prime Minister and Sovereign'.[38] Russell had to get the cabinet to endorse both the dismissal of Palmerston and the nomination of Granville, because of the political situation.

Unfortunately the purity of Russell's Whig constitutionalism was obscured when on 3rd February 1852 he came to explain the dismissal to Parliament. He could speak with assurance, and with the assurance of success, for he had the goodwill of the Court, the approval of most Tories and Peelites, a majority of the Radical M.P.s and many Whigs and Liberals. But, now that the excitement of the December days had passed, and the French democracy had endorsed the President, and good relations with the President were vital, Russell's case against Palmerston in regard to the coup d'état did not look so impressive. It would have looked decidedly frail but for Palmerston's letter to Normanby of 16th December. Even as it was, Russell evidently did not think it was very strong, for to make up the balance he threw in the text of the royal memorandum of August 1850, which constituted a sort of 'terms of engagement' for Palmerston. The Queen required of the Foreign Secretary:[39]

1. 'That he will distinctly state what he proposes in a given case, in order that the Queen may know distinctly to *what* she has given her Royal sanction.'
2. 'Having *once given* her sanction to a measure, that it be not arbitrarily altered or modified by the Minister; such an act she must consider as failing in sincerity towards the Crown, and justly to be visited by the exercise of her Constitutional right of dismissing that Minister.'

This part of the memorandum was (though neither Russell nor parliament were ever told so) based on a draft made by Stockmar in March 1850. The Queen in August corrected the English grammar and smoothed the style, and added:

3. 'She expects to be kept informed of what passes between him and the Foreign Ministers before important decisions are taken, based on that intercourse.'
4. '[She expects] to receive the Foreign Despatches in good time' and
5. 'to have the drafts for her approval sent to her in sufficient time to make herself acquainted with their contents before they must be sent off.'

Palmerston attached little importance to the memorandum, regarding it as a paltry attempt to extract some compensation for the failure to get rid of him. When its terms were revealed by Russell to the House of Commons in February 1852, many were amazed that Palmerston had consented to stay in office under such conditions. They would have been the more amazed if they had known that he had sought an interview with the Prince, at which he wept, and said that if he was guilty of disrespect for the Queen, he was almost no longer fit to be tolerated in society.[6] He stood at the time triumphant after the 'Civis Romanus' speech and serious would have been the repercussions if he had resigned in protest against the memorandum. This he did not fail to point out to Russell's brother, the Duke of Bedford, when protesting that Russell's citation of the memorandum was 'unhandsome by me, and very wrong by the Queen'. He had submitted to it in August

1850, he said, because 'the paper was written in anger by a lady as
well as a Sovereign' and he had no reason to suppose that it would
ever be seen by, or known to, anybody but the Queen, Russell and
himself. To resign would have been to bring 'for decision at the
bar of public opinion a personal quarrel between myself and my
Sovereign — a step which no subject ought to take, if he can
possibly avoid it'.[40]

Palmerston had not, when Russell sent him the memorandum,
resigned, brought down the government and injured the monarchy.
He had said that he would not fail to attend to these directions.
But, apart from this generality, his letter to the premier — and this
seems to have been overlooked by most commentators — was
concerned with point 4 of the memorandum, the least important
of the five. With an additional clerk or two, he said, he could revert
to the ancient practice of having the dispatches copied for the
Queen as soon as they reached the office.[41] Only one of the points
— 2 — carried a clear threat of dismissal. In its way it was the
most important of all. But it was also the one most likely to
produce legitimate misunderstandings and genuinely conflicting
interpretations, on which it would hardly have been right to base
an extreme use of royal prerogative. No doubt Palmerston felt he
could rely on a member of the House of Russell to resist the
unconstitutional pretensions of the House of Hanover. If one
wishes to be pedantic, one may remark that, as the Walewski
conversation *preceded* the cabinet's decision on instructions to
Normanby, the only technical violation of point 2 was the dispatch
of 16th December, which also violated point 5. Possibly the
interview with Walewski violated point 3. But Palmerston would
never admit the necessity of retailing to the monarch what he had
said to an ambassador as his personal opinion.

Palmerston complained, privately, that in citing the memorandum in the House, Russell was dragging the Queen into the
discussion 'and making her a party to a question which constitutionally ought to be, and before Parliament could only be, a
question between me and the responsible adviser of the Crown;
and . . . that this mention of the Queen as a party to the transaction
had given rise to newspaper remarks much to be regretted'. He
alleged that he had no idea that Russell proposed to use the
memorandum; Russell said that he had informed him it would be
used.[42] The explanation is almost certainly that Russell had

originally intended to say only that the Queen had asked for an explanation of the apparent discrepancy between the language to Walewski and the instruction to Normanby. The Queen told him he might add that 'I had frequently to complain of similar delays.'[43] That would have been bad enough for Palmerston, but the reading of the memorandum was ruinous. He sat as though pole-axed while Russell read out the memorandum and added that 'the noble lord's course of proceeding in this matter he considered to be putting himself in the place of the Crown, and passing by the Crown, while he gave the moral approbation of England to the acts of the President of the Republic of France, in direct opposition to the policy which the Government had hitherto pursued'.

Well might Russell report to an indecently delighted Palace that 'Lord Palmerston made no case, and was not supported by any considerable party in the House.'[44] Palmerston could have answered with some effect as well as impudence if the royal letter had not been introduced. He did succeed in drawing laughter when he alleged (on the authority of Walewski) that Russell himself had expressed opinions on the internal affairs of France in Palmerston's own house, and had repeated the offence two days later, and that Lansdowne, Wood, Earl Grey and even Earl Granville were all guilty of it too. Apparently any minister might state his view except the Foreign Secretary, who 'is to remain silent like a speechless dolt or the mute of some Eastern Pasha' when an envoy comes to tell him he has news.[A] But in general his attempts at flippancy were unconvincing, even pathetic. The Marylebone Liberals, whose first reaction to the news of his departure from the government was to contemplate asking him to become their M.P., said that a man who did not answer the Queen's letters would receive no address from them. 'There *was* a Palmerston' said Disraeli.[45] And there was to be a Palmerston again. He who had so often 'got away with murder' now seemed to have been murdered politically. But he was to rise again, all the stronger, because the verdict of justifiable homicide pronounced by the Court, the cabinet and the Commons was so joyfully echoed by the illiberal courts in Europe, whom the British people knew instinctively to be wrong about everything. It was very unwise of Schwarzenberg to give a ball to celebrate the fall of Palmerston. A piece of doggerel

[A] The other ministers explained that their comments were confined to wishing Napoleon, after his coup d'état, good fortune in his struggle with the Socialists.

published by *Reynolds' Weekly*, a Chartist, Radical, pro-Kossuth newspaper convinced that his dismissal was 'an unworthy concession to the Court at Vienna', was perverse, because it was so anti-French, but it was, in its broader prophecy, justified[46] —

> ... For small Lord John has been and gone
> And turn'd adrift Lord Palmerston,
> Amongst the lot the only don
> Who didn't take care of number one;
> Out spoke Home Secretary Grey,
> I wish old Palmy were away,
> Aye, turn him out they all did say,
> > For he's the people's darling.
>
> In every foreign Court his name,
> Upheld Old England's glorious fame,
> And all our enemies were tame
> > Because he kept them under.
> But now in Austria's tyrant Court,
> They did chuckle all in glee and sport,
> Because they've heard the glad report.
> Says young Napoleon 'that's your sort';
> But let them laugh who win the day,
> He'll live to make them dearly pay,
> That aught against him they did say:
> > And if he don't I'll wonder.
>
> Whene'er doth meet the Parliament,
> The Whigs to pot will straight be sent,
> That humbug of a Government
> > Won't live a moment longer.
> Then Palmy he'll be at our head,
> And keep the tyrants all in dread,
> Austria and France will wish him dead,
> And for a milksop in his stead,
> Haynau and the Russian Tsar
> Will curse him in their realms afar.
> And on their feelings it will jar.
> > To find old Palmy stronger. . . .

Section D

Towards Supremacy, February 1852 – January 1855

CHAPTER XVI

TITS AND TATS

IN March 1850 the Palace had agreed with Russell that Palmerston was 'very popular with the Radical part of the House of Commons as well as with the Protectionists, so that both would be ready to receive him as their leader'.[1] Rarely has a politician been in such a position. There were Radicals (of the Manchester School) who, asked which minister they most detested, would have answered unhesitantly — Palmerston. There were other Radicals, impressed by his concern for the protection of trade and the expansion of markets, his patronage of Liberalism and his abuse of tyrants, who, asked which minister they most admired, would have answered — Palmerston. There were some Tories who, answering honestly the question which minister they least liked voting against, would have answered — Palmerston; there is always a sort of Tory that likes to hear the lion roar. And there were more Tories — including leading Tories — who, asked which Whigs they would most like to secure as allies in order to achieve a Tory majority, would have put Palmerston at the head of their list.

As early as 1841–2 Melbourne and Greville had agreed that, in the event of a dislocation of parties, Palmerston was free to take any course. He was accustomed at Tiverton to defend in standard party terms the record of the administrations of which he had been a member, neatly gearing his appeal to local circumstances. When his Chartist opponents and hecklers attacked those administrations, Palmerston pointed to parliamentary and municipal reform with the words 'We know the difference here' (1847). Tiverton had been a close borough whose self-perpetuating corporation returned two members to the Commons under the influence of Lord Harrowby; after 1832 it returned two Whigs and the local Chartist butcher, Rowcliffe, was twenty years a councillor. Palmerston disarmed those who attacked him as a Tory in disguise by his 'happy knack of referring to the Tory party as if their opinions and his were wide as the poles asunder'[2] — as, indeed, on the question of being rude to foreign powers on grounds of their illiberality and injustice, he was. But there is no reason to believe that in 1852 or at any other time he was prepared to make any major concessions on domestic policy to acquire or to keep a Radical following. He saw no need for any more parliamentary reform, and was prepared to resist, to the point of resignation, any considerable one.[A] But there was no prospect of him approving the re-imposition of a Corn Law in order to facilitate his reunion with the Tories. For a moment, indeed, in 1846 it looked as though Palmerston, one of two ministers who protested against the *Edinburgh Letter* in writing, might emerge as the leader of a centre party standing for a moderate corn duty, and his brother-in-law, Beauvale, regretted that he did not do so for it was 'quite on the cards that the reasonable men of all parties would have turned to him'.[3] But Palmerston, though rarely far in advance of public opinion on any issue, was rarely far behind it, and though as a landlord his attitude to the Corn Laws was ambivalent, he was a political realist. He did not think Peel in the past had gone far enough; he thought that now Russell and Peel had gone too far, but he sensed that a great matter had come to issue, to be decided once and for all. He joined to help Peel's bill through, convinced that graceful concession was the best means of preserving the political influence of the aristocracy, to which he attached great importance.

Once Repeal was on the statute book, Palmerston was loyal to it. Speaking immediately after Peel, when Sir Robert announced his resignation, Palmerston capped Peel's famous tribute to Cobden, saying that Cobden was not only a great improver of the commercial code but a great result of the Reform Bill.[4] He thus showed that he saw the Repeal in perspective, and was later entitled to cite the Reform and the Repeal together, with other measures, as responsible for the avoidance of revolution in 1848. Men would continue to cite 'his old Protectionist leanings' as an explanation of Palmer-

---

[A] He always held that the necessity for Reform, if it existed, arose principally if not solely from declarations (especially that of 20th Feb. 1851) made by Russell without previous concert or agreements with colleagues (Walpole, ii. 196). Palmerston and Lansdowne helped other ministers prevent a ministerial bill in 1850 (ibid. 102–3). On 20th Jan. 1851 the cabinet had vetoed a bill that year (ibid. 123). Probably Palmerston, while stressing his objections to the bill in course of preparation at the time of his dismissal, and introduced in 1852, did not think it necessary to threaten to resign, for Lansdowne's objections (withdrawn only at the last moment) seemed conclusive against the bill passing even if it were introduced (ibid. 130, nn. 1, 2). In December 1853 the roles of Palmerston and Lansdowne were to be reversed — see below, p. 336[A].

ston's popularity with the Tories and the possibility of his rejoining them. No doubt he would have welcomed the passage of those 'compensations' to the landed interest for which Disraeli pressed after Repeal. But he was no putter back of clocks. He sensed that the rise of business activity and living standards, especially after 1849, would be attributed (justly or not) to the fiscal revolution. In 1851, finding 'the labouring classes fully employed ... and better off than they have been for a very long period', and seeing that 'all things considered neither the owners nor the occupiers of land [had] any great cause to complain', he told the electors of Tiverton to expect a return to Protection when the Exe flowed up from the sea.[5] At the general election of mid-1852 he told them that the protection of the landed interest lay in the happiness and contentment of the people, and that the Chartist fiasco of 1848 had shown the popular feeling that 'the course of legislation had been directed towards the general good'.[6] Derby (formerly Stanley), who became premier in February 1852, hoped to get Palmerston with Gladstone and other Peelites to join him and give him a majority or the prospect of one. His refusal to repudiate Protection *before* the election made this impossible. 'I do not say mean to say that, irrespective of the question of Protection, I should have been much disposed to join him in any case', Palmerston explained privately, 'but if his Government had been framed on a comprehensive principle, and Protection had been thrown overboard, the matter would have required considera- tion.'[7]

It was profoundly irksome to the Palace to find Derby proposing, within three weeks of the debate on Palmerston's dismissal from the Foreign Office, that he be offered the Chancellorship of the Exchequer and the leadership of the House of Commons. Accep- tance by Palmerston would have come as a great relief to many Tories as involving the deposition of their improbable leader, Disraeli. Albert inquired 'whether Lord Derby fancied he would remain Prime Minister any length of time, when once Lord Palmerston had got the lead of the House of Commons'.[8] It had been for some three years a nightmare to the Prince that Palmer- ston might emerge as prime minister. A monarch usually had very little control over who became prime minister at the time of the appointment. So, Albert argued, 'a sagacious sovereign ... would look forward and take his share in the preparatory arrangements of party organization, whenever he could, in order to have those presented to his choice in times of emergency whom he had before recognised as eligible'. Palmerston must therefore be blacklisted as a candidate for the leadership of the House, even if it had to be done on the ground that the Queen could never accept 'as her chief adviser and confidential counsellor in all matters of State, religion, society, Court etc etc' a man who had tried to rape one of her ladies.[9] The royal pair were certainly more long-sighted than Russell in objecting to Lord John's plan of 1849 and early 1850 to take the Foreign Office himself and go to the Lords, leaving Palmerston to lead in the Commons. Russell (aged fifty-seven) said that Palmerston (aged sixty-five) was 'too old to do much in the future'; the Palace feared that if the Whigs went into opposition Palmerston would become their real leader and force himself on the Queen as prime minister.[10] Russell, was, of course, reluctant to let Palmerston loose to become a critic of the government; the Palace preferred it to the risk of seeing him displace Lord John. For the Queen and the Prince never gave Palmerston the credit of having any principles, scruples or regard for consistency, and attributed to him so strong a desire for place that they believed he would accept War and Colonies, or some other cabinet post (without the leadership of the House) or the Lord Lieutenancy of Ireland, just to stay in office. But Palmerston always took the view that his leaving the Foreign Office would involve 'a loss of character . . . which he could not be expected to submit to'[11] and when, on 17th December 1851, Russell, in the letter intimating his dismissal, offered him Ireland, with or without a British peerage, or, by implication, another office, his reply was tart. A week later it was tarter still. Palmerston parted from Russell in anger. When Russell referred to the past week as being the most painful of his life, Palmerston retorted: 'I, on my part, feel that just indignation which the whole transaction has produced on my mind.'[12]

Towards Granville Palmerston, when handing over the Office, was amicable, but in his remark that the work was very interesting, but laborious, involving seven or eight hours' work a day on current, besides the extraordinary and parliamentary, business, there was a barb. Palmerston remembered his old friend's son, who had only recently entered the cabinet, as an idle youth who had not efficiently performed the work of Under-Secretary at the Foreign Office in 1840–1. His only qualifications appeared to be that his family lay at the heart of the 'Sacred Circle of the Great-Grand-motherhood' of Whiggery, that he was courtly, and admired at Court. Palmerston could hardly regard the appointment as other than an insult, and though he was polite enough to Granville, the next day's *Morning Post* (henceforward the organ of Palmerston's political views) was, in Greville's words, 'malignant' about the Government from which Palmerston had been extruded.[13]

Granville himself said that he would be attacked on grounds of 'my incompetency; the neglect of strengthening that which is weakened by the loss of an able man; the adoption of Lord Aberdeen's policy, now that the only man is gone who cared for the popular cause in Europe; and that the whole is the result of a Court intrigue to displace one who was too powerful to be influenced, and to replace him by one under the influence of the Court. The first two objections are strong. I hope that we shall be able to show that the last two are not true'.[14] To show this was both difficult and necessary. It was difficult because, as Russell had told the Palace, 'many of those who dislike and distrust Lord Palmerston would have England take up a position totally different, viz of intimate and cordial alliance with Austria and Russia and sullen peace with France'. How could they be shown to be beaten if relations with Austria improved? In fact, relations with France deteriorated as a result of the circumstances of Palmerston's dismissal, and relations with Austria were not improved. Granville's circular of 13th January 1852 was no doubt more conciliatory in tone than if Palmerston had framed this reply to a Note from the Powers on the subject of refugees in Britain, received before Palmerston left the Foreign Office. But it was unacceptable to Schwarzenberg, who published his answer to it in the Vienna newspapers before Granville had received it. He threatened restriction on 'Roman citizens' visiting the Habsburg domains unless an Aliens Bill satisfactory to Austria was passed in Britain. The crisis temperature of relations between London and Vienna did not fall until a *Tory* Foreign Secretary, Malmesbury, in a dignified reply to a violent outburst by Buol, explained 'that no Government which complied with such demands could exist a month in England'. Granville tried to avoid public, publishable, or even private acrimony, but he could not allow himself to be trodden on, and his last act was to return, as unacceptable, notes from Modena and the Papal States, passed on by the Austrian ambassador.ᴬ Rumour even had it that *Granville* threw them on the floor in front of Buol.¹⁵

The net effect of all this was to make Austria more unpopular in Britain than before, to exculpate Palmerston from responsibility for bad relations with her, and to enhance the prestige of the politician who had so often rebuked and sometimes baited her. No doubt this was more than a little unfair on Russell and his colleagues, who had striven to show how unjust was the general verdict of Europe that the substitution of Granville for Palmerston was 'a triumph for the Absolute and a blow for the Liberal cause'; a victory for the Palace as against the government; a sign that, as Disraeli assumed, or said he assumed, the foreign policy of Britain was to be entirely changed. The Queen and the Prince were not slow in trying to ensure that there should be more than a change of mere tone, that there should be a very considerable change of slant. Russell resisted them, arguing as always that 'it was only the *personal manner* of Lord Palmerston in conducting the affairs which could be blamed'. The letter from the Palace on 28th December, asking for a 'reconsideration' of the principles upon which foreign affairs had been conducted since the beginning of 1848, certainly implied criticism of Russell and the cabinet as well as Palmerston, and an intention to secure a change in policy if possible. The Queen required 'a more specific definition ... a regular programme', something more than 'the mere assertion of abstract principles such as "non-intervention in the internal affairs of other countries", "moral support to liberal institutions", "protection of British subjects" etc etc'. Russell told her that it was 'very difficult to lay down any principles from which deviations may not frequently be made', and Greville described Granville's paper (which he was invited to sample) as 'a series of commonplaces', to every word of which either Palmerston or Aberdeen might subscribe.¹⁶ There were some implied criticisms of Palmerston's proceedings, partly dictated, no doubt, by reports that the

---

ᴬ These were notes, addressed to Vienna and handed or sent to Granville by Buol on 7th and 21st January 1852 respectively, demanding the extradition of refugees. On 23rd Granville, about to leave office, returned both, accompanied by a dispatch circulated to British envoys, as a retort to the publication in Vienna of Schwarzenberg's dispatch. Granville later denied that he was 'guilty of any personal discourtesy to Count Buol'. Malmesbury declined to receive the Modenese and Roman notes and told Buol he would not bear a repetition of the 'most coarse and insolent manner' with which he addressed him on being told this (M., pp. 234–5, 240; G., 72–4, 77).

name of England was so odious on the Continent that the only protection was to cry 'Civis Romanus non sum'. All considerations of a higher character were not to be roughly pushed aside for the mere sake of supporting British traders in every case. There was a duty to protect British subjects engaged in innocent pursuits abroad, to demand redress in strong but dignified language, followed when necessary by corresponding measures, but if they subjected themselves to the penal laws of foreign countries they could expect only 'good offices' and it was no duty of the Foreign Office to give assistance 'if they fell into difficulties through their own wanton folly or misconduct'.

Yet embedded in the conciliatory phrases there was a rich deposit of Palmerstonian doctrine. While acknowledging that, justly or unjustly, Britain's foreign policy had obtained the reputation of interfering too much, Granville repudiated the Cobdenite notion that diplomacy was obsolete and the Foreign Office should show no interest in what passed in other countries. Because 'internal' affairs often had international consequences, no general rule could be uniformly applied. Britain might often have an interest in the establishment of liberal institutions and the reduction of tariffs. Her Majesty's representatives abroad should press for these only when it was opportune, but they should be furnished with the government's views with respect to these and other internal affairs of foreign countries. 'With the countries which have adopted institutions similar in liberality to our own, it ought to be the endeavour of H.M.'s Government to cultivate the most intimate relations. In this connection the duty of H.M.'s Government should be to keep them informed of everything which might expose them to danger, and to give them, when required, frank and judicious advice; and also to exert its influence to dissuade other Powers from encroaching on their territory or attempting to subvert their institutions. But cases might occur in which the honour and good faith of this country would require that it should support such allies with more than merely friendly assurances.' On the strength of that passage alone in Granville's memorandum, Palmerston was entitled to feel that he had not lived in vain.

* * * *

Granville occupied the Foreign Office for a mere two months, after which Palmerston was to be found informing Malmesbury

'You have no idea till you know more of your office what a power of *prestige* England possesses abroad, and it will be your first duty to see that it does not wane.'[17] No one was more conscious than Palmerston that the one thing fatal to this prestige was that foreigners should hold, as Metternich had, that Britain 'cannot make war for any of the ends which she pursues'. She must have no Achilles' heel. Equally important, she must be known not to have one; she must not seem 'the most tempting and the worst guarded prey that ever invited the robber instincts of military aggression'. Since the Tahiti affair, Palmerston, out of office and in office, had pressed more consistently than any other leading Whig (except perhaps Clarendon) for an increase in the number of ships and men available or able speedily to be made available for the defence of the British Isles (while a large fleet was maintained in the Mediterranean to keep a large part of the French fleet there); for fortifications to defend the arsenals and dockyards (even if this cost one million pounds, he said in 1846, it was 'a matter of indispensable necessity'); for a militia. To do him justice, Russell was only less forward than Palmerston because of the difficulties of the political and financial situation. He accepted the danger of a descent by the French on Britain. His memorandum on national defence of 10th January 1848 was described by Palmerston as very clear and able. Indicating that he would resign if not supported on this vital matter, Russell could hardly demur at Palmerston's letter saying that if the Chancellor could not find £100,000 for a militia, the government was unable to perform its duty to the country and ought to go out, or at his subsequent threat of resignation on the issue (February 1848). Any expedient was better, said Palmerston, than proclaiming to France and to Europe that Britain was too poor and distressed to be able to defend herself. Russell introduced, in February 1848, a budget raising the income-tax from sevenpence to one shilling, of which one-fifth of one penny was to go to providing £150,000 for the foundations of a militia. The House of Commons would not look at this increase in the income tax, and Palmerston was able to acquiesce in the abandonment of the militia scheme and the reduction of the naval estimates, after the French Revolution of 1848 made an attack on Britain unlikely, and indeed for as long as there was 'no ground for alarm in the Channel'.[18] But early in 1852 the grounds for complacency vanished. Louis Napoleon was master of France. He was not very well disposed to Britain after the dismissal of Palmerston. He was irritated by British (and Belgian) press attacks on him, especially those in *The Times* which, Reeve alleged when Granville expostulated, were partly intended to drum up public support for rearmament. He was thought likely to move in one direction or another — against Belgium, Switzerland (where the activities of refugees annoyed him), Italy or even the Rhineland. Granville, pacific as he was, did not ignore these rumours; the uneasiness was shared by others normally pacific, including Aberdeen. Russell thought the time ripe to introduce a Militia Bill. And on it Palmerston turned him out (20th February 1852). Less than three weeks after the humiliation of the debate on his dismissal, he had the pleasure of noting, as one of the reasons for Russell's resignation, 'the almost insulting manner towards him [Russell] in which the House, by its cheers, went with me in the debate'.[19]

It was now Russell's turn to be indignant. He considered the vote one of censure. It was 'an entirely unprecedented case not to allow a Minister of the Crown even to lay his measure on the Table of the House'. He further alleged conspiracy — 'there seemed to have been a pre-arranged determination between Lord Palmerston and the Protectionists to defeat the Government; . . . the Peelites also had agreed to vote against them'. No doubt Palmerston's action seemed evidence that, as Graham and Aberdeen had predicted, he would be 'bent on revenge',[20] and it was with relish that Palmerston wrote to his brother: 'I have had my tit-for-tat with John Russell, and I turned him out on Friday last.'[19] But there had been no conspiracy. Palmerston had drawn his bow at a venture. He was probably speaking the truth when he said that he had not expected the government to resign if beaten. His intention had been 'to persuade the House to reject his foolish plan and to adopt a more sensible one'. Despite appearances, this was no act of faction. Palmerston had always disagreed with Russell and his adviser on military matters, Fox Maule, as to the sort of militia required. He thought it important that a militia (ideally numbering at least 150,000) should be genuinely and avowedly available for *national* defence. His successful motion of 20th February was to leave the word 'Local' out of the title of the bill. He was a tower of strength to the new Tory administration when it proposed (and carried into law) its own Militia Bill. He supported it the more readily because its opponents were the Manchester School (Hume,

Milner Gibson, Cobden and Bright) and Russell. Lord John first expressed a preference for an increase in the regular army and then demanded a ballot and compulsory service, while the Tories proposed a system of bounties, with compulsion reserved as a last resort. As Disraeli, the new Leader of the House, reported to the Queen: 'Your Majesty's Government, about to attempt to reply to it [Russell's speech], gave way to Lord Palmerston, who changed the feeling of the House, and indeed entirely carried it away in a speech of extraordinary vigour and high-spirited tone.'[21] The second reading was carried against Russell by 315 to 165.

*   *   *   *

The strength of Palmerston's tactical position lay in the fact that, in the parliament of 1847–52, neither the Whig government nor its Tory successor had a working majority, and that in the new parliament elected in the summer, the Tories, though stronger, were still short of a majority. But behind the man was a popularity based on memories of Don Pacifico, Haynau and Kossuth. Even Greville admitted that at Brooks's (the Whig club) there had been 'a great deal of sulky disapprobation at Lord Palmerston's dismissal'.[22] Now that he was out of office, Palmerston was still more popular outside parliament than within. Two books on Palmerston and his policy were published in 1852, and were reviewed, in July, in the *Westminster*. The books, and the review, portrayed a hero hated by kings. By implication, they attacked royal interference in British policy. Albert annotated the review in savage detail.[23] In the new parliament Palmerston admitted that not more than twenty M.P.s were 'disposed to look to me'.[24] 'Lord John will never again unite us', said Roebuck. 'Lord Palmerston, though popular, wants the support of the sedate portion of politicians.'[25] Palmerston was not inclined to win this at the expense of popularity. Though he came to the aid of the Tories on the Militia Bill, he attacked Malmesbury's handling of the case of a British subject maltreated in Tuscany by an Austrian officer (even though Russell did so too) and (unlike Russell) expressed the view that the Austrians ought to leave Italy. He was 'loudly cheered and greatly admired by his Radical friends', noted Greville; he was 'dealing largely in those Liberal clap-traps which have always been the chief part of his political stock-in-trade' and did not omit to attack

Granville and Russell as well as their successors.[26] He was still 'being himself'.

'He had no political adherents whatever', wrote Greville, 'but he is very popular and finds any amount of cheering in the House of Commons.'[27] There the Tories were the most coherent group, but they could not see how to get a majority without the help of Palmerston and the leading Peelites. These, however, Derby deterred by refusing to abandon Protection before the election. The overtures which Palmerston declined in February were made, perhaps, not with the expectation that they would be accepted, but to propitiate him. They were defended to the Palace on the ground that if Palmerston, one of the ablest debaters, were excluded from office, 'he would become dangerous and might in fact force himself back at the head of a Party with a claim to the Foreign Office'.[28] Palmerston, privately, repudiated any desire to become Foreign Secretary again. But he did want to become prime minister, and thought himself no more wanting in the necessary qualities than Derby or Russell or any available candidate. He thought he would be able to form a government. He saw that, because of the feeling at Court, he was unlikely to be asked, but he could help prevent Russell's return to No. 10, having, he said, lost all confidence in his judgement and discretion and loyalty to colleagues.[29] He could try to make sure that if there took place that conjunction of Whigs and Peelites which Albert had planned (and had tried prematurely to secure in February 1851), it should be under Lansdowne rather than the Peelite Aberdeen, so that, while its tendencies in domestic policy would be conservative, its tendencies in foreign policy would not be Tory. Palmerston was the prime mover in the effort to 'draft' the reluctant Lansdowne. He thought that under him Russell might hold the Foreign Office as a peer and Palmerston himself the Home Office with the leadership of the House of Commons. And he did not doubt that, with such a position, he would be able to outbid Russell for the succession. Lansdowne, aged seventy-two, would not last long. Palmerston, who had his sixty-eighth birthday in October, was cheerfully confident of his own energies and abilities.

Those who saw in Palmerston's sponsorship of a Lansdowne administration a sinister conspiracy to secure an all-party administration excluding Disraeli and Russell, to pass a 'sham' Reform Bill, misrepresented him. Palmerston did not want the

Tories to go out until it was certain Russell would not come in. He preferred a 'sham' Reform Bill to a real one; he would more readily tolerate the continuance of the Derby government if it introduced a 'sham' bill. He hoped a Lansdowne government would have the support of some of the Derbyites. But there is no evidence to suggest that he wanted an alternative government excluding Lord John. He wanted one excluding Lord John from the premiership and, if possible, the leadership of the Commons, and excluding Aberdeen from the Foreign Office and, if possible, from the premiership.[30] There is no evidence that Palmerston ever seriously considered joining the Tories. He told his brother that he had neither intention nor inclination to enlist under Derby, of whom he did not think highly as a statesman. It would not answer, and would not be agreeable to 'go slap over to the opposite camp' merely on account of 'a freak of Lord John Russell's which the whole Whig party regretted and condemned'.[31] But he encouraged, by a 'studious silence' on the matter, the continuance of speculation, which kept his name in the forefront of affairs, and he left the way open to serve under Derby if his government were comprehensively reconstructed to include himself and the Peelites (especially Gladstone). As a popular man, he found very agreeable a situation in which everyone except the Court ('cold, though civil') and, of course, the Manchester School, was 'well-disposed and civil', not wishing to offend him; in which 'the Government and the Liberals, wishing to get me on their side, are vying with each other in civilities'; in which, 'being free to act individually, I can express my own opinions without caring for others, and those opinions have generally been lucky enough to meet with concurrence'.[32] His wife was very proud of his clever election speech at Tiverton, where he parried the question which administration he would join with the jest that it would not be 'a Rowcliffe Administration'. He was strong against the folly of taxing the food of the many for the benefit of the few, firm on the necessity of building up the national defences, conservative on Parliamentary Reform. Members of the government put out feelers to him, but met no response. In the new parliament he could expect, owing to the Tory gains which made the result of a confidence or no confidence vote uncertain, to occupy a key position. That he did so was admitted on all sides, and he showed it in connection with the ceremonial abandonment of Protection as a political issue.

John Morley, the biographer of Cobden and of Gladstone, says of this incident: 'It did not suit Lord Palmerston that the Government should be turned out too soon. His plans for the succession were not ripe. A hurried crisis might make Lord John Russell again Prime Minister.' And he sneers at the House of Commons 'always ready to be captivated by anything that wears the air of moderation and compromise'.[33] This is unfair. As to a new government, Palmerston now thought he 'saw daylight'. For Russell, having pondered Palmerston's frank statement that he could serve with him but not under him, on 20th October said that he would serve under Lansdowne.[34] And there was nothing statesmanlike in the Manchester School's desire to carry through the new House of Commons by a smaller majority than could have been obtained in the old a form of words (hailing the repeal of the Corn Laws as 'just, wise and beneficient') for which few ministerialists could vote. Disraeli's motion was, indeed, too tepid for convinced Free Traders to support, but Charles Villiers' full-blooded amendment was defeated by 336 to 256 and Palmerston's amendment was accepted, in the small hours of 26th November 1852, by 468 to 53. Thus was Protection dispatched, by a decisive majority, into the limbo of lost causes.

'I believe the Derby Government rather calculate upon inducing me to join them when Protection has had its public funeral', wrote Palmerston in April.[31] Late on 24th November Disraeli asked Palmerston to go and see him for the purpose, Derby thought, of trying to secure his adhesion, with that of Gladstone, Herbert and other Peelites. The premier received, at Windsor, permission to approach them, but not to offer Palmerston the leadership of the House which, it was thought, might have been decisive with Gladstone, who 'wished to be on the liberal side of the conservative party, rather than on the conservative side of the liberal party' but could not enrol under Disraeli. Palmerston and the Peelites were, to a degree, acting together; Palmerston's amendment on Free Trade was originally Graham's. But Palmerston told Disraeli that he was not in concert with Gladstone and Herbert and that they evinced no desire to join the government. Disraeli (who had no wish to be demoted) made no proposals and when Derby saw Gladstone he was tentative and Gladstone non-commital. It was known to be no good inviting either Palmerston and Gladstone alone, and it was generally accepted that Palmerston would not join

Derby except on terms which (as Cornewall Lewis said) would virtually make Palmerston prime minister.[35]

All now hung on the result of the division on Disraeli's ingenious budget introduced in a speech which wrung grudging admiration even from Gladstone, who followed with a splendid denunciation. At 3 a.m. on 17th December 1852 the Tory government was defeated on this issue of confidence by a majority of nineteen. Palmerston took no part in the debate or division. Very damp weather had taken its toll. He was crippled by gout. But so was Lansdowne, who did not want the premiership and virtually shifted the work of forming a Whig–Peelite coalition on to Aberdeen.

This coalition could be formed without Palmerston, who, indeed, when offered the Admiralty or any other office except the leadership of the House, the Foreign Office or the Exchequer, refused. It could not be formed without Russell, and it was he who, complaining of 'degradation', made the difficulties.[36] But it was generally felt that, though the coalition could be formed without Palmerston, it could not last without him. At the first crisis, he would hold its fate in his hands. The Court's hostility had been mitigated a little by Palmerston's good offices in the matter of burying Protection, and Aberdeen agreed that it would be imprudent to leave him to coalesce with Disraeli. After toying wistfully with the unrealistic vision of a Palmerston residing at Viceregal Lodge, Dublin, Aberdeen went to make his offer. But Palmerston was reported to be 'disgusted' that Aberdeen, not Lansdowne, was to be premier and none too pleased that Russell was to lead the House. He said that, if there were no other objection, his reluctance to agree to any further reform of parliament would be an insuperable one. He declined to join the cabinet on the ground that the long hostility between himself and Aberdeen on foreign affairs would make his acceptance liable to misconstruction.[37]

There seems no justice in Graham's assertion that Palmerston who, if he did not join, would place himself at the head of Opposition, 'thus shows us the point of his sword and hopes by threats to prevail'.[38] The Grahams of British politics would traduce Palmerston equally for joining or not joining. Lady Palmerston, however, was anxious to see her lord back in harness. 'I am out at grass, and grass to an old horse is like mother's milk to a baby', he had said a few months before. But this, even if sincere, was a passing whim.

Estate matters had now been brought into order. The head-
gardener at Broadlands, who had deteriorated into a smoking sot,
had been replaced. The Ascot Stakes had been won.[39] Out of office
Palmerston would be restless, mischievous in effect if not in intent.
Lansdowne begged him to reconsider. So did Clarendon, who
made much of the fact that the Foreign Office was to be in the
hands either of Russell or himself. Palmerston admitted that he
would find political solitude 'little agreeable'. There would be
much to interest him at the Home Office, including responsibility for building up the militia. And he could hardly be kept from
playing an important part in the formulation of the foreign policy
of any cabinet of which he was a member. So Greville was able to
write on 24th December: 'The great event of yesterday was
Palmerston's accession to the Government.'[40]

Palmerston defended himself in a letter to his brother-in-law,
Sulivan, who thought he had done the wrong thing[41] —

... I have for the last twelve months been acting the part of a very distinguished tight-rope dancer and much astonishing the public by my
individual performances and feats. ... So far, so well; but even Madame
Sacqui, when she had mounted her rope and flourished among her
rockets, never thought of making the rope her perch, but prudently came
down again to avoid a dangerous fall. ...
... I must either have been left alone between earth and heaven with
the imputation of nourishing implacable personal resentments, and from
my new position have lost much of my influence in the House of Commons; or I must have accepted the invitation which the 310 Derbyites
were preparing to make to me, to place myself at their head as Derby's
Lieutenant and Disraeli's chief. If I had been a reckless adventurer,
without principles to restrain me, without friendships to care for, without
character to lose, such a course would have been a clear one. ... [But]
what would the great Liberal Party, not in the House of Commons, nor at
Brooks's, nor at the Reform Club, but in the United Kingdom, have said
of such a course; ... what would that party at Tiverton by whom I have
so long been returned have said, and how should I have been sure of not
having to go abegging like Graham from one place to another!

Palmerston makes no pretence that he does not like office. He wants
to be in the government or virtually leader of the Opposition. But
he shows a regard for consistency and still more for reputation, and
most of all for the goodwill of that Liberal public opinion which
most spontaneously applauded the characteristic extravagances of
his foreign policy.

The new Peelite ministers, whether recently hostile (like

Graham) or friendly (like Gladstone) rushed to 'shake hands and congratulate'. Palmerston received Graham coldly, and Gladstone warmly. They were congratulating themselves, rather than him, for his refusal to join them had been, Gladstone said, 'a serious blow . . . without him, or rather with him between us and the Conservatives, I cannot but say the game will be a very difficult one to play'. Palmerston, Graham said, appeared to think opposition would be formidable, and Sir James asked 'What would it have been if he had led it, in concert with Disraeli?'. Sitting beside him in cabinet, Clarendon thought he meant the government to last, that he meant to 'run true'.[42] When, indeed, Gladstone revealed to his colleagues the plan of his first, momentous, budget, Palmerston criticized it as opening too many points of attack, and unlikely to pass, and he objected, strongly and persistently, in correspondence with the Chancellor, to the new succession duties, as an attack on landlords. But he admitted that the budget was a great plan, and his doubts as to its passage through the House were widely shared in the cabinet, which was surprised by its popularity. Palmerston gave no public or private sign of disloyalty during a session which strengthened the administration in the House of Commons.

Superficially, this strengthening of the administration should have meant a weakening of Palmerston's own position. This, however, did not occur. We find Aberdeen writing to the Queen on 11th September 1853 urging her to invite the Home Secretary to be minister-in-attendance before she left Balmoral, because the public and press would not fail to attribute the lack of an invitation 'to the jealousy and ill-will of Lord Aberdeen . . . and would convert this neglect into the ground of the most hostile and bitter attacks'. Moreover, 'the situation of Lord Palmerston is peculiar. Unless he should continue to be a cordial member of your Majesty's Government, he may very easily become the leader of the Opposition. . . . Your Majesty may perhaps be aware that there is no amount of flattery which is not offered to Lord Palmerston by the Tory party, with the hope of separating him altogether from the Government'.[43] Palmerston's bargaining power had been enhanced, rather than diminished. We must see why.

CHAPTER XVII

RESIGNATION AND RETURN, 1853

THE real subject of Kingsley Martin's notable book, *The Triumph of Lord Palmerston*, is the development in the Britain of the 1850s of a chauvinism which forced a reluctant government into what the premier, Aberdeen, called 'a war for and with a barbarous government which had declined to follow our advice'. It is remarkable that so little of a book with such a title is concerned strictly with what Palmerston said or did. It is the story of how public opinion 'came round' to Palmerston, and made him its not reluctant champion, the embodiment of patriotic sentiment. It was because complex issues of foreign policy were rationalized in terms of a contest between Palmerston and Aberdeen that the latter stressed the importance of Palmerston having 'no personal or private cause of complaint against Lord Aberdeen'.[1] For in keeping Palmerston in the government rested the prime minister's only hope of preventing war with Russia.

In 1852–3 the most unpopular of foreign Powers was, in general, Austria. Granville, Malmesbury and Clarendon in succession declined to take, at the behest of foreign governments, especially the Austrian, measures against refugees that would hardly be tolerated even for the security of the United Kingdom itself. Clarendon was distinctly Palmerstonian when Austria, blaming the activities in Britain of Mazzini and Kossuth for a rising in Milan and an attempt on the life of Franz Josef, threatened that foreign governments would take steps 'for their own protection as well as to mark their sense of the wrong done to them by England'. As Clarendon reported to the Queen, his discussion with the envoy of Austria 'became rather warm, and [he] thought it right to remark that too much importance might be given to these proclamations and too little to the causes at home which might lead the subjects of Austria to manifest their discontent by revolutionary outbreaks, nor could we conceal from ourselves that the complaints about the refugees were occasionally directed against the free institutions which gave them protection, and that we were not always viewed with favour as presenting the single but prosperous exception to that system of government which otherwise would now be almost uniform in Europe'.[2] It was the Tory Lord Ellenborough who most lucidly expounded the doctrine of right of sanctuary for political refugees. Yet it was significant that the adjective which sprang, and springs, to mind to describe such defiance of continental attempts to secure new curbs on the activities of refugees and tightening of British passport regulations is 'Palmerstonian'.

That there was some ground for an impression existing, as King Leopold said, not only in Austria and Prussia and France, but among the Belgian workers, that 'in England a sort of menagerie of Kossuths, Mazzinis, Legranges, Ledru Rollins etc is kept to be let loose occasionally on the Continent to render its quiet and prosperity impossible'[3] Palmerston discovered as Home Secretary. After the Foreign Office passed on reports from Berlin of the discovery of rockets made in England for purposes of sabotage and outrage, the police descended on a factory at Rotherhithe frequently visited by Kossuth and seized forty cases of rockets believed to be destined for Rostock and 6,000–8,000 explosive devices completed or in process of manufacture. It was Palmerston's duty to pass the papers on to the Law Officers of the Crown for an opinion as to prosecution for conspiracy to levy war upon a foreign sovereign. But he hardly disguised his opinion that it was the business of threatened governments to intercept letters, couriers and arms coming in from outside.[4] He responded, of course, as public opinion responded, to news of indignities offered to Cives Romani travelling or residing abroad. Malmesbury, who had to deal, and dealt toughly but temperately, with the Mather and Murray cases, suspected that the Civis Romanus doctrine encouraged British people to behave irresponsibly. At Florence the young Mr Mather wilfully impeded an Austrian officer and was struck on the head with a sword; at Rome Mr Murray was probably implicated in a murder.[5]

In November 1852 the Austrians touched British feeling in the raw when they declined to send officers to the funeral of the Duke of Wellington, in revenge for the insult to Haynau. In 1853, when war with Russia was likely, and co-operation with Austria was important either to avoid or to wage it, all that was Liberal and Radical in public opinion was anti-Austrian as well as anti-Russian — and anti-Roman as well. But many elements not specifically

anti-Austrian were also anti-Romanist, and, as the agitation un-
leashed by Russell's letter to the Bishop of Durham had shown,
vehemently so. In 'the Protestant cause' both the Court and Derby
were 'sound'. It seemed to the latter as well as to Russell closely
connected with the cause of liberty; Derby thought Lord John's
talk of 'an organized conspiracy against the liberties of Europe' by
the priestly party justified and read in that context the closing of a
Mr Hamilton's school in Naples, the prosecution of the Madai in
Florence for proselytizing Protestantism, and many of the designs
of Napoleon III. Palmerston, like Russell and unlike Derby, stood
consistently for the civil equality of Catholics in the United
Kingdom, and the Nonconformist ministers of Tiverton knew
only too well from his dusty answers to their representations
against the state endowment of the seminary at Maynooth in
Ireland that his dislike of the Romanist system did not influence
his views on domestic issues. Though closely connected with his
wife's son-in-law, Lord Shaftesbury, a narrow Anglican Evangelical, Palmerston would never have written the Durham Letter nor
made the speech against Romanism which Russell made in a
debate in 1853; this the prime minister had to disavow in order to
prevent the resignation of Catholic members of his administration.
But Palmerston had achieved a corner in the political credit
accruing from national indignation against Austria and her satel-
lites, and hence incidents such as the arrest in September 1853 in
Florence of a Scottish Presbyterian, Miss Cunningham, for
propagating the Protestant faith, helped his popularity.

Such incidents also intensified warlike feeling. It is quite
illogical that Russia, Austria and Rome should have become almost
interchangeable terms of abuse — except that all were synonymous
with illiberality. By the mysterious alchemy of hatred, the unpopularity of Russia turned the Turks, in the public estimation, into para-
gons of virtue. The public joyfully accepted the Palmerstonian thesis
of 1833, that the maintenance of the Turkish Empire was essential to
the interests of Great Britain. As a matter of course, it accepted,
with it, the much more disputable thesis that this empire was
perfectly capable of being transformed into a civilized and efficient
state. To the cause of reform in Turkey Stratford devoted himself
unceasingly and with undoubted nobility. He was forced to admit
that the results were very disappointing. Palmerston never perhaps
hoped, in detail, for such results as Stratford did, and on occasion

wrote sharp dispatches about Turkish cruelty and oppression, like that of 18th December 1850 (apropos of Syria and Bosnia) in which he said: 'If the Christian subjects of the Sultan are to be liable to become the victims of such abominable crimes Christian Europe will come to the conclusion that the existence of the Ottoman Empire is an evil, and that its overthrow would be conducive to the general interests of the human race.'[6] But he was committed to the view that the system of Turkey was 'progressively liberal',[7] because unless it was Turkey could never be a respectable ally. In 1853 public opinion came round to this view, helped by memories of Turkish resistance to Austria and Russia over the surrender of the refugees. Kingsley Martin points the paradox: 'In a palace on the Bosphorus sat the Sultan, a fleshy and irascible debauchee, usually intoxicated and always lethargic, surrounded by a group of Mohammedan fanatics of whose plots to supplant him he was dimly aware and whose ability to rouse the fury of a priest-ridden mob kept him in abject terror and peevish submission. In England were public halls, crowded with respectable shopkeepers, evangelical maiden ladies, and stolid artisans enthusiastically proffering their lives and money in the service of this obese little tyrant in a fez, whose name they could not pronounce and whose habits of life were as unknown to them as those of a prehistoric monster.'[8] By January 1855 they were to make Palmerston prime minister, as the man to win the war.

Public opinion had been bellicose in 1852, when the expected enemy was Napoleon; it was more bellicose in 1853, when the expected enemy was Nicholas, war with whom involved a French alliance. Palmerston welcomed the change of villain, and welcomed it the more for the prospect of alliance with the emperor of the French (for on the anniversary of the coup d'état President Buonaparte became Napoleon 'III'). In 1852 only Malmesbury (a personal friend of Napoleon) seemed immune from the general 'presentiment', as he called it, that French ambitions would lead to war. Palmerston was 'evidently very distrustful of his friend the Emperor's pacific intentions' and determined to exploit the 'scare' to get on with the two or three year task of putting the country into a state of defence.[9] Yet, in standing against the tide and urging a French alliance, the *Morning Post* represented Palmerston's own preference.

It was the French, not the Russians, who revived the Eastern

Question. Palmerston had warned Malmesbury that France sought the principal influence in the East, that France and Britain were like two men in love with the same woman.[10] One of his last dispatches had warned the Turk against offending the Russian Colossus, when Napoleon revived eighteenth century claims on behalf of the Latin monks at the Holy Places which could not be granted without derogation of the rights of the Greek clergy whose protector was the Tsar. British opinion, official and unofficial, was against France, seeing in the action another sign of deference to the 'parti prêtre'. One of Malmesbury's last dispatches warned France that the question, roughly handled, could lead to war — 'it is giving Russia an opportunity of bullying and degrading the Porte'. After he left office he told the Emperor, most astutely, that every country had its subject on which no concession could be made — 'the Holy Places in the East was that of Russia, the Refugees was ours'.[11] And this is the answer to the question, often rightly and reasonably asked, why the French claims, which were in fact withdrawn, should have led to the Crimean War — that, as Malmesbury said, the Tsar would as soon grant a Russian House of Commons as surrender his prestige among the populations of the Orthodox faith by any appearance of concession on this claim. When the Russians dispatched Menschikoff to Constantinople to complain against and undo the Turkish concessions to the French, the British hastened out Lord Stratford de Redcliffe via Paris and Vienna to watch the Russian, guide the Turk and moderate the French. He procured a graceful French withdrawal, but Menschikoff did not wish to leave empty handed, and deemed it an affront to Russian honour when he had to.

Those who have blamed the Turk for 'causing' the Crimean War have really blamed, often explicitly, Stratford, as 'the real Sultan'. They were right, of course, to see in him, even more than Palmerston, the champion and indeed the author of the theses of 1833. He felt more strongly than Palmerston the importance of securing some Russian admission that the multilateral agreements of 1840–1 had affected Russia's special position in the Danubian Principalities. He chafed at Palmerston's statesmanlike refusal to exploit the 1848 revolutions there to reinsert Turkish influence at the expense of Russian, and regarded as a major diplomatic defeat the Turkish Act of Balta Liman (1849) which, if anything, strengthened Russian rights.[12] But the ambassador himself mainly drafted the instructions handed him by Russell, dated 25th February 1853,* and they were unexceptionable in their assertion that the Russian claims in regard to the Holy Places were 'superior to the French'. Ministers who later railed against him as an agent provocateur (but dared not recall him) overlooked the moderation shown by Stratford until he knew of the Russian determination (end of May) to occupy the Principalities as a 'material guarantee' for satisfaction on the wording of an agreement on the Tsar's special rights in the Ottoman Empire.[13]

The whole cabinet, had it been consulted, would have approved the conciliatory tone of Stratford's instructions. None of the ministers wanted war with Russia; none wanted a crisis over Turkey, for even those who believed the days of Turkish power in Europe were numbered thought the disintegration of the empire a more remote contingency than Nicholas had implied in his recent conversations with the British envoy, Seymour.[14] None of the ministers thought that Nicholas wanted war. 'Had Nicholas been weak, Aberdeen strong, or Mensikov tactful, there might have been no war.'[15] But Menschikoff was tactless and domineering. He dealt in ultimatums, and, indeed, in insults. He left in dudgeon in May, with claims to a special protective role for the Tsar over twelve million of the Sultan's subjects unsatisfied. Precisely what those claims implied — whether a mere reassertion of rights under existing treaties, or an advance on them — the Tsar does not seem to have asked himself, at least until too late. He seems to have been surprised to find that the Menshikoff mission had brought Russia to the brink of war with the Western Powers, and a breach with Austria. Had not Russell, perhaps unwisely, admitted in a dispatch to St Petersburg that with regard to the Ottoman Christians Russia had rights of 'exceptional protection . . . no doubt prescribed by duty and sanctioned by Treaty'? When the Four Powers sent to St Petersburg the Vienna Note, and it was accepted, the crisis seemed over. But this Note had not been submitted to the Turks, and they proposed amendments unacceptable to Russia, which raised the vital issue — hitherto evaded — of what precisely the Tsar's rights had been, and what they were to be. These Turkish propositions also exposed deep divisions within the British cabinet.

*   *   *   *

The Home Secretary expounds strategy to the Aberdeen Cabinet

Charles Wood   Argyll Clarendon J. Russell Granville Cranworth G. Grey Sidney Herbert
J. R. G. Graham W. E. Gladstone Lansdowne Aberdeen Palmerston Newcastle
William Molesworth

THE ABERDEEN CABINET, formed in 1853

There was much disposition in the cabinet to be tough with the Turks. Aberdeen loved peace. He disliked, and was known to dislike, Napoleon. He liked and trusted, and was known to like and trust, Nicholas. Ever since 1813 he had thought of Russia (as of Austria) as an 'ally'; he had got on well with Nicholas and Nesselrode in England in 1844; he had admired Russia's dignified stance in 1848 and approved her action in Hungary in 1849. Though, in deference to the Duke, he had from 1828 to 1830 submerged his philhellenism and tenderness for Russia and played (ineffectively) the role of Sultan's friend, he loathed and despised the Turks and their régime in Europe. He believed it was the aim of these 'barbarians' to cause a war, to play off one Power against another, to divide them, not in order to rule, but in order to survive. He believed that, if war came, there would be Christian risings in the Balkans.[16] In Aberdeen, Argyll and Gladstone this belief almost contained an element of hope, but they were very fearful of having to help suppress Christian populations as the allies of an oppressive Sultan-Caliph. Even Russell was sufficiently moved by their arguments to make a distinction between fighting as a principal and as an auxiliary; he tried to find a way of acting 'not for the Sultan, but for the general interests of the population of European Turkey'.[17]

Palmerston had no such qualms. His reply to these distractions from the central Balance of Power theme on which, alone of all the ministers, he kept his eyes fixed, was crushing. If, he said, one wanted to play the Polish drama over again, and expel two million Moslems, including the army and most of the landowners, one ought to fight with Russia against Turkey.[18] But who was to fill the vacuum? Lansdowne had suggested that Britain tell Russia that in the event of a catastrophe, England would consider the Greek nation the natural heir of the Mahometan power.[19] But the Greeks, Palmerston pointed out, were a minority and could not be the ruling race, a verdict which a hundred years more Balkan history hardly invalidates. And the Slavs, though the majority, were unfitted for that role. So 'a reconstruction of Turkey means neither more nor less than its subjection to Russia, direct or indirect, immediate or for a time delayed'. Palmerston insisted that there would be no Christian risings. He had some evidence to go on, in that (as Stratford never ceased to stress) the Turkish generals who occupied the Principalities in 1821–4 were regarded by the

M

Christian inhabitants as liberators from the Russian despoilers, and the viceroy Sulieman was welcomed by the Wallachians in 1848. But he was bound to take this attitude, because he was irretrievably committed to the proposition that Turkey was a reforming and reformable state. His mode of arguing it was not one which appealed to Aberdeen, for he said that there were many Christians in Russia, Austria, Rome and Naples would be glad to be as well treated as the subjects of the Sultan.[18] But by incorporating in a dispatch to Stratford the suggestion that, to avoid Christian uprisings, aid to the Turks should be made conditional upon reforms, Clarendon, the Foreign Secretary, virtually committed the government to the view that Turkey was reformable. Palmerston thought this all to the good, but it did not make much sense if one thought, as he did, in terms of simple confrontation with Russia. Turkey was to be supported, not on her merits, but in the general interest of Europe. That had been his theme in 1833–41; it was his theme now. Not that he wished for war. Not that he thought Nicholas wished for war. Not that he thought Nicholas other than a gentleman who could be trusted. But he knew, what those colleagues who had been attracted and impressed by the Tsar when he visited England in 1844 overlooked, that even the Supreme Autocrat of all the Russians could not personally control foreign policy in all its detail; could not be guaranteed immune from the temptation to 'take a chance'; could not be relied upon to be infallible in his judgements of the reaction, in given circumstances, of all foreign Powers, still less of the influence of particular individuals such as Aberdeen. Even he, perhaps, did not suspect that Nicholas, of whom they all thought so highly, might prove to be, as Gavin Henderson said, a blunderer. But Palmerston was sure that war could be avoided if the probing antennae met resistance. 'If others are firm they will stop or recede; if others recede or falter, they advance and rush in', he had written of the France of Louis Philippe and Guizot.[20] In May 1853 he wrote to Clarendon: 'The policy and practice of the Russian Government has always been to push forward its encroachments as fast and as far as the apathy or want of firmness of other Governments would allow it to go, but always to stop and retire when it is met with decided resistance.'[21]

All that was required, then, was firmness and clarity. Russia must be told that Britain would fight, as a principal, and as an ally of France and Turkey, if Russian claims were not confined to what

'Europe' would allow. And Russia must be told what that limit was. The Tsar, Palmerston believed, was a rational man, who would take such firmness without rancour. But other ministers pondered the fact that if the Tsar was prudent, he was also proud. As Argyll put it, his resolute will was always fearless and might be fierce; accessible to argument, he would never yield to menaces. Palmerston, they said, was too fond of bullying to be a safe guide. But Palmerston knew, in great crises, the difference between firmness and bullying. What infuriated him was that every belated approach by the cabinet towards firmness and clarity was eroded by Aberdeen in his conversations with the Russian envoy, Brunnow.[22] 'Nicholas believed that whatever happened, Aberdeen would prevent his colleagues from going to war', concluded Professor Temperley.[23] That was fatal. 'Every single step tending to make war inevitable was taken in advance by Russia; . . . we only followed with slowness and reluctance', boasted Argyll. Palmerston put it differently — Russia 'was led on step by step by the apparent timidity of the Government of England', by the belief that its policy was peace at any, or almost any, price.[24]

With Aberdeen and his friends on the one hand and Palmerston and Russell on the other virtually cancelling one another out, control of policy was in effect left to Clarendon, whose only lodestar was the survival of the ministry. He had an evident distaste for alliance with Turkey, but his was 'the fatal mediation' which sent the fleet to Besika. He was swayed by public opinion. It was public opinion, rather than pressure from this or that colleague, which overcame Aberdeen's passionate attachment to appeasement. It is true that Temperley describes as 'a fateful decision' the inclusion of Palmerston, from late March onwards, originally at the suggestion of Clarendon, in the 'inner cabinet' which dealt with foreign affairs, and consisted of Aberdeen, Russell (who remained Leader of the House when he gave up the Foreign Office to Clarendon late in February), Clarendon and Palmerston, and sometimes Graham, First Lord of the Admiralty.[25] To have left him out would have been an insult, certainly leading to trouble via the *Morning Post*, and probably to a resignation and a cabinet crisis. To include him meant that Aberdeen could not have his way consistently. But it is inconceivable that the premier could, in any circumstances, have prevailed, and, as Aberdeen himself attested, in the letter to the Queen in September, Palmerston 'has been recently more than once thwarted in his endeavours to press a hostile policy on the Cabinet'.[1] When it became evident that there were two alternative policies in conflict within the cabinet, it was generally assumed that the principal antagonists were Aberdeen and Palmerston. Thus when Walewski contrasted Palmerston's assurances to him that Britain would fight and Aberdeen's assurances to Brunnow that she would not, Malmesbury told him that the stronger man, Palmerston, would prevail. But then Malmesbury was in opposition, and was rationalizing on the basis of Palmerston's frank and private admission to him at the end of May that he agreed with the criticisms of the Government.[26] The evidence is certainly that up to and after 1st June, when the cabinet (with Aberdeen protesting but acquiescing) decided to send the fleet to Besika Bay in the wake of the French (which had gone in March), Palmerston, involved in the discussions and decisions, was no trouble-maker. He was, moreover, less vehement and querulous in correspondence and interviews with Aberdeen and Clarendon than was Russell, who had decided as early as March that the Russians aimed at the destruction of Turkey and must be resisted. It was, indeed, possible for Lord John's biographer to write of the conflict as between Aberdeen and Russell, with Palmerston sometimes intervening.[27] But those who were not in the cabinet had no doubt, on account of Palmerston's record and the tone of the *Morning Post*, that Palmerston was the champion of the patriotic cause in the cabinet, and to be exempted from the mounting charges of 'childish obstinacy' and 'senile hesitation' levied by the press against his contemporary, Aberdeen.

To Clarendon Palmerston was helpful and respectful, and the frankness with which he expressed his views to Walewski, Malmesbury and others was, at the worst, merely doing what Clarendon had done in 1840. Not until September did the premier avow that 'it has been reported to Lord Aberdeen that he [Palmerston] has expressed himself in terms of great hostility'. He had the grace to add: 'This cannot perhaps be avoided, and is only the result of taking different views of the public interest'. Aberdeen could hardly complain that he had to read the *Morning Post* to find out what Palmerston's views were, when Palmerston had to read *The Times* to discover Aberdeen's. The prima facie case to be made against Palmerston is not one of disloyalty to Aberdeen, whom he scarcely respected ('We have our own wretched pasha at

home'), or Clarendon, but that he did not join forces with Russell
to press his demands for action, for firmness, for clarity on their
colleagues, and that he did not do so because of personal ambition.
This works both ways. Russell was ambitious too. If Palmerston
had no wish to turn out Aberdeen just to put Russell at the head of
the same cabinet (and knew that the colleagues would resist such
substitution), Russell had no wish to turn out Aberdeen if the
alternative was to be a different government, under Palmerston,
and probably including Tories, in which Russell, if he was
included, would find his position (already, in his view, degrading)
highly uncongenial. Whatever the explanation, the fact is clear,
that Palmerston and Russell pressed for more vigour, but did so in
alternation, rather than in harness. Putting the matter at its crudest,
each of the rivals wanted a more manly policy, and each wanted
power, which could only be obtained at the expense of the other.
Of the two, Palmerston behaved with the greater restraint, and
hence with the greater claim to be regarded as a good colleague,
loyal to the concept of coalition; perhaps he was confident that
public opinion would do his work for him, and give him the credit.
That might mean an unnecessary war. Palmerston would have liked
to avoid war, but he had to realize that, because of his reputation
for 'bullying', he would defeat his own objects by pressing too
strongly too often. By contrast Russell, who lacked Palmerston's
popularity, and was consumed by ambition for the premiership,
was restless and intemperate, though his pressure was of such a
nature as to be concealed from the public and indeed from most of
the cabinet. It was in general surreptitious, and was dealt with
surreptitiously.

At the time that the French fleet went to the East Palmerston
was reported as 'ready to join in more stringent and violent
measures if they had been proposed'. They were not, and it is
likely that he did not know that Russell was, to Clarendon, 'full
of very wild talk of strong measures to be taken, and a fleet sent to
the Baltic to make peremptory demands'.[28] Russell did not support
Palmerston when in mid-June he urged that a Russian move into
the Principalities should be regarded as a *casus belli*.[39] It was not
until 28th June that Palmerston, at last convinced (by the tone of
Menschikoff) that Russia was 'bent on a stand-up fight', began a
fortnight's sustained attempt to persuade his colleagues to agree
that, as soon as Russian troops moved, the fleet should go into the

Bosphorus and Stratford have authority to send it into the Black Sea. This would encourage the defensive operations of the Turks and discourage revolt, it would act as a wholesome check on the Tsar and assist the efforts of Austria and Prussia to bring him to reason. 'I am confident that this country expects that we should pursue such a course', he wrote to Aberdeen.[30] As to the strength of public opinion, Aberdeen knew it as well as Palmerston — 'there could not have been more agitation in Rome when Caesar crossed the Rubicon than in England when the armies of Nicholas crossed the Pruth', says Argyll. But Aberdeen said that in such a case he dreaded popular support. He had not Neville Chamberlain's excuse for appeasement, that it was popular, but he had all his temperamental and personal aversion to the Churchillian mode. Twice in vain Palmerston wrestled in cabinet, arguing that 'nothing is to be gained with the Russian Govt, or indeed with any other, by anything which looks like doubt, hesitation, or fear, while on the other hand, a bold firm course founded on right, and supported by strength, is the safest way of arriving at a satisfactory and peaceful result'.[31] When the Russians moved into the Principalities, and Nesselrode had the nerve to say that they had gone there because the Western fleets were at Besika, Palmerston circularized the cabinet in vigorous condemnation of excessive forbearance which was taken for irresolution. The robber was saying he would not leave the house till the policeman retired from the courtyard. Nesselrode should be told that the squadrons would go up to Constantinople as a reply to his note. But on 15th July Palmerston agreed to 'share the responsibility' of submitting to insult in order to see what came of the negotiations at Vienna.[32]

*   *   *   *

The Vienna Note did not provide for the immediate evacuation of the Principalities, and was therefore denounced by the *Daily News* and by Urquhart (in the *Advertiser*), sure that the cabinet was in Russian pay. But when the Tsar accepted it, the press in general, and even the *Morning Post*, said that the Eastern Question was settled. Such was the situation in the closing days of the parliamentary session, during which the government had a very rough passage on foreign affairs and, in the opinion of some, was saved because 'Lord Palmerston was roused . . . [and] fell upon Cobden with great vigour and success'.[33]

When the Turks insisted on amendments to the Note, the general opinion of the cabinet was that they should be forced, by a threat of abandonment, to accept the Note in toto. This attitude looked foolish when there was published on 7th September Nesselrode's interpretation of the Note (later known as 'the violent interpretation'). This justified the Turkish reservations and showed that the Powers had been outsmarted by St Petersburg. The Powers could not admit that they had accepted Nesselrode's extreme version of the rights acquired by the Tsar at Kutchuk Kainardji, that they had, in acknowledging old treaties, acknowledged, in effect, the new pretensions which Menschikoff had made at Constantinople. To Palmerston, even before this publication, his colleagues' attitude was just plain stupid, for to abandon Turkey was to abandon a British and European interest. He did, however, draft a proposed dispatch to the Powers urging Turkey to accept the Vienna Note, trusting to the Powers to insist on an interpretation in line with the Turkish. Aberdeen found his 'comical'.[34] The cynic will say that Palmerston did this in the assurance that such a note to Turkey would never be sent, and in fact the Austrians declined to accept it. But it was the only feasible compromise, if somewhat illogical after the Powers had submitted the Turkish modifications to Russia, and seen them rejected. The Tsar's repudiation, when he met Franz Josef at Olmutz, of Nesselrode's interpretation, made the initiative look promising. In putting it forward, Palmerston took the great personal risk of having Russell resign and accuse the government of acting shabbily and abandoning British interests. For Lord John argued that, having forwarded to St Petersburg the Turkish objections, 'we surely cannot again present to him [the Sultan] the same note unamended, with whatever explanations we may accompany it'. He hoped the Turk would instantly reject the proposal which 'the fatal facility of the electric telegraph' had led Aberdeen, Clarendon and Palmerston to make during Russell's absence in Scotland. But even Turkish rejection could not wipe out the shame of the proposal, and if the dispatch was ever sent to Constantinople, he did not see how he could stay in the cabinet.[35] This threat was given point by Russell the same night, 19th September, in a speech at Greenock, where he said that peace without honour was not peace.

Palmerston, though he risked seeing Russell emerge as the champion of the popular mood, was being disingenuous, for even

Clarendon admitted that the Sultan could not accept the Vienna Note unamended without losing his throne and perhaps his life. It must, however, have surprised Palmerston that on 23rd September Aberdeen and Clarendon, without consulting anybody else, accepted the French suggestion that the fleets pass the Dardanelles. They did this because they feared public opinion and the resignation of Russell and perhaps Palmerston as well, and because, owing to weather prospects, the fleet had to go somewhere less exposed, and must go forward rather than back. 'Russell triumphed', says Temperley;[36] 'Palmerston has triumphed' said the public, which, Clarendon complained, 'seems to think there is nothing to do but to declare war against Russia, just when she is yielding the point in dispute, and back the Turk, just when he acts contrary to our advice'.[37] For Turkey, owing, Aberdeen and Clarendon believed, to the malign influence of Stratford, was about to declare war on Russia. Palmerston had no part in the decision, and Stratford was most reluctant to pass on the order to the admiral, and delayed doing so until peremptorily ordered after a cabinet on 8th October (the first since late August). The movement of the fleets removed Stratford's power to restrain the Turk, and it blew sky-high the attempt of Buol, with Napoleon's approval, to reinstate the Vienna Note with explanations which *ought* to have satisfied Turkey though they were rather more conciliatory to Nesselrode than Palmerston's draft.

Among those who credited to Palmerston the decision of 23rd September was David Urquhart, for once trusting Palmerston and transferring his suspicions to Prince Albert. Of Palmerston he wrote: 'The man who can over-reach his own sovereign is surely qualified to put down that of Russia.'[38] But the Palace was for the moment in tune with public opinion. The Queen forwarded to Aberdeen a memorandum by the Prince stating that Russia had laid bare her intention to 'acquire *new* Rights of interference which the Porte does *not* wish to concede and cannot concede, and which the European Powers have repeatedly declared she *ought not* to concede'.[39] Clarendon said as much in his note of 30th September* — Russia had shown 'a total disregard for the feelings and interests of the European Powers . . . who . . . cannot see with indifference that Russia should thus surreptitiously seek to obtain a virtual Protectorate over the Christian Subjects of the Porte'. This was all Palmerston could have desired, but there was still much shilly-shallying around him. Russell had inopportunely discovered qualms about the fate of the Christian subjects of the Porte; Clarendon abused the Turks for declaring war; Aberdeen, whose only reason for staying in office was to maintain peace, resented Palmerston's earnest request that he maintain to Brunnow a mysterious uncertainty as to what aid would be given to Turkey (a request made because it was idle to get any stalwart talk out of the premier) and sent the same day for Delane of *The Times* to say that he would resign rather than agree to war.[40]

In these circumstances, compromise was the only alternative to a political crisis caused by resignations. The order to the fleet to pass the Dardanelles and the decision that if the Russians crossed the Danube or attacked the coasts of Turkey it should enter the Euxine (8th October) were concessions to Palmerston's demand that the Western fleets should detain and hand over to the Turks any Russian warships in the Black Sea found out of port, and that the Foreign Enlistment Act should be suspended, a demand vigorously resisted by Aberdeen and Gladstone.[41] Russell, who had 'faintly supported' Palmerston in cabinets on 7th and 8th,[42] the next day demanded the recall of parliament, which Aberdeen refused as likely to make war certain. Indeed, the premier only waited for the dispersal of the cabinet ministers, to try to secure a compromise Note which Turkey and Russia might accept, with the old, stupid threat that if the Turks were obdurate, Britain and France would leave them to their fate, a gambit condemned in advance by Clarendon, who pointed out that 'we should still have to help them, because otherwise Russia would be established at Constantinople in a twelvemonth'.[43] Aberdeen was still stubbornly refusing to face facts, especially the facts inseparable from the basic nature of the relationship between the Western Powers and Turkey. Clarendon, worn out by the premier's incessant interferences intended to blur every decision made by the cabinet or the inner group, now realized that the present anomalous and painful position might have been avoided by firmer language and a more decided course in May. For here they were drifting into war (as he unwisely told the Lords) at a pace to be determined by the issue of battles between Turkey and Russia at land or sea and the pressure of public opinion.

Aberdeen was encouraged in his latest efforts by a protest from Albert which would have made Palmerston smile[44] —

... Here were decisions taken by the Cabinet, perhaps even acted upon, involving the most momentous consequences, without her previous concurrence, or even the means for her to judge of the propriety or impropriety of the course to be adopted, with evidence that the Minister, in whose judgement the Queen placed her chief reliance, disapproved of it. The position was morally and constitutionally a wrong one. The Queen ought to have the whole policy in spirit and ultimate tendency developed before her to give her deliberate sanction to it, knowing what it involved her in abroad and at home. She might now be involved in war ... chiefly by the desire of Lord Aberdeen to keep his Cabinet together. ...

The dispatches were sent off without submission to the Queen. She too disliked feeling that Britain's commitments fell to be determined by 'the hundred and twenty fanatical Turks constituting the Divan at Constantinople'. Aberdeen admitted that the decisions had been taken because otherwise the cabinet would have been broken up by Russell and Palmerston. But it looked as though Russell, profoundly discontented with his personal subordination, would go anyway; if he did, Aberdeen thought, Palmerston, Lansdowne and even Clarendon would go too.[45] The premier withdrew his new proposals because Palmerston apparently now, for the first time, made a positive threat of resignation. Palmerston and Russell, for the moment in concert, or at least in close correspondence, accepted, indeed, that a last attempt at a settlement should be made, before the Turks began active operations. The inner cabinet agreed to ask the Turks to abstain from military action, but Russell procured the insertion of the addendum 'for a reasonable time'. That was interpreted, says Kingsley Martin bitterly, as two weeks.[46]

★   ★   ★   ★

Palmerston thought the gold and silver age of notes was all but passed, and the age of bronze and iron about to begin.[47] It was all so unnecessary. 'If the Russian Government had been plainly told that the moment a Russian soldier set foot on Turkish territory ... the combined squadrons would move up to the Bosphorus, and, if necessary, operate in the Black Sea, there can be little doubt that the Russian Government would have paused. . . .'[48] As to conditions and qualifications and half-measures towards Turkey when she was at war with Russia, 'we passed the Rubicon when we first took part with Turkey and sent our squadrons to support her, and when England and France have once taken a third Power by the hand, that third Power *must* be carried in safety through the difficulties'. As to the argument that it was humiliating that Britain's action should be determined by Turkish action or fortunes, it was pointless to repine. *'We support Turkey for our own sake and for our own interests, and to withdraw our support, or to cripple it so as to render it ineffectual, merely because the Turkish Government did not show as much deference to our advice as our advice deserved, would be to place our national interests at the mercy of other persons.'*[49] Happy indeed was his knack of exposing the absurdities of a case in a short, crisp parody of it.

Aberdeen seemed to forget that the Russians were already in Turkish territory. He made it a point of merit to Russia that she had not declared war, while to Palmerston this was only an example of trying to gain simultaneously the advantages of war and of peace.[31] The argument that there could be no objection to seizing the territory of a country to hold it as a 'material guarantee' for the enforcement of other demands, if those demands were unreasonable in the eyes of Europe, was subversive of international order. On 10th December Palmerston urged that Russia be told that her ships would be denied the use of the Black Sea as long as her troops remained in the Principalities. Aberdeen said he would prefer a declaration of war to that kind of 'pressure'.[50] From him this was an unequivocal refusal. On 14th December 1853 Palmerston submitted his resignation.[51] Downing Street forwarded to *The Times* Aberdeen's gloss on the reasons for the resignation, and that paper therefore attributed it to Palmerston's opposition to Russell's draft Reform Bill. Only two other newspapers followed suit, and they, unlike *The Times*, deplored the resignation. Palmerston himself wrote to Borthwick of the *Morning Post* a skilful letter, really non-committal as to the reason he had left the cabinet, but couched in the form of a refutation of *The Times*'s account. The *Post* leader of 20th December said that everyone would judge for himself according to his estimate of the man.[A] Everyone did — and agreed with the *Post*'s own verdict that Palmerston had resigned on the Eastern Question, and probably as a result of monarchical pressure.

[A] Kinglake, in *The Crimea*, parrots this general reaction — '. . . He was gifted with the instinct which enables a man to read the heart of a nation, and he felt that the English people would never forgive the Ministry if nothing decisive was done after the disaster at Sinope' (quoted A. ii, p. 55).

The private record — Palmerston's letters to Aberdeen and other ministers — was certainly compatible with the 'official' version of his resignation published in *The Times*. Indeed, the Palace, convinced that Palmerston would 'be a source of mischief as long as he lives' marvelled that instead of finding 'a popular question of his own choosing, for which he has plenty of ingenuity' he had chosen 'an unpopular ground, on which he will expose himself to the condemnation of his former Radical admirers'. This showed a defective understanding of public opinion. For plenty of Radicals war with Russia (a symbol of oppression), even in alliance with the Turks, was *the* question of the day. The sentiment represented in parliament by Layard and Lord Dudley Stuart (a great champion of the Poles), who 'inveighed against Russia, and attacked the Government for their unwillingness to enter upon the conflict' was, a historian of Radicalism woefully admits, 'overwhelming . . . [and] all but universal'.[52] Palmerston had known what he was doing when he intervened in the debate on 16th August to answer Cobden's argument that 'the independence and integrity of the Ottoman Empire' was an empty phrase, that the corrupt tyranny of the Sultan must not be supported, that Britain's interest was in peace. Britain, Palmerston had said, was accustomed to go to war for the liberties of Europe, not to gain so much per cent on her exports. He contrived to make the honest passivism of the Manchester School, which some hold to have been noble, sound like a cheap and blinkered commercialism, and chauvinism sound noble and unselfish. Even the Palace and Aberdeen could see that Palmerston's resignation must be greeted with suspicion as well as jubilation. That was why Albert stressed the importance of securing a declaration *in writing* 'so as to make all future misrepresentation or equivocation impossible'. (This would also help protect the Court against innuendo!)[53]

Palmerston wrote a short letter to Aberdeen, enclosing a long letter to Lansdowne. The latter dealt almost wholly with Reform, and indeed remarked (as did Palmerston in letters to his relatives) that he thought the presence in cabinet 'of a person holding the opinions which I entertain as to the principles upon which our Foreign Affairs ought to be conducted, is useful in modifying the contrary system of Policy, which, as I think, injuriously to the interests and dignity of the Country, there is a disposition in other quarters to pursue'. But what a text that would provide for a resignation speech, introduced by way of explaining why he had not resigned before! And the covering letter to Aberdeen urged that the Black Sea should at once be denied to Russian ships of war![54] Aberdeen saw at once how 'dexterous' this was — 'P. has stolen a march on us by combining the Eastern Question with Reform. Truly he is a great artist'.[55] In the method of his resignation, not basing it on foreign affairs, but not denying in public that they were the real matter in dispute, Palmerston was indeed ingenious. His opposition to Reform pleased the Tories and some of the Whigs; his resignation horrified many of the Whigs, Liberals and Radicals. His objection to Reform appeared to ensure that if anyone went with him, it would be Lansdowne and not Russell.[56] Aberdeen cynically declared that Palmerston's departure 'would tend greatly to the improvement of Lord John's Foreign Policy'.[57] This was to assume that Russell would stay, in return for assurances that his Reform Bill would be pressed forward virtually unaltered — the assurances, given by Aberdeen and Graham, which Palmerston used as the peg for his resignation. There was, in fact, a danger that Russell would not stay, but would attempt to trump Palmerston's ace. 'It would be very awkward for you if Palmerston quarrels one day with you about Reform, and I the next about Turkey', he said to Aberdeen.[58] As one who according to the premier was 'looking for an opportunity to break up the Government on some popular ground'[59] Russell, for all his devotion to Reform, must have been sorely tempted by the outcome of the cabinet of 17th December. He asked his colleagues to say quite clearly that Britain would fight if the Russians crossed the Danube and would convoy Turkish troops and supplies in the Black Sea.[60] His colleagues, however, tried to behave as though they had not heard on the day of Palmerston's resignation (14th) that the Russians had sunk the Turkish fleet at anchor at Sinope on the northern coast of Asia Minor, an incident described by the public as 'a massacre' and by Clarendon himself as 'an outrage' (though Turkey had declared war on Russia early in October).

Palmerston's position after his resignation must in any case have been a strong one. The public reaction to Sinope made it fearsomely so. The Queen and the Prince, Aberdeen and Graham, were disconcerted to find that the whips and 'all the people best conversant with the House of Commons stated that the Government had no chance of going on with Lord Palmerston in opposition', and that almost every member of the cabinet showed what Aberdeen called 'cowardice' and Russell 'shabbiness' and urged that he be induced to return.[61] They knew that unless he did they were doomed. The means of preventing Palmerston's return seemed to be to leave the decision to Russell. Surely he would be staunch — for Palmerston had written to Lansdowne that he did not choose to be dragged through the dirt by John Russell,[62] and Lord John described his resignation as 'treachery', which Aberdeen had the grace to see was unfair, since Palmerston's opposition to the sort of Reform Bill being planned had always been frankly avowed.[58] Russell was not willing to make any significant concessions on Reform, and assurances that he would not be asked for them constituted half the pound of flesh he demanded for staying in himself. But he was prepared to admit, what he could not reasonably deny, the right of the cabinet to an examination of the details.[63] The rest of his price was decisive action in the East. On 22nd December the cabinet deliberated for five and a half hours on the Eastern Question, Reform and Palmerston. It was decided to send the fleet into the Black Sea and inform the Russians that any ship caught out of harbour would be seized or sunk. And it was decided that any overtures from Palmerston to return would be favourably received. Aberdeen was unable to resist 'the general weight of the Cabinet' either on the Eastern Question or the return of Palmerston. And Russell could not deny that his return was 'a political necessity'.[64]

Lady Palmerston (it is not known with what encouragement from her spouse) had made it known that overtures would be well received.[61] What the cabinet decided on 22nd was that the overtures should come, in form, from the prodigal but that Newcastle, the Secretary of State for War and Colonies, should contrive them.[64] Palmerston wrote on 23rd to say — what was not strictly true — that he found he had been mistaken in thinking the details of the Reform Bill were finally settled, and that therefore he could not decline to comply with the wish of many members of the government that he should withdraw his resignation.[A] Missing no

---

[A] Technically, it could not be the case, as Palmerston now wrote that he had mistakenly inferred, that the details 'had been finally settled by the Government, and that no objection to any part of those details would be listened to', for the cabinet had not approved the measure in a final shape. But Palmerston's letters to Lansdowne (the first written on 8th Dec.) of which he forwarded copies to Aberdeen, and his interviews with Aberdeen, showed that he 'differed so entirely

trick, he added: '. . . the decision, which I am informed the Cabinet came to yesterday, to accede to the proposal of the French Government, whereby the British and French squadrons will have the command of the Black Sea, greatly enters into the considerations which have led me to address this letter to you'.[65] Thus a decision made to keep Russell, save the French alliance and appease an enraged public opinion, though Aberdeen deplored it as making war certain, allowed Palmerston to return with honour. The public was convinced that the cabinet had taken him back on his own terms, and that the decision about the fleets represented those terms. This view confirmed the general impression that the Eastern Question was the real cause of his resignation. Without having made any public pronouncement whatever on this point, he emerged as the accredited champion of the national mood.

Whistling to keep up their spirits, the Queen, Aberdeen, Russell and Graham told one another that Palmerston had repented on finding he had chosen an unpopular ground; that he had 'done for himself' by a sacrifice of 'opinions, principles and consistency', so that, according to Aberdeen, not a member of the cabinet respected him. The incident, Russell said, would have ruined anyone but Palmerston.[66] This was all moonshine. War was now almost certain, and war would almost certainly kill the Reform Bill; if it did not, Palmerston could always resign again. Greville and Delane, men who loved not Palmerston, thought he had played a high-minded

in all the elements of our Reform Bill' that there seemed no chance of agreement. Aberdeen thought his objections conclusive, and also indicative of a desire to 'take the lead of the War Party and the Anti-Reformers in the House of Commons, who are essentially the same' (6th Dec.). The Prince warned that 'should Lord Palmerston have stated his objections with the view of having the Measure modified it will be right to consider how far that can safely be done' (9th Dec.). But on 12th Aberdeen, Russell and Graham agreed that no material alterations were to be made, and the premier so informed Palmerston, whose resignation followed. 'Albert thought this serious, particularly as Lord Lansdowne shares the greater part of Lord Palmerston's objections' (Queen's Journal, 15th) and Aberdeen then indicated that modifications might be made to meet Lansdowne's views. Lansdowne on 16th rebuked Russell, saying that a full cabinet should have been summoned before Palmerston was told that 'his suggestions could not even be taken into consideration' and that he himself would not attend a cabinet until he had ascertained 'how far there is any chance of those who are making themselves responsible for the whole measure consenting to any modification of its provisions'. So on 20th Aberdeen's position was that 'concessions would have to be made to Lord Lansdowne, which might satisfy Lord Palmerston'. On 23rd he informed the Queen that, though no important concession could be made, certain details could be submitted to a fair discussion, it being understood that Palmerston would 'do his best to come to an understanding with his colleagues'.

and disinterested part in not basing his resignation on foreign policy; Kingsley Martin, though deducing a large element of self-interest, grudgingly concurs.[67] The last word may be yielded to Lady Palmerston. 'The manner in which Palmerston's resignation has been received is most flattering', she wrote to Monckton Milnes on 22nd; 'the despair of the Whigs and friends of the Government, even Radicals and Reformers (the fact is, nobody wants Reform); none pleased but the Tory party, and those most exulting.' A few days later Milnes wrote to his wife: 'Lady P writes: "Every event in which P. is concerned ends in his standing higher than he did before." There is a fine deluded wifie for you, though I think she is right for this once.' Palmerston's luck ran true.

CHAPTER XVIII

'THE FITTEST MAN', 1854

According to John Bright, 50,000 men died to make Palmerston prime minister. He meant to blame Palmerston for the war, which he regarded as a product of the Balance of Power 'delusion' and of the Palmerston spirit. Yet it is far from certain that there would have been a war if the policy of the Aberdeen coalition had been more Palmerstonian, or, indeed, if the premier had been anyone but Aberdeen. The Queen herself remarked that 'Lord Palmerston's mode of proceeding always had that advantage, that it threatened steps which it was hoped would not become necessary, whilst those hitherto taken started on the principle of not needlessly offending Russia by threats, obliging us at the same time to take the very steps which we refused to threaten.'[1]

It was in the Crimea and the pestiferous hospitals at Scutari that men died, and many more suffered, needlessly. Was Palmerston primarily responsible for the decision to fight in the Crimea? Gladstone congratulated him on concentrating the mind of the cabinet on operations at Sebastopol.[2] But the naval authorities were earlier clear that Sebastopol, 'the eye-tooth of the bear' must be drawn,[3] and once it was clear that the Western troops would not have to fight on the line of the Balkan Mountains, and Palmerston's argument that they should not fight on the Danube was accepted, the choice of the Crimea was so obvious that it cannot be credited to any one man. The choice was, moreover, strategically sound, and, around this central operation, Palmerston sketched a plan of campaign which gave promise of a merry Christmas and a happy New Year.[4] It was not his fault that the expedition failed to achieve its objective in 1854. He pressed for haste, and there was delay. Nothing could have saved Sebastopol if the Allies had landed a few weeks earlier, before the Russians began to transfer men from the Principalities (which were to be garrisoned for the duration of the war by the Austrians). Nothing could have saved Sebastopol if the Western navies had interrupted Russian movement through the bottle-neck of Odessa or by combined operations on the isthmus of Perekop and at Kerch isolated the Crimea from the rest of Russia. Nothing, indeed, could have saved Sebastopol if, when at last enough transports had been gathered to move the Allied armies (British, French and Turkish) from the Bulgarian port of Varna in mid-September, the operation had proceeded as Palmerston had envisaged. His estimate that Sebastopol would fall in six weeks by assault via the commanding ridge to the north was reasonable; his assurance that 'an invested fortress always falls', which struck Argyll as characteristically boyish in its optimism, ought not to have been over-sanguine.[5] After the Allied landings at Calamita Bay north of Sebastopol, the Russians began to evacuate a large part of the garrison of the port to link up with the field army. The Allies failed to attack them as they moved across the line of advance. Yet the Alma and Inkerman had shown the tactical inferiority of the Russians, who massed their troops in such a way as to maximize the effect of superior fire-rate of the British muzzle-loaders and good markmanship, provided discipline was sound (as it was). Communications between the Crimea and the rest of Russia were never cut. And the assault on the northern redoubts of Sebastopol was never attempted. The artilleryman, General Burgoyne, fatally miscalculated the efficacy of his own arm. Elaborately and slowly, an all-day cannonade of Sebastopol from a distance was prepared. It was totally ineffective. The British army then proceeded to regain contact with the fleet at Balaclava, having marched round the three landward sides of its objective. This was not at all what Palmerston had had in mind when urging an expedition to the Crimea.

The Allied dispositions were now grotesque. The whole expedition had been held up because the French lacked sea-transport, but the French had plenty of wagons, horses and mules. They occupied a compact coastal position at Kamisch. The British, short of supply transport (and of supplies, which had been left at Varna), were strung out along ridges six to eight miles from the wharves of Balaclava. When on 25th October the Russians struck towards Balaclava, between the French and the British, all the ingredients of the catastrophe which was to make Palmerston prime minister (by convicting the existing government of incompetence) were assembled. The British base and army were saved by the thin red line of the 93rd Sutherland Highlanders and the flank charge of the Heavy Brigade of cavalry, though it is the suicidal charge of the

Light up the wrong valley which is remembered. But the Russians retained the vital Vorontzov ridge, commanding the only road between the British lines and Balaclava that might have survived military use in winter. The French general, Canrobert, came to the rescue of the British in a pell-mell scrimmage in the fog at Inkerman, but he would not throw everything in to retaking that ridge and opening that road. Yet the Allied troops were now condemned to winter in the Chersonese, unless the British commander-in-chief Raglan and Napoleon III accepted the advice of the old Radical war-horse, General Sir de Lacy Evans, 'My Lord, raise the siege and save your army.' Such a decision would certainly have caused the fall of the British cabinet and probably of the régime of Napoleon III. It was not considered. Yet Raglan took no steps to build a road to the lines, and though he asked for reinforcements and hutting, he did not ask for forage for his (in any case inadequate) supply animals. The cabinet never grasped that the key to all the calamities that followed was the loss of control of the road, and was slow to realize that the medical arrangements, thanks to the qualities of the chief medical officer, Dr John Hall, would have been inadequate even if the campaign had gone according to plan. They were assured by Hall that all was well both in the Crimea and in the main hospital at Scutari opposite Constantinople.

When they first read, in private letters and the reports of the newspaper correspondents, of conditions in the lines and in the hospitals, ministers assumed that the trouble was due to the great gale of 14th November. This was, indeed, a crowning misfortune for the men in the field and, politically, for Aberdeen and Newcastle, the Secretary of State for War. It wrought havoc in the Crimean camps and littered the harbour of Balaclava with wrecks. Worse still, it sent to the bottom of the Black Sea many transports conveying stores from Varna, including the new and capacious *Prince*, laden, inter alia, with warm clothing. But ministers were wrong in assuming that, if they scraped together all the transports, men and stores they could find, and sent them as quickly as incompetent arrangements permitted, all would be well with an army only half of which was, by the end of the year, effective. For within a week of the great storm all the 'roads' to the British lines were quagmires on which waggons would have been of little use even if anyone had thought to provide them. For the pack-animals there was little forage. The quays at Balaclava became choked with supplies, but all that could be got up to the lines were irregular issues of rations and ammunition. In the opposite direction jolted the wounded and the far more numerous sick, destined for unbelievable and unnecessary horrors at Balaclava and en route to Scutari, thanks to the criminal negligence and almost utter stupidity of Hall and his representative at the port. The survivors were scarcely to be congratulated on reaching Scutari, for, as Florence Nightingale, sent out by Sidney Herbert, the Secretary at War, with the first women nurses ever attached to the British army, found, the basic stores needed at Scutari had been sent to Varna and the scandalous deficiencies in the hospital had been concealed from the government by Hall, whose worthy local representative, Dr Menzies, did not feel that he could expose the mendacity of his superior. He could only give his life in a losing battle against disease.

Behind the errors of Raglan, Canrobert, Burgoyne, Hall and others in the East, magnified in their effect by the absence of any directing personality to co-ordinate and to cut through red-tape, lay administrative muddle and red-tapism at home, magnified in its effect by the incapacity of Aberdeen as a war premier. It was merely symptomatic that nobody at Scutari could discover the dividing-lines between the authority of the purveyor and the commissary; that when much needed and long overdue stores did arrive there their distribution was held up by want of a Board of Survey to inspect and release them; that the men shivering before Sebastopol without warm clothes, hutments or tentage, without fuel, received green coffee which they had scant means of roasting, while tea and limejuice provided by *The Times Fund* piled up at Balaclava, no one having thought to add tea and limejuice to the warrant governing rations. At home it was nobody's business (unless poor Aberdeen's) to knock together the heads of the Ordnance officials responsible for packing and the Admiralty officials responsible for stowing equipment, so as to reduce delays. Each of the too many departments and services, at home and in the field, was left to itself, usually with totally inadequate staff, while the Treasury, under the penny-wise Gladstone and Trevelyan, frustrated more than one of the rare attempts of supply officials to make precautionary dispositions.

No exculpations can make the tale anything but one of appalling neglect and incompetence, the extent of which might have been concealed if the Allies had occupied Sebastopol by the beginning of November, as they could have done by bold strokes which seemed to Raglan and Canrobert too reckless. Every member of the cabinet which tolerated the continuance of muddle must bear not merely a formal constitutional responsibility but a moral responsibility for allowing loyalty to Aberdeen, gentlemanly feeling towards New-castle, loyalty to the concept of coalition, to stand in the way of public duty. It is only a partial defence that the cabinet did not know the full extent of the chaos, and could not account for it, because Raglan was so uninformative and uncomplaining (he was a gentleman too!); that in this bitter winter two-thirds of the Russian reinforcements destined for Sebastopol never reached their destination, although the Allies did nothing to stop them; that despite their many advantages the French fared proportionately worse than the British. Certainly these comparisons could not save the government, for the facts about the Russians and the French were concealed from their peoples, while Britain had correspon-dents at the front and Scutari and freedom of speech and of the press at home. The accounts of suffering and incompetence, sent especially by W. H. Russell of *The Times*, were known from Wick to Penzance (and eagerly reproduced in St Petersburg). They, and the gist of 'letters home', fully justified Delane's leader of 23rd December 1854, stating that 'the noblest army ever sent from our shores has been sacrificed to the greatest mismanagement' at the camps, at Balaclava, at Scutari 'and how much nearer home we do not venture to say'.

Palmerston was a member of the government, and must share the responsibility. But what was he to do? To resign, without bringing down the government, if that were possible, would merely make it less effective. To bring it down, by resigning, might be to replace it by one which, if it consisted mainly of Tories, was likely to be no more impressive. And to resign would be to expose himself to the taunt of self-seeking. This he must shrink from doing, if not on grounds of care for his reputation, then on grounds of self-interest. The public might want him, did want him, to have the management of the war. But governments were composed of parliamentarians bound to one another by peculiar ties irrelevant to the war situa-tion, and it required at least a minimum of Court acquiescence to be in a position to form one. Suffering from the great disadvantage of being known to agree with the public that he would be a better prime minister or war minister than the existing incumbents, Palmerston had to be very careful to show himself a good colleague, if he was to exercise any influence in the cabinet on the matters he thought most important.

Russell's position was similar, his reaction different. He wanted to be prime minister, and he seemed to think he could achieve this ambition by constantly railing against Aberdeen and threatening resignation if this or that course was not adopted. Consequently, nearly everything he proposed — and it was usually something that could have been advantageously adopted — failed to receive the attention it merited. It was written off by his colleagues as just more evidence of his self-seeking. Among his demands was the replacement of Newcastle by Palmerston, who did not reciprocate by demanding the substitution of Russell for Aberdeen, a change that would have been obnoxious to all his colleagues and to himself. So it was Russell who pressed, usually in vain, the things the public imagined Palmerston must be pressing. And Palmerston ended the year with the reputation of a good colleague, though a dissatisfied one, while Russell ended it with the reputation of a thoroughly bad colleague.

* * * *

In the first months of 1854, Aberdeen was the one minister who, because he thought war an act of insanity, utterly disgraceful to all concerned, did not admit its inevitability as soon as the campaigning season drew near. His evident feet-dragging made him very unpopular. 'Is there some person among you who has mistaken his mission, or who is treacherous to the cause?' asked Layard, the warlike Radical who had discovered Nineveh; 'I say then, throw your Jonah overboard; if you do not, your vessel will be wrecked.' Others, including Urquhart, found a traitor in higher quarters and the year began with a very nasty campaign in the Tory and Radical press against Prince Albert which, sometimes by implication, sometimes overtly, exalted Palmerston as the true patriot. It fell to Aberdeen and Russell, ex officio, to defend the Prince when Parliament met, and to Russell to defend Aberdeen, though his own 'May God defend the right' speech was woundingly contrasted with the tone of Aberdeen and Clarendon in the Lords.

Ellice cynically observed that Russell made this speech to prevent Palmerston having a monopoly of the public favour. Certainly Palmerston's own speech at the dinner at the Reform Club in honour of Sir Charles Napier on the eve of his departure with a fleet to the Baltic matched the popular mood. When Bright protested in the House at its levity and cock-fighting tenor, Palmerston fell mercilessly, and popularly, upon 'the honourable and reverend gentleman'.[6] In June, more than two months after the declaration of war, a speech by Aberdeen in the Lords caused Layard to table a censure motion in the Commons, and drew protests from the Palace. The Queen hoped that Aberdeen would not again 'undertake the ungrateful and injurious task of vindicating the Emperor of Russia from any of the exaggerated charges brought against him and his policy at a time when there is enough in it to make us fight with all might against it'.[7] Such a speech did indeed match ill the misrepresentation of the Tsar's talks with Seymour as to a possible division of Turkey which was achieved by its inclusion in the Foreign Office Papers laid before parliament on the eve of the war.

It is hard to forgive Aberdeen, who had said that he would resign rather than go to war, for his decision to stay in office as long as the war lasted. He entirely lacked the qualities required of a war premier, even if he had believed in the cause. Russell was justified in complaining that 'the great want of all is of a head of the English Cabinet. . . . The Government, in fact, wants direction; and in wanting direction wants everything that is essential', and that there was 'discordance and indecision; no question is put before us in a shape to bring about a definite result'.[8] Russell's frank desire to succeed him, and the public demand that Palmerston conduct the war, merely brought out the stubbornness which was Aberdeen's basic characteristic. To tell him (as Gladstone and others did) that Russell and Palmerston were contending for the succession, and that Palmerston was likely to win, was to convince him that he must stay.[9] For to his deep and chronic distrust of Palmerston, and contempt for the public opinion which extolled Palmerston, was added the conviction that Palmerston would make war as long as possible instead of making peace as soon as possible. Aberdeen resisted stubbornly military alliances (for example, with Sweden) which, while increasing the pressure on Russia, would tend to extend the objects of the war. These, as far as he was concerned, had really been achieved when the Russians evacuated the Principalities. Significantly, he deplored the Austrian occupation, not because it released Russian troops for other theatres, but because, by involving Austria with the Allies, it weakened her position as a mediator. What then must he think of the cabinet paper of 19th March 1854 in which Palmerston sketched as his 'beau idéal' the restoration of Poland; the junction of Finland with Sweden and Norway instead of with Russia; Austrian tenure of the Principalities instead of Lombardy and Venetia; the enlargement of Turkey in the Crimea and Georgia; the aggrandizement of Austria and Prussia in a Germany freed from the thraldom of the Tsar. Aberdeen complained of a plan for a thirty years' war.[10]

When on 10th April Aberdeen begged Russell not to resign, he used the argument that Palmerston must not be enhanced. If Russell ceased to be Leader of the House, Palmerston must succeed him or Palmerston would resign. As Aberdeen would not allow him Russell's place, Lord John would be breaking up the government, for 'the Country persisted in thinking [Palmerston] the only able War Minister' and would, if Palmerston resigned, 'cry out at the imbecile old Head of the Government having it now all his own way'. Russell had submitted his resignation (in fulfilment of a threat of 24th March) because the cabinet would not go on with his Reform Bill, which the House of Commons did not want. He withdrew it, when promised that all the ministers other than Palmerston would support its reintroduction whenever Lord John gave the word. But he changed his mind again, his attitude being that 'a Cabinet in which Lord Palmerston's objection to Reform had prevailed was not one in which he ought to remain'. It was Palmerston who changed his mind back again, to staying, by saying that *he* ought to be the one to go; this 'very clever' letter from Palmerston begging Russell not to desert the Queen and country would have 'floored' Lord John completely if leaked to the press or parliament.[11]

Russell, back in the cabinet, rightly concentrated for some weeks on demanding improvements in military arrangements, for which he argued in a paper of 12th April. He had long agreed with two Whig former Secretaries at War, Earl Grey and Fox Maule, that all responsibility ought to be concentrated in a Secretary of State answerable to parliament, and assisted by a Board of War on Board of Admiralty lines. This plan was abhorrent to the Queen as exalting civilian and parliamentary control at the expense of the Commander-in-Chief at the Horse Guards and of the royal prerogative. Russell therefore now proposed that the separate departments be retained, but the Secretary of State be given co-ordinating power. Aberdeen was reluctant to put this before the cabinet, and it was a month before it was agreed in principle even that the Secretary of State for War and Colonies should be relieved of the responsibility for non-military colonies. It is doubtful whether action would have followed if the debate on 28th May had not made it clear, as Palmerston drily remarked, that this was at least a parliamentary necessity.[12] Royal approval was secured only when Russell threatened to go down to the House and vote for the whole Whig plan, as moved by Henry Rich, and Aberdeen told the Prince that Rich's motion would be carried if nothing was done, and also that expressions would be dropped 'in favour of Lord Palmerston's taking the conduct of the War in his hands'.[13] Russell had himself proposed this, but the Duke of Newcastle was allowed to be Secretary of State for War, Sir George Grey taking the Colonies. Aberdeen said it would be 'unjust' to remove the Duke against his will; though even he acknowledged that Sidney Herbert (currently Secretary at War) would be more efficient, he dared not suggest this to the cabinet, for the public reaction to a change would infallibly be: 'Why not Palmerston?'[14] That worthy was said by Malmesbury to be furious that Newcastle was to have the War Office 'because he wanted it, and certainly would have been the fittest person'.[15] The Queen and the Prince and the pedestrian premier congratulated one another on how few personal and administrative changes they had had to concede (it took Newcastle another five months to prise the Commissariat out of the stingy hands of the Treasury). They looked forward thankfully to the parliamentary vacation.

With the advantage of hindsight, we can see that in failing to make Palmerston Secretary of State for War Aberdeen lost the last chance of saving his government. If Palmerston had succeeded, the government would not have fallen, and if Palmerston had failed, he could hardly have been accepted so generally as the man to win the war. But then in June there had been no disaster. Even when cabinets began again in October, their main business was diplomacy, especially the effort to rivet Austria to the Western side. But by the end of November the hearts of ministers were weighed

down by ominous tidings and prognostication and in December,
though Palmerston pronounced vigorously against leaving it to the
military commanders to decide whether to abandon the Crimea,
had reluctantly to admit that such a course was not entirely
out of the question.[16]

*   *   *   *

The news from the Crimea and Scutari in November, December
and January exasperated the public. Malmesbury on 11th December noted in his journal: 'The deplorable state of our troops in the
Crimea is described and repeated in all the private letters that
arrive. It is impossible for this country to bear these accounts with
patience, for every kind of negligence is attributed to . . . those
responsible.' In a notable cabinet paper of 30th December Russell
assembled the data and drew the inescapable conclusions. 'There
must have been great mismanagement to cause the want of clothes';
'there must have been negligence' and should be an inquiry about
forage; there was a want of concert between the various departments, especially the naval and the military. Graham too saw that
there must have been neglect by the Commissariat and the Quartermaster-General and urged Lyons (who had recently succeeded
Dundas in the chief naval command) to overstep his province and
try to work out improvements with Raglan.[17] But the responsible
ministers seemed totally unaware of any failure on their own part
(except the basic failure to anticipate a winter campaign). When in
December Newcastle warned his colleagues that the army might be
lost, and Palmerston, half rising in his place, asked 'But why should
this be?', none could answer. It seems that they did not understand
the importance of the Vorontzov Ridge until they received Raglan's
letter of 20th January reluctantly criticizing the Commissariat and
the Treasury in order to defend his own staff. 'We were kept in
complete ignorance of the causes', says Argyll. 'The silence of
Lord Raglan was positively excruciating. Nothing came from him
but the driest facts.'[18]

Oppressed by Wellington's dictum that civilians at home could
not judge officers on distant fronts, the cabinet was totally lacking
in ruthlessness towards commanders or specialists and, of course,
its own members. The First Lord sprang to the defence of the
prayerful but inactive Admiral Dundas when the Foreign and War
Secretaries urged his replacement by Lyons. Newcastle bowed for

months to Raglan's reluctance to dismiss the inept Airey from the post of Q.M.G., and sent out a replacement only under strong pressure from Hardinge, the Commander-in-Chief. Raglan himself was protected by his reputation as a conscientious gentleman and 'incomparable and indispensable in our relations with the French army', though certainly, as Argyll confesses, by January 'a general impression was gaining ground' in the cabinet 'that in the faculty of organizing Raglan was deficient'. But, he adds, 'there was no General of whom we knew that would be better'.

The general impression was also gaining ground in the cabinet that there could be a better Secretary of State than one who had waited more than three months for the report of a commission to inquire into the medical services in the East and confessed to the Queen that he had protested repeatedly, in the strongest terms, about 'the condition of the Hospital at Scutari, and the entire want of all method and arrangement in everything that concerns the comfort of the Army' but had been fobbed off with lies.[18] 'Newcastle is awfully slow, and his department seems to be in as much confusion as the Headquarters at Balaclava', complained Clarendon.[19] Russell was, of course, convinced that the heads that should roll were those of Aberdeen and Newcastle. Fired by a letter from Minto ('We are playing for too great a stake to allow any personal scruples or considerations to lose us the game')[20] he demanded on 17th November the abolition of the office of Secretary at War and the presence in the Commons of the Secretary of State to present and defend Estimates and 'to satisfy the House upon points which are determined by military officers sitting in the Horse Guards'. But he ruined the chance of persuading Aberdeen to adopt this means of prising the War Office from the hands of Newcastle by insulting Aberdeen. For he continued:[21]

... We are in the midst of a great war. In order to carry on that war with efficiency, either the Prime Minister must be constantly urging, hastening, completing the military preparations; or the Minister of War must be strong enough to control other departments. ... In the present case it seems to me that the last example is the most applicable. If, therefore, the first considerations here presented lead to the conclusion that the Secretary of State for the War Department must be in the House of Commons, the latter considerations point to the necessity of having in that office a man who, from experience of military details, from inherent vigour of mind, and from weight with the House of Commons, can be expected to guide the great operations of war with authority and success. There is only one person belonging to the Government who combines these advantages.

My conclusion is that, before Parliament meets, Lord Palmerston should be entrusted with the seals of the War Department.

Here Russell says, in effect, that in the absence of a prime minister capable of doing his duty to a nation at war (a prime minister such as Russell), that duty must be delegated to Palmerston. Lord John deserves credit for proposing the elevation of his rival, which, even now, might have saved the government. But he had exhausted his credit and most of his capital by his frequent threats of resignation and Aberdeen replied coldly that even if the secretaryship at war was abolished, the Secretary of State need not be in the Commons. Moreover, he said, no one could do the work of both Newcastle and Herbert and 'Palmerston, within a few months, is as old as I am; and, without disparaging his inherent vigour of mind, he possesses no immunity from the effects of age'.[22]

Russell reiterated his theme — 'What you want . . . is a Minister of War of vigour and authority. Let Parliament and the country be assured that you have placed the conduct of the war in the hands of the fittest man who can be found for that duty.' Aberdeen replied that such changes, unless absolutely necessary, tended only to weaken a government and this was a change of doubtful advantage to the public and an act of unfairness and injustice towards a colleague.[23] He did not add that his endemic distrust of 'the fittest man' was increased by Palmerston's recent visit to Paris at Napoleon's invitation, which he and the Court were sure impended an 'intrigue'.[24] Russell appealed to the cabinet. But he was lost unless Palmerston supported him. Palmerston joined him in pressing a short December session to ensure that everything necessary could be done for the army in the Crimea, and he said that he would accept the War Office if the cabinet desired it. But he professed to doubt the expediency of abolishing the secretaryship at war and saw no broad or distinct grounds for the dismissal of Newcastle which would justify breaking up the government.[25] When he became premier, Palmerston amalgamated the secretaryship at war with the secretaryship of state. But it was vital to keep a Secretary at War as long as Newcastle stayed at the War Office. For, as Gladstone said, 'the Duke of Newcastle's staff being in truth very little competent, Herbert strained himself morning, noon and night to invent wants for the army, and according to his best judgement or conjecture to supply them'.[26]

Russell must have thought Palmerston very unfeeling. At a

cabinet dinner at Aberdeen's house on 6th December Lord John, when challenged, 'made it quite clear that it was Lord Aberdeen he wished to have removed'. He would resign now or shortly, giving as his reason his weakness in the House of Commons. Palmerston said that if that was to be the test, it should be the Home Secretary who resigned, and that his only criticism of general policy was the delay in going to the Crimea, which was the fault of Russell. Argyll's account continues: 'Aberdeen was not given to jokes in his conversation, still less was he disposed to indulge in chaff. But when Palmerston told us how completely he had failed in legislation in the previous session, Aberdeen could not resist the comical aspect of the situation, and he gravely interpolated the remark that the failure must have been due to a want of vigour in Palmerston. The laughter raised by this sally on the part of our generally very solemn chief lightened the tension due to a very odious dispute, and . . . not a single member of the Cabinet said one word in support of Lord John.'[27] Aberdeen now rather hoped Russell would resign, for he could not go on with a Leader of the House who kept telling him to his face that he was incapable. At the next cabinet encounter, Palmerston was almost brutal to Lord John, asking him 'how he could expose the Country to such fearful risks at such a moment'. Russell said he would support the government out of office. 'You will support it at the head of a very virulent Opposition', Palmerston is quoted as retorting, 'and when you have succeeded in overthrowing the Government, which has difficulty enough to hold its ground even with your assistance, what will you say to the Country? Will you say: "Here I am. I have triumphed, and have displaced, in the midst of most hazardous operations, all the ablest men the Country has produced; but I will take their place with Mr Vernon Smith, Lord Seymour, Lord Minto and others! . .".' Later at the same meeting there was a bitter exchange between the two men on Reform.[28]

The result of Lord John's attempt to get Palmerston into the War Office was that Palmerston was designated to succeed Russell as Leader of the House. 'Disagreeable as this must be . . . to Lord Aberdeen, and dangerous as the experiment may turn out, we agreed with Lord Aberdeen that he should make the offer to him with the Queen's assent', minuted Prince Albert. Aberdeen dwelt upon 'the long antecedent and mutual opposition between him and Lord Palmerston' and 'the fact that Lord Palmerston loved war

for war's sake, and he peace for peace's sake' but 'consoled himself
. . . at last by the reflection that Lord Palmerston was not worse
than Lord John in that respect, and, on the other hand, gave greater
weight to the consideration of what was practicable' — by which
he meant that Palmerston had not lately made a nuisance of
himself.[28] We can only speculate as to the accuracy of Aberdeen's
family theory that Palmerston desired the maintenance of the
existing arrangements because that 'suited his game far better than
Lord John's decided pre-eminence would'.[29]

Palmerston was not, however, to become Leader of the House in
1854. Russell again cancelled his resignation, pressed for inquiry
into the deficiencies of the specialized services in the East (30th
December), wrote but did not send another resignation on 1st
January, went to Paris and saw the Emperor, walked into a cabinet
meeting on 16th babbling of Poland, attended cabinets on 18th
and 19th on domestic measures, and was thought by Aberdeen's
son to be reasonable on the question of negotiations with Russia,
leaving Palmerston, Newcastle and Lansdowne as 'the fire eating
war party'.[29] On 20th the cabinet agreed to establish an Army
Board of the Secretary of State, the Commander-in-Chief, the
Master-General of the Ordnance and the Secretary at War to
secure 'more unity of action in these Departments'. With this to
be announced, ministers might hope to meet parliament satisfactorily, especially if, as now seemed likely, Newcastle sacrificed
himself and Palmerston succeeded him. 'It must, under existing
circumstances, be Palmerston', noted Aberdeen's son, Arthur
Gordon, because this was the only change that would give real
confidence, though Herbert would have filled the office better.[29]
When Roebuck put down a motion for a select committee to
'inquire into the condition of our army before Sebastopol, and into
the conduct of those departments of the Government whose duty
it has been to minister to the wants of that army', one thing only
seemed certain, that ministers were safe from a Russell resignation.
Whoever heard of a minister refusing to stand with his colleagues
to meet a vote of censure directed against them collectively? But
on 23rd Russell wrote to Aberdeen that he did not see how the
motion was to be resisted, and that 'as it involves a censure upon
the War Department, with which some of my colleagues are
connected, my only course is to tender my resignation'.[30]

*   *   *   *

Russell robbed his colleagues of any chance of surviving the Roebuck motion. He made it possible for Disraeli to exclaim: 'When the debate is commenced by the secession of the most eminent member of the Government, and when we are told by him that the conduct of the war is entrusted to a minister who he thinks is unequal to the task, I ask the country — I ask Ministers themselves — whether they can complain that a member of the Opposition should give his vote according to the belief which he entertains.' The immediate reaction of ministers was to resign before the debate, though Newcastle begged them to give his office to Palmerston 'who possessed the confidence of the nation' and Palmerston said that though he did not expect to do half as well as the duke, somehow or other the public had a notion that he would manage the War Department better than anyone else, and he was willing to try, as the break-up of the government would be a real calamity at this moment.[31] But, at the request of the Queen, they stayed to meet the motion, to be driven out rather than run away, and they could not, in the circumstances, sacrifice Newcastle. So it fell to Palmerston, as Leader of the House, to reply, on 26th January 1855, to his predecessor's resignation speech. The effort was 'singularly unsuccessful' (Aberdeen), 'wretched' (Gladstone). 'And this is to be our leader!', muttered Wood.[32] To do Palmerston justice, he had suggested that Gladstone should follow Russell, as Lord John was taking his stand on Aberdeen's refusal to make Palmerston war minister, but the cabinet ruled otherwise. The debate was adjourned to 29th, when Palmerston reported that Gladstone had made a masterly speech which 'would have convinced hearers who had not made up their minds beforehand'.[33] But the result was inevitable. Only four non-ministers spoke against the Roebuck motion, and none really expressed confidence in the ministry. How could one when the latest reports from the Crimea gave effectives as 18,000, with 14,000 dead and 22,000 sick, and Russell had said he could neither affirm that the evils complained of did not exist nor that arrangements had been made to remedy them? Ministers were beaten, after midnight on 29th–30th January, by the incredible margin of 305–148.

Palmerston had wound up unimpressively, but his stock was unimpaired. In the search for an alternative government, he would hold the key. Derby, to whom the Queen first repaired, did not bother to communicate with the Peelites Gladstone and Herbert except through Palmerston, for whom, the Tory leader told the Queen, the whole country cried out as the man who could win the war and whom the French government wanted. Derby said he did not think the ignorant public right — Palmerston was seventy-one (actually he was seventy), very deaf and very blind and totally unfit for the task; his day had gone by, though he still kept up the sprightly manners of his youth.[34] Palmerston did not agree with this estimate, and told Gladstone that there was 'another result' which he considered would be agreeable to the country, but that if he refused Derby's offer of the leadership of the House (as Lord President of the Council) he would be accused of self-seeking. He therefore named as his price the retention of Clarendon at the Foreign Office. With Gladstone and Herbert in as well, said Malmesbury, Palmerston would be the real premier and omnipotent in the cabinet. The price was unacceptable, and Palmerston wrote to say that he did not think his adhesion would bring a Derby government the stability it required. A messenger posted off at midnight on 1st–2nd February to Malmesbury in Hampshire to say that Derby had failed, 'Lord Palmerston having thrown him over'.[35]

It was thought that Derby expected that the Queen would have to come back again to him later; Aberdeen thought him inevitable, 'because he is the only man who has a party'.[36] But the public and the House were so much for Palmerston that when on 1st February the coalition chief whip, Hayter, rose to move a by-election writ, it was imagined that it would be for Tiverton on Palmerston's appointment as First Lord of the Treasury. There was an explosion of laughter when Hayter named New Radnor. The Queen and the Prince, after Derby's failure and Lansdowne's explorations, 'observed that the whole matter seemed to resolve itself into two alternatives — to send either for Lord John, or for Lord Palmerston'.[37] To reach that point was really to opt for Palmerston, for nobody outside Lord John's immediate entourage thought he could succeed, though Lansdowne thought it necessary to go through the ceremony of letting him try. On 3rd February Russell, asked to try, met Palmerston and offered him the War Department or the Leadership of the House, Russell going to the Lords. Palmerston said he would accept the latter suggestion, and that 'although the general voice of the public had pointed him out as the person who ought to form a Government, he had no

Henry John Temple, 3rd Viscount Palmerston

pretensions for himself or personal views'. Russell did not see the significance of Palmerston's request — 'that, if the Queen would see him, now that she had seen Lord Derby, Lord John and Lord Lansdowne, it would remove any impression that there were personal objections to him entertained by the Queen'. He attached no importance to Palmerston's stipulation that Clarendon stay at the Foreign Office, and remained optimistic even when the Peelites refused to serve.[38] But when Palmerston went to the Palace he said that he had just heard *from Walewski* of Clarendon's refusal to serve, and 'he must say that if Lord Clarendon persisted he must himself withdraw'. Lord John found himself in the curious position that of all his coalition colleagues only Palmerston had agreed, even conditionally, to serve under him. Clarendon, following Palmerston to the Palace, was vitriolic about Russell and warned the Queen that the impression had spread that she was trying to avoid having Palmerston as premier. He 'hoped for that for her own sake, and to prevent false impressions taking root in the public mind, the Queen would give afterwards Lord Palmerston his fair turn also, though he could not say that he would be able to form an Administration'. The Queen said that such was her intention and that she had never expected that Russell could succeed.[39]

On 4th February 1855 the Queen wrote from Windsor to ask Palmerston whether he could undertake to form an administration which would command the confidence of Parliament and efficiently conduct public affairs 'in this momentous crisis' and commissioning him to undertake the task if he thought he could. He replied: 'Viscount Palmerston has reason to think that he can undertake with a fair prospect of success to form an Administration which will command the confidence of Parliament and effectually conduct public affairs in the present momentous crisis, and . . . will at once take steps for the purpose.'[40]

'I had no other alternative', the Queen explained to Uncle Leopold on 6th, adding the note: '*Six o'clock* p.m. — One word to say that *Lord Palmerston* has just *kissed* hands as *Prime Minister*. . . .' 'I am l'inévitable', wrote Palmerston to his brother. Lady Palmerston had been 'very much out of sorts' when she believed 'it would end in Lord Lansdowne'. Now 'the première' was as happy as a child with a new toy and 'she really may rejoice in thinking how fairly and honestly he has won the prize'.[41]

N

SECTION E

First Premiership, February 1855 – February 1858

CHAPTER XIX

THE WAR PREMIER, 1855

FOR a moment it looked as though Palmerston would have to form a Whig government, though without the Whig leader, Russell (who refused the presidency of the Council and leadership in the Lords). For, round the sickbed at the Admiralty of Graham (between whom and Palmerston there was a personal dislike), the Peelite cabinet ministers decided to refuse to serve. This decision was taken under the influence of Gladstone, after Aberdeen, who favoured the Peelites joining, had said that he could not himself make the 'painful sacrifice' and suffer the 'gratuitous indignity' of joining, and replied to the question whether he could express confidence in the foreign policy of a Palmerston government that he could say he would hope for the best. But time was on Palmerston's side. It was fortunate, after all, that time had been wasted in attempts by Derby and Russell, for now the Duke of Wellington's maxim that 'the Queen's government must be carried on' was quoted on all sides. Peelite ministers of less than cabinet rank felt that those who had met at the Admiralty were out of touch with public opinion, and Cardwell, Lord Canning and Lord Elcho agreed to serve. Aberdeen himself saw the validity of Palmerston's argument that the Peelites would be much blamed and that it would be said that he was trying to keep a party together to recover power, and, though unwilling himself to accept membership of the cabinet, induced the Peelites to place themselves in his hands.[1] So, on 7th, Palmerston was able to hand the Queen his cabinet list, and presided over his first cabinet on 9th. He himself replaced Aberdeen as prime minister and Russell as Leader of the Commons; Granville replaced Aberdeen as leader in the Lords; Russell's candidate, Panmure (formerly Fox Maule) succeeded Newcastle at the War Office; the Peelite Lord Canning entered the cabinet.

Argyll said he could not help feeling that it was rather ridiculous, for 'it seems to be the same identical ship, with the same crew, excepting only a new captain and a new mate'.[2] But it was the captain and the mate who had been most criticized, and were, ex officio, most deserving of criticism. Account had to be taken of political realities. If the Peelites had not joined, Palmerston said, there would have been just as many discontented, 'but they would have consisted of more able men'.[3] He would very much have liked to include Russell, especially if he would go to the Lords. But Palmerston's coalition cabinet was short-lived. In less than a fortnight after its first meeting three of the five Peelite cabinet ministers (Gladstone, Graham and Herbert) announced to their colleagues that they must retire, and some of the Peelite ministers outside the cabinet followed them.

This fortnight had seen a flood of decisions, many made by Palmerston himself, and most of them flowing from his initiative — the sort of thing which the public expected of him. Palmerston himself was not over-anxious to make Russell Britain's representative at the Four Power conference in Vienna, but Clarendon suggested it and the elder statesmen Lansdowne and Aberdeen commended it, and it got Lord John out of the way.[4] A placatory gesture was made to the United States and a stiff message sent to Naples, saying that relations with Britain could not return to a friendly footing unless the king changed his system of policy, foreign and domestic.[3] A letter went to Napoleon III declaring that the alliance had originated in the 'loyalty, frankness and wisdom' of the Emperor, who could always count on the loyalty and frankness of the Palmerston government, and that Palmerston would be honoured to receive from Napoleon direct any communication too confidential to be put in official dispatches. Communicated to the Queen after it had been sent, this missive did not please the Court, and the Prince wrote:[5]

This letter gave us great uneasiness.... The sort of private correspondence which Lord Palmerston means to establish with the Emperor Napoleon is a novel and unconstitutional practice. If carried on behind the back of the Sovereign, it makes her Minister the Privy Councillor of a foreign Sovereign at the head of her affairs. How can the Foreign Secretary and Ambassador at Paris, the legitimate organs of communication, carry on their business, if everything has been privately preconcerted between the Emperor and the English Prime Minister? What control can the Cabinet hope to exercise on the Foreign Affairs under these circumstances? ...

Circumstances alter cases. The conduct of French diplomacy was chaotic precisely because it depended on the momentary whim of Napoleon III, a man of conflicting motivations and unsteady purpose. Palmerston's contact with him was valuable, as was Winston Churchill's direct line to Franklin Roosevelt. When allied to the acquisition by the ambassador, Lord Cowley, of an imperial confidence denied to Napoleon's own ministers, it became a matter of complaint for French notables rather than the British cabinet or Court.

Palmerston's letter to Napoleon spoke, in the premier's fluent French, of 'the bad state of the English army' and declared: 'We are going to put a little order into our camp before Sebastopol.' The new cabinet agreed at the outset that there were sound constitutional, administrative, political and diplomatic grounds for resisting the actual appointment of the Roebuck Committee.[6] But if this was to be done, Palmerston must be able to go to the Commons and say, like Richard II to the rebels, 'I will be your leader', to promise that the cabinet itself would act as the House's committee.[7] New brooms must be seen to be effectively at work. So no Secretary at War was named; his functions were to be merged with those of the Secretary of State. Panmure was told to prepare a memorandum for abolishing the Ordnance, allotting discipline and promotions in the Artillery and Engineers to the Horse Guards, the rest of its functions to the War Office. An Admiralty Transport Board would be set up to take over the relevant functions of the Navy Victualling Department (overworked and incompetent). A regular shuttle service of ships carrying casualties one way and stores the other was ordered. At the suggestion of Lady Palmerston's son-in-law, the humanitarian Shaftesbury, a Sanitary Commission was sent out, with the utmost expedition, to see what was wrong with the medical services, initiate remedial measures and see them to completion. Palmerston was satisfied that there had been much avoidable suffering and sickness. Another commission under Sir John McNeill would go out to inquire into the deficiencies in the supply services in the Crimea, and, in effect, superintend the reform of the commissariat and also provide the answers it was so difficult to extract from Raglan. An active and intelligent officer would go out as Chief of Staff to relieve Raglan of many details 'which require an attention and direction which he has failed to give them'. And Panmure made it clear to Raglan that both the Adjutant-General and the Quartermaster-General should be replaced.[8]

Even this impressive activity could not, however, prevent the nomination of a Commons committee of inquiry. When convinced that it was inevitable, Palmerston at first hoped to direct or limit its terms of reference, but by 20th he had concluded that even this was impossible, and that the only politic course was to ensure as favourable a composition of the committee as possible. The alternative, after all, was another political crisis, and an incapable Derby government. But Gladstone had never liked joining a Palmerston administration. He abominated the committee of inquiry as aimed at Aberdeen and Newcastle, and held, with some reason (but little sense of proportion), that if it were granted it would be impossible for the Executive ever to resist the most absurd and preposterous demands for inquiry and the steady encroachment of the legislature on the executive sphere. He carried Graham and Herbert with him for resignation. When they announced this to the cabinet, Palmerston, with some difficulty, kept his temper, indicated that he had agreed with Roebuck a list of names which, all things considered, was unobjectionable, and said that he would consult the cabinet on replacements for the retiring ministers. This deference to colleagues, which was not required by constitutional convention, surprised Argyll as much as the fact that Palmerston proved as good a listener as Aberdeen, though, of course, more prone to suggest initiatives.[9]

The resignation of Herbert enabled Palmerston to offer the Colonies to Russell, who accepted while en route for Vienna. The loss of the Peelites weakened the calibre of the administration mainly by the loss of Gladstone's powers of advocacy and financial understanding. His successor, Sir George Cornewall Lewis, was a worthy and respected man, with an encyclopaedic knowledge of everything *except finance*. It is certainly a count against Palmerston that he proposed to deprive the new Chancellor of his exceedingly able coach, the Financial Secretary, James Wilson, who was to go to the Board of Trade to assist the new President, Stanley of Alderley, a narrow-minded Whig, formerly chief whip, much given to intrigue and safer to have in the government than out. This disastrous move was avoided only because Wilson was unsure of re-election to the House.[10]

Palmerston, losing notable Peelites, had to strengthen his hold on Whiggery by the appointment of Russell (*vice* Herbert), Stanley of Alderley (*vice* Cardwell), Vernon Smith (at the Board of Control *vice* Wood, who succeeded Graham at the Admiralty) and the dispatch of Lord Carlisle to Viceregal Lodge, Dublin. He did not think highly of these colleagues. But he was loyal to his class. He ostentatiously refused to accept the allegation of the Administrative Reformers that incompetence had been due to the aristocratic origins of the officials and officers. He agreed with Argyll that 'there was not the smallest reason to believe that there were in the House of Commons, or in the country, neglected men of the middle classes who would have conducted affairs better. . . . We never heard anything about it in the Cabinet, except occasionally as a joke'.[11]

Palmerston had, indeed, initially offered the upstart Layard, who shared his views on Russia and Turkey, the under-secretaryship at the War Office, for which the public had marked him out, but substituted the under-secretaryship for the Colonies after the Queen and Gladstone made strong representations.[12] *The Times* championed Layard, complaining of 'the cold shade of aristocracy blighting the energies of the nation' and Layard on 19th February said there was no reason to trust the new government more than the last. Instead of commissions, he said, there should have been sent to the East men of the stamp of the members of the French Assembly after the Revolution, 'who had no party considerations, who cared not for aristocratic influence, who went out determined to sacrifice those who were guilty, regardless of persons'. It was a positive insult to the common sense of the country to say that one could not find a man to put in order the harbour of Balaclava, unless one wanted a man 'seventy years old, a member of Brooks's, . . . who had always voted with the Government'. Palmerston's protest at vulgar declamations against the aristocracy, and reference to the charge of the Light Brigade, were hardly an answer to accusations which did not impugn the gallantry, but only the intelligence and education of the upper classes. But Layard defeated himself by his violence. At Liverpool on 21st April he complained that all the old Whig scum had come again to the top of the pot and attacked (not altogether accurately) the promotions system and the Commander-in-Chief, Hardinge, who replied in *The Times*. Three hundred members turned up in the Commons on a Friday to bay at Layard and cheer Palmerston's tribute to the public spirit and manly feeling of the gentlemen of England.[13]

Meanwhile, Roebuck and Layard had been defeated on the Committee of Inquiry, which adopted the report of the Whig ex-minister, Lord Seymour, blaming the system not the men, except that Roebuck carried by his casting vote a condemnation of the dispatch of the expedition to the Crimea without proper military intelligence reports. But though his friends reminded him that 'Cobbett, O'Connell and Cobden have all tried to rule Parliament *out* of Parliament and have all failed', this is what Layard aimed to do through the Administrative Reform Association launched in the City in April and hailed by *The Times* on 1st May as 'designed to upset the whole system of corruption and favouritism, and to introduce into public matters the energies and enterprise of private management'. A great meeting at the Drury Lane Theatre on 13th June provided a popular middle class background to the debate of two days later, when Layard moved 'that this House . . . is of opinion that the manner in which merit and efficiency have been sacrificed in public appointments to party and family influence, and to a blind adherence to routine, has given rise to great misfortunes, and threatens to bring discredit upon the national character and to involve the country in grave disasters'.

Layard's motion was parried by 359 to 46, a vote which owed something to Palmerston's spirited rejoinder to a personal attack made by Layard at Drury Lane ('I never jested at the sufferings of the people; I never made light of their unfortunate condition') and his argument that Layard's own career (he rose from paid attaché at Constantinople to Under-Secretary of State for Foreign Affairs) was a recognition of merit. Yet it was thought the government might have been defeated if it had not accepted Bulwer Lytton's amendment, as an alternative to Layard's motion. The resolution, as passed on 21st July read: 'That this House recommends to the earliest attention of Her Majesty's ministers the necessity of a careful revision of our various official establishments, with a view to simplify and facilitate the transaction of public business, and, by instituting judicial tests of merit, as well as by removing obstructions to its fair promotion and legitimate rewards, to secure to the service of the State the largest available proportion of the energy and intelligence for which the people of this country are distinguished.' Lytton said that Layard had proved the baneful effects of aristocratic privilege, but must be defeated because he sought to overbear the House by outside pressure, disparaged the Commons and called into question the fundamental principles of the electoral system. It has long been recognized that Palmerston well served the aristocracy and the established political order by his resistance to parliamentary reform after 1832. It is less often remembered that in 1855 he endangered his popularity by resisting demands for administrative reform couched in terms of fundamentalist condemnation of the aristocracy and linked with demands for the extension of the suffrage and the ballot.

Yet Palmerston was no mere obstructionist, and the Lytton resolution was not without fruit. The Minute had already been issued establishing the Civil Service Commissioners, not as yet to conduct open competitive examinations for entry to the public service, but to examine the fitness of candidates put up by the departments. Civil service pay was increased. There is evidence that Palmerston abetted Trevelyan in legislating by Treasury Minute procedures for the conduct of government departments, thereby advancing Trevelyan's notions of Treasury control.[14] Palmerston recommended for the Regius Chair of Greek at Oxford Benjamin Jowett, one of the prime movers in the exploitation of the Trevelyan–Northcote Report as the charter of a reformed curriculum in the public schools and universities which would prepare the able offspring of the middle class for careers in the public service (as Haileybury was doing for the Indian service).[15]

Adept at making small concessions, Palmerston promoted Sir Benjamin Hall, influential in the metropolis, to be President of the Board of Works ('Big Ben') and Matthew Talbot Baines, influential in the West Riding, to the cabinet. He 'wished to make Gregg of Manchester and Marshall of Leeds, peers, they being representatives of the manufacturers of Lancashire and Yorkshire'.[16] But the movement for administrative reform in the first months of his administration impaired Palmerston's image in middle class eyes. Class solidarity, official patronage and hope of it, and the tenderness of the Peelites for Aberdeen's reputation (and their own) could beat off in the House, on 19th July, Roebuck's motion to 'visit with its severe reprehension every member of the [late] Cabinet'. But, when all the members of that cabinet except Aberdeen and Newcastle had been, or were still, in the present one, it was hardly a glorious victory to carry by 289–182 'the previous question' on the motion of a member of the Opposition, General Jonathan Peel. And Palmerston could not, because of the demand for administrative reform, appeal, as he would otherwise have been inclined to do, from the House to the nation. He would have liked to have an election in the hope of excluding the petulant Peelites and the currently discredited Cobden and Bright from the House. But 'Layard would be returned for London, and every Layardite would come in'.[17] Layard was a War Radical, but he was also an anti-aristocratic one, and a champion of Parliamentary Reform. Palmerston preferred the present House, for the parliamentary sequel to the Vienna Conference showed that it was sound on the main point of continuing the war until a satisfactory peace could be secured.

★   ★   ★   ★

The deep reason for Peelite hesitations as to whether to join Palmerston and for Peelite secessions in February was a mistrust of Palmerston's foreign policy. This was part of their Tory heritage and yet, in the case of Gladstone and Graham, constituted an important link with the Manchester School. Was not Palmerston the one leader of whom it could be hoped, even by Layard, that he would extend the objects of the war to give hope to the oppressed nationalities of (non-Turkish) Europe, and the Circassians? Gladstone had said that Aberdeen was being excluded from the premiership because 'of leanings and sympathies with respect to peace, and of opinions with respect to the State and institutions of Turkey, in which I share'. This was true only in the sense that Aberdeen's crass incompetence as a war premier was partly derived from his conscience-stricken attitude to the war. Palmerston met Gladstone squarely on this point. '. . . To speak plainly and forcibly you distrust my views and Intentions, and you think that I should be disposed to continue the War without necessity for the attainment of objects unreasonable in themselves, or unattainable by the Means at our Command, or not worth the Efforts necessary for their attainment.' This was a just summary of the views stated and implied in Gladstone's letter of refusal of 5th February, which Gladstone retracted, against his inclination, when Aberdeen received Palmerston's pledge repeated to Gladstone in the following terms — 'If by a Stroke of the wand I could effect in the Map of the world the changes which I could wish I am quite sure that I could make arrangement far more conducive than some of the present ones to the Peace of Nations, to the progress of Civilization, to the Happiness & Welfare of Mankind but I am not so destitute of Common Sense, as not to be able to compare Ends with Means, and to see that the former must be given up when the latter are wanting! And when the Means . . . consist in the Blood & Treasure of a Great Nation, those who are answerable to the Nation for the Expenditure of that Blood & Treasure must well weigh the value of the objects which they pursue, and must remember that if they should forget the just Proportion between Ends & Means the good sense of the People whose affairs they manage will soon step in to correct their Errors, and to call them to a severe account of the Evils of which they would have been the Cause.'[18]

This honest pronouncement, meaning no more than that Palmerston would not for any large objects continue the war after it became unpopular, could not really satisfy one concerned that every opportunity for peace should be sought 'and husbanded to the utmost'. Had not public opinion forced the government to war? Was not public opinion, as Burke had said, often 'outrageously wrong'? Had it not been outrageously wrong in rejoicing at Aberdeen's fall and Palmerston's rise? When Herbert declined the Colonial Office on Molesworth's death in October 1855 he told Gladstone that the Government's popularity rested on 'its *supposed* war-at-all-price leanings' and that Palmerston had not considered what a just peace would be.[19] Was it not sinister that Palmerston should raise to the cabinet a Tory, Lord Harrowby, whose main claim to distinction was that he was an enthusiast for the liberation of Poland? But it did not follow from the Gladstonian suspicion of Palmerston that the Peelites had done right to leave him. Herbert received this offer of the Colonies because it was an open secret that he thought they had done wrong, that 'to make Palmerston useful or even harmless his Ministry should have been leavened and not opposed'. Aberdeen had pressed this argument, with temporary success, in February. But Gladstone never deviated from the view that 'the first time he and the leaven disagreed about a question on which he had the popular side (he was perfectly sure to have or take the popular side of all questions) the leaven would go to the wall'.[20] By the time of the breakdown of the Vienna Conference, Gladstone had 'argued himself into a fever of antagonism and suspicion of Palmerston, as determined to fight for a mere victory, when everything substantial as to terms had been or could be gained'.[20]

This was not true. Britain had reluctantly, indeed, almost

accidentally, endorsed the Four Points which originated with Drouyn and Buol. The Russians accepted them, unconditionally, in November 1854. But everything hinged on their interpretation, and especially on the meaning of Point 3. In December 1854, while Aberdeen was still premier, Britain and France had bound themselves to the view that it involved the demolition of Russian fortifications on the Black Sea and the reduction of Russian warships there to four. But on 28th December Britain, France and Austria adopted the phrase 'Russian predominance in the Black Sea should be brought to an end.' What did this mean? Palmerston was always clear that it meant very few Russian warships in the Black Sea, though as long as the Peelites were in his cabinet he agreed that the destruction of the works at Sebastopol should be insisted on only if that port were taken.[3] On 28th March Palmerston dismissed as a 'mauvaise plaisanterie' the Buol–Gorchakov proposal that Russia be allowed to keep her pre-war fleet if she accepted that the Straits should be open to British and French warships at all times.[22] The cabinet agreed. But Buol lured the French foreign minister, Drouyn de Lhuys, into acceptance of the suggestion that if Russia increased her Black Sea fleet an equal Turkish fleet could be reinforced by British and French fleets each half the size of the Russian. He threw in an Anglo–French–Austrian treaty of 'guarantee' of Turkey. Palmerston did not put any trust in Austrian engagements, and Drouyn's action in Vienna was treason to the Anglo-French alliance, for he had just, in London, bound himself to the British proposal of 'limitation' or his own new idea of the 'neutralization' of the Euxine as the only alternatives. Both of these were rejected absolutely by Russia on 21st April. Whereupon Drouyn accepted Buol's proposal of 'counterpoise'. *And Russell accepted it too.*

Palmerston had feared some action by Russell characteristic only in its unpredictability. But he had hardly imagined that Lord John would approve a proposal which he admitted would bring not peace but an armed truce and was justified only on the conclusion that the security of the Porte was not a vital question for Britain like the independence of Belgium and Portugal. The proposed arrangement, said Palmerston, would be dangerous and dishonourable; it was really 'a mockery'. No government in Britain could accept it unless the alternative was clearly abandonment by France; it was, muttered Palmerston in cabinet when Russell, on

2nd May, explained himself, 'capitulation'.[23] On 3rd, however, it looked as though ministers might have to accept, though even Granville, a pacific man, said he would do so with 'sorrow and almost shame', and they would probably be hooted out of office.[24] They were saved by Cowley's intervention with Napoleon, assisted, according to Russell, by 'very strong language' from Palmerston through Walewski. Most ministers, a majority of both Houses of Parliament, and, by all the signs, the mass of the British public were relieved that ministers did not go to parliament and ask it to accept terms that would have been accepted before the armies left Varna, on the argument that since then they had achieved nothing and could not be sure of achieving anything. 'The House had voted for Palmerston as the Minister who would prosecute the war vigorously, not as the Minister who would listen to shabby terms of peace'.[25]

When Drouyn, disowned by the Emperor, resigned, Russell declared that 'his resignation entails mine'. But he allowed himself to be dissuaded, for the atmosphere of London was different from that of Vienna and the unpopularity of the Peelites and Manchester School was striking. He saw that resignation on such an issue 'would injure my reputation — perhaps irretrievably'. On 28th May Palmerston was able to write a personal letter to Napoleon recording a majority of 100 against Disraeli's accusation that 'we occupied ourselves with a useless and hardly honourable negotiation, when we ought to be solely occupied with the war'.[26] Russell had made a sprightly speech, very anti-Russian, describing the Austrian terms (which he had secretly advocated) as 'nugatory and meagre'. His attitude at Vienna was then made known to the world in a circular dispatch by Buol, and when Russell was forced to admit its accuracy, 'the hound-element in the House of Commons' (and the press) 'fell upon Lord John with a savage bay'.[25] The cabinet was prepared, if Lord John insisted, to sink with him; the junior ministers, possibly encouraged by Palmerston, sent in a round-robin demanding his resignation. 'My continuance in office would only embarrass and endanger your Administration', wrote Russell to Palmerston on 13th July; 'neither the Crown nor the country would derive any benefit from my resistance to the present clamour.' Palmerston could only reply: 'You have judged rightly. . . . But juster feelings will in due time prevail.'[27]

Truly the wheel had come full circle. It had been customary, and right, to say that no Liberal government could survive without Russell in it; now Palmerston's could not stand unless he left it. But it was still true that Russell had not enough magnanimity to support a government out of office. By early August he was in Gladstonian terms attacking the government for not accepting the Vienna proposals, even implying that the Allies were keeping the Turks in the war against their will. 'In all my political experience I remember nothing so bad', commented Clarendon. 'He filled up the measure of mischief, and with malice prepense did all the harm in his power to every English interest', introducing 'that apple of discord, Italy' in order to 'set us ill with France and Austria'.[28] It was difficult enough to prevent the French and the Austrians from getting on too well with one another at the expense of British views.

It was difficult, too, to reach agreement with France on operations against Russia. Napoleon's proposal, described by Palmerston to the Queen as 'wholly unnecessary' and not unlikely to be 'attended with the most lamentable consequences', to command in the Crimea himself was abandoned after, perhaps in consequence of, his state visit to Britain in April.[29] But it had given the cautious Canrobert, who had a higher opinion of Raglan's 20,000 effectives than his own 70,000 (an estimate British subalterns and men most indiscreetly showed the French they shared) excuse for procrastination. There was a week's heavy bombardment of Sebastopol in mid-April, but the expected assault, which might have succeeded, did not follow. Not till June was the British cabinet heartened by the first Allied success since the Alma — the destruction of Russian steamers and transports and vast stores of grain by the descent upon Kerch, on the Sea of Azov. The expeditionary force had started off on 3rd May, only to be recalled by the Emperor by telegraph; it sailed again when Canrobert was succeeded by the intrepid Pélissier, an admirer of Raglan, a man bold enough to defy the Emperor.

On 28th May Palmerston wrote to Napoleon an appeal to be staunch against subtle diplomacy.[26] He feared the consequences in England if the Allies were again plunged into the Viennese labyrinth, simply to serve Austrian purposes. 'Victories in the Crimea will command for us the friendship, perhaps even the sword of Austria; without success in the Crimea, we shall not even have her pen'. In a few weeks they could be masters of Sebastopol

and the Russian fleet. But could they? Early in June the French
took the Mamelon and the British the Gravel Pits, but on 18th
both armies met disastrous set-back, the French at the Malakhoff
redoubt, the British at the Redan. Cholera was spreading through
the camp, and on 28th Lord Raglan died. The telegram announcing
the capture of the harbour of Sebastopol did not arrive until 10th
September, three weeks after the failure of the massive Russian
onslaught on the French and Piedmonters at Tchernaya. And then,
to Palmerston's fury, no attempt was made to clear the Russians
out of the Crimea. The generals, he complained, seemed content
with 'quiet winter quarters'. But they had not even assured
themselves of these while the Russians held the northern heights
beyond Sebastopol, so that 'we have half Sebastopol in our hands
. . . which we dare neither leave nor live in, with a large army in
our front undefeated'. The stroke at Kherson on the Dnieper in
October was the one sign of life after the entry into Sebastopol,
and no action followed against the main Russian arsenal and depot
of Nicholaiev up river.

★   ★   ★   ★

Palmerston was a better Leader of the House than Russell, but
that was not saying much. He showed, as premier, more activity
than Aberdeen, but that was not saying much either. Colleagues
who were sure that he would have been a better war minister than
Newcastle had doubted whether he could fulfil half the hopes
which public opinion placed in him on the strength of his patriotic
and belligerent spirit and contempt for infirmity of purpose, and
they soon realized that Panmure was no better than Newcastle.[A]

[A] 'I had known him personally for a good many years . . . but it never
occurred to me that he was a man to resort to in any great crisis of administrative
affairs', writes Argyll (pp. 533–4). Granville described 'Mars' as a Scotch divinity
perhaps more fit to direct a campaign in the General Assembly of the Church of
Scotland than on the shores of the Black Sea (*G.*, 102) and for his other criticisms
see ibid. 137 — 'Mars was very much at sea today; there was a strong feeling
against him shown by his colleagues'; 172. — 'the god of war is not yet found out
as to want of capacity by the public'. Clarendon wrote in Sept. 1855: 'It is all
very well running down Mars's ability, but there is no other single member of
the Cabinet who can defy the Prime Minister, all his colleagues, excepting
perhaps Charles Wood, and the Court itself: you will see that he will retain
Simpson in command in spite of us all. . . . Mars, who is a much more wily
creature than he used to be when he was so easily caught by a brother god, will
slip through all our nets' (ibid. 114). The full flavour of Panmure's massive
powers of procrastination and incomprehension is well brought out in Cecil

Palmerston and Panmure started off, indeed, with a roar, and it would be wrong to give the impression that the first fortnight of vigour was without effect. The Sanitary Commission, said Florence Nightingale, 'saved the British army'. Palmerston was vehement about it, writing to Raglan on 22nd February 1855:[30]

This will be given to you by Dr. Sutherland, Chief of the Sanitary Commission . . . whom we have sent out to put the hospitals, the port and the camp into a less unhealthy condition than has hitherto existed, and I request that you will give them every assistance and support in your power. They will, of course, be opposed and thwarted by the medical officers, by the men who have charge of the port arrangements, and by those who have the cleaning of the camp. Their mission will be ridiculed, and their recommendations and directions set aside, unless enforced by the peremptory exercise of your authority.

But that authority I must request you to exert in the most peremptory manner for the immediate and exact carrying into execution whatever changes of arrangement they may recommend; for these are matters on which depend the health and lives of many hundreds of men, I may indeed say of thousands. It is scarcely to be expected that officers, whether military or medical, whose time is wholly occupied by the pressing business of each day, should be able to give their attention or their time to the matters to which these commissioners have for many years devoted their action and their thoughts.

But the interposition of men skilled in this way is urgently required. The hospital at Scutari has become a hotbed of pestilence, and if no proper precautions are taken before the sun's rays begin to be felt, your camp will become one vast seat of the most virulent plague. I hope this commission will arrive in time to prevent much evil, but I am very sure that not one hour should be lost after their arrival in carrying into effect the precautionary and remedial measures which they may recommend.

Panmure gave 'full authority' to Alex Soyer, the superlative chef of the Reform Club, who, with Miss Nightingale, performed miracles at Scutari. But when that formidable woman moved to the Crimea, she found, especially after Raglan's death, obstruction and ill-will on all sides. Panmure derided her plans for reducing intemperance among the soldiery. Palmerston was more enlightened than his war minister, a former captain in the Life Guards, on the question of whether the soldier was 'a remitting animal', and more enlightened than his wife in his attitude to the Nightingale Fund for training nurses, which she thought 'a great humbug'.[31] Palmerston was interested in public health, and his concern for the improvement of

Woodham-Smith's *Florence Nightingale*, especially in regard to the Sanitary Commission promised in October 1856 but not appointed (under the chairmanship of Herbert) till seven months later.

barracks and military hospitals at home carried over into his second administration of 1859–65 was to involve him in struggles with Gladstone at the Exchequer.

In matters of army health Palmerston was seen at his most Churchillian. Thus he wrote to Panmure on 10th June 1855:

This is capital news from the Sea of Azoff, and the extensive destruction of magazines and supplies in the towns attacked must greatly cripple the Russian army in the Crimea. I am very sorry, however, to see so sad an account of the health of the Sardinians, and I strongly recommend you to urge Raglan, by telegraph today, to move the Sardinian camp to another and healthier situation.

Such prevalence of disease as the telegraphic message mentions *must* be the effect of some local cause; and I am as sure as if I was on the spot that these Sardinians are put down in some unhealthy place, from which they ought without the loss of a day to be removed. Our quartermaster-generals never bestow a thought about healthiness of situations, and, indeed, they are in general wholly ignorant of the sanitary principles upon which any given situation should be chosen or avoided; but if Raglan were to consult Dr. Sutherland on the subject, I am confident he would get a good opinion. At all events, these men ought to be removed from where they are without loss of a day; and no excuse of military arrangements ought to be accepted as a pretence for delay.

As the cholera seems to be increasing among the troops, I should advise you to send for the doctor I mentioned, and who would give you useful suggestions as to the treatment of the disease, and as to the best way of administering sulphuric acid, which seems now to be the most effectual remedy, and which, if taken in time, seldom fails in stopping the attack....

Palmerston had brooded over the problem of cholera as Home Secretary, and had no respect for those who regarded epidemics as acts of God. The following letter bears the authentic stamp of the man who wrote for Metternich in 1841 that elementary instruction in the case for constitutionalism. Bearing the signature of the Under-Secretary, Henry Fitzroy, M.P., it reads:[33]

Whitehall Oct 19 1853.

SIR — I am directed by Viscount Palmerston to acknowledge the receipt of your letter of the 15th inst, requesting, on behalf of the Presbytery of Edinburgh, to be informed whether it is proposed to appoint a day of national fast on account of the visitation of the cholera, and to state that there can be no doubt that manifestations of humble resignation to the Divine Will, and sincere acknowledgements of human unworthiness, are never more appropriate than when it has pleased Providence to afflict mankind with some severe visitation; but it does not appear to Lord Palmerston that a national fast would be suitable to the circumstances of the present moment.

The Maker of the Universe has established certain laws of nature for the planet in which we live, and the weal or woe of mankind depends upon the observation or neglect of those laws. One of those laws connects health with the absence of those gaseous exhalations which proceed from over-crowded human beings, or from decomposing substances, whether animal or vegetable; and those same laws render sickness the almost inevitable consequence of exposure to those noxious influences. But it has at the same time pleased Providence to place it within the power of man to make such arrangements as will prevent or disperse such exhalations so as to render them harmless, and it is the duty of man to attend to those laws of nature, and to exert the faculties which Providence has thus given to man for his own welfare.

The recent visitation of cholera . . . is an awful warning given to the people of this realm that they have too much neglected their duty in this respect, and that those persons with whom it rested to purify towns and cities, and to prevent or remove the causes of disease have not been sufficiently active in regard to such matters. Lord Palmerston would, therefore, suggest that the best course which the people of this country can pursue to deserve that the further progress of the cholera should be stayed, will be to employ the interval . . . between the present time and the begin-ning of next spring in planning and executing measures by which those portions of their towns and cities which are inhabited by the poorer classes, and which, from the nature of things, must most need purification and improvement, may be freed from those causes and sources of con-tagion which, if allowed to remain, will infallibly breed pestilence and be fruitful in death, in spite of all the prayers and fastings of a united but inactive nation. When man has done his utmost for his own safety, then is the time to invoke the blessing of Heaven to give effect to his exertions.

The letter of 10th June 1855 praising a victory and urging 'action this day' for the improvement of the health prospects of the troops is Churchillian both in the range of its interests and the vigour of its purpose. It goes on to explore means of raising more men, to take steps to see that liaison with the principal ally shall be profitable, to point out what is obvious to an intelligent layman but which the experts may well overlook —

. . . We are 40,000 men short of the number voted by Parliament, and we shall be without the shadow of an excuse if we do not resort to every possible means and every possible quarter to complete our force to the number which Parliament has authorized. Let us get as many Germans and Swiss as we can; let us get men from Halifax [Nova Scotia]; let us enlist Italians and let us forthwith increase our bounty at home without raising the standard. Do not let departmental, or official, or professional prejudices and habits stand in our way. We must override all such obstacles and difficulties. The only answer to give to objectors on such grounds is, the thing *must* be done; we *must* have troops. . . . We are now getting on in the month of June, and no time is to be lost.

I wish you would send General Ashburnham to me before he goes to Paris, that I may talk over with him the matters he will have from time to time to discuss, according to his instructions, with the French Government.

Do not forget to suggest to our commissariat people in the Black Sea that large supplies of oxen to be eaten, and of horses to be ridden or to draw, may be derived from the country on the eastern shore of the Sea of Azoff, from whence these animals might be brought down to the port of Taman, near the Straits of Kertch, and be from thence carried coastwise to Balaclava; and it would be well also to point their attention to the projecting neck of land or island called Krassnoi, in the Bay of Perekop, which is said to abound in sheep and hay. It lies north-west of the coast of the Crimea.

The spirit was willing. The flesh had great reserves. Although he appeared to be ageing rapidly, and, over-worked, 'napped' frequently in parliament and made ill-prepared and sometimes well-nigh incoherent speeches, Palmerston never shirked work. Noticing that the Home Secretary, Sir George Grey, was showing signs of strain from handling the Colonies while Russell was away in Vienna, the premier took over the Colonial Office himself, welcoming, he said, an opportunity to get to know the business.[22] But he was, after all, older than Chatham had ever been, and as old as Winston Churchill at the *end* of the 1939–45 war. He was faced by formidable difficulties which he did not overcome. No pretence can be made that he was very effective as a war premier. There is not the ghost of a justification for comparing him with the elder Pitt or Churchill, except in spirit. In part his difficulties were institutional. A mid-nineteenth century prime minister had not the power acquired by a Lloyd George or a Churchill, or inherited by an Asquith or Chamberlain. He was hedged about by distrust of executive government, habits of official routine, traditions and conventions not lightly overcome, vested interests both obtrusive and subtle. Chatham had overcome these, but he had able officers to inspire, and Palmerston could not, without the most drastic purges, overcome the disastrous effects of forty years' peace, which left the British army with no assets save its regimental system, its discipline, and the reckless bravery of its aristocratic officers, so often squandered by the inertia of the staff. Palmerston was not ruthless enough to insist on the removal of the Commissary, Quartermaster and Adjutant-Generals, although he came into office convinced they were incompetent and that their dismissal was necessary both to appease the public and improve the morale of the troops.[34] Panmure gravely mishandled the affair. On 12th February he addressed to Raglan a strong and just rebuke on the score of his failure to give full information and explanations of the deficiencies and breakdowns. But he defeated his own objects by his further remarks. It was one thing for Palmerston to tell Panmure 'he must do something to satisfy the House of Commons', [35] quite another for Panmure to tell Raglan 'Your staff must be changed, as the least that will satisfy the public' and worse still to accuse Raglan of ignorance because he did not visit the troops enough (which was untrue) and to say that his staff was as ignorant as himself.[36] This missive roused the most uncomplaining of men to bitter complaint, and enhanced his sense of loyalty to his immediate subordinates, who rallied round him to resist the attacks of the newspapers and Whitehall.

Raglan was able to resist demands for dismissals because the government was sending out General Simpson not only to act as chief of staff but to inspect and recommend dismissals. Simpson was a disastrous choice. The hostility with which he was met soon evaporated when it was discovered that he too was a creature of routine and, moreover, so conscious of his lack of social connexions as to be over-anxious to please those who had them. On 16th April he reported that he had no fault to find with anyone. By this time the cabinet was sure that Raglan, as Palmerston said, was 'not much of a hand at forming opinions or inventing plans'.[37] The premier was dissatisfied that, falling heir to the immense exertions made by ministers under Aberdeen, especially Herbert, in December and January, he had been able to achieve little more than the improvements in the medical department procured by Sutherland and in the supply services procured by McNeill and Tulloch, who were, however, much handicapped by the fact that a war minister who admitted that it would be necessary to go very far down in the commissariat to find able and energetic officers was not willing to go very far down.[38] Palmerston was right to be dissatisfied when even the meek Granville asked for some dismissals before a censure motion tabled by Ellenborough was debated in the Lords.[39] On 1st May Palmerston had written to Panmure: 'I for one cannot undertake to stand up in my place and defend an inactivity which would leave our Army . . . the victim of that knot of incapables who in the last eight months have been the direct cause of the disability and death of thousands.' Now he wrote again: 'I clearly foresee that unless you should be able to say that more efficient men . . . are appointed the debate will be as damaging to yourself and to the Govt as the continuance of these men in their several places is detrimental to the welfare of the Army. . . . I have often urged these things upon you without effect; we shall now see what our opponents will make of them.' It was perfectly evident that Raglan would never of his own accord make any change — 'We must cut the knot.'[40]

It does not argue success on the part of a premier that the Opposition should be making in public the demands that he had in vain made in private. His reputation would have stood higher with posterity if he had taken the gamble urged upon him by Granville, and promoted comparatively junior officers with Crimean experience to the chief responsibilities.[38] Was it, in any case, much of a gamble, when, in his view, the existing incumbents were so unfit? But the government easily survived the Ellenborough debate, in which the mover bitingly recalled Wellington's low estimate of Palmerston a quarter of a century ago ('It was not for me to fire great guns at small birds') and taunted the sparrow grown into an eagle — 'the man of the situation . . . carried into power by an impulse of individual admiration, so common in this country, and so soon followed by frigid indifference'. The knot remained untied till the Great Reaper cut it. Raglan and Estcourt died; Brown came home ill. Panmure did then contrive to dislodge Burgoyne, whose devotion to text-book routine positively invited his brilliant opposite, Todleben, to snatch the key position of the Mamelon in no-man's-land from under his very nose. Markham from India was given a division. But when on Raglan's death Simpson asked that a general of distinction be appointed, 'personal prejudices and gossip' (according to Argyll) influenced the cabinet's decision not to appoint Sir Colin Campbell.[41] Simpson was given the command. He was a man with all Raglan's defects and none of his virtues and none of his prestige. He had an infectious conviction that Sebastopol would not fall.

Everyone (except the War Office) now realized that Panmure had been a disastrous appointment. Known for his shaggy appearance as 'the Bison', he showed that the soubriquet was apt. As lacking in finesse as in a sense of humour, he proved slow and thick of skin. After initially going on the rampage, he became merely a bulky obstruction. He found the work of the War Office easy because, unlike the plodding Newcastle, he made no attempt to keep up with it. He fell increasingly into the hands of the officials, especially the Permanent Under-Secretary, Benjamin Hawes (formerly a Radical M.P. and junior minister), who was a master of evasions and delays. By 23rd April Panmure was complaining *to Raglan* that Palmerston 'listened too much to the people'; on 1st June he assured him that he would press changes of personnel no more.

Panmure was the choked conduit in which Palmerstonian impetus was dissipated. Yet Palmerston did not remove him even when a wonderful opportunity offered. Men were short; if the war was popular, recruiting was not (and who, in view of the well-publicized conditions in the field, could be surprised at that?). The Secretary of State accordingly announced in the Lords the doubling of field-pay. His colleagues read of this in the newspapers; he had consulted neither the Treasury nor the premier.[42] One supposes that Palmerston did not dare dismiss a leading Whig when Russell's own forced retirement was imminent. He had all the time to look over his shoulder at the parliamentary situation. But this is to say that he fell below the level of events. For a premier to be occupied in prodding the Bison, and usually prodding in vain, was not only vexatious to Palmerston, it was contemptible. The best way of securing support from Parliament would surely have been to take bold measures calculated to bring success, and if the parliamentarians had failed him, Palmerston could with a good conscience have appealed to the country. In the view of the present author, Palmerston should have tried to get a coalition with the Tories, for the duration of the war, making Ellenborough, who had formidable energy if little tact, and was in many ways a natural ally of Palmerston, either Secretary of State for War or First Lord of the Admiralty. Or, without a coalition, he should have dismissed Panmure and taken the War Office himself. He could have left the routine of Commons leadership to Sir George Grey and the routine of the War Office to a trusty lieutenant (his stepson William Cowper, perhaps) devoted enough to transmit unpalatable instructions to the civil servants and the military. Palmerston himself could then have composed and signed peremptory dispatches to the Crimea.

★   ★   ★   ★

God knows what would have happened if Sebastopol had not fallen. There is little evidence that another winter campaign would have found the army better administered and supplied than the year before. On coming into office Panmure had said that 'the system by which an army should be provisioned, moved and brought to action . . . is non-existent'.[43] Were things better now? It seems not. The regenerative effects of the McNeill and even of the Sutherland Commission were wearing off. Florence Nightingale, once bitten, refused to return to the Crimea until Panmure signed a dispatch asserting her status, which was published in General Orders by Simpson's successor, Codrington (to find whom Palmerston went only a very little way down the Army List). She met all sorts of petty obstructions and annoyances from Hall (who ought to have been hanged, but was knighted); the chief purveyor denied her party rations. She said that in point of routine versus system 'everything in the Army . . . is just where it was eighteen months ago . . . Nous n'avons rien oublié ni rien appris'.[44] McNeill came home to say that the commissariat in the Crimea was still rotten from top to bottom and that not one of his recommendations for reform had been acted on.[45] Lyons said that the (land) Transport Corps was a complete failure, so that the army could not march a mile, though the French and Sardinians could, and that there was still no system of local intelligence.[46] 'Everyone agrees that roads should now be made, the railway repaired, and certain sanitary arrangements carried out, not to mention field works', Granville had written in August, but he heard of none of this being set in hand nor of any attempt to get the 2,000 sappers who would be required.[47] Yet at that time Simpson expected another winter campaign, and doubted whether morale would stand it. He complained that the French had regular lines and his men none. Whose fault was that?

Of course, as far as securing operational activity was concerned, the ministers were handicapped by the fact that a large majority of the troops in the Crimea were not British, and the French had a natural veto on everything. 'We have generals whom we do not trust', said Granville. 'The French generals seem worse than ours.' But when the humble Simpson ventured to propose, as the emperor Napoleon had done, that a French general should be given overall command, he was told that if he was not fit for his duties he should resign.[49] The problem of securing congruent instructions to the

British and French commanders was never solved. Ministers in London spent much of their time trying to maintain diplomatic accord with the French. This was not easy when the British government and the British people were more anxious to continue the war than their French counterparts but the British military contribution was too small to call the tune in the field. Under Simpson, the British army became suspect in quality as well as quantity, and when, early in September, the assault on the Redan was made with stale troops, and essential equipment such as ladders was lacking, there were ominous signs that discipline was beginning to crack under the weight of incompetent leadership. The best that can be said of this shambling fiasco is that it may have helped the French in their difficult task of taking the Malakhoff, but comments at home were disturbing. 'We shall lose as much character by the victories of our allies as by the resistance of our enemies' it was said, and whatever was done by the military authorities '*seems* ill done, and generally is so'.[50] Comments abroad were unfavourable too. Napier's dictum that the British were 'a warlike but not a military people' seemed apt. Apparently they were no longer capable of making the sort of contribution which Wellington in the Peninsula had made to the defeat of Napoleon. British prestige had taken a nasty knock. It became vital for Palmerston and Clarendon to invalidate the opinion, all too common on the Continent (as the Queen complained) that Britain was properly to be regarded as 'a political and diplomatic Contingent of France'.[51]

CHAPTER XX

THE PEACE OF PARIS, 1856

'OUR danger will then begin — a danger of peace, and not a danger of war. Austria will try to draw us again into negotiations for an insufficient peace, and we shall not yet have obtained those decisive successes which would entitle us to insist on such terms as will effectually curb the ambition of Russia for the future.'[1] Thus wrote Palmerston in August 1855, in anticipation that the Russians would shortly be cleared not only from Sebastopol but the whole of the Crimea. As they were not, his target of reaching before the winter a good position from which to negotiate was far from being reached. Indeed, the Russians in November took Kars, the fortress town beyond which only Erzerum barred the way to the heart of Asia Minor and the upper valley of the Euphrates. The Turkish force there had resisted with much gallantry under the effective command of General Fenwick Williams and the Hungarian Klapka (one of the 1849 refugees) until famine forced surrender. Its neglect by the Allies is one of the most shameful features of the Crimean War; they regarded it as a side-show, but the Russians did not. The British government's only defence, ministers admitted, lay in throwing the blame on others. The Sultan, as Palmerston complained, wasted in 'extravagant prodigalities' (palaces, pashas, wives and concubines) much of the £5 million British loan extracted with difficulty from the House of Commons, while the brave army at Kars received no provisions or munitions (or pay).[3] Simpson, Stratford de Redcliffe and even Layard (who was engaged with Stratford in founding the Ottoman Bank and received frantic appeals from the medical superintendent at Kars, Sandwith, which he failed to use as ammunition against the authorities) bore much blame. So did the Emperor and Pélissier, who obstructed the departure of Omar Pasha and some of the Turkish troops from the Crimea to relieve Kars. 'We are foresaken now by all the world', wrote Sandwith on 25th August; 'I suppose you are all grouse shooting now.' It would be difficult to explain to parliament why Stratford, whose inactivity was criminal, was retained, and why no troops were sent from India.[4]

Palmerston, Granville, Sir George Grey, Clarendon and Vernon Smith all wanted to send 10,000 British troops to Trebizond, the port across the mountains from Erzerum, but most military opinion was against this.[5] The first three of these, with the two service ministers, formed the War Committee of the cabinet, set up in September 1855.[6] It had little effect in improving military organization, though it may have galvanized Panmure into sending that rough message to Simpson which caused his resignation. Once again the cabinet rejected Colin Campbell, and, lighting on General Codrington, paused only to ponder whether he could be held personally responsible for the disaster at the Redan.[7] The Committee did, however, consider war plans for 1856, having in mind as possible theatres of operations Kars, Georgia and Circassia. The cabinet decided on 2nd February 1856 to ask Napoleon to approve an expedition of 40,000 British troops (who were not available) to Georgia,[8] but this was merely part of 'the peace game' to which Russia came with the possession of Kars as a strong card.

The War Committee also considered operations in the Baltic. Early in the war Napier had demolished the fortifications at Bomarsund in the Åland Isles, the pistol pointed at Stockholm, and later, Sweaborg (Palmerston asked what was the point of 'knocking down some stone walls'). When it was suggested that Kronstadt might be assailed in 1856, the First Lord said it would be very hazardous, though it would have been perfectly possible in 1855! Men out of, and in, the cabinet, who viewed Palmerston with suspicion, were on the watch for entanglement in grandiose operations in the Baltic. Palmerston's project for an Anglo-French 'guarantee' of Sweden and Norway was checked in the cabinet in May 1855 but bore fruit in November. Unlike the treaty Aberdeen had vetoed, it would not involve Sweden in the existing war; it merely bound her not to cede any territory to Russia (such as a Norwegian fjord for use as a North Sea naval base). But it was a departure from the British tradition of keeping 'guarantees' to a minimum, and a last-minute insertion appeared to bind Britain and France to bear the whole cost of any operations by them to defend Scandinavia against Russia.[9] To Palmerston this treaty was part of 'a long line of circumvallation to confine the future extension of Russia even if the events of the war should not enable us to drive her outposts in at any part of her present circumference'. He very much hoped to deprive Russia of the Crimea, Georgia and Circassia, and opposed French talk of an indemnity. Russia, he said, would resist financial demands just as strongly as a cession of territory, and the latter ('wresting from her . . . sallying-points for attacks upon her neighbours') would 'lastingly diminish her means and power of aggression'.[10]

While Russell had been at Vienna, Palmerston provocatively declared in the House of Commons that 'the kingdom of Poland, as at present constituted, and at present occupied, is a standing menace to Germany' and asserted, in that context, that Britain and France had 'reserved to themselves the right . . . of adding in the future to these Four Points any other stipulations which they may think essential for the future security of Europe'. But he covered himself by saying that it would be for the German Powers to decide, if they found themselves fighting Russia, whether it was in their interest to change the position of Poland. And when peace-talks were resumed, neither Poland nor Finland featured among the points Britain insisted on her right to make at the peace conference, though the Åland Isles and Circassia did. Palmerston, we may be sure, would never chase the Polish hare unless it became fair game. But who knew what might not be possible if Russia were well and truly 'licked'? There would have been considerable enthusiasm in France for a war for Polish independence, and Napoleon III had a genuine sympathy with Nationalism and a strong desire to undo the treaties of 1815. Palmerston meditated offering the French a free hand in the Baltic theatre in 1856 in return for a free hand for the British in the Black Sea area. But it is unlikely that he meditated the march of French armies through Germany.

Poland was kept in the picture because Granville reported from Paris in October a feeling that if France continued the war it should be for larger objects than the Four Points. But the general preference in Paris was for peace, while in Britain it was for continuing the war for larger objects. Palmerston himself was against agreeing too closely with France the terms of peace, because they would certainly leak to Russia via Austria (or more directly via Morny 'and all the other Russian agents acting on the French Government', the 'cabal of stock-jobbing politicians' surrounding the Emperor). If they were unacceptable to Russia they would be said to be insincere; if otherwise, they would be taken as an overture. 'If we want to discuss anything, let it rather be the best way of carrying on the war', he said. 'Russia has not yet been beat enough to make peace possible. . . . We shall find all our steadiness and skill required to avoid being drawn into a peace which would disappoint the just expectations of the country, and leave unaccomplished the real objects of the war.'[11] Indeed, the only hope of a satisfactory peace lay in convincing Napoleon that an unsatisfactory one would fracture the alliance; while using him to strengthen the terms approved by Austria, the British could also use Austria to strengthen certain of the terms of direct interest to Vienna. In his agreement with Bourqueney on 14th November, Buol proposed that Russia be asked to cede part of Bessarabia, to cut her off from the mouths of the Danube, and this was to be part of the treaty although Napoleon grumbled at being asked to embarrass the financial and other resources of France for a few marshes on the Danube.

Buol was moved to this new initiative, which involved a return to Drouyn's plan (abandoned by Drouyn at Vienna in the summer) for the neutralization of the Black Sea, by the fear of direct talks between France and Russia, cutting him out of the picture (and virtually cutting out Britain too). Such talks were favoured by Morny at Paris and Gortchakov at St Petersburg, and the spectre of the rapprochement between the two enemies exercised a powerful influence over what followed. Palmerston himself did not believe that France would go to the lengths of alliance with Russia *directed against Britain* and he did believe that Napoleon would be impressed by British firmness and, in the last resort, by the threat to tell Parliament that Britain had been forced by French defection to accept shabby terms of peace.[12] Diplomacy must be called in to cancel out the weakness of Britain's military contribution, and a high tone of equality with France, involving, in the last resort, a veto on unsatisfactory terms, should be maintained. Thus, of the agreement of 14th November in Vienna, as to terms which Austria would be prepared to send to Russia as an ultimatum, breaking diplomatic relations with Russia if it were rejected, the British prime minister wrote sharply to the French ambassador, Persigny, on 21st November:[13]

. . . There has been in Vienna a negotiation in which we have not partici-pated; . . . a protocol has been signed . . . for us, but without us; . . . [it] has been communicated to us confidentially, to take or leave it, we being told to reject or accept it immediately, good or bad, without discussing the drafting and the details.

This manner of acting in an affair so grave does not suit us. We desire to conform to the wishes of the Emperor, but we must keep the rules with regard to our Parliament; and we cannot subscribe to a peace proposal to be made in our name, to Russia, unless we agree entirely on the form and substance of such a proposition. It is therefore indispensable that we should have a proposition in writing, whose wording we can well examine, before we can give Austria the authorization which she demands of us, to speak to Russia in our name.

I say 'speak in our name' because, although Austria must appropriate to herself the démarche which she would wish to make to Petersburg, she proposes to say that she knows in advance that her proposition would be adopted by France and England, if it were to be accepted by Russia.

The English nation would be delighted with a good peace which would assure the objects of the war; but rather than be dragged into signing a peace with inadequate terms, she would prefer to continue the war with no other allies than Turkey, and she feels wholly able to sustain the burden. . . . Submit, I pray, these observations to Walewsky.

Since this letter would not appear on the public record, Clarendon instructed Cowley to inform Walewski that he must learn that Britain was a principal, not 'a political and diplomatic Contingent' of France.[14]

Palmerston's letter and Clarendon's dispatch have, indeed, to be read in the light of the anterior cabinet decision of 20th November. The Foreign Secretary had put, at the Queen's bidding, her view (which he shared) that the threat to continue the war without France was an idle one and that it was only common prudence to follow Napoleon 'fairly and unreservedly' in any negotiations. But the cabinet would insist on certain conditions, especially the inclusion of the neutralization of the Black Sea in a general European treaty; Buol had proposed that it be left to a Russo-Turkish agreement. When Persigny came on 25th to argue this, Palmerston was adamant: 'I can fancy how I should be hooted in the House of Commons if I were to get up and say that we had agreed to an imperfect and unsatisfactory arrangement about one of the most important parts of the whole matter, as a personal favour to Count Buol, or to save the *amour-propre* of Russia. I had better beforehand take the Chiltern Hundreds.'[15] On this central issue Napoleon gave way, but the French objected seriatim to all other British stipulations and reservations. However, at length they agreed to add a Fifth Point, which Austria would not be called upon to incorporate in her ultimatum, not merely reserving the right to demand 'particular conditions' but giving notice of intention to do so. Britain was fully and properly consulted by Austria before she accepted amendments and sent the ultimatum on 15th December 1855. And Austria was neither to communicate nor entertain any Russian counter-proposals.

Although at the cabinet of 20th November Palmerston gave way 'without much fight', the whole transaction went against the grain and there is no doubt that he hoped the Russians would reject the proposals, on account mainly of the British addenda and stipulations.[16] The Russian reply was, however, equivocal. Buol rejected it, not because he had promised to do so, but because he was afraid of losing his *locus standi* in the negotiations, as Prussia had already done. Nesselrode induced the Tsar to accept the ultimatum. There would be an armistice and preliminary treaty and the definitive peace would be negotiated at a congress in Paris. It was necessary to agree that the preliminary treaty should exclude the Fifth Point, as Walewski complained that the British were trying to sabotage the negotiations by 'a second ultimatum'. But Britain kept up the pressure by a strong diplomacy directly inspired by Palmerston, who took a far greater part in the conduct as well as the formulation of foreign policy than any premier since Wellington, and the younger Pitt before him. A very sharp letter to Seymour in Vienna on 24th January declared: 'We know the exhaustion, the internal pressure, difficulties, and distress of Russia quite as well as Buol does; but we know better than he does our own resources and strength. . . . We are quite prepared to go on if [essential] conditions cannot be obtained. The British nation is unanimous in this matter. I say unanimous, for I cannot reckon Cobden, Bright and Co. for anything; and even if the Government were not kept straight by a sense of our public duty, the strong feeling which prevails throughout the country would make it impossible for us to swerve. So pray let Count Buol keep his *threats* for elsewhere, and not send them over here.'[17] Some colleagues did not approve of the tough tone of even Clarendon's official notes to Vienna. They were obsessed by the basic fact that 'Russia will yield if France is faithful to us, and we must yield if France throws us over.' They were afraid that dispatches taking a line from which they might later have to retreat would embarrass them when laid before parliament. But they agreed that some things should be insisted upon as *sine quibus non*, including the

restoration of Kars to Turkey and the demilitarization of Bomarsund (whereby Sweden in 1856 secured the paper guarantees she
had sought in vain at Vienna in 1814–15), and that certain other
matters (not including either Poland or Finland) must be matters
of discussion at the congress. What these timid ministers could not,
apparently, see, was that the stronger Britain's tone, the more
France would be prepared to stand for, in order to get peace
without dishonour; they tended to forget that, if operations
resumed in the spring, the Russians could expect to lose at least
the Crimea. Palmerston insisted on an ostentatious continuance of
military planning, and secured French assent to the armistice
being for a limited time only (to 'put a screw' on Russia) and to a
speedy meeting of the congress.[18] And Clarendon went to the
congress forearmed by his declaration in the Lords that 'should any
attempt be made to deprive us of the conditions which we have a
right to demand, and to which we have already agreed, then I
believe the people of this country would be as one man'.[19] Palmerston was intent upon having it understood that, while Britain
fighting on without France might be military nonsense, British
public opinion did not accept this assessment and could not usefully
be presented with too meagre terms.

An initial British intransigence was very necessary, given the
British government's conception of the minimum acceptable
terms, because Clarendon found in Paris that everyone except the
Emperor was prepared to make 'ANY peace'; that peace was
'unavoidable'; that 'everybody was against us, our motives were
suspected, and our policy was denounced'. The absolute determination of the British delegation to resist Russian attempts to
barter Kars for the erosion of the Austrian conditions about
Bessarabia paid dividends. Russia lost the Danube mouths, as well
as losing her cumulative treaty rights to protect the Christian
subjects of the Sultan and her right to keep a war fleet in the Black
Sea. Clarendon even secured a specification of the light coastguard
vessels permitted to her. These great points, and the demilitarization of the Åland Isles, being gained, Clarendon could be, and
indeed had to be, conciliatory, for he warned his colleagues that the
fate of the Anglo-French alliance, as well as the conditions of
peace, was 'en jeu'.[20] He could not insist on the demolition of all
fortified posts on the Black Sea or on any territorial concessions
there (Bessarabia apart).

o

Even the pacific Lewis admitted that Palmerston was generally 'moderate and reasonable' on the reserved questions which were only discussed at Paris because Britain insisted. He was apt to bluster, and some colleagues were alarmed that he controlled the telegraph to Clarendon; on his own authority he answered 'yes' when Clarendon inquired whether he should press for Circassian independence. At the last Clarendon was prepared to defy Palmerston and sign the treaty on 30th March 1856 without the prior authority of the cabinet, which was to meet on 31st.[21]

'Greater and more brilliant successes by land and sea might probably have been accomplished if the war had continued', wrote Palmerston to Victoria, 'but any great and important additional security against future aggressions by Russia could only have been obtained by severing from Russia large portions of her frontier territory, such as Finland, Poland and Georgia . . . and to have continued the war long enough for these purposes would have required greater endurance than was possessed by your Majesty's Allies, and might possibly have exhausted the good-will of your Majesty's own subjects.'[22] He did not pretend, except in public, that the peace was satisfactory, or more than 'satisfactory for the present'. But it was something to have gained so much without a breach either with France or Austria, to have gained enough for peace to be tolerated by the British public and to have made peace before the war became unpopular. The peace could not be popular. The heralds who proclaimed it were hissed at Temple Bar and extremists called Palmerston a traitor. Propaganda, official and unofficial, had depicted Russia as the tyrant of Europe, and no one, except perhaps the Turks, had been liberated from her. Some Radicals deplored the peace on that account; they and others regretted that it had come before any thoroughgoing administrative reform had been secured. There was wide resentment that it had come before the British army had won victories to restore its shattered prestige. Palmerston and Clarendon regretted that it had come a year too soon.[23] But it would have been fatal to adopt an apologetic tone in public. Conservative and Radical attacks were withstood. The Government was positively helped by the Mancunian and Gladstonian argument that peace had come in despite of Palmerston. It was true, but such was his reputation that the conclusion was drawn that the peace must be necessary and that it could not be discreditable, else he would not have accepted it.

This verdict was, perhaps, even more important when related to the Declaration of Paris, which resulted from discussions begun after the Treaty was signed, and which the Tories attacked, on the whole, more strenuously than the Treaty. It defined international law governing the conduct of war at sea. On one issue — the status of cargoes in neutral ships trading with the enemy — Britain had long been at odds with most of the world, and especially, since 1793, with the United States. During the Crimean War differences in British and French interpretation and practice had proved inconvenient and, though Britain adopted a tough line with some German maritime states, practical concessions had had to be made to neutrals.[24] But at Paris in 1856, in Article 2, Britain accepted, for the first time, the doctrine that 'free ships make free goods' (other than such goods as were automatically contraband of war). The signatory states, including France, and states later adhering to the Declaration, accepted (by Article 3) the British position that the cargo of an enemy ship might in some circumstances be 'neutral'. Britain's price for Article 2, a price unacceptable to the United States with her large commerce and small navy, was Article 1, outlawing the practice of privateering. Article 2 made a large concession to international opinion. Article 4 concealed another. Britain's 'paper blockades' had long been unpopular with the international community, and the 'effective' blockade stipulated by Article 4 as the only one valid at international law was clearly envisaged as the 'close-cordon blockade'. Britain 'agreed, more or less willingly, to confirm declarations of neutral rights . . . against which, as the world's strongest naval power, she might have been expected to struggle'. Lord Salisbury in 1871 said that as a result of 1856 'the fleet, valuable as it is for preventing an invasion of these shores, is almost valueless for any other purpose'.[25]

It was remarked at the time that the Declaration of Paris made very good sense on the assumption that in most wars Britain would be the greatest neutral carrier. But this was a proposition more applicable to a Cobdenite foreign policy than a Palmerstonian one. Judgement is difficult for us, who cannot expunge from our minds the knowledge of the difficulties which beset Britain in 1914–18 in trying to conduct 'economic warfare' against Germany within the rules of 1856. It may be felt that she aggravated those difficulties by failing adequately to distinguish between long-range contraband control and blockade. In any case, we have to remember that in

1856 the steamship had made 'close-cordon blockade' feasible as with sail it was not feasible, and that Palmerston had no conception of submarine warfare; of national economies mobilized for war in a way that made academic the distinction between what was public and what was private; of twentieth-century techniques of coastal defence or even the enormous development of artillery which took place in the second half of the nineteenth century.

*   *   *   *

While peace was being arranged with Russia, there was a considerable danger of war with the United States. Before Sebastopol fell, Clarendon had received an 'insolent' dispatch from the Americans demanding the recall of the British minister, Crampton, on the ground that the enticement of American citizens to British North America to be recruited under the Foreign Enlistment Act was contrary to American law. The dispatch also protested against the reinforcement of the British fleet in the North Atlantic (allegedly to deal with Russian privateers) and accused Britain of breach of treaty in Central America.

This last matter was as complex, in law and fact, as could be. Britain was a Caribbean Power, with island possessions, a fixed determination that the United States should not take Cuba from Spain, and (British Guiana apart) rights, some established, some merely oft reiterated, but all ill-defined, on the mainland of ex-Spanish America. These became contentious when the purely defensive and window-dressing Monroe Doctrine began to grow the milk teeth of 'Manifest Destiny'. Having occupied California during the recent Mexican War, the Americans projected a canal along the line of the San Juan River to link the Atlantic with the Pacific states and facilitate the trade of the former with the Far East. On this isthmus Cornelius Vanderbilt already operated a transit company. And there now appeared on the scene the famous filibusterer, William Walker of Tennessee. Intervening in the internecine strife of five successor-states of Spain, and the internal strife of Liberal and Conservative which convulsed them, he carried out a coup (May 1855) in conjunction with the Liberals of Nicaragua, which made him virtual dictator of that republic. Below Belize on the Honduras coast (which Britain had never formally annexed but where she had long-established rights of occupancy) stretched an unpalatable shore long subject to intermittent British intrusion, terminating in the 200-mile 'Mosquito Coast' (including the mouth of the San Juan), looked upon in London as a British protectorate.[A]

During Palmerston's third tenure of the Foreign Office, British officials reappeared on the Mosquito Coast and British troops occupied Greytown on the mouth of the San Juan. The Americans could not now build a canal without British assent. But both countries had every reason to desire to add to the treaties of 1842 and 1846 settling the boundaries between the United States and British North America an agreement on Central America. The Clayton–Bulwer Treaty of 1850 provided that any isthmian canal

[A] See map p. 563.

THE CARIBBEAN DISPUTE OF THE 1840s AND 1850s

The whole of the coast of Central America was for centuries under the nominal control of Spain. But British buccaneers, logwood traders and settlers from Jamaica had in the seventeenth century established themselves round Belize and the whole coast from there to the San Juan had been subject to intermittent British intrusion.

Spain was never formally ousted by Britain. The settlements on the Honduras coast and the strategic Bay Islands were considered a sort of concession; a British superintendent was sent to Belize in 1786 and a Spanish attack beaten off in 1798. The British considered the 200-mile *Mosquito* (*or Miskito*) *Coast* a quasi-protectorate derived from a seventeenth-century compact with the 'king' of the Miskitos, who were a mixture of Amerindian and Negro. London certainly in the second half of the eighteenth century regarded the Coast as a British dependency, though the Spaniards in 1780 foiled an attempt to ascend the San Juan and secure control of the whole isthmus. In 1844 a British Resident was sent from Belize; a formal protectorate was proclaimed in 1847 and the Nicaraguan authorities were expelled from San Juan (renamed Greytown) in 1848. The Clayton–Bulwer Treaty (1850) forbade exclusive influence by the U.K. or U.S. over any part of Central America, including the Mosquito Coast; Britain had in 1848 refused to take Costa Rica, and in 1855 refused to take Guatemala, under protection. In 1859 part of the Mosquito Coast was transferred to Honduras and in 1860 the rest was recognized as Nicaraguan, subject to rights of autonomy which were abrogated in 1905.

British Honduras, though not formally annexed till 1862, after the settlement of its boundary with Guatemala, was treated as a dependency, governed from Jamaica, with settled institutions (1839). The superintendent of Belize occupied the largest of the *Bay Islands* in 1839 and they were formally annexed in 1852. In 1859 they were ceded to the republic of Honduras *on condition that they were never to be ceded to any other power.* English remains the chief language of the (mainly Negro) inhabitants.

should be neutralized, any other form of transit across the isthmus of San Juan should be protected by both Powers, and that neither would occupy or dominate a canal, a canal zone or any part of Central America. Depositing the British ratification, Bulwer appended Palmerston's declaration that the abnegatory clause did not apply to (British) Honduras and its dependencies. The American State Department (but not the Senate) accepted that it did not apply to (British) Honduras and its neighbouring small islands. When in 1852 Britain (while Palmerston was out of office) annexed the strategic Bay Islands, regarding them as dependencies of (British) Honduras, the Americans claimed, with much reason, that they were not the neighbouring small islands of the State Department document. They also claimed that the abnegatory clause deprived Britain of any special rights on the Mosquito Coast, to which neither the Foreign Office declaration nor the State Department declaration had referred.

To the 'insolent' American note, Clarendon sent a 'hot and not well-guarded' reply and Palmerston had ships sent to the San Juan. He would 'not allow these blackguards to bully us'. But he was prepared to substitute a joint Anglo-American protectorate of the Mosquito Coast for a British one, and to submit the matter of the Bay Islands to arbitration. When the trouble with America was raised in parliament in February 1856 his tone was moderate and reasonable, the American reply to Clarendon having been moderate (and cogent). Granville, no chauvinist, thought the next British note, revised by Palmerston and considered at two long cabinet meetings, 'an able document', and, with the Treaty of Paris near, hope of a peaceful settlement with America seemed good. But reinforcements were sent to Bermuda and Canada, and Palmerston, requesting the United States to reconsider the demand for the withdrawal of Crampton, told Dallas, their minister in London, that it was for them to decide between peace and collision. If he fell upon Roebuck in the House of Commons, calling him 'the mouthpiece of calumnies . . . uttered by interested parties in the United States against Her Majesty's Officers', he had reason, for the attacks of Cardwell and Roebuck helped the Americans to assume that Palmerston was bluffing. Washington resented his implication that Crampton had given no cause for offence and, even more, his suggestion that the American Secretary of State had accepted British explanations on the enlistment question. Crampton was given his passports, and the Walker-dominated régime in Nicaragua recognized (May 1856). Palmerston's predictable reaction was to wish to expel Dallas and interdict American trade with the isthmus. But Dallas stayed and though a British fleet surrounded the American frigate off Greytown, it received no orders to interfere with trade, but only to stop Walker occupying the port. On 16th June Palmerston told the House of Commons he hoped to avoid a break with America, and an apology was offered about enlistment. The crisis died away.[26] The Peelite ex-ministers alleged that Palmerston had retreated in deference to the House, but this hardly squares with Gladstone's complaint that 'he made the House drunk on ginger-beer'. The evidence confirms Argyll's claim that the cabinet restrained Palmerston — 'His first impulse was always to move fleets and to threaten our opponents, sometimes on trivial occasions, on the details of which he had not fully informed himself by careful reading. Then, on finding his proposals combated, he was candid in listening and inquiring, and if he found the objections reasonable, he could give way to them with the most perfect good-humour. This was a great quality in a man so impulsive and strong-headed as he was, and so prone to violent action. It made him a much less dangerous man than he was supposed to be . . . [provided] he had colleagues who understood him, and were not afraid of him.'[27]

In 1857 Vanderbilt financed the expulsion of Walker from Nicaragua by the neighbouring states and the Conservative opposition. In September 1860 Capt. Salmon, R.N., handed Walker, attempting another filibuster, over to the Republic of Honduras for execution. To that republic Britain in 1859 ceded the Bay Islands, and she achieved with Guatemala a favourable boundary settlement for British Honduras, which was formally constituted a colony. In 1860 Britain recognized Nicaraguan sovereignty over the Mosquito Coast. A Palmerston government thus completed, by bilateral agreements with small republics, what was in effect a compromise settlement of the points in dispute as a result of the loose drafting of the 1850 treaty.

*   *   *   *

The government attributed the unexpected truculence of the United States *after* the end of the Crimean War to the fact that Britain's relations with Russia were not restored and those with

France were deteriorating. On 7th May 1856 ministers and ex-ministers had a 'dinner of reconciliation' with Brunnow at the Palace and Granville was commissioned to go to Russia in style for the Tsar's coronation. But he was nearly recalled en route because the Russians, instead of evacuating Kars, destroyed the fortress but increased their garrison, and he arrived to find Gorchakov very irritated because British ships had arrived to prevent any further Russian landings on the Island of Serpents, whose lighthouse was essential to navigation in the mouth of the Danube. Palmerston's comment was that Gorchakov 'must not be surprised if we continue to act . . . [alone], whenever any occasions for doing so should arise, inasmuch as we consider that we have a right to do so, and we know that we have the power to do so'. The premier's first interview with the new Russian ambassador, Chreptovitch, was very stormy, Palmerston entering on to a string of grievances, because Russia had in some instances broken her engagements and in others evaded them. At Ismal and Reni in Bessarabia, which were to go to Turkey, the Russians, as at Kars, had destroyed the forts — a childish ebullition of ill-humour and revenge, as the Turks would only rebuild them on a better plan. Chreptovitch was told that 'if he did not choose to listen to me, he had better go back to Petersburg'. The Isle of Serpents must go with the Danube. Then there was the case of Bolgrad. At Paris the original area of cession in Bessarabia had been modified in favour of the Russians, and they had produced a map on which the new line was clearly and plainly described, showing 'Bolgrad' (to be retained by the Russians) north of it. When the commissioners arrived to demarcate the frontier, 'the Russians started a new Bolgrad on the allies'. This was 'an unworthy deception which cannot be acquiesced in'. Russia was using it to delay demarcation and keep her troops in the ceded land. When Chreptovitch fell back on the time-honoured device of blaming subordinate agents, Palmerston said that the Russian government was despotic, and could get its orders obeyed, and was responsible. He added that the ambassador's long delay in taking up his appointment must be considered a want of respect to the Queen, and he would not be taken to Osborne to present his credentials.[28] Chreptovitch's report to St Petersburg arrived before Granville, who was himself instructed to say that British dissatisfaction at the non-compliance with the treaty had reached a climax. At the official reception of the diplomats, the Tsar told Granville sharply that evidently Her Majesty's present advisers did not wish to restore Anglo-Russian relations to their old footing.[29] In fact, Gorchakov and Morny were working for a secret agreement between France and Russia to erode the Treaty of Paris. Palmerston and Cowley repeatedly warned Napoleon that Russia's main aim was to divide Britain and France, or to exploit Britain's anxiety to maintain the Western alliance so as to secure for Russia concessions not granted at the Congress. Britain would not, for fear of the former, consent to the latter. What Palmerston said to Russian ministers he said equally to French. In 'a really old Roman letter . . . to Walewski in the Roman hand itself' he stated that Russia would never get the Isle of Serpents 'as long as England has a ship of war' and the pretension 'substituting for the Bolgrad of the Map . . . this new town of Bolgrad of which the Congress never had any cognisance [was] equally inadmissible'. Austria and Turkey were entirely with Britain on these questions, but 'France would seem to wish to change sides and associate herself in everything with Russia.' The English nation was not well pleased with the Treaty of Paris 'and I should not dare to present myself to Parliament next session, and have to say that I had consented to any sacrifice whatever of the terms'. If they were not executed, the House would be told the reason why.[30] Palmerston was jauntily confident that if Britain stood firm, Napoleon would yield, and when the French came to heel over the Serpents' Isle he would not hear of sending Bolgrad to arbitration.[31] He assented to a conference on Bolgrad only when it was settled that it should be a 'sham' conference, at which Britain, Austria, Turkey and Piedmont would outvote Russia, Prussia and France. Palmerston remarked that he would rather have had the conference at St Petersburg, as less Russian than Walewski's house. But he had won. He had, moreover, rescued British prestige from the criticism of the War Radicals, that Britain hung on the coat-tails of the French usurper. One of their organs claimed in February 1857 that Russia's current diplomatic defeat was more significant than the Treaty of Paris itself.

★　　★　　★　　★

Palmerston would have liked to do something for Cavour, the liberal leader who brought Piedmont into the war against Russia to win Western goodwill at the expense of hesitant Austria and to give Victor Emmanuel's army battle-training. There was talk in

London as well as Paris of offering Austria the Legations if she would yield Lombardy to Victor Emmanuel or of getting him at least Parma and Modena. But the Austrians were not in the market. Queen Victoria thought it should be recompense enough for Piedmont to be a full member of the Congress when Prussia was not brought in until the negotiations were over. Palmerston told Cavour he might say to Napoleon that for every step he took in Italian affairs he would probably find 'us' ready to take one and a half. Buol was to understand that in a war with Piedmont brought about 'as it will be' by Austria's fault, Piedmont would not be alone like last time.[32] Russell gathered from 'Palmerston's newspapers' that he thought a war of nationalities would come, but not yet,[33] and wanted both the Italians and the French to know that Britain was not uninterested in Italian affairs and would not give France a free hand there even if Russia did.

Palmerston, of course, remained as convinced as ever of the need for constitutionalism in Italy and would have liked to see the Pope 'reduced to the condition of the Greek patriarch of Constantinople' even if part of his territories went republican.[34] But it was with Bomba that his patience was exhausted, as with Otho in 1849–50, and he made the same mistake again, of thinking that ninety-nine out of a hundred of his subjects must be discontented and that a slight push would unseat him. His response to a petty slight to the British minister was to write that they ought to insist on the immediate dismissal of the minister of Police and his permanent banishment from public life, the demand to be made when the reserve squadron had anchored opposite the King's palace and embarked the embassy and consular staff. If within two hours of a boat putting out from the flagship it had not returned with 'King Bomba's' acceptance of the ultimatum, 'the palace should share the fate of Sweabourg; e poi dopo, if that should not be sufficient'.[1] But the cabinet would discuss this after Clarendon returned — he was currently (August 1855) with the Queen and Prince on a state visit to Napoleon and Eugénie and the reserve squadron was at Boulogne waiting to escort them. What Clarendon transmitted to the Queen as a proposal from the cabinet was a naval demonstration (not bombardment), to secure the dismissal of the police minister *and* the liberation of political prisoners.[A] But Victoria and

---

[A] Azeglio admitted to Malmesbury that the principal Whigs subscribed to a fund got up to finance a descent by Garibaldi to release Poerio (for whose libera-

Albert were not impressed by the argument that Bomba was bringing the monarchical principle into disrepute 'and might place weapons in the hands of the democracy'. They pointed out that if Britain interfered to secure changes in *the internal system of Government* of the Kingdom of Naples' she would have to undertake a continuing responsibility. This was the old argument against such intervention in Portugal, and it had point. And if, as the French predicted, such interference led to revolution, would it not be humiliating to Britain to have Bomba put it down in the presence of her fleet? And was this not likely if the régime was as unpopular as Palmerston alleged?

Palmerston was restrained by the Palace and cabinet, and the net outcome was a 'good and dignified' note of protest.[35] The condition of Naples was discussed at the Congress of Paris, where even Austria could not defend it but, of course, took a non-interventionist stand. The communiqué, in which Naples was 'alluded to with reserve', did not satisfy Palmerston, and he talked of a London conference on Italy to admonish the Pope and Bomba and set a term to French and Austrian occupation of parts of the papal dominions. This was a still-born project. As for coercing Bomba, on that Palmerston and Clarendon stood alone in the cabinet, but they contrived a joint Anglo-French note worded as though it were certain the wish of the Allies would be fulfilled. Bomba replied, in effect, 'Mind your own business.' The Foreign Secretary lamented: 'We shall cut a very foolish figure for having barked at such a wretch . . . and then not ventured to bite him.' The British and French ministers were withdrawn, and fleets blustered in the Bay of Naples 'pretending to be ready to bombard the Town'. The Bourbon king ignored their presence; there was no insurrection. It was, as Granville said, 'a very foolish affair'.[36] But perhaps it paid political dividends. Derby found it difficult to rally his full strength against 'a Conservative minister working with Radical tools, and keeping up a show of Liberalism in his foreign policy'.[37]

Palmerston's liberal and humanitarian instincts were as genuine

tion Malmesbury at Potsdam asked the Neapolitan minister to Prussia in August 1858) and other political prisoners — 'a strong measure on the part of a neutral country and its leading statesmen', the Tory called this (Malmesbury, p. 446). Poerio and others were, however, released, on parole to go to America not Europe. They bribed the captain and were landed at Cork, whence they passed through London en route for Turin on the eve of the war of 1859, Shaftesbury forming a committee to subscribe for them (ibid. 468).

as ever, even if they were paraded for political advantage. The suspicion that he had moved nearer to sponsorship of Nationalism as an 'ism', outside Italy, rested, however, on frail evidence. If he would have liked to detach Finland from Russia, it was to add it to Sweden; he demanded the demilitarization of the Ålands, not their cession, though their population was Swedish. If he would have liked to free Poland, it was to get Russia out of central Europe. If he would have liked to deprive Russia of Circassia and Georgia (as well as the Crimea) it was to protect Turkey and the route to India. Certainly in 1856–7 Palmerston was no more a champion of Roumanian nationalism than in 1848, and in 1862 no more a champion of Serbian independence than in the 1830s. He wished to maintain Turkish sovereignty in Serbia and the Principalities, so that they were covered by the umbrella of the European 'guarantee' of the Ottoman Empire confirmed by the Treaty of Paris.[A] It was with him a main concern that Russia, whose cumulative treaty rights in regard to the Sultan's Christian subjects were cancelled by that Treaty, should never be able legally to act alone in the Principalities on the pretext of acting in the name of Europe, as one of the co-guarantors.[38] The visible sign that the Principalities had passed from arrangements concocted between

---

[A] Serbia first received a degree of international recognition by the Treaty of Bucharest, 1812, between Russia and Turkey, which gave Russia certain protecting rights; the degree of autonomy was enlarged by the Treaty of Adrianople, 1829, and confirmed by a Turkish edict of 1830, making Serbia an autonomous but tributary principality and confining Turkish garrisons and residents to six towns. A strong constitutional movement from 1835 received the support of Russia, and was therefore opposed by Britain and France and Austria. The Turks, however, favoured limiting the power of the prince and granted a limited constitution 1838. The prince from 1842 to 1858, Alexander Karageorgević, was pro-Austrian (and, in the ferment of 1848–9, anti-Magyar); he preserved neutrality during the Crimean War, to avoid Austrian occupation, though his people was pro-Russian. By the Treaty of Paris 1856 Serbia was given full autonomy under the collective guarantee of the Powers; the Turkish garrisons were forbidden to interfere in the affairs of the country without the consent of the Powers. Michael Obrenović (1860–8) was anti-Turk, and, while no Russian puppet, a potentially formidable threat to the Ottoman Empire in Europe, from whose activities Russia might profit. After the Turkish garrison bombarded Belgrade in 1862, Britain and Austria prevented international agreement on the withdrawal of the garrisons, though they were limited to four and the Turkish civil population was to be evacuated. The garrisons left in 1867 (when Stanley was Foreign Secretary); Serbia became independent by the Treaty of Berlin, 1878.

Palmerston declared that the Polish revolt of 1863 was a judgement on the Russians for plotting trouble in Turkey's Balkan empire.

Russia and Turkey as a result of the pressure of the Tsar on the Sultan to the status of a ward of Europe was the presence in Bucharest, under the provisions of the Treaty of Paris, of an international Commission to revise the constitutional statutes.

The Commission was to be advised of the opinion of the inhabitants by Wallachian and Moldavian divans *ad hoc* summoned and dissolved by the Sultan. There is every ground for saying that the inhabitants wanted a union of the principalities under an imported monarch, with a constitution modelled on the Belgian. This was approved by France (such a constitution would be worked by Roumanian politicians who had spent their exile in France), by Prussia and Piedmont (who had a vested interest in encouraging nationalism and embarrassing Austria) and soon by Russia as well. It was not approved by Turkey, nor by Austria (whose empire was based on a negation of nationalism and contained many Roumanians in Transylvania), nor, after some wobbling by Clarendon, by the British government. Palmerston feared that a united Roumania would become a puppet of Russia or France or become 'another Greece', and he wished to uphold both Turkish and Austrian interests in Danubia.[39] So Stratford sponsored if he did not organize, the fraudulent elections which produced an anti-unionist divan in Moldavia, in protest at which the envoys in Constantinople of the Powers which favoured union 'struck their flags'. Napoleon invited himself to Osborne to discuss this problem (August 1857) and a compromise resulted. The fraudulent elections were anulled, but there were to be separate Moldavian and Wallachian hospodars and assemblies, though there might be a joint commission; Clarendon, in opposition, co-operated with Malmesbury to draw its teeth (1858).[40] The Roumanians had to gain Roumania by electing the same man hospodar of both principalities. Palmerston returned to office in 1859 to find that the Tory government had reconciled itself to accepting this *fait accompli*, and when at last in December 1861 the Turks did the same, Roumania could be proclaimed. It was small thanks to Palmerston.

Nevertheless, Mr A. J. P. Taylor can describe as 'the real achievement of the Treaty of Paris' the transformation of Roumania into a 'genuine buffer-state' guaranteed by the rivalry of her two great neighbours, Austria and Russia.[41] That interest in the Balkans which Metternich had always professed was confirmed by the temporary Austrian occupation of the Principalities during the Crimean War and lasted as long as the Habsburg empire. Given the assumptions on which British policy towards the area rested, this was a valuable development. And although the 'prized achievement' of 1856 — the ban on a Russian fleet of war in the Black Sea — proved temporary, it was none the less important. It was important symbolically, because it was humiliating, and Gladstone condemned it as an 'immoral' restriction on Russian sovereignty. It was certain that Russia would not tolerate this restriction when she felt strong enough to denounce it; 'the Black Sea closed to all the guns and opened to all the commerce of the world' would be a temporary phenomenon. But it gave Russia a diplomatic priority to concentrate upon, and in doing so she relaxed her pressure upon Europe and upon Turkey. She turned in on herself to recoup her strength (sapped by the war) and remedy her weaknesses (revealed by the war). All of which convinced Palmerston, that though the Treaty of Paris had come a year too soon, the Crimean War had not been fought in vain. Q.E.D.

CHAPTER XXI

'THE TRITON AMONG THE MINNOWS', 1856

IN 1856 Palmerston's ascendancy seemed complete. However much the competitors for power — Derby, Disraeli, Russell — and the convinced opponents of the Palmerstonian spirit — Cobden, Bright, Gladstone — regretted it, there was no sign of 'the bursting of that bubble which the cockney clacquers have been so industriously blowing up for the last few years'. Cobden's prediction that he could not last two months after peace was made was shown to be over-optimistic.[1] Gladstone could only console himself with the thought that Palmerston had failed to cash his popularity cheque by dissolving after the Peace of Paris.[2] This the premier had been urged by many advisers to do, but he accepted the advice of the chief whip, Hayter, given presumably on the principle of 'better the evil one knows', and taken, perhaps, on the theory that when one's vogue outside parliament is greater than it is within, a potential dissolution may be as advantageous as an actual one.[3] There were certain aspects of the 1855 campaign, given publicity in 1856 — Kars; the second McNeill Report incriminating officers recently decorated;[A] the publication of Panmure's telegram to Simpson (on the latter's appointment) bidding him look after the Secretary of State's nephew — better left to the blurring processes of time. And the indicators pointed to economic prosperity, always an asset to a government at a general election

A The second report of McNeill and Tulloch by clear implication accused Cardigan, Lucan, Airey and other senior officers of negligence. The cabinet, Feb. 1856, agreed to follow the precedent, set after the Convention of Cintra, of a General Board of Officers at Chelsea, which duly 'whitewashed' the culprits. But mud was stirred up. Admiral Sir Charles Napier in March moved for a committee into his own conduct of the Baltic fleet in 1854, as a means of attacking Graham and Adm. Berkeley (ex-Civil Lord of the Admiralty); de Lacy Evans took this opportunity to attack Crimean mismanagement (March 1856). Palmerston on behalf of the government accepted Sidney Herbert's motion for a humble address for the honouring of McNeill and Tulloch and, 'borne in triumph on the arms of the people', the former was made a privy councillor, the latter K.C.B. There was still the debate on Kars to come. Fenwick Williams, released by the Russians, received the K.C.B. (like Hawes and Panmure!), a parliamentary pension of £1,000 p.a. and the Freedom of the City.

even in times when government was not expected to do very much about securing economic prosperity.

Meanwhile, Palmerston's relations with the Court had improved. The Queen and the Prince had shown a strong hostility at the time of his resignation, and its retraction, in 1853, not abated by the press campaign against the Prince in January 1854. The *Morning Post* was not quick to reprove its competitors, and it even crossed the mind of Albert and of General Grey that Palmerston might be behind the campaign.[4] Towards the end of 1854 there was unease at the Palace on account of Palmerston's visit to Napoleon and his close relations with Walewski. *They* showed Derby, at the audience at which he told them he could not form a government, a letter from Walewski to Albert saying that Palmerston and Clarendon were indispensable members of any ministry. It showed, Albert said, 'to what state of degradation the British Crown had been reduced by the efforts on all sides for Party objects to exalt the Emperor Napoleon, and make his will and use the sole standard for the English Government'.[5] The Queen accepted Palmerston as prime minister because she had no other alternative. She had become dissatisfied with Aberdeen, because of his inertia, but 'to change him for Lord Palmerston is somewhat of a trial', she confessed; 'the latter certainly does owe us many amends for all he has done'.[6] But throughout 1855 and 1856 there was a growth of mutual confidence or, at least, an ebbing of mutual mistrust. Palmerston cultivated a courtly touch, shown, for instance, in his letter of 26th April 1855 on the Vienna terms: 'Viscount Palmerston presents his humble duty to your Majesty, and begs to state that the Members of the Cabinet who met yesterday evening at the Chancellor's were of opinion that the Austrian proposal adopted by M. Drouyn de Lhuys, even with his pretended modification, could not be described more accurately than in the concise terms of H.R.H. Prince Albert, namely, that instead of making to cease the preponderance of Russia in the Black Sea, it would perpetuate and legalize that preponderance, and that instead of establishing a secure and permanent Peace, it would only establish a prospective case for war. Such a proposal therefore Your Majesty's Advisers could not recommend your Majesty to adopt . . .'.[7] The Palace's dislike of Palmerston's personal link with Napoleon evaporated as Palmerston brought the Queen and the Prince into the consolidation of the alliance almost as Aberdeen had brought them into the consolidation of the entente with Louis Philippe, and Palmerston's letter to Victoria on her return from her state visit to the Emperor would not have disgraced Disraeli himself. As long as the war lasted, the Prince, full of ideas on military organization and planning, found Palmerston receptive and Panmure and Simpson were prodded, even harried, from the Palace as well as from No. 10. The premier had no objection, in 1856, to the Queen stirring up the Admiralty to make permanent improvements in dockyard facilities. Despite old, and basic, and persistent differences of attitude to Prussia and Austria, Victoria and Albert liked no more than Palmerston the pusillanimity of the former and the un-reliability of the latter. And though the Queen saw more readily than Palmerston at the end of 1855 the inevitability of peace, she was as firm as he on the need for tough diplomacy, both to secure the best possible terms and to see that they were enforced.

In such circumstances, and with Palmerston not insisting (as *They* had made Russell insist) that written communication between the Palace and the Foreign Office go through the premier, the relationship between the monarch and the Foreign Secretary was one of proper, and valuable, mutual restraint. If the Queen and the Prince queried proposals and secured the modification of dispatches (such as a querulous and indeed hardly explicable one to Austria in September 1855 demanding her evacuation of the Principalities), Clarendon modified the over-severe terms of Victoria's letter to Napoleon's empress on the relations between France and Russia in September 1856. Palmerston could trust Clarendon as Russell had not been able to trust Palmerston. Some of the more pacific members of the cabinet, indeed, like Gladstone outside, thought that Clarendon played too readily and aptly the role of His Master's Voice.[8] The private correspondence of Albert with Granville, the Leader of the House of Lords, was potentially rather than actually sinister as giving the Palace a window into the cabinet. There were, inevitably, some brushes between the government and the Queen on matters of prerogative, but Victoria and Albert found in Palmerston the only safe shield against administrative reforms which would have trenched upon pre-rogative, and were as appreciative as it was in their nature to be. Above all, Victoria and Palmerston became used to one another as a result of day-to-day correspondence on the business of the House of Commons, cabinet decisions and on multitudinous matters ranging from strategy and high diplomacy to bands in the parks, cleansing the lake at Buckingham Palace and holidays for Eton and Harrow to celebrate the peace. There seems a genuine warmth in the Queen's letter offering Palmerston the first Garter conferred on a member of the House of Commons since Castlereagh's, 'as a public token of her approval' and of her satisfaction 'as to the manner in which . . . the honour and the interest of this country have been maintained, by the zealous and able guidance of Lord Palmerston'.[9] Even the knowledge that, as Melbourne had said, there was 'no damn'd merit' about it, that Newcastle had been offered and Aberdeen taken a Garter in 1854 (in congratulating Aberdeen, Russell had said he was glad *he* had refused one!) did not spoil the miracle.

'He has no colleagues to fear or to upset; he has attained the object of his ambition; he can't act upon his impulses at the Foreign Office; he is more immediately responsible to Parliament than he ever was before, and he is proud of having, as he thinks, overcome the repugnance of the Court.'[10] When he wrote that, in September 1855 Clarendon was asking Granville to warn the Court that, though with his altered position, Palmerston could not wish to get into trouble, he required to be 'delicately handled' and would not bear to be 'brusqué or put down by authority'. Now, in 1856, there seemed no need for this warning, and Palmerston had 'overcome the repugnance of the Court' to a greater degree than might have been expected. This reflected credit on both sides, for realism if not magnanimity, a quality which came more easily to Palmerston than to Victoria or Albert. As for parliament, the position of the government was not, in absolute terms, enviable. There were many defeats in both Houses. Majorities were obtained, as in 1855 Disraeli had sneered, God knows how and God knows why. One wonders at the strength of contemporary tributes to Hayter, with his 'invaluable watch', who, the Attorney General said, had put his hook in the nose of the House of Commons and 'led that many-headed monster like a tame Beast',[11] unless one appreciates both the extreme instability of 'the Liberal Party' and the fact that Palmerston's ascendancy, based on popularity outside rather than inside the House, encouraged members to make a show of their independence[12] because they could see no prospect of an alternative government with a stable, working majority. The official Opposition did not offer such a prospect; of those outside its ranks only Gladstone and perhaps a very few other Peelites hankered after reunion with the Conservative Party while a very few Irishmen, unforgiving since 1850, would prefer Derby to Russell or even to Palmerston. The 'ministerialist' forces were divided between Peelites, such as Graham and Herbert, who now regarded themselves as Independent Liberals; Whigs, some Palmerstonian, some still Russellite; Liberals so diverse as to elude categorization; Radicals, some Mancunian and devotedly anti-Palmerston, some uncritically pro-Palmerston, some broadly favourable to the premier despite strong inclinations on their own part or that of their constituents to domestic reforms in which Palmerston was not interested, or was interested only to thwart; and Irishmen of every political complexion and none. There was not the material here for steady day-to-day majorities. But Palmerston was described as a Triton among the minnows by one who thought him not naturally of a capacity superior to the average churchwarden.[13] Of his competitors, Derby was neither active nor attractive to middle-of-the-road men; Disraeli was disliked and mistrusted almost as much within his party as outside it; Gladstone, querulously and tentatively drifting towards reunion with Derby, had no following at all; Russell was discredited, wayward, pathetic; Lansdowne was old and semi-retired; Clarendon and Granville were harnessed, the former willingly enough, to Palmerston's car; George Grey was a loyal lieutenant and a quietly efficient Home Secretary. Nobody else counted. It would be easy enough to defeat Palmerston if the Tories, following their whips, were joined by Liberals who did not regard themselves as in any way bound to keep Palmerston in. But his resignation would only make confusion worse confounded. Probably he would not resign, but appeal to the country. And his enthusiastic reception at the end of the year both in the City of London and at Manchester and Liverpool did not give his Tory and Radical opponents much hope of profit if he did that.[14]

Palmerston's approach to foreign affairs evoked a favourable response from those who adhered to Balance of Power precepts and also from those who adopted, at this time very articulately, what to Cobden and Bright was 'the equally unsound and mischievous line of our so-called "democrats" ' on behalf of Mazzini and the nationalities. In the Northern cities especially popular enthusiasm seemed to be reserved for the defeated but persevering leaders of

European nationalisms.[13] If Palmerston was not practically a supporter of the cause of national independence he was still the patron of constitutionalism on the Continent. He had checked Russia; he had rebuked the Habsburgs for illiberality and brutality and he wanted them out of Italy; he denounced papal misrule; he itched to coerce Bomba. Sadly Cobden and Bright, heard during the war more tolerantly inside parliament than without, confessed that there was no out of doors support for the party of peace and non-intervention. Indeed, there seemed 'to be no party having an intelligible principle or policy in which any considerable body out of doors [took] an interest'.[16] The only disturbances in London consisted of demonstrations against the carriage-folk on Sunday afternoon in the Park when Lord Robert Grosvenor was promoting his bill against Sunday trading (which Palmerston persuaded him to withdraw).[17] That state of equilibrium which suggested to Professor Burn the title of his fascinating book *The Age of Equipoise* had been reached. The main aspirations of the politically conscious middle classes had been achieved, so that, as a whole, they were now devoid of reforming zeal. The repeal of the Corn Laws and the passing of the Ten Hours Act had drawn the sting of Chartism. Prosperity was seeping down into the working classes. For them it was a time of preparation for political influence rather than the premature exercise of it, though the growing pains of an effective trade union movement were being felt. Palmerston was well suited to preside over the nation's affairs at such a time, for though he was an aristocrat, and proud of it, and intent upon maintaining the political influence of the aristocracy, he was capable of striking sparks from middle, and indeed working, class opinion, by virtue of his pride in the British system of government, his protection of British traders, travellers and missionaries, his care for the expansion of markets. And, more clearly than any contemporary, he spoke in a language everyone could understand the sentiments — often platitudinous, sometimes crudely chauvinistic — which many people felt. The Palmerston of the Tiverton elections, who drew to that Devon market town representatives of the foreign as well as of the British press (and timed his speeches so that the reporters could catch the evening train back to London), was as intelligible a politician as it was possible to have in days when speeches by major politicians in the country were still (except at election time) few and far between and, in the absence of newspaper photographs, the cartoon probably played a major part in creating 'political images'. Palmerston well understood the advantage of newspaper publicity. He also understood the limitations of the power of the press. He did not complain, as Derby did, that the newspapers sought the powers of an estate of the realm without showing a due sense of the attendant responsibilities. When the Queen commended Panmure's idea of an 'anti-Times League', urging a social boycott by ministers of the owner, editor and chief contributors, Palmerston retorted that newspapers lived by circulation, and would always change their tune to suit the public mood.[18] A boycott would be an acceptance of The Times's own estimate of its importance. Palmerston ranked it as a sort of primitive public opinion poll merely reflecting — sometimes very reluctantly — public opinion.

★   ★   ★   ★

Though Palmerston was not anxious to facilitate the dissemination of political information among the unenfranchised classes, his personal appeal was of such a nature that he probably gained more than any politician from the rapid spread of provincial daily newspapers which followed the repeal of the stamp duty in 1855, as previously from the boost to the metropolitan press by the abolition of the advertisement duty which was forced by the House of Commons in 1853. Unlike many Tories and some Whigs, he did not fear the spread of education in the narrower sense. He looked to it as a means of moral and material improvement, and openly deplored the sectarian jealousies which so long impeded the spread of popular education. He deemed it highly creditable to the House of Commons that it voted overwhelmingly, just before an election (that of 1847) for a large increase in the education grant to voluntary schools, most of them Anglican, although the Dissenters were up in arms.[19] The Nonconformists in Tiverton demonstrated at elections perhaps more to impress Palmerston than to overawe the Tories, but he spoke frankly of his wish for state endowment of Catholic priests in Ireland, though adding soothingly that he saw no prospect of it.[20] He desired regular diplomatic relations with the Holy See, though he was not prepared to have a curial ecclesiastic holding court in London. He had, with some difficulty, secured a concordat with the local Roman bishop in Ireland as a preliminary to opening schools on his Sligo estates with papist teachers. As home secretary under Aberdeen he authorized the appointment of Nonconformist and Roman Catholic prison chaplains, and made the new cemeteries required by his burial regulations open to all denominations. He even, as prime minister, so far weakened over church rates as to be willing to relieve non-Anglicans from the obligation to contribute towards the services as distinct from the fabrics. But he would not have welcomed the *Record*'s description of him as 'a man of God', earned by his choice of bishops (influenced by Shaftesbury).[21] It was certainly a novel test of eligibility for a bishopric that the nominee would be popular with the Nonconformists, and even the Queen (fiercely hostile to the Anglo-Catholics) thought the appointment of Bickersteth as first bishop of Ripon 'extreme'.[22] The Palace preferred sound or rather 'modernist' Erastians to Evangelicals. Palmerston himself, a child of the semi-pagan rationalism of the eighteenth century, had no more affinity to the Evangelical enthusiasts, whether Anglican like Shaftesbury or Nonconformist, than to the High Churchmen of the Oxford school (to which, incidentally, many of the Peelites, including Gladstone, adhered). The plaudits of the Evangelical press will have struck him, inter alia, as in bad taste. They were also undeserved, for, as an early biographer said, 'judged by the standard of Exeter Hall or Mr Spurgeon's Tabernacle, we must confess that Lord Palmerston could scarcely be called "a religious man" '.[21] He was evidently surprised to find his proposal to adjourn a cabinet meeting until Sunday morning questioned because some of his colleagues wished to go to church.[23]

Palmerston never pretended to be better than he was, and at first sight this makes him a strange candidate to be 'the representative man' of a Victorian age on which middle-class Nonconformity was ever-increasingly writing its canons of moral conduct. His was a manly contempt for cant. His assertion that the loyal subject and the statesman working for the common weal illustrated some of the best aspects of Christianity convinced the Nonconformist ministers of Tiverton that he was never 'converted'.[24] His remark that children were naturally good, but corrupted by their environment, gave offence to the Evangelicals, because it appeared to leave no room for Original Sin.[25] It is to be understood, surely, as the comment of one of Nature's fathers deprived (by his refusal to marry until he could marry Emily) of the chastening experience of having his children grow up in his house. He frankly regarded dogma as a disturbing and obstructive force in society, the Church of England as a useful institution of the realm,[A] and religion as a moral and social cement. Louis Philippe, he wrote, had fallen because he 'worked at the superstructure of monarchy without taking care of the foundation. Education and religion have been neglected'.[26] The letter to the presbytery of Edinburgh explains the quip that 'he treated God as a foreign Power'.[27] It is a good quip, but it must not be misunderstood. The point is that he had no patience with God's ministers when from obscurantism or prejudice or vested interest they seemed to him to oppose the common good. Asked to exempt ecclesiastical dignitaries from his regulations prohibiting intra-mural interment, he inquired 'what special connection is there between church dignities and the privilege of being decomposed under the feet of survivors?'. To a petition from the canons of Ely, passed on by Gladstone, he retorted that 'in almost all these Cases the real Question is one of Fees, & though I am sorry to interfere with Ecclesiastical Emoluments which are far from being generally too great yet Regard to Rules of Health must supersede pecuniary Considerations'.[28]

Palmerston's commonsense attitude to practical problems is seen in his plans for his estates. His junior branch of the Temples of Stowe, diverging in the days of Elizabeth, had made a fortune in Ireland, producing in successive generations a provost of Trinity College, Dublin; a Cromwellian Master of the Rolls who became Restoration Vice-Chancellor of Ireland; a Speaker of the Irish House of Commons; a Walpolian politician. This last, becoming an Irish peer as Baron Temple of Mount Temple in the County of Sligo and Viscount Palmerston of Palmerstown in the County of Dublin, completed the re-Anglicization of the family, but half the third viscount's inherited income, and two-thirds of his income from landed property came, in 'good years', from Ireland, and principally from 10,000 acres round Mullaghmore on the northern coast of Sligo. His father had been a classic example of an absentee landlord who never found an agent to transform his good

---

[A] 'My opinion is that, unless kept very tight and within the narrowest bounds, Convocation would become a nuisance, and I should not be disposed to consent to any alterations which would tend to give them a more real and practical existence. . . . Aberdeen, who was not addicted to unnecessary vigour of action, sent them about their business one time when they were beginning to be meddlesome' (Palmerston to Sir George Grey, 24/5/865, A. ii. 268).

intentions into fact. Nor could any agent have done so without capital, and the second viscount spent capital as well as income not in Ireland but on the embellishment of his London houses and the mansion and gardens of Broadlands near Romsey in Hampshire, leaving his son financially embarrassed, with Broadlands mortgaged and stripped of much of its timber and the Northamptonshire and part of the Yorkshire estate sold.[29] Visiting Sligo in 1808 Palmerston found it 'wholly unimproved' and drew up an ambitious plan for the regeneration of the district —

1. To restore the parish church (a signal example of the conventional priorities of a Protestant landlord).
2. To establish three or four good schools (necessarily with Catholic teachers).
3. To make roads.
4. Where possible, to get rid of the middlemen who stood between the landlord and the sub-tenant.
5. To introduce a Scottish farmer to demonstrate improvements.
6. To 'establish a little manufacturing business'.
7. To build a pier and small port.

He could not afford to do any of this until the mid-twenties, when he went to Ireland four years running (1825-8), got his schools started, opened a linen market at Cliffony and a lime-kiln and a harbour at Sligo and began reclamation. At the same time he put in hand plans for a railway to render more competitive a North Welsh slate quarry in which he had a large interest and to build up the Cornwall and Devon Mining Company. A visit to Fairbairn in Yorkshire led to the opening of a lime-kiln and a vain search for coal. The purchase of a neighbouring property improved the economy and amenities of Broadlands, and Palmerston was active in promoting a national school at Romsey.[30]

Within the limits of a landlord outlook which made him the author in his old age of the memorable adage that 'Tenant Right is Landlord's Wrong',[31] and of absenteeism, Palmerston was a good landlord, for many years ploughing back the greater part of his rents, as well as using borrowed capital, for improvement in Sligo. His opponents at Tiverton never alleged otherwise, though they wrongly imagined that he was drawing quick returns, and complained that he did not subscribe enough to the poor of Tiverton.[32] But Palmerston saw very clearly that the evils of subdivision, which accentuated the basic inefficiency of the economy of a region of poor land, could be cured only by a drastic reduction of population, and few Irish landlords were more active in shipping tenants off to North America in the Famine years. That it was inhumane to exploit the Irish poor in this way never occurred to one convinced that opportunity awaited them elsewhere and that unless they left neither he, nor those who stayed, could make a good thing of the Sligo coast. The disgusting conditions of the passage from Liverpool, exposed by Mrs Cecil Woodham-Smith in her impressive book, *The Great Hunger*, must be blamed rather on the 'reputable' firm of agents employed than on the busy Foreign Secretary, who had paused from the dispatches to order a 'sweetener' to be given to every captain and rum rations to the passengers (until the protests of Father Mathew's Temperance movement compelled the substitution of coffee).[33]

Within the limits of the landlord outlook, then, Palmerston was hard-headed and not hard-hearted. Similarly, within the limits of the *laisser-faire* attitude, he made room for humanitarianism at home as well as abroad. He was, of course, influenced by Lord and Lady Ashley and by Emily's son (perhaps her son by him) William Cowper, who had Christian Socialist leanings. Palmerston supported Ashley's Mines Bill in 1842 and attacked the Peel government for yielding to the mine-owning peers on the details; children, he informed Russell, were not free agents and seemed entitled to protection against the combined cupidity of parents and masters. On the eve of the vote on Ashley's Ten-Hour amendment to Graham's Factory Bill Palmerston received, without appointment, 1844, two delegates from the millworkers and put their tale of the children's hardships to the test, using two chairs in the dining-room at Carlton House Gardens to simulate the action of 'Old Ned', the spinning mule. Then he accepted the statement that the children serving the machines had to walk or trot 25 or 30 miles a day, and the scars and callouses on his visitors' hands and knees made sense. He was among the minority which supported the Ten Hours Bill in 1846 and the majority that passed it in 1847. When he became Home Secretary, he was as convinced as ever that to restrict the hours of labour of adult males was 'a vicious and wrong principle' and reluctant to disturb the compromise settlement of 1850. But he was persuaded that, though this settlement left women and 'young persons' adequately protected, the loopholes left for the exploitation of young children 'must entail such evils that no one could be surprised at their extreme mortality'. There must be a bill, even if it meant, in effect, limiting the hours of adults.[34] It became law on 20th August 1853. The same year he passed a Truck Act. And under Palmerston's premierships began the process of extending the Factory Acts to trades not at first covered.

From a sheer practicality, rather than any study of the lore of the Utilitarians, Palmerston derived a concern for the moral and material health of the community which deserves emphasis, perhaps even over-emphasis, to counterbalance the better-known picture of a man who floated with the tide of reform until it became safe to resist it and was at the end himself a main impediment to its flow. To problems of public health he brought a sensible pragmatism not unmixed with that zeal for 'world-bettering' which he was often said to lack. He sincerely regretted the delay in passing, and the emasculation of, his colleague Morpeth's Health of Towns Bill. Immediately after the general election of 1852 he was off to tell the Sussex farmers, bewailing the shortage of Peruvian guano, that the dirt of their own towns ought to be on the fields. 'The country should purify the towns, and the towns should fertilize the country. . . . We allow decomposed substances in towns to pollute the atmosphere, to ruin health, to produce premature misery, to be pestilent and destructive of existence.'[35] As Home Secretary he entered with some enthusiasm into a project for diverting London sewage from the Thames to tunnels where it could be trapped for processing into 'home made guano'. To his brother he wrote: 'I shall try to compel at least the tall chimneys to burn their own smoke. . . . I am shutting up all the graveyards in London. . . . [This is] absolutely required for the preservation of the health of the town.' When his prohibition of the 'barbarous' practice of intra-mural interment evoked strong criticism, he retorted that 'no great measure of social improvement can be effected without some such temporary inconvenience to individuals . . . . England is, I believe, the only country in which, in these days, people accumulate putrifying [sic] dead bodies amid the dwellings of the living; and as to burying bodies under thronged churches you might as well put them under libraries, drawing-rooms and dining rooms'.[36] Florence Nightingale at the end of the Crimean War found Palmerston more receptive than Panmure of her criticisms of the design for the new hospital at Netley, though nothing came of his interventions because too much money had already been committed.[37] That there was a real regard for personal convenience, and not merely an abstract regard for sanitation, is shown by a letter to the War Office urging decent provision of facilities for soldiers in barracks at night. And Palmerston's whole character prevents us from regarding his ambition to close all the beershops in London, because they demoralized the lower classes, as that of a kill-joy.[39]

Palmerston's first administration was responsible for useful, or potentially useful, measures, many of which constituted unfinished business from his period at the Home Office. Having visited prisons (and written a sensible paper on the ventilation of cells) Palmerston stressed the need for an element of hope in the treatment of criminals. He is entitled to credit for the introduction of the 'ticket of leave' system. He would have been as surprised to learn that penal servitude (provided for in the act of 1857 which virtually put an end to transportation) could ever be regarded as other than a progressive reform as he would have been appalled to learn that trade unions would rise to sufficient power to prevent competition from useful prison labour. Palmerston was concerned to rescue the children of the criminal and depressed classes. By acts of 1855 and 1857 local authorities were permitted to send the children of people on outdoor relief, and vagrant children, respectively, to industrial schools, for the promotion of which the Privy Council was from 1856 entitled to make grants. By another act of 1857, local authority grants to reformatory schools were authorized.[40] That these powers were optional, and not widely used, was a fault of the time and its ethos. Though Granville's ambitious schemes for national education, endorsed by the Palmerston cabinet,[41] failed to secure the approval of parliament, Palmerston recognized the importance of the Privy Council's educational responsibilities — its grants now amounted to half a million pounds per annum — by the appointment of a Vice-President of the Council (and of its committees) to sit in the Commons. The first holder of this office was William Cowper, who had been the parliamentary head of the General Board of Health since August 1855. The Board had been established as an extra-parliamentary body in 1847 and had become highly controversial because of the bureaucratic Benthamism of Edwin Chadwick and the hostility of a wide variety of vested interests and of opponents, interested or doctrinaire (or both), of central control and initiative. The Board was saved by sacrificing Chadwick, and reprieved by

Palmerston's initial continuance of Sir Benjamin Hall, the champion of the localists, as parliamentary head. Even Hall's bills were important to sanitary reform and advanced central control. Cowper, on appointment to the Board of Health, at once made the eminent sanitarian John Simon its Medical Officer. His biographer says, fairly enough, that the Whig government was dilatory and lukewarm on sanitary matters but 'its chief, Lord Palmerston . . . possessed a genuine social concern, and the responsible minister, William Cowper . . . proved zealous, competent and knowledgeable'.[42] As much cannot be said of their Tory successors; Disraeli had not yet discovered that sewage was a matter of life and death to the common people. An annual struggle was necessary to save the Board of Health, and Cowper's public health bills did not pass. When he saw that the Board was doomed, Palmerston explored with Arthur Helps, the sanitary reformer (whom in 1860 he made Clerk to the Privy Council in succession to Greville), ways of preserving its work, by transferring its medical functions (and Simon) to the Privy Council. The resultant bill failed to pass, but the transfer was accomplished on a temporary basis by the Tories in 1858 and Palmerston secured its permanent ratification (by a small majority) in 1859.

The notion that Palmerston was an idle Home Secretary is as misguided as was the hope attributed to the Tsar and the Palace that the drudgery of that busy department would prevent him from playing any part in the formulation of foreign policy. Too much may be read into the famous reply of the Home Secretary to the Queen, to an inquiry whether he had heard any more news of labour troubles in the Potteries, 'No, Madam, I have heard nothing: but it seems certain that the Turks have crossed the Danube.' Even the grudging Professor Bell writes: 'Only long investigation would make it possible to say that he neglected his duties.'[43] Palmerston certainly entered upon this new department with characteristic impatience at its methods, at once sending a clerk over to the Foreign Office to learn about filing. He entered it with a clear interest in some aspects of its work, but without the knowledge and authority he had long had of Foreign Office matters, to find that it was the lot of a Home Secretary to be bombarded with memorials and harrassed by deputations[44] and questioned in the House of Commons on a multifarious range of topics, on some of which he was frankly at sea.[45] But it is unfair to compare him with his successor, Sir George Grey, because he had also been his predecessor and had acquired over five and a half years a very extensive acquaintance with office affairs and the reputation of a 'heaven-sent' Home Secretary. Indeed, the criticism of Palmerston as Home Secretary appears to rest largely on a statement by Robert Lowe (a valuable, if unpopular, junior minister) which is really an assertion that Palmerston as Leader of the House and George Grey as Home Secretary was a superior arrangement to Russell as Leader and Palmerston as Home Secretary.[45] George Grey greatly added to his reputation and to the morale of the government in the House of Commons by his successful steering of the Police Bill in 1856, one of those Palmerston had failed to pass. It made a police force obligatory everywhere, the Home Secretary having a veto of appointment of chief officers and changes in regulations and establishments and power to pay a quarter of the cost of police pay and uniforms if satisfied, on the report of Inspectors of Constabulary, that a force was efficient. A majority of 268–106 was secured for the second reading although Liberal members attacked the Bill as introducing a continental system of centralization repugnant to the feelings and habits of Englishmen, a despicable despotism more fitted to Naples than England.[46]

That it would be wrong to imply that Palmerston was not interested in reforms, simply because he was not interested in Reform, is shown by his threat in 1855 to keep the House sitting into September, if necessary, to pass the first of two Partnership Bills which together constitute 'the crucial step for Britain in the evolution of the modern joint stock company'. Official and legal opinion was on the whole against making so generally available the security of limited liability, and Professor Smellie has ascribed the main credit for it to Palmerston and George Bramwell.[47] And it seems that it was Palmerston himself who took the initiative of having Chief Baron Parke made a life peer (as Lord Wensleydale) for the purpose of expediting and improving the hearing of appeals.[48] (Bramwell filled the vacancy on the Exchequer Court.) This, as it turned out, was ill-advised, for the Lords — for a variety of reasons — declined to receive life peers as members, and it may be that Palmerston's precipitate action hindered statutory provision for legal life peers. But it was well-intended, and deserves mention as yet another example of an attitude to what the Queen's

Speech of 1856 called 'internal improvement' which modifies the validity of complaints at 'the curious spectacle of the least Liberal of the Whigs receiving Radical support at the expense of his colleagues, who were genuinely in favour of domestic reform' because he 'continued to persuade the democracy that he was a revolutionist, whilst the aristocracy knew him to be *their* safe friend'.[49]

*   *   *   *

For all the poor sight and hearing, the ill-fitting false teeth and the visibly dyed side-whiskers, which caused Disraeli to call him 'the old painted pantaloon', Palmerston in 1856 appeared in great form as well as in his perpetual good heart. 'You may see the breed, but the action and power are gone', Disraeli had said, and in 1855 Palmerston's friend, Monckton Milnes, deplored signs of failing energy.[50] But this no longer appeared true as, after a meeting of ministerialist M.P.s had given him, in April 1856, a better reception than Derby had from his supporters, Palmerston made one of the most effective speeches of his long parliamentary career on the awkward subject of Kars and emerged radiant despite a bad attack of gout.[51] He had in February resisted with contempt the idea of a regular adjournment at midnight, and though he may have looked unimpressive as he sat slumped on the Treasury Bench, his hat over his eyes (and often asleep), the picture changed if one walked behind him and noted the straight back and soldierly step which conveyed the impression of impatient energy or remarked his unwearied diligence in parliamentary business. Granville, thirty years his junior, complained of a shoot at Broadlands on New Year's Day 1856: 'It was hot walking, we went fast, still Pam trudged along with wonderful energy. It was a bad feeling, but I was almost grateful when I saw him begin to limp a little.'[52]

Much work fell to Palmerston, for it was, in truth, as Disraeli said, 'a government of all the mediocrities' whose cabinet members began the habit of meeting not, like their predecessors, mainly at the Foreign Office, but in the famous room at No. 10.[53] If, however, the government depended on one man, that man was 'master of the situation'. He need not quake before a multitude of divided opponents, for his secret friends outnumbered his covert enemies. 'Palmerston's popularity is very great with the country gentlemen', reported Herbert. 'His old Protectionist leanings, his unconcealed aversion to Gladstone's financial policy, his objection to Parliamentary Reform, in any shape or degree, and his noisy foreign policy, which they understand the use of on a hustings as well as he, combined with the distrust they feel to their own leader, all incline them to support him. Many who sit opposite to him would like to sit behind him, and no doubt would do so, were it not that the old machinery of party is stronger than its spirit, and the club in London and the attorneys in the country prevent them'.[54]

CHAPTER XXII

TRIUMPH AND SET-BACK, 1857–8

EARLY in the session of 1857 Disraeli and Gladstone strove together to topple over Palmerston. It was a strange concatenation of competitors, for Gladstone's main attraction to Tories was that they could not bear Disraeli, and Disraeli's chief security was that there were other Tories who could not bear Gladstone. And each strove to outmanœuvre the other, Disraeli getting in an amendment on the budget to anticipate Gladstone, who insisted on amendments before he would support it. Gladstone defeated them both, and saved Lord Derby difficult decisions, by an over-vehemence which gave the ministers an impressive majority[1] and reserved their defeat for an issue which Palmerston could make more attractive to the country than resistance to Gladstonian retrenchment and complaint of faction.

One should not be surprised at the temporary alliance of Gladstone with Disraeli in defence of Gladstone's financial scheme of 1853, under which the income tax was to perish in 1860 and the tea and sugar duties to be nevertheless reduced. It was difficult for the Opposition to find a good issue on which to fight 'a Conservative Minister working with Radical tools and keeping up a show of Liberalism in his foreign policy'.[2] Tories could hardly complain that the Queen's Speech included 'no reform, excepting in the law'.[3] Was not the cause of the stagnation in domestic policy, of which Gladstone complained, precisely that, as Herbert replied when Gladstone accused Palmerston of 'demoralising' the House of Commons, the old controversies were dead, and the choice simply between two parties each offering to do the same thing better?[4] This condition of things exposed the Peelites to the fissiparous tendencies which afflict 'middle parties' most when they do not themselves stand clearly by inheritance or habit for anything that can be deemed relevant and distinctive. Stuart Wortley had just rejoined the government. Cardwell wanted to. Herbert wished they had never left it. Graham sighed for the policy of Peel and Aberdeen, of Conservative Reform at home and nonintervention abroad, but could not approve Gladstone's increasing predilection for Derby.[5] Gladstone's belief that Derby would be a better minister than Palmerston was simply a rationalization from his conviction that Palmerston was the worst minister it would be possible to have. 'For all the purposes for which I value Liberalism', he said, 'the Liberal party is dead. The Government is Liberal because it palters with one or two Liberal measures, and because Hayter gives places to Liberals; its Conservative side, I suppose, is that of its inaction and extravagance. . . . On the back of all this comes the foreign policy, which with Palmerston is in the blood and in the grain.' Powerless for good while Palmerston held the reins, the Liberal party might be made valuable and effective in opposition to a Tory government.[6] Whether Gladstone — violently opposed to the project for allowing the courts to decree divorce which was one of the 'one or two Liberal measures' comprehended under the term 'law reform' — would have long continued to hold this attitude as a Tory minister may perhaps be doubted.

Herbert tried to counter Gladstone's preference for Derby with the argument that the Tories required 'regeneration, if not absolute creation' and that this was the task of years, which would meantime have disposed of Palmerston 'in the way, not of all ministers, but of all flesh'. Graham pointed out that in the spring of 1856 the Opposition had been more warlike than Palmerston, that Ellenborough had schemes of Asiatic conquest and for a large standing army, that Gladstone must not expect the Tories to carry out the policy he wanted any more than Palmerston.[7] This policy which was, Gladstone said, going a-begging, was 'the general policy which Peel took office in 1841 to support — the policy of peace abroad, of economy, of financial equilibrium, of steady resistance to abuses, and promotion of practical improvements at home; with a disinclination to questions of organic change gratuitously raised'. From Palmerston they might expect 'a foreign policy keeping us in perpetual hot water; large establishments which will undoubtedly be needed to sustain it; the utter ruin of the financial policy of 1853; and general legislative inefficiency. Here are "Four Points" with a vengeance'.[8] It is, of course, artificial to make a distinction between foreign policy and financial policy when they are linked via defence expenditure, but it would evidently be wise to appeal more to the pockets of the people than to their morality, because, as Graham argued, Palmerston's 'foreign broils and warlike propensities [were] unfortunately . . . congenial to the temper and spirit of the nation'.[9] Palmerston must be fought not on the full-blooded Mancunian doctrine but on finance.

Ministers expected trouble over the income tax, which it was proposed to lower at once below the level Gladstone had planned, but to hold at a uniform rate for three years, instead of reducing it annually for abolition in 1860–1. So, when the service ministers, upheld by the Defence committee of the cabinet (which meant, in effect, by Palmerston) and by the Palace, proposed estimates of twenty-four million pounds — seven and a half million above the last year of peace — they were told to cut them to twenty million pounds and, despite Palmerston's optimism, Lewis would not propose an eightpence income tax. He asked for sevenpence. He was well-received, and Gladstone, in two speeches, was so indecently (though of course sincerely) violent in his attack on 'the worst proposition I had ever heard from a minister of finance', a plan for gross, glaring and increasing deficiency undoing the blessed work of Peel, that there was a reaction in favour of the chancellor, the author of a book called *The Usage and Abusage of Political Terms*, who protested, with genuine surprise, at Gladstone's 'downright, wilful deception'.[10] On the night of 23rd–24th February 1857 the Disraeli–Gladstone motion was defeated by 286–206. The news was received with delight at the Palace, and, of course, at the Treasury. There, however, Wilson noted: 'Matters look very queer about China. I doubt whether we shall come off so well on that subject.'[11]

He was right. Lawyers in the Commons were shaking their heads about the action of Sir John Bowring at Canton, as weak in international law. The Attorney-General, summoned to advise the cabinet, shook his head too, and Derby tabled a motion. Under ultimatum from Bowring, who was Chief Superintendent of Commerce on the China Coast, Commissioner Yeh had surrendered all the Chinese pirates or smugglers taken off the lorcha *Arrow*. But instead of apologizing and giving assurances for the future (which Bowring well knew would have been valueless in any case) he insisted that the European authorities had no right to protect Chinese criminals and that the *Arrow* was not a British vessel. Since its licence had expired, this was technically true, though the Chinese did not know it when they boarded. Bowring, however, impelled by the exasperation natural to a hot-blooded man (he was a Radical) in face of a steady Chinese refusal to treat Europeans as equals or carry out fully the terms of the Treaty of Nanking, reacted as Palmerston had done over Don Pacifico. He ordered the admiral to bombard Canton. In the cabinet, Granville had 'great doubts whether it is the best policy to treat Orientals in a way inconsistent with all the principles of justice'. In the Commons Russell would complain that they heard too much of the *prestige* of England, instead of her character, reputation and honour, and Gladstone invoke both international law and the higher ground of natural justice which binds man to man, older than Christianity, broader than Christianity, to which Christianity itself appealed. But Argyll 'did not care to ask whether the conduct of Sir John Bowring had or had not been more high-handed than was absolutely necessary. It was enough for me to see that the disavowal of our Commissioner . . . would throw into confusion the whole system on which our commerce rested in that part of the world'. The assumption 'that our representative officers on the Canton River were bound by the same highly complex rules of so-called International Law which governs the relations of the civilized nations of the Christian world . . . appeared to me absurd'. He was sure that 'this common-sense view would be taken'.[12] In the cabinet it was, but not in the Commons.

It goes without saying that Palmerston, hobbling on his crutches at Broadlands (the gout had struck again!) was also convinced 'that the Government will be deemed to have acted right in advising your Majesty to approve the proceedings, and to direct measures for obtaining from the Chinese Government concessions which are indispensable for the maintenance of friendly relations between China and the Governments of Europe'.[13] He thus, incidentally, put the issue on the general ground of the relations between China and the West, preparing the way for the demand that embassies be received by the Son of Heaven in his capital, and for French co-operation in the China War (the overt ground of which was the death of a missionary in the interior). When Lord Elgin arrived as plenipotentiary, he made in his ultimatum no reference to the *Arrow* affair which he privately described as 'a scandal to us, and so considered . . . by all except the few who are personally compromised'.[14] But it served its turn at home. The Queen's Speech informed parliament that 'acts of violence, insults to the British flag, and infraction of treaty

rights committed by the local Chinese authorities at Canton, and
a pertinacious refusal of redress, have rendered it necessary . . . to
have recourse to measures of force to obtain satisfaction'. It was
perfectly true that the Chinese had evaded, at Canton, per-
tinaciously, the conditions prescribed by the Treaty of Nanking for
European trade in all the treaty ports, and enforced elsewhere. But
the ministerial emphasis was on 'insult' and the Blue Book now
issued was called 'Insults in China'.

Disraeli was now hoist on Derby's petard; after the motion in
the Lords he could not refuse to support Cobden's motion
declaring that the papers laid did not justify the violent measures
taken and calling for a select committee on commercial relations
with China. That motion needed to be moderately worded, for it
would be highly dangerous for Palmerston's opponents to defeat
him unless they did so by such a majority that he did not dare to
dissolve. But though Cobden's motion was moderate, his speech
was not; it deterred members 'very much provoked at Bowring's
conduct' for it 'condemned our whole case as against the Chinese'.[15]
Indeed, there was in the Opposition the violence of desperation —
Russell was 'very telling' but 'unnecessarily savage'; Disraeli, who
summed up the complaints as 'no reform (!), new taxes (?), Canton
blazing, Persia invaded', was bitter and personal; Gladstone was
moved by crusading zeal to great eloquence, for he was convinced
that 'we have lived into times, politically more disastrous to the
honour of the country, than any we have formerly seen — For the
first time is her government guided by a man without convictions
of duty; by a man who systematically panders to whatever is
questionable or bad in the public mind, who lives simply on the
dissension of those who disapprove of his policy, and who now
seems at last to have overshot his mark'. But now he, who yearned
for the restoration of the two-party system of 1835-45, complained
that party considerations intervened.[16] On the government side,
the pointed references of the whips to the absence of an alternative
government, and the broad hint of Palmerston at a party meeting
that parliament would be dissolved if the government lost, gave
Hayter hopes of a majority of thirty. For only 150 of some three
hundred Tory M.P.s turned up at their party meeting to hear a
petulant Derby (peeved at desertions on the income tax) threaten
to throw up the leadership if the party presumed to dictate to him.
But in the end, Palmerston went down to the House knowing he

might well be beaten. Still suffering from gout, he was 'weak in body and mind' and his speech was a sad anti-climax following Gladstone's. It was full of claptrap about the safety of English lives and property in the East and the 'honour' of the country, interspersed with jibes at Gladstone for having long ago (on the First China War) defended the Chinese for poisoning wells and at Cobden for being un-English as usual.[17] Nearly 150 members absented themselves and or abstained from voting. Cobden won by 263–247.

*   *   *   *

'There was a crowd in Westminster Hall which cheered the victors, Cobden, Gladstone, Dizzy etc, as they went out, but the cheerers did not represent England.'[18] Indeed they did not. Disraeli, in for a penny, in for a pound, urged the noble lord who talked (as usual when challenged) of 'conspiracy' not only to complain to the country but to appeal to it. When the vote was taken, Palmerston had in his pocket a letter from the Prince saying that the Queen, who was expecting her ninth child, could not face a ministerial crisis and 'would prefer any other alternative'.[19] With little hesitation, the cabinet dismissed the old Whig notion of Sir Charles Wood that it would be right to resign to come in stronger; if the fortress were abandoned, it would have to be retaken. Palmerston was confident that it was better to have an appeal to the country as a result of a defeat in the Commons than in the ordinary course of things at the end of a session 'without any particular event out of which a distinction between opposing parties could have been drawn'.[20] For the only time in British history since the Reform Bill of 1832 a government appealed to the electorate from the House of Commons and triumphed. Palmerston was sure it would. Less than four days after the vote it was noted: 'Lord Palmerston is in great spirits, everything looking in his favour, the Country declaring for him against the House of Commons.' 'You have not given us a chance', complained Cardwell to Argyll when he heard of the dissolution.[21]

The 'cockney clacquers' had most of the press on their side, and Palmerston's, for, as the *Daily Telegraph*, the most successful of the new penny newspapers, knew, this was the side for the circulation and hence the advertisements and the profits. Maccoby, the historian of Radicalism (or, at least, the chronicler of Radical diversity) complains of 'the unlovely spectacle of a press drunken with its new power and with the profits of war-excitement'; John Bright said at the time that 'Palmerston and his press are at the bottom of the excitement.'[22] Cobden thought that the Palmerstonians would try to escape the China issue, and that their opponents 'must rub their noses in it'.[23] He could not have been more wrong. It may be true that Downing Street 'leaked' false news of peace in China as well as bona fide news of peace with Persia to influence the elections. But he made China, or rather the China vote, the central issue. His address to Tiverton proclaimed that 'an insolent barbarian . . . had violated the British flag, violated the engagements of treaties, offered rewards for the heads of British subjects . . . and planned their destruction by murder, assassinations and poisons'. He seized eagerly on exaggerated and often unfounded stories in *Punch* of Chinese habits of torture and in the *Illustrated London News* (whose proprietor was among the Palmerstonians elected) of widespread poisoning of wells and of bread at Hong Kong and the murder of the crew of a mail steamer by assassins who boarded as passengers. There could be but one answer to the question of whether a middle class electorate approved of Chinamen poisoning 'respectable English merchants'. The government press indicated that if one was not a Palmerstonian one was a 'Yehite'. Palmerston paraphrased the *Illustrated London News*, which asked whether Cobden, Derby and Graham were not ashamed of their 'clients'; he by implication accused Derby, Gladstone and indeed Russell, of trying to 'make the humiliation and degradation of their country a stepping-stone to power'. Derby had reason to complain that the blood of 'unwarlike and innocent' people had been shed. But he could not carry conviction as the self-styled 'advocate for weakness against power, for perplexed and bewildered barbarism against the arrogant demands of overweening, self-styled civilization . . . for the feeble defencelessness of China against the overpowering might of Great Britain'.

The result showed, Bright confessed, that the country was not ripe for squaring its policy with the maxims of commonsense and plain morality. 'Disraeli will say he was right; we are hardly of the English type, and success, political and personal success, cannot afford to reject the use which may be made of ignorance and prejudice among the people.'[24] Of course, the Palmerston victory was not due to mere chauvinism, which can flourish, and often flourishes most (and is most exploited), when times are bad internally, providing an escape-channel for discontent. In 1857 the country was prosperous beyond all precedent.[25]

Agriculture had entered into its 'golden age'. Even in Ireland the decline of emigration and evictions, especially evictions for non-payment of rent, indicated a relative improvement. In counties and country towns the Palmerston cult was marked. Herbert had noticed this more than a year ago, when he said that 'the regular old-fashioned country gentlemen who are not Londoners enough to come within the vortex of the Carlton are Palmerstonian pur et simple', thinking the premier the only man who could make peace and ward off democracy.[26] Now the member for North Lincoln-shire (whose colleague, a privy councillor, yielded his seat without a struggle to a Palmerstonian Whig who, significantly, had still been at the last election a protectionist) reported to the Tory chief whip that in that constituency Derby was not popular, D'Israeli (*sic*) was unpopular, Lord John Russell very unpopular, Gladstone extremely unpopular, and Palmerston *very popular because* he carried out the Russian War — Lord Derby unpopular *because* he did not carry out the Russian War & because the *farmers* think he *dropped them* in '52'.[27] But the popularity of Palmerston was not confined to the rural districts. Looking at the urban returns, Cobden feared that a trend was setting in which would continue as long as exports continued to increase markedly, and would eventually return a Tory government. Prosperity, he said, increased the number of Tories and cooled down to a genteel tone the politics of the Whigs, especially where businesses were on a large scale and the great capitalists formed an influential 'aristocracy' cut off from natural intercourse with the working classes. The base snobs at Manchester, converted by prosperity into little better than Tories, found Bright, an earnest Radical who was one of themselves and defended his order against all assailants, not sufficiently genteel for their taste, though he was mainly responsible for the prosperity.[28]

Certainly Palmerston in 1857, as during the Crimean War, was conspicuously popular in the great commercial and manufacturing cities as well as in the metropolis and home counties, and among the Palmerstonians carried in for such places and some smaller boroughs were men of substance and business achievement who had not yet, or only just, broken into the squirearchy and member-ship of Brooks's as had some of the Palmerstonian members elected for the more industrialized county divisions. But well over half the Liberal gains in 1857 were in county seats and the victors, Palmerstonian almost to a man, were generally from the classes that had always supplied county members. It was twenty-two years since the Whigs had held so many county seats. That they did so was in no small degree due to Palmerston's membership of the landed aristocracy, his essential loyalty to it, his instinctive reflection of the prejudices of the gentlemen of England (with which, however, he combined a stronger sense than they of the importance and the consequences of industrial and commercial growth). In sum, the parliament which met on 30th April 1857 had the first professedly non-Conservative majority since 1841 and the largest Liberal majority since the first reformed parliament was dissolved in 1834. But the transfer of seats from Tory to Liberal was only half the tale. 'We have gained nearly forty, *independent of Government Liberals*, who have turned out Bright and Milner Gibson and so on', noted Granville.[29] There was a quite unusual turnover of Liberal personnel, because Liberals who opposed Palmerston in the China vote threw up the sponge or went down to defeat at the hands of Palmerstonians. *The Times* noted nine of the Manchester School and three Independent Irish among the victims. Two ostentatiously Palmerstonian Liberals defeated Bright and Milner Gibson at Manchester; another beat Cobden who, abandoning the West Riding to the like-minded Lord Goderich, sought to hold the former's seat at Huddersfield. The Under-Secretary at the Home Department beat another Mancunian at Salford; the Quaker W. J. Fox fell at Oldham. From Wick and Aberdeen, from Galway Town and Cardiff, as well as from metropolitan districts, came news of anti-Palmerstonians giving way to supporters of the premier. *The Times* rejoiced that a dozen Peelites would be missing from the new House. Three were beaten by Liberals in Oxford (Cardwell), Brighton and Lanarkshire; three, having abandoned their constituencies, stood in vain elsewhere; some did not stand at all. In this strange elec-tion, with so many net Liberal gains assured, there were Tory gains which brought nothing but pleasure to Palmerston and Hayter, for they removed from the House Layard (Aylesbury), Miall of the *Nonconformist* (Rochdale) and two Independent Irishmen —

Richard Swift (Co. Sligo) and Tristram Kennedy (Co. Louth) — who were victims of vote-splitting by Palmerstonian Whigs. The Queen remarked to Palmerston that it was very excellent and very striking that Bright, Gibson, Cobden, Layard and Walmsley were out, though she regretted that one of the worst, who would be very troublesome and mischievous in every way — Conningham (sic) was the victor at Brighton.[A] Palmerston agreed that a few had been elected who would have been better away, and a few (including three junior ministers) defeated whom they would have wished to keep. But, enclosing the new Dod's *Parliamentary Companion*, he rejoiced that many objectionable members (including, Lewis pointed out, many bores) had been thrown out and more gentlemen and men of character and substance returned than was usually the case.[30]

The personal nature of the triumph was indisputable. 'Palmerston has had a great triumph', noted Granville. 'The elections have turned entirely on him personally . . . The whole country in

---

[A] William Coningham, M.P. for Brighton 1857–63, was a Palmerstonian Radical who decisively beat the Peelite ex-minister Lord Alfred Hervey at Brighton. He had published in Feb. 1854, at the height of the popular run against Prince Albert, a pamphlet called *Lord Palmerston and Prince Albert, together with the Suppressed Pamphlet entitled 'Lord Palmerston: What has he done?'* with the motto, from Blackstone, 'The husband of a Queen Regnant is her subject: and may be guilty of high treason against her.' The suppressed pamphlet was, allegedly, written by S. Phillips (for £100 and a cask of golden sherry) in the form of an open letter to Lord John Russell, commissioned by Sir John Easthope on information supplied by Palmerston after his dismissal. It ascribed the dismissal to Coburg intrigues with despotic Courts, and the story was that it was suppressed by Palmerston himself after a copy had been sent to Windsor, and was written for that purpose; hence Palmerston became the honoured guest of Royalty and eligible for the highest office.

At about the same time, Urquhart wrote, but did not publish until 1857 (under the title *The Queen and the Premier*), a slightly different version, alleging that Palmerston provoked his dismissal by insulting the Queen, and, his calculations upset by Russell's revelation of the royal memorandum, countered by causing the suppressed pamphlet to be prepared. Hence, according to Urquhart, Derby's otherwise inexplicable invitation to Palmerston to be Leader of the House in Feb. 1852. Urquhart's theme was that both Prince Albert and Palmerston had all along been Russian agents, but had quarrelled, and that Palmerston survived the quarrels to become prime minister because he had 'knowledge', i.e. by blackmail.

In March 1854 Coningham joined Urquhart's Turkish Association and paid his hotel bill of £20. When Urquhart said this was not a personal loan but a subscription, and Coningham called him a liar, Urquhart challenged him to a duel, and was bound over by the Brighton magistrates to keep the peace (*Morning Advertiser*, 22nd and 25th Jan. 1855).

England and Scotland is Palmerstonian.' 'We see approbation of
Lord Palmerston, more or less qualified, but no approbation of
Lord Anybodyelse', declared *The Times*.[31] Derby, no tactician —
and himself handicapped, as the letter from North Lincolnshire
shows, by the feeling that he had 'funked' becoming war premier
when those who had not funked failed — did not improve matters
by a bitter personal attack on Palmerston in the Lords on the eve
of the dissolution, when he declared, inter alia, that his colleagues
were mere appendages and cyphers.[32] What were his own, other
than Disraeli? The prospective recruit, Gladstone, was a distinct
liability in the eyes of Tories always distrustful of unconventional
and unpredictable men. Whatever Palmerston was, he was a man
the ordinary man could understand, earthy, plain-speaking,
evidently good-humoured and with a boisterous sense of fun, with
neither the complexity nor the dogma of the intellectual. And
whatever Gladstone was, he was not that. Those Tories who hated
Palmerston did so, not because of his views, but because of his
success. They had little in common with the Peelite and Radical —
and 'conscience Whig' — members of what Palmerston called,
when they denied combination or 'conspiracy', the *'fortuitous*
concourse of atoms' that formed the Commons majority on the
China motion. The election turned on Palmerston, if only because
the 'combination among all the scraps and debris of parties which
had resulted from many fractures . . . had . . . in common . . .
(only) an unreasoning antipathy to Palmerston'.[33] In this statement
of Argyll the adjective alone can be queried. One may imagine how
Palmerston's frame-shaking laugh rang out when he read how
many Conservatives, as well as Liberals striving to hold their seats,
protested that they had not joined the fatal vote, or had done so
without thought of winning it or that if they did win it ministers
would resign, and/or professed their willingness to give Palmerston general (though, of course, independent) support. Many of
the new Conservative candidates who won seats (usually from
anti-Palmerston Liberals) complained that the China vote had
been factious and said they would support Palmerston whenever
they could do so consistently with their Conservative principles.
Some did not even enter this caveat, and the appellation *Liberal-
Conservative*, used in the crucial election of 1835, and since 1846
employed to differentiate from the Protectionist ruck both genuine
Peelites and Tory candidates holding that Protection should not be

restored, was again pressed into service. It now indicated a
Conservative with a penchant for Palmerston or seeking election by
deferring to such a penchant among his constituents.[34]

*   *   *   *

'Our foes are scattered like chaff before the wind', commented
Argyll. 'The Peelites are smashed as a party, which is good',
remarked Granville, though he thought the government had 'gone
too fiercely against many people who for conscience sake voted
against them'. 'The League has disappeared from Parliament'
crowed *The Times*. 'There is reason to hope that a better class of
men will be returned and returned to support the Government, not
a particular cry of this or that . . .', the Queen had written to Uncle
Leopold.[36] But would the men support the government? Had
Palmerston, in an improbable way, restored the two-party system?
And would Palmerston live? When he went to Windsor to ask for a
dissolution he looked very ill from a renewal of the gout, though 'in
excellent pluck', and as the session began Lady Palmerston
wondered whether he would stand the strain.[37]

The strain did not, however, seem likely to be great in a fore-
shortened session ushered in by a Queen's Speech described by a
leading Tory as the tamest he had ever read.[38] Only Gladstone's
obstruction of the bill to permit divorce without a special act of
parliament in each case made necessary the threat to sit in September. In the latter part of the session the Government was sustained
by the crisis in India called by British historians 'the Mutiny' and
by Indian 'the Great Revolt'. So far as north-east and north-
central India, up-country from Calcutta, were concerned, it was
something between the one and the other. The sudden loss of
Meerut (10th May 1857) and Delhi, where a Mogul prince was
enthroned, showed that the government at home had been living in
a fool's paradise of complacency over India, from which two
European regiments had been withheld because of the Crimean
War, and six had been recently sent to Persia, leaving only five in
an eight hundred mile stretch of the Ganges. Neither in London
nor Calcutta had the psychological effects of the policy of the
Peelite governor-general, Dalhousie, and of the unexpected
appointment as his successor of Lord Canning (because he was his
father's son and a Peelite who had stayed in the cabinet when
Gladstone and the others seceded), been understood. In Indian

eyes, Dalhousie had mounted a deliberate attack upon Indian customs and customary relations between the Company government and the Indian princely states and families culminating in the annexation of Oudh (and the promulgation of a land settlement there which, though to Western eyes just and beneficent, offended the feudatories without winning the allegiance of the emancipated peasants) and Canning's reduction of the dignities and stipends of 'mediatized' royal houses, including that of Delhi. Canning looked, from London, the very man to prevent Indian revolt, had the notion of one been entertained. Instead of that, he unwittingly provoked it, though it was plain bad luck for him that the grooved bore rifle should be introduced on the centenary year of Plassey (when Hindu prophecy said British rule was to end), and require a new form of cartridge. The cartridge grease was of uncertain origin, but had to be bitten; the story spread that it was intended to defile Hindu or Moslem or both, and was believed partly because Canning had been preceded by the rumour that he came to attack the religions of India. In fact, Canning's respect for, and benevolence towards, Indians alienated the Europeans in Calcutta, whose contempt for Indians horrified him as much as the blundering proselytism of some missionaries, teachers and officers of native regiments. It was easy to see, when the Mutiny came, that he had underrated the loss of morale of the sepoy regiments, but to suggest that he ought to have disbanded more of them was, with the shortage of European troops, unrealistic. Unlike the public at home, he never forgot that India must be garrisoned and governed (and, at need, reconquered) mainly by Indians. And how could he foretell which regiments would remain loyal, which desert, and which turn on European officers and civilians with murder in their eyes, when until the moment of choice the Indians did not know themselves?[39]

Canning's calmness was justified by the fear that panic measures would spread the mutiny, but it meant that the news of Meerut and Delhi struck a home government and public totally unprepared for it. Even now Canning did not think that troops from home could arrive in time to be of use (except those he had asked for on 22nd April), for it was not foreseen that Delhi (accessible to Lawrence's troops from the Punjab) would remain in rebel hands till mid-September and that the garrisons and civilians in Lucknow, the capital of Oudh, though reinforced by Havelock on 25th

September, must wait till late November to be relieved. Judgement at home was clouded by these inexplicable delays and by news of the two massacres, first of the men, and then of the women and children, in Cawnpore as Havelock approached. Canning complained that the Government at home did not give him and did not express in public its full confidence, and the fact that the main defence against Disraeli's attack on the policies which had caused (and, he implied, justified) what he called a national revolt came (27th July) from Russell, not Palmerston, might certainly be taken to indicate that a premier whose habit it was to seek public acclaim was to some extent dissociating himself from the viceroy. Palmerston did not speak out for Canning until Clarendon, as well as Granville (a close friend of Canning), urged him to 'stop the run' against the proconsul, which he alleged was due to the Gagging Act promulgated by Canning (mid-June) against European as well as native newspapers in Bengal, since they constituted a security risk and inflamed racial hatred to an extent that made Canning ashamed.[40] The Calcutta Europeans deluged their friends at home with complaints against Canning as a 'nigger-lover' and in October memorialized the East India Company for his recall. By now public opinion at home was nearly as bad as in Calcutta. Middle-class journals called for the sack of Delhi and the indiscriminate massacre of prisoners; officers talked of the work of blood as of hunting animals; the services on Wednesday 7th October (a Day of National Prayer and Humiliation) showed few signs of genuine Christian charity towards 'the heathen in his blindness'. On 17th October *The Times* dubbed the lonely, proud, maligned governor-general 'Clemency Canning' and *Punch* with a cartoon and the *Daily News* with virulent abuse reinforced the attack. Press comment could hardly have been more violent if Canning had promised free pardon and pensions to the murderers of Cawnpore on whom General Neill, the avenger, exacted awful retribution. The public anger is understandable when even Cobden, who stood against the tide, called the rebels 'these monsters who have startled the world with . . . deeds' unparalleled since the slave revolt in St Domingo, and when Lord Shaftesbury, no less, attributed, without justification, to Lady Canning an atrocity story which had no foundation.

We, who know that what *The Times* called a 'silly proclamation' was no proclamation at all; that it was not, as believed at home, imposed on Canning by his Council but a product of his own maxim 'I will not govern in anger'; that it implied no mercy to those taken with arms in their hands or blood on their records or even belonging to units so tainted; that it imposed no check on the systematic burning of villages on the line of march (which was economic stupidity) or on the military's practice of killing suspects with or without the formality of a drumhead court-martial — we must remember that for weeks after Canning's instructions of 31st July to civilian officials (some of whom were behaving like mere butchers) had leaked to the press, Palmerston knew none of these things. Thinking it a 'proclamation', he (privately) condemned it as 'twaddling' and 'ill-timed'.[41] But when the cabinet met, he substituted for Vernon Smith's draft expressing modified disapproval another expressing approval in principle but asking for information and justification, neither of which Canning had furnished, apparently not understanding that though the document was confidential it was so widely circulated as to be bound to be published.[42] Palmerston here followed his usual course of shielding public servants, though he frankly shared the public criticism of the 'Clemency proclamation', which was so violent that thirty years later Granville described the diners at the Mansion House in honour of the Duke of Cambridge (the Queen's cousin, who had become Commander-in-Chief) as the most hostile audience he had ever faced.

From Calcutta on 11th December Canning complained that 'the head of the Government has never held out a little finger to me, although not for want of opportunities. This is not like him'.[43] We must agree. The wonted magnanimity had failed. But a few hours earlier Granville had written to Canning: 'I am annoyed at thinking that all your accounts from England will be of an unsatisfactory character till you receive Pam's speech.' For at Guildhall Palmerston, in a speech described by Granville as judicious, spat out in a most decided manner his confidence in Canning and by Christmas Eve Lady Canning could write: 'Lord Palmerston's good stout support has quite changed the tone of the newspapers here', which had been daily predicting her husband's recall.[44] Conspicuously absent from Canning's complaints is any suggestion that the troops sent him from home were defective in numbers or equipment. As a result of his request of 22nd April (received late May) 8,000 men were under orders from India when his graver tidings were received. They began to leave at once (1st July). Within a week the decision was taken to send four more regiments, and by the end of the month it was decided to send 20,000 in all, with artillery, and get horses in the Cape and Asia Minor. Sensible consideration was given to the question of acclimatization, and there was more to be said for the Admiralty's preference for sail over screw transports than appears to the modern eye. A particular point was made of sending out those officers most frequently mentioned for high positions if there had been some particular spectacular purge in the Crimea. The performance in India of Mansfield and Ashe Windham and even of Sir Colin Campbell (Commander-in-Chief) offered no strong proof that they would have transformed the situation before Sebastopol. Only Sir Hugh Rose, operating from Bombay, showed (though he lacked any Indian experience) a proper appreciation of the importance of mobility.

In his Guildhall speech Palmerston praised the fortitude and resource of individuals and knots of his countrymen — and countrywomen — scattered over India, and claimed that 'the Government at home . . . may justly pride themselves on not having been unequal to the magnitude of the occasion'. He had been criticized by the Tories for delays in sending the troops. He had been criticized, more validly, by the Palace, where it was felt that the army had been run down too quickly to too low a peace time level. The Queen and the Prince, and Clarendon too, were 'woefully disappointed' by Palmerston's 'system of hoping and believing', his lack of urgency and vigour. What they feared was that European Powers might take advantage of the defencelessness of Britain after the troops had gone to India.[45] The apprehension was reasonable, though in fact the Powers behaved decently and Napoleon III allowed troops bound for India to proceed by rail to Marseilles, thus settling the dispute over whether it was better to send them via the Cape or Suez. Clarendon was a pessimist, who believed the British would lose India after a protracted struggle — a prospect which never crossed Palmerston's mind — and his complaints of Palmerston's optimism must be read in the light of this pessimism. No weight can be attached to his complaint that Palmerston refused to use Prussian officers and 10,000 Belgians because the suggestion was 'out of the beaten track'.[46] Palmerston had been willing enough to use Germans and Swiss in the Crimea. Clarendon was alarmed when, at the Lord Mayor's banquet, the premier said: 'If any foreign nation ever dreamed in its visions . . .

that the time had arrived when a different bearing might be exhibited towards us from that which was safe in the moment of our strength, the manner in which the spirit of the country has burst forth, the manner in which our ranks have been filled, the manner in which our whole force has been replenished, will teach the world that it would not be a safe game to play to attempt to take advantage of that which was erroneously imagined to be the moment of our weakness.' The Foreign Secretary deemed this an affront to France for the sake of loud and prolonged applause at Guildhall. Palmerston noted in his pocket book: 'gave much offence at Compiègne — can't be helped — il n'y a que la vérité qui blesse'. He explained to Clarendon that the speech was aimed at the whole Continent 'where, for the last six months, we have been talked of, and written of, and printed of as a second-rate Power'. That was why he had insisted from the first that it was essential to win in India 'off our own bat';[47] this was not mere bravado, but statesmanship, the more necessary in view of Britain's sorry record in the Crimea.

The Indian Mutiny clouded relations between Palmerston and the Palace which, rightly contemptuous of Panmure and undervaluing (as parliamentarians did as well) Vernon Smith, accused the cabinet of living from hand to mouth and Palmerston of failing to instil into administration planning and urgency. 'The Queen ... must say that if she had been in the House she would have joined in saying that the Government were not doing enough to "reorganize a defensive force for home service".' There is a certain irony in Palmerston, the champion of a large national militia, being rebuked for backwardness in mustering one, and having to defend himself by arguments in favour of a phased build-up without undue interference with the harvest or with recruiting for overseas service. By 3rd September the Queen was acknowledging 'the first indication of their desire to exert themselves to meet an extraordinary emergency by extraordinary means'. They were scraping the barrel across the Atlantic; by a calculated risk which had worried the Palace Palmerston had already stripped the Mediterranean. On 1st and 2nd October the cabinet decided to lower the height and age standards for recruits and raise the militia to 25,000. At Guildhall on 9th November Palmerston could claim that 'we have now under arms in the United Kingdom as many fighting men as we had before the news of the Mutiny reached us'. He did not, of course, claim that they were equal in training and discipline to those who had gone to the East, but it was now the Queen's turn to deploy the argument he had used against her, and stress the importance of cadres upon which expansion could be based, rather than mere numbers.[48]

*   *   *   *

Palmerston was able to speak as he did at Guildhall, with confidence and to applause, because it was known that Delhi was retaken and Lucknow reached. When on 27th July in the House he had praised Russell for striking the keynote of public opinion, what he really appreciated was Lord John's appeal to the country to rally behind the government. Now the security of crisis was passed, but it seemed that the security of success had replaced it. Opposition attacks in December were partly provoked by the unfairness of the fact that, before the troops from home had made any contribution, 'people talk[ed] of our victories in India as being proof of Lord Palmerston's glorious administration'. Granville wrote to Canning on 23rd December that the taking of Lucknow 'completes the good fortune of Palmerston and his Government, for which nothing could be more favourable than the short session which we have had',[49] a session made necessary by the action of the Treasury and the Bank to stay a serious financial crisis. Of the February debates Canning was told that they had witnessed the signal discomfiture of his enemies.[50] Two days before the main debate *The Times* admitted that Canning had made a valid defence to the main charge against him and that 'at any rate India was in the extreme of peril six months ago; it is now safe and returning to tranquillity'.

But the government, as it turned out, was not safe. Explanations of its fall must be treated with reserve, because they are ex post facto, and the fall was unexpected. It was a case, we are told, of hubris. Palmerston had become overbearing and dictatorial, and his admission to the cabinet of Clanricarde, 'a reprobate' (Prince Albert), 'a man universally and justly disesteemed' (Gladstone), was held to prove it.[51] It is difficult to see why Palmerston should have allowed success to go to his head, and run his luck too hard, nearly a year after, rather than on the morrow, of his dramatic, almost plebiscitary, success in the 1857 election, especially as his health was now better. His defeat on the Conspiracy to Murder Bill was so marginal that anything may be held to be decisive which offended a handful of members — even the appearance of Clanricarde in the gallery during the debate, or the hectoring violence of parts of Palmerston's speech. He could have been saved if he had circulated assurances on Reform, or if he had offered a different India Bill. By the same token, it may be said that he fell, not because Clanricarde was a man whose reputation could not stand recent rough handling in an Irish court case, so that his appointment offended the Victorian ethos, but because Lady Clanricarde was the sister and stalwart champion of Canning. The governor-general was still unpopular at home, though the great debate in February went in his favour owing to the efforts of three Conservatives after a bad beginning. But the real explanation of Palmerston's defeat early in 1858 is surely either more pedestrian or more portentous. *The Times* had presciently remarked that Palmerston's majority was 'a snow giant'. It was always likely to melt away if climatic conditions produced another 'fortuitous concourse of atoms' to which some Palmerstonian Radicals (to say nothing of Palmerstonian Whigs and Palmerstonian Tories) felt bound to adhere because Palmerston had acted out of character.

At a crucial moment, the vaunted Hayter nodded, over a hundred of his flock being absent with no idea that the government was in danger.[52] It proved to be in danger because Palmerston, as at the time of the coup d'état of December 1851, put the long-term interests of the country above temporary popularity, and affronted his most strident admirers. Russell (whom Palmerston had grown into the habit of discounting, with strong reason, but to his cost) had been immensely encouraged by his signal personal victory in the City elections in 1857. He believed that he could wrest the leadership of the Liberals from Palmerston if only he could get him out of No. 10. In December 1857 he complained that 'any attempt to overthrow Palmerston on his sins of omission and commission in India, Persia and China, would only strengthen his hold on the country'. Palmerston, he avowed, was a dangerous minister 'from his over-confidence and light way of giving offence to foreign powers, where no interest is at stake'. He regretted that 'the people of England, inspired by *The Times*, have not found this out, and attribute to cabal, to jealousy and to intrigue every just criticism or censure upon the Government'.[53] But he had learned in December 1851 that it was possible to take advantage of offence given to the people of England because the interests of foreign policy required it. And when George Grey indicated to Russell the intention of ministers to alter the law of conspiracy in deference to French reactions to the attempt by Orsini on 14th January 1858 to kill Napoleon and Eugénie, he thought he saw his chance. He declared at once that their attitude was incompatible with national dignity, and 'in that shame and humiliation I am determined not to share'.[54]

Ministers had imagined that they might have great difficulty with their India Bill, defeat on which need not, however, be fatal to them. On 18th February it was read a first time by 318:173, a majority, Palmerston said, 'even greater than had been expected [which] proved how little credit is to be given to reports which circulate in clubs and drawings rooms'. Walking home through the night the Attorney-General, Bethell, told Palmerston that, like a Roman consul at a triumph, he needed someone to remind him that he was (as a minister) not immortal.[55] Within a week Palmerston was a minister no longer, Bright and Milner Gibson walking up to the table of the House of Commons 'to pass sentence upon that venerable political sinner',[56] as tellers for Gibson's amendment to the motion for the second reading of the Conspiracy Bill, carried by 234 to 219.

The premier's first reaction to French protests had been to seek from parliament power for the Home Secretary to expel undesirable aliens. The Conspiracy Bill was a modest substitute. It would have converted conspiracy within the Queen's dominions to commit murder elsewhere from a misdemeanour into a felony. Because men such as Granville and Malmesbury took seriously the danger of war with France 'at this moment when . . . we are not in a position to have war with anyone',[57] Russell carried into the lobby with him against the first reading (in conscious imitation of Palmerston on the Militia Bill six years before?) only a hundred companions, mainly Radicals — fewer than Orsini's bomb had killed and wounded in Paris. The Government triumphed by 299-99, with the support of the Leader of the Opposition. But Palmerston was ill-received, the Liberals being very angry with him, and the ministry was thought 'very shaky' because, as the Queen told Uncle Leopold, 'people are very indignant here at the conduct of the French officers, and at the offensive insinuations against this country'.[58] The colonels' protestations of loyalty to the Emperor were couched in very violent terms; one of them begged for orders to destroy for ever 'the infamous haunt in which such infernal machinations were planned'. Palmerston argued that it would be unworthy to be turned from a proper course by 'any paltry feelings of offended dignity or of irritation at the expressions of three or four colonels of French regiments, to act the childish part of refusing an important measure on grounds so insignificant and trumpery'.[59] But the 'idle vapourings of irresponsible swash-bucklers' assumed an added gravity when some of the addresses were published in the official *Moniteur*. John Bull's blood was up at the idea that Palmerston of all people should ignore the gauntlet thus flung down. The French ambassador's apology did not appease public opinion, which was scandalized by the publication of Walewski's dispatch asking for 'a guarantee of security which no state can refuse to a neighbouring state, and which we are entitled to expect from an ally'. This seemed reasonable to a minister who regarded the French alliance as the linch-pin of his foreign policy and a safeguard against the bugbear of a Franco-Russian alliance. To the press in Britain it seemed an insult. Milner Gibson's motion read:—

That this House hears with much concern that it is alleged that recent attempts on the life of the Emperor of the French have been devised in England, and expresses its detestation of such guilty enterprises. That this House is ready at all times to assist in remedying any defects in the Criminal Law which, after due investigation, are proved to exist, yet it cannot but regret that Her Majesty's Government, previously to inviting the House to amend the law of conspiracy by the second reading of the Bill at the present time, have not felt it to be their duty to make some reply to the important despatch received from the French Government, dated Paris, 20th January 1858. . . .

The ministerial case was, in substance, that the bill was the answer to the dispatch. The Government's defence of the bill was ably conducted by Baines, the Lord Advocate and the Attorney-General (who lied to save his colleagues), but the weight of debating talent was against the cabinet, and this was decisive when public opinion believed that, as an answer to the dispatch, the bill was craven and undignified. Some said that it was not until Derby, sitting under the gallery, noted the effect of Gibson's speech, that he gave the order to charge, which was to make him prime minister.[60] By the time Palmerston followed Gladstone and a confident Disraeli, he scented defeat, and by being 'actually rabid' in 'a most bewildered and uncertain house' perhaps assured it.[61] Only one ministerial back-bencher had risen to defend the Government whole-heartedly. Palmerston reciprocated 'the very bitter feeling against Pam on the part of Radicals, Peelites, Johnnians and ex-placemen'. He 'made a very intemperate speech, and actually shook his fist at the Manchester clique'.[61] Now, if ever, indeed, he was entitled to complain of factious combination. The hostile motion was presented by Mancunians who ought to have been the last people to thrust Britain on to, perhaps over, the brink of war with France, the country's unreadiness for which was in no small part due to their persistent propaganda against the Estimates. It was supported by Gladstone, defending the national honour. It was instigated, some thought, by Graham. It was framed, in the general belief, by Russell. It was carried by the junction with these of the Tories, whose leader had supported the bill. Palmerston was ousted as Peel was ousted in 1846, with this distinction, that the public applauded the decision of the House. He was hooted by the crowd in the Park after the vote.[62] He had risen and triumphed by reflecting, exploiting, sometimes pandering to, public opinion. And by affronting it he fell.

CHAPTER XXIII

FIGHTING BACK, 1858-9

ALMERSTON loved office, and many of his critics alleged, and
sometimes believed, that for it he would forsake all principles
(if they allowed him any) or consistency. He can hardly have
relished the prospect of Derby forming a government which, even
when Gladstone, Newcastle and Earl Grey had refused to join it,
was as 'tolerably presentable' as its predecessor, and which was only
the third government in fifty years of public life that Palmerston
had not been asked to join. Yet, though Palmerston could probably
have secured a small majority on a straight vote of confidence, he
made no response to the Queen's request to his cabinet to reconsider its unanimous decision to resign. There was no ground
for Disraeli's suspicion that he believed Derby would fail to form a
ministry; there could be no assurance that the four hundred
Liberals in the House of Commons, not half of whom had rallied
to keep him in, would join to put him back. The disarray of the
majority was evident from physical dispositions in the House.
Palmerston and his colleagues occupied the front Opposition
bench, and Cardwell sat behind them. Russell sat with Bright and
the Radicals below the gangway. Opposite, below the gangway on
the ministerial side, after as before the change of government, sat
Gladstone, Graham and Herbert, of whom only the first definitely
preferred Derby to Palmerston.

The leading men below the gangway could prevent the unity of
the Opposition under Palmerston. But they could not procure its
unity under anybody else. For Palmerston was the ostensible
leader of the Opposition. He maintained a shadow-cabinet and he
summoned party meetings. The minority government was therefore likely to have a clear run, unless it provoked its ruin by some
gratuitous folly. This it nearly did, twice, through the agency of the
egregious Lord Ellenborough, President of the Board of Control.

The Palmerston government had introduced an India Bill to
abolish the Board of Control, the East India Company's Court of
Directors and the Court of Proprietors ('a mob of holders of

Indian Stock assembled for three or four hours three or four times a year', Palmerston called them) and confer the government and army of India upon the Crown, to be exercised by a secretary of state with a council. Ellenborough's substitute was 'a clap-trap, and denounced as such by Palmerstonians, Peelites, Radicals and Russellites'. In a 'profligate and reckless bid for popular favour' he proposed that part of the Council for India should be chosen by five great city constituencies in Britain.[1] This was opposed even by those (such as Gladstone and Graham) who hoped that the council would act as a check on the minister, and was repugnant to Palmerston on the opposite ground that the council should be non-political, consisting of men of Indian experience acting as an advisory wing of the Executive. While the 'shadow-cabinet' was pondering the political prospects of a motion against the second reading, Russell indicated that *he* would move such a motion. The front bench agreed to support him.[2] Bewaring the Greeks bearing gifts, Russell retreated, in concert with Disraeli, to the halfway house of committee resolutions as a basis for a third India Bill. Disraeli deceived the Queen as to his pourparlers with Russell, but he was sincere enough in ascribing Lord John's action to a wish 'to defeat the prospects of Lord Palmerston, and himself to occupy a great mediatory position'. There was, he reported from the House on 12th April 1858, 'a marked discordance between Lord John and Lord Palmerston, not concealed by the latter chief, and strongly evinced by some of his principal followers . . .'.[3]

Russell, playing *vis-à-vis* the second Derby administration the role Palmerston had played in 1852 *vis-à-vis* the first, had let the Tories off the hook. But Ellenborough soon put them back again, by a peremptory dispatch denouncing Clemency Canning for a proclamation on the settlement of Oudh incompatible with the Government's wish to 'see British authority in India rest upon the willing obedience of a contented people'. This dispatch, which was unknown to the Queen, the cabinet and the Directors, was 'leaked' to Bright in order that he might give Disraeli an opportunity to express in the House thorough disapproval of Canning's policy. Probably in order to force the governor-general to resign, the dispatch was laid on the table of the Commons unexpurgated, containing an offensive passage stating that Dalhousie and Canning had been tyrannical and misguided in their land-settlement in Oudh and implying that the annexation of that friendly state was based on fraud or deception. This made the matter a party issue with a vengeance, and the shadow-cabinet decided that motions of censure, based on the unhappy effect of the dispatch in India, should be moved in the Lords by Shaftesbury and in the Commons by Cardwell. Palmerston expected to win, even after Ellenborough resigned, exculpating his colleagues, because the Queen let him know that she had refused to pledge herself to dissolve parliament (if Derby asked her to) 'in order to support such tricks' as the collusion of Disraeli with Bright. His supporters went about confidently asserting this.[4] Palmerston and Russell were brought together by Ellice ('they have shaken hands and embraced, and hate each other more than ever' commented Russell's sister-in-law) and Lord John delivered a fine speech in defence of Canning.[5] But Gladstone and Graham saved the government. The former, by persuading Aberdeen to defect, saved ministers in the Lords debate; the latter became the medium by which the Queen's intimation to Derby (consequent on the advice of Aberdeen) that a dissolution would not be refused, was surreptitiously circulated.[6] There occurred, on the evening of 21st May, 'the utter explosion of a well-constructed mine, under the feet, not of the assailed, but of the assailants'. With 626 M.P.s in attendance, 400 of them Liberals, it became evident that if the Opposition forced a division, ministers would win it, perhaps by thirty. Disraeli sat with a sardonic smile as member after member opposite rose and begged Cardwell to withdraw his motion, which after discussions with Palmerston and Russell, he did.[7]

Few leaders of the Opposition have ever been made to look more foolish. The election of 1857 had been held in such unusual circumstances that more members than usual had reasons, other than merely financial ones, for fearing another election. And while some members, like the Queen, disliked the idea of an election turning on Reform, with 'violent pledges' given, some, like Argyll, who genuinely wanted a not illiberal settlement of that question, preferred to give Derby a chance of settling it. A visit to Knowsley by Russell early in the winter even gave some ground for hoping that the rivals who had broken from one another in 1834 might co-operate over it.[8] For, if Palmerston had lost control of the Opposition, Russell had not won it. 'Palmerston has lost all influence in the House of Commons and all his popularity in the country . . . Johnny has not profited in the least by the descent of his rival', commented Granville.[9]

Palmerston's failure in the House of Commons is easy to explain. Seventy-three is a great age to start learning the trade of a leader of the Opposition, a position Palmerston had never held before, and the divisions in the Liberal party were beyond Hayter's control. Impatient to be back in office, Palmerston was much influenced by colleagues, especially Vernon Smith, who 'look[ed] upon office as their birthright, and upon those who deprive[d] them of it as brigands who [had] robbed them of their property'.[10] As in 1841–6, Palmerston in Opposition showed vigour rather than judgement. But, above all, Palmerston for a decade had been the representative of public opinion, and now it failed him. The one strong scent — antipathy to France — he nobly refused to follow. When the Tory ministers bowed to the pledge of Russell and Gladstone 'with 140 men, to interrupt *any* bill, in *any* way, and for *any* time' and sought accommodation with the French without concession, by concocting with Persigny a reply to Walewski's dispatch whose tone might be described as one of 'cordial protest', Palmerston and Clarendon joined Malmesbury and Cowley in pressing moderate counsels upon the Emperor.[11] When the Commons reassembled on 12th March the government was able to announce that painful misconceptions between the two countries had been terminated in a friendly spirit. Palmerston and his friends 'compensated' by allegations that Malmesbury was being 'soft' to Bomba over the *Cagliari* affair.[A] The ex-ministers did not pretend

---

[A] The *Cagliari*, a Sardinian ship that had worked for the Italian nationalists, was taken into custody by the Neapolitans. In Malmesbury's view, it had been on its way to Calabria to land nationalist agents to promote revolution, and he told the Lords it was the intention of the Turin government and its supporters in Britain by such means to provoke war. This was fraught with such danger to Europe that he was determined to thwart them, and to settle the two issues arising out of the seizure without reference to Sardinia.

The first issue was the detention of two British engineers, Watt and Park, who had been aboard; though Britain had no diplomatic relations with Naples, Mr Lyons was sent to procure their release. The Law Officers of the Crown held unanimously that their detention was illegal.

This was a purely British issue. The other — whether the Neapolitans were entitled to retain the ship — concerned all the maritime Powers 'and therefore Great Britain first', but the judges consulted held, by 4 to 3, that the detention was legal.

On 16th April 1858 Disraeli announced that £3,000 compensation would be demanded for Watt and Park, already released, and on 11th June Malmesbury announced that the £3,000 was to be paid and that Naples had agreed to render

to be pleased when in June Disraeli was able to announce that this matter had been satisfactorily settled.[12]

Palmerston had been embarrassed in the weeks after his fall by Persigny's arrant partisanship against the Tories,[13] and was relieved that Persigny resigned his embassy. It was a dubious privilege for Palmerston and Clarendon to be invited by the Emperor to visit him at Compiègne, just after the Queen, the Prince and Malmesbury had been at Boulogne. They went (November 1858), feeling that 'such visits serve as links to main tain and strengthen the English alliance' although they knew the Radicals would not like it and Clarendon's sister, the wife of Lewis, said that Palmerston had placed another large nail in the coffin of his premiership. Russell hoped that this was so, and wrote that Palmerston and Clarendon 'must thereafter be considered rather as courtiers of the Tuileries than as subjects of St James's'.[14] Malmesbury was amused to hear of Palmerston stag-hunting on a very wet day, the only one of the party not weather-proofed, remarking 'rien ne perce un habit rouge'. He was less amused when he heard that Persigny was to return to London, presumably to intrigue against Her Majesty's ministers.[15]

Prince Albert, in a memorandum of 4th September, could find no rational explanation of Palmerston's 'extraordinary un-popularity'[16] —

... A House of Commons, having been elected solely for the object, and on the ground of supporting Lord Palmerston personally (an instance in our Parliamentary history without parallel) holds him suddenly in such abhorrence, that not satisfied with having upset his Government, which had been successful in all its policy, and thrown him out, it will hardly listen to him when he speaks ... The man who was without rhyme or reason stamped the only *English* statesman, the champion of liberty, the man of the people, etc, etc, now, without his having changed in any one respect, having still the same virtues and the same faults that he always

---

up the ship and the Sardinian crew to Britain. When Disraeli announced this in the Commons, amid enthusiastic cheers, 'the ex-Ministers and their adherents were completely taken by surprise, and would not even pretend to be pleased that a quarrel which at one moment threatened a general war should have terminated in a manner so satisfactory' (M., 424-38).

Malmesbury had remarked to Cowley in April: 'I am made Minister on purpose to resist interference on the part of France with our laws, and I am also expected to keep up a quarrel with Naples in support of interference with their institutions. What a set we are!' (ibid. 429-30). This was a reference to the general quarrel with Naples, which he wished to bring to an end as soon as the *Cagliari* question was settled.

had, young and vigorous in his seventy-fifth (sic) year, and having succeeded in his policy, is now considered the head of a clique, the man of
intrigue, past his work etc etc — in fact hated! and this throughout the
country. I cannot explain the enigma except by supposing that people had
before joined in a cry which they thought was popular without themselves
believing what they said and wrote, and that they now do the same; that
the Radicals used his name to destroy other statesmen and politicians, and
are destroying him now in his turn . . .

Lord Palmerston himself remains, outwardly at least, quite cheerful,
and seems to care very little about reverses; he speaks on all subjects, bids
for the Liberal support as before, even at the expense of his better conviction (as he used to do), and keeps as much as possible before the public;
he made an official tour in Ireland, and is gone to visit the Emperor
Napoleon at Paris; his Chinese policy upon which the Dissolution had
taken place in 1857 has just been crowned by the most complete success by
the advantageous treaty signed at Pekin by Lord Elgin; and yet even for
this the public will not allow him any credit. Lady Palmerston . . . is said
to be very unhappy and very much hurt.

Greville thought that Palmerston's career was drawing to a close.
Gladstone, with an anonymity rendered specious by the distinc-
tiveness of his style, rejoiced in the October issue of the *Quarterly*
that sufficient of his former followers had 'written this sentence on
the tables of their hearts *Come what may, Lord Palmerston shall not
again be Minister*'. But it never occurred to Palmerston to retire
from active politics, or even to go up to the Lords. He was
confident, or at least hopeful, that a reaction would come, and
Granville thought it would 'if he maintains his health and strength,
but he is seventy-four'.[17]

*   *   *   *

The main parliamentary business for 1859 would be a Reform
Bill. Since Russell had reopened the question in 1849, Palmerston,
satisfied with the Constitution under which he was born (as he told
the men of Tiverton)[18] had threatened to resign over the bill being
prepared for 1852 and had resigned over the bill prepared for 1854,
which Russell so reluctantly abandoned at the beginning of the
Crimean War. He denied that he was opposed to all Reform, but
held that any considerable disfranchisement of boroughs or
liberalization of the borough franchise would overbear intelligence
and property by ignorance and poverty and undo what it had been
the peculiar merit of 1832 to do.[19] Now that he had been Home
Secretary, he more than ever feared the domination of the seats of
manufacture and trade by trade unions if there were too many

working class voters. 'Palmerston hates Reform as he hates the Devil', said Herbert. 'He only dislikes peace because it must lead to it.' There is little doubt that Palmerston hoped to die, full of years and honours, in office if possible, with no change in the settlement of 1832. Peace came in 1856, but no Reform Bill was proposed for 1857. When he secured a dissolution after the China vote, he was pressed by some of his colleagues to say something, however equivocal, about Reform in his address, but was unwilling to make any clear reference to Parliamentary Reform at all.[21] Yet the Palmerstonian victory seemed, paradoxically, to bring Reform nearer. 'Nothing but a Transatlantic or Continental War . . . could save the Premier from the absolute necessity of attempting at least to solve the question', declared the *Leader* on 11th April 1857. 'The country has returned a Parliament to support Palmerston and Reform, and the two must be brought into harmony, or the former will go to the wall', wrote Herbert the following day. 'Palmerston has the sense to know it, and colleagues who are, I suspect, determined to drag or drive him in that direction.'[22] 'The House of Commons is sure to be apathetic about Reform. The country does not care a great deal about it', wrote Granville, 'but would be very angry if it was thought that the Government was anti-reforming.'[23] After the election, indeed, a smaller proportion of the enlarged ministerial party in the Commons really desired Reform, but a party majority of about a hundred removed the main argument for inertia. Palmerston had to promise to bring in a measure in 1858 (unless, as he put it to the Queen, 'other more urgent and important matters should justify them in abstaining from doing so').[24]

In mid-October 1857 Palmerston informed the Palace that he had asked George Grey to prepare proposals for the cabinet. He made it clear that what he wanted was a measure which would greatly disappoint the Radicals and greatly satisfy all reasonable men, though many a member would be bound to cry out that it fell short of what justice and propriety demanded, because he had 'unguardedly and needlessly' made wild pledges to some few radicals in his constituency.[25] The Queen's Speech of December 1857 indicated that Parliament would be invited to consider what amendments might 'safely and beneficially' be made in the law relating to representation. Palmerston's attitude to Argyll's pressure for some disfranchisement of small boroughs strongly suggests that he had not made up his mind that it was necessary to introduce a bill at all or seriously try to pass one. He hoped that something would turn up, other than the defeat of the government, to make it unnecessary. The India Bill was given precedence and might consume the session. Argyll, asking on 14th January for a bill to be drafted, found the premier still 'shy of the subject' and procrastinating. 'Oh, there will be time enough for that', he said; 'we cannot introduce it before Easter.'[26]

Before Easter the Palmerston government fell, and impatience about Reform on the part of 'Palmerstonian Radicals' may conceivably have decided the issue in the close vote on the Conspiracy Bill. It now fell to the Derby government to make an attempt to settle the question, with the goodwill, Russell feared, of many 'shabby' people. Bright's winter campaign against the aristocracy made this more likely — 'Bright disgusts all, and opens the way for a mild Reform', noted a junior minister.[27] Some feared the result of bid and counterbid, that the Tories would be 'ready to sacrifice the monarchy that they may keep their places', that 'if Derby goes for universal suffrage, Palmerston and Johnny will produce the women and children'.[28] Others speculated as to a Derby–Palmerston coalition, at the expense of Disraeli and Malmesbury; others again feared that the Government would 'be safely floated over the question and the session . . . by the rivalries' of Palmerston and Russell.[29] Palmerston, not wanting any Reform at all, expecting a moderate bill with some Disraelian absurdities, and believing Russell wanted to add a million voters (swamping intelligence and property), was for remaining 'quite still', making no attempt at an understanding with Russell or 'anybody else'. Lord John, bursting to produce a plan of his own to forestall Disraeli, was himself forestalled by Bright, causing Russell to call him a dangerous man. Palmerston supposed 'this means he thinks him a dangerous ally'.[30]

At last, after much research, heart-searching and two resignations from the cabinet, Disraeli produced a bill. Russell, as well as Bright, was bound to declare against it, for it hardly touched the working classes, though it accepted in principle the assimilation of the county to the borough franchise (at ten-pound occupancy). Lord John was bound to move rejection. But he would not win without the Palmerstonians who, at the introduction, were 'still and impenetrable'. Palmerston's only real objection to the bill was that, while adding 200,000 ten-pound occupiers to the county electorates, it subtracted some half that number of county electors who were forty shilling freeholders resident in parliamentary boroughs.[31] This would strike at the prospects of Liberal county members. But a reasoned amendment to the second reading, based on that ground alone, would be unsatisfactory; the government might give way. And the Opposition dare not allow the bill to get into committee, for there the differences between Palmerston, Russell and Bright would be embarrassingly exposed. In the end, Russell moved an amendment to the effect that no bill could settle the question which did not lower the franchise qualification in the boroughs. For this, as no figure was named, Palmerston could vote. He took the precaution, however, of appealing to those Liberal members who thought that some sort of bill could emerge from committee, by 'counselling a degrading submission to the House', whereupon the Government obligingly replied by dispelling such hopes.[32] If ministers were beaten, they would resign or dissolve. In the small hours of 1st April 1859 Russell's motion was carried by 330:291, in the largest House since January 1835. To Russell's chagrin and Palmerston's delight Derby asked for a dissolution. If ministers had resigned, Russell would have had a certain *locus standi* as the mover of the amendment that turned them out. The Conservative gains in the election made it clearer than ever that no bill would pass 'which [did] not suit the taste of Lord Palmerston and Lord Derby'. Graham thought these two might join forces, for there was not much between the former Whig turned Tory and the Whig who in some ways had always remained a Tory at heart. Gladstone too talked of this solution, and perhaps dreamed of himself as Foreign Secretary under Derby, with Palmerston as leader of the House (shades of 1852!).[33] Such a conjunction would appal Lord John. It might make him leader of a Radical Opposition, but he was sixty-seven and longed to return to office.

Palmerston, in his seventy-fifth year, was no less impatient, and was especially anxious to control policy because Italian affairs were now coming to crisis, Napoleon III having promised Cavour the year before that he would expel the Austrians from Italy as soon as a suitable *casus belli* arose or was engineered. Until the election, Palmerston's public attitude did nothing to justify Malmesbury's suspicions that he was misrepresenting the Government's policy to the French emperor.[34] Borthwick, indeed, in the *Morning Post* obeyed Napoleon's injunction to write down Malmesbury who

Q

'has leagued Germany against me and is entirely opposed to my policy', but the closest student of Britain's policy towards Italy at this time speaks of that newspaper as 'once Palmerstonian, but now thoroughly Bonapartist'.[35] It is doubtless true that Napoleon hoped for a Palmerston government which would be more friendly to action against Austria in Italy, but it is hardly (as Malmesbury suggested) an adequate explanation of his delaying tactics. Napoleon believed that Malmesbury was more completely pro-Austrian than he was, because the Foreign Secretary was so simple-minded as not to see that the dispute over Lombardy and Venetia could not be settled peacefully, and because (as Palmerston saw) British diplomacy at Paris was inept — it alienated but it did not deter.

Palmerston's personal attitude to the Italian crisis was explained, with his usual clarity, in a letter to Granville[36] —

I am very Austrian north of the Alps, but very anti-Austrian south of the Alps. The Austrians have no business in Italy, and they are a public nuisance there. They govern their own provinces ill, and are the props and encouragers of bad government in all the other states of the Peninsula, except in Piedmont, where fortunately they have no influence. Their claim of 'ancient rights of possession' is groundless. Their title goes no further back than their Treaty of Vienna of 1815. . . . They are overstepping any rights which the Treaty of Vienna gives them, by their military occupation of the Papal States. . . .

I should therefore rejoice and feel relieved if Italy up to the Tyrol were freed from Austrian dominion and military occupation.

But . . . the Austrians cannot be driven from their Italian provinces without a desperate struggle, and however desirable their expulsion would be, those who might make or recommend or encourage a war for that purpose would incur a heavy responsibility. . . . A war begun to drive the Austrians out of Italy would infallibly succeed in its immediate object . . . but if [Austria] was deeply engaged in a conflict in Italy, the Hungarians would rise, and Russia would threaten the Galician frontier, and instead of seeing Italy freed, and nothing more, we might find Austria dismembered. But even if this were not to be, the bloodshed and destruction of life and property consequent upon such a war would far more than counterbalance the good that would be accomplished. . . .

Palmerston therefore hoped that peace would be maintained, and was quite sure that if war should break out, the only course for England was neutrality. 'We must stand aloof. Public opinion would not allow the Government to declare war against France, Sardinia and Russia, in order to maintain Austria in Italy, and, of course it is out of the question that we should take part against

Austria', there being no pretence for 'violating or disregarding' the treaties of 1815 to which Britain was a party.

Malmesbury was entitled to point out that all Napoleon and Cavour required of Britain was neutrality, and that they had grounds for hoping that under a Palmerston government the neutrality would be more friendly to them than under the Tories. But policy depended to a marked degree on public opinion. Because, though not without Italian sympathies, the press (suspicious of France and her relations with Russia) disapproved the designs of Napoleon and Cavour, both Palmerston and Russell heeded the counsel of Clarendon that 'political capital would be lost and not made by a warlike tone or by sympathy in Italian grievances pushed to its extreme limits'.[37] Then, after the dissolution was announced, the Austrian ultimatum to Piedmont took the Foreign Office by surprise. A surge of public feeling impelled Derby himself to denounce a 'criminal act' by which Austria 'forfeit[ed] all claim upon the support or sympathy of England' and made it politic for Palmerston to speak his mind, or much of it, at Tiverton.[38] He defended the Conspiracy Bill. He defended the French alliance and accused Malmesbury of wantonly wrecking it. He strained credulity by pretending that 'nobody, that I am aware of, had meant to wrest from Austria the territories in Venice and Lombardy which she possesses by virtue of the treaties of 1815', speaking as though the issue was confined to Austrian intervention elsewhere in Italy —

... Territories were given to Austria in Italy which I believe she did not herself then wish to have, but the possession of which has been a source of infinite misery to the people of the whole of that Peninsula. For Austria, not content with ruling her own provinces in her own way — and Heaven knows that hers was a way that no right-minded Government would have persevered in — ... exerted influence over and exacted treaties from all the other States of Italy ... by which in all those countries ... the most abominable system of misgovernment has been supported by the confidence which their Governments felt that ... Austria was there by an overwhelming military force to compel obedience. Now that which Austria ought upon the present occasion to have conceded ... was her consent for the future to confine herself within her own rightful limits.

This was a shrewd appeal to the instincts of British Liberalism, and to the hatred of the Pope and Bomba which stemmed from anti-popery, and it was calculated to confuse the champions of non-intervention by the emphasis which it placed on Austrian

interference in central and southern Italy. The continued occupation by Austria of Lombardy and Venetia was, Palmerston implied,
to be condemned not so much on the ground that it was an element
of insecurity in the European balance (inciting action by Piedmont
and France), or that it involved misgovernment there, but because
those provinces were the strategic base upon which depended all
the political, diplomatic and military operations required to maintain odious misgovernment throughout Italy, except in Piedmont,
that progressive, liberal, free-trade (and anti-clerical) state.
Palmerston did not advocate British involvement; he did not
praise French intervention; he admitted, of course, the danger that
the war might spread. But he clearly hoped that the war could be
both limited and decisive. Lombardy and Venetia were Austria's
by right, and the judgement, though not the sympathies, of
Europe affirmed that she was entitled to keep them. *But* —

. . . those who, like myself, think it an object of great European advantage
that there should be in Germany a considerable power like Austria, as a
barrier between the east and the west, to maintain the liberties and independence of Europe, must deeply lament a course which tends, I fear,
to results that may alter materially the future position and condition of
Austria. If the war is confined to Italy, if the consequences of Austria's
aggression should be that she should be compelled to withdraw to the
north of the Alps and leave Italy free to the Italians . . . every generous
mind will feel that sometimes out of evil good may flow, and we shall
rejoice at the issue, though we may regret the miseries which may have
preceded it.

★　★　★　★

Palmerston's speech was important because it outbid Russell
(who had chided the Palmerston government for inactivity over
Italy but was now very restrained) and because of its effect on
Gladstone, but it attracted more attention abroad than at home,
and it is difficult to fault the considered judgement that the Italian
question was not decisive in the general election.[39] For there was
no clear-cut issue between the parties, and Palmerston at Tiverton
based his argument on Malmesbury's own ground that the overt
issue in dispute with Austria was one which 'Austria ought to have
settled peaceably, amicably and freely'. Palmerston did not think it
would be wise to stake the battle with the government on the
Address on foreign policy (among other reasons because Irish
Catholic M.P.s were worried about the future of the Pope). On

16th May 1859 Russell received via Lewis a message that Palmerston would deprecate an amendment on foreign policy, or one censuring the dissolution, or one insisting on Reform (Lord John could get little support for his view that the House should regard itself as a constituent assembly elected to pass a Reform Bill). Palmerston suggested a straight vote of no confidence, and accepted Russell's idea that it should be a repetition of Peel's after the election of 1841.[40]

* * * *

The two rivals thus set in train a development which has received far less attention and emphasis than it deserves — the deliberate re-creation in 1859 of the two-party system which had broken down in 1846. They saw that they must strike at the earliest opportunity, when members were coming up from the constituencies in partisan mood, for the Tories were as near to half the House as in 1852. They saw that they must act in unison. They saw, indeed, that they ought to be able to say they had agreed on an alternative government, but while Palmerston was willing to indicate that he would serve *in the Commons* under his rival if the Queen should send for him, Lord John would not reciprocate.[41] Meanwhile, others urged upon them that even if this difficulty was overcome, success in the crucial division could not be guaranteed. They must 'take the whole Liberal party into counsel, discuss the risks to be run, and the objects to be attained'. It fell to the gentlemanly Herbert to explain to the Whig chieftains that 'the party . . . are very independent in habits and feelings, and the time is gone by when they will vote like a flock of sheep for whatever some half-dozen men may concoct in a library'.[42] A Whig might retort that the Peelites, with so few followers, were as familiar as any politicians with this use of libraries and resent the fact that they were always putting themselves up to auction and buying themselves in. But the margin was now so close that, whether the Whigs liked it or not, the Peelites counted.

Palmerston had become used to meetings of M.P.s, summoned by himself as leader, regarding them as safety-valves, but he did not like the idea of having one now, when his grip on the party was less than at any time since he became premier and the need for the meeting was a sign of disunity. But Hayter advised it. The meeting of 280 M.P.s at Willis's Rooms on 6th June 1859 may legitimately be regarded as the formal foundation of the Liberal Party.

On the platform, Palmerston had the priority, and it was thought symbolic that he helped 'Little John' up the step. Both Herbert and Graham had told Lord John that Palmerston would have a better chance of forming a government without Russell than Russell without Palmerston, and of maintaining a government, with or without Russell, because of the Tory preference for him.[43] Palmerston 'said that he and Johnny were at one (great cheering). Then there was a pause and a call for Lord John, who . . . said . . . if the vote succeeded . . . and if the Queen sent for Pam, he, Johnny, would cheerfully co-operate with him in the formation of a Government — broad basis etc — and then Pam whispered to him, and he added as much for Pam'. Herbert spoke for the handful of Peelites and Bright for the Mancunians and the members agreed overwhelmingly to support the motion of censure the next day, to be moved (on Palmerston's invitation) by the young Lord Hartington.[44] At 2.30 a.m. on 11th June it was carried by 323–310. Derby at once resigned.

Russell had wanted to be prime minister or, at the least, Leader of the Commons with Palmerston as premier in the Lords. Palmerston wanted to be premier and get Russell off to the Lords. He had no intention of going there himself, even if the worst happened and Russell became premier in the Commons. Seeking to avoid 'the very invidious and unwelcome task' of choosing between the two veterans, both ex-premiers, the Queen sent for Granville. Significantly she desired him to make Clarendon Foreign Secretary and Palmerston Leader in the Commons.[45] She thus indicated that she rated Palmerston's claims above Russell's and brought the latter to see that he could not be the first man in the state and could be the second man only under Palmerston. She would have liked Granville to succeed, because the arrangement she proposed would have deprived Palmerston of the direction of foreign policy. His name, she said, would have a bad effect in Europe 'after the speeches he had made . . . bad and mischievous speeches'.[46] It had not escaped the (pro-Austrian) Palace that the French and Sardinian envoys had wildly cheered Palmerston as he emerged from the Commons chamber after the vote. But Granville did not really have a chance. Palmerston, as was his custom on such occasions, said he would co-operate, provided a strong government was formed. All the prospective ministers hoped Russell would join, but only Milner Gibson said his presence was essential. Lord John would not consent to be third man in the state. Granville's attempt merely brought Palmerston and Russell to the common position that each would serve if the Queen sent for the other, which meant quite simply that Russell would serve under Palmerston. The latter, 'having the largest following', made it clear that he would not go to the Lords. But he could not insist on Russell doing so, nor deny him the Foreign Office. Palmerston took comfort on the fact that, on 12th June, he was distinctly commissioned to form an administration. There was no question of 'equality' with Russell, and no question of a joint commission.[47]

So hostile a critic as John Morley (the biographer of Cobden and Gladstone) declares that Palmerston was 'designated for the first post by a voice which the sovereign of a free country cannot pretend to ignore'.[48] This seems less clearly true of 1859 than 1855, but it is the case that Palmerston was more capable than any other leading politician of representing the current consensus. The historian of Radicalism wrily remarks, of the decade 1855-65, that 'by degrees the Conservatives and Whigs, without entering into a coalition, formed a working combination, which left office in the hands of Palmerston and power in those of the old governing classes'.[49] There is some resemblance between the situation of 1859-65 and that of 1835-39, though with the marked difference that Derby was no Peel and that Palmerston had a strength of will and liking for initiative which Melbourne had lacked and also had a palpable public appeal. Palmerston could usually feel confident that, if the Radicals were unduly pressing, Tories would fly to his aid. But the other side of the picture is apt to be overlooked. As soon as the euphoria induced by the Italian Question was dispersed, it became increasingly clear that Palmerston could not rely on carrying the cabinet and the Liberal party with him in all things, especially foreign affairs. He was haltered by the compact made at Willis's Rooms, which dictated the composition of his cabinet as the Lichfield House compact of 1835 had not dictated the composition of Melbourne's.

Palmerston confessed to Cobden that he would rather have gone on as before with his old friends, but that no government could have sufficient prospect of duration or be satisfactory to the country unless it contained representatives of all sections of the Liberal party.[50] He had to offer Cobden office 'as of right' and the leader of the Manchester School, landing at Liverpool on 29th June from America, in ignorance of Willis's Rooms and what followed, found awaiting him a letter from Palmerston offering him the Board of Trade, and a letter from Russell saying:[51]

An attempt has been made, more or less wisely, to form a government from various sections of Liberals. Recent speeches have prevented the offer of a cabinet office to Mr Bright. This is much to be regretted, but if you accept, his accession may take place hereafter. If you refuse, I do not see a prospect of amalgamating the Liberal party during my life-time.

When Cobden visited No. 10 Palmerston did not pretend to share Russell's regret about Bright, whose 'attacks on *classes*', whose conception of British diplomacy and empire as a gigantic system of outdoor relief for the aristocracy, made him ineligible. But the premier did press Cobden to join the cabinet, and thus influence the secret diplomacy of which he had so long complained. Despite the pressure of many of his friends, Cobden remained convinced that it would be 'monstrous' for him to accept. 'I believed you to be warlike, intermeddling and quarrelsome', he told Palmerston, 'and that your policy was calculated to embroil us with foreign nations. At the same time I have expressed a general want of confidence in your domestic politics.' He had meant, and still meant, what he had said.[50] So, not Cobden, but Charles Villiers joined Milner Gibson as a representative of the Manchester School in the cabinet.

How little freedom of action Palmerston had in his cabinet-making in 1859 is shown by the close similarity between his appointments and those which Russell had intended to make if he received the commission.[52] Apart from Granville and George Grey, who were automatic choices, the cabinet included only three of Palmerston's colleagues of 1858 — Cornewall Lewis, Argyll and Wood. Russell had intended to appoint 'two or three of the Palmerston set'. Palmerston could do no more, for he was forced to have three Peelites (it would have been four if Graham had not pleaded age) and two Manchester Radicals, and Russell. He had to depart from that equal distribution of cabinet ministers between the two Houses which in 1855–9 he had held to be proper. Only six of the sixteen were in the Lords — Granville, Newcastle, Argyll, Campbell, Somerset and Elgin. Of these, only Argyll and Elgin (both ex-Peelites) were in any real sense Palmerstonians, and

Argyll wanted Parliamentary Reform and Elgin was ashamed of the *Arrow* incident. There was not one full-blooded Palmerstonian among the premier's nine cabinet colleagues in the Commons, and when Russell at last took a peerage in 1861, Palmerston's heir-presumptive in the Commons was — GLADSTONE.

In all the ways in which he was liberal, bar one, Gladstone was Cobdenite. Between Palmerston and all right-thinking men, he had written in 1858, was a quarrel that was no lover's quarrel. 'The proscription is no personal proscription. It is the determination of a great and serious issue, too long neglected and misunderstood . . . the proscription . . . of a system of misgovernment at home and abroad; of a system which, because it despised or made light of rights, was sure to mismanage interests; a system which at home was favourable neither to permanence nor to progress, and which abroad united the dangers of violence with those of poltroonery; . . . which . . . has left for itself a bad memorial in remembered slights and insults, in the uneasiness and suspicion which it has introduced or aggravated in the whole range of European diplomacy, and in the spirit of jealousy and even of hatred which it has engendered towards England.' But the one burning issue in Gladstone's mind was now Italy. 'The most brilliant stroke . . .', Aberdeen avowed, 'was Palmerston's speech at Tiverton. His declared wish to see the Germans turned out of Italy by the war has secured Gladstone, who is ready to act with him, or under him, notwithstanding the three articles in the *Quarterly* and the thousand imprecations of late years.'[53]

Gladstone had earnestly desired the reconstruction of the two-party system of 1835-45 which, in his growing isolation, he had come to idealize. But he had made no contribution to it when it took place. He had been to the Ionians on a special mission for the Tory government. He had not been at Willis's Rooms. He had talked of a Derby–Palmerston junction, and would have assisted it. He had voted with the Tory government against the Hartington motion. But, when asked, he at once accepted office, choosing the Exchequer. He had no mind to be 'the Ishmael of the House of Commons'. His position was very like Palmerston's at the time of the foundation of the Aberdeen coalition in 1852. Like Palmerston then, he joined a government of whose chief he had a low opinion in hopes of influencing cabinet policy in the matter which interested him most, of doing useful work through an important department, and, eventually, of securing the premiership himself. Because of Italy, he could write with sincerity: 'I am in real and close harmony of sentiment with the new premier and the new foreign secretary.'[54] The ill-judged Austrian ultimatum to Piedmont to disarm had released Palmerston from the necessity of pretending that he did not want a localized war to expel the Austrians from Italy and Gladstone from the dilemma of deciding whether or not it was permissible to desire such a war. 'It may be better or less bad that war should come *now*, than that the ails of Italy should go on festering and should accumulate more and more. . . . The worst is, that as matters now stand, war may easily pass into European confusion.'[55] Only the style identifies the writer as Gladstone rather than Palmerston.

CHAPTER XXIV

THE TRIUMVIRS, 1859–60

'IT was not by a deliberate verdict on foreign policy that the pro-Italian triumvirate — Palmerston, Russell and Gladstone — was placed at the head of affairs.'[1] But it was Italy that had created the triumvirate, and it was the triumvirs who, in Italian policy, provided the impetus to initiatives, with Gladstone, however, leaning to caution. Palmerston and Russell proposed. Often, however, they were not able to dispose — 'The spirit of the two old statesmen was willing; the Cabinet's flesh was weak.'[2] Palmerston, at Willis's Rooms, had had to promise Bright a policy of peace and neutrality. He and Russell argued that neutrality was not the same as impartiality, but their colleagues tended to the view that it should be, and that the aim should be peace rather than any particular solution. Even when they approved the end, they sometimes burked the means. The Court, disapproving the end, intervened assiduously — often, barely properly, through Granville, who kept the Prince posted on cabinet deliberations and the views of individual ministers — to ensure that the obstructive tendencies of the cabinet should prevail over Palmerston. For it was Palmerston who counted; he 'brilliantly managed' Russell.[3] He flattered him by allowing plans which originated with the premier to appear as those of the Foreign Secretary. He used him to fly kites. He exploited his impatience with the Court, his dislike of deferring to the cabinet, his tendency to disregard (often from sheer inattention rather than malice prepense) the spirit of cabinet wishes. He no doubt observed with amusement that Russell at the Foreign Office was a veritable caricature of Palmerston, though without his grasp of fact or his fixity of purpose, of which Lord John spoke with admiration.

Palmerston's was the directing mind. He strove consistently for the exercise of self-determination for the Lombards and Venetians, and for as many other Italians as possible, believing they would all gather under the wing of Piedmont, and that by their doing so the best interests both of Italy and Britain would be served[5] —

461

... It is surely for the interests of England that there should be created in Northern Italy a State as independent as possible of foreign dictation, and as likely as possible to consult its own interests, which would lie in commerce and peace. But, the weaker a state is, the more dependent it is on its neighbours: and the stronger it is, the more able it is to have a policy of its own. It seems, then, to be for our interest that there should be in Northern Italy a State as considerable, and therefore as strong, as circumstances will permit; and such a State must be built up on the present Kingdom of Sardinia.

... A State possessing Genoa and Venice would of necessity make commerce its vital principle, and having two seaports, both of which might, in case of war with England, be blockaded by British squadrons, such a State would have a double inducement against a rupture with England. How far south the new Sardinian territory should go must depend on events, but I think it probable that Parma and Modena at all events would be included, and possibly Tuscany. I have no doubts ... that no English Minister ought to sign a treaty of peace that does not provide efficient reforms for the States of the Church. ...

He backed without hesitation Russell's rejection of the Prussian suggestion for peace on the basis of the status quo ante — Austria must surrender territory. Though Russell and Gladstone did not agree with him, he refused, at first, to put to the Austrians the French suggestion that Venetia be given to an archduke, since this would 'fall far short of the wishes and expectations of Italy and lay us open to the accusation of betraying and disappointing' the Italians (which he suspected to be the French motive). This would make Venetia another Tuscany and probably perpetuate Austrian interference in central Italy. He was willing to propose it to Austria only when Napoleon opted for an armistice at Villafranca and peace preliminaries. The Queen congratulated herself on saving the premier from falling into a French trap, and proposing a bigger sacrifice than the French asked the Austrians.[6] But neither Victoria nor Palmerston can have expected that Napoleon, having won Magenta and Solferino, would agree to Austria's retention of Venetia, to Austrian participation in a Confederation under the presidency of the Pope (the old plan of 1847, which wore a different aspect now that Pio Nono was so illiberal) as well as the restoration of the client rulers south of Lombardy, ejected by their subjects.

Palmerston's immediate reaction was characteristic. 'Deeply mortified and annoyed', he cast in Persigny's teeth the Emperor's talk of Northern Italy liberated from sea to sea. England must protest in the face of Europe against Austria having any political or military influence beyond her borders. 'England could never associate herself with such a bad arrangement' as was proposed. She could not attend the proposed European Congress on such a basis.[7] He was determined, in particular, to prevent, if he could, the restoration of the Austrian clients, and, though the cabinet weakened (15th August) Britain's official protest to France and Austria, he always insisted that it committed her to 'the principle that no force should be employed for the purpose of imposing upon the people of Italy any form of government or constitution, that is to say, that the people of Italy, and especially of Central Italy, should be left free to determine their own condition of political existence'.[8] And he moved Russell to prepare a dispatch proposing the annexation of the disputed territories to Piedmont (as their peoples desired), the heir of Parma being compensated by appointment as papal viceroy in the legations.[9] When the Queen put the view that true neutrality involved abstention from such expressions of opinion, sparks flew, for this doctrine struck at the root of Palmerston's conviction, held throughout his long career, that . . .[10]

England is one of the greatest powers of the world, no event or series of events bearing on the balance of power, or on the probabilities of peace or war can be matters of indifference to her, and her right to have and to express opinions on matters thus bearing on her interest is unquestionable; and she is equally entitled to give upon such matters any advice which she may think useful, or to suggest any arrangements which she may deem conducive to the general good.

The cabinet, consulted by the Queen's command, thwarted him, finding the draft too vehement and offensive to France as well as Austria. Even Gladstone swung round.[11] The pro-Italian Argyll thought that 'all goes well in Italy', perhaps better than 'if we interfere too actively'.[12] The policy of genuine non-interference won a signal victory. Palmerston's request for fuller powers during the recess was met by his distrustful colleagues with 'a general assurance of readiness to come up by night trains'.[13] But Granville did not pretend that 'a schism very dangerous to the Court and to the Government' had been more than 'postponed'.[14] And Palmerston, though checked, was not mated. It was accepted that Britain's moral influence should be used, at the proper time, to prevent recourse to force in Italy. Palmerston saw that he could win if he could only persuade the French, having ratted on the Italians over

Venetia, to rat on the Austrians over Central Italy. He found Persigny willing (3rd September) and asked that, since Court and cabinet had thwarted formal British initiative, Paris should propose the annexation of Parma and Modena to Piedmont and the division of the papal territories between Victor Emmanuel and the Neapolitan Bourbon.

This private initiative produced great tension between Balmoral and Broadlands, for Walewski, Napoleon's foreign minister, protested vigorously at the proposed bargain and tendered his resignation (which was not accepted). Once again the issue turned on Palmerston's favourite distinction between formal and informal approaches. 'What is the use of the Queen's open, and she fears, sometimes wearisome correspondence with her Ministers, what the use of long deliberations in the Cabinet, if the very policy can be carried out by indirect means which is set aside officially?', asked the Court. The reply was firm. '. . . If your Majesty's meaning is that Viscount Palmerston is to be debarred from communicating with Foreign Ministers except for the purpose of informing them officially of formal decisions of the British Government, Viscount Palmerston would beg humbly and respectfully to represent to your Majesty that such a curtailment of the proper and constitutional functions of the office which he holds would render it impossible for him to serve your Majesty consistently with his own honour or with advantage to the public interest.' Russell had to instruct Cowley to inform Walewski that no opinions were those of Her Majesty's Government 'except those given in the official and regular way'. That left the 'two dreadful old men' (as the Queen would later call them) free to make or respond to private overtures.[14] And by October Napoleon came out against the use of force in Central Italy and a close Anglo-French understanding began to look feasible. On 26th November the cabinet left unaltered not one sentence of a draft dispatch, yet allowed it to be said that Britain would not object to a central Italian kingdom being formed and would prefer it to be ruled by a prince of the House of Savoy.[15]

This project for a separate kingdom, long favoured by the French and by many British ministers, including Gladstone and sometimes even Russell, was never to Palmerston more than a poor substitute for annexation, for which he continued to strive. Indeed, on 3rd January 1860 he unfolded to a shocked cabinet a project for a triple alliance with France and Piedmont to allow the peoples of central Italy to determine their own destiny. If Gladstone's conception of the alliance was not Palmerston's, the triumvirate was nevertheless now seen in action trying, as Clarendon, out of office and very anti-French, said, to cram a policy down the throats of twelve colleagues, with threats of resignation to coerce the cabinet and of dissolution to coerce the Commons. Palmerston was absolutely confident that he could carry parliament and the country, and Gladstone said that for such a noble cause they ought to stake their positions.[16] The moment was favourable, for Napoleon had simultaneously approved the principle of Cobden's commercial treaty with Britain and inspired an article very hostile to Austria and the Pope.

Granville told Palmerston that many ministers had 'insuperable objections to our engaging ourselves to give material assistance'. But he added that all, or nearly all, would 'agree to great moral support to France and to strong moral pressure upon Austria in order to prevent armed interference in Italy'.[17] Palmerston was always irritated by the pusillanimity of people unwilling to threaten action because they deplored action, when he was sure that the threat would make the action unnecessary. He wrestled mightily with his colleagues, in a memorandum circulated to them,[18] which took as its text the assertion that —

the English Government might have determined that, in regard to Italian affairs, England should abdicate its position as one of the great Powers of Europe. We might have said that we live in an island, and care not what may be done on the Continent; that we think only of making money, and of defending our own shores; and that we leave to others the task of settling as they like the affairs of the continent of Europe. . . . But we rightly considered that what is at issue is . . . the interests of the people of Italy, and, through them, the welfare and peace of Europe. . . .

and that Britain was concerned with these. Therefore she had accepted an invitation to the Conference, and indicated the policy which she would strive to get adopted at it. The only question was how best to make that policy prevail, and the obvious answer was to come to an understanding with France and Sardinia, as the Powers 'most able to sway the course of events in Italy and to bring them to the result we wish for . . . for the purpose of common and united action with them'. To wait until the Conference met would be unbusinesslike and dangerous. If such an agreement led to war with Austria, Britain's part would be confined to action by the squadron in the Adriatic, with perhaps service by a couple of regiments there if she were asked for them and saw fit to lend them. But it was in the highest degree probable that the engagement would be the most effective means of preventing war. It might be affirmed 'as confidently as anything can be affirmed as to a future event, that . . . the triple alliance, while it would be honourable to England (I might say, the only course that would be honourable to England), would secure the continuance of peace in Italy, and thereby avert one danger to the general peace of Europe'. If the congress did not meet, the necessity for the alliance was all the greater, and he was sure 'that it would be highly approved by the country, upon the double ground of its own merits, and of its tendency to avert a rupture with France, and to secure the continuance of peace with our neighbour'. In any case, 'I would far rather give up office for maintaining the principle upon which the course I recommend would be founded, than retain office by giving that principle up.'

There was bluster here, for the fall of Palmerston and Russell would not help the Italians, which was the object. Palmerston did not prevail. The cabinet vetoed the treaty. But Austria and France were formally requested in a dispatch of 15th January to abstain from armed interference in Italy, and although this dispatch proposed that new plebiscites be held in central Italy, it thereby upheld the principle of self-determination, destroyed the project for a separate kingdom there, and imposed, by implication, a moral obligation to protect, if necessary, annexation by Piedmont after the plebiscites. For Palmerston and Russell this was an adequate, though disappointing, response to the main proposition put to their colleagues. But France, who had never accepted annexation, was left unrestrained by formal engagements (except to Austria, which she broke), and made it clear that her price for accepting the aggrandizement of Piedmont in Central Italy would be the price surreptitiously agreed at Plombières for procuring the annexation to Piedmont of Lombardy and Venetia. France was to annex Savoy and Nice, after plebiscites which British opinion refused to accept as bona fide. That opinion now became vehemently anti-French.

*   *   *   *

The hostility of British opinion towards France at the time of Palmerston's fall in 1858 obscured its sympathy with the Italians

until the Austrian ultimatum. Then opinion was pro-Italian but
not pro-French. Villafranca enraged all those politically conscious
Britons who were not pro-Austrian, and yet confirmed all the
suspicions of those who had deprecated British favour for Cavour
on the ground that he was merely the unwitting instrument of
French ambitions. Their view was that Napoleon had beaten
Russia with British aid, and then made friends with her; that he
had beaten Austria with British concurrence, and now made
friends with her; that he hoped to use both 'in any subsequent
quarrel with us'. The Prince Consort thought it was Napoleon's
aim next to make war against Prussia on the Rhine, and so become
master of Europe. He concluded that Britain ought to have nothing
to do with France over Italy.[19] Palmerston drew the opposite
conclusion. There was, he said, much to be said for choosing allies
according to the mischief they could do. Austria, usually spoken of
as 'the natural ally' could 'do us no possible harm as an enemy;
France could injure us severely'.[20] Common prudence dictated a
rapprochement with France.

This, we have seen, Palmerston attempted, and partly contrived.
Gladstone was much attracted by this policy, to which the
Cobden treaty would be his own particular contribution. He
approved the idea of a triple alliance, knowing that it was Palmerston's view that it would 'remove to a greater Distance that Rupture with France which sooner or later must be looked to as a
possible if not probable Event'.[20] The reaction of the public, and
of Palmerston, to Savoy and Nice set the commercial treaty in a
different light. It imperilled it, and yet left it, splendid, if alone, as
a sedative and counter-irritant to the prevailing francophobia. It
caused a serious difference of opinion between Palmerston and
Gladstone, and yet, for reasons we shall see, made a breach
between them for the moment less likely.

There has been a tendency to assume that Palmerston's
indignation at the French project of annexing Savoy and Nice was
assumed, because Palmerston was determined not again to fall (as
he had fallen in 1851 and 1858) for failing to give expression to
current hatred of France and because he wished to use the francophobia to secure approval of defence expenditure which Gladstone
opposed. But the indignation was real; it was, indeed, a natural
reflex. Palmerston disliked the annexation; he disliked the
plebiscite even more; he disliked the manner of the announcement

most of all. Since the French declined to enter into any engagements for the continued neutralization (prescribed by the Treaty of Vienna) of the districts of Savoy which abutted Switzerland, he was bound to view the annexation (to which the signatories of Vienna were not invited to assent) as he had viewed the Austrian annexation of Cracow. But the heart of the Vienna Treaty was a series of elaborate arrangements for the containment of France; to this everything else had been subordinated. Napoleon professed to find British vehemence inexplicable — what interest could England have in Savoy, he asked. Had he protested when the British occupied Perim in the Red Sea in 1857?[21] He did not understand the chronic British uneasiness at the fact that the destinies of the foremost military Power on the Continent were ultimately dependent on a man who, though not (as the Prince Consort thought) a cunning planner driving systematically towards the domination of Europe and the reversal of Waterloo, was a plotter and the prey of conflicting emotions, sentiments, judgements, counsels and whims; that he ruled a people whose martial predilections were perhaps only partially counterbalanced by dislike of paying taxes; that he ruled despotically a middle class whose desire for political freedom might have to be diverted, for the safety of the régime, into the channels of chauvinistic adventure. No doubt the evidence cited for the current designs of Frenchmen, partly catalogued by Palmerston in a draft cabinet minute in May,[22] and ranging from the Saar and the Rhenish Palatinate through the Balearics, Genoa, Liguria and the island of Sardinia to Morrocco and Syria, was little stronger than similar evidence in 1859. But in 1859 such moderate men as Herbert and Lewis thought war with France not unlikely in 1860.[23] The aspect was more sinister now. Savoy and Nice smacked of 'natural frontiers' and brought the Saar and the Rhineland, even French-speaking Belgium, into the reckoning. The other designs attributed to the French seemed to confirm Clarendon's fear (which made him seem pro-Austria) that the French war in Italy would prove, like the first Napoleon's, only the prelude to a sustained attack on Britain's position in the Mediterranean, and hence on her empire in the East.[24] A French-sponsored Suez Canal was on the Emperor's agenda. French troops actually went to Syria later in 1860. In such circumstances it was wise to warn the Emperor off by martial talk and diplomatic gambit. That it was wise does not mean that it was not both spontaneous and sincere.

On 26th March 1860 Russell publicly doubted whether a nation so warlike as the French would not call for other acts of aggression, and stated that Britain must be ready to act with other European nations. When, the next day, Flahaut went to No. 10 to seek crumbs of comfort to carry to Paris, Palmerston offered only stones. The Foreign Secretary's speech, he said, represented the unanimous feeling of the country. He (Palmerston) had lost all confidence in Napoleon. People feared schemes and views which tended to war and to array Europe against France. If war was forced upon England she would cheerfully accept it, even alone. The country would rise as one man.[25] When the Queen asked Palmerston to embody in a cabinet minute the policy now to be pursued, he had only to expand what Russell and he had said on 26th–27th March. 'A great and serious change in the aspect of European affairs and in the prospect of European tranquillity' had come about because alliance between Britain and France was possible only so long as French policy was not directed towards territorial aggrandizement, and the general opinion was now that this condition no longer obtained. The French establishments were 'rapidly assuming such a condition as could not be required for peace' and French diplomacy was directed towards separating the Powers from one another. To diagnose was to prescribe. There should be 'a full and frank communication between the Powers' and 'in the meanwhile, it is incumbent upon the British nation to collect its strength, to place its military and naval establishments in the most efficient state of organization, and to secure the means of rapid augmentation'.[26]

The cabinet did not endorse the memorandum. It was more willing to make hostile noises against France than it had been against Austria, but no more willing to make formal engagements against France than a little while ago with her. Nor were such possible. What was possible the cabinet agreed to do. An understanding was reached with Austria and Prussia that any of the three Powers would communicate to the others any overtures from France tending to disrupt the territorial settlement of Europe, and in such a case to discuss what measures should be taken. This was a reiteration of the doctrine of Castlereagh, a reminder of Britain's habitual interest in the Balance of Power. It was Palmerston living up to the prediction of the Austrian foreign minister, Rechberg, who saw in his return to power 'a guarantee to us that he will not lend a hand to establish the preponderance of France in the concert of Europe, already so much to be feared by its military power and the quite extraordinary development of its marine in the last years'.[27] For the foreign minister of the Habsburgs to say this of Palmerston at such a time shows a somewhat belated, but welcome, recognition in Vienna of Palmerston's basic loyalty to the Treaty of Vienna. But, if the French action forced Palmerston to change, for the moment, the tone of British diplomacy, he did not abandon his belief that the best way to restrain France was by co-operation and it was not long before his colleagues had to restrain him from expressing in public his trust in the Emperor.[28]

One minister especially deplored the changed diplomatic posture because he said that, taken with the armaments programme, it made a conflict with France more likely by inviting mutual national hostility.[29] Gladstone had been waiting for something to turn up to prevent the resurrection of the fortifications projects which he hoped he had killed in December 1859;[30] instead, events enabled Palmerston at least partly to prevail. As Palmerston was evidently as sincere and uncompromising on the need for rearmament as was Gladstone on the need for retrenchment and fiscal reform, each was, naturally, suspicious of the other. Gladstone thought as early as January that Palmerston's attitude to the Cobden treaty was 'neutral'.[31] But January was the month when Palmerston pressed for a treaty with France on Italy. Palmerston's attitude to the commercial treaty may, indeed, be described as somewhat detached (Russell's was plain indifferent).[32] If it could be signed and ratified, well and good; it would be a sign not only of imperial enlightenment but of imperial control, at Paris. But he did not believe, as Cobden and Gladstone hoped, that it would mark a major breakthrough towards a continental triumph of Free Trade — the aggrandizement of Piedmont would be a greater victory for that cause. And, of course, he did not accept the Mancunian assumption that the commercial intercourse of peoples necessarily fostered international friendships which rubbed off on to governments. But there is no adequate ground for accepting Bright's allegation that Palmerston did all he could to make the treaty miscarry.[33] It was not of the treaty that he was suspicious, but of its citation by Gladstone to strengthen his argument that an armaments programme was unnecessary, because of French goodwill, an argument which sometimes seemed to slide from the platitude that

Britain's ultimate strength lay in her wealth to the controversial proposition that a defence programme, because it diverted wealth from productive investment, positively weakened the country.

Gladstone did not always bear sufficiently in mind that his colleagues and his chief, somewhat against their judgement, had allowed him to introduce 'measures . . . sufficient to stamp a character on the Session'.[34] By the end of February the main features of the budget, and the treaty, had been approved in principle by the Commons by encouraging majorities. The tariff was to be confined to less than fifty good revenue-earning duties, at the cost of a penny on the income tax. At the moment of the French declaration on Savoy and Nice, Gladstone's parliamentary programme was interrupted, not by Palmerston, but by Russell, who insisted on introducing the Reform Bill indicated for 1860 at the time of the formation of the government. It was based on a compromise agreed between Palmerston and Russell on the eve of Willis's Rooms. Palmerston had then seen some point in trying to settle the question on this basis. [36] He now saw no need to settle it all, but he was not obstructive, and even suggested a procedure for removing a major impediment to the passage of a bill — the dislike of members for a third dissolution in four years.[36] But he was, of course, not displeased when the apathy of the House, and of the country, killed the bill decisively enough for Russell to admit, in the winter, that there was no point in trying again and to go off, in 1861, to the Lords. Nor was Palmerston displeased that Russell's interruption of Gladstone's financial measures, together with some minor delays imposed by the premier himself, held up the verdict of the House on that part of Gladstone's budget which not more than one of his colleagues really liked — the repeal of the paper duties — until European tension, national feeling against France and the British share in the Anglo-French expedition to Pekin provided a colourable case for 'postponing' the repeal of the paper duties while keeping the penny on the income tax.

At the end of April Palmerston proposed to the cabinet that the Paper Duties Bill should be dropped. He was overruled, when Gladstone said he would meet part of the China costs by wines and spirits taxes.[37] But Gladstone secured a third reading to the bill by a majority of only nine. Palmerston then spoke for three-quarters of an hour in cabinet against the Paper Bill being sent up to the Lords. Again he was overruled, but Lady Palmerston was in a cheering gallery when the peers, by a majority of 89, ignored the ministerial argument that to defeat the bill would be contrary to the constitutional conventions which governed parliamentary control of finance.[38] Gladstone did not take kindly Palmerston's letter of commiseration[39] — 'Of course you are mortified and disappointed, but your disappointment is nothing to mine, who had a horse with whom I hoped to win the Derby, and he went amiss at the last moment.' The horse, it seems, had been 'got at'. Gladstone felt that his budget had been got at, and demanded the vindication of the rights of the Commons, if necessary by a special session in which the bill would be reintroduced. Palmerston, with much support from colleagues, wished, as Gladstone complained, to close the controversy by abandoning the privileges of the Commons with some meaningless words as garniture. Whatever the constitutional position, he said, 'the opinion of the great majority of the public is that the Lords have done a right and useful thing . . .', and he agreed with the public.[40] But Russell as well as Milner Gibson backed Gladstone, rather to the latter's surprise, for, though Lord John had warned Palmerston that he must take a more serious view than Palmerston of a Lords' defeat of the Paper Bill, he had said that he would 'endeavour to come to the same conclusion' as the premier (that a struggle between the Houses should be avoided), causing Gladstone to complain that 'Lord John leans so much upon Palmerston in regard to foreign affairs that he is weaker in other subjects when opposed to him, than might be desired'.[41] When Malmesbury conveyed to the Palmerstons Tory assurances that if he lost Russell over Reform and Gladstone over the paper duties the Opposition would protect the government against the Radicals, they said they did not wish to lose Russell.[42] To keep Lord John, Palmerston 'with middling grace' agreed to move for committees of the Commons to search the journals and muster the precedents. When he did so, he told the Commons he had no view to hostility against the House of Lords; he virtually said, Gladstone protested, 'We mean nothing.' The outcome was a series of three resolutions introduced by the premier in a speech described by the Speaker as a great success but 'rather too much of an apology for the Lords to have been spoken by the Leader of the House of Commons'. Derby called it 'the best tight-rope dancing he ever saw'.[43] The metaphors of sport and entertainment which tripped so naturally from the tongue or pen of Palmerston and Derby seemed to the Chancellor of the Exchequer to betray a shameful levity on such sacred subjects as sound finance and constitutional ethics. Gladstone had verbally, on 2nd July, submitted his resignation, demanding action, not tepid resolutions. But he contented himself with speaking after Palmerston, denouncing the action of the Lords as 'a gigantic innovation', and explaining to his colleagues that while he could never have been a party to a statement that the rights of the Commons would not be vindicated he could agree, reluctantly, to abstaining from vindication at the present.[44] He stayed in office, but 'on the half-cock of resignation'[45] to fight the battle of the fortifications.

* * * *

'England will not be listened to in Europe, and be powerless for the preservation of the general peace . . . if she is known to be despicably weak in her military resources', wrote the Queen to Derby in January 1859.[46] Palmerston thoroughly agreed, and told Gladstone that he had but two public objects left in view, the extinction of the Negro slave trade and putting the country into an adequate state of defence by naval building and fortifications.[47] Gladstone, who had found on arrival at the Treasury (Tory) Estimates providing for 'a scale of expenditure . . . far more prodigal and wanton than I had ever charged upon Lord Palmerston's first government' said (but not to Palmerston) that he would not have joined the administration had he known of the premier's views on rearmament.[48] Gladstone, as is well known, believed that wealth should fructify in the pockets of the people. Palmerston believed that national wealth without defences merely offered the butcher a well-fatted calf instead of a well-armed bull's head.[49] By the end of 1859 a Royal Commission had reported that ten million pounds should be spent on the landward defences of the main dockyards and naval arsenals. Palmerston pressed for action at once, but agreed to desist until Gladstone's budgetary scheme was well and truly launched.[30]

France's annexation of Savoy and Nice, Palmerston said, had only two compensations — it exposed the hollowness of the Emperor's professions of disinterestedness in helping the Italians, and 'it would make People here more ready to complete our Defences'.[50] He might have added a third, arising out of the second. If in December 1859 he had insisted on a decision to launch a ten-million-pound programme, he would, almost certainly, have prevailed, and it is perhaps likely that Gladstone, for the sake of the Cobden treaty and the budget, would have stayed in office. But of this there was doubt. The 'panic' which started in March, and led to fear of invasion, Gladstone said, 'by men usually rational', made it all but certain that Palmerston would be able to initiate the programme *with Gladstone in the cabinet*. The Chancellor, for all his protests, knew in his heart that the government could survive his resignation and that to go on this issue would be to court unpopularity. Even Graham thought 'the risk of being taken off our guard . . . very serious'.[51] French actions and attitudes deprived Gladstone's main political argument, that it was foolish to display simultaneously trust and mistrust, of its force. The argument had never impressed Palmerston, who wondered at the naïveté of those who could not see that if, while professing trust, one takes precautions in case the trust proves misplaced, the trust is the more likely to be well-founded. When seeking the maximum co-operation with France, Palmerston wrote to Russell that 'the only expression we ought to give or anything like suspicion should be in the activity and scale of our defensive arrangements. In regard to them . . . we must not be overruled by financial economy'.[52] If Her Majesty's dispersed forces were to be capable of concentration to defend London should some part of the French army of 600,000 succeed in landing, and the maritime bases to play their vital role in a counter-blow, then Portsmouth, Plymouth, Chatham and Cork must be put in such a state as to be capable of defending themselves by land and sea. Nine to eleven million pounds must be spent on fortifications as quickly as possible, that in three or four years the country might be entirely secured. The money was to be raised by borrowing, partly because if the work was begun out of current revenue there was more likelihood of it being left unfinished. Palmerston allowed Gladstone to proceed with his budget only after satisfying himself that there would be money available to meet the charges on the first part of a loan.

In February Gladstone told Palmerston that to propose a loan for fortifications would be 'on my part with the views I entertain, a betrayal of my public duty'.[53] In April the Chancellor was sticky about finding £150,000 to keep the militia embodied, a step deemed necessary in view of the deterioration of relations with France. He retreated only when Sidney Herbert, the Secretary of State for

War, resigned. 'We must not part with him for so small a sum. He is by far the best administrator of Army Matters I have ever known', wrote Palmerston, adding that any successor would be bound to take the same view.[54] In July the issue of the fortifications could no longer be avoided, for the end of the session was at hand. Gladstone argued that it could be postponed till next year. But Palmerston said that would be 'a breach of our public Duty'.[55] He had all along been resolved to get a start in 1860. He would rather lose Gladstone than risk losing Plymouth and Portsmouth. 'There might be some Persons in the House of Commons with peculiar notions on Things in General and with very imperfect notions as to our National Interest', he declared, 'who will object to the proposed Measures, but I cannot bring myself to believe that the Majority of the present House of Commons, or the House of Commons that would be elected on an appeal on this Question to the People of the Country would refuse to sanction Measures so indisputably necessary.'[56] Gladstone's friends warned him that 'if you ride a high horse, objecting to the whole principle of making the great dockyards into strong places, . . . you will not be supported by public feeling'.[57] He left the ground of 'insuperable objection' and began to parley, stating at last that 'concessions have been made beyond my expectation at the last moment and under great pressure'.[58] The main concession was that annual authorization by parliament should be sought. This would enable Gladstone to fight the good fight again next year. Palmerston thought this was childish; it would only mean a repetition of 'ineffectual opposition and ultimate acquiescence'.[59]

Gladstone could not bring himself to attend the House when Palmerston announced a four year programme to be met by terminable annuities of nine million pounds in all, two million of which parliament was now invited to authorize for the twelve months to July 1861. Having read this speech, he at once complained that it was not in the spirit of their agreement. Palmerston's retort was sharp: 'I never intimated that I should not open the whole Scheme to Parliament, and endeavour as far as my speech and the Debate in the House could go, to pledge Parliament to the Adoption of the Whole.'[60] As the session came to a close, workmen began to lay the foundations of those fortifications at Plymouth and Portsmouth later known as 'Palmerston's follies'. Everyone remarked how wonderfully well and fresh the veteran looked, 'after his horrible Session's work', by comparison with his jaded Commons colleagues.[61] It is true that, thanks to Gladstone and Cobden, more of the Commons programme than usual was financial, true also for the first time since December 1851 (except for a very few months in 1855) the Foreign Secretary was in the Commons. But Palmerston was unwearying in attendance, in constant concert with the whips, assiduous in inspecting the Orders of the Day, on the look out (not to put too fine a point on it) for signs of Gladstone 'pulling a fast one'. The Queen thanked him for his nightly reports, always interesting, she said, and sometimes very amusing.[62] Certainly his humour did not flag. The latest toast of the young men-about-town was a delicious young lady known as 'Skittles' Waters. When Elgin inquired whether he might take (Admiral) Bowles to China with him, Palmerston replied: 'By all means, but I think you'd find Skittles pleasanter.' Asked to hold a Day of Humiliation because the harvest had been ruined, he said that if it was ruined it was past praying for.[63]

Gladstone, overlooking what he had been able to achieve, 'subsided at last into repose by the sea-side' in a mood of disgruntlement. He complained of the feebleness of the government, due to the want of an effective head, and of the timidity and vacillation of his colleagues. 'It is a vile precedent to give away money by remission, and borrow to supply the void', he groaned, certain that the 'void' was due to the policy of Palmerston and Russell.[64] He might have reflected that the cabinet which supported Palmerston against him (on the fortifications and the quarrel with the Lords) had supported him against Palmerston (on the Paper Duties Bill) and that he himself, with his treaty and his budget, had been the chief beneficiary of the relatively free hand given to departmental ministers when there was a 'want of an effective head'. Palmerston believed in a light rein except on matters on which he felt especially strongly. He had much cause for good spirits as the session ended for, as Granville said, everything really wanted had been done (except for bankruptcy law reform) and much that nobody wanted had been left undone.[65] Palmerston had tried to squeeze (from Gladstone) time for the Bankruptcy Bill, describing it as 'a Measure of very great importance to all the trading and Commercial Interests . . . the only one of the three great Measures of Law Reform which were announced in the Queen's Speech that we have any chance of passing'.[66] At the very end of the session he sent directly to Derby to secure the reversal by the Lords of a vote against Gladstone's Savings Banks Bill.[67] The future was (after Palmerston's death) to be Gladstone's, but he was not yet 'the People's William'. The Palmerstons' short tour of the Yorkshire cities was triumphant. Granville thought the premier decidedly the most powerful man in the country, and doubted his losing his prestige until his strength failed him, unless there was serious discontent due to bad trade and another bad harvest.[68]

CHAPTER XXV

THE LORD WARDEN, 1861–3

R ADICAL delight at the victories of Garibaldi in Sicily and Naples and the Piedmontese invasion of the Roman States made Palmerston's visit to Yorkshire in October 1860 timely. He, and Russell, and Gladstone were all in close and friendly touch with Italian emigrés and envoys in London, and it was widely argued then, and since, that at Shaftesbury's 'house of call for refugees', a conspiracy had been forged by Azeglio, Lady Palmerston and Shaftesbury to poison the premier's mind against Napoleon as an enemy of Italy united under the House of Savoy.[1] But Cavour himself was for months uncertain whether Garibaldi was working for the House of Savoy or not. Even as late as 28th September Palmerston insisted that the government in Turin 'ought to treat Garibaldi as an ally and not an enemy'. Always attracted, as was the British people, by the heroism of Garibaldi's exploits, he was prepared to say (though serious indeed would be the implications for the peace of Europe if he were wrong): 'I believe in the honesty of Garibaldi, and in his singleness of purpose. He wants to unite all Italy under Victor Emmanuel. . . .' He had the advantage of reports from his private secretary, Evelyn Ashley, whom he had dispatched to the South after the end of the session.[2] By 26th October Palmerston felt it safe to speak at Leeds of the successful action of opinion, but of opinion only, in the affairs of Italy, and safe also to approve the astonishing dispatch from Russell, dated the next day, which welcomed in extravagant terms an outcome which Britain had never officially blessed and had sometimes publicly deprecated. On 9th November Garibaldi sailed from the Bay of Naples in a British warship, with his bag of seed-corn, bound for his island retreat of Caprera.

What Palmerston did not say at Leeds was that in January he had thought a triple alliance necessary to secure that 'liberation of the Italian people from a foreign yoke' which, as Russell informed the Queen on 9th February in a letter which Palmerston had to get him to withdraw because of the Queen's objection to its tone, was 'in the eyes of Lord Palmerston and Lord John Russell, an increase of freedom and happiness at which as well-wishers of mankind they cannot but rejoice'.[3a] He did not reveal that, as part of a consistent effort to prevent the involvement of Venetia (still under the foreign yoke) Russell (with the assent only of the Queen) had on 31st August sent a strange dispatch reminding Piedmont that Britain had interests in the Adriatic,[3b] or that nearly three months earlier Russell had privately assured Azeglio of British support against an Austrian intervention.[3c] He did not say that he had vainly urged on Russell in May that Piedmont be offered a British alliance with the threat to support, if necessary with the navy, a reformed Bourbon monarchy if Turin failed to comply, and vainly repeated the proposal in July when, the Bourbon king having proclaimed the reforms urged on him (as on his father before him) by Britain and France, the most appropriate British policy would seem to have been to try to secure co-operation between Piedmont and Naples. This policy was, indeed, officially commended by both Britain and France and was toyed with by Cavour,[3d] but Russell did not like it. For though Palmerston continued to assure the Queen that it would be better from an English point of view to have a separate kingdom in the South,[3e] Russell acted, and talked, as though he had never declared in August 1859 that the unification of Naples and Sicily with the North was a 'wild and foolish' dream which, if it came true, 'would make a despotism instead of a free government, an unwieldy power instead of a compact one, and . . . increase tenfold the European difficulties'.[3f] Palmerston left his auditors to assume that a consistent policy of non-intervention had been willingly and deliberately followed by him and Russell with the intention of producing the result which the arms of Garibaldi and Victor Emmanuel had by now achieved, although Russell had informed Cowley on 23rd July that he did not wish to see the crown of the Two Sicilies on the head of the King of Sardinia. He did not say that this same dispatch urged Anglo-French good offices to reconcile the Houses of Savoy and Bourbon.

There is, however, an element of consistency, not only in the official policy as approved by the Queen (out of dislike for Cavour and Garibaldi and a conviction that the former was always to be looked upon, as Russell once said, as Prefect of the Department of the Po) and by the cabinet (out of passivity), but in the attitudes of Palmerston and Russell. What Azeglio reported to Turin on 14th

April — that 'Italy is still for them what it was before, a favoured land whose progress and education they watch with the liveliest sympathies' — was pre-eminently true of Palmerston and Russell. If it was not yet quite true that they wished 'for nothing better than to see us annex the whole peninsula' it was only because that seemed, until Garibaldi went to Sicily, an idle dream, unless circumstances arose in which 'it is no longer Italy which is at stake but the peace and balance of all Europe'.[39] But on 17th May Palmerston wrote to Russell that there was no strong objection to the unification of all Italy into one monarchy and Russell replied enthusiastically that 'one must expect that Umbria and the Marches as well as Naples will fall and proclaim Victor Emmanuel'. He informed a sceptical queen that another Prussia in the south of Europe would 'in all probability be a new guarantee for the Balance of Power'.[3h] The two old men were clearly prepared to welcome what in fact ensued, *provided that* non-intervention was the policy of all the Powers, not merely Britain, and provided especially that there were no more compensations for France. It was for fear of these that Palmerston was willing to intervene diplomatically, in a way that might have led to a commitment to defend a reformed Neapolitan kingdom, and Russell to recommend an Anglo-French policy of reconciling Victor Emmanuel and Francis. But Russell especially was profoundly unwilling to thwart a unification which, miraculously, became possible without French aid to Piedmont, and which France clearly did not desire. Should the Anglo-French good offices fail, he said in his dispatch to Cowley of 23rd July, the Powers should leave the people of Southern Italy, as they had earlier left those of Tuscany, etc., to determine their own future. Thus he welcomed the cabinet's rejection of the French proposal for joint armed mediation in the Strait of Messina, which was virtually an invitation to stop Garibaldi invading Naples. It has been said of this 'refusal to concert with France' that 'there can have been few negative actions producing greater results'.[1] In fact, the cabinet's decision was not to stop Garibaldi, but also not to stop the French stopping Garibaldi, and Napoleon's decision that he desired that 'Italy pacify itself, no matter how, but without foreign intervention'[3i] was not an automatic response to a British veto, though it was, among other things, a recognition that Britain must not for a second time be allowed to appear the one dis-interested friend of Italian cause. That is why a British policy of non-intervention, the exercise of the power of 'opinion only', was effective. The central fact about the Italian Question in mid-1860 is, as Mr Mack Smith has said, that 'in order to prevent Italy emerging as a client of France, Russell was ready to vie with Napoleon for Cavour's favour and gratitude. The mutual distrust between Britain and France was an invaluable fact, easily exploited in emergencies, and one more indication that fate was on Italy's side'.[3j]

The French reservations about recognizing a kingdom of Italy excluding only Venetia and the city of Rome, allowed her to play again that role. So Russell framed the famous and extraordinary dispatch of 27th October 1860,* which read more like a proclamation than a formal diplomatic document, and was, to the horror of the Queen, published by Cavour as such.[4a]

This manifesto is, from one point of view, the *locus classicus* of that British patronage of constitutionalism which distinguished Palmerston's diplomacy from that of his predecessors. It avowed that the peoples of Southern and Central Italy had looked forward to the overthrow of their rulers as a necessary preliminary to the improvement of their condition and had deemed that they could secure their independence from foreign control only by forming one strong government for the whole of Italy. The Italians themselves were the best judges of their own interests and, as it was evident that they had good reasons for rising against their rulers, on the 1688 parallel Britain could not pretend to blame the King of Sardinia for assisting them. Moreover, the Italian revolution had been conducted with singular temper and forbearance; there had been no outburst of popular vengeance and the extreme views of the democrats had nowhere prevailed. 'The venerated forms of constitutional Monarchy have been associated with the name of a Prince who represents an ancient and glorious Dynasty. . . . Her Majesty's Government can see no sufficient ground for the severe censure with which Austria, France, Prussia and Russia have visited the acts of the King of Sardinia. Her Majesty's Government will turn their eyes rather to the gratifying prospect of a people building up the edifice of their liberties, and consolidating the work of their independence, amid the sympathies and good wishes of Europe.' Here is enshrined the Palmerstonian concept of Britain as the enunciator of the public opinion of Europe in defiance of the other great Powers of Europe. But Palmerston did not write the dispatch, and it is redolent of

Palmerston addressing the House of Commons

Russell's Foxite Whiggery — though he wrote a dispatch exhorting Cavour, on grounds of policy, not to intervene in the South, and admitted to the Queen that intervention for purposes of acquisition would be criminal, he insisted that intervention at the behest of the peoples concerned would not be morally wrong, even if the effect was acquisition, and cited with a repetition which Victoria found tedious the legist Vattel's approval of the actions of William of Orange in 1688.[4b] The dispatch also goes nearer to approving nationalism, or at least an Italian nationalism, as an *ism* than Palmerston can have liked, for it was impossible to deny that what applied to Central and Southern Italy would apply also to Venetia and Rome.

Indeed, what alarmed Palmerston about the unification of Italy was that it was unfinished business, so long as Rome and Venetia were outwith the monarchy of Victor Emmanuel. The implications, for the peace of Europe, of Italy, Russia and Prussia, as well as, presumably, France, all having ambitions unattainable except by war involving at least two Great Powers, were alarming. Palmerston never accepted the view that in the long run an Italy united and free of Austria would be a mere pawn of France. But the German Nationalists were not inclined to allow Austria to be driven from Venetia by force, and it was not easy to see how Venetia could be joined to Italy without a dangerous European war fought on the Rhine as well as in the Alps. British diplomacy after 1860 had therefore to work against war in Venetia. But until Venetia was free, Italy was apt to be tied to France, as the only Power who could free it. And, as Russell proposed to say, in a 'hands off' dispatch to Paris against which the Queen protested (3rd November) and which the cabinet killed, 'if France were to sway the united navies of Genoa and Naples, and Great Britain to look on from fear or apathy or excessive love of peace, she might soon to have to defend her possessions of Malta, Corfu and Gibraltar'.[5] Once again, therefore, Palmerston suggested that Austria surrender Venetia freely, at a price which would enable her to fortify her new frontier. But the cabinet (December 1860) refused to make a formal approach. And the Austrians were, as ever, insensitive to argument on the matter.

* * * *

A fluid and uncertain diplomatic situation strengthened, if that were possible, Palmerston's determination to improve the defensive

R

power of Britain. The fact that a confrontation between Britain and France over Southern Italy had been averted in no way weakened his belief that a good understanding between them was possible only as long as British naval superiority was maintained. Even Cobden pointed out in Paris that an insane rivalry which, he feared, could only lead to war, had been initiated by the French naval programme.[6] Setting little store by the iron casing of wooden ships already taken in hand in Britain ('paste-board construction', he called it), Palmerston insisted that future conversions must be superior in strength and technique and that in future iron ships must be built. Moreover, he declared that unless action was taken at once, in 1861, the French fleet would be, by the end of 1863, for practical purposes, stronger than the British.[7] This conviction necessarily involved him in controversy with Gladstone. Indeed, the Chancellor's first reaction when the premier raised the question in February 1861 was to draft (but not send) a letter of resignation, because of 'the unseemliness of my renewing during the present Session a series of struggles such as were those of last year upon the Fortifications, the Paper Duty and the Question of Taxing Bills'. He had always known, he said, that the fortifications loan would become a precedent for unsound finance, and, though he approved (tacitly) the issue of more terminable annuities for forts, he resisted the suggestion that part of them be used for ships.[8]

Gladstone could not have been kept in the cabinet if he had not been allowed to propose the repeal of the paper duties and adopt the device (used ever since) of a single Finance Bill incorporating all the budgetary proposals, which, by convention, the Lords would not be able to amend (and which, till 1909, they never took the risk of defeating). Palmerston was beaten easily in cabinet on this. But Gladstone, partly from a sincere attachment to retrenchment, and partly from a well justified fear that an amendment to substitute a reduced income tax for the repeal of the paper duties would be carried in the Commons with the not altogether secret approval of the premier, proposed to postpone the operation of repeal for six months in order to reduce the income tax. Palmerston condemned this Gladstonian finance as irresponsible, because it left no slack for contingencies. According to Gladstone, he lost his temper for the first time in cabinet, and though he yielded gracefully on 13th April, he wrote, the following day, to the Chancellor a letter described with reason by its recipient as 'strange and painful'. The prime minister informed the Chancellor of the Exchequer in writing that he disapproved the budget proposals to which he had 'acquiesced reluctantly' in cabinet, and was unwilling to make it a question of confidence.[9] This extraordinary epistle is scarcely palliated by the fact that Gladstone, at the beginning of the year, had tried to arm himself for the battle with his colleagues over the Estimates by soliciting a round-robin in favour of economies from Liberal M.P.s.[10] Gladstone sent a soft answer to turn away wrath, and in the crucial debate on Horsfall's amendment to reduce the tea duties instead of repealing the paper duties, Russell made 'a capital speech' and Palmerston weighed in with a fierce attack on Father Daly's attempt to blackmail him into restoring the subsidy on the Galway transatlantic packet service by threatening that Irish votes would be withheld that night in the lobby.[11]

The Government majority of 15 caused mixed feelings at Cambridge House, for the Tories had made it clear that their object was not to replace Palmerston by Derby but to relieve him of Gladstone and Milner Gibson. Malmesbury had come in January to repeat the Opposition's pledge not to 'enter into combinations and cabals to embarrass the government', while reserving the right to criticize Russell's diplomacy (which was, in detail, slapdash and crude). He asked in return only that Palmerston would protect the Tories from a 'democratising' budget.[12] The knowledge, or suspicion, that Palmerston had Opposition assurances of support if the chief champions of retrenchment left the cabinet was bound to operate as a curb on Gladstone, provided he was granted his chief priorities and was met by compromise on other financial points. There was, as usual, a compromise on the Naval Estimates. But less than a month later, Palmerston asked urgently for cabinet approval of a three million pound loan which, he reckoned, would just enable the Royal Navy to float twenty-seven heavy iron ships to France's twenty-six in 1863.[13] As on fortifications in 1860, the crisis came in July. On 19th Palmerston was in a rare (and perhaps assumed) rage, because, after Gladstone's criticisms of the estimates on which William Cowper had based the ministerial bill for the reconstruction of the Law Courts had been overruled in cabinet, Gladstone submitted to the House a minute repeating those criticisms. Palmerston astutely claimed the prerogatives of Peel, in Gladstone's eyes the perfect premier. 'I have not made it my Practise to interfere with the detailed Business of the Board of Treasury of which I am the Head', he wrote, 'but I wish it to be clearly understood beween us that I do not intend to be set aside as I have been on this occasion, and to be made without my Knowledge and Consent a virtual Party to Proceedings of which I intirely disapprove.' Rubbing in his advantage, the premier wrote the same night: '. . . The Naval Question is extremely pressing and important. . . . It is absolutely necessary that we should take immediate and active Measures to keep Pace with the French.'[14]

Palmerston had always despised the recurrent argument that as long as Britain was rich she was strong. 'No doubt a full Exchequer is a good Foundation for National Defence', he wrote, 'but if the superstructure is wanting, the Foundation would be of small avail and if the French had the Command of the Sea they would soon find the means to make a full Exchequer empty.'[15] He also parried the ingenious argument that technological change was now so rapid that the only sensible policy was a 'standstill'. The imminent inferiority of the navy was mainy due to the caution with which the authorities had turned over to iron, as previously to screw. His thoughts were not on the eventual design of the great iron ships, but on the gap which threatened within two or three years to give Napoleon an unexampled opportunity to strike at Britain with hope of commanding the Channel. And the danger he feared was real — too real to merit any notice being taken of the perennial argument of Gladstone and Cobden that a naval programme would irritate the French, to Palmerston the most stupid of the appeasers' cries. There was, however, enough point in the argument about rapidly changing design to justify Palmerston reducing his demand for three million pounds at once to one million, which would allow for continuing experiment in improved armour and projectiles, the results of which might be incorporated in all but the first of the new ships. Gladstone accepted this compromise, privately admitting that, on the defence question, Palmerston more nearly represented national opinion than he did himself.[16]

*　　*　　*　　*

Once again, it was noted that Palmerston began the session 'stronger than ever . . . in political position' and ended it 'retain

[ing] a great hold on the country, both from his merits and his faults'. 'I saw him the other night', reported Granville, 'looking very well, but old, and wearing a green shade, which he afterwards concealed. He looked like a retired old croupier from Baden.'[17] He was more worried about his wife's health than his own, and thought that a summer stay at Walmer Castle near Deal, his official residence in his new capacity as Lord Warden of the Cinque Ports (a title in the royal gift), did her good. No doubt he himself relished sitting at Pitt's desk at Walmer, where that devoted premier (whom Palmerston at 21 aspired to succeed as member for Cambridge University) had mused on invasion prospects sixty years before as Winston Churchill (later himself Lord Warden) did eighty years after. But as the year ended Lady Palmerston began to wonder for the first time whether he could live to see the crucial year of the naval race (1863). Considering the story of the relations between the two men, he seemed disproportionately distressed by the death of the Prince Consort, of typhoid fever, at the age of forty-two. Granville had never seen him so low in spirits. And in less than a week the rumour spread that Palmerston was dead. This was premature, but he had his worst attack ever of gout in hands and feet, and since, in severe attacks of gout, when the kidneys have been affected, blood pressure mounts and there is risk of seizure, colleagues expected hourly to hear of a seizure. Immediately after Christmas he was reported better, in the New Year recovered though very lame, in mid-January, well. 'His death at this moment would be a national misfortune, when we consider who the men are who are likely to succeed him among the Whig party', commented Malmesbury.[18]

The Radicals of the Mancunian brand naturally did not agree. Bright and, less clearly, Cobden in concert with Persigny, had made, in 1860, overtures to the Tories to turn Palmerston out. Now, as 1861 gave way to 1862, they were convinced, at first that Palmerston and Russell were willing to rush to war with North America, leaving the country exposed to the French; then that Palmerston was revelling in 'brinkmanship' ('Palmerston likes to drive the wheel close to the edge, and show how dexterously he can avoid falling over the precipice'); then that, though he knew there would be no war, he and the *Post* kept alive 'the wicked passions in this country' in order to secure 'reckless expenditure'. This, Cobden said, 'was like the man, and that is the worst that can be said of it'.[19] These strictures are, in the main, unjust, as an examination of the crisis in relations with the Northern states, engaged in civil war with the South, reveals. In particular, it must be said that no minister could 'know' there would be no war unless he had complete reliance on the disposition of President Lincoln and some of his cabinet to resist the irresponsibility of Seward, the Secretary of State, a virulently anti-British press and a scarcely less virulent Congress, a reliance which no man in his senses could feel. The Northerners did not seem to understand that Europe could, except from animosity to them, regard the Confederates as other than mere rebels, or why, when Congress empowered the President to close by proclamation any port in Confederate hands, Russell should so promptly indicate that Her Majesty could not acknowledge 'that ports in the complete possession of the (so-called) Confederate States, and which are not blockaded, shall be interdicted to the commerce of Her Majesty's Subjects' by mere municipal law of the United States.[20] The British Proclamation of Neutrality of course recognized, in effect, two belligerents, so that the Northern blockade had to be 'effective' to be recognized in International Law. It was indeed soon effective enough (the South having virtually no navy) as to produce a severe cotton famine in Lancashire, and a considerable public demand for the diplomatic recognition of the South based on the misapprehension that this would cause the cotton to start flowing across the Atlantic again.

Palmerston and Russell knew, of course, that this was not so. But their class was, in general, sympathetic with the South or, at least, hostile to the North as representing a noxious combination of plutocracy and democracy, Protectionism and a nationalism that threatened Canada. They (like Gladstone) thought, and (unlike Gladstone) hoped, that the North would fail to subdue the South. All the triumvirs thought that in due course Europe — and effectively Britain and France — would have to mediate. The French early wished to go further, to recognize the South and forcibly break the blockade. Russell, in October 1861, was attracted by the notion. He suggested to Palmerston that Britain and France might propose terms of pacification that seemed to them fair and equitable and join the party which accepted them (presumably the South) against the party that rejected them (i.e., the North, fighting to maintain the Union). But Palmerston said that it would be an infringement of national independence thus to interfere, only rarely to be justified by danger to the interfering parties themselves. It would not be justified by the want of cotton, unless the distress in the manufacturing districts grew worse than seemed likely (and he stirred up the Board of Trade to scour the world for alternative supplies). He saw that a correct attitude must be maintained if mediation was ever to be acceptable to both parties. 'The only thing to do', he said, 'seems to be to lie on our oars, and to give no pretext to the Washingtonians to quarrel with us, while, on the other hand, we maintain our rights and those of our fellow-countrymen.'[21]

Thanks to Palmerston's sense of responsibility, the Radical historian Grote was able to write of this war as 'the single case in which the English Government and public — generally so meddlesome — have displayed most prudent and commendable forbearance in spite of great temptations to the contrary'.[22] This was the more remarkable since, as Cobden pointed out to Senator Sumner, John Bull had never before been neutral when great naval operations were in train and did not take kindly to the experience.[23] The Americans, moreover, so keen on 'the freedom of the seas' and 'neutral rights' and hostile to 'paper blockades' when they had been neutral as between Britain and France, now showed an arrogant disregard for the niceties of international law. The S.S. *San Jacinto* (U.S.A.) early in November 1861 took off the British mail packet *Trent*, homeward bound from Havanna, Mason and Slidell, the envoys accredited by the Confederate Government to Britain and France. Since, when the *San Jacinto* was hanging about the Channel to intercept the envoys, the Law Officers had given the cabinet a clear opinion that to remove them and allow the ship to proceed was clean contrary to international law, the cabinet at once concluded that this was 'a gross outrage and violation of international law' for which reparation and apology must be required. In a furious burst of energy before his serious illness, Palmerston stopped the export of arms to the North and rushed further reinforcements to Canada. He had to take the matter seriously, for public opinion did, and he had only recently received assurances from the Federal envoy that the war steamer had orders not to meddle with any vessel under a foreign flag.[24] It was on this assurance that Prince Albert, as his last intervention in public affairs, seized to amend the draft dispatch to Washington, so that the Americans were given the plainest of hints to reply (as they did) that the captain had not acted on instructions and that they would restore the envoys to British protection. It is possible that the Prince's amendment made all the difference, but Russell wrote privately on 1st December to Lyons in Washington that it was 'the disposition of the Cabinet ... to accept the liberation of the captive commissioners, and to be rather easy about the apology'.[25] Cobden warned his American friends that there must infallibly be war if the Americans asserted the doctrine that a belligerent had the right to remove enemy personnel from neutral ships, which would have rendered a Kossuth passing into exile liable to be removed from a British ship by the Austrians or a Pole by the Russians.[26]

The Federals were soon to have cause to protest that British neutrality was not 'strict and impartial', as it professed to be.[27] While Northern seapower enabled the North to import weapons and material from Britain almost at will, the only hope the South had of breaking this power lay in procuring ships abroad. After due inspection, the British authorities at Nassau in the Bahamas had released a ship which, as the Confederate privateer, *Florida*, preyed on Northern shipping and frequented British colonial ports. At the time of the *Trent* affair, the Federal minister, Adams, drew Russell's attention to 'no 290' on the stocks at Laird's shipyard at Birkenhead. Britain's Foreign Enlistment Act allowed the authorities to detain a vessel if there were a prima facie case that it was being equipped for the purpose of making war on a friendly Power. In June and July the customs officials at Liverpool ruled there was no such case. On 28th July, while the Law Officers in London were considering documents submitted by Adams, including the opinion of R. P. Collier, Q.C., that it would be difficult to find a stronger case of violation of the Act, 'no. 290', incomplete and without a regular crew, slipped away for 'sea-trials', missed a detention order by a few hours, and was fitted and commissioned in the Azores as the Confederate warship *Alabama*. It is not possible to say with certainty that there was no 'tip-off' from a government office, but there is no evidence that it came from, or with the connivance or knowledge of, any minister.

In the autumn of 1863 the Government detained, and the Admiralty bought (at Palmerston's suggestion) two ironclads being built on the Mersey whose purpose could not be in doubt, as

they were 'rams'. But it was some years before Russell was willing
to admit that he ought to have ordered the detention of 'no.
290' pending the Law Officers' report. He himself, indeed, supported by the pro-Northern Argyll, was willing to order her to be
detained if she touched at any part of Her Majesty's dominions, but
this gave rise to a 'perfect insurrection' in the cabinet.[28] In
November Adams formally solicited 'redress for national and
private injuries' inflicted by the *Alabama*, and 'a more effective
prevention of any repetition of such lawless and injurious proceedings in Her Majesty's ports hereafter'. The government
rejected both demands, and continued, as long as Palmerston lived,
to refuse either compensation or reference to a foreign arbitrator.
Palmerston always held that, since everyone was jealous of Britain's
wealth and power, no arbitration involving her could ever be
impartial. Russell said that 'trumpery cases' — such as whether
some British naval officers gaoled after an incident in a Brazilian
inn had been sober and insulted or drunk and insolent — might be
submitted to arbitration but that he would rather pay twenty
million pounds direct to the United States than submit to a foreign
Power the question whether the government, Law Officers and
parliament had acted properly. Palmerston would certainly have
protested, as Russell did, against the submission of the *Alabama*
claims to arbitration by Gladstone and Granville, which resulted
in an award against Britain (1871).[29]

*   *   *   *

No doubt Palmerston rejoiced that the *Trent* affair kept up his
popularity at the beginning of the 1862 session and impeded
Gladstone in his opposition to the increases in the Army Estimates
demanded by Cornewall Lewis, who had succeeded the dying
Herbert at the War Office. In presenting his budget, however,
Gladstone said that 'the epoch of retrenchment [had] commenced'. Disraeli said that statistically this was untrue and that it
was politically immoral for Gladstone to hold his office while
perpetually insinuating that he disapproved the expenditure for
which he budgeted. Palmerston complained similarly to the
Chancellor that his speeches invited agitation to force his colleagues
to retrace steps they had taken deliberately and responsibly. He
denied Gladstone's thesis that the country had forced the government to high (and, by implication, unnecessary) expenditure by

'panics' (Cobden's term). There had been, on the part of all, he said — country, parliaments, governments — an 'apathetic Blindness' and lethargy, and all shared the *merit* of having awakened to the danger from France, 'not indeed to rush into exravagant and uncalled for Exertions, but to make up gradually for former omissions'. But Gladstone was incorrigible. The English people, he said, had proved their spirit but shown less than their usual high degree of political intelligence and self-possession. There had been some panic, and much precipitancy, and a misreading of the spirit and intentions of France. He held that Palmerston was feeding not only expenditure, but the spirit of expenditure, which was far worse, and a Chancellor who saw real public danger in the course of things had a duty to improve as far as he could public opinion on these topics.

There was perhaps something to be said for Gladstone's view when one remarked how early in April the Commons 'ran wild' about iron-cased floating batteries for coastal defence in view of the havoc wrought by the Confederates' turreted iron-clad, *Monitor*, before her inconclusive but promising engagement with the *Merrimac*, which relied on broadsides. This caused the government to halt the recently begun batteries at Spithead. The enormous cost of total and sweeping changes in maritime construction, which nevertheless bordered on construction for obsolescence, had already caused Disraeli in a speech of July 1861 hailed by Cobden as most able and statesmanlike to glance at the possibility of an agreement with France on limitation, an idea brushed aside by Palmerston as Utopian when Cobden had urged it.[32] Now, in June 1862, Disraeli thought it expedient to raise the note of economy. He extolled past expenditure to discourage new. It was difficult, he said, to see how any country could be in a position more completely secure and for Palmerston to keep on talking about being prepared against some midnight foray by a cordial ally confounded civilization; it was 'a mystification too monstrous for belief'. The Enfield rifle had replaced the smooth-bore Brown Bess; all the regulars, militia, volunteers and the forces in Canada had the new weapon. All the overseas garrisons, home garrisons and field artillery had the Armstrong. 'From the siege-train to the ambulance England was never so profusely and so effectively furnished as at the present moment. . . . The time has come . . . when a considerable reduction may be made in our naval and military expenditure without the least impairing our home defence or the efficiency of those forces which defend our interests abroad.'[33]

This speech by the Leader of the Opposition was music in the ears of Gladstone, who, when he claimed that the day was near when both political parties would run a race for possession of the word 'retrenchment' had had little to justify his faith. Disraeli spoke to a motion concocted at the house of W. E. Forster of Bradford and moved by Stansfeld of Halifax, 'that in the opinion of this House the national expenditure is capable of reduction without compromising the safety, the independence, or the legitimate influence of the country'. Palmerston wanted to support Horsman's amendment, asserting that the sums spent on defence had not been greater than required, and implying the continued need for defence as well as economy. Gladstone would have nothing to do with this as it stood, and said that if he was to vote for it even with an addendum of his own, he would have to indicate his disagreements with Palmerston by a difference of tone which would be very disparaging to the government. Palmerston agreed that Horsman's amendment 'might be taken by some of our Friends below the Gangway as a Slap in the Faces, richly deserved indeed but which it might not be useful in a Party sense for us to administer'. But he could not accept Gladstone's alternative, which implied that a considerable reduction of the service estimates was possible. Those, including junior ministers, who complained that Palmerston took a great risk in submitting a government resolution which might have been defeated did not grasp that Gladstone left him no choice.[34]

Palmerston's resolution read as follows: 'That this House, deeply impressed with the necessity of economy in every department of the State, is at the same time mindful of its obligation to provide for the security of the country at home, and the protection of its interests abroad. That this House observes with satisfaction the decrease which has already been effected in the national expenditure, and [trusts that such further diminution may be made therein as the future state of things may warrant].' The Tories met at Derby's house, and concocted an amendment to be moved by Walpole, substituting for the words in brackets the following —
'trusts that the attention of the Government will be earnestly directed to the accomplishment of such further reduction, due regard being had to the defence of the country, as may not only

equalize the revenue and expenditure, but may also afford the means of diminishing the burthen of those taxes which are confessedly of a temporary and exceptional character'. Although this was disliked by Gladstone as purporting to dictate the priorities of tax reduction, it was possible that enough Radicals might vote for it to defeat the Government. Palmerston therefore tested the Tories with a direct challenge, and they broke and fled. When moving the adjournment over Derby Day, he indicated, in a very peremptory way, that Walpole's amendment would be treated as a matter of confidence. If it were carried, he would resign or go to the country. Before Stansfeld even spoke, it was clear that Walpole, to Disraeli's disgust, would withdraw his motion. It was left for Disraeli to describe as a supper to satisfy even an Opposition Palmerston's declaration that he was 'deeply impressed with the necessity of economy' ('that is the first time I ever heard he was') and to invite the sympathy of those who might find tomorrow that their favourite had bolted.[35]

Stansfeld's motion was defeated by 367–65. Cobden was disgusted. Palmerston was spending millions more than the Tories and there was literally no opposition, he said. The Government, violating the principles of retrenchment, non-intervention and reform, was an imposture that had better be ended. 'If there is nobody but the noble lord to mislead us and mock our principles instead of enforcing them', he said at the end of the session, 'let us [the Radicals] go into opposition, and there we shall find leaders who will rally us to some principles.'[36] Palmerston was as serene as ever, sure that if faction prevailed in the House, an appeal to the country would succeed. Cobden was gloomier than usual, complaining of the old man's 'terrible run of good luck'.[37] But the tide was on the turn. Much of what Disraeli had said was superficial and unconvincing, the knock-about of party polemics, but it was significant that he thought that public opinion had changed since January 1861, when he told the Prince he had three hundred men who thought solely of strengthening the government in a patriotic sense against the intrigues of the Tuileries with the Radicals and would to a man help Palmerston resist retrenchment.[38] In November Gladstone told his wife that he thought that, thanks to the Palmerston Resolution carried unanimously in June, he would get in the Great Estimates with far less trouble or even by spontaneous acknowledgement far more saving than in the former years it had cost a life and death struggle to obtain. He was right, and was able in 1863 to reduce sugar to 'the peace point' and income tax as well. And soon the worst of the depression in Lancashire was over, and the prosperity of the country raised the government's stock.

After the dispute on the Resolutions, Palmerston had a full year free of major disputes with Gladstone. On America, Palmerston and Gladstone were virtually as agreed as they had been on Italy in 1859. When, in the summer of 1862, it looked as though the Southerners would capture Washington and Baltimore, Gladstone wrote: 'Lord Palmerston has come exactly to my mind about some early representation of a friendly kind to America, if we can get France and Russia to join.'[40] But Russia would not, and the South failed to win the expected victories. It was now that, on 7th October, at Newcastle, Gladstone made his notoriously indiscreet speech accusing the Northern states of trying to avoid the cup which all the rest of the world saw that they must drink, because Jefferson Davis and his colleagues had 'made a nation'. There seemed no point in saying this unless to foreshadow recognition of Southern independence. Russell was presented with a much-longed-for opportunity to chide in private a colleague who was always chiding him (in private) for irresponsibility of tone and language. He went to Walmer for discussions with Palmerston, who put up Cornewall Lewis to say at Hereford that the South, not having established its independence de facto, was not entitled to recognition.[41] When in November Napoleon pressed for joint mediation 'Lord Russell rather turned tail . . . Palmerston gave . . . a feeble and half-hearted support'.[42] After 1862 the possibility that the North would win gradually became a certainty and there was no more talk of mediation or of recognition of the South. Argyll, the pro-Northerner, was able to remain in Palmerston's cabinet and even point out at Edinburgh on 1st April 1863, with the premier on the platform, that Palmerston at his installation the day before as Lord Rector of Glasgow University had not implied that they were entitled to censure the American government for going to war with the South.

Palmerston was much cheered in Scotland, not only by the burgh councils presenting addresses ('privileged flunkies', Cobden called them), not only as 'the Feargus O'Connor of the middle classes', but ('the most singular and inexplicable of public incidents') by working men in large numbers.[43] His health was, of course, anxiously watched, the more so as the fashionable Dr Ferguson complained that he refused to bother about keeping dry and persisted in riding during attacks of gout. He rode down from Piccadilly in the pouring rain to open the new library at Harrow and then rode back again (1862). In the winter of 1862–3 he had no violent attack of gout, and he strode firmly about on his spring visit to Scotland, climbing Arthur's Seat, as he said, with hardly more difficulty than when a student living with Dugald Stewart sixty years before. He was still capable of going through one of the Saturday-evening receptions at Cambridge House without sitting down, and worked by preference standing at a desk, the Blue Books all around him. Nor could the Speaker find many signs of intellectual decay. His 'form' in the House in 1862 was good, as though his physical recovery had, in more than the literal sense, given him a new lease of life. In the budget debate of 7th April Disraeli had done Gladstone some damage. 'Lord Palmerston saw that he must reply. He kept himself awake.' Refreshed by a nap during an intervening speech, he made, after nearly six hours' sitting, 'a capital speech, fairly smashing Disraeli', 'playing' with his subject and his victim. In the debate on Stansfeld's resolution he was even better. 'It is not that the House respects a public servant who has done great service; that they are indulgent to advanced years', noted the Speaker. 'It is that he still can make a better and more effective speech than any other man, taking the House between wind and water with wonderful skill; that he has more vigour and force about him than the younger men.'[44]

After the death of his contemporary, Aberdeen, in 1860, the younger people were dying all around him — first Graham and then five who were young enough to have been Palmerston's children, the Prince Consort, Lady Granville, Sidney Herbert, Lord and Lady Canning, followed in 1863 by Cornewall Lewis and in 1864 by Newcastle, who lived a life of pain. When Herbert, before his death, had to leave the War Office, the doctors said that George Grey was not strong enough for the work. Considerations of health entered into Russell's decision to go to the Lords at the end of the 1861 session. Lady Palmerston protested at his 'deserting' her husband, whose work was necessarily increased, and who therefore insisted, against the strongest opposition from the Queen and the Prince, on appointing Layard as Under-Secretary at the Foreign Office.[45] Despite past differences, Layard was generally

Palmerstonian in his outlook on foreign policy, he was energetic, he was member for a great metropolitan constituency (Southwark) and he loved not Gladstone, who impeded his grandiose schemes for a great Central Hall of Antiquities at the British Museum. The contrast between these two men came out in a debate on 29th May 1863 when Gladstone had, reluctantly, to deputize for the gout-stricken Palmerston, and Cobden was much struck by the altered feeling of the House towards the Turks — 'they have not a friend except Palmerston and his partial imitator, Layard' [46] Because the gout recurred, Palmerston could not go to the House for the debate, early in July, on the future of the Exhibition building of 1862 in South Kensington. On this the House (to the indignation of the Queen) preferred aesthetics to economy and, snubbing Gladstone, rejected the conversion of the existing structure in favour of a new building on the site. Of all the deaths we have recorded, the one that proved most troublesome to Palmerston was that of the Consort. It revived in Victoria memories of old contentions. It inflicted on ministers, especially the premier, tedious references to the All-Wise departed and floods of self-indulgent grief, and involved them in embarrassments over the form and financing of the many memorials to Albert which the Queen desired. Palmerston's own preference for the Classical over the Gothic, which consigned the design for a new Foreign Office to serve for the St Pancras railway station, was a sign of conservatism which posterity may deem more admirable than his almost incredible statement that the procedure of the House of Commons was incapable of improvement. [47] The procedure of the House of Commons is always capable of more improvement than its members are willing to accept.

At the end of 1863 Palmerston, about to enter his eightieth year, had his premiership threatened, not by death, but by being cited as co-respondent in a divorce suit. Palmerston's gallantries were well known in Society, and annually at Broadlands old 'Poodle' Byng regaled Chichester Fortescue with tales of his own, and Palmerston's, adventures with women, some of which showed a thorough and not very admirable acceptance of the maxim that all is fair in love as in war. [48] But it seems that this aspect of the prime minister's life was not generally known to the public [49] and, the double standards of the middle class in the High Victorian Age being what they were, there were two opinions as to the effect of any disclosures on the old man's position. When the Conservative Whip said 'We've got him' Disraeli replied that Palmerston would sweep the country. But Gladstone's correspondence seems to show that, apart from the embarrassment of Lady Palmerston and her descendants (some of whom did not like to be reminded that they were probably, if not lawfully, his as well), the political danger was rated seriously on the Liberal side. Palmerston, however, replied to O'Kane's citation and notice of suit for £20,000 damages with an affidavit that the action was undertaken for the purpose of extorting money, and as the allegedly aggrieved husband found he would have some difficulty in proving his marriage, he dropped the case.[50] Gladstone would have to wait for Palmerston to die.

CHAPTER XXVI

FADED MAGIC, 1863-4

PALMERSTON had always believed that the right way to restrain France was to co-operate with her. Though he was bitter about French protection of the Bourbon King Francis in his last stronghold of Gaeta, and Russell kept nagging about the French troops in Rome protecting the Pope, there were fairly good relations between London and Paris in 1862 and much of 1863. The French having co-operated with the British in the expedition which extracted a treaty from China at Peking, and having gone to Syria with British approval (and, better still, left), the British joined with the French and Spaniards in action on the Mexican coast, in the interest of government bondholders (whom generally Palmerston, unlike his successors, refused to back with force, holding that they had loaned their money knowing the risks).[1] But Palmerston professed neutrality in the Mexican civil war[2] and the British did not accompany the French in their ill-fated intervention in the interior which ended in tragedy for their Habsburg client, the 'emperor' Maximilian, in 1867. Generally speaking, Britain and France had a common attitude in the American Civil War, though the French were more anxious for intervention than any British minister save Russell.

Complications, however, flowed from Russell's dispatch of October 1860, regarded, not only by the Prince-Regent of Prussia (soon to be William I), as 'a declaration on the part of England, that wherever there exists any dissatisfaction among a people, they have the privilege to expel their sovereign with the assured certainty of England's sympathy'.[3] There were in 1862-4 three revolts of subjects against their sovereigns in which the consistency of Russell's outlook was tested and the whole cabinet was grateful that a Venetian rebellion was not among them. The revolt of the Greeks against King Otho in 1862 was applauded by the British government only when it had succeeded. It raised serious problems of international diplomacy from which Britain emerged triumphant, without having alienated either of the co-guarantors of Greece,

France and Russia. But the rising of the Poles against the Tsar damaged relations with Russia because the government would not condone her actions and relations with France because the government would not fight and restrained the French from fighting for the Poles. And the rising of the Holsteiners and the Germans of Schleswig (against the King-Duke) supported by Prussia and, with less enthusiasm by Austria, exposed British isolation and weakness. It provided not only a major triumph for Bismarck, the new master of Prussia, but a major humiliation for Palmerstonian diplomacy. No one can pretend that it was anything less.

Deeply as he disliked the Neapolitan Bourbons, Palmerston was in 1860 prepared to support them, if they reformed, for the sake of European peace and the containment of France. Deeply as he disliked Otho of Greece, Palmerston was in 1861–2 prepared to give him 'moral support', if he reformed, for the security of Turkey and the containment of Russia. He feared that, if Otho was deposed, Russia's candidate, Leuchtenberg, would succeed him, and/or a war for Greater Greece would begin. 'Neither King nor insurgent must attack Turkey', wrote Russell at the time of the abortive revolution of February 1862. The Three Guarantors pressed Otho, successfully, to grant an amnesty and initiate reforms, but the mission of Russell's turcophil brother-in-law, Sir Henry Elliot, was further to discourage a policy of aggrandizement and to secure the Bavarian succession. When Queen Victoria objected to his detailed advice to Otho on the procedure for introducing constitutional government, Russell replied that 'unless we have made up our minds to abandon Turkey, we ought to employ all the influence of Your Majesty's Government in preventing a revolution in Greece'.[4] There was a colourable ground for such a policy, at least if pursued by the Three Powers in concert, as a revolution would be directed against the succession as guaranteed by the London Conference in 1832. But Otho, whose chauvinism had led to an Anglo-French occupation of the Piraeus during the Crimean War, saw that he could only save himself by an anti-Turkish policy; his agents were everywhere — in Serbia, Montenegro, Roumania, the Ionians, Turin and Paris — drumming up support against the Turk, and Garibaldi himself was daily expected. After Russell had made it clear that an attack on Turkey would lead to Otho's deposition and that his further sponsorship of agitation in the Ionians would involve a reckoning with Britain,[5] Otho was overthrown by revolution in October.

There now occurred a disagreement between Palmerston and Russell. The latter desired to accept the Russian suggestion of a Three-Power Conference in London; Palmerston said this was unnecessary and that the Russians would raise the 1856 Treaty, from which it was still their principal diplomatic aim to escape. And Russell wished to preserve the Bavarian succession. Palmerston knew that to suggest this now would forfeit British influence in Greece, and drafted a dispatch declaring:[6]

... The Kingdom of Greece having by the transactions of 1832 been acknowledged as an independent State, the people of Greece are entitled to exercise the rights of national Independence; and one of the rights which belong to an independent nation ... is that of changing its governing dynasty upon good and sufficient cause. Her Majesty's Government cannot deny that the Greeks have had good and sufficient cause for the steps they have taken.

Russell might have objected that Greece's independence was, in fact and in international law, highly qualified by the rights of the Guarantors, and that Palmerston did not mean to say that the Greeks could have the king they chose unless he was acceptable to the Three. But the Foreign Secretary saw the parallel with October 1860 in Naples and, despite Victoria's strong objection, signed and sent it. Palmerston had just told his principal Greek confidant that a republic in Greece would be contrary to the interest of Europe, but that if the Greeks found a king acceptable to Britain, the Ionians (except, perhaps, Corfu) might be ceded to them. But the king must be neither Leuchtenberg (or Prince Romanoffsky, as Palmerston called him) nor the British prince Alfred, the popular candidate in Greece, where he was known as 'the widow's son'. Palmerston later became inclined to support Alfred,[7] because the Russians had refused to say whether or not Leuchtenberg was a member of their Imperial Family excluded by the Protocol of 1830 or to extend the prohibition on members of the dynasties of Britain, France and Russia to 'persons connected with them'. The Queen vetoed Alfred's candidature (though in February 1863 he was overwhelmingly elected by plebiscite in Greece) and on 4th December 1862 Britain and Russia signed a self-denying ordinance, the latter admitting that this excluded Leuchtenberg. The search for a king for Greece acceptable to the Three now ranged far and wide, though tending to concentrate round various German connexions of Queen Victoria or of the Russian Imperial family.

A definitive British policy was forged, under Palmerston's impulse, at a cabinet of 8th December.[8] Provided Greece was a constitutional monarchy, and a king was elected who was likely to favour religious liberty, constitutional freedom and peace with Turkey, Britain would cede the Ionians, including Corfu, provided the Ionian legislature and the signatories of the Treaty of Vienna concurred. Further, Elliot was privately and secretly instructed to suggest that the Turks cede to Greece Thessaly and Epirus. 'They will do it if we advise it', said Palmerston, but the Ottomans could no more see that it was in their interest to cede Mount Olympus than the Habsburgs that it was in theirs to cede Venice, and the Porte peremptorily refused the suggestion (1st January 1863). Palmerston was clearly seeking stability by compromise between the Turks and the Christians, though in the long run there could be none and the Turk was probably right to feel that with every success Greek appetites would grow.

Meanwhile the search for a king for Greece had not prospered, and of the period after the election of Alfred and his mother's refusal of the honour it is written: 'It seems that but for Palmerston's firmness Great Britain would have lost control of the election ... Russell was inclined to let matters take their own course.' On 16th March 1863 Palmerston produced Britain's last card, and Russell played it, inviting the Greek assembly to elect Prince William of Denmark, brother of the Princess of Wales, after securing the concurrence of the Three. This the assembly did on 30th March, though the lad's father withheld his assent for two months. On 5th June the London Conference, under the presidency of Earl Russell, recognized Prince William as George I, 'King of the Greeks', a style changed (after Turkish protests) to 'King of the Hellenes'. By the Treaty of London, 13th July, ratified on 3rd August, Greece was declared under the hereditary sovereignty of Prince William and the guarantee of the Three Powers, a monarchical, independent and constitutional state (still bound by the financial provisions of 1832 and 1860), to which in due course the Ionians would belong.

★   ★   ★   ★

The peaceful settlement of the Greek succession by concert of Britain, France and Russia was a considerable achievement though not unattended with tension between Britain and France, especially when the latter seemed to lean to Leuchtenberg. And the folly of the local British minister in Athens, Campbell Scarlett, could easily have led to serious diplomatic strain before Prince William ever arrived, owing to an incipient civil war between the Greek parties of the Mountain (pro-French) and the Plain (pro-British). From the restraint imposed on Scarlett from London it almost looked as though Palmerston had learned some lessons from his futile partisanship in Spain and Portugal in the 30s and 40s.[10]

By this time, the Franco-Russian entente, which had long ceased to alarm Palmerston, had cracked over Poland. Those who took seriously the apparent implications of Russell's dispatch of October 1860, coupled with the Palmerston–Russell dispatch on Greece of November 1862, asked how the British Government could fail to applaud the attempt of the Poles in January 1863 to discard their sovereign, the Tsar, or could criticize foreigners who helped them. After all, Britain had held in 1831, through Palmerston himself, that the liberties which, in her view, were assured to the Poles by the Treaty of Vienna were unaffected by the earlier revolt, and that the Tsar's legal, as well as moral, title to Poland was impaired by their violation, which had now reached the point of extinction. It was not publicly known that Clarendon had desisted from raising Poland at the Congress of Paris in 1856 only when he received private promises, never carried out, of constitutional concessions.

Palmerston, and the British public, did applaud the Poles, and the last sustained diplomatic campaign which Palmerston may be said to have conducted personally throughout was intended to persuade Russia that the danger of general war was great enough to make it politic for her to restore Poland to the dispensation of 1815. Neither the Queen nor his colleagues quite trusted him to avoid going over the brink. The Russians, in April, thought it 'evident that France is determined on war unless she is prevented by England, and we do not feel confident that England will do so'.[11] Apponyi, for Austria, felt the same, and was entitled to do so when Palmerston suggested to him that Austria might give up her Polish provinces to an independent Poland under a Habsburg and rid Europe of the muscovite promontory which jutted into the centre of civilization.[12] But Palmerston was not prepared to renew the war against Russia for a 'beau ideal' unobtainable in 1856, and he did not wish to see France go to war for Poland and, of course, 'compensations'. His brinkmanship was devised to bring the maximum pressure on Russia, but he was entirely sincere in assuring Apponyi that it was his policy to go with France up to a certain point in order to 'group and control' her.

Palmerston's caution was evident as soon as the French reacted with alarming alacrity to the Alvensleben Convention for co-operation against the Poles on the borders of Prussian Poland which was pressed on a sceptical St Petersburg by the new prime minister of Prussia, Bismarck, and was a sign of his inexperience rather than his calculation. Prussia was a power whom France could fight, and hope for the goodwill, if not the assistance, of Austria in fighting, for Austria in this year staged her last great effort to consolidate her hold on Germany by institutional reform. Even the most pacific ministers admitted that the state of public opinion made a British protest to Berlin inevitable. But Palmerston made no protest when they etiolated Russell's draft and inserted the hint (which Bismarck took) that Prussia could extricate herself by saying that the Convention would remain a dead letter. He approved a dispatch to Paris intended 'to slacken the too rapid movements of the French Government'. He did not want the French seizing the Rhineland and it was no part of British interests to help the French authorities divert the emotion of their people from Russia to Prussia. He therefore opposed a collective démarche in Berlin, suggesting, however, that Austria, France and Britain should make one in St Petersburg. It was contemptible, he said, to protest to the incidental accomplice and not to the real culprit.[14]

Austria vetoed a collective note. Instead, different notes were delivered simultaneously in St Petersburg. The Austrian note was mild. The French, Palmerston said, in very measured language implied a great deal; it was 'a pretty intelligible Threat of War about Poland'. The British note, as Professor Mosse says, in very unmeasured language implied extremely little.[15] Russell repeated the unmeasured language in an interview which Brunnow described as menacing and astonishing, as well he might, for Russell said that the difficulty in giving representative institutions to Poland might be solved by giving them to All the Russians. What would Canning have thought of that? Not surprisingly, Brunnow found Palmerston more intelligible and realistic, though very strong in his language about Russian conduct in Poland.[16] It was Palmerston's aim to make Russia believe that he would allow France to drag Britain into a war with Russia to be fought mainly at France's risk and expense, and Gorchakov was warned on 27th May not to count on the indifference or neutrality of England if France went to war. This was on the eve of the presentation of new notes recommending an amnesty and the 1815 constitution. Russia was certain to reject them, and Apponyi feared that Palmerston had too strong a dose of British pride to remain inactive under such a blow.[17] Palmerston, on the contrary, now that the bluff had been called by the Russians, was concerned only to make sure that it went down into history simply as a bluff that had been called. He declined a French proposal that the Three Powers agree on their intentions and reserve the right to take measures other than diplomatic. He repelled Drouyn's persistent demand for an identical note to Russia; it would mean war or unnecessary humiliation for the West, he said.[18] When Drouyn's draft was circulated to the cabinet, with a note by Russell inviting ministers who agreed with him that it should be rejected to sign accordingly 'nearly all, including Lord Palmerston, signed'.[19] For the third time, each Power sent its own note. Britain reiterated her view that the condition of Russian Poland was a matter of international contract, on which all the signatories of the Treaty of Vienna were entitled to be consulted, to confer and to make representations. Gorchakov was bound to repudiate this, but when Russell wished to continue the angry controversy, Palmerston asked pithily what advantage was to be gained by forcing the Tsar to say bluntly that he held Poland by his 'own Strong Hand and Stark Sword' and that it was no more Britain's business than Moscow or Siberia.[20]

The closing dispatch was therefore such that Gorchakov thanked Russell for the friendly disposition and moderation it revealed. This did not please the Foreign Secretary, who replied to Russian appeals for a *cordon sanitaire* against France that co-operation was impossible unless the Poles were better treated. But that St Petersburg should make such a suggestion showed that the Franco-Russian entente had foundered. So, now also, did the Franco-British entente. The French were very angry at what they considered British pusillanimity over Poland, and those at Paris who made pointed reference to the last years of Louis Philippe and

Guizot, and asked why France should value a connection esteemed by Palmerston only as a means of preventing France from achieving any of her objectives, were strengthened in influence. When Napoleon proposed to hold a European Congress, and Britain refused to attend, he threatened to go on with it whether she went or not.

The British riposte to this proposal was an effective answer to the criticism made, in Prussia and elsewhere, at the time of Russell's dispatch of October 1860, that Russell and Palmerston were playing, for the pleasure of momentarily outplaying him, the game of Napoleon III, who was generally regarded, and was sometimes proud to be regarded, as the champion of both nationalism and of territorial revision in Europe. Ever since 1848 British statesmen had feared the day when Louis Napoleon would seek to translate into fact the thesis of Lamartine's Circular. Explaining the difference between the British and French representations to St Petersburg in April 1863, Palmerston said 'the French hint Threats which we are not prepared to make, and we appeal to the Treaty of Vienna which the French would wish to tear to Tatters'.[21] The French emperor's invitation of November 1863 to the sovereigns of states which had signed the Treaty of Vienna was to attend a congress based on the assumption that the 1815 settlement had no longer effect. Russell was hesitant, but Palmerston was quite ready to 'bell the cat', as Russia urged, and under his stimulus the British cabinet rudely shattered Napoleon's dreams of a peaceful revision of 1815 achieved by his initiative and implying a recognition of his hegemony in Europe.

Palmerston's case against a congress was simply that, whereas in 1814–15 Europe had been a 'political waste, and required the action of a body of inclosure commissioners to allot the lands and give holding titles' and in 1856 four of the five Great Powers were directly concerned in an attempt to end a war involving three of them directly and the other partially, no such situation now obtained. Some of the infractions of 1815 which were *faits accomplis* had undoubted validity, and the others would not receive general endorsement. There were, indeed, many difficult questions requiring settlement, and if the congress could reach one without altering the Rhine frontiers or the 1856 treaty, it would be a well-doer. There were plenty of unfulfilled aspirations — Italy wanted Rome and Venetia; Greece wanted Thessaly and Epirus; Spain

wanted Gibraltar; Denmark wanted to integrate Schleswig;
Sweden wanted Finland; the larger German states would like to
mediatize the smaller, etc., etc., to say nothing of the ambitions of
France and Russia. But how were decisions to be reached? And
how could they be enforced without a European gendarmerie?
'What a Babel of Tongues and What a Confusion of Interests'
there would be. The result could only be to record and render more
irreconcilable fundamental differences of opinion and interest. The
cabinet accepted this view on 19th November and Russell's note
conveying it was scathing. It was, moreover, published in the
London Gazette on 27th November *before* the French Foreign
Minister received it.[22]

*   *   *   *

'In this manner, without perhaps fully realizing the gravity of
their decision, British Ministers took the step which ended the
French alliance.' It was 'a landmark in the history of European
diplomacy'. It isolated France — 'Napoleon ceased to be the
arbiter of Europe'. But it isolated Britain too, and meant that she
'could play but a modest role in continental affairs'.[23] The invincible criticism of British policy over Schleswig–Holstein in
1864 is quite simply that it showed an inadequate awareness of this
crippling limitation. Palmerston and Russell endeavoured to deter
the Germans from overturning the King of Denmark's power in
the Elbic duchies (confirmed by the treaty of 1852 which though
settled by Malmesbury, was a Palmerstonian conception), by
raising the spectre of a war in which the French would be the chief
allies of the Danes. But this spectre had no substance. The French
would not dance to the British tune, and Bismarck was sure he
could rely on Napoleon's indecision, if not on his goodwill.
Moreover, everybody knew that, at bottom, the British would
dislike the French on the Rhine more than the Germans on the
Eider and the Schlei. The Foreign Office briefing to Cowley on
the last occasion during the Polish crisis when it looked as though
France might fight indicated that 'Britain would insist on certain
conditions in favour of the integrity of Germany and against
encroachments on the part of France, before she consented to be
neutral'.[24] This was no doubt foolish, as there was no prospect of
Britain fighting with Russia against France and Poland, but it
showed a due regard for the Balance of Power, granted the

assumption universally made, and perhaps still true in 1864 (though not within a year or two) that the French army would beat the Prussian. Russell seemed to overlook it when in mid-February he suggested that, if Austria and Prussia refused to accept Anglo-French mediation or the verdict of the mediators, a strong British squadron should go to Copenhagen and a strong French corps stand by on the Prussian frontier. Palmerston very sensibly retorted that these actions would not be effective unless they were steps to something more and that 'it might not be advisable nor for our own interest to suggest to France an attack upon the Prussian Rhenish territory . . . the conquest of [which] . . . would seriously affect the position of Holland and Belgium'.[25]

Palmerston knew it was foolish to invite a major shift in the Balance of Power to avoid a lesser one, which even the annexation of Schleswig and Holstein by Prussia would be. And the Germans knew that he knew it — 'Palmerston will not decide to cross the Sound for he does not wish Napoleon to cross the Rhine', they said.[26] So Russell's hectoring notes could only irritate German opinion, and the British were seriously at fault in not making it clear to the Danes that they must meet reasonable demands. Palmerston was especially at fault, for in the House of Commons on 22nd July 1863 he said that he, and other reasonable men, including those in France and Russia, desired that the independence, integrity and rights of Denmark should be maintained. 'We are convinced — I am convinced at least', he added, 'that if any violent attempt were made to overthrow those rights and interfere with that independence, those who made the attempt would find in the result, that it would not be Denmark alone with whom they would have to contend.' It is mistaken to attack this as a pledge of aid to Denmark by Britain which was later broken. He was simply applying his standard technique of threatening Power A with counter-action by Powers B and/or C. But in the circumstances of 1863–4 the threat was idle. For Russia, though she stood for the Treaty of 1852 longer than any other Power, would not go to war for it. Austria became an aggressor in Prussia's wake because to do otherwise would be to abdicate to Prussia the leadership of Germany. The threat made sense only if France was eager to march into Germany, and Palmerston would have been very worried if that had been the case. As it was not, there was only Sweden as a possible ally for Denmark. The error of Palmerston and Russell was to threaten

Denmark's enemies and avow the essential rightness of the Danish cause, as based on the sanctity of treaties, so that any chance there might have been (and perhaps it was not great) of the Danish nationalists adopting a conciliatory attitude towards the Germans was lost.

For the crisis of 1863 arose, like the crisis of 1848, from the determination of the Danish nationalists to detach Schleswig constitutionally from Holstein with a view to incorporating it into Denmark proper. This was contrary to engagements made by the King-Duke on the strength of which the Powers, including the principal members of the German Confederation, but not the Confederation itself, signed or adhered to the Treaty of 8th May 1852, under which Prince Christian of Glucksburg was recognized as heir to Schleswig-Holstein as well as Denmark, although the lawful heir to the duchies was probably the Duke of Augustenburg or possibly the Tsar, with reversion to the Duke of Oldenburg. The March Patent of 1863 marked a large step towards the Danish design, and within a few days of his succession as Christian IX in November, Glucksburg had to ratify another or lose the throne. The response of the people of the duchies, and of public opinion in Germany, to this virtual incorporation of Schleswig in Denmark was even fiercer than in 1848, not only because it was a violation of the previous king-duke's post-1848 engagements, but because neither peoples nor diets had been consulted on the succession in or before 1852 and they wanted (as did the King of Prussia and Queen Victoria, but as did not Bismarck) Augustenburg. Underrating Bismarck partly because they thought he was still insecure in the saddle, Palmerston and Russell did not understand that he could add to his security by making Prussia the spearhead of German nationalism.

The Federal Diet conducted an 'execution' in Holstein, and Augustenberg set up court at Kiel. But it was the Prussians and Austrians who occupied Schleswig, to hold it as a 'material guarantee' for the performance by Christian IX of his predecessor's engagements. Only subsequently did it emerge that Bismarck had recognized the sovereignty of Christian in the duchies (as Prussia was bound to do by the Treaty of 1852) in order to be able to deprive him of them 'legally' by forced cession. The 'just' solution would, of course, have been self-determination, conducted so as to leave North Sleswig to Denmark. Napoleon always hankered after this and asked the British in the spring of 1864 how he could pursue one policy on the Eider and a diametrically opposite one (self-determination) on the Po. But not till both duchies were wholly in German hands and Denmark proper invaded did the British, with great reluctance, talk seriously of this solution, when it was too late for the neutral Powers to insist on a good military frontier for Denmark, and that Rendsburg should not become a Federal fortress and Kiel a Federal port. These conditions Bismarck scorned. The war was renewed. The Danish mainland was occupied. Denmark ceded the whole of both duchies to Prussia and Austria, and Bismarck used the question of their destiny to provoke the war with Austria which in 1866 made Prussia master of Germany.

Behind the dislike of self-determination was a fear that a reduced Denmark would become incorporated into a Scandinavian kingdom under the francophil king of Sweden and Norway; this Russia also feared. Britain and Russia both took the line that the treaty of 1852 barred all signatories from suggesting the dismemberment of the Danish monarchy, and that if so awful a thing happened, 'all Treaties might be thrown into the fire as waste paper, or used to wrap up cartridges, and English interests would be endangered by the keys of the Baltic being in the hands of a single Power'.[27] Palmerston was standing for the public law of Europe. When Queen Victoria referred to the seizure of Schleswig as 'a natural and legitimate proceeding', he inevitably recalled the Russian occupation of the Principalities and pronounced, fairly enough, that 'there cannot be a principle more dangerous to the maintenance of peace, or more fatal to the independence of the weaker Powers, than that it should be lawful for a stronger Power, whenever it has a demand upon a feebler neighbour, to seize hold of part of its territory by force of arms, instead of seeking redress in the usual way of negotiation'. The day might come when such a principle, established by Prussia, 'might be fatally retorted upon her by France, by the seizure of the Prussian Rhenish provinces . . . [and] the whole French nation would be as clamorous for the Rhine as the Germans are for what they call Schleswig-Holstein'.[28] But it would have been better to secure a compromise than allow Bismarck to establish the precedent by force. Palmerston alternated between a world of romance in which the Balance of Power operated according to theoretical specification and the realm of reality in which it did not, and lingered long in a half-light of bluff which failed to deter the Germans but encouraged the Danes to be stubborn, they hoping for a war between France and Germany which he did not want.

Some of the cabinet regarded the treaty of 1852 as an embarrassment from which they would have been glad to escape. The Queen and Prince had always hated it as an unjust transaction, the fruit of Russian intrigue and/or Palmerstonian contrivance. As in 1848–9, Victoria abused her ministers for having one attitude to Italian aspirations and another to German. It was too like the Holy Alliance to dispose of peoples without their consent as might suit the convenience of Britain or even of Europe, she said.[29] So pro-German was she that Palmerston on 4th January 1864 went so far as to remind her that she was queen of Great Britain and that her conduct must be guided by the honour of the Crown and the interests of her dominions. How many of the territories held under the Treaty of Vienna, he asked, were assigned to states subject to popular appeal? None! What sovereign, Her Majesty not excluded, had not in part of his or her dominions a set of factious demagogues acting from without as well as from within, who might raise a local cry for separation and transfer? The theories now put forward in Germany 'might be applied to break into fragments every European State'.[30] All this was true, but yet the Queen's point that a war would be a war 'to impose upon those people a Sovereign whom they violate no engagement or allegiance in rejecting' was not met. At the end of the day Palmerston was reduced to admitting that 'if the Duchies had forced themselves from Denmark by their own exertions, they would have acquired the right to dispose of themselves', but arguing that once the occupation had taken place no true test of opinion could be taken.[31] But was that not as true of Lombardy when she acceded to Sardinia in 1848 or the Romagna, Umbria and the Marches in 1860? The Holsteiners did not recognize Christian, did recognize Augustenburg, and would in any case have had to be conquered by the Danes before they accepted either the March Patent or the Glucksburgs. Before the invasion of Schleswig, the German officials there had refused to swear allegiance to Christian IX. In these circumstances, to denounce the pretensions of Augustenburg as 'a bare-faced attempt at usurpation, doubly scandalous because his family received money compensation for [their] renunciation' of their claim in 1852 was pedantic. Yet Russell wished to ask the Powers to say they 'would feel bound to afford assistance to Denmark in opposing so evident an act of aggression' as his installation.

The Danes had ground for feeling that Britain had encouraged them, only to let them down, although there was no specific official commitment on which she could be said to have defaulted. Russell on 19th December gave it as his personal view to Apponyi that England might consider the invasion of Schleswig a *casus belli*. When Palmerston's anti-German outburst of 4th January to the Queen sent Granville scurrying to Broadlands, he concluded that the irritable tone was due to the gout, since Palmerston assured him there was no question of England going to war. But the premier told the Queen that he heartily concurred in Russell's opinion that Britain 'could not let Denmark perish', an opinion communicated to Prussia.[33] The invasion of Schleswig began on 1st February. Palmerston told the Commons on the strength of assurances extracted from Prussia by Russia that the purpose of the occupation was not the dismemberment of the Danish monarchy.[34] He may have believed Bismarck; if not, he had to pretend to. The reply to Denmark's official request for assistance was that Britain would not act except in conjunction with France and Russia, and the Danish envoy was told on 19th February that there was no prospect of them giving material support. There came a moment, indeed, on Sunday 20th February when British policy was active and decisive and looked as though it might be fruitful — when news of the invasion of Denmark proper was accompanied by rumours that an Austrian fleet was heading for the Baltic. Britain would be laughed at, said Palmerston, if the Germans were allowed to dictate peace in Copenhagen. The Admiralty was asked to send a squadron, as soon as the season permitted, to prevent an attack on the island of Zealand. France and Russia were told that the Channel Fleet would go to 'watch the enemies of Denmark' and invited to join with Britain and Sweden in a naval demonstration.[35] Russia, though grateful that her ships were frozen in till May, was likely to agree if France did. For the first time it seemed that Napoleon would come into line. Bismarck was never so near to being curbed. But Russell hesitated and was lost. At Paris the opponents of co-operation with Britain rallied. At home the Queen and cabinet, not consulted on 20th, intervened. Only Lord Chancellor Westbury, besides Palmerston, supported Russell's démarches. He was forced to cancel them.[36] It is possible that the vigour of that Sunday contributed to German acceptance of a conference in London. It met at the end of April, with the British and French still at loggerheads, and broke up at the end of May in disorder and controversy, having settled only that the treaty of 1852 was dead, denounced by Prussia and the diet and tacitly abandoned by the Powers.

*   *   *   *

Russell at the end of February 1864 was compelled to accept 'the doctrine of the cabinet' that Britain could not effectively make war against Germany alone. And though in the debates of that month almost every speaker was pro-Dane and the Government was criticized for not giving Denmark more support, it was clearly the doctrine of the country that at that moment she *should* not make war. Sir Charles Wood assured the Queen that the premier was 'quite as strong against war' as Wood himself.[37] But as long as war was being fought in Denmark, there remained a risk that Palmerston and Russell would send a fleet to the Sound. When Palmerston told Russell that the country and the cabinet were not *as yet* ready for active interference, he encouraged his rasher colleague to believe the time might come when they would be. And he did so with his eyes open, because he felt that there were limits to the patience of the public, which coincided with his own[38] —

... It is quite intelligible and reasonable that the British government should hesitate to send 20,000 troops, and more could not be got together, to face the hundreds of thousands which Germany, if united, could oppose to us. . . . But that England, the first and greatest Naval Power, should allow an Austrian fleet to sail by our shores, and go and conquer and occupy the island capital of a friendly Power, towards which we are bound by national interests and Treaty engagements, would be a national disgrace to which Viscount Palmerston, at least, would never stoop to be a party. It makes one's blood boil even to think of it; and such an affront England, whether acting alone or with Allies, ought never to permit.

There was a time when even the pacific Clarendon feared that public opinion would make the dispatch of a fleet to the Sound unavoidable, whatever government was in office.[39] To some it has seemed that sense can be made of British policy over Schleswig-Holstein only by regarding it as the mere reflection of public opinion. Palmerston and Russell represented the nation's desire to count in the counsels of Europe, its antipathy to Germany, its reflexive impulse to use the fleet, which could certainly save the whole of Denmark from being overrun. The Queen (accidentally, because she was pro-German), Wood, Granville and Gladstone represented an inner shrinking from war which was sometimes submerged. The government represented public opinion when it used strong language; it represented it also in doing nothing when foreign nations ignored that language. The result, Derby said, was meddle and muddle. The nation had taken too literally Palmerston's boast that, in Italy, 'moral influence' had prevailed, as though it could be assumed that things would always turn out as Britain wished without her having to fight or threaten to fight. Palmerston had always said that if neutrality was taken to mean abstention from advice, 'Great Britain would, by her own act, reduce herself to the rank of a third-class European State'. He was as anxious as ever that Britain should 'count' in the transactions of the continent. In this spirit the Government acted over Poland. The public would not have tolerated silence and it would not have tolerated war. It accepted Palmerston's explanation that there was a middle course between 'an ignominious silence' and 'broadsides of shot and shell', that it was sometimes right to try moral pressure without intending to go to war if it failed.[41] What Schleswig-Holstein in the end showed the public, if not Palmerston, was that if moral pressure was not likely to be effective, it would be more dignified to use it very sparingly. Palmerston was reluctant to accept this lesson, because it meant that unless Britain was closely allied with a European military Power she had ceased to count as a first-class state in Europe. But by and large his colleagues were coming to accept it. They always found it easier to decide to do nothing than to do anything. Even in January 1860 when most of them were willing to agree to 'great moral support to France and to strong moral pressure upon Austria in order to prevent armed interference in Italy' many of them had 'insuperable objections to our engaging ourselves to give material assistance'. By 1864 their tendency to negativism had become even more pronounced. Palmerston and Russell told one another how much pleasanter it would have been if the cabinet had been under their control.[42]

Russell wanted to strengthen Britain's hand at the London Conference by sending the fleet to the Baltic at the end of April. The cabinet prevented it.[43] Palmerston, as he told Russell, 'was so little satisfied with the timidity and weakness of the Cabinet . . .

Henry John Temple, 3rd Viscount Palmerston,
photographed late in life as Prime Minister

that I determined to make a notch off my own bat'. He sent for Apponyi and told him that Denmark had been harshly and unjustly treated and that 'the integrity and independence of the State which commands the entrance to the Baltic [were] objects of interest to England'. Britain's direct interests had not been sufficiently engaged to make direct action indispensable, but there were things which could be suffered, and things which could not. He knew it was generally thought in Germany that England was cowardly and would avoid war at any price. But the intervention of the Austrian fleet in the Baltic would be an affront and insult which could only lead to a collision with Britain. For he could not stay in office unless a superior squadron was sent to the Baltic, and he would remind Austria that she was vulnerable in the Adriatic and that other enemies waited to fall upon her. He would like a formal assurance in writing that the Austrian fleet would not intervene. Apponyi duly recognized British naval power; he was not, he said, attracted by the notion of Austrian ships being fired on by British or compelled to retrace their steps on the summons of a British admiral. But he said that Germany could never be made to understand that a dozen plenipotentiaries had the right to sit round a green table and dispose of the fate of a million compatriots contrary to pre-existing rights of succession and without consulting the estates or the Bund. And he gave no hope of formal assurances about the fleet.[44]

Palmerston had been speaking 'for myself, personally, and for nobody else', in an 'explanation as between friends' but reported the conversation to the cabinet. The encounter was discussed 'with the respect and deference due to Palmerston', but the premier received little support, and Russell was told to strike out of his dispatch to Vienna a threat to send the fleet to the Baltic in certain circumstances. When, as a second best, he added an account of Palmerston's talk with Apponyi, there was a 'general row', for the cabinet wished to retain 'freedom of action'. Russell blustered. Either the policy of Palmerston's conversation must be endorsed or it must be repudiated. 'Of course I shall not be a party to such repudiation' he said and Palmerston would have to decide whether *he* could be responsible for any other policy. But it was agreed that the dispatch should not be communicated to the Austrians.[45]

'All this naturally increases the feeling of distrust with which Lord Russell has contrived to inspire her Majesty', wrote General

s

Grey to Granville. 'She relies upon the Cabinet, and particularly upon yourself to save her from being dragged unnecessarily into this miserable war.'[46] Palmerston deeply resented the fact that the German conviction that Britain would not act was due to reliance on the Queen and the majority of the cabinet checking Russell and himself. On 10th May he complained to the Queen that indiscreet expressions from persons about Her Majesty gave currency to the view that her personal opinions had embarrassed the course of the government. 'He has a singular want of knowledge of what may or may not be said', wrote Phipps to the Queen, and once again an 'impertinence' was ascribed to gout.[46] But Grey admitted the indiscretions of the Queen's Household. He himself unashamedly canvassed ministers on the Queen's behalf and he and his brother-in-law, Wood, who was in the cabinet, were as thick as thieves.[47] The Queen herself virtually admitted the validity of Russell's charge, made in his 'coldest, hardest style',[A] that her German

[A] On 25th May 1864 Granville reported to the Queen that Ellenborough in the Lords had 'alluded to an impression abroad, that, with regard to German politics, this country was now not in the condition in which it was when George III declared himself to be an Englishman, and that the German sympathies of his two predecessors would not influence the policy of his Government, which should be guided by English interests'. Russell had replied that the Queen had feelings of sympathy with the country of the Prince Consort's birth, in which two of her daughters were happily married, but that as regards public policy she had but one wish, 'the maintenance of the honour and interests of this country'. She certainly required on important matters due consideration and deliberation, but, whenever the government had come to any deliberate decision, had 'always adopted with cordiality the advice of [her] responsible advisers'.

(The complaint of Palmerston and Russell was, of course, that royal influence in the cabinet prevented deliberate decisions, and that reliance on royal preferences in Germany blunted the effect of decisions when they were made.)

The Queen wrote to Russell, on 27th, thanking him for 'having spoken the *truth*', defending 'the highest in the country from base calumny' as he had in 1854. Was it not enough that she should have to see her country 'hurried on by the Press and by many public men into violent and passionate excitement against our *natural ally*, abusing that great country till she returns it in the same manner — that country from which *everyone* nearest and dearest to the Queen has come, and to which she is bound by every possible tie . . .', and to work to prevent further mischief and a war in which Britain might be isolated, without being exposed to base and ungentlemanlike insinuations. From these 'her terrible misfortunes, her unprotected position without a husband to stand by and protect her, her known character for fearless straightforwardness, her devotion *now* and ever to her country (a proof of which is her weakened health and strength)' ought to have protected her?

Russell replied on 31st that 'it was to be lamented that your Majesty's relations in Germany have allowed rumours to go forth that in the present contest your Majesty was disposed to take part with the Germans and against the Danes' and relations made her views known,[48] when she wrote to Granville: 'That Germany felt and feels confidence in the Queen's impartiality and her determination to prevent any of those dangerous steps which Lord Palmerston and Lord Russell would on several occasions have plunged us into, there can be no doubt of.' When her brother-in-law, the Duke of Coburg, wrote: 'Germany knows well what it owes to your mild views and your firm will', she replied that she must protest against being spoken of separately from her government — 'Albert would never have allowed that.' But the relations of the Queen with Granville were barely proper even in terms of the constitutional conventions of that day. It was excusable, even perhaps legitimate, to use him to check up on Russell's reports of cabinet decisions, which were often misleading and sometimes wildly inaccurate, and to make sure that her remonstrances were read to the cabinet when she had so instructed. But the only ground for defending her permission to Granville to show her correspondence with Coburg *to any ministers other than Palmerston and Russell* is that the end justifies the means.[49]

Palmerston was entitled to complain that he did not receive from the monarch the 'confidence' (it is a technical term) which a prime minister was, by the 1860s, entitled to claim as his right. But if the cabinet was for the moment the Queen's as much as, if not more than, Palmerston's, it was only because the great majority, though not pro-German like the Queen, was against war. The Queen 'shuddered' when on 11th June Russell claimed that the cabinet had endorsed a pledge by Britain alone to give material aid to the Danes if the Germans refused arbitration on a frontier across Schleswig and renewed the war. Granville and Wood assured her that this was quite erroneous.[50] At the cabinet on 15th Gladstone found his colleagues very united and pacific in tone. Palmerston did not stand by Russell; though he might talk big, Granville explained, he was quite aware of the folly of war.[51] The Queen herself found the premier, at Windsor on 21st, 'very sensible,

that others, such as Beust, are stated in the newspapers 'to have received from your Majesty the assurance that your Majesty's Government would never take part in the war in favour of the Danes'. No doubt what the Queen had said had been 'perverted and misrepresented'.

On 1st June General Grey wrote to Granville saying that the Queen was 'deeply hurt by a cold dry letter from Lord Russell, quietly assuming that she may, inadvertently, have given occasion to the attacks which are made against her'. (*V.L.*, 2nd series, i. 196-7, 197-8, 208-9; G. 466-7.)

wonderfully clear-headed and fully alive to the extreme dangers'. Of these the greatest, he said, was that the French would undertake a campaign for the Rhine and perhaps revolutionize all Italy.[52] The cabinet had to decide on 24th not to make war single-handed if the invasion of Denmark was resumed, and, having decided that, whether to pay the high price of checking (and punishing) German aggression — France's price. There could be little doubt of the answer. It only remained on 25th to decide not to send the fleet to Copenhagen and not to warn Austria against sending hers, but to preserve freedom of action should circumstances change.[53] Palmerston and Russell informed parliament on 27th that the breakdown of the Conference left Britain with no moral obligation to help the Danes and that neutrality would be maintained and that no decision had been made to send the fleet. When Palmerston referred in a menacing way to the possibility of the fleet going later to Copenhagen, he was greeted with some derision.[54] Disraeli gave notice of a vote of censure. An Opposition could hardly do less.

* * * *

A. J. P. Taylor and Professor Mosse both regard the cabinet of 25th June 1864, with the debate on the vote of censure, as a landmark in the history of British foreign policy, and it was seen so at the time. Lord Robert Cecil (later Lord Salisbury) repeated Disraeli's assertion that if foreign affairs had been conducted on the principles of Cobden and Bright the results would have been the same but the position of the country would have been more consistent and dignified.[55] Lord Stanley (another future Foreign Secretary) claimed that a policy of neutrality and non-intervention could be safe, honourable and respectable. Radicals rushed to endorse these Tory views. W. E. Forster, who was to serve in Gladstone's cabinets, demanded a shift from 'that meddling, dishonest system of apparent intervention . . . which is really non-intervention' to an 'honest, dignified and plain-spoken system of non-intervention'. Cobden talked of 'a revolution in our foreign policy' and ascribed the cabinet's decision to do nothing to a decisive veto on war coming up from the great centres of manufacture and commerce.[56] It is possible to over-dramatize. On 25th June eight of the fifteen ministers (though only one of them besides Palmerston belonging to the House of Commons) were in favour of saying something specific about the security of Copenhagen,[57] and the public might have demanded action if the Austrian fleet had gone there. But, if the Palmerston government (to general surprise) survived the motion of censure (by eighteen votes) the Palmerston policy hardly did. For the 'triumph' was obtained by substituting for Disraeli's indictment of the government Kinglake's amendment congratulating it on keeping out of war! Apponyi recorded that Palmerston 'won a victory by making an immense draft on his old popularity, and by tactics worthy of an old parliamentary hand. He dwelt on the thriving state of the finances. Men hardly believed their ears'.[58] To Cobden and his friends such arguments were a sweet revenge on the poor old man who had to use them to stay in office.

Palmerston had failed to appreciate that, in a world of advancing nationalism, 'Germany' had become a reality not to be ignored, and that in Bismarck there had arrived an opportunistic and unscrupulous practitioner of *Realpolitik*. Whatever elements controlled German policy would, indeed, have had to wrest Holstein and southern Schleswig, effectively if not nominally, from Denmark. It had seemed in 1862 that William I, worsted in the constitutional struggle with the Liberal Prussian parliament over the army, would abdicate in favour of his son, and the Liberal Germany of Prince Albert's dreams take form under the leadership of his son-in-law. With such a Germany Palmerston could, perhaps, have conducted a fruitful dialogue. But Bismarck was a different proposition. Even so, Palmerston could claim that, while British prestige had taken a knock and international law had been cynically disregarded, neither British interest nor the Balance of Power had suffered from the German conquest of Schleswig-Holstein. Only a month before his death he penned a calm appraisal of the new situation.[59] Denmark had been grossly ill-treated, but it was better for the interests of Europe that the duchies should go to increase the power of Prussia than be added to 'the cluster of small bodies politic which encumber Germany and render it of less force than it ought to be in the general balance of power in the world. . . . With a view to the future it is desirable that Germany, in the aggregate, should be strong, in order to control those two ambitious and aggressive powers, France and Russia, that press upon her west and east. As to France, we know how restless and aggressive she is, and how ready to break loose for Belgium, for the Rhine, for anything she would be likely to get without too great an exertion. As to Russia, she will in due time become a power almost as great as the old Roman Empire. She can become the mistress of all Asia, except British India, whenever she chooses to take it and when enlightened arrangements shall have made her revenue proportioned to her territory, and railways shall have abridged distances, her command of men will become enormous, her pecuniary means gigantic, and her power of transporting armies over great distances most formidable. Germany ought to be strong in order to resist Russian aggression, and a strong Prussia is essential to German strength'.

Lord Salisbury, never an admirer of Palmerston, declared that 'if we do not intend to carry out by arms our threats and measures, we must abstain from the luxury of indulging in them', and on that note the long dialogue on the meaning of 'non-interference' to which Palmerston made his first controversial contribution in 1829 ended, with the verdict against him. But Temperley and Penson, at the end of a section highly critical of Palmerston, quote his last views on the future balance of power as evidence that 'he set aside all querulous complaints, and viewed the question in a large way, with an eye on the future. . . . Even humiliation cannot blind him to reality or prevent his view from being statesmanlike. . . . In the moment of defeat, Palmerston, unlike the Queen or Russell, shows a certain greatness'. And it was true that, as long as Prussian aggression had limited objects, as against Austria in 1866 and France in 1870, or was foresworn, as in the following twenty years, the rise of a strong German state was advantageous, rather than otherwise, to the Balance of Power. Hence it was safe for a new generation of British statesmen to follow public opinion which, as Salisbury said in 1866 (when he was Lord Cranborne) was, largely as a result of the experience of 1864, 'in favour of abandoning the position which England held for so many years in the councils of Europe'.[60] Hence it was possible for him in later years to call isolation 'splendid'. But when in the twentieth century Germany began to appear in another guise and to reproduce, by combining naval development with massive military power, the sort of menace France had seemed to presage in 1860, British statesmen were driven to rekindle the lights by which Palmerston had practised diplomacy. Some may think they would have been wiser to practice the Palmerstonian technique of alliance with the most likely disturber of the peace in order to control her. Others may approve the entente with her potential victims on the Continent. What is clear is that they were driven back to the principles of the Balance of Power, just as, after 1947, the West was driven to them again, on a global basis, in the form of the Balance of Terror.

CHAPTER XXVII

'REST AND BE THANKFUL'

B Y 1864 it was apparent that only paralysis or death could unloose 'the great bundle of sticks'[1] which only Palmerston could hold together. But, though he started the session in fine trim, the gout, accompanied by severe colds, became chronic. He soldiered on, sitting night after night in the House till all hours, struggling up the steps at Harrow on the arm of Sir Robert Peel, ignoring the advice of friends and colleagues not to tire himself by going to Cambridge to meet the Waleses and receive an honorary degree. Uneven parliamentary performances were nothing new with him. On 1st March 'Lord Palmerston was roused. He rose with great vigour and energy, and made a most telling and effective reply . . .' to an unexpected attack by Disraeli on foreign policy. The Speaker noted on 20th June: 'Within the last fortnight he has shown symptoms of failure. He does not catch the point of questions, and when a question refers to two or three particulars, he does not keep them in his memory. These failings are quite new to him. On the motion of censure on the Ashantee War he spoke much below the mark.' But he corrected himself on 27th — '. . . He seemed quite strung up to the occasion; there was no appearance of age or failure. . . . His voice was strong and clear. The statement was excellent; a better narrative of events could not have been given. It was distinct and forcible; enough was said and not too much. Many parts were run over with a light hand. I was much struck with it, as a remarkable parliamentary performance', though he admitted that the end 'was not good'.[2] As often happened when his back to the wall, Palmerston failed to shine when winding up on the vote of censure on 8th July. There seemed no fight in him, and 'his jolly way of looking at disaster'[3] failed him. 'There was a great appearance of physical weakness. . . . The effects of age were more apparent than they had been on any former occasion.'[4]

Palmerston was, naturally, depressed at his failure to carry his colleagues with him and at the very real prospect of defeat on an issue on which an appeal to the country might not succeed. And it had been a session of petty annoyances, including the necessity of getting an Act of Indemnity because the Marquess of Hartington sat in the House of Commons as an under-secretary while disqualified, and the forced resignation of two other junior ministers, Robert Lowe and James Stansfeld. Palmerston in February 1863 had been delighted when the Duke of Devonshire gave his son permission to take office, for, he said, it was 'highly conducive to the working of our Constitution' that young men of high aristocratical positions should take part in the administration of public affairs 'and not leave the working of our political machine to classes whose pursuits and interests are of a different kind'.[5] Hartington, who was to be the last Whig leader, was, characteristically late for his first parliamentary engagement as a minister, the moving of a bill to provide permanent services for the Volunteers. It will have pleased Palmerston to hear him extol, with references to the Confederates (whom he had just visited) the capacity of enthusiastic amateurs to thwart trained regulars (such as the Yankees and, by implication, the French). The Tories were gentle with Hartington, who was a gentleman, and whose offence was technical, but they were savage with Lowe and Stansfeld, two middle-class professional men. Lowe's resignation after Lord Robert Cecil had pressed a charge of 'doctoring' inspectors' reports was the culmination of the Church Party's campaign against the 'conscience-clause' which allowed children at Church schools to escape instruction in the Anglican creed and against the Revised Code, which was seen as a blow at the aided schools, mostly Anglican. On the principle of making the poacher a gamekeeper, Palmerston had appointed Stansfeld to the Admiralty with instructions to investigate the dockyards, and chuckled to find him reporting that no overall economy was possible.[60] Stansfeld had to resign when the House all but carried a motion criticizing the government for not taking seriously allegations made at a political trial in Paris that he had allowed his house to be used as an accommodation address for Mazzini and other Italian revolutionaries, and that he, or his wife, had acted as banker for, or subscribed to, the funds of conspirators, including would-be assassins of Napoleon III.

In the spring of 1864 Garibaldi visited England and foreign governments saw with amazement the lionizing by High Society of one who openly declared his wish to lead attacks on Venetia, Rome and Russia, was currently *persona non grata* to the Italian and

French as well as the Austrian Papal and Russian governments and whose reputation was almost enough to re-create the Holy Alliance. The colourful guerrilla leader had all the qualities required to make him a public idol in Britain, but the Stafford House set, including Shaftesbury, were 'temporarily a little out of their mind' about him. He was the only person ever allowed to smoke in the boudoir of the Dowager Duchess of Sutherland, long the Mistress of the Robes. The Queen herself complained that ministers lavished on Garibaldi honours usually reserved for royalty. They frankly admitted, what Cobden perceived, that although (or because) the visit was offensive and ridiculous to foreign rulers, it was very useful at home. Palmerston and Garibaldi had few views in common. Indeed, said Cobden, it would be difficult to show that Palmerston had any views at all 'beyond the wish to hold office by following the popular passions of the time'. Good harvests and (outside Lancashire) full employment provided the bread, Garibaldi the circus. Palmerston was the ringmaster. Granville said that the aristocratic auspices took the democratic sting out of the visit; Palmerston that the nation would take the sponsorship as proof of the community of feeling of all classes. As John Bright looked down on hordes of working men cheering Garibaldi in Westminster he asked sadly why they did not make a few demonstrations for themselves. The government took elaborate precautions to keep the guest out of the hands of agitators and to stop him visiting the large cities and repeating the offences of Kossuth in 1851. The amenable Dr Ferguson wrote an opinion that such visits would be bad for his health (a verdict publicly challenged by Garibaldi's own doctor) and the hero returned prematurely to Caprera on the Duke of Sutherland's yacht. 'This is on every account a good arrangement', commented Palmerston.[7]

Among the cities most anxious to receive a visit from Garibaldi was Bradford, the scene of one of the longest-lived of Urquhart's Foreign Policy Committees, also considered by Bright a promising centre in which to agitate for Parliamentary Reform in 1859. A visit from Lord and Lady Palmerston in the recess was evidently not regarded as adequate compensation. There was a certain coolness about the public meeting. The official addresses praised the Cobden treaty and urged closer relations with France; one M.P., Forster, talked of retrenchment and Parliamentary Reform and another, Crossley, spoke of his pain whenever Palmerston gave the cold-shoulder to a proposal for reform in Church and State. These were signs that the middle-class intelligence was becoming impatient with the Palmerston freeze. To set against them was the notable failure of an organized attempt to have the working-men maintain a disapproving silence during Palmerston's reception; 'those who were to have kept silence were loudest in their hurrahs'.[8] In London the Garibaldi Committee staged a demonstration in protest at the curtailment of the hero's visit. Among its members (including the prominent trade unionist Applegarth) were the men who early in 1865 founded the National Reform League. But Cobden could not 'see how any material improvement in public affairs [was] possible, so long as this old man at the head [could] contrive to use all parties for his own ends', and Palmerston returned from these 'August peregrinations, not sought for by me' convinced that they had been 'successful not simply as regards myself, but as relates to the Government'.[9] After Bradford, the Palmerstons had gone to milady's estates in Northamptonshire (the death of Lord Beauvale had left her as the last of the Lambs) and the premier had cut the first sod for a new railway line at Towcester with jocular platitudes on what was, after all, the most important revolutionary change in his lifetime. The Tory county member had remarked on the unusual feature of Palmerston's reputation — 'the people, it is evident, are determined to give him all the half-pence, and the rest of the Ministry all the kicks'. After presiding at the inauguration of a memorial at Hereford to Cornewall Lewis, Palmerston was seen at the racecourse at Tiverton, dressed in a rusty green swallow-tailed coat, a check neckerchief, coarse striped trousers and an old white hat, a cheery smile playing over furrowed features. He spoke at the race dinner. In September he was at Wilton to inspect the Volunteers.[10] He loved inspections and when the Queen set the seal of royal approval on the Volunteer movement inaugurated in 1859–60 as part of the anti-French 'panic', and sedulously encouraged by Palmerston, by inspecting a parade in Hyde Park, he explained that the body odours of which she complained were what was meant by 'esprit de corps'. On his eightieth birthday in October, he left Broadlands at 8.30, returning at 6.00, having ridden round the South Downs fortifications.

On a cold November Sunday after lunch he pulled a ferry boat across a stream and took a two-hour walk, falling over a tree stump in the dusk.

* * * *

This was Palmerston's Indian summer, when everyone was waiting for him to die, knowing that 'things would never be the same again', for, like Melbourne before him, this leader of the Liberal forces left no obvious successor to be the champion within the progressive party of the Conservative Cause. There could be no honesty in public life, said Cobden, as long as Palmerston had Gladstone and Milner Gibson in his cabinet and the tacit connivance of a section of the Tories.[11] Palmerston knew himself that soon politics would be dominated by the strife and competition of Gladstone with Disraeli, and there would be much anxiety and confusion.[12] His own cabinet was the oldest in the record books, with an average age at his death of over sixty, the only newcomer to cabinet rank admitted after 1859 being the refreshingly unorthodox Earl de Grey and Ripon, one of the principal champions of administrative reform in 1855, who would have qualified for description as a Mancunian if he had not been so friendly to trade unionism and something of a Christian Socialist. This champion of economy was given the War Office; with his record, even Gladstone must find the Army Estimates persuasive. But where was the *vis inertiae* of the Liberal party to come from after Palmerston's death? Hartington was young and not yet in the cabinet. Hardly older, and not yet in office, was Goschen, the new member for the City of London who has left a valuable record of his interview with Palmerston after he had been invited in 1864 to second the Address in reply to a Queen's Speech which referred to only one domestic topic — the report of a commission on clerical oaths.[13] Goschen's speech would bring a gleam to the old man's eye, for it was an attack on the Manchester School —

... That does not seem to me necessarily a warlike policy, which contemplates the possibility of strong measures for the coercion of disturbers of the peace; or that necessarily a peaceful policy which by laying down beforehand the doctrine of absolute non-intervention, almost holds out a temptation to aggression. ... The Country cannot comprehend how, whilst the barriers separating different nations are being thrown down every day ... the first utterance of England on the approach of a European danger should be to proclaim an utterly selfish and isolated policy, repudiating not only her international obligations, but also, I may say, her international interests. It seems to me as impossible, as it would be inconsistent and impolitic, for England, in the face of Europe, to lay down a rule of absolute non-intervention. Those professing to desire peace at any price seem often unwilling to pay the heavy price which might be asked for it — and that is war itself.

When he saw Palmerston —

. . . The Old man's manner to me was one of extraordinary cordiality, and full of life. . . . He ran through the various points of foreign policy that required to be touched. They were sufficiently numerous and important. When he came to a stop as if he had finished his instructions, I asked with becoming diffidence, 'What is to be said about domestic affairs and legislation!'. 'Oh', he gaily replied, rubbing his hands with an air of comfortable satisfaction, 'there is really nothing to be done. We cannot go on adding to the Statute Book ad infinitum. Perhaps we may have a little law reform, or bankruptcy reform: but we cannot go on legislating for ever. . . .

This view had recently received startling endorsement from Lord Russell, who, at Blairgowrie in September 1863 declared:

. . . With regard to domestic policy I think we are all very much agreed, because the feeling of the country, and of those who have conducted great reforms, is very much like that of a man who, having made a road in your own highlands, put a stone on the top of the mountain with an inscription 'Rest and be thankful'.

But Gladstone was restless. He was in his middle-fifties, and tired of waiting for the old soldiers to fade away. He was also sufficiently unpopular with right-wing, and even with moderate, Liberals to require some popular stimulus to sustain him. Perhaps not wholly consciously he set out to emulate Palmerston's achievement of 1849–51 and compensate for weak support in the House of Commons by identifying himself with a growing mood among the people. Unlike Palmerston, however, he did not build his popularity primarily on his attitude to foreign affairs, and unlike Palmerston he did not do it by being, only more ostentatiously than before, the man he had always been. He remained, indeed, to his dying day the champion of economy and of *laisser-faire*, but he emerged now as a champion of reform, and of those aspects of reform to which he had previously, to the distress of the Manchester Radicals who admired him as the practitioner and prophet of fiscal reform and retrenchment, been cool — the reform of the electoral system and of the ecclesiastical establishment in Ireland. This implies no hypocrisy, because Gladstone's whole political career, unlike Palmerston's, was one of change and development, each stage preceded by long critical self-examination by the light of a keen intellect and an active conscience, though revealed to the world apparently through sudden enthusiasm or political impulse, not, however, without giving his critics ground for supposing calculation. In 1864 Baines's annual proposal for the extension of the borough franchise provided an opportunity for Gladstone to bid for Liberal approval in the country, and yet to claim that he had done no such thing.

On the day of the debate Palmerston was too ill to attend the House, but sent a note to Gladstone. It was true, he said, that there were unenfranchised working men fit to exercise the franchise, but unfortunately in the great towns they were under the control of Trade Unions, which were themselves controlled 'by a small Number of directing Agitators'. He hoped that Gladstone would leave everything open, committing neither himself nor the government to any figure. Palmerston's private feeling was that the six-pound householder represented the lowest he could accept, and Gladstone, *after* his speech, reported that he had said he was for a considerable but not excessive enlargement, on the lines of 'our proposal' of 1860. But when he read *The Times* next day, Palmerston found that Gladstone had stated the number of electors he wished to see enfranchised. And he had done worse than that. He had said that every man was entitled to come 'within the pale of the Constitution' who was not presumptively disqualified by personal unfitness or public danger and 'called on the adversary to show cause'. Gladstone would attempt to pass this off to colleagues as mere platitude, but it was not so taken. 'We knew pretty well what he really meant, viz that when he had the chance, he would produce a real Reform Bill' notes Wilfrid Lawson, the Cobdenite Radical nephew of Graham.[14] Palmerston knew it too. The heir presumptive had offended against the cardinal precepts which Whig and Tory alike accepted, that the vote was a public trust; that it was a privilege not a right; that a man could not be considered eligible for it unless he had a substantial 'stake in the country'; that it was always up to the advocate of Reform to show that considerable numbers were excluded who could with safety and advantage be admitted; that the concepts of 'elector' and 'citizen' were not logically connected, except that one could not be an elector unless one was a citizen.

The Opposition said that Palmerston was the man to answer Gladstone. He did not oblige in public, but in private he was scathing[15] —

. . . I have read your speech and I must frankly say with much regret as there is little in it that I can agree with, and much from which I differ. You lay down broadly the Doctrine of Universal Suffrage which I can never accept. I entirely deny that every sane and not disqualified man has a moral right to a vote — I use that expression instead of 'the Pale of the Constitution' because I hold that all who enjoy the Security and civil Rights which the Constitution provides are within its Pale — What every Man and Woman too have a Right to, is to be well governed and under just Laws, and they who propose a change ought to show that the present organization does not accomplish those objects. If every Man has a Right to have his Share in chusing those who make Laws, why should he not have a Right to express his own opinion on Laws to be made. . . . ?

. . . If you will not take it amiss, I would say, that it was more like the Sort of Speech with which Bright would have introduced the Reform Bill which he would like to propose than the Sort of Speech which might have been expected from the Treasury Bench in the present State of Things. Your Speech may win Lancashire for you, though it is doubtful but I fear it will tend to lose England for you. It is to be regretted that you should, as you stated, have taken the opportunity of your receiving a Deputation of working men to exhort them to set on Foot an Agitation for Parliamentary Reform — the Function of a Government is to calm rather than to excite Agitation.

Palmerston understood what Gladstone had done and understood better than Gladstone (whose fantastic power of self-deception was already a subject of remark) why he had done it. Gladstone's replies, insisting that his proposition was neither strange, nor new, nor extreme, were disingenuous, for he admitted that 'it required . . . to be construed', and therefore proposed to publish the speech with an explanatory preface designed to remove 'strange misconceptions' and curb (he said) 'the applause which I do not deserve', which, he claimed, vexed him at least as much as the criticism. Palmerston begged him not to do so, for if a number of ministers committed themselves in advance on an issue, it would be difficult for a government to survive by the normal processes of give and take.[16] Exactly twenty years later Gladstone, as premier, similarly begged a Radical colleague, Joseph Chamberlain, not to enter so freely in public into 'matters not proximate'.[17]

'I have no desire to force the question forward', protested Gladstone, though the effect of his speech was to do so. He believed, he said, that 'the party which supports your Government' had suffered, was suffering, and would much more seriously suffer from the part played on the franchise question and 'such influence as argument and statement without profession of political intentions can exercise upon the public mind, I heartily desire to see exercised in favour of an extension of the franchise, that the question may if possible be disposed of for another generation to come' (i.e. for the rest of Gladstone's probable political career, should he live to be as old as Palmerston) 'while it remains manageable and before it runs the risk of becoming formidable'. As to the allegation of exciting agitation, he had only told the workmen that one of the main causes of parliament's indifference was that it could be said that the working classes were themselves indifferent. Palmerston dismissed this as sophistry; what he had said was tantamount to an invitation to agitate. The speech, he said, had produced an unfortunate effect 'even upon many of the Liberal Party and upon all Persons who value the Maintenance of our Institutions'.[17] The Queen, 'deeply grieved at this strange and independent act of Mr. Gladstone's', hoped the premier's gout — to which she ascribed recent 'impertinent' communications of which it must be said that Palmerston seems to have been right constitutionally on the matter if somewhat crisp in matter — was better.[18]

Palmerston knew that Gladstone was urging ardent Liberals to look to him for 'a good time coming'. There would be strange doings, he said, 'when Gladstone has my place'. He was 'a dangerous man; keep him in Oxford and he is partially muzzled, but send him elsewhere and he will run wild'.[12] Palmerston himself had, as member for Cambridge University, survived support for Catholic Emancipation in 1829 but not support of the Reform Bill. Gladstone's speech on Reform made it, as Palmerston did not fail to point out, more likely that he would win South Lancashire but more likely that he would lose the Oxford University parsons. He clinched his defeat at Oxford by his speech on Dillwyn's motion against the Irish Church in March 1865. Gladstone opposed the proposition that the state of the Establishment in Ireland called for the early attention of Her Majesty's Government, but accepted that it was 'unsatisfactory'. 'His argument went to all establishments' and was vociferously cheered by Radicals and voluntarists, commented the Conservative who was to defeat him at Oxford University. Palmerston had tried to dissuade Gladstone from speaking. He did not know, he said, what Gladstone's views were, but if he aired them from the Treasury Bench were his colleagues to air their own or stay silent?[19] When, in the general election of 1865, Gladstone lost Oxford he unconsciously used Palmerston's own metaphor, and told the Lancastrians he came among them 'unmuzzled'.

In the winter, the question of expenditure 'lay . . . like a nightmare' on Gladstone, and in October he fired off a letter which was meant to be moderate but might 'lead to consequences' by February unless Palmerston concurred, which he would only do 'through apprehension'. Independent members, he told the prime minister, would in 1865 agitate the questions of expenditure and taxation with vivacity. He was proud to have halted the upward trend of civil expenditure and brought the service estimates down to below 1860–1 though still above 1858–9. But he could not maintain that it was really necessary to spend £26½ million on a peacetime establishment, now that rearmament, reconstruction and sanitary improvement had gone so far, and they must resume the process of reduction begun in 1863–4 under the impulse of the Economy Resolution.[20]

Palmerston's reaction justified the obituary comment that 'to the last he fought as a contemporary, claiming no favour and requiring none'.[21] He kept Gladstone, who was keyed up for conflict, waiting two weeks before he answered him. Then he said that no doubt before the dissolution there would be some 'Clap-Trap Motions' intended to help members in their constituencies. But he was sure that there were two strong feelings in the national mind — 'the one a Disinclination to organic Changes in our representative System; the other a steady Determination that the Country shall be placed and kept in an efficient Condition of Defence'. It was as demonstrable as any proposition in Euclid that 170,000 Volunteers would not have come forward if they did not believe that the country might at any moment be in danger and that the establishments on their own were insufficient to meet that danger. He could not see what 1858–9 had to do with the question nor what was 'the necessary and inherent Connexion between any arithmetical sum and the wants of the various services'. There could be no material reduction in the navy and the home garrisons were not too large. Some marginal saving might be possible in New Zealand and India, but though, from sound policy and true economy they had been attending to the comforts and general condition of servicemen, he was sorry to say that much remained to be done to provide healthy and sufficient accommodation for the home garrison and some of the barracks in colonial stations were extremely injurious to health. The premier then entered into details of weapon-development in the past decade. There were enough rifles, though many needed to be converted for breech-loading. There were enough Armstrong field-pieces 'as good . . . as any Nation's'. But there were not enough up-to-date land batteries and it was going to cost a lot to produce enough high-calibre cannon to deal with iron ships, 'and yet efficient guns, it is evident, we must have'. He objected to leaving the fortifications incomplete and abstaining from issuing more terminable annuities; to finance fortification by loans was only to do what a landowner did for purposes of capital developments and a businessman when building a mine or harbour.

Gladstone retorted that he had always felt that the present level of estimates was beyond the reasonable wants of the country, and was now sure it would injure the government in the elections. Significant cuts could be obtained only as the result of a policy decision for which he now asked, pointing out that 'the Finance Minister is, after the Prime Minister, specially responsible for the sum total of these estimates taken together'. He had assented to the Estimates in the past partly in consideration of the wants and partly of the opinions and feelings of the nation. Now he felt bound to say that *'it is your own personal popularity, and not the public conviction or desire, that would alone keep the Estimates at their present high level'*.[22] This notable tribute to his personal influence Palmerston repudiated in characteristic terms. Gladstone was confusing cause and effect. The British nation was not one 'disposed to bear unnecessary Burthens out of Regard for any individual Man' — *'. . . if I have in any Degree been fortunate enough to have obtained some Share of the Good will and Confidence of my Fellow-Countrymen, it has been because I have rightly understood the Feelings and Opinions of the Nation, and because they think that I have, as far as any Scope of Action of Mine was concerned, endeavoured to maintain the Dignity and to uphold the Interests of the Country abroad, and to provide for its security at Home. . .'.* And this was the only way of obtaining the only popularity worth having, 'and of that Popularity I sincerely wish you the most ample share'.[23]

After providing this outstandingly apt text for his own obituary, Palmerston continued to play the heavy father. Of course there would be a difference in 'abstract ideas' on national expenditure between chancellors taking a departmental view and prime ministers taking a general view; the broader view must of course prevail, and he could not accept the constitutional theory that the Chancellor was entitled to come to an arbitrary conclusion on the amount of the service estimates and impose his will by a threat of resignation. Gladstone asked for the correspondence to be circulated to the cabinet. The meeting of 19th January 1865 was 'about as rough as any of the roughest times' and his opinions on naval expenditure were 'manifestly in a minority'.[24] After the service departments had made 'inadequate' concessions of detail in the usual way, Palmerston expressed from Brocket on 31st January his satisfaction and conviction that the Commons and the country would not expect 'any greater Reduction of Force than that which is thus agreed upon'. He then went on to the offensive over the budget, breaking into verse —

> When Gladstone gleans from each Man's Yearly Hoard
> How much more free the workman than the Lord
> Safe Skulk the Poor beneath the taxing Power
> And leave the wealthier Grumbler to look sour.

But his complaint was, professedly, that taxes on common consumption (tea, sugar, coffee, beer, spirits) should have priority for reduction, rather than income-tax, which the poor did not pay, especially as a 4d. income-tax would be taken as a proclamation to abolish it as soon as possible.[25] Gladstone admitted that he felt himself bound to place parliament in the position as at 1853 of being free to decide whether to part with the income-tax or not.[26] Palmerston suggested that a reduction in the malt-tax would please the rural interests and help in the elections. From Brocket on 18th April he expressed alarm at rumours that Gladstone was planning a new house-tax. If it fell on owners it would be unjust double taxation, for the Dukes of Bedford and Portland, Sir John Ramsden, etc., already paid income-tax on their house rents. If it fell on occupiers, all the ten-pound householders would rise against it. When Gladstone explained that it was to be a tax on owners in lieu of the tax on fire-insurances, which the House, against his advice, had rejected in 1864, the old man was severe. 'You are too ingenious in your complications', he said. He would come up to London for the final cabinet on the budget.[27] There Gladstone won his main point — a 4d. income-tax was combined with reductions on pepper, timber and tea. But Palmerston, despite evident physical decay, was not less in control of affairs than in any other year of this government. In March he did not fail to point out to Gladstone that the debate on the naval estimates, so far from reinforcing Gladstone's urgent but unavailing demand to reduce the number of seamen, had been marked by criticism of the reduction of boys and marines and demands for more ironclads, guns and docks. He added a blistering comment — 'shallow Streams run with the most violence and Noise' — on Cobden's letters to the premier criticizing measures for the defence of Canada as futile and provocative to the United States.[28]

In April Cobden died, at sixty. His view that Canada was indefensible was put by Lowe ('a very absurd speech' remarked Palmerston to the Queen) at a time when at least one cabinet minister expected war.[29] But the government was careful in its relations with the victorious Federals, whose hostility was helping to create the climate which made possible the confederation of British North America in 1867. The Queen thought Russell took too low a tone with Seward. 'Ought your Majesty's Government to refuse to do right . . . because swaggering and insolent men will say that Great Britain is frightened by the successes of the Federal Government?', he replied.[30] Quebec and Montreal were being fortified. In the last defence debate in which he participated (the first had been fifty-five years ago) Palmerston deprecated the suggestion that the Americans would attack. But, he said, Canada could be defended, and must be defended, and there was no intention whatever of withdrawing British troops.[31]

*　　*　　*　　*

Without any personal ill will, Derby, who in the winter had seemed likely to predecease Palmerston (fifteen years his senior) wished that Palmerston might drop dead before the influence of his name condemned the Tories to yet another minority.[32] The premier, free from gout, started the session in great form, seeming at the afternoon pre-Session dinner on 6th February particularly well and less deaf. This was the occasion on which[33] —

. . . he ate two plates of turtle soup; he was then served very amply to cod and oyster cause; he then took a pâté; afterwards he was helped to two very greasy-looking entrées; he then despatched a plate of roast mutton (two slices) . . . there then appeared before him the largest, and to my mind the hardest, slice of ham that ever figured on the table of a nobleman, yet it disappeared just in time to answer the inquiry of the butler, 'Snipe, or pheasant, my lord?' He instantly replied 'Pheasant', thus completing his ninth dish of meat at that meal. . . .

And he went on to pudding, jelly, dressed oranges and half a large pear. It should be explained that Palmerston habitually had only one considerable meal a day (as was the custom) and that, always moderate with the bottle, he drank on this occasion seltzer water, one glass of sweet champagne late in the meal, and a glass of sherry at dessert. At the end of March, when the Speaker asked him if he had some comfortable arrangement for getting home in the cold weather, he replied: 'Oh yes; I often take a cab, and if you leave both windows open you get nearly as much air as if you walked.' 'A through draft [sic] and a north-east wind! And in a hack cab! What a combination for health!' commented his questioner.[34]

Palmerston took evident delight in defying the enemy of all men, and until the Easter vacation all went well. But at Brocket the gout assailed him and was not improved by his riding a rough mount. The letter to Gladstone of 18th April is in Lady Palmerston's hand. Too ill to attend the House on budget day, the premier for the remaining two months of the session went down usually only for questions. The gout was chronic, and prevented him sleeping. When walking he leaned heavily on William Cowper. The head slumped on the chest. His skin had the transparency of age; its colour told a tale of failing kidneys. There was bladder-trouble. The end was not far off. But first there was an election to be won. On 16th June the House heard Palmerstonian banter for the last time, as he recited the ancient arguments against Berkeley and Bright on the ballot — to get his name in the papers and conceal how ill he was, the Opposition thought.[35] For the Tory leaders were very angry at the prospect of an election on the theme 'Leave it to Pam' when he was unlikely to be alive to meet the new parliament. Their whips were optimistic as to the result, but they suspected that the old wizard would win the day.[36] On 27th June Palmerston gave notice of dissolution. When he explained the date by saying that the harvest was early, and they must have the election over before it started, many thought he had the activity of the Great Reaper in mind. On 5th July 1865 he spoke for the last time in the House of Commons, which he had entered nearly fifty-eight years before, sitting on a Front Bench above the gangway for all but three years. There were no parting tributes, for he would not admit that he would not be there in 1866.

* * * *

The rhyme went round Tiverton 'Hearty he looked — bold he spoke, his eye twinkled with fun. There are older men at sixty-two than he at eighty-one'. But he was visibly worn out, and the crowds from the Devon and Somerset villages, Bristol and Exeter came to take a last look at him and to hear his last brush with Rowcliffe, whom he chaffed for voting for Sir John Walrond, the Tory. 'I did not vote for you, my lord, for if I had, I should have voted for a Tory' came the apt reply.[37] When Sir John beat his Liberal colleague Denman by three votes, Palmerston bowed stiffly to him. He was not sure whether Denman's defeat was the accidental result of Tory goodwill towards Palmerston or whether, in warning the Liberal agent that Palmerston himself was in danger because electors wishing to split their votes had been told to go for Walrond and Denman, the Tory agent had deliberately contrived the gain. But from the country as a whole the results of a languid election fought without clear issues between the parties were all that could have been wished. The Liberal majority was greatly increased. Certain of the gains were Radical, but Palmerston's prestige checked Conservative advance in the sort of seats where it might have been expected. Twice only between 1832 and 1955 did a party in office increase its majority at an election. The dates were 1857 and 1865. On both occasions Palmerston was prime minister.

From Tiverton Palmerston went for the last time to Broadlands and then to Brocket, easier of access for doctors (and messengers) from London. His mind was still clear and his language forceful. The opposition to a general half-day on Saturdays for the civil service, he wrote to Gladstone on 23rd August, reminded him of the attitude of the master-manufacturers to a ten-hour day. He had no patience with it. Morale was important; men were not machines but moral and intellectual agents. Let a Saturday shift-system — like naval watches — be tried out for six months. Gladstone, whose meanness over candle-ends was proverbial, was not convinced; it would lead to demands for increased establishments, he said. A month later Gladstone was seeking to parry with predictions of trouble in parliament the premier's demand for a larger salary for the Civil Lord of the Admiralty, whose responsibility had been increased by recent reforms. Palmerston wanted to give the office to a businessman, while Gladstone wanted to save money by having some of the naval lords in the House. Then Palmerston heard that his friend Sir Arthur Helps was wilting under the extreme pressure of the Privy Council's emergency responsibilities due to cattle plague. On 3rd October Palmerston informed Gladstone: 'I have told Helps that, as head of the Government, I authorize him to take, without any delay, such steps as may be necessary to procure additional assistance for his office.' And the Queen would have to put up with some Home Office clerk officiating at a Council at Balmoral instead of Helps.[38]

Gladstone was not the only minister to be reminded that Palmerston was not yet to be spoken of in the past tense. Reports coming in from consuls in the United States, as well as from Ireland, indicated that the Fenian conspiracy might be coming to a head. For growing discontent in Ireland — aggravated he believed by the priests, partly from self-interest and partly under instructions from a pope protected by French bayonets[39] — Palmerston had no remedy except to send the Prince of Wales to open the Dublin Exhibition in February 1865 (the Queen would not let the Princess go) and to reinforce the garrison. This was his concern on 3rd October 1865, when he asked for a regiment of cavalry to be sent at once to inspire confidence in the loyal and deter the Fenians. It mattered nothing to him that the Commander-in-Chief in Ireland did not think this necessary. 'Sir Hugh Rose has been accustomed to walk over everything and everybody opposed to him; but in this case final success is not the only thing to be provided for.' If the Fenians did not heed the warnings, trouble would take the form of a series of scattered outbreaks, and cavalry would be needed. At the same time the War Office was enjoined to inquire about stores of arms and ammunition in Canada, where Fenian outbreaks or incursions from the United States were likely, and to consider, apropos of a possible American invasion in the future, whether the armament of the Quebec defences should not be heavier than planned.[40]

Palmerston's last important letter to the Queen was written on 4th September, rejoicing at the fraternization of the British and French navies in the Channel. The cordiality of the British, he said, would shake the French belief that the English nation entertained a settled hatred of France and Frenchmen. Of course, it was not unnatural that the French navy should be better disposed towards the English than the army, for the French had always looked on naval reverses as in the natural order of things, and not a cause for wounded pride or mortified vanity as well as the pain of national disaster — 'added to which, it may be said that there is less of vanity and more of simplicity of character belonging to the naval than to the military profession'. Some may feel that Palmerston himself was a sea-dog manqué; it has always seemed to the present writer that he would have enjoyed being first lord of the admiralty.

The meeting of the navies was, Palmerston pointed out, not only a good sign for Anglo-French relations. It could not fail to have a wholesome effect on the other side of the Atlantic, 'for there is nothing which the North Americans dislike more, as an obstacle to their schemes, than a cordial union between England and France . . . and . . . as the tendency of the human mind is always to exaggerate the bearing and importance of events not clearly understood', the Americans would think the meetings a sort of preliminary to a defensive alliance and be less likely to pick a quarrel with either Power. But he did not weaken in his hostility to the French project for a Suez Canal, a hostility less obscurantist than it seems to us, for the original schemes made no sense except as a device for securing a large French concession in Egypt, and the canal was a commercial success only because of technological developments which were very new when Palmerston died.[A] He

---

[A] Argyll writes that the Suez Canal project was first mentioned in cabinet on 20th August 1855 as a French idea urged by Napoleon III. 'Palmerston surprised me and others by the most vehement opposition.' He was supported only by Clarendon. The other ministers all thought the proposal could not be creditably or successfully opposed, and urged that the canal should be built as an international enterprise and run under international control. 'But Palmerston remained as hostile as ever. He seemed quite ready to risk a quarrel with France rather than to consent to any such canal' and, this being conveyed to Napoleon, the project was dropped for the moment (*Arg.*, i. 568–9).
At first sight Palmerston's attitude is unbelievably obscurantist and narrow, for we think of the Suez Canal as having been safely in British hands (and used for Britain's ends) from 1882 until the arguments of Eden triumphed over those of Churchill in 1954. Palmerston realized clearly enough that 'any great work which would shorten considerably the voyage to India, would be advantageous to all nations trading by sea to Asia', and to Britain on political and military grounds, as well as commercial, provided it were not in hostile hands. But he presumed that 'Thouvenel did not expect 'us' to receive 'except with a decently suppressed smile' the proposal to forbid passage to ships of war, as at the

was sure that it was 'the standing Policy of France . . . to make the Mediterranean a French Lake' and as prevention was better than cure, 'our Business consequently ought to be to unravel their Plots, to see through their Intrigues, and to defeat their schemes by Counteraction steadily and Systematically applied'.[41]

The lucidity and force of the letters of the last months of his life justify Clarendon's verdict that he went at the best moment for himself, 'in the plenitude of his political and intellectual power, just after the triumph accorded to him by the country in the elections, without suffering or change of habits or loss of consciousness, and plucky and "Palmerston" to the last moment'.[42] It never

Dardanelles. In the first week of war between England and France 15,000–20,000 Frenchmen would take possession of it. (To Russell, 8th Dec. 1861, A. ii, pp. 325–8.) He contended, as in 1855, that the Canal would form a strong military frontier between Egypt and the rest of the Turkish empire, enabling the Pasha to declare his independence, 'which would mean his being a dependent of France'. It would 'place British interests in Egypt and in India at the mercy of France' (1855). The 'political objects of the enterprise . . . are hostility to England in every possible modification of the scheme' (1861). He would have nothing to do with the 'plausible' proposal for a Franco-British-Austrian commision to inquire into the practicability of de Lesseps's scheme. He obviously thought the French were renewing in a different form the great plan he had thwarted in 1840. He did not want to make Egypt a British possession, but he feared that a canal, or even an abortive canal project, would make Egypt in fact actually or potentially a French possession.

There was more ground than we can easily realize for Palmerston's confident assurance that 'as a commercial undertaking, it is a bubble scheme, which has been taken up on political grounds, and in antagonism to English interests and English policy'. He could not see how the canal could be built at anything like the estimated cost, or how, if it was built, it could ever pay, the Red Sea being a very difficult piece of water attractive, as compared with the Cape route, only to 'very powerful steamers'. It might be that the canal would never be built, and the whole thing end up as a gigantic French land speculation giving France permanent 'pretences for interfering in all the internal affairs' of Egypt.

On these points it must be said, in defence of Palmerston: 1. That the Egyptian concessions were so extensive and unpopular that only strong French pressure saw the scheme through amid growing Egyptian irritation and British and Turkish discouragement, and they contributed materially to the collapse of public credit which resulted in Anglo-French control of the finances of Egypt (and Disraeli's purchase of the shares of the bankrupt Khedive) which in turn stimulated Egyptian nationalism, answered by British occupation in 1882. 2. That when the Suez Canal was opened in 1869 its success was 'automatically assured by *technological developments far beyond its planner's imagination*'. Of these the principal were the perfection of the screw-propeller as a substitute for the paddle-wheel and the development of the compound engine, which in the 1860s revolutionized the economics of the shipping lines. Only these developments clearly made the pure steamer a superior proposition to the steam-assisted sailing-ship, and removed reservations about the navigation of the Red Sea. (Marston, *Britain's Imperial Role in the Red Sea Area*, 385.)

occurred to Palmerston to resign, and on 7th October he fixed 10th November for the first of the cabinets to consider the business of the new parliament. But soon bulletins were being issued. People said that the last illness could have been avoided by elementary caution and deference to medical advice, but the fatal 'chill' was almost certainly fever due to heightened blood-pressure owing to the rapid degeneration of the kidneys.[A] Without vitality he had no wish to linger on — he stole out of the house to climb the high railings and back again to see whether he was still capable of it. 'When a man's time comes, it is no use repining', he said. The family could not wish him to linger on when to infirmity were added signs of senility — a few minutes after he had quoted from Vergil's *Georgics* the symptoms of the current cattle plague he lapsed into inordinate laughter at recollections of stone-throwing at Harrow. On Sunday 15th October, as the Queen decided that Russell should succeed him at his death, Palmerston greeted with monosyllabic aquiescence in the proposition that all men are sinners and that Christ died for them a physician's attempt to stage a Victorian deathbed scene. He preferred the Belgian Treaty to the Gospels. 'Read the sixth Article again', he said on the Tuesday; 'that's article 98, now go on to the next.' On Wednesday 18th at 10.45 a.m. he died, prime minister of Great Britain, as he had intended that he should, with an open dispatch box by his side and a half-finished letter before him.

[A] I am indebted to Dr J. S. Frew and Dr Charles Rizza for information on the medical significance of Palmerston's symptoms so far as they are recorded.

AND HIS WORKS DID FOLLOW HIM

THE death, at a great age, of eminent persons kept to the last before the public eye by position (like Queen Victoria) or prestige (like Sir Winston Churchill), inevitably attracts talk of 'the end of an era'. In the historical perspective we can see that the death of Palmerston was not merely a case of 'the last candle of the eighteenth century going out'. It did coincide with the end, or nearly the end, of a phase in the triumphant career of British industrial capitalism, before the disappearance of surpluses of exports over imports, before the dark clouds gathered over agriculture, before the bite of foreign competition on Britain's overseas markets pierced the flesh, before the dread power of a military machine based on conscription, railways and mass-produced armaments of steel was revealed. But the death of Palmerston was not merely symbolic. It was of practical importance. For he was still prime minister, and an active one. His disappearance was expected to make a difference. Some rejoiced at his passing, with no like-minded successor to take up his mantle, no man who would consciously lead Liberalism from right of centre or, as Radicals put it, from behind, no man trusted by the Tories to maintain the *Conservative Cause* while frustrating the Conservative Party. Others waxed apocalyptic, like Lord Shaftes-bury — 'We must now be prepared for vast and irrevocable changes. Palmerston was the great pillar appointed, under God's Providence, to which all the vessels of the State were linked, and so the fleet was held to its moorings. It is now cast down: the ships are set afloat without rudder or compass.' But all agreed that 'the exceptional sway of Lord Palmerston could not be reproduced by any other statesman, or any combination'. The most that could be hoped or feared was that the House of Commons elected under his auspices, which he never met, would not be a willing instrument in the hands of Gladstone, and that its successor would have a majority conservative in party as well as a majority conservative in opinion. If that were so, it would mean that Palmerston had not held up reforms, but merely prevented Conservative victory.

543

Palmerston's death transferred the onus of providing a brake for Liberalism from No. 10 Downing Street to the Whig aristocracy and the smoking-room of the House of Commons. Even before Palmerston was accorded the Abbey funeral which, at first, Russell did not think to recommend, Gladstone wrote: 'As to politics, there is in the Cabinet all the disposition that can be desired.'[1] Soon the lobbies buzzed with talk of the activities of the new Lord Lansdowne against the ministerial Reform Bill; then with the news of a wrecking amendment to be moved by Earl Grosvenor, M.P., and seconded by Lord Stanley, the Tory leader's son, and of another to be moved by Lord Dunkellin, the heir of Clanricarde. And this was carried, by the desertion of right-wing Liberals christened 'Adullamites'. Horsman, who was one of them, expressed their discontents: 'Lord Palmerston would never have been weak enough to be persuaded that England would be governed from Manchester or the Liberal party dominated over by the member for Birmingham. The wise and tranquil policy of Lord Palmerston was to be reversed, the days of truce and compromise were over, and so was the reign of moderate Liberalism behind the Treasury benches.' The Chief Whip agreed: 'The Whigs hate Bright; moreover many distrust Gladstone. Lord Russell is very unpopular; since Palmerston died he has greater proclivities for Bright. . . . The fact is, we have been resting too much on the Radical leg. Palmerston's plan was to rest upon Whig support, and the Radicals had no choice but to follow. Russell's plan has been to rely on Radical support, and the Whigs immediately take fright and desert to the Tories.' There was talk of a coalition between the Tories and the dissident Whigs (which would have involved, inter alia, the deposition of Disraeli).[2] But Derby formed his third minority government, in 1866, Disraeli and Gladstone crossing the floor as leaders of their respective parties in the Commons. Before the end of 1867 Russell, the old soldier, faded away (though he lived till 1878) and early in 1868 Derby yielded the premiership to Disraeli. Later in 1868 Disraeli, accepting the verdict of the electorates before parliament met, yielded the premiership to Gladstone, a Liberal leader of whom it could certainly not be alleged that he stood for 'conservatism and lethargy'. He appealed to 'great social forces . . . mov[ing] onwards in their might and majesty' and increased Palmerston's majority by gains in the Celtic fringe won on an anti-landlord cry. The Gladstonian majority differed in tone from the Palmerstonian. And the Gladstonian cabinet differed in style from Palmerston's. Of eight cabinet colleagues in the Commons, only one — Cardwell — had sat in cabinet with Palmerston. There was a great series of reforms paralleled only in the 30s. But there was also a drift to the Tories (in the 80s it became a flood) not only of Whig nobility and gentry but, as Cobden had sorrowfully predicted, of moneyed men. Both leakages it had been a prime achievement of Palmerston to delay. After his death many men of substance, hitherto Liberal in profession, concluded with the Widow of Windsor that 'Lord Palmerston was *not* wrong when he said to the Queen "[Gladstone] is a very dangerous man" '.[3]

Since power in Britain became ministerial instead of monarchical, her history has no parallel to those last years when everyone was waiting for an old man to die, persuaded that many things would change with, and because of, his death. But it is probable that the immediate effects of his death have been misunderstood. The events of, and after, 1868 followed a democratic Reform Act of 1867 which was the child of a mésalliance between Disraelian contrivance and Liberal majority, not desired by most Tories (if any) or by most Liberals in the House of Commons and bearing little resemblance to the much more modest bill of Russell and Gladstone defeated in the same House in 1866. The constituent basis of the House was radically changed by the admission to the electorate of hordes of working men in parliamentary boroughs, and not merely the more prosperous working men moulded in the bourgeois and Liberal image. Over-dramatizing the effect of Palmerston's death, commentators have emphasized the speed with which Russell, 'an old man in a hurry', concerted with Gladstone his Reform Bill, and have sometimes left the impression that all that followed did so inexorably.[A] This must be challenged by

---

[A] Historians have been almost as prone as journalists to over-dramatize on the lines of the *Daily Telegraph* obituary: 'The two imperial sections have positively waited, with weapons in hand, to let him pass from public life in quiet and honour. . . . It was as if the two great sects of State had made a lane for him to pass to his grave — as if the Armageddon of principle had been put off by mutual consent, because the great Chief must first be grandly buried.' Even G. M. Young, in the present writer's most respectful opinion, implicitly over-dramatizes (*Victorian England*, pp. 80–81, 103–6) — though it is factually true that 'the notion that a party should enter office with a ready-made list of things it meant to do, begins to take hold in the years just after Palmerston's death' (ibid. 134) ,probably as a result of the Reform of 1867. Young shrewdly balanced

emphasizing that, if Russell and Gladstone introduced a bill, they also failed to pass it, because the House elected in 1865 was still cast in the Palmerston mould. It must be suggested, quite seriously, that Palmerston, though from 1861 to 1865 he was the decisive influence against the production of a ministerial bill, and though he had failed between 1855 and 1865 to pass (as he could have done) a much more moderate measure than the act of 1867, would, if he had lived, have introduced a bill in 1866 or promised, in 1866, a bill for 1867. After all, it had been accepted both in 1857 and 1859 that a Liberal majority meant a reform bill. It is not improbable that, this time, he would have introduced it with the intention that it should pass. It is very likely that, if he had done so, there would have been no considerable Adullamite revolt, and as certain as anything can be that the secessions would have been inadequate to kill the bill. With Palmerston as premier, no one could have said that Bright governed, though he did not reign. The Russell–Gladstone bill was defeated because men distrusted the intentions and inclinations of ministers and because Gladstone lacked Palmerston's easy manners in the smoking-room, lacked the finer arts of conciliation, and did not work sufficiently closely with his chief whip.

*   *   *   *

Unlike Palmerston, Gladstone was far more interested in domestic affairs than in foreign. Where the older man's most characteristic lecture was on the merits of the British constitutional system and spirit as export commodities, the younger's standard

the verdict: 'Till his death at eighty-one . . . in the eyes of the world and his country Palmerston was England and England was Palmerston' with the reminder that 'the unfriendly and mistrustful union of Palmerston and Gladstone . . . is typical of the poise of the age' (ibid. 80, 83).

Bagehot, writing the introduction to the second edition of his *English Constitution* in 1872, put his finger upon a factor which goes far to explain why it was that 'in so short a period there have rarely been more changes. . . . The change since 1865 . . . is a change not of particular details but of pervading spirit.' To attribute this to the Reform of 1867 was, he said, a complete mistake; it was too soon to measure the effects of that Act. 'There has', he wrote, 'been a change of the sort which, above all, generates other things . . . a change of generation. . . . Lord Palmerston to the last retained great prohibitive power. Though in some ways always young, he had not a particle of sympathy with the younger generation; he had brought forward no younger men; he obstructed all that young men wished. In consequence, at his death a new generation all at once started into life; he pre-'32 all at once died out. . . .'

political sermon extolled public thrift and private self-reliance. Long convinced that intervention abroad should be 'rare, deliberate, decisive in character, and effectual for its end', and now prone to argue that intervention was not morally justifiable unless it could be effectual (thereby he distinguished the case of Poland from the case of Italy),[4] his dislike of expenditure fortified his rejection of the Palmerstonian method in diplomacy. But overdramatization of the consequences of Palmerston's death must be avoided 1859 inaugurated a decade of change in Europe which required of Britain either a costly involvement which, when it came to the crunch, her people would not face or a dignified withdrawal for which, in time, the people and the politicians opted, allowing Cobden to claim a notable victory. There was a period of not very dignified confusion, caused by Palmerston's unwillingness to recognize facts. Temperley and Penson describe as 'pathetic' Palmerston's claim to Apponyi to divine the instincts of the public that had deserted him. The national option was made before he died. He had outlived the popular mood which had been his sustaining medium. If Palmerston's spirit was willing, the popular, as well as the cabinet, flesh was weak. The time was ripe for men who would not kick against the pricks, who would foreswear the bullying tone ever since associated with Palmerston.[5] Palmerston's death meant simply that, as Seton-Watson has said, a 'deliberate abstention from Continental affairs . . . (became) equally the policy of both the great political parties'.[6] The Queen complained in almost Palmerstonian terms in 1866 of the appointment to the Foreign Office of Stanley, described by Apponyi as one of 'that school of statesmen who make a dogma of the most complete nonintervention', a school which, he admitted, 'enjoyed all the sympathies of the British public'. He was the first Foreign Secretary to regard the *guarantees* of the Treaty of Vienna as obsolete and its obligations outworn; significantly, he was the first Foreign Secretary or prime minister to have been born since the Treaty was signed.[7] In 1869 the Queen protested at the policy of Clarendon, though he had been Foreign Secretary under Palmerston. She feared that now even Belgium and Portugal would feel they could rely on nothing more than 'moral' support from Britain.[8] In conscious repudiation of Palmerstonian techniques and outlook, Stanley, in his first interview with Apponyi, said that the right to advise foreign governments had lately been abused, and the

T

country had lost and not gained by it. Gladstone held that Britain's authority in Europe was a fund to be accumulated and used only sparingly and thriftily; she must beware of seeming to lay down the law by her own authority.

But Gladstone was a Palmerstonian in foreign affairs by comparison with Granville, whom he appointed to the foreign office in 1870. For Granville, cosmopolitan in life, was isolationist and passivist in policy, while Gladstone, a more insular person, was more cosmopolitan in his outlook on world affairs. In his own way he, too, believed that opinions were mightier than armies. He saw it as Britain's duty and mission to rely on, and to help develop and mature, a European opinion to serve as the best bulwark against wrong. He even hoped that the governments of the Powers, despite their evident shortcomings in terms of righteousness, would form together a misted image of the ideal, and he would have liked to restore the Congress System. The efficacy of his prescriptions was not fairly tested, for Bismarck despised him as a sermonizing intellectual. But Gladstone protested at the notion that 'the dominion of Force' should be 'the sole power acknowledged and regarded'. When Russia seized the occasion of the Franco-Prussian War to denounce the Black Sea clauses of the Treaty of Paris, Lord Odo Russell posted from the Foreign Office to Versailles to tell Bismarck that Britain would 'have to go to war with Russia, with or without allies'. This Palmerstonian sting was rapidly retracted, and Gladstone complained that 'some crude ideas have been floating about even within the precinct of the Cabinet'.[9] But Bismarck (for his own reasons) proved an ally, and Russia, isolated, was compelled to submit herself, in form, to a European conference, at which Granville declared, for the record, that there was 'no foregone conclusion'. This was not true, but even Disraeli admitted that it bore 'a semblance of dignity'.[10] Angered at the annexation of Alsace-Lorraine by the Germans, without even a reference to self-determination, justifying the act in terms solely of German security, Gladstone wished to protest. But Granville said that Palmerston had wasted by his brag the moral strength that Britain had gained from the great war and that to lay down general principles when no one would attend to them would be to waste the strength now derived from moral causes — such as the arbitration of the *Alabama* claims and of the dispute over the boundary between the United States and British Columbia at San

Juan. Of the former Gladstone said that the 'fine', though 'harsh in extent and unjust in basis' was dust in the balance compared with the moral value of the example.

For a decade after his death Palmerston was a prophet without honour in his own country. In his famous Manchester speech of 3rd April 1872 Disraeli said: 'The very phrase "foreign affairs" makes an Englishman convinced that I am about to treat of subjects with which he has no concern', though on them depended the state of taxation and of the economy. He foreswore a turbulent or aggressive diplomacy. He 'acknowledge[d] that the policy of England with respect to Europe should be a policy of reserve, but proud reserve'. At Glasgow in November 1873 he declared grandiloquently that it was 'very probable that the future of Europe depends very greatly on the character of the next Parliament of England' and in his election address in 1874 he asked for 'a little more energy in our foreign policy and a little less in our domestic legislation'. But this was mere party politics, not fundamental criticism. The following year Evelyn Ashley, completing the official *Life* of Palmerston, could write: 'We appear to be removed by a vast interval from the epoch of active interference in the affairs of other countries.'

Yet there was more continuity than at first sight appears. The Palmerstonian policy of vigilance with regard to America, France and Russia persisted, although accompanied by the Gladstone's government's sustained attempt to settle questions at issue with the United States and to agree with Russia that Afghanistan should form a neutral, insulating belt between the British and the advancing Russian empire in Asia. The Canadian defences were strengthened. Cardwell, as secretary of state for war in 1870, boasted that he had the largest force at home available for service since 1816 (except for 1855-6) and that it was susceptible of rapid expansion and backed by growing reserves. Bright's complaints against Gladstone's government were veritable caricatures of Gladstone's against Palmerston's. He denounced the level of military expenditure as 'scandalous and wicked', complaining that 'we seem not to know that Economy in a state is the main security for permanence and peace'.[11] France's military weakness was exposed to a surprised world in 1870. But her naval building long continued virtually to determine the rate of British building. Her African (and Asian) ambitions (encouraged by Bismarck) were watched with jealousy by Britain, determined that Suez and the Strait of Gibraltar should be kept open. When at length Lansdowne traded Morocco for Egypt, the British had been occupying the latter for twenty years. The second Gladstone government which Bright left in 1882 because of the bombardment of Alexandria (directed against the nationalist leader Arabi Pasha and followed by a 'temporary' occupation of more than half a century) reacted in a Palmerstonian manner to a Russian threat at Merv on the borders of Afghanistan in 1885, as though its leaders had not attacked Disraeli hip and high for his own Afghan war. The Russians took Samarkand and Bokhara in 1868. They promised in 1869 not to control or attack Afghanistan. They promised in 1873 not to advance beyond the Oxus or take Khiva — and took Khiva later the same year. In 1875 they took Khokand. Again they promised to retire beyond the Oxus, and to respect the neutrality of Afghanistan, whose ameer's attempt to secure a British alliance was repulsed. He gravitated into the Russian orbit, and was attacked from India on Palmerston's principle — 'We have long declined to meddle with the Afghans . . . but if the Russians try to make them Russian, we must take care they become British.' Disraeli attempted to add only the new concept of a 'scientific frontier', wanting to keep Kandahar.

Professor Seton-Watson obviously believed that Disraeli accepted Palmerston's dictum: 'Our baffling on so great a scale the intrigues and attempts of Russia cannot fail to add greatly to the moral weight and political influence of England and thus to help us in other European questions', for he wrote: 'Thanks to our strong colonial and naval position, nothing could happen outside Europe without us, and Disraeli wished this to be true of Europe also.' When the Eastern Question flared up again, he trod consciously in the steps of Palmerston — he 'inherited and upheld the Palmerstonian tradition in the Eastern Question, and like the elder statesman profoundly misunderstood the forces at work in the Balkan Peninsula'.[12] It should in fairness to Palmerston be said that in his time the forces at work were less patent and impressive (Bulgaria had not been heard of), and in fairness to Disraeli that in his time it became impossible to uphold 'the Palmerston doctrine of Turkish independence and integrity', and in fairness to both that in a peninsula of such mingled nationalities with clashing aspirations nationalism was not an evident prescription for stability. Disraeli dismissed the considerable British sympathy with the Christian rebels (felt by some of his colleagues, including his two Foreign Secretaries) as 'coffee house babble'. He minimized Turkish atrocities. He embraced the Palmerstonian illusion of the reformability of the Turk, but would not help Europe force him to reform, and thereby avoid a Russian attack. But it was common ground among men of the centre that the Turks must keep Constantinople, and public opinion applauded the movement of the fleet to the Sea of Marmara when Russian troops were near the city. It applauded, too, the calling up of Cardwell's reserves when the Russians refused to submit to a European Congress their treaty of San Stefano with Turkey. Defending this, Disraeli (by now Earl of Beaconsfield), to play the Palmerstonian tune, pulled out all the stops save, significantly, 'integrity and independence'. From this there was retreat. By the Treaty of Berlin two Bulgarias came into existence. They were in effect independent and soon they were also one. Bosnia and Herzegovina and Novibazar passed, in effect, under the Habsburgs, confirming an Austro-Hungarian counterpoise to Russia in the Balkans. The Russians regained their Bessarabian loss of 1856 down to the most northerly of the Danube mouths, and kept Batum, although Beaconsfield had said that these gains made the Black Sea as much a Russian lake as the Caspian. But to compensate for the abandonment of 'integrity' were the Austrian counterpoise; a British commitment to defend Asia Minor against Russia, with Cyprus as 'a place of arms' and a pretty clear statement by Britain that, despite the Straits Convention and the treaties of 1856 and 1861, she would send her ships of war into the Black Sea at need with or without the Sultan's assent. Britain could not have fought Russia without a continental ally, but she was able, because the Turkish defence of Plevna exhausted the Russian army, to extract a peace treaty by and large favourable, and certainly indicative of a Palmerstonian determination to control the Eastern Mediterranean and the routes to India.

★ ★ ★ ★

'What our duty is at this critical moment is to maintain the Empire of England', said Disraeli on 11th August 1876. Gladstone and Salisbury, unlike Disraeli, lacked Palmerston's relish for the high-handed action, but Asian and African historians may be pardoned for feeling that, for all their reluctance, they put their predecessor in the shade as imperialists. The business classes which, at the end of Cobden's life, opted for non-interference in Europe did not, as he hoped, abandon their penchant for force as the opener and preserver of non-European markets, and the political and economic pressures for imperialist courses mounted all the time.

Before the acquisition of the African empire of Britain, however, the Cobdenites had lost a major battle in which, at the time of Palmerston's death, they scented victory. 'Through the labours of Molesworth, Roebuck and Hume, more recently supported by us, and by Gladstone, every article in the creed which directed our Colonial Policy has been abandoned, and now men actually abhor the notion of undertaking the government of the Colonies; on the contrary, they give to every Colony that asks for it, a Constitution as democratic as that which exists in the United States' — so wrote Bright to Cobden in 1857.[13] The fact, as regards the colonies inhabited by white settlers, was true, though it would have been more just to attribute the victory to the constructive Colonial Reformers — Durham, Edward Gibbon Wakefield, Buller, Earl Grey — with whom Palmerston, a member of British governments which granted self-governing institutions in North America and Australasia, could have some sympathy. Like the Manchester School, these Colonial Reformers believed in Free Trade, against which Palmerston made no stand, though he must have regretted the decision of the cabinet of which he was a member (1846–51) to dismantle the remaining colonial preferences on sugar, coffee, etc., and provide, in effect, an incentive to slave cultivation in Brazil and Cuba and help continue the slave trade. They could see, too, the case for the reduction of imperial garrisons in the self-governing colonies. With this matter Palmerston was directly concerned when he was Secretary at War, and in it he was closely interested as Foreign Secretary and prime minister. For he applauded Wellington's peace-time strategy of keeping in being a larger regular army than parliament wanted by dispersing it ('hiding it away') among colonial stations, available to augment the establishment at home in case of danger of invasion, or to contribute to campaigns in the Crimea or India. In face of mounting demand, Earl Grey, as Colonial Secretary 1846–52, reduced the garrisons in the colonies as low as he thought safe or proper, and they were further reduced during the Crimean War. Thereafter, they rose, especially in Canada. Cobden linked with his attacks on obsolete naval construction and gigantic and abortive experimental expenditure on dockyards and arsenals an onslaught on 'colonial expenditure by which we fool away millions yearly for the defence of communities . . . twice as competent to pay for their defence as we are for ours'. The House of Commons passed without a division, on 4th March 1862, a resolution calling on the self-governing colonies to pay for their own internal security and to contribute to the cost of their external defence.

There was a strong case for such a policy. But those who pressed most aggressively for an end to the 'tribute' paid by the British taxpayer to the settlers hoped, quite avowedly, for the separation of the colonies from Britain, holding that they were 'an excrescence of our Empire, rather than an important element of its prosperity: an encumbrance rather than a material source of strength: a source of commercial and political loss rather than of national wealth'.[14]

Their arguments were formidable and persuasive, and there was some excuse for the implication that only Palmerston stood in the way of a general acknowledgement of self-evident truth. Earl Grey had reported in 1849 that he was sorry to say that there was beginning to prevail in the House of Commons and the highest quarters the erroneous opinion that there was no interest in preserving their colonies and that no sacrifice to lose them; the leading Peelites shared it, and some cabinet ministers were not free from it.[15] Cornewall Lewis, before he became a minister, proved conclusively that, *in the circumstances of the time* all the assets ascribed to empire were illusory, save possibly that of prestige. As Palmerston's Secretary of State for War he stated (25th July 1862) that he looked forward without apprehension or regret to the independence of Canada as soon as she was strong enough to assert it. Bright wrote, just after Palmerston's electoral triumph of 1857, as though only Palmerston, who 'will not last long as Minister or as man' and had no one around him to inherit his mantle, stood between the Manchester School and victory. Goldwin Smith, publishing in 1863 the most extreme example of Separatist propaganda, thought the same — 'It is not to be expected that an inch of the Empire will be given up by the present Premier. Though youthful in bodily vigour, he is old in ideas and unconscious of the great moral and material changes which have taken place in Europe since he first entered public life. But he will be succeeded, probably, by statesmen more imbued with the ideas, and more alive to the exigencies of our own age; and depend upon it, such statesmen will be disposed to retrench our Empire in order to add to our security and greatness.'[16]

After Palmerston's death, it looked as though Mancunian optimism was entirely justified. 'What is the use of these colonial deadweights which we do not govern?' asked the Leader of the House of the premier on 30th September 1866. The writer was Disraeli, more than a decade earlier the author of the famous description of the colonies as 'millstones round our necks'. 'They want to get rid of us', wrote the Canadian statesman, Galt, on 1st January 1867. On 21st March 1869 Granville, as Colonial Secretary under Gladstone, sent to New Zealand a dispatch which would have been offensive if directed to a foreign Power with whom Britain was on bad terms. He told the House of Lords that 'many thoughtful men' looked forward to amicable separation. Gladstone described his policy as not aimed towards separation, but as intended to make sure that it should be amicable if (in effect, when) it came. Lowe, now Chancellor of the Exchequer, had never made any secret of his view that trying to defend Canada was nonsense. In April 1870 the principal architect of the Dominion of Canada, Sir John A. Macdonald, threatened to appeal from the British government to the British people. But the danger melted rapidly away. John Edward Jenkins's warning that 'we are exposed to the possibility of waking up unexpectedly to find our Empire slipped away in a night, cut loose by our statesmen', sounded fantastic within months of its being uttered. Professions of belief in the future of empire became the politicians' stock-in-trade; professions of pride in its extent and greatness became common. 'Who talks now of casting off the colonies?', asked W. E. Forster in 1875, the year in which, but for ill fortune, he might have become leader of the Liberal Party. 'What more popular cry than the preservation of our colonial empire?'. And at the Mansion House in August 1881 Gladstone himself, as prime minister, set the seal of respectability upon the abandonment of the Cobdenite position. 'The business of founding and cherishing those colonies is one which has so distinctly been entrusted by Providence to the care of the people of this country, that we should almost as soon think of renouncing the very great duties . . . imposed upon us with regard to the more distant, but not less dear, portions of this great British Empire.'

It was only fifteen years since Disraeli had complained of 'these colonial deadweights' and proposed to leave the Canadians to their own devices and give up the West African settlements (and the African Squadron). It was only eleven years since the Gladstone government contemplated giving the Gambia to France whom Cobden had said, was welcome to the whole of the African continent if she was fool enough to take it. What had wrought this marvellous change? Simply the response of the public of Britain and of the colonies to suggestions that the moment for action on the lines of Cobdenite orthodoxy had arrived, the instinctive reaction that cutting colonies adrift would be 'the end of England's greatness'. Back in the late 40s, Roebuck had complained that the people continued irrationally to believe that the colonies were useful, although, if that had ever been true, Free Trade and self-government had made it patently false, and Cobden deplored the fact that 'there is as much clinging to colonies at the present moment amongst the middle classes as among the aristocracy: and the working people are not wiser than the rest'. But they were sure that this was due to 'want of information and instruction upon armaments, colonies and taxation and so forth'.[17] If the truth was but preached, it would make Britain free of the baneful burden of colonies. Nothing could have been more wrong-headed than this prediction, based on a conviction that the Mancunians could triumph by 'arguing through the pocket', by 'playing off John Bull's acquisitiveness against his combativeness'. The decisive response of public opinion in 1869–71 *preceded* the Great Depression and the Scramble for Africa which provided economic incentives to 'belief in empire'. It was as unsophisticated and simple as Palmerston's own assumption that for Britain to be an imperial Power was part of the natural order of things. In this too the weight of 'informed' opinion merely concealed how representative he was of the unarticulated assumptions, or prejudices, of his people. This the popular newspapers realized in 1869–70 when the *Spectator* and the *Beehive* rapidly changed their tune to accommodate themselves to their readers, and *The Times*, more ponderously, returned to its earlier theme that empire had its advantages and that in any case the colonists were British subjects 'and as long as they choose to remain so the mother country has no right to deprive them of their heritage'.

Palmerston's attitude, having been unchanging — he repeated

against Bright (and Gladstone) in 1865 the defiance he had given to Joseph Hume on the defence of Canada almost half a century before — may rightly be described as old-fashioned and un-intellectual. He talked in the 60s of 'ships, colonies and commerce as men had done in his youth, when mercantilism was generally accepted, and as they had done (against his party, and policies with which he concurred) when this became a partisan cry of the Pro-tectionists in his later middle age. Adhering to the outlook of Huskisson — of whom it is written that 'he was first and foremost an Englishman, and enlightened national self-interest was the mainspring of his policy'[18] — he made no fundamental reassess-ment of national self-interest to take account of the British adoption of Free Trade and the grant of colonial self-government, followed (in 1859, when Palmerston was premier) by Canadian tariffs on British imports. Any disposition to consider seriously the arguments for the abandonment of colonies was quelled by the names associated through his career with its advocacy — Joseph Hume and Sir Henry Parnell; Grote, Roebuck and Warburton in the 30s; Brougham, Cobden, Bright, and Goldwin Smith sub-sequently. Morley writes of Cobden that from 1846 until the year when both died (1865) 'his political history . . . is one long antagonism to the ideas which were concentrated in Lord Palmer-ston'. The attack of the Manchester School on the colonial connexion was part of their demand for retrenchment — on 26th February 1849 Cobden moved to reduce military and naval expenditure to the level of 1835 (i.e. virtually to halve it), admitting that it could not be done at once only because 'the changes in our distant colonies will take time'. It was part of their attack on diplomacy, on the attempt 'to regulate the affairs of the world', on the tendency of 'ambitious ministers when they cannot win the heart of the nation by good measures at home to win it by swagger-ing abroad'. Three and a half months after the motion noted above, Cobden moved for the adoption of a system of international arbitration (which Palmerston repulsed with the cynical remark that one could not stop people quarrelling) and then went off to attend the pacifist congress in Paris. The Mancunians argued that the colonies increased the danger of war with other Powers and kept the country involved and committed in every quarter of the globe. As to Canada, some of them said that the only danger in her relations with the United States came from the British connexion;

all that Britain had no substantial interest in guaranteeing three million North Americans against the other North Americans; most that British blood and treasure should not be spilled to protect the Canadians from the consequences of their unreasonable hostility towards the Americans. Palmerston sincerely believed that this propaganda encouraged the Americans to expect British North America to fall like a ripe plum into their eager hands. He never questioned that Canada could and should be defended.

The attack of the Mancunians on colonies was also part of their attack on tradition, on aristocracy, and on Palmerston as the embodiment of both. To them empire was a fabric of 'reckless and useless expenditure, which the ambition of former days reared, and the blindness of these days upholds'. They spoke of colonies as among the 'accessories to our aristocratic government', retained partly from a senseless vanity, partly as a rich field of patronage, partly because the aristocratic régime flourished on distant wars and home panics. Palmerston fought them, unyielding to the last. He refused to show, and did not feel, that 'servile fear of the United States' which, according to Galt in 1867, made the politicians 'rather give us up than defend us, or incur the risk of war with that country'.[19] He did not mourn, but rather rejoiced, that the burden of empire kept 50,000 soldiers in the colonies and 125 ships on colonial stations with half the personnel of the Royal Navy aboard, at a cost of some six million per annum (the figures relate to 1867). Let the Little Englanders prove by the balance-sheet that colonies did not pay; he recked not. Obligation apart, there was the point that 'England's loss will be other nations' gain'. Unless emancipated colonies were to be defended still, but from outside, they might be added to the aggressive strength of potentially hostile Powers. And better tariffs against all, including the mother country, than tariffs against all save one competitor of Britain, as John Stuart Mill said. And, of course, as Mill also said — though unlike Palmerston he consciously thought of the empire as a step towards universal peace and friendly co-operation among nations — empire 'added to the moral influence and weight in the councils of the world, of the Power which, of all in existence, best understands liberty'.[20] That, for Palmerston, was the invincible argument. One cannot doubt that the fact that the age in which regard for empire reached its lowest ebb was the age in which Palmerston stood sentinel helped preserve the empire, for what future Palmerston never inquired. After his death, imperial sentiment became common, and numerous and various portents — diplomatic, political, social and economic — supplied increasing arguments with which to justify it. But even before most of them had been perfected, Disraeli, at the Crystal Palace in June 1872, having gauged the movement of public opinion, and sniffed on the wind his long elusive victory, declared the time approaching when Britain must decide between the cosmopolitan principles of Liberalism and national principles. He declared as the objects of the Tory party not only the maintenance of the institutions of the country and the elevation of the condition of the people, but the upholding of the Empire of England, which, he said, Liberalism had for forty years tried continuously, subtly, energetically, ably to disintegrate — and nearly succeeded. Thus, like Palmerston, he held up Cobdenism to scorn, and bid his auditors choose between 'a comfortable England . . . meeting in due course an inevitable fate' and a great country — an Imperial country', and to deliver to their posterity 'a land of liberty, of prosperity, of power and of glory'. Somewhere a half-forgotten laugh rang out and a mouth wrinkled in a familiar, puckish grin.

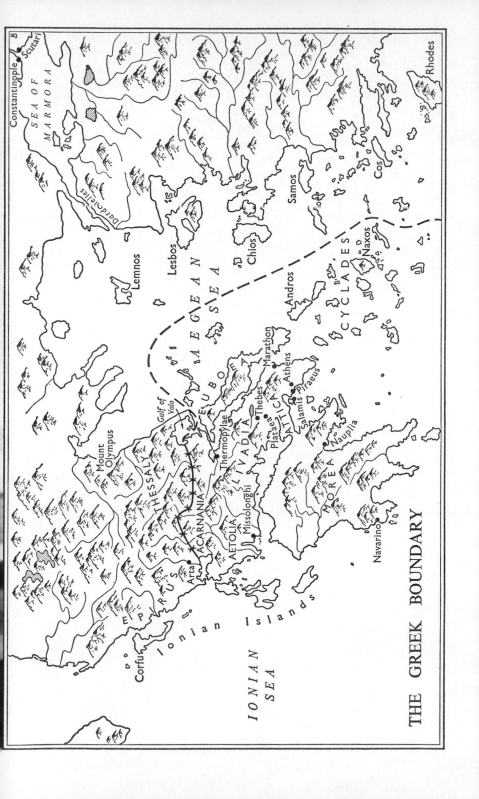

THE GREEK BOUNDARY

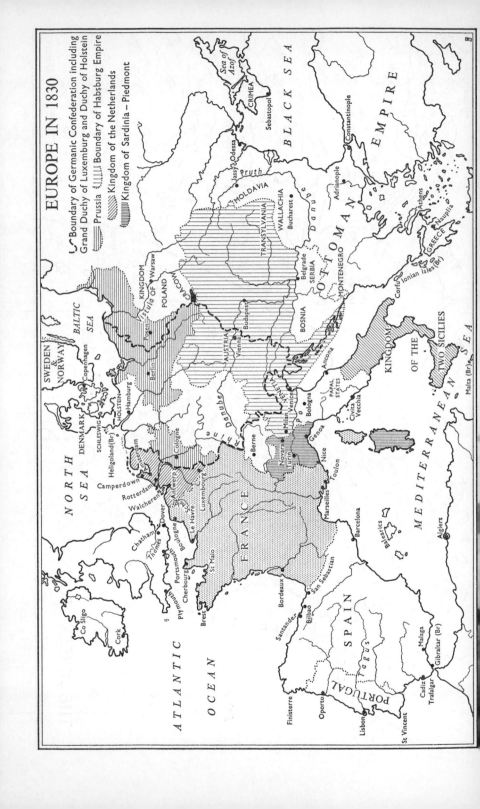

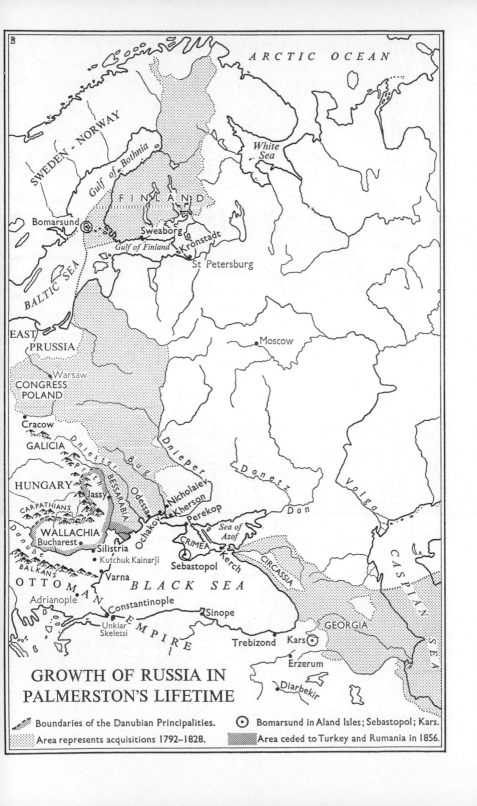

GROWTH OF RUSSIA IN
PALMERSTON'S LIFETIME

Boundaries of the Danubian Principalities.
⊙ Bomarsund in Aland Isles; Sebastopol; Kars.
Area represents acquisitions 1792–1828.
Area ceded to Turkey and Rumania in 1856.

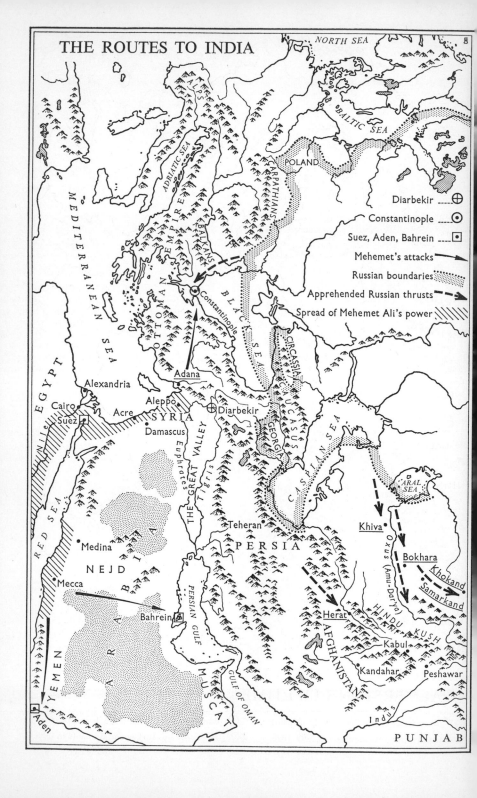

THE ROUTES TO INDIA

NORTH SEA

BALTIC SEA

POLAND

MEDITERRANEAN SEA

ALPS
CARPATHIANS
ADRIATIC SEA
BALKANS
OTTOMAN EMPIRE
BLACK SEA
CIRCASSIA
CAUCASUS
GEORGIA

Constantinople

Adana

Diarbekir ____ ⊕
Constantinople ____ ⊙
Suez, Aden, Bahrein ____ ⊡
Mehemet's attacks ____ →
Russian boundaries ____ ⋯⋯
Apprehended Russian thrusts ____ ⇢
Spread of Mehemet Ali's power ____ ╱╱╱

EGYPT

Alexandria
Cairo
Suez
Acre
Aleppo
⊕ Diarbekir
SYRIA
• Damascus

NILE
RED SEA

THE GREAT VALLEY
Euphrates
Tigris

CASPIAN SEA
ARAL SEA

• Medina

NEJD

• Mecca

ARABIA

Bahrein

PERSIAN GULF

• Teheran

PERSIA

Khiva
Oxus (Amu-Darya)
Bokhara
Khokand
Samarkand
HINDU KUSH

Herat
AFGHANISTAN
Kabul •
• Kandahar
• Peshawar

YEMEN
Aden

MUSCAT
GULF OF OMAN

Indus

PUNJAB

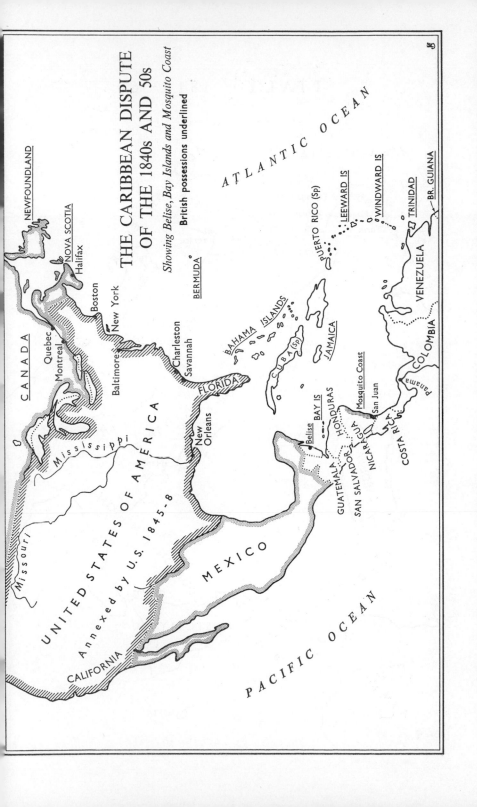

THE CARIBBEAN DISPUTE
OF THE 1840s AND 50s

Showing Belise, Bay Islands and Mosquito Coast
British possessions underlined

ATLANTIC OCEAN

NEWFOUNDLAND

NOVA SCOTIA
Halifax

Boston

New York

Baltimore

Quebec
Montreal

CANADA

Mississippi

Missouri

UNITED STATES OF AMERICA

Annexed by U.S. 1845-8

CALIFORNIA

MEXICO

Charleston

Savannah

FLORIDA

New Orleans

BERMUDA°

BAHAMA ISLANDS

CUBA (Sp)

JAMAICA

PUERTO RICO (Sp)

LEEWARD IS

WINDWARD IS

TRINIDAD

BR. GUIANA

VENEZUELA

COLOMBIA

Panama

COSTA RICA

NICARAGUA

San Juan

Mosquito Coast

HONDURAS

BAY IS

Belise

GUATEMALA

SAN SALVADOR

PACIFIC OCEAN

5

ITALY 1815-60

SWITZERLAND

SAVOY

PIEDMONT

LOMBARDY

FRANCE

Magenta
• Milan
Custozza
Turin
Solferino
Verona
Villafanca

VENETIA

AUSTRIAN EMPIRE

Venice

LIGURIA

PARMA

Genoa

MODENA

Ferrara

Nice

Bologna

ROMAGNA

LUCCA

Leghorn

Florence

MARCHES

Ancona

TUSCANY

ELBA

UMBRIA

ADRIATIC SEA

CORSICA (Fr)

Civita Vecchia

PATRIMONY

Rome

NAPLES

SARDINIA

Gaeta

Naples

BOURBON KINGDOM

MEDITERRANEAN SEA

Messina

Palermo

SICILY

AFRICA

MALTA

REFERENCES

INTRODUCTION

1. David Urquhart, *The Queen and the Premier — A Statement of Their Struggle and its Results*, 1857 (written earlier, during the Crimean War).

2. *Two Great Statesmen — A Plutarchian Parallel between Earl Russell and Viscount Palmerston, M.P.*, 1862.

3. James Grant, *Random Recollections of the House of Commons*, 1st series, 1836.

4. See P. J. V. Rolo, *George Canning*.

5. Trollope, *Lord Palmerston* (1882), 213–14.

6. *V.L.* ii. 377, Albert memo. 3/3/1851.

7. G. M. Young, *Victorian England — Portrait of an Age*, 80.

8. T. Macknight, *Thirty Years of Foreign Policy* (1855), 359.

9. A. J. P. Taylor, *The Italian Problem in European Diplomacy, 1847–9*, 32.

10. *Illustrated London News*, 27/12/1851.

11. Maccoby, *English Radicalism 1832–52*, 371.

12. J. Ewing Ritchie, *Palmerston* (in 'Modern Statesmen' Series) (1861), 13.

13. Quoted A.J.P.T., 84.

14. Macknight, op. cit. 287. The same point is made by G. M. Young in *Victorian England*.

15. Trollope, op. cit. 200.

16. Bright to Crawshay 3/10/1855 and 25/9/1855, quoted by Urquhart, *Materials for the True History of Lord Palmerston* (Nov. 1865), 11.

17. Sir Archibald Alison, cited Walford, 50; Ritchie, op. cit. 10.

18. Ritchie, ibid. Cf. *The Times* obituary: P. 'fell short of that heroic character which we associate with a few — a very few — historical names' such as Chatham, Pitt, Peel, 'yet he was a great man, unless that title be confined by an arbitrary limitation to a prescribed class of moral and intellectual virtues'.

19. *V.L. 2*, i. 279, H.M. to King Leopold 20/10/1865: '. . . He was very vindictive, and *personal* feelings influenced his political acts very much. . . .'

20. There was much indignation (and a debate in the House) about the ministerial patronage of the last great prize-fight of the old sort (which was also the first international heavyweight boxing-match) staged at Farnborough on 17th April 1860 between the Englishman Tom Sayers (149–155 lb.) and the U.S. champion John C. Heenan (195 lb.). The Englishman, known as 'The Little Wonder' had been beaten only once in his career (at the end of 61 rounds) and started 2–1 favourite. The contest went to 42 rounds in 2 hours 20 minutes and ended in a riot (and a draw,

Sayers having injured his right arm). A public subscription of £3,000 was made to Sayers.

21. A. ii. 316. Earl of Shaftesbury to Evelyn Ashley 6/1/1876.

22. *Daily Telegraph* obituary. Cf. M. 609: 'He was *English* to the backbone'; Earl Russell at Guildhall Nov. 1865. 'His heart beat ever for England.'

23. *P.P.* 310–13, P. to Gladstone 7/11/1864.

CHAPTER I THE EMERGENCE OF PALMERSTON

1. Greville, i. 296, 11/6/1829. Cf. ibid. 274 19/3 — 'a speech from Palmerston which astonished everybody . . . an imitation of Canning, and not a bad one'.

2. B. 90–106.

3. This was the eloquent but timid Pemberton Milnes, father of Richard Monckton Milnes, Lord Houghton.

4. B. i. 107. Cf. 1808, of mismanagement of the campaign in Spain: 'If I were in the Cabinet, I would have Dalrymple shot.'

5. B.i. 202 and 204–6, 19/10, 27/11, 4/12/1827.

6. Lorne, 56–57, to Sulivan 7/10/1829.

7. B. i. 215–31, 246–8.

8. B. i. 329, 334, 30/3 and 14/6/1829.

9. Temperley, *The Foreign Policy of Canning* (*1925*), 64–65.

10. T.–P., 82–84, to A'Court 18/9/1823.

11. Ibid. 65, 85, 87 n., speech 28/4/1823.

12. Ibid. 66–67, speech 12/12/1826.

13. Ibid. 86–87, memo. 4/12/1824.

14. H. of C. 3/11/1830.

15. Rolo, *George Canning*, 220, 222, Canning to Liverpool 15/10/1824, to Granville 21/1/1825.

16. Ibid. 202–3, Liverpool speech 30/8/1822.

17. B. i. 239–46.

18. H. of C. 5/2/1830.

19. Airlie, 172–4, 1/8/1830, to Sulivan.

20. Rolo, 247, July 1826, Canning to Princess Lieven.

21. B. i. 220, 18/1/1828.

22. H. of L. 19/6/1829.

CHAPTER II THE MAN OF CONFERENCE

1. H. of C. 16/2/1830; 1/6/1829, 5/2/1830; C. W. Crawley, *The Question of Greek Independence* (1830), 187, 203.

2. N. Kaltchas, *Introduction to the Constitutional History of Modern Greece* (New York, 1940), 68, 38 ff.; chap. iv, 92.

3. Crawley, 53–54, calls this 'the first *positive* departure from the system of the European Alliance . . .'.

4. Ibid. 220.

5. T.–P., Doc. 1, Grenville to Chauvelin 31/12/1792.

6. Balfour, i. 260–4, circular dispatch.

7. W. 80–81, P. to Chas. Grant 17/8/1830; ibid. 337, to Melbourne 1/3/1836.

8. Balfour, i. 271–2, Aberdeen to Bagot (Holland).

9. Palmerston, H. of C. 7/12/1831, 26/1/1832.

10. Balfour, i. 282–4, 290–1, to Bagot 6/10 and 25/10/1830.

11. B. ii. 53–57, P. to Granville 18/3/1831; cf. ibid. 51/53, 15/3/1831.

12. W. 142, P. to Granville 21/2/1832.

13. W. 158, P. to Lamb 9/9/1832. Palmerston's *Theme* was in fact unpopular in the City of London.

14. W. 166, P. to Matuszewic 6/6/1832; H. of C. 26/3/1832.

15. B. ii. 57–60, P. to Granville 25/3/1831.

16. Ibid. 36–37, P. to Granville 2/2/1831.

17. W. 108, P. to Ponsonby 15/4/1831.

18. B. ii. 108–10, P. to Granville 17/8/1831 (T.–P., no. 14).

19. W. 108, 143, P. to Adair 18/10/1831, to Leopold 20/10/1831.

20. W. 145, P. to Granville 11/12/1831.

21. Lorne, 69–70, 65–66.

22. W. 111, 12/11/1831. Cf. *re* the representatives of the Three Courts, ibid. 113.

23. Lorne, 67–68, 16/11/1831.

24. W. 114–15, Minto to Palmerston 24/1/1833.

25. H. of C. 16/7/1832.

26. H. of C. 15/2/1833.

CHAPTER III THE PATRON OF LIBERALISM

1. W. 187, P. to Heytesbury 3/5/1831.

2. W. 128, n. 1, 28/2/1831.

3. W. 202, April 1831.

4. B. ii. 27–29 7/1, 51–53 15/3, 53–57 18/3, 65–70 13/4, 120–3 26/8/1831, all to Granville.

5. Ibid. 39, 8/2/1831, to Granville.

6. Ibid. 53–57 18/3/1831, to Granville.

7. W. 244, P. to Chad 3/12/1831.

8. W. 246, to Lamb 19/2/1832, to Chad 7/2/1832.

9. B. ii. 48–50, to Granville 9/3/1831.

10. W. 166.

11. W. 152.

12. W. 80–81, P. to Chas. Grant 17/8/1830.

13. W. 226–7, P. to Lamb 30/6/1832.

14. W. 243, late 1831.

15. W. 242, P. to Granville Aug. 1831.

16. W. 249, P. to William Russell mid-1832.

17. W. 191.

18. W. 367, *re* occupation of Frankfort May 1834.

19. H. of C. 10/3/1830.

20. W. 224, Lamb to P.

21. W. 235, P. to Lamb 28/8/1832.

22. W. 232.
23. W. 358–9, P. to Lamb 18/6/1833.
24. W. 356, P. to Minto 1/6/1833.
25. A.J.P.T., 31–32.
26. Balfour, ii. 11–12.

CHAPTER IV EASTERN QUESTION AND WESTERN ALLIANCE

1. W. 751. Cf. 11/7/1833, H. of C. P. doubts whether Russia seeks partition or ruling class would relish the shift of authority to Constantinople.

2. Temperley, *The Crimea*, 4.

3. B. ii. 144, to William 21/3/1833.

4. For Mehemet in Arabia see T. E. Marston, *Britain's Imperial Role in the Red Sea Area 1800–78*, Shoe String Press, Hamden, Connecticut, 1961.

5. *Russia*, 1836; Morley's *Cobden*, 101 ff. and 63–67.

6. W. 282, P. to Granville 6/11/1832.

7. *The Crimea*, chap. i.

8. B. ii. 144–5, to William 21/3/1833.

9. Ibid. 'the Sultan may hold his ground', with help; ibid. 145, 154 on the difficulties. On 6/11/1832 he had explained that the Sultan was a reformer from principle, conviction, and political motives and Mehemet only as mere commercial speculation.

10. Crawley, 212.

11. G. M. Trevelyan, *Lord Grey and Reform*, 355–6, Grey to Holland 1/1/1833.

12. W. 282, P. to Granville 6/11/1832.

13. See Temperley, *The Crimea*, 64; C. J. Bartlett, *Great Britain and Sea Power 1815–53*, 88–95; Webster, 282–5.

14. B. 223–5, P. to William 25/3/1828.

15. B. ii. 144, 21/3/1833, to William. Mehemet was to have Southern Syria only, and not hereditarily.

16. W. 283–4, to Lamb, 22/5/1838 and memo. 8/3/1840.

17. *The Crimea*, 73–74; Crawley, preface.

18. Hence, for sidelights on his character see O. W. Hewett's . . . *and Mr. Fortescue* (A selection from the Diaries of . . . Lord Carlingford, K.P.).

19. For Canning's hint to Princess Lieven on P.'s speculations see Guedalla's *Palmerston*.

20. *The Journal of Mrs Arbuthnot*, ii. 322–39, entries of 5/1, 27/1, 9/2, 19/2, 22/2/1830.

21. e.g. H. of C. 5/2 and 16/2/1830.

22. See especially Urquhart, *Materials for a True History of Lord Palmerston*, reprinted from the Free Press, May–Nov. 1865, esp. at 3, 7–13, 16–18.

23. *Lord Palmerston and the Jesuits*, by a Protestant Whig of 1688 and An Administrative Reformer of 1855. Its theme was that 'Peelism, Puseyism and Jesuitism are all one'; that Palmerston's cabinet, even when the three leading Peelites left it, was 'the Pope's Cabinet still'.

24. Balfour, ii. 13–14, Nov. 1833.
25. W. 252, 275, to Lamb 5/12/1832, 16/2/1833.
26. W. 364, to Granville 7/11/1833.
27. W. 372, 383.
28. W. 385–7, to William Russell, 11/12/1833.
29. H. of C. 18/2/1831.
30. W. 358–9, 8/7/1833.
31. W. 364, to Granville 7/11/1833.
32. W. 390, to Villiers 11/2/1834.
33. B. ii. 180–2, to William 21/4/1834.
34. Ibid. 186, to William 12/5/1834.
35. W. 306, to Minto 23/9/1834.

CHAPTER V WILL HE RETURN?

1. *The Journal of Mrs Arbuthnot*, ii. 129, 17/6/1827; cf. 162, 19/2/1828.
2. B. i. 178–9, to William 21/10/1826; cf. ibid. 171, 17/7/1826 and speeches 1813, 1824–5–6.
3. B. i. 178–9, *lit. cit.*
4. Ibid. 153–5, 161–70.
5. Lever, 146; Airlie, i. 131–2 and B. i. 171–2, to Lady Cowper 20/6/1826 and to William 17/7/1826.
6. Lorne, 56–62, P. to Sulivan 7/10/1829. Palmerston put the attempt down to Eldon and H.R.H. The Duke of Cumberland, patron of the Orangemen outraged by Catholic Emancipation. On contact between Cumberland and 'the Huskisson party' through the Princess Lieven, Lady Cowper, and Frederick Lamb, see Greville, i. 262, 311, March and August 1829.
7. B. i. 190–1, to William 4/5/1827 (cf. 189, 19/4); 220, to same 18/1/1828.
8. Ibid. 62–63, 215–18, 242.
9. Ibid. 188–97. Canning had mentioned the Home Office, but the King wanted a 'Protestant' there and Herries at the Exchequer. Cf. above, 68, n. A.
10. Greville, ii. 33, Aug. 1830. Another reason for Palmerston's aloofness was a determination not to be regarded as a follower of the unimpressive Goderich.
11. B. i. 195–6, to Sulivan 14/8/1827.
12. *Vide The Journal of Mrs Arbuthnot*, ii. entries 5/2, 16/2, 10/3, 16/7, 30/9/1830.
13. Mrs Arbuthnot, ii. 389 (26/9/30), says the second approach to Palmerston was made at her suggestion and was a cabinet decision. The emissary was Lord Clive (B. i. 361–3).
14. B. i. 363–4; *The Journal of Mrs Arbuthnot*, ii. 393–5, 23/10, 30/10/1830; Greville, ii. 56, 63, 91.
15. B. i. 361–4; *The Journal of Mrs Arbuthnot*, ii. 397–9, 4/11/1830.
16. Greville, ii. 233–4, 7/1/1832.
17. J. R. M. Butler, *The Passing of the Great Reform Bill*, 320.
18. On Palmerston and the Waverers and the creation of peers, see

ibid. 140–5, 319, 321, 343, 366; Greville, ii. 123, 214–15, 220, 228, 223–4, 256–61, 290–3; *Melbourne Papers*, 140–1, P. to Melbourne 20/11/1831.

19. B. ii. 48, to Granville 9/3/1831.

20. *Lieven Letters*, 359–60; *Grey–Lieven Correspondence*, 421–6.

21. They were not invited to the congratulatory dinner to Althorp and Russell.

22. B. ii. 162, to William 25/6/1833.

23. W. 407, Granville to P. 31/10/1834.

24. W. 409, P. to Granville 11/11/1834.

25. B. ii. 48, P. to Granville 9/3/1831.

26. Ibid. 120, to William 26/8/1831.

27. Ibid. 203–6, to William 15/7/1834.

28. Ibid. 206–7, to William 1/11/1834.

29. W. 409; B. ii. 207–11, 16/11/1834.

30. Ibid.

31. Ibid. H. of C. 20/3/1822.

32. Greville, iii. 145, 157.

33. B. ii. 150–1, 155–6.

34. Ibid. 176–7, 184–5.

35. Ibid. 213–14, to William 25/11/1834. On 1/8/1835 he explained to his brother that he would not go to the Lords because the House of Commons was the place where a man *out* of office could make himself of consequence (W. 421 n. 1).

36. Greville, iii. 24–25, 33–34, 19/3 and 11 and 12/5/1834. Greville describes the speech on Turkey (17/3) as 'wretched . . . pitoyable' and refers to that on Portugal early in May as a 'woful exhibition' of which Peel said that Palmerston seemed bereft of his senses and had miserably failed at 'a new line' — that of humour.

37. Walpole, i. 231–2, 12/4/1835 (*E.C.J.R.*, no. 216).

38. B. ii. 222, Bulwer's comment.

39. W. 195, Lieven to Nesselrode 1/10/1832, Lamb to P. 12/9/1832.

40. B. ii. 160, to William 7/5/1833.

41. Ibid. 180–1, eodem, 21/4/1834.

42. e.g. Airlie, i. 142, Jan. 1828.

43. Greville, ii. 399, 20/7/1833.

44. H. of C. 11/7/1833.

45. B. iii. 6, to William 21/4/1835.

46. B. ii. 180–2, to William 21/4/1834.

47. Greville, iii. 10–12, Jan.–Feb. 1834. 'A pretty Secretary of State in such times', says Greville: 'He does nothing.' Mrs Petre, whom Palmerston proudly exhibited in the Commons gallery, was thought to have kept her virtue and became mother-superior in a Belgian convent (Fortescue, 135).

48. But cf. Greville, v. 2, 11/1/1842.

49. Greville, iii. 302–3, 7/8/1836.

50. Ibid. 86, 23/9/1834. Quizzed by Melbourne on Palmerston's relations with envoys, Greville said the complaints were so general that there must be cause for them.

51. *E.C.J.R.* ii. 108, 24/4/1835, Lord William to Lord John Russell.

53. For details of the attempt to exclude Palmerston in 1835 see W. 417–21 and correspondence with Melbourne, ibid., Appendix C, April 1835; Melbourne Papers, 266, Melbourne to Grey 14/4/1835; *E.C.J.R.* ii. 107, 11–12/4/1835.

CHAPTER VI PLOUGHING THE SANDS

1. W. 437.
2. Balfour, ii. 245–6, Aberdeen to M. Barbecue.
3. H. of C. 10/3/1830.
4. H. of C. 19/4/1837.
5. H. of C. 24/6/1835.
6. H. of C. 10/3/1837.
7. T.–P. no. 19, note on a draft of 9/6/1836.
8. A.J.P.T. 30–31.
9. H. of C. 11/7/1833.
10. W. 390, to Villiers 11/2/1834.
11. W. 787; cf. ibid. 271, 30/9/1834 to Lamb.
12. W. C. Atkinson, *Pelican History of Spain and Portugal*, 278.
13. Maxwell, i. 102, 13/12/1835; cf. W. 464, 13/1/1838, same to same, 'liberty is at present but little understood and still less appreciated'.
14. W. 475–6, to Aston, Sept. 1840.
15. Ibid. 435, to Granville 24/11/1835.
16. Morley's *Cobden*, ii. 64.
17. Ibid. ii. 8–10, Cobden to Bright 24/10/1846.
18. H. of C. 1/3/1848.
19. H. of C. 27/2/1844.
20. H. of C. 10/8/1843.
21. Lorne, 92, Sept. 1846.
22. B.–A. 242–57. The former dispatch is at 245–6, dated 16/3/1848.
23. T.–P. 104; Pemberton, *Lord Palmerston*, 63.
24. Atkinson, op. cit. 278–9.
25. Kaltchas, op. cit. 104–7.
26. T.–P., nos. 23, 24, to Granville 19/3/1841.
27. W. 509, to Erskine 20/2/1839.
28. H. of C. 16/2/1830.
29. Kaltchas, op. cit. 102–3.
30. W. 507, to Erskine 11/5/1837.
31. As Lamb constantly complained to Palmerston, 'unnecessary ill-blood' was created over Greece, W. 505–7 especially 21/10/1837.
32. W. 495.

CHAPTER VII EASTERN ANSWER AND WESTERN QUARREL

1. B. ii. 169–71, to William 8/10/1833.
2. W. 841, to Melbourne 8/6/1835.
3. W. 603, n. 1, to Granville Mar. 1836.
4. B. ii. 179, to William 3/3/1834.

5. W. 850, 854, Melbourne to P. Jan. 1836, 29/4/1837.
6. B. ii. 179 and 182–3, to William 3/3/1834, 21/4/1834.
7. W. 563, to Melbourne 30–31/10/1835.
8. B. ii. 248–9, to Granville 3/2/1837.
9. H. of C. 21/6/1838.
10. H. of C. 14/12/1837.
11. H. of C. 18/3/1836.
12. W. 605, to Ponsonby 17/5/1837. The last such protest was 15/3/1839 (T.–P., no. 28). Ponsonby did not like these instructions and (W. 596) saw the illogicality of trying to win the Sultan's favour while transmitting threats that if the Sultan attacked Syria, Britain would find means to protect her interests without regard to those of a government which selfishly brought on a general war.
13. H. of C. 20/4/1836; cf. 11/7/1833, 19/2/1836.
14. T.–P., no. 26, to Campbell 7/7/1838.
15. B. ii. 281–2, to Granville 13/9/1838.
16. B. ii. 270, to Granville 6/7/1838.
17. W. 631, to Beauvale 20/6/1839.
18. W. 643 and 641.
19. B. ii. 299–303, to Bulwer 24/9/1839.
20. W. 594.
21. B. ii. 266–70, to Granville 5/6, 8/6, 6/7/1838.
22. B. ii. 299–303, to Bulwer 24/9/1839.
23. To Granville 9/2/1836. This was a never-ending refrain — cf. below, Chap. XXVI, n. 42 (11/9/1864).
24. W. 657, to Ponsonby 29/10/1837.
25. *V.L.* i. 255, 8/12/1839. For the wooing, see Tresham Lever's *Letters of Lady Palmerston* (1957) and Airlie (1922).
26. B. ii. 305, to Granville 6/12/1839.
27. W. 851–7, 10/2/1836, 29/2/1836, 14/6/1838, 4/9/1840.
28. Maxwell, 184 ff.
29. Accounts of the opposition to Palmerston from the participants are to be found in Maxwell's *Clarendon*, i. 184–218; Greville, esp. under dates Aug. — 3/11/1840; Walpole's *Russell*, i. 346–63.
30. Walpole, i. 347–51, gives Ellice to Spencer, Spencer to Bedford 25/8/1840, Spencer to Russell 20/9, 23/9, Hume to Russell 26/9. It is not suggested that Spencer, who was in retirement, behaved in an underhand way. Ellice to Melbourne is in *The Melbourne Papers*, 472 (16/9/1840), Holland to Melbourne, ibid. 483.
31. B. ii. 323 14/3/1846.
32. B. ii. 356–61, to Melbourne 5/7/1840.
33. W. 843–5, 30/10/1835, 7/1/1836, 24/5/1836; Melbourne, 340–8, May 1836, 18/7/1836.
34. B. ii. 315–18, to Bulwer 21/7/1840; cf. ibid. 310–11, 16/4/1840.
35. B. ii. 307–9, to Granville 11/3/1840.
36. B. ii. 318–19, to Bulwer 22/7/1840.
37. B. ii. 361–3, to Melbourne 6/7/1840.
38. The main convention and annexes are given in B. ii. 420–7.

39. B. ii. 307–9, to Granville 11/3/1840, 315, to Bulwer 21/7/1840.

40. Quotation from Aberdeen cited in Balfour, ii. 147–8.

41. Walpole, i. 348–50, Russell to Melbourne 10/9, 15/9, 17/9; Melbourne Papers, 475–9. P. to Melbourne 16/9, Melbourne to Russell 19/9; W. 713 Melbourne to Palmerston 17/9.

42. Walpole, i. 346 ff.

43. e.g. at dinner at Holland House 8/9 (Greville, 283) after Palmerston had sent him away with the assurance that everything was going splendidly.

44. Walpole, i. 349–50, Russell to Melbourne 17/9/1840, 353 28/9.

45. D. ii. 312–14.

46. Walpole, i. 352, Russell to Melbourne 27/9/1840.

47. *V.L.* i. 294–6, Leopold to H.M. 2/10/1840.

48. B. ii. 343–4.

49. Ibid. 324–31, Bulwer to P. and P. reply 22/9; also Appendix, ibid. 428–30.

50. See *V.L.* i. Melbourne's letters of 1/10, 2/10, 9/10, 10/10, 11/10/1840; Walpole, 351–7, Russell to Melbourne daily 26–29/9, 8/10, and to Palmerston 10/10, and P. to Russell 9/10; W., Appendix C, Melbourne to Palmerston 29/9, 30/9, 10/10, 12/10/1840.

51. Walpole, i. 359–62, Russell to Melbourne 31/10, 1 and 2/11, P. to Russell 6/11; W., Appendix C, Melbourne to P. 12 and 18/10, P. to M. 26/10; Maxwell, 214 Clarendon to M. 27/10; *V.L.* i, M. to H.M. 9–13 and 16/10, P. to H.M. 9/11 and reply.

52. W. 621.

53. B. ii. 333–5, to Granville 5/10/1840.

54. Melbourne Papers, 475, 16/9/1840.

55. B. ii. 344–6, to Granville 5/10/1840.

56. W. 731. Beauvale quoted this to the Queen, Jan. 1846 (Lorne, 105).

57. Lorne, 58, Lady P. to P. Jan. 1841; Lever, 234, Lady P. to Beauvale 12/10/1840.

58. Walpole, i. 362, P. to Russell 4/12/1840.

CHAPTER VIII ENCIRCLING THE GLOBE

1. B. ii. 327–31, to Bulwer 22/9/40.

2. Quoted Bartlett, op. cit. 58.

3. Michael Lewis, *History of the British Navy* (Penguin), 176–8.

4. H. of C. 23/7/1863.

5. T.–P., no. 33, P. to Clanricarde 11/1/1841.

6. e.g. H. of C. 19/3 and 21/6 and 6/8/1839, 10/8/1842.

7. H. of C. 26/2/1836.

8. H. of C. 20/3/1843.

9. B.–A. 31–3, 35–40, to William 13/3, 20/4, 13/5, 13/7/1840.

10. For the use of the navy in Canning's time see Bartlett, *Great Britain and Sea Power 1815–53*.

11. For Morocco, see Flournoy, *British Policy Towards Morocco in the Age of Palmerston*, including 127, Palmerston to Hay 21/2/1848 and 118,

Hay to P. 4/11/1846. Assurances demanded and received from France *re* Morocco and Tunisia 1836 and 1837 (pp. 55–60) were revealed to the House of Commons, 13/2/1838. They were repeated July and Sept. 1841.

12. Maxwell, ii. 300, P. to Clarendon 1/3/1857.

13. *Speech of Lord Viscount Palmerston to the Electors of Tiverton on 31st July 1847* (2nd ed.), 35. Pointing to an investment of £150 million by British subjects on which no interest was being paid, he warned that it was 'very possible' that the time would come when popular indignation and the pressure of the House of Commons might 'compel the Government of England to use stronger language, and perhaps resort to other means of obtaining justice for so many . . .'.

14. Graham was being consistent. As First Lord of the Admiralty (and Palmerston's colleague) he expressed in 1831 the Government's 'fixed determination to uphold the predominance of our power, which is so much founded on opinion in your Eastern regions', but blamed the supercargoes for trouble, insisting that 'our Factory there can only thrive by ready compliance with the laws, the prejudices, and even the caprices, of a nation which we seek to propitiate' (to Lord William Bentinck, Parker, i. 150–1). Palmerston's speech in the China debate was described by Greville as 'capital' (iv. 261) and Palmerston relished the general praise (B.–A. 37, 20/4/1840).

15. *V.L.* i. 327–34, 552–3; B.–A. 119–21, P. to William 8/12/1842.

16. B.–A. 178, to William 6/9/1845.

17. B.–A. 376–8, to Sir John Davis, 9/1/1847.

18. H. of C. 10/5/1838.

19. H. of C. 8/8/1839.

20. H. of C. 21/3/1843.

21. T.–P., no. 114 — 31/7/1862 (63?) P. to Russell. For a brief statement on the diminution of the Brazilian trade see Bartlett, op. cit. 268–9, citing C. Lloyd's *The Navy and the Slave Trade*.

22. T.–P., no. 116 — note for Layard 29/1/1865. But Palmerston, returning to office in 1846, thought what Aberdeen and Guizot had begun as a measure to coerce the Argentinian ruler Rosas and continued as a 'blockade' forcing Argentina to import her goods through Montevideo in Uruguay, 'a bad business', not blockade but 'piracy', illegal from first to last (to Normanby, two letters given in B.–A. 325–7).

23. T.–P., no. 112 — to Russell 4/5/1863.

24. A. ii. 227–8.

25. 19th March 1850. Greville, vi. 211 — 'They have determined (of course in obedience to Palmerston's will and pleasure) to stake their existence on it; and they have been moving heaven and earth to obtain support'; 211–12 'people came away furious' from a party meeting harangued by Russell and Palmerston. Palmerston's letter of congratulation to Russell is in Walpole, ii. 107.

26. T.–P., no. 115, to Crampton 17/2/1864.

27. Robinson, Gallagher, and Denny, *Africa and the Victorians*, 34.

28. J. D. Hargreaves, *Prelude to the Partition of West Africa*, 26–71; quotations from pp. 37–38 dated 1864–5.

29. *Tiverton Election Speech, 1841.*

30. For these views see above, pp. 552–8.

31. For these views see G. D. Bearce, *British Attitudes Towards India 1784–1858.*

32. A. ii. 124–5, P. to Cowley 25/11/1859.

33. Temperley, 12 (22/2/1836) and 92–93 (8/7/1839).

34. Marston, *Britain's Imperial Role in the Red Sea Area 1800–78*; quotations ibid. 55–56, P. to Campbell 8/12/1837 and (p. 60) 24/5/1838 and (p. 61) 29/11/1838.

35. Maxwell, i. 186 ff.

36. W. 586 23/1/1836.

37. For the trade with Persia via Turkey see, inter alia, Morley's *Cobden*, i. 74-80, Cobden from Smyrna, Jan. 1837, and Disraeli (as Earl of Beaconsfield), H. of L. 8/4/1878.

38. W. 749, P. to Clanricarde 24/1 and 24/3/1840.

39. W. 741, P. to Durham 27/10/1835.

40. W. 747, P. to Lamb 13/7/1839.

41. e.g. *Lord Grey and Lord Palmerston* (1846), 21: '. . . I cannot forget the Afghan Papers. I might endure the forms of the Constitution and of International Law being trampled under foot, but I cannot forgive *false pretexts* for any thing, least of all for gigantic injustice to others and fearful danger to ourselves. I cannot forgive fraudulent — nay, almost literally *forged* documents — *the true words expunged from his dispatches and their contrary meaning infused.* . . . A LIE — a lie long and elaborate — that has cost the deceived assailant £20,000,000 and 15,000 lives: the assailed, who can count what woes. . . .'

42. *V.L.* i. 411–14, Ellenborough to H.M. gives the terms of the dispatch from the Secret Committee (sent 6/9/1841) suspending the Instruction of 4/6/1841 to take Herat.

43. Ibid. In arguing that the advance on Herat would have rendered more difficult of accomplishment the intention to withdraw as soon as Shah Suja was 'firmly established' Ellenborough showed his incomprehension, not only of the facts, but of his predecessor's diplomatic strategy.

44. *V.L.* ii. 233–4, Gov.-General's Minute 30/9/1848. The Queen rejoiced (ibid. 262, 26/5/1849) that the government concurred with the viceroy. This it did rather reluctantly. But Palmerston backed the Duke of Wellington in a strong letter to Russell, 9th June 1847 (A. i. 23–5), arguing that 'if the Khyber Pass is the only gate to India, and if it is there that we are to defend India, we ought to have, and must have, military occupation of the country up to that gate . . .'.

45. W. 739 to Hobhouse 14/2/1840.

46. Maclagan, *Clemency Canning*, 51–55, etc.; cf. Palmerston to Russell 9/6/1847 (A. i. 23–25) — 'Persia must, I fear, now be looked upon as an advanced post for Russia . . . [and] a Russian force . . . might convert Afghanistan into the advanced post of Russia . . .'. *V.L.* iii. 37–38, Dalhousie to H.M. 2/10/1854. For Palmerston's insistence on Persia repudiating pretensions to Herat see A. ii. 128–9, P. to Clarendon 17/2/1857.

CHAPTER IX PALMERSTON THE INTEMPERATE

1. W. 414, P. to Howard de Walden 20/5/1836.
2. Greville, iii. 343–7, says that when Granville asked for a reference to France in the Speech, Palmerston retorted that as they could not speak with praise they had better be silent; H. of C. 10/3/1837.
3. W. 853–4, Melbourne to P. 6/2/1837.
4. Walpole, i. 357, Russell to P. 10/10/1840.
5. Ibid. 354.
6. B. ii. 339–40 to Granville 8/10/40.
7. *V.L.* i. 302–4, Melbourne to H.M. 12/10 and 13/10/1840.
8. Ibid. 305–6, H.M. to Leopold 17/10.
9. Ibid. 307–9, Leopold 20/10, H.M. 23/10; W. 722–3; B. ii. 341–3.
10. Greville, too, stresses that Palmerston was given the credit, not the government — e.g. iv. 309, 345.
11. e.g. *V.L.* i. 286–7 26/7/1840; 294–6, 2/10; 315–17, 26/11.
12. B. ii. 346–9, to Granville 29/10/1840. P. claimed (to Melbourne 26/10/40, W. 848–9) that his colleagues wanted him to make a *submission* to France.
13. Greville, iv. 274–5 28/8/1840 on reading Palmerston's letters to Clarendon.
14. Walpole, i. 359, Russell to Melbourne 31/10 and 359–60, 1st and 2nd Nov.
15. Ibid. 360–2, Russell to Melbourne 2/11, Palmerston to Russell 6/11.
16. B. ii. 363–7, letters of 26/11, 30/11, 8/12.
17. T.–P., no. 31, P. to Beauvale 10/5/1841.
18. Ibid., no. 33, to Clanricarde 1/1/1841.
19. B. 346–9, to Granville 29/10/1840.
20. *V.L.* i. 311–12, 11/11/1840.
21. *V.L.* i. 286 and 315–16.
22. Bell, i. 316–17; B. ii. 376–83 to Bulwer 13th and 17th Aug. 1841.
23. Greville, v. 9; cf. iv. 332–3.
24. Greville, iv. 138 (Mar. 1838) wrote that Palmerston 'enigmatical . . . detested by the Corps Diplomatique, abhorred in his own office, unpopular in the House of Commons, liked by nobody, abused by everybody, still reigns in his little kingdom of the Foreign Office . . . apparently not troubling himself about the affairs of the Government generally . . .'. Melbourne told him in January 1841: 'He has no intimacy, no interchange of thought and complete openness with anybody' (ibid. 344–5).
25. H. of C. 5/2/1830, 7/8/1832, 15/8/1833, 17/8/1835, 6/6/1836.
26. *V.L.* i. 346–7 13/5/1841.
27. B.–A. 50–52.
28. Greville, v. 9.
29. *V.L.* ii. 79–82, Palmerston to Melbourne 26/12/1845, for the Queen's eye.
30. Greville, iv. 344–5, Jan. 1841.
31. Ibid. v. 34–36; B.–A. 125.
32. Maxwell, i. 223, Clarendon to Granville 31/12/1841.

33. Greville, v. 14, 29, 19/2 and 1/9/42; Walpole, i. 385, V. Smith to Russell.

34. H. of C. 10/8/1842.

35. H. of C. 9/2 and 10/8/1842.

36. B.–A. 92–112, letters of 8/2, 16/2, 30/9/1842.

37. Greville, v. 9.

38. Lever, 263, Lady P. to Beauvale 6/5/1842.

39. Greville, v. 35–37.

40. Ibid. 34–37, 56; B.–A. 111, 120; *V.L.* i. 470–1, Melbourne to H.M. 17/1/1842 on press.

41. II. of C. 5/8/1836.

42. Lorne, 114–15, P. to Bancroft.

43. Lever, 248, Lady P. to Beauvale Feb. 1841.

44. Maxwell, i. 228, Clarendon to Lady Granville 25/5/1842; Greville, v. 35, 63–64; Melbourne Papers, 515; L.C.J.R. i. 59, 61–62; B.–A. 113–18.

45. H. of C. 7/8/1844. Even Melbourne thought (3/2/43) that the Speech showed too great an anxiety for peace and fear of war with America — *V.L.* i. 577. On Spain see *V.L.* i. 436, 438, 558.

46. *V.L.* i. 610–14, Aberdeen to H.M. 15/8/1843, 619, H.M. to Aberdeen 9/10/1843.

47. H. of C. 7/8/1844.

48. *V.L.* ii. 25, H.M. to Leopold 15/9/1844.

49. Maxwell, i. 258, Clarendon to Dr Ferguson 9/9/1845.

50. B.–A. 147–9, to William 29/8/1844.

51. H. of C. 7/8/1844; to Russell, L.C.J.R. i, 248–54; cf. B.–A. 139–49, 162–4, 175, 179–80.

52. See especially Palmerston's memo. on the National Defences Dec. 1846 B.–A. 390–402.

53. Bartlett, 172.

54. Bell, i. 351; H. of C. 7/8/1844.

55. Greville, v. 226, 21/8/1845.

56. Maxwell, i. 259–60, 18/12/1845.

57. *V.L.* ii. 70, Albert's memo. 20/12/1845; Walpole, i. 414, P. to Russell 19/12/1845.

58. Walpole, i. 412–16, gives Grey to Russell 16/12/1845 and 19/12/1845. Greville, v. 274–6, 284–6, shows the part played by Ellice and Grey's strange assertion that though he had 'purposely abstained from naming Palmerston . . . it was impossible J. R. could have any doubt about his meaning'.

59. Walpole, i. 416, 21/12/1845.

60. Lever, 274, Lady P. to Mrs Huskisson 19/3/1846.

61. *V.L.* ii. 99–100, Albert memo, 30/6/1846.

Chapter X Palmerston Encounters the Prince

1. Greville, v. 257, 16/12/1845, 338, 13/8/1846.

2. *V.L.* ii. 67–68, Louis Philippe to H.M. 16/12/1845, 69–71 Albert memo 20/12/1845.

3. Ibid. 79–82, P. to Melbourne 26/12/1845.

4. Ibid. 62–63, Peel to H.M. 10/12/1845.

5. Ibid. 92–93, Louis Philippe to H.M. 5/5/1846.

6. Ibid. 103–4, H.M. to Leopold 7/7/1846.

7. *V.L.* ii. 69–71, 79–82.

8. *Lord Grey and Lord Palmerston*, 20.

9. *V.L.* ii. 123, Stockmar to H.M. 18/9/1846.

10. Ibid. 121–3, H.M. to Leopold 14/9/1846.

11. Bulwer's own account shows that, despite some ineptitude in detail, he usually had a closer grasp than P of what was practicable in Madrid. But it does not explain, still less exculpate, his gaffe in handing Narvaez the dispatch of 16/3/1848, of which lady P. wrote in amazement to her brother.

12. *V.L.* ii. 115–17, P. to H.M. 19/8/1846.

13. Greville, v. 371, 24–25/12/1846; *V.L.* iii. 118–19, 125–6, H.M. to Leopold 7 and 29/9/1846.

14. *V.L.* ii. 113–14, 17/8/1846 H.M. to Russell.

15. Ibid. 118–19, 121–3, 124–5, H.M. to Leopold 7/9, 14/9, 21/9/1846; Greville, v. 357, 20/11/1846.

16. Greville, v. 344.

17. *V.L.* ii. 128, 118–19, 121–3, 124–5, H.M. to Leopold 6/10, 7/9, 14/9, 21/9/1846.

18. Greville, v. 350, 24/9.

19. A. i. 53–54, 69–75, 110–12, P. to Minto 24/2/1848, Normanby to P. 13/3/1848, P. to Normanby 12/11/1848.

20. Greville, v. 397–406, 414.

21. *V.L.* ii. 138–9, Leopold to H.M. 15/1/1847.

22. Ibid. 79–82, 26/12/1845; Gavin Henderson, essay on Foreign Policy of Palmerston in *Crimean War Diplomacy, etc.*, 193–5.

23. Greville, v. 359, 23/11/1846.

24. For Switzerland, see Ann G. Imlah, 'Anglo-Swiss Relations 1845–60', *Bulletin of the Institute of Historical Research*, xxxvi, no. 94, Nov. 1963; A. i. 13 to Canning 18/12/1847.

25. A.J.P.T. 25–27.

26. Ibid. 76–77, Dietrichstein to Metternich 10/3/1848.

27. *R.* v. *P.* 63–64, P. to Albert 31/8/1847; Albert memo. 29/8/1847.

28. *V.L.* ii. 113–14, H.M. to Russell 17/8/1846.

29. e.g. *R.* v. *P.* 49, 50–51, 61, 27/11/1846, 14/12/1846, 3/12/1847.

30. *V.L.* ii. 156–7, H.M. to Russell 18/10/1847.

31. Ibid. 293–4, Russell to H.M. and reply 21/6/1850.

32. Ibid. 157–8, P. to H.M. 30/10/1847.

33. Ibid. 115–16, 19/8/1846 — *re* the famous (divided) dispatch to Bulwer shown to Jarnac.

34. Ibid. 128–9, H.M. to Leopold 17/11/1846.

35. Ibid. 204, H.M. to P. 1/5/1848.

36. Ibid 128–9, 152, H.M. to Leopold 17/11/1846, H.M. to P. 9/10/1847.

37. Ibid. 128–9, 137–8, 132, H.M. to Leopold 17/11/1846, to Russell 7/1/1847, to P. 28/11/1846.

38. Ibid. 140–1, 132, 137–40, H.M. to Russell 14/3/1847 and 7/1/1847, to P. 28/11/1846, to Russell 14/2/1847.

39. *Speech of Lord Viscount Palmerston to the Electors of Tiverton on 31st July 1847*, 2nd ed., 35; *R.* v. *P.* 58, P. to H.M. 6/8/1847.

40. *V.L.* ii. 140–1, 156–7, H.M. to Russell 14/3/1847, 18/10/1847.

41. Ibid. 211–12, H.M. to P. 15/6/1848.

42. Ibid. 207–8, H.M. to P. 23/5/1848.

43. *R.* v. *P.* 78–80 (*V.L.* ii. 212–14), 16–18/6/1848.

44. *R.* v. *P.* 83–89, H.M. to P. 1/7/1848, long reply 2/7/1848.

45. *V.L.* ii. 125–6, H.M. to Leopold 29/9/1846.

Chapter XI The Peace-Keeper

1. *V.L.* ii. 161–3, Frederick William IV of Prussia to H.M.; *R.* v. *P.* 114–17, Albert to Russell 2/4/1850.

2. See Imlah, art. cit.; A. i. 7–16, P. to Minto 11 and 17/11/1847, to Canning 18/12, to Ponsonby 20/11 and 21/12/1847.

3. A. i. 63–65, P. to Ponsonby 11/2/1848; cf. ibid. 13–15, same to same (*re* Switzerland) 21/12/1847.

4. A.J.P.T. 19–20; ibid. 36, dispatches of 2/8/1847.

5. Ibid. 24–29, 39–41.

6. Ibid. 30, 23/9/1847.

7. Ibid. 90, 16/4/1848.

8. Minto's instructions A. i. 34–37; *V.L.* ii. 150–1, H.M. to Russell 3/9/1847; Palmerston's defence of the mission *R.* v. *P.* 84–5, 2/7/1848.

9. A.J.P.T. 40–41, Albert 29/8/1847, P. to Ponsonby 11/9/1847.

10. Ibid. 44, 61, Metternich to Dietrichstein 20/12/1847 (for Albert's eye) and 28/2/1848.

11. Ibid. 90, 77, P. to Ponsonby 31/3/1848, Dietrichstein's account of meeting on 10/3/1848.

12. Ibid. 80, 79.

13. Ibid. 69, Metternich to Dietrichstein 23/2/1848.

14. Ibid. 61; A. i. 63–67, P. to Ponsonby, Abercromby, etc., 11–12/3/1848.

15. A.J.P.T. 60 n. 2.

16. Ibid. 71, 29/2/1848.

17. A. i. 93–94, to Normanby 11/4/1848.

18. A.J.P.T. 77, Dietrichstein's report of meeting on 10/3/1848.

19. *R.* v. *P.* 7—72, P. to H.M. 18/4/1848.

20. A. i. 90–91, P. to Normanby 31/3/1848.

21. *S.M.E.* 14–15; A.i. 82, Leopold to P. 23/1/1849.

22. A.J.P.T. 118.

23. *V.L.* ii. 177–9, 27/2/1848.

24. A. i. 76–78, to Normanby 26/2/1848.

25. Ibid. 82, 80–82, to Normanby 28/2/1848.

26. A. 83–84, P. to Westmoreland and Ponsonby 29/2/1848.

27. *S.M.E.* 5; A.J.P.T. 75, draft of 7/3/1848.

28. A. i. 86–87, P. to Clarendon 9/3/1848; *S.M.E.* 6; A.J.P.T. 75.

29. See *S.M.E.* 8–11 and Mosse, *The European Powers and the German Question*, 13–18; A. i. 91–92, P. to Bloomfield 11/4/1848.

30. *S.M.E.* 14.

31. A.J.P.T. 73.

32. A. i. 78–80, 90–91, P. to Normanby 27/2/1848, 31/3/1848.

33. A.J.P.T. 218, 240–2; Gavin Henderson, op. cit. 195–6, did not agree.

34. Greville, vi. 31/3/1848.

35. A.J.P.T. 84 n. 1, 28/2/1848.

36. Ibid. n. 2, Ponsonby to P. 20/3/1848.

37. Ibid. 88–89, 94.

38. Ibid. 86–87.

39. Ibid. 42 n. 3, account of talk with Palmerston at Broadlands 6/10/1847, Dietrichstein to Metternich.

40. Ibid. 93–94.

41. Ibid. 93–94, Dietrichstein's account of interview of 15/4/1848; A. i. 101–4, P. to Ponsonby 21/4/1848.

42. A. i. 96–99, P. to Leopold 15/6/1848.

43. A.J.P.T. 8.

44. Ibid. Taylor's appreciation 105–10; Walpole, ii. 40–42, Russell memo. 1/5/1848; A.J.P.T. 109 n. 2, Hummelauer's report 4/6/1848.

45. Ibid. 101–5, 120, 132.

46. *R. v. P.* 75–76, P. to H.M. 25/5/1848.

47. A.J.P.T. 111–16; *S.M.E.* 18.

48. Ibid. 83; cf. 82 n. 1, Abercromby to P. 18/5/1848.

49. Ibid. 118 n. 4, 117.

50. Ibid. 132.

51. Ibid. 135, 138–41.

52. *S.M.E.* 19, 21; A.J.P.T. 139–40, 144, 218.

53. A.J.P.T. 154; P. to Russell 30/8/1848; 155, 160–1; *S.M.E.* 22.

54. A. i. 107–110, P. to Ponsonby 31/8/1848.

55. *R. v. P.* 93–94, H.M. to P. 4/9, P. to H.M. 9/9/1848.

56. A.J.P.T. 186–7, Beaumont to Bastide 23/10/1848.

57. Ibid. 177–8, 186.

58. A. i. 112–14, P. to Abercromby 28/12/1848.

59. A.J.P.T. 181–2 and 187, P. interview with Koller 20/11/1848.

Chapter XII Palmerston and the Nations, 1848–9

1. Greville, vi. 102–3; Mosse, Appendix A.

2. Mosse, 15–16, memo. 16/9/1847.

3. Ibid. 22, Strangways to P. 12/7/1848.

4. Ibid. 4, 5, 8.

5. See F. G. Weber, 'Palmerston and Prussian Liberalism 1848', *Journal of Modern History*, xxxv, no. 2, June 1863.

6. Mosse, 19–20 and 20 n. 3; *V.L.* ii. 215, H.M. to P. 1/7/1848 *re* his dispatch to Bunsen.

7. Ibid. 24, Strangways to P. 28/6/1848 and Cowley to P. 21 and 27/8/1848.

8. Ibid. 16, P. to Strangways 23/3/1848.

9. Ibid. 23–24, P. to Cowley 29/7/1848.

10. *V.L.* ii. 250–1, H.M. to Leopold 13/9/1848; Mosse 24, P. to Cowley 8/9/1848.

11. *S.M.E.* 16–17.

12. A. i. 55–57, P. to Minto 28/3/1848.

13. Ibid. 107–10, P. to Ponsonby 31/8/1848.

14. A.J.P.T. 179, P. to Ponsonby 11/11/1848.

15. Ibid. 93–94, at interview with Dietrichstein 15/4/1848; cf. A. i. 100–4, P. to Ponsonby 21/4/1848.

16. A. i. 96–99, P. to Leopold 15/6/1848.

17. A.J.P.T. 217.

18. Ibid. 98, 69.

19. Ibid. 189, P. to Ponsonby 20/11/1848.

20. Ibid. 190–1, Schwarzenberg to Werner 4/12/1848.

21. A. i. 101–10, P. to Ponsonby 30/4, later letter (104–5), 31/8/1848.

22. Sproxton, *Palmerston and the Hungarian Revolution* 11–12, 20–21.

23. Ibid. 43–46, 11/12/1849.

24. Ibid. 38.

25. *S.M.E.* 33.

26. T.–P. 160–1, P. to Bloomfield 14/4/1848.

27. See Florescu, 'Stratford Canning, Palmerston and the Wallachian Revolution of 1848', *Journal of Modern History*, xxxv, no. 3, 1963.

28. T.–P., no. 36, P. to Westmoreland 14/3/1848; cf. ibid. 155 minute on Switzerland 2/10/1847

29. *V.L.* ii. 215–16, H.M. to P. 1/7/1848, 206–7, undated.

30. Ibid. 235–6, H.M. to Russell 7/10/1848.

31. *V.L.* ii. 216–17, H.M. to P. 5/7/1848; *R.* v. *P.* 141, Albert memo. 14/7/1852.

32. A.J.P.T. 105–10; *R.* v. *P.* 82–83, H.M. to P. 28/6/1848 and reply 29/6.

33. *R.* v. *P.* 83 (*V.L.* ii. 215–16) H.M. to P. 1/7/1848.

34. *V.L.* ii. 206–7; *R.* v. *P.* 76, 90, 25/5/1848, to Palmerston, 27/7/1848 to Russell.

35. *R.* v. *P.* 92–93, H.M. to Russell 26/8/1848, to Palmerston 30/8/1848.

36. *V.L.* ii. 183, 204, H.M. to P. late Feb. and 1/5/1848; *R.* v. *P.* 69, H.M. to P. 10/3; *R.* v. *P.* 72–73, P. to H.M. 30/4 and (80–81) 19/6 and (81–82) reply; *R.* v. *P.* 91, H.M. to P. 8/8/1848.

37. *V.L.* ii. 224–7, 8–11/8/1848 and *R.* v. *P.* 91–92, 10–11/8/1848; *V.L.* ii. 245–6, H.M. to Russell 22/12/1848.

38. *R.* v. *P.* 90, H.M. to P. 22/7/1848.

39. Ibid. 92, H.M. to Russell 11/8/1848.

40. Ibid. 94, H.M. to P. 7/9/1848.

41. Ibid. 94–95, reply 9/9/1848.

42. *R.* v. *P.* 100–2, 26/9–6/10/1848; cf. *V.L.* ii. 227–8, H.M. to Russell 21/8/1848.

43. Walpole, ii. 37, Russell to Wellington 12/3/1848; cabinet memo. 1/5/1848, ibid. 40–2.

44. *R.* v. *P.* 104, Russell to H.M. 28/1/1849.
45. Greville, vi. 187 (Sept. 1849).

CHAPTER XIII A SOURCE OF CONTENTION

1. Greville, v. 256 (13/12/1845).
2. A. ii. 319, Earl of Shaftesbury to Evelyn Ashley 6/1/1876.
3. B. ii. 266, P. to Granville 5/6/1838 (cf. to same, 9/2/1836).
4. *Lord Grey and Lord Palmerston — A Letter Addressed to Macaulay on the occasion of His Letter to M'Farlane, from a Free Trader* (London, 1846), 18–19.
5. Greville, vi. 200.
6. Ibid. v. 403–4, 406, 409–10, 418–26, and especially 426–7 (Feb. 1847).
7. Ibid. vi. 55–56 (30/4/1848).
8. Ibid. 60–61 (13/5); Walpole, ii. 44–45, Grey and Wood to Russell, 28/5/1848.
9. Walpole, ii. 46–47, Russell to P. 1/10/1848.
10. *V.L.* ii. 279–82, Albert memo. 3/3/1850.
11. Walpole, ii. 47–49, Russell memo. 18/10/1848.
12. *V.L.* ii. 237–8, H.M. to Leopold 10/10/1848; Walpole, ii. 49, Russell to P. 2/12/1848.
13. *V.L.* ii. 213 (*R.* v. *P.* 80) H.M. to Russell 17/6/1848.
14. Ibid. 213–14, reply, 18/6/1848.
15. The minute of 19/9/1848 on this conversation is given *R.* v. *P.* at 96–98, including the allegation of trickery omitted from the officially published *V.L.* ii. 231–3.
16. Maxwell, i. 341, Clarendon to Geo. Cornewall Lewis 26/12/1851.
17. Walpole, ii. 46–47, P. to Russell 25/9/1848 and reply 1/10/1848; *R.* v. *P.* 114–17, Albert to Russell 2/4/1850.
18. *R.* v. *P.* 114–17, Albert to Russell 2/4/1850.
19. Ibid. 123–6, Albert memo. of interview with P., August 1850.
20. Fulford, *The Prince Consort.*
21. *R.* v. *P.* 114 (*V.L.* ii. 282) Stockmar memo. 12/3/1850; cf. note 18 and *V.L.* ii, 315, H.M. to Russell 12/8/1850.
22. *R.* v. *P.* 120–1, Albert memo of talk with Russell 11/7/1850.
23. *V.L.* ii. 213–14, Russell to H.M. 18/6/1848.
24. Greville, vi. 125 (5/11/1848).
25. Ibid. vi. 128; Walpole, ii. 47, P. to Russell 25/9/1848; A. i. 110–12, P. to Ponsonby 12/11/1848.
26. A.J.P.T. 190–3.
27. *V.L.* ii. 245–6 H.M. to Russell 22/12/1848; A. i. 112–14, P. to Abercromby 28/12/1848; Greville, v. 421–2 (Feb. 1847).
28. A.J.P.T. 188, P. to Ponsonby 9/10 and 14/11/1848.
29. For the question of the Sicilian arms see Walpole, ii. 51–52 (Russell to Palmerston and reply 20–22/1/1849); *V.L.* ii. 250–2 and *R.* v. *P.* 104–5; Greville, vi. 149–50, 159–61, 164–6.

30. *R.* v. *P.* 105–6, 22/2/1849 (H.M. to Russell) and A.J.P.T. 212.

31. Greville, vi. 171–2 (30/3/1849); A. i. 115–17, P. to Russell 9/4; *R.* v. *P.* 106–7, P. to H.M. 2/5/1849.

32. A. i. 115–17.

33. A.J.P.T. 226, 235; *R.* v. *P.* 106–7, P. to H.M. 2/5/1849.

34. Mosse, 28–31; *S.M.E.* 36–7; *V.L.* ii. 264–5, H.M. to P. 21/6/1849; *R.* v. *P.* 108–10, 21–26/6/1849.

35. Greville, vi. 167 (16/3/1849).

36. Ibid. 177–8 (21/5/1849).

37 Walpole, ii 53 (18–22/6/1849); *V.L.* ii. 262–4; *R.* v. *P.* 107

38. Walpole, ii. 53–54.

39. *Speech of Lord Viscount Palmerston to the Electors of Tiverton on 31st July 1847*, 2nd ed., p. 23.

40. T.–P. 171.

41. Greville, vi. 165–6, 187.

42. Greville, vi. 180, 183; A.J.P.T. 69, Metternich to Dietrichstein 23/2/1848.

43. A. i. 137–8, P. to Ponsonby 20/8/1849, 139–41, P. to Ponsonby 9/9/1849.

44. Walpole, ii. 54–55, P. to Russell 28/9/1849; A. i. 142–3, 155–7, P. to Normanby 29/9, 2 and 23/10/1849; Walpole, ii. 55, Russell to Minto 2/10/1849.

45. A. i. 150–3, P. to Stratford 2/10/1849.

46. A. i. 144–53 memo. of conversation with Brunnow 2/10/1849 and P. to Normanby 2/10 and to Stratford 2/10.

47. A. i. 158–61, P. to Ponsonby Stratford 7/11/1849; 165–7 same to same 22/11/49; 171–3 P. to Bloomfield 27/11/1849.

48. Ibid. 167–71, P. to Ponsonby 27 and 30/11/1849.

49. Ibid. 173–5, P. to Stratford 10/2/1851.

50. A. i. 138.

51. A. i. 257–60; Morley's *Gladstone*, 389–401; Balfour, ii. 165–6.

52. Sproxton, p. 58.

Chapter XIV 'The Minister of England', 1850

1. See A. i. 183–209.

2. Walpole, ii. 56–59; *V.L.* ii. 272, 276–8; Greville, vi. 203–8, 211.

3. *V.L.* ii. 279–82, Albert memo. 3/3/1850; *R.* v. *P.* 114–17, Albert to Russell 2/4/1850.

4. *R.* v. *P.* 114–17, Albert to Russell.

5. Walpole, ii. 59–69; A. i. 201–4, P. to Normanby 17–19/5/1850; Greville, vi. 213–16, 218; A. i. 208–9, P. to Bloomfield 24/5 and 205–8, P. to Russell 22/5; *V.L.* ii. 287–8, Russell and H.M. 18/5/50.

6. Walpole, ii. 60–61; *V.L.* ii. 289–90, Albert's memo. 20/5.

7. *R.* v. *P.* 118–20, H.M. to Russell 8/7/1850 and reply 10/7; *V.L.* ii. 312–14, Albert memo. 8/8/1850 on Russell's talk with Palmerston. Cf. A. i. 224–6, to William 8/7/1850.

8. Walpole, ii. 56 Russell to P. 12/1/1850; Baring to Russell, 19/10/1850, quoted Bartlett, 266

9. Walpole, ii. 56–57, P. to Russell 26/1/1850.

10. Trollope, p. 201.

11. e.g. Gavin Henderson, op. cit. 205–6; G. M. Young, *Victorian England*, 80.

12. Quoted Walford, *Memoir of Rt. Hon. Viscount Palmerston* (1865), 34.

13. Greville, vi. 165 ff.; Bagehot's *Biographical Studies*.

14. Walford, op. cit. 34.

15. *Daily Telegraph* obituary; J. Ewing Ritchie, *Palmerston* (1861), 6.

16. A. i. 180–1, P. to Bloomfield Aug. 1847.

17. Ritchie, op. cit. 415.

18. Lorne, 140–3.

19. *R*. v. *P*. 65, Albert to P. 11/12/1847; A. i. 181–3, P. to Normanby 20/4/1847; *R*. v. *P*. 64–65, P. to Albert 19/9/1847; ibid. 65–66, P. to Albert 31/12/1847; *R*. v. *P*. 102–4, H.M. to P. 8/10/1848 and reply, and again 14 and 16/10/1848; *R*. v. *P*. 83, H.M. to P. 1/7/1848 and 89, P.'s long reply 2/7/1848; P. sums up to Normanby 1/2/1850 (A. i. 184–7).

20. A. i. 196–7 to Bloomfield 27/3/1850.

21. *V.L.* ii. 293–4, Russell to H.M. and reply 21/6/1850.

22. Ibid. 299–300, Russell to H.M. 26/6/1850.

23. Greville, vi. 232–4.

24. Ibid. 252–3 (11/8/1850).

25. A. i. 223–6 to Normanby 29/6 and to William 8/7/1850.

26. Greville, vi. 234.

CHAPTER XV THE DEMAGOGUE DISMISSED, 1851

1. *R*. v. *P*. 121–2, Russell to Albert 11/7/1850; Greville, vi. 233, 253.

2. *R*. v. *P*. 120–1, Albert memo. of talk with Russell 11/7/1850.

3. Greville, vi. 261–2.

4. A. i. 242–4, P. to Cowley 22/11/1850.

5. *V.L.* ii. 295–8, H.M. to P. 22/6/1850, P. to Russell 23/6, H.M. to Russell 25/6/1850.

6. *R*. v. *P*. 122, H.M. to Russell 28/7; *V.L.* ii. 307–8, H.M. to Russell 31/7; *R*. v. *P*. 123–6, Albert's memo. of 17/8/1850 on interview with P.

7. *V.L.* ii. 328–30, H.M. to P. 18/11/1850 and reply, same date.

8. L.C.J.R. 35–36, P. to Russell 26/11/1850; A. i. 242–4, P. to Cowley 22/11/1850.

9. S.M.E. 37; Mosse, 42.

10. L.C.J.R. 34–35, Russell to Stockmar 22/11/1850.

11. *V.L.* ii. 330–1, H.M. to Leopold 22/11/1850 and 333, H.M. to Leopold 3/12, reporting her 'plain speech' to Russell.

12. Mosse, 40 n. 5, P. to Westmoreland 3/12/1850 and see n. 10 above.

13. *V.L.* ii. 330–1, H.M. to Leopold 22/11/1850.

14. *R*. v. *P*. 127, H.M. to P. 10/9/1850 and 4/10; ibid. 127–9 (and *V.L.* ii. 319–21) P. to H.M. 8/10/1850.

15. A. i. 239–41, P. to Sir Geo. Grey 1/10/1850; P. to H.M. 8/10 see above. This she sent to Russell *V.L.* ii. 321–2 11/10; ibid. 322, H.M. to P. 12/10, 324–5 to Russell 19/10/1850.

16. *V.L.* ii. 392, H.M. to Russell, 24/10/1851, not forbidding a private meeting of P. and Kossuth (*V.L.* ii. 392, Russell to H.M. same date). But *R.* v. *P.* 131–2, H.M. to P. 31/10/1851 (*V.L.* 394) forbidding the meeting was not sent, because Russell withdrew his advice (ibid. 392–4) despite P. to Russell 30/10 (Walpole, ii. 133). Walpole, ii. 134, Russell to P. 1/11 (copy to H.M. *V.L.* ii. 395). Russell's speech at the cabinet is given in Walpole, ii. 134–6, and *V.L.* ii. 396, H.M. acknowledges the matter settled (3/11).

17. *V.L.* ii. 397 and 400, H.M. to Russell 20 and 21/11; *V.L.* ii. 398–9, Russell to H.M. 21/11; Walpole, ii. 136–7, P. to Russell 28/11 and reply 29/11, J. R. to H.M. on cabinet 4/12.

18. Walpole, ii. 139–40, Russell to P. 17/12/1851.

19. A. i. 285–6, P. to Normanby 24/1/1851.

20. A. i. 289–92, P. to Normanby 3/12/1851; ibid. 287–8, memo. 29/9/1858; ibid. 292–4, P. to Normanby 6/12 and 300–6 to Russell 16/12/1851.

21. *V.L.* ii. 404–5, Russell to H.M. 4/12; A. i. 294–6, P. to Normanby 5/12, Normanby to P. 6/12.

22. *V.L.* ii. 406–8, Lady Normanby to Col. Phipps 7/12/1851.

23. A. i. 292–4, P. to Normanby 6/12/1851; *V.L.* ii. 409–12, Lady Nby to Phipps 9/12/1851.

24. *R.* v. *P.* 133 H.M.'s journal 11/12; *V.L.* ii. 412, P. to Russell 13/12; Walpole, ii. 138, Russell to P. 14 and 16/12/1851.

25. *R.* v. *P.* 135, Maule's explanation; Greville, vi. 324; A. i. 300–6, P. to Russell 16/12/1851.

26. *V.L.* ii. 412 n. 1, Lady Normanby.

27. Walpole, ii. 137, Russell to P. 29/11/1851.

28. A. i. 296–9, Normanby to P. 15/12 and reply 16/12/1851.

29. Walpole, ii. 140–1, P. to Russell 18/12/1851.

30. A. i. 307, Russell to P. 19/12/1851.

31. Greville, vi. 315–16, 320; M. 217, Derby to Malmesbury 25/12 (wrongly dated 5th), 218 diary 26/12.

32. Walpole, ii. 142 (1875).

33. Parker, ii. 144, Graham to Aberdeen.

34. Greville, vi. 317–20, on Lady Palmerston's indignation and resentment 25/12; Walpole, ii. 141, Russell to Lady P. 28/12; A. i. 311–18, P.'s account, dated 22/1/1852; Ashley, ibid. 308.

35. William Coningham, *Lord Palmerston and Prince Albert*, Feb. 1854.

36. A. i. 308–9.

37. Walpole, ii. 141, Russell to Lady P. 28/12/1851; A. i. 325–30, P. to Lansdowne, Oct. 1852; *V.L.* ii. 413–15, Russell to H.M. 18/12 and 19/12 and H.M. to Russell 20/12/1851; *R.* v. *P.* 133–4, H.M.'s journal 20/12; cf. *V.L.* ii. 417, H.M. to Leopold 23/12/1851.

38. *V.L.* ii. 415–16, H.M. to Russell 20/12/1851.

39. *V.L.* ii. 315, H.M. to Russell 12/8/1850; cf. *R.* v. *P.* 114.

40. A. i. 325–30, P. to Lansdowne, recounting conversation with Bedford Oct. 1852. On 21/2/1852 Russell told the Queen he 'had heard that Lord Palmerston had said that there was one thing between them which he could not forgive, and that was his reading the Queen's Minute to the House of Commons' — *V.L.* ii. 446.

41. Walpole, ii. 63.

42. *V.L.* ii. 458–9, Phipps, 10/3/1852, said Palmerston was still making this unfounded allegation. Greville, vi. 334, assumed that P. had been unprepared for the reading, but by 26/3/1852 (336) says that though P. was still complaining of surprise he had been informed by Russell three days before of his intention to read it.

43. *R. v. P.* 135, Journal 26/12/1851.

44. *V.L.* ii. 438–9, Russell to H.M. 4/2/1852.

45. See also A. i. 325–30, P. to Lansdowne Oct. 1852; ibid. 311–18, P. to William 22/1/1852; A. i. 331–2, Bulwer's account.

46. Quoted Kingsley Martin, pp. 70–71.

Chapter XVI Tits and Tats

1. *R. v. P.* 113–14, memo. 3/3/1850.

2. Snell, 71.

3. Mabell, Countess of Airlie's *Lady Palmerston and Her Times*, ii. 100, Beauvale to Lady P., Jan. 1846.

4. H. of C. 29/6/1846.

5. A. i. 244–5, to William 27/1/1851.

6. Ibid. 351–62.

7. Ibid. 334–6, to William 24/2/52 and Sulivan, same day.

8. *V.L.* ii. 447–8, Albert memo. 22/2/1852.

9. *R. v. P.* 120–1, memo. 11/7/1850.

10. Ibid. 113/17, memo. 3/3/1850 and Albert to Russell 2/4/1850.

11. *V.L.* 312–14, memo. 8/8/1850 on Russell's talk with Palmerston after the Pacifico debate.

12. Walpole, ii. 140–1, Russell to P. 18/12/1851; A. i. 307–8, P. reply 23/12/1851; *V.L.* ii. Albert memo. 27/12/1851.

13. Greville, vi. 322.

14. *G.* 45, Granville to Lansdowne 23/12/1851.

15. *R. v. P.* 119–20, Russell to Albert 10/7/1850; *G.* 70–77; M. 234–5, 240.

16. *V.L.* ii. 425–7, H.M. to Russell 28/12/1851 and 427–8 reply, 29/12; *G.* 49, Russell to Granville 29/12/51; Greville, vi. 330. Granville's statement is at *G.* 49–52.

17. M. 238.

18. See especially C. J. Bartlett, *Great Britain and Sea Power 1815–53*. For Palmerston's views see, inter alia, his Memorandum on the National Defences Dec. 1846 (B.–A. 390–402) and (Jan.–Feb. 1848), Walpole, ii. 18–24 and Bartlett, 250.

19. A. i. 334, to William 24/2/1858.

20. *V.L.* ii. 445–6, Albert's memo. 21/2/1852; Parker, ii. 143, 159, Graham to Aberdeen and to Lady Graham 25/12/1851 and 10/1/1852.

21. *V.L.* ii. 469–70, Disraeli to H.M. 19/4/1852. For the clash with Russell and Maule see Walpole, ii. 16–24 and for insistence on provision for a militia A. i. 252–3, 24/1/51, Palmerston to Wood.

22. Greville, vi. 329; cf. Parker, ii. 148, Graham to his wife 9/1/1852.

23. *R.* v. *P.* 139–43.

24. A. i. 368–9, to William 17/9/1852.

25. Parker, ii. 161–2, Roebuck to Graham 20/7/1852.

26. Greville, vi. 344, 7/7/1852.

27. Ibid. 366, late Oct. 1852.

28. *V.L.* 447 8, Albert's memo. 22/2/1852 and Derby to H.M. that day.

29. Greville, vi. 337, 26/3/1852; A. i. 336–41, to William 30/4/1852.

30. A. i. 364–77 especially 371–3 to Fitzwilliam 24/9/1852. See Southgate, *The Passing of the Whigs*, 232–33.

31. A. i. 336–41, to William 30/4/1852.

32. Ibid. 336–43, to same, 30/4 and 23/5 and 347–50, 20/6/1852.

33. Morley's *Cobden*, ii. 124–5.

34. Walpole, ii. 158–9, Lansdowne to Palmerston 22/10; Parker, ii. 175, Russell to Graham 23/10; Bowood MSS. 24/10/1852 cited Bell, ii. 65; Greville, vi. 367, 3/11/1852; A. i. 377–9, to William 17/11/1852.

35. *V.L.* ii. 488–90, Derby to H.M. 25/11/1852; 491–2, Albert's memo. 28/11; Morley's *Gladstone*, 434–5; Parker, ii. 175–6, 25/10/1852 Lewis to Graham; Greville, vi. 366; M. 281–2.

36. See Southgate, *The Passing of the Whigs*, 233–43.

37. *V.L.* ii. 502–4 and 510 12, Albert's memos. of 19/12 and 22/12/1852; Greville, vi. 351, 378, 382; Parker, ii. 195, Graham's journal 21/12/52.

38. Parker, ii. 192, journal 2c/12/52.

39. Letters to William of 30/4, 23/5, 30/6, 24/7/1852.

40. A. ii. 1–4, to William 22/12 and Sulivan 24/12/1852; Greville, vi. 383.

41. Lorne, 151–3, to Sulivan 31/12/1852.

42. *Gladstone to his Wife*, 95–97 and 101, 21st, 23rd, 31/12; Parker ii. 197, 23/12; Maxwell, i. 361, Clarendon to Lady Clarendon 10/1/1853

43. *V.L.* ii. 548–9.

CHAPTER XVII RESIGNATION AND RETURN, 1853

1. *V.L.* ii. 548–9, Aberdeen to H.M. 11/9/1853.

2. Ibid. 534–5, Clarendon to H.M. 25/2/1853.

3. Ibid. 545–6, Leopold to H.M. 3/6/1853.

4. *R.* v. *P.* 146–7, April 1853; A. ii. 12, to William 3/4/1853.

5. M. 246–7, 250, 253–9, 275.

6. Kingsley Martin, 135–6; M. 269–71, 274, 286; Temperley, 198, 218–19, 223–43, 268–70.

7. A. ii. 36–40, P. to Herbert 21/9/1853.

8. Kingsley Martin, 164–5.

9. M. 272–3; Stanmore, ii. 179–80; A. ii. 6–7, to William 31/1/1853.

10. M. 238.

11. M. 287–8, to Cowley 20/12/1852; 297–302, Journal 20/3/1853.

12. See Florescu, art. cit.

13. On this compare Temperley with many of the anti-Canning letters of Clarendon printed in Maxwell.

14. T'.–P. 134, Russell's dispatch 9/2/1853.

15. Temperley, 305.

16. Walpole, ii. 178–9, Aberdeen to Russell 15/2/1853; Maxwell, ii. 15, to Clarendon 29/6/1853.

17. Walpole, ii. 191–4, memo. 4/10/1853.

18. A. ii. 43–49, P. to Aberdeen 1/11/1853.

19. Walpole, ii. 182, June 1853.

20. Gavin Henderson, 12, cites P. to Clarendon 11/4/1853 that the Tsar was 'ambitious and grasping, but he is a Gentleman'; on France, cited Bartlett, op. cit. 188.

21. A. ii. 25, P. to Clarendon 22/5/1853.

22. Hence A. i. 40, P. to Aberdeen 4/10/1853.

23. Temperley, 299–300.

24. *Arg.* i. 451; A. ii. 32–34, Palmerston's cabinet circular 12/7/1853.

25. Temperley, 311–12.

26. M. 307–10, entries 29/5, 3/6, 11/9/1853.

27. Walpole, ii. 181, Russell to Clarendon 20/3/1853, stressed by Temperley and Henderson (Gavin Henderson, op. cit. 11–12) as uncharacteristic of the government in general and based on the misapprehension that the Seymour Conversations were a case of Russia acting under the Nesselrode Memo. of 1844 before setting about the disruption of the Ottoman Empire.

Argyll, in good faith, describes Spencer Walpole's account as almost pure fiction.

28. Greville, vii. 56; Kingsley Martin, 103.

29. Temperley, 336, on cabinet of 18/6/1853.

30. A. ii. 26–31, P. to Aberdeen 4/7 and to Russell 7/7/1853.

31. *Arg.* 459; A. ii. 28–29, Aberdeen to P. replying to 4/7; Temperley, 337. P. to Clarendon 28/6/1853.

32. A. ii. 32–4, 35–6, P.'s cabinet circular 12/7, P. to Aberdeen 15/7/1853.

33. Kingsley Martin, 123; Maxwell, ii. 16, Graham to Clarendon 16/8/1853.

34. Walpole, ii. 183–5, Russell to Clarendon 20/7, 20/8, Aberdeen to Russell 25–26/8; Maxwell, ii. 16–17, shows preparations to supersede Canning, but Clarendon (20, to Lewis, 12/9, saw that this was impossible); Walpole, ii. 189–90, Aberdeen to Russell 16/9 and later.

35. Walpole, ii. 186–7, 189–91, Russell to Aberdeen 30/8, memo. for cabinet committee 3/9, to Clarendon 17/9, to Aberdeen 19/9, to Clarendon 23/9 (or 22/9, Maxwell, ii. 23 and ibid. 23/9 as well); Maxwell, ii. 23, to Clarendon and Aberdeen 27/9/1853.

36. Maxwell, ii. 20, Clarendon to Lewis 12/9/1853; Temperley 353.

37. Kingsley Martin, 139–40.

38. *The Advertiser*, 29/9/1853. See Kingsley Martin, 130–4.
39. *V.L.* ii. 550, 25/9/1853.
40. Kingsley Martin, 168; A. ii. 40, P. to Aberdeen 4/10/1853.
41. A. ii. 41–42, P. to Aberdeen 7/10; *V.L.* ii. 551–2, Aberdeen to H.M. 7/10; Martin, 140.
42. *V.L.* ii. 552–3 note, Aberdeen to Graham 8/10/1853.
43. Maxwell, ii. 20, Clarendon to Lewis 12/9/1853.
44. Aberdeen had first used the term 'drifting fast towards war' to Clarendon 7/6/1853 (Maxwell, ii. 15); *V.L.* ii. 552–4 Albert memo. 10/10/1853
45. *V.L.* ii. 555–8, Albert memo. 16/10/1853 on talk with Aberdeen.
46. Kingsley Martin, 143–4.
47. A. ii. 49–51, P. to Russell 24/10/1853.
48. Ibid. 32–33, P.'s cabinet circular 12/7/1853.
49. Ibid. 43–49, P. to Aberdeen 1/11/1853.
50. Ibid. 52–54, P. to Aberdeen 10/12/1853 and reply, 13th.
51. *V.L.* ii. 569–70, Albert memo. on talk with Aberdeen on 15/12; Walpole, ii. 199–200, Russell to Lansdowne 15/12/1853.
52. On the resignation and return, see Kingsley Martin, 153–62, 170–8. The Queen to Aberdeen 7/12 is ibid. 154–5; Harris, *The History of the Radical Party in Parliament*, 402.
53. *V.L.* ii. 568–9, Albert to Aberdeen 9/12; ibid. 567 n., P. to Lansdowne 8/12.
54. Ibid. 567 n., P. to Lansdowne 8/12, sent to Aberdeen on 10th with Lansdowne's reply; Palmerston had previously seen Aberdeen about it (ibid. 567–8, Aberdeen to H.M. 6/12). On 13th Aberdeen informed Palmerston there would be no material alterations in the Reform Bill (Walpole, ii. 198).
55. Aberdeen to Graham, 10/12, quoted Kingsley Martin, 158.
56. H.M. to Aberdeen, quoted Kingsley Martin, 156.
57. *V.L.* ii. 567–8, Aberdeen to H.M. 6/12/1853.
58. Ibid. 569–70, Albert memo. on talk with Aberdeen 15/12/1853.
59. Ibid. 555–8, Albert memo. on talk with Aberdeen 15/10/1853.
60. Walpole, ii. 200–1.
61. *V.L.* ii. 573–4, Albert memo. on talk with Aberdeen 24/12/1853.
62. Ibid. 567 n., P. to Lansdowne 8/12/1853.
63. Walpole, ii. 201–2, Aberdeen to Russell; *V.L.* ii. 573–4 (see n. 61).
64. *V.L.* ii. 573–4 (see n. 61); Reid's *Milnes*, i. 489.
65. Quoted, with Aberdeen's reply of 24th, Kingsley Martin, 160–1.
66. H.M. to Aberdeen, quoted Kingsley Martin, 155–6; M. 320 report, 25/12 of Peelite comments alleged by Disraeli; *V.L.* ii. 573–4 see n. 61.
67. Kingsley Martin, 159; Delane cited ibid. 175.
68. Reid's *Milnes*, i. 488–91.

CHAPTER XVIII 'THE FITTEST MAN', 1854

1. *V.L.* ii. 572–3, H.M. to Clarendon (undated).
2. A. ii. 68 Gladstone to P. 4/10/1854.

3. Kinglake's attribution of the decision to *The Times* leader of 15/6/1854 is as misleading as his implication that half the cabinet slept at the *decisive* cabinet. Argyll has a good account, 464–5. Aberdeen said all the cabinet agreed on the destruction of Sebastopol and the Russian fleet as soon as possible (Balfour, ii. 240, memo. June 1854). For Admiralty views see Parker, ii. 226, 242–3, 253.

4. A. ii. 60–67, P.'s memo. for cabinet 15/6 and P. to Newcastle 16/6/1854.

5. *Arg.* i. 478.

6. Layard, H. of C. 17/2 and 31/3/1854; Aberdeen and Russell H. of L. and H. of C. 31/1/1854; Palmerston at Napier dinner 7/3 and H. of C. 31/3 (and see A. ii. 55–59).

7. H. of L. 19/6/1854; Balfour, ii. 238, H.M. to Aberdeen 26/6/1854.

8. Maxwell, ii. 44, Russell to Clarendon 10/5/1854; Walpole, ii. 217–19, Russell to Aberdeen 5/5/1854 and to Lansdowne 28/5/1854.

9. Morley's *Gladstone*, 493, on conversation of 22/2/1854.

10. Gavin Henderson, 199 — the paper was a commentary on Russell's (Walpole, ii. 213–14); Balfour, ii. 205–6, Aberdeen to Russell 27/4/1854.

11. *V.L.* iii. 27–28, Albert's memo. 10/4/1854; Walpole, ii. 208 Palmerston to Russell; *V.L.* iii. 29–30. Albert memos. 10 and 11/4/1854.

12. Balfour, ii. 226, P. to Aberdeen.

13. *V.L.* iii. 42–43, Albert memo. 8/6/1854.

14. Walpole, ii. 219, Russell to Aberdeen 29/5/1854, *re* two of three possible courses; ibid. 219–20, Aberdeen to Russell 30/5/1854.

15. M. 333.

16. *Arg.* i. 506–16.

17. M. 343; Walpole, ii. 233–5; Parker, ii. 258–9, Graham to Lyons 19/1/1855.

18. *V.L.* iii. 78–79, Newcastle to H.M. 22/12/1854.

19. Maxwell, ii. 55, Clarendon to his wife 11/1/1855.

20. Walpole, ii. 228, Minto to Russell 16/11/1854.

21. Ibid. 229, Russell to Aberdeen 17/11/1854.

22. Ibid. 230, Aberdeen to Russell 21/11/1854.

23. Ibid. 230, Russell to Aberdeen 28?/11/1854, reply 30/11.

24. *R.* v. *P.* 156, P. to H.M. 3/10/1854; Balfour, ii. 255, H.M. to Aberdeen, 275, Aberdeen to H.M.; cf. Walpole, ii. 236, Russell to Aberdeen 3/1/1855; Balfour, ii. 286, Stanmore 22/1/1855.

25. Walpole, ii. 231, Russell to Aberdeen 3/12/1854; ibid., P. to Russell.

26. Morley's *Gladstone*, ii. 809–10.

27. *Arg.* i. 509–10.

28. *V.L.* iii. 74–76, Albert memo. 9/12/1854.

29. Balfour, ii. 286, journal of Hon. Arthur Gordon (Lord Stanmore) 22/1/1855.

30. Walpole, ii. 237; *V.L.* iii. 91.

31. *Arg.* i. 516–17; *V.L.* iii. 91–93, Albert memo. 25/1/1855.

32. *V.L.* iii. 97–98, Aberdeen's report 27/1/1855; *Arg.*, 520; Morley's *Gladstone*, 523.

33. *V.L.* iii. 99–100, Palmerston's report 2 a.m. 30/1/1855.
34. Ibid. 102–4, memo. 30/1/1855.
35. Morley, 525–6, Gladstone memo. 31/1/1855; A. ii. 73/74, P. to Derby; H.M. iii. 104–5, Derby to H.M. 31/1/1855; M. 348.
36. Maxwell, ii. 56, Clarendon to Lewis 30/1/1855.
37. *R.* v. *P.* 157–8, journal 2/2/1855.
38. *V.L.* iii. 111–13, Albert memo. 3/2/1855, 113–14, H.M. to Russell 3/2, 114–16 Russell's narrative; Morley, 530–1; A. ii. 76–79, P.'s narrative to William 15/2 — note his remark: 'Besides, he broke with the late Govt because the War Department was not given to me.'
39. *V.L.* iii. 116, memo. 3/2 and 116–18, cf. 119–21 on earlier interview with Lansdowne; *R.* v. *P.* 158–61.
40. *V.L.* iii. 122–3; *R.* v. *P.* 161.
41. *V.L.* iii. 128, H.M. to Leopold 6/2/55; A. ii. 76–79, P. to William 15/2; Reid's *Milnes*, i. 505.

Chapter XIX The War Premier, 1855

1. See Southgate, *The Passing of the Whigs*, 263–4, 279–83.
2. *Arg.* i. 533.
3. A. ii. 76–9, P. to William 15/2/1855.
4. Maxwell, ii. 63, P. to Clarendon 8 and 10/3/55; *V.L.* iii. 132–3, Clarendon to H.M. 10/2.
5. *V.L.* iii. 133–4 and enclosure, P. to H.M. 10/2/55, P. to Napoleon, iii. 8/2/1855.
6. *R.* v. *P.* 166–8, P. to H.M. 10/2/1855.
7. H. of C. 16/2/1855.
8. *R.* v. *P.* 10/2/1855 (see n. 6); *Arg.* 533–6 on cabinets of 6 and 9/2/1855.
9. *V.L.* iii. 134–5, P. to H.M. 16/2/55; *Arg.* i. 536 on cab of 17/2; *R.* v. *P.* 168–70, 20/2; *V.L.* iii. 136–9, Albert memo. and P. to H.M. 21/2/1855; *Arg.* i. 537 on cab of 21st, 539 on cab of 22nd.
10. *V.L.* iii. 138–9, P. to H.M. 21/2 will consult cabinet, which, says Arg. i. 539, was 'unusual, if not wholly unprecedented'. Argyll says that on 22/2 P. put to them the alternatives of 'advances to Lord John and the Whigs, or . . . to the Tory Opposition'. On P.'s offer to Shaftesbury see *Arg.* i. 541, *V.L.* iii. 147. On Wilson see Barrington, *Servant of All*, 266–7.
11. *Arg.* i. 559.
12. *R.* v. *P.* 161–4, clearly 6th (not 5th) Feb. royal memo.
13. See Waterfield, *Layard of Nineveh*, 254–76.
14. Barrington, ii. 48, Wilson to Lewis 7/4/1857; i. 312–14, Lewis to Wilson, Sept. 1856.
15. *V.L.* iii. 187–8, P. to H.M. 22/9/1855.
16. *R.* v. *P.* 184, P. to H.M. 16/7/1855; *V.L.* iii. 190, P. to H.M. 10/11/1855; *G.* 127–8, Granville to Canning 27/11/1855; ibid. 139, 8/1/1856.

17. Reid's *Milnes*, i. 513. That P. intended to dissolve at the end of the session is shown by A. ii. 76–79, to William 15/2/1855.

18. A. ii. 79–80, P. to Gladstone 6/2/1855.

19. *V.L.* iii. 189–91, P. to H.M. 10/11/1855; see Stanmore's *Herbert*, i. 433.

20. Stanmore, ii. 59–60, correspondence of 18–20/11/1856; cf. ibid. i. 424 ff., remonstrances to Gladstone May 1855.

21. *Arg.* i. 556 ff.

22. For the Four Points, etc., see Gavin Henderson, 'The Two Interpretations of the Four Points', Dec. 1854, and the 'Diplomatic Revolution of 1854', in *Crimean War Diplomacy*. For Palmerston's reluctance to take the Four Points seriously see ibid. 103 (Argyll to Clarendon 25/10/1854); on his concession to the Peelites see ibid. 37, Colloredo to Buol 24/2/1855 and A. ii. 76–78, P. to William 15/2/1855. For his reception of the 'mauvaise plaisanterie' (and his temporary assumption of the Colonies) see ibid. 84–88, to Russell 28/3/1855.

23. *V.L.* iii. 152–3, P. to H.M. 26/4/1855; *Arg.* i. 553.

24. *G.* 106–8, Granville to Argyll 3/5/1855.

25. Gavin Henderson, op. cit. 60–61; *Arg.* i. 549, 553–4, 557. Sidney Herbert admitted that a government approving these terms would have been hooted from office — Stanmore, i. 426, to Aberdeen.

26. A. ii. 92–94, P. to Napoleon 28/5/1855.

27. *R.* v. *P.* 182–4; *V.L.* iii. 166–8, 12–14/7/1855; Walpole, ii. 267–8, Russell to P. and reply.

28. Gavin Henderson, op. cit., rightly concluded that the first six months of 1855 were 'decisive in [the] careers' of P. and Russell; Maxwell, ii. 87, Clarendon to Cowley 11/8/1855.

29. *R.* v. *P.* 173–5.

30. Woodham-Smith, *Florence Nightingale*, 156; A. ii. 81–82, P. to Raglan.

31. Woodham-Smith, 187; *G.* 133, 136.

32. A. ii. 97–99.

33. Ibid. 13–14.

34. *R.* v. *P.* 166–8, P. to H.M. 10/2/1855.

35. C. Hibbert, *The Destruction of Lord Raglan*, 257, P. to Panmure 19/2/1855.

36. Ibid. 254, P. to Raglan 12/2/1855.

37. Ibid. 252, P. to Panmure 11/7/1855.

38. *G.* 116–17, memo. citing and criticizing Panmure.

39. Ibid. 109–10, Granville to P. 7/5/1855.

40. Hibbert, op. cit. 257 and 281–2, P. to Panmure 1 and 8/5/1855.

41. *Arg.* i. 585–7.

42. *R.* v. *P.* 179–80, P. to H.M. and reply 29/6/1855.

43. Hibbert, op. cit. 253.

44. Woodham-Smith, 194–7.

45. *G.* 142, 15/1/1856.

46. Ibid. 137, 4/1/1856.

47. Ibid. 115.

48. Ibid. 106–8, Granville to Argyll 3/5/1855.

49. *Arg.* i. 567.

50. Reid's *Milnes*, i. 521, Delane to Milnes 9/9/1855, ii. 3, Milnes to C. J. MacCarthy 21/2/1856.

51. *V.L.* iii. 194–6, H.M. to Clarendon 23/11/1856.

CHAPTER XX THE PEACE OF PARIS, 1856

1. A. ii. 100–1, P. to William 25/8/1855.

2. *R.* v. *P.* 174, 9/4/1855 — complete blockade in the Baltic, capture of Sebastopol, destruction of the Russian Black Sea fleet, expulsion of Russians from Georgia and the Circassian coast.

3. A. ii. 91–92, memo. P. 16/12/1855.

4. Waterfield, 279, Sandwith to Layard; *G.* 133–4, 137, 25/12/1855 and 4/1/1856.

5. Ibid. 136–9.

6. *G.* 127. See J. Mackintosh, *The British Cabinet*.

7. *Arg.* i. 584–7.

8. *Arg.* i. 602; *G.* 136–8, 162.

9. *Arg.* i. 563, 570, 591; *V.L.* iii. 169–70, H.M. to Clarendon 27/7/1855. For the important impact of this treaty on Russia see Mosse, *The Rise and Fall of the Crimean System*, 22.

10. Bell, ii. 138, P. to Clarendon 25/9/1855 and 9/10/1855, Lorne, 174–7.

11. But when after the fall of Sebastopol Walewski proposed to make the restoration of Congress Poland a condition of peace, Palmerston (to Clarendon 16/9/1855) demurred — Mosse, *Crimean System*, 17; Lorne, 174–7.

12. *S.M.E.* 79–80, P. to Clarendon 1/12/1855. For the negotiations see Henderson, op. cit. 87–93, Mosse, *Crimean System*, 17–32, *S.M.E.* 78–81.

13. A. ii. 103–4, cf. Maxwell, ii. 118, Clarendon to Granville 12/3/1856.

14. *V.L.* iii. 194–6, H.M. to Clarendon 23/11/1855; *V.L.* iii. 191–3, 13 and 19/11/1855; *S.M.E.* 80, Clarendon to P. 18/11; Maxwell, ii. 118 Clarendon to Granville 12/3/1856; cf. Henderson, 91, Albert's views 29/11 and 12/12 and Palmerston's impatience with them 13/12 (ibid. 91–92).

15. A. ii. 104–5. Russia at first (6/12) wished to insist on a Russo-Turkish convention only.

16. *Arg.* i. 597; Henderson 88–89, P. to Clarendon 20/11; *G.* 133, 135.

17. A. ii. 105–7.

18. *G.* 143–7; Lorne, 179–80.

19. H. of L. 31/1/1856.

20. Maxwell, ii. 117–18, Clarendon to P. 29/2 and 3/3/1856 and to Granville 8/3/1856; *G.* 168–70. The specification of light vessels was left to a Russo-Turkish convention but this was to have the same force and validity as if it were part of the general treaty.

21. *Arg.* ii. 22–23; Henderson, 95–96; *V.L.* iii. 228–9, H.M. to P. Mar. 1856.

22. *V.L.* iii. 232–3, P. to H.M. 30/3/1856.

23. *S.M.E.* 78, P. to Clarendon 16/10/1855; Maxwell, ii. 115, 118, Clarendon to Reeve 26/1/1856, to Granville 12/3/1856. Granville, untypically, says, 'peace has been wonderfully well received in the country' *G.* 175, 7/4/1856, but admits the hissing at Temple Bar (ibid. 178, 29/4).

24. On this see Gavin Henderson, paper on problems of neutrality in *Crimean War Diplomacy*. He shows that despite a professed, and novel, acceptance of the 'free ships make free goods' doctrine, Britain, so far at least as the Hanse ports were concerned, 'took away with her left hand what she gave with her right', partly as a way to pointing out to Prussia her vulnerability to maritime power.

25. A. ii. 108–10. Henderson, however, concludes, in contrast to Salisbury (H. of L. 6/3/1871), that it was understood from Crimean War experience 'that she might safely consent to the Declaration without her maritime preponderance being any less useful to her in the future' because of 'a strict interpretation of contraband trade, an extension of the doctrine of "continuous voyage" and a widespread enforcement of blockades' ibid. 237. Admiral Sir Herbert Richmond, in *Statesmen and Sea Power*, says of the Declaration of Paris that while 'nothing was gained in security, shackles were imposed on the action of sea power' (267).

26. See Bell, ii. 141–5, 154–7; *Arg.* i. 591, ii. 47–48, 51–52; *G.* 177–8; *R. v. P.* 194–5; M. 380; A. ii. 123. Cf. G. F. Hickson, 'Palmerston and the Clayton–Bulwer Treaty', *Cambridge Historical Journal*, iii. 295–303. On 20/1/1848 Palmerston had proposed to Russell an arbitration treaty with the U.S. (A. i. 59–60). In September 1851 the Admiralty sent orders to co-operate with the Spaniards against American filibusters in Cuba, which were strengthened under the Tories, and in 1853 the British invited the French and the Americans to sign a mutual self-denying ordinance over Cuba (Bartlett, op. cit. 275).

27. Stanmore, ii. 46; *Arg.* ii. 49, 65.

28. M. 380–3; A. ii. 111–17, memo. on talk with Chreptovitch. For a full account of these incidents see Mosse, *The Crimean System* 55–104.

29. For Granville's own account see *G.* 185–212.

30. A. ii. 117–21, P. to Walewski 10/9/1956 — for Granville's comment 'a really old Roman letter' see *G.* 216, 30/9/1856, Granville to Canning.

31. Maxwell, ii. 133, Clarendon to his wife 24/10/1856; M. 383.

32. For schemes of redistribution usually involving the removal of the heiress of Parma to Modena and other transfers to Roumania or even Greece see *S.M.E.* 87 and notes — Cavour to Azeglio 11/8/1856, P. to Clarendon 30/4/1856 and 27/5/1856. Cavour reported that Clarendon had said the British would 'gladly and with great energy' help when war came. When this was published after Cavour's death, Clarendon wrote: '. . . it is absolutely false that I ever told him or led him to suppose that we should go to the relief of Piedmont if she would declare war against Austria. . . . I should never have thought of committing the English Government to such a course without instructions — OR WITH THEM' (Maxwell, ii. 258). But it does look as if Clarendon was temporarily carried away in 1856 by Palmerston's enthusiasm. By 1859 he felt very differently, because of his

alarm about France — e.g. 197 ibid. to Granville 13/9/1859 — 'Pam is inclined to go the whole hog about Italy, and is in a fool's paradise about the Emperor of the French'.

33. *G.* 132, Dec. 1855.

34. Bell, ii. 152, P. to Clarendon 29/6/1856.

35. A. ii. 101, P. to William 25/8/1855; *V.L.* iii. 178–9, 182–4, H.M. to Clarendon 3/9, Granville to Clarendon 14/9.

36. Maxwell, ii. 123, Clarendon to Cowley 28/6/1856; *G.* 217, 30/9/1856; Barrington, i. 304–7, Lewis to Wilson 5 and 21/10/1856, Wilson to Lewis 26/10; M. 384, 13/11/1856. For Palmerston's refusal to send back the British minister 17/3/1857 and Clarendon's very violent language about Naples to Apponyi 2/1/1858 see T.–P. 213. Malmesbury, who wished to restore diplomatic relations, said the King was only too glad to be rid of the English and French ministers (M. 451).

37. M. 385 Derby to Malmesbury 15/12/1856.

38. Lorne, 174–7, P. to Clarendon 9/10/1855. Argyll stresses this as an issue at the cabinet of 29/11/1855 (*Arg.* 599–600). The Triple Treaty of 15th April 1856 was, inter alia, intended to be a security against this.

39. Austrian resistance to a united Roumania was a strong factor — Mosse, *The Crimean System,* 51; *S.M.E.* 94–95.

40. *G.* 229, Granville from Paris 8/4/1857; Maxwell, ii. 144, Clarendon to his wife 14/8/1857; M. 403–4. For Clarendon to Malmesbury 13/6/1858 see M. 438–9. On 7/9/1858 Malmesbury authorized Cowley to show Palmerston the 'Principalities Reform Bill' and the dispatches on Turkey and Montenegro, saying, 'I have only followed in his wake' (ibid. 447). On 27/11/1858 P. wrote to Clarendon 'I am glad to hear that Derby adopts and approves all our foreign policy' (Maxwell, ii. 173).

41. *S.M.E.* 85–86.

CHAPTER XXI 'THE TRITON AMONG THE MINNOWS', 1856

1. Morley's *Cobden,* ii. 171, 178, to Bright 11/2/1855, to Chevalier 5/10/1855.

2. Milnes, ii. 6, 3/5/1856 'the rumours of a dissolution increase'.

3. *G.* 171, Granville to Canning 18/3/1856.

4. Fulford.

5. *V.L.* iii. 106–7, Albert memo. 1/2/1855.

6. *R.* v. *P.* 163, H.M.'s journal 5/3/1855.

7. *V.L.* iii. 152–3, P. to H.M. 26/4/1855.

8. *Arg.* i. 568–70. Gladstone had predicted that Palmerston would have everything his own way — 'the leaven would go to the wall'.

9. *V.L.* iii. 237, H.M. to P. 11/4/1856.

10. *G.* 120, Clarendon to Granville 16/9/1855.

11. Barrington, ii. 8–9, Bethell, Oct. 1856.

12. Stanmore, ii. 53, 22/10/1856, Herbert to Gladstone, cf. ibid. 55–6, 26/10/1856.

13. Palmerston's vogue at this time is well described in Asa Briggs, *Victorian People,* 90–92.

14. *G.* 218, Granville to Canning 24/11/1856.

15. Morley's *Cobden*, ii. 171 to Bright 11/2/1855. Lewis wrote 13/12/1851 of 'the solidarity of peoples which lately excited so much enthusiasm at Birmingham' (Maxwell, i. 330).

16. Ibid. 190, Cobden to Lindsay Dec. 1856.

17. Barrington, i. 275, *re* riots 18th and 24th June 1855. Burn, *Age of Equipoise*, cites these demonstrations as evidence of a 'vast casual rowdyism' (82). Puritanism continued to irk the general public, Palmerston and the Queen. Permission for bands to play in the Parks, given in 1855, had to be withdrawn in 1856 after representations from the Archbishop of Canterbury, because, as Palmerston informed the Queen (10/5/1856), 'the Scotch members and the Dissenters are violent upon the subject' (see *V.L.* iii. 172–3, 202–3; *Arg.* ii. 49–50).

18. *R. v. P.* 186–7, H.M. to P. and reply, 6 and 9/10/1855. The House of Commons had compelled Gladstone to drop the advertisement duty in 1853, to the great benefit of the metropolitan press, but it was not until 1855 that the newspaper stamp was abolished and 1d. postage granted to newspapers. It was in that year that the *Daily Telegraph* was founded and the *Scotsman* and *Manchester Guardian* became dailies.

19. A. ii. 21–22, P. to Normanby 23/4/1847.

20. Snell, *Palmerston's Borough*, 67 (*re* 1837); *Speech of Lord Viscount Palmerston to the Electors of Tiverton on 31st July 1847*, 2nd ed., 1847, 16.

21. Walford, *Memoir of Rt Hon Viscount Palmerston*, 31–32.

22. *V.L.* iii. 276, H.M. to P. 24/11/1856; cf. ibid. 529–31.

23. *G.* 177, 26/4/56, Granville to Canning.

24. For relations between P. and the Rev. W. H. Headebruck or Heudebourck see B.–A. 165–71; Snell, *Palmerston's Borough*, 67.

25. A. ii. 15–16, Speech to the Romsey Labourers, 1854.

26. A. i. 96–99, P. to Leopold 15/6/1848.

27. Quoted above, 373 — A. ii. 13–14, 19/10/1853.

28. Ibid. 16–18, P. to Stanley of Alderley 3/1/1855; *P.P.* 99, P. to Gladstone 1/10/1854.

29. For the fecklessness of his cultured, dilettante father see Brian Connell, *Portrait of a Whig Peer*, 1957. When Palmerston's marriage to Lady Cowper was bruited, Melbourne commented: 'The thing is what his circumstances are: some say he is very much indebted, and then they might both be poor together were he to be out of office' (Mabell, Countess of Airlie, *Lady Palmerston and Her Times*, ii. 31).

30. B. i. 157, 174–8, 200, 203, 308; B.–A. 172, 178; Trollope, 12, 23–24, 42; Lorne, 37–39; Airlie, ii. 69; Ritchie, *Life and Times of Lord Palmerston*, 431; Tiverton speech 1847.

31. *V.L.* 2, i. 255–7, P. to H.M. 24/2/1865.

32. *Speech of Lord Viscount Palmerston, 31st July 1847*, 2nd ed.

33. Lorne, 91; Ritchie, *Life and Times*, 431, and above, n. 31.

34. See J. T. Ward, *The Factory Movement 1830–1855*, indexed references; *V.L.* i. 399, Melbourne to H.M. 6/9/1841; B.–A. 102–3, 127; L.C.J.R. 54; *Tiverton Speech, 1847*, describing the Ten Hours Bill as 'that measure . . . greatly desired by the working classes' also expressed the

view that the Poor Law was 'a matter with regard to which we have not, I think, even yet arrived at final conclusions' (15, 19).

35. *Tiverton Speech, 1847*, 15; Lewes speech A. i. 362–4.

36. For his H.O. programme see A. ii. 9–10 to William 3/4/1853; cf. Lady P. to Monckton Milnes: '. . . when Palmerston has ended all his Herculean labours by draining the valley of the Thames, and making all the furnaces and grates consume their own smoke, then, indeed . . . London will be worth living in. He is really sanguine enough to hope to see this day' (Reid's *Milnes*, 487, 2/12/1853). Professor Finer, in his *Edwin Chadwick*, writes: 'His ability to handle a department is well-known, but in addition Palmerston had the habit, rare among Whig statesmen, of finding things out for himself, then making up his own mind, and sticking to it. He had this great advantage too, that electioneering held no terrors for him: he did not have to bend to public opinion because he was its incarnation' (456).

37. Woodham-Smith, *Florence Nightingale* (Penguin) 213–16, etc.

38. This letter to Sidney Herbert, buried somewhere in the official Life, escapes me — D. G. S. Cf. his severity to Hall about keeping people off the grass in the Parks ('When I see the grass worn by foot traffic, I look on it as proof that the park has answered its purpose') and on the shrubberies in Green Park ('. . . Your iron hurdles are an intolerable nuisance. . . . I must positively forbid the prosecution of (the shrubberies and plantations) scheme. . . . I do not choose to be responsible for things which I disapprove' — B.–A. 413–15, 31/10 and 12/11/1857.

39. *P.P.* 95–96, P. to Gladstone 20/10/1856.

40. For the Penal Servitude Acts, 1853, 1857, 1864, the Criminal Procedure Act, 1865, the Prisons Act, 1865, the Act for the Better Care and Reformation of Youthful Offenders, 1854, the Act for the Education of Children in Receipt of Outdoor Relief, 1855, the Industrial Schools Act, 1857, and the Privy Council Minute of 2/6/1856 see Burn, *The Age of Equipoise*.

41. *G.* 145–6, 162, Jan.–Feb. 1856.

42. Cowper combined the Education and Health posts except for the period Feb.–Aug. 1857 when the Board temporarily lapsed. Hall had been first parliamentary head of the reconstituted Board (Aug. 1854) after the anti-bureaucratic Lord Seymour (for whom see Southgate, *The Passing of the Whigs*, 153–4) had induced the Commons to destroy the old Board consisting of Chadwick, Southwood Smith and Shaftesbury in what Palmerston called 'the foulest vote I have ever known in all my parliamentary experience'. The Home Secretary snubbed the House by assuring the Three of 'the full approbation of Her Majesty's Government of the zealous, able and indefatigable manner in which you have performed [your] important duties . . .' —see Finer, op. cit. 464–74. The tribute quoted in the text is from Royston Lambert, *Sir John Simon and English Social Administration*, esp. p. 222. Bell (ii. 79) quotes P. to Russell, 1/12/1853, objecting to replace the zeal and activity of the Board of Health by 'the jog-trot routine of a Government office'.

43. Bell, ii. 72, from Martin's *Life of the Prince Consort*; *P.P.* 43; Bell

ii. 75. Those who have conducted 'long investigation' into special subjects which Palmerston touched as Home Secretary are less grudging. Professor Burn calls P. 'probably the most "progressive" Home Secretary of his day'; Professor Finer 'an astonishingly able Home Secretary'.

44. A. ii. 9–10, to William 3/4/1853. He defined a deputation as 'a noun of multitude signifying very little'. But he bore, for instance, with a deputation of a hundred vestrymen and eight metropolitan members pursuing their remorseless vendetta against the Metropolitan Commission for Sewers.

45. *G.* 175.

46. Ibid. 171, Granville to Canning 18/3/1856; see Burn, *Age of Equipoise*.

47. K. B. Smellie, *Great Britain since 1688*, 155; Bell, ii. 134–5 — 'It is a question of free trade against monopoly,' he said.

48. *V.L.* iii. 184; *Arg.* ii. 10–20. There is a good account of the battle in the Lords in *G*.

49. Harris, *History of the Radical Party in Parliament*, 411; Morley's *Cobden*, ii. 178, Cobden to Chevalier 5/10/1855.

50. Milnes, i. 23/2/1855, 503.

51. *G.* 178, 180, Granville 28/4 and 2/5/1856; *Arg.* ii. 50.

52. Bell, ii. 117–19; *G.* 136.

53. See J. P. Mackintosh, *The British Cabinet*.

54. *G.* 218, Granville 24/11/1856; Stanmore, ii. 69, Herbert to Graham 27/1/1857. Palmerston confirmed to the Queen 13/1/1857 Granville's conclusion (*G.*) that he had decided he could do without Russell.

Chapter XXII Triumph and Set-back, 1857–8

1. The voting was 286–206. See *R.* v. *P.* 211–12, P. to H.M. 23/2/1857; cf. ibid. 208–11; Parker, ii. 297–302, Morley's *Gladstone*, 558–9, Maxwell's *Clarendon*, ii. 138; M., 390.

2. M. 385, Derby to M. 15/12/1856.

3. Ibid. 388, 4/2/1857.

4. Stanmore, ii. 55–56, 26/10/1856. Gladstone's article *The Declining Efficiency of Parliament* was published in the *Quarterly* in Jan. 1857.

5. For Peelite positions see especially Parker, ii. 288–309 and Stanmore, ii. 52–88.

6. Stanmore, ii. 54, 67–68, Gladstone to Herbert 24/10 and 23/12/1856; Parker, ii. 288–95, Gladstone to Graham 10/11, 29/11, 2/12.

7. Parker, ii. 297, 3/12/1856.

8. Ibid. 291–2, 295–6. 2/12 and 29/11/1856.

9. Ibid. 298–9, 6/12/1856.

10. See especially Barrington, ii. 21–51. Also *R.* v. *P.* 208–11 and *V.L.* iii. 285–7; *Arg.* ii. 72–74; M. 389–91; Morley's *Gladstone*, 559–62; Fortescue, 103.

11. Barrington, ii. 27–28, 22/2/1857.

12. *Arg.* ii. 67–69; *G.* 225 and cf. 246 (Canning to Granville 4/5/1857); Barrington, ii. 29.

13. *V.L.* iii. 285–7, P. to H.M. 13/1/1857.

14. Cited Barrington, ii. 30, 32–3.

15. Fortescue, 104; *V.L.* iii. 288–9, P. to H.M. 28/2/1857. M. 391, speaks of Disraeli's reluctance to use the China question against Palmerston.

16. Barrington, ii. 31–32; Fortescue, 103–4; M. 391; *G.* 227; Maxwell, 139. For Gladstone's verdict, *Gladstone to his Wife*, 114 (28/2/1857 to Sir S. Glynne).

17. M. 391; Barrington, ii. 28; *V.L.* iii. 288–9; Fortescue, 104; *G.* 227.

18. Fortescue, 104.

19. *V.L.* iii. 290, 3/3/1857.

20. *R.* v. *P.* 213–14, 4/3 and 6/3/1857.

21. Fortescue, 104–5, 7/3/1857; *Arg.* ii. 70–71.

22. Maccoby, *English Radicalism 1853–86*, 59–63; Cobden, ii. 195 (Bright, 16/4/1857). Cf. Stanmore, ii. 80, Herbert's comment: 'It is mortifying to see a sensible nation so Press-led.'

23. Parker, ii. 303, Cobden to Graham 16/3/1857.

24. Cobden, ii. 194–6.

25. Ibid. 219–20 (to Lindsay, 23/3/1858): 'The great prosperity of the country made Tories of us all'; Barrington, ii. 47 (Wilson to Lewis 7/4/1857): 'As long as people are as well off as they are now, the economical fit in the House for Party purposes will find no response out of doors.' Wilson (ibid. 21, 15/1/1857) had forecast commercial stringency; in Nov. 1857 Granville reported to Canning that it had arrived (*G.* 267, 24/11/1857).

26. Stanmore, ii. 3; cf. ibid. 69, 27/1/1857 to Graham.

27. Cited Jones's *Derby*, 218 note (Stanhope to Taylor, 19/4/1857).

28. Cobden, ii. 197–200 to Moffatt and to Parkes 7/4/1857 and to Hargreaves 9/8/1857.

29. *G.* 227, Granville to Canning 8/4/1857.

30. *The Times*, 13/4/1857; *R.* v. *P.* 214–16; Barrington, ii. 50 Lewis to Wilson 11/4/1857.

31. *G.* 227, Granville to Canning 8/4 and 10/3/1857; *The Times* 16/4/1857.

32. *V.L.* iii. 291, Granville to H.M.; cf. Jones, 217. For Derby's considered view on China, see M. 397–8 (6/5/1857).

33. *Arg.* ii. 70.

34. See *The Passing of the Whigs*, 287–9.

35. *Arg.* ii. 74; *G.* 228, Granville to Canning 8/4/1857 and 227 10/3/1857; *The Times* 30/3/1857.

36. *V.L.* iii. 193, 24/3/1857.

37. On Palmerston's health see Jan. *R.* v. *P.* 208; recurrence of gout and effect on China speech *G.* 227 (10/3), cf. Fortescue, 104 (3/3) and *R.* v. *P.* 213, H.M. 4/3. On 30/4 Malmesbury (395) recorded Lady P.'s anxiety, P. being so weak that he could neither walk nor ride for exercise; she dreaded the session. *R.* v. *P.* 216 (21/5) makes it clear the leg was bad again in May. On 10/6 Granville (250) noted: 'He is beginning to fade a little in looks' but (ibid. 258) wrote on 26/8/1857: 'He, Pam, is younger

and healthier. . . . His very laborious work in the House has positively done him good.'

38. M. 397 (6/5/1857).

39. For Canning in India see Maclagan, *Clemency Canning*, and Canning's frequent letters in Fitzmaurice's *Granville*. For his attitude see especially ibid. 245–6 (9/4/1857) on causes of outbreak; 248 on the surprise of 'those who know the sepoys best' (19/5) and 275 (11/12/1857) and Canning to H.M., esp. 25/9/1857 (*V.L.* iii. 315–20).

40. Canning's reports were optimistic till 19/5/1857 after Meerut and Delhi, news described by Argyll (*Arg.* 80) as 'a clap of thunder out of the blue'. Until 9/9 (*G.* 257) inclusive Granville was assuring Canning of the full support of the cabinet and public opinion, but he could not write favourably again till 10/11 (*G.* 265). He defended him in the Lords against Ellenborough 9/10. For Clarendon's attitude see Maxwell, ii. 154 (to Lewis, 5/10, and to Palmerston, 4/11). On the press law Granville had doubts (*G.* 268–9, but cf. 20/6, 250–1).

41. On Canning and his Council see Maxwell, 155 (P. to Clarendon 6/11/1857); *G.* 258 Granville to Canning 26/8; Lady Canning to Granville (ibid. 271, 10/12/1857). Later the Tories falsely alleged disagreements between Canning and Colin Campbell. For reactions to the 'Proclamation' see *G.* 261 (Granville to Canning 24/10), 263 (9/11), 263–4 (9/11) and 292 (to Argyll 19/2/1887); M. 407 (18/10/1857). On 10/11 (*G.* 264–5) Granville told Canning that Palmerston and Vernon Smith were both inclined to be wrong about the 'Proclamation' and that he could not say in public all he would have liked. By 24/11 (ibid. 267) he was able to tell him that 'even Shaftesbury' was praising Canning (267). For Lady Canning's defence (10/12) see ibid. 271–2, and for Canning's 273. Not till now (12/12) did he dispatch a formal explanation of the instructions.

42. On the cabinet see *G.* 263 9/11/1857, Granville to Canning; for Canning's amazement that disapproval should have been considered ibid. (24/12) 280.

43. Ibid. 276 (11/12). Canning said only Granville, Smith, and Argyll had publicly helped him. He ascribed Palmerston's attitude to dislike of the diversion of Elgin's troops, to which Palmerston had, as Granville reported 10/7 (251), objected. Elgin handed them over on his own responsibility. Wood, for the government (Palmerston absenting himself) made the cabinet's lack of enthusiasm evident in the House — see M. 400–1 (11/7), Granville deplored this and announced government approval in the Lords (ibid. 253–5) and got Palmerston to send greetings to Canning (25/7/1857).

44. Ibid. 269 (10/12/1857) and 264 (10/11); 284, 24/12 (Lady Canning to Granville).

45. Granville never ceased to assure his friend Canning that all he asked for would be sent. For the decisions see especially *R.* v. *P.* 217–19 and *V.L.* iii. 297–8, 308. For Tory criticism of delay see M. 411, and for the royal allegation *R.* v. *P.* 224–5. For royal criticism of demobilization and low estimates see *R.* v. *P.* 199–200, 215–16, 220, *V.L.* iii. 299. For

Clarendon's criticisms see Maxwell, ii. 152–3. For apprehension as to foreign powers see *V.L.* iii. 306–7, 311–12; *R.* v. *P.* 219.

46. Maxwell, 144–6; *G.* 259; Maxwell, 152.

47. Report of speech in A. ii. 138–40 and P. to Clarendon 16/11 (ibid.).

48. *R.* v. *P.* 220–3 (royal memo. 18–7–1857); *G.* 261, Granville from Balmoral to Canning 24/9; *R.* v. *P.* 219 H.M. to P. 17/7; *R.* v. *P.* 219–20, *V.L.* iii. 306, 311 n., *R.* v. *P.* 224–5 18/9/1857; ibid. 225–6 (2/10/1857); *V.L.* iii. H.M. to Panmure 18/12/1857 (ditto) 330, 29/12/1857.

49. M. 411 (27/11); *G.* 268 (10/12) and 277 (23/12), Granville to Canning.

50. *G.* 289–90, Granville to Canning 9/2/1858.

51. Palmerston's strong position is stressed by Granville (*G.* 249–50 10/6/1857, 269 10/12 and 287–8 26/1/1858) and Graham, who (Parker, ii. 325) wrote 19/12/1857 of the 'unabated subserviency' of what Cobden christened 'the Servile Parliament'. The unexpectedness of the defeat is attested by Ashley (A. ii. 146), the Queen (*R.* v. *P.* 20/2), Granville (*G.* 293, 24/2), Gladstone (*Gladstone to his Wife*, 120, 21/2). Fortescue (122–3) says Gibson said his motion 'would do the Govt no harm'. It was on 2nd March, *after* the vote, that Granville says that Palmerston's manner had recently become rather overbearing and dictatorial (*G.* 294); and Ashley accepts this.

52. On 10th Nov. Granville noted that Palmerston was 'a good deal knocked up by his speech' (*G.* 265) and on 19th the Queen was worried in case he might die (Maxwell, ii. 157). But Granville had spoken highly of his fitness in August (see above, n. 37) and in December Russell said that his physical strength was unimpaired though his mental vigour was decreasing (Parker, ii. 325). Greville's gloomy account of Palmerston's condition appears to be a sweeping generalization based on his falling asleep more frequently.

The conspicuous presence of Clanricarde is referred to by the Prince (*V.L.* iii. 337–8). The mismanagement of the House during the actual debate is stressed by Argyll (*Arg.* 110 to Aberdeen 2/3/1858) and Lewis (Barrington, ii. 74, 26/2), who thought the Speaker should have ruled Gibson out of order (on this see Denison, 11–18). The optimism of the ministers till the last is stressed by Fortescue, 123. Hayter's miscalculation is avowed by Palmerston (*V.L.* iii. 335–7, 19/2/1858). That Canning was still unpopular was shown when the inclusion of his name in an address of thanks to the officers in India had to be accompanied by explanations that this did not prejudge consideration of complaints against him. That there was suspicion that Palmerston intended to 'dodge' Reform needs no proof when some of his cabinet colleagues shared it.

53. Parker, ii. 325–6, to Graham 21/12/1857; ibid. 317, 11/10/1857. After his return in 1857 Russell made speeches at South Molton, Sheffield, and Birmingham, defending himself over the Vienna Conference and demanding educational and parliamentary reform, economy and (bravely) the removal of Jewish disabilities. His correspondence with Graham in the winter shows him as afraid to incur the charge of faction, until he cast off his doubts and, ignoring Graham's advice, attacked the India Bill *ab initio*.

54. Walpole, ii. 295, 2/2/1858 to Geo. Grey.

55. *R. v. P.* 231; for Bethell's remark see A. ii. 142 and cf. *G.* 287–8 (26/1).

56. Cobden, ii. 218.

57. A. ii. 144; M. 415 (1/2).

58. M. 415 (9/2); *G.* 289 (8/2); *V.L.* iii. 335 (9/2).

59. Others, by contrast, thought the measure insignificant, and therefore ignominious — 'all Europe would laugh at our degradation' (Parker, ii. 336, Graham to Russell 4/2/1858).

60. Fortescue, 123 (19/2); *G.* 293 (24/2) — repeated by Ashley; seemingly implied by Palmerston to the Queen (*V.L.* iii. 335–7, 19/2) attributing Derby's decision to the 'marked effect' of Gibson's speech, and openly alleged by him at Tiverton in the 1859 election.

61. *Gladstone to his Wife*, 120–1, 21/2/1858.

G. 294 (2/3); M. 417 (20/2). Cf. Fortescue, 123: 'a bad speech . . . very angry and abusive of Gibson & Co' (19/2).

62. *G.* 293 (24/2); *Gladstone to his Wife*, 121 (22/2). Derby's expression of surprise at his victory may have been genuine; his attribution of the plot to Russell and Graham 'in the interest of the Radicals', with Gladstone's accession 'accidental' was clearly an *argumentum ad feminam* (*V.L.* iii. 338, 21/2) but was not necessarily untrue for all that.

CHAPTER XXIII FIGHTING BACK, 1858–9

1. Barrington, ii. 77–78 Lewis to Wilson 30/3/1857 — cf. ibid. 75–76, Wilson 'Disraeli's extraordinary proposition'; *Gladstone to his Wife*, 122, 'imaginative and not workmanlike'; Cranbrook, i. 116 (Hardy, a junior minister, 'What a mess altogether!'); *Arg.* ii. 111–12, Argyll to Granville: 'I am boiling over — foaming at the mouth.'

2. *G.* 299–300; *Arg.* ii. 112–13.

3. Russell's unsent letter to Derby is in Walpole, ii. 297–8. Disraeli to Queen 12/4/1857 *V.L.* iii. 354–5.

4. Before Ellenborough's resignation on 10th the shadow cabinet expected a majority of a hundred (*G.* 306); afterwards Hayter promised one of about fifty (ibid. 306–8). The Queen declined to promise dissolution on 11th (*V.L.* 359–60). Cf. M. 434–5; Fortescue, 128–9.

5. M. 436 (16 and 17/5). Malmesbury expected to be beaten, and Derby told the Queen the adverse majority would be 15–35 (cf. *G.* 308, 17th, 35–50) unless he could let it be known that a dissolution would not be refused.

6. *G.* 307–9; *V.L.* iii. 363–6, Phipps's talk with Aberdeen; Parker, ii. 343, Disraeli's three letters to Graham of whom Fortescue says (130) 'hatred of Palmerston probably decided his course'. Graham's anti-Canning speech, praised by Disraeli to the Queen (*V.L.* iii. 368–9), indicated his allegiance to Russell. Graham and Gladstone in turn were offered Ellenborough's office, but refused.

7. *V.L.* iii. 369–71, Derby to Queen 23/5/1858.

8. 'We cut rather a foolish figure' (*G.* 308); 'the farce of the evening'

(Fortescue, 130). For fear of dissolution, and hatred of Palmerston by Peelites and Manchester School, and the effect of the knowledge that in India Outram had attacked the original Oudh Proclamation (causing Canning to amend it) see ibid. and Cranbrook, i. 119. For the hope that Derby would settle Reform see *Arg.* 122–4, 132–3 and Barrington, ii. 96–98.

9. *G.* 310 (25/6/1858) — cf. 311, 10/7, 'Both are determined not to give way and neither of them can be put aside.' Wilson on 15/10 found an arrangement between them as distant as ever (Barrington, ii. 93). Granville thought there was still a feeling for Palmerston in the country and none for Russell.

10. M. 423, cf. 433, 439; *G.* 304, 311 and 299 (1/4/1858) — 'Pam has no time to wait.'

11. M. 420–1; A. ii. 148–9, P. to Clarendon 1/3/1858.

12. M. 424 and *V.L.* iii. 347–8; see footnote.

13. M. 420–5, 458–61, cf. 480 (26/4/1859 a propos of Persigny's return — 'He will go and repeat everything I say to Lord Palmerston'), 483, 491 (allegation that in 1859 Persigny spent money in the British elections). It must have seemed significant that Lady Shaftesbury (Lady Palmerston's daughter) organized the presentation of a bracelet to la Persigny when she left.

14. A. ii. 149–50, P. to Sulivan; Maxwell, ii. 162, P. to Clarendon 31/10/1858; ibid. 165, Russell to Wood and 167, Lady Theresa Lewis to Clarendon, 24/11/1858. Cf. Barrington, ii. 96–101, Wilson's comment 21/11/1858. At Tiverton in 1859 Rowcliffe said that Palmerston was well known to be a pet of the Emperor of the French (A. ii. 152).

15. M. 455 and 460.

16. *V.L.* iii. 381–2.

17. *G.* 310 (25/6). Cf. Fortescue, 139 (28/11/1858), did not think that Palmerston could form a government again or act under anyone else 'but he expects it'.

18. A. i. 359.

19. *V.L.* ii. 567 n. 2, P. to Lansdowne 8/12/1853; *Account of the Tiverton Election* (29/4/1859), 11; *P.P.* 279–80, P. to Gladstone 11/5/1864.

20. Stanmore, ii. 89–90, Herbert to Aberdeen 12/4/1856.

21. *Arg.* ii. 76–77.

22. Stanmore, op. cit.

23. *G.* 227–8, Granville to Canning 8/4/1857.

24. *R. v. P.* 227–9, 18/10/1857.

25. Ibid. Granville early in November said he had seen Palmerston's plan, which would certainly not destroy the British Constitution (*Arg.* ii. 94; *G.* 265); on 23/12 he said that it would give more than expected from Palmerston, though he was still opposed to any general lowering of the £10 household test in boroughs (*G.* 277–8; cf. *Arg.* ii. 95–97).

26. *Arg.* ii. 94–98. Both Granville and Argyll believed Palmerston was using India to damp Reform but Palmerston denied it to Argyll (*Arg.* ii. 95–97, 26/11/1857).

27. Cranbrook, i. 125, 15/12/1858 — cf. Barrington, 96–98. Clarendon

said that Derby paid glowing tribute to the service Bright rendered him (*Arg.* ii. 128; Maxwell, 173). Bright backtracked (Barrington, ii. 106–17). For fears of Liberals voting for an over-modest bill see *Arg.* ii. 134 (8/3/1859) and Barrington, ii. 132 (20/2/1859, Hay to Wilson). The shabby people were expected to include Palmerston if the bill was reasonable — Arg. ii. 113–14 (P. to Argyll 31/3/1858), Barrington, ii. 115–16 (Lewis to Wilson 27/12/1858).

28. *Arg.* ii. 121–2, Herbert to Argyll 13/3/1858.

29. Parker, ii. 359–60, 1/9/1858; cf. 382, 9/5/1859; Maxwell, ii. 172, Clarendon to Lewis 20/12/1858.

30. Maxwell, ii. 174, P. to Clarendon 27/11/1858; 175 same to same 19/12/1858. Russell found it difficult to get others to discuss details with him; for his ideas see Parker, ii, especially 359–60 (Sept. 1858). For Russell on Bright see, inter alia, *Arg.* ii. 131, Fortescue, 139, Parker, ii. 364, Barrington, ii. 130–2. On 19/1/1859 he informed Graham that he was against Bright's bill and would bring in his own if Derby's was unsatisfactory (Parker, ii. 367).

31. Cranbrook, i. 128 (2/3/1859); cf. Fortescue, 145 (28/2/1859), who says Russell's speech smacked of the Bright school. The phrase used by Russell 'a great body of the working classes' upset Palmerston, whom Argyll thought would have supported the government but for the 40s. clause (*Arg.* ii. 134, 8/3/1859 to Geo. Grey).

32. Cranbrook, i. 130. Fortescue (146) describes his speech as 'very adroit and wonderfully young'. There is some mystery as to Palmerston's attack on a dissolution; it can have been sincere only if he feared the Tories might win an election. He denounced the dissolution on constitutional grounds at Tiverton (*An Account*, p. 7). It was, of course, quite astute to attack the Tories for not settling the question when they could have done. Russell, in a feeble speech, outlined his own bill (4/4/1859), which was moderate (Cranbrook, i. 132, Parker, ii. 377–8; Fortescue, 147).

33. Parker, ii. 382, Graham to Russell 9/5/1859; on Gladstone, see Morley, i. 623–4, Journal of R. J. Phillimore, 18/5/1859 and 31/5/1859.

34. That the Emperor 'detests the Derby Government, and pines for Palmerston and Clarendon' (*G.* 324, 9/2/1859 from Paris) was an open secret, though Walewski hated England and those two especially (so Shaftesbury told Fortescue, Fortescue, 137, 3/11/1858). For Malmesbury's suspicions see M. 460, 471.

35. M. 426. On 26/1/1859 (460–2) he thought the connection with Palmerston clear and on 25/3 (471) wrote of the *Post* as 'the organ of the Emperor, Palmerston and Azeglio'. But see Beales, 49–50.

36. *G.* 325–7, 30/1/1859.

37. Twice 'Johnny and Palmerston, especially the former, . . . much modified what they intended to say' — *G.* 324, Granville to Canning 9/2/1859; M. 477; Fortescue, 145; *V.L.* iii. 414, Queen to Leopold 1/3/1859. Malmesbury attributed the moderation to Clarendon, who 'approved my Italian policy'. For Clarendon's advice see Clarendon to Cowley 2/2/1859 (cited Beales, 52–53).

38. The cabinet was unanimous (*V.L.* iii. 418–19, 21/4, Derby to H.M.). For the Tiverton speech of 29/4/1859 see *An Account*.

39. Russell's election address attacked ministers as pro-Austrian and said that our honour demanded that Britain should not assist in riveting chains on Italy, but that interest required peace. The Queen (3/5 to Leopold, *V.L.* iii. 423–4) contrasted his 'moderate and prudent language' with Palmerston's. On the electoral impact of the war see Beales, 75. But Malmesbury (M. 481) and the Tory managers (according to the Liberal manager, Parkes, see Barrington, ii. 151) thought otherwise and Evelyn Ashley accepted their verdict (A. ii. 154)

40. Parker, ii. 381–3, Russell to Graham 7/5/1859 and 17/5/1859; cf. *G*. 329–30, Granville to Palmerston 27/5/1859.

41. On need for speed, *G*. 329–30 and Barrington, ii. 156–9. The two rivals, whose competition was described by the party manager Parkes as 'unpatriotic and scandalous' (ibid. 153) met on 20th May and agreed on Reform, foreign policy and the general composition of a government, but not on the lead (Parker, ii. 386–7, Russell to Graham 23/5). Russell's indecisive mood at Wilton was described by his host, Herbert, to Granville on 27th (*G*. 327–9), whereupon Granville saw Palmerston, who permitted him to propose to Russell that they agree each to serve under the other (*G*. 330–1, 29/5). Russell declined (31st, ibid.), and never fairly put to Palmerston his view that he (Russell) must be either premier or Leader of the House of Commons (for which see Parker, ii. 384–8; Stanmore, ii. 181–2).

42. *G*. 327–9, Herbert to Granville 27/5/1859.

43. Ibid., Stanmore, ii. 195–6, and Parker, ii. 385–6, Graham to Russell 18/5/1859. Granville agreed that Palmerston could get on better without Russell than vice versa (*R.* v. *P*. 256–8).

44. Stanmore, ii. 198. This agreement between Palmerston and Russell did not bind either to serve under a third person (A. ii. 155–6, Palmerston to the Queen 12/6/1859).

45. Many felt that there could be no peace while there were two kings of Brentford in the Commons (e.g. Parker, ii. 340–2), but Palmerston never contemplated making or accepting the condition that one or other should go to the Lords.

46. *R.* v. *P*. 255–6, *Journal*, 11/6/1859. Granville did not tell Palmerston this (*V.L.* iii. to the Queen, 12/6, 2 a.m.) and Clarendon said that Palmerston would 'resent this public proof of her want of confidence in him given in the face . . . of Europe' (*G*. 335–6, 11/6 to Granville). Russell did not agree with Clarendon or Granville about foreign affairs either.

47. For the cheers see M. 490, 492. For accounts of Granville's negotiations see his report to the Queen at 2 a.m. on 12th (*V.L.* iii. 440–1) and his summary letters to Palmerston and Russell on 26th (*G*. 340–1) and *V.L.* iii. 438 ff. and *G*. 332–9. For Russell's view that 'concert' between the two in the choice of ministers was essential see Parker, ii. 384–5 (17/5). For Palmerston's commission and his report that he was 'sorry to say' that Russell insisted on the Foreign Office (he would have liked him to take

India) see *R. v. P.* 256–8 and *V.L.* iii. 442. It is not clear whether Clarendon was at all justified in saying that Palmerston as well as the Queen wanted *him* at the Foreign Office (Fortescue, 151).

48. Morley's *Cobden*, ii. 226.

49. Harris, 410. Wilson (Barrington, ii. 167) on 11/6 declared that Russell was nowhere as to rank-and-file support as against Palmerston. He told his father-in-law, Minto (Walpole, ii. 296), on 16/3/1858 that he would not be insensible to the honour of again leading the Whig party, but would not cabal with Peelites and Radicals. This he had often seemed to do, but he could not simultaneously anchor himself on the Whigs of Brooks's and the Peelites (they disliked one another) and his flirtations with the Radicals had only harmed him (e.g. Stanmore, ii. 195–6 Herbert to Gladstone 28/5/1859).

50. Morley's *Cobden*, ii. 229–34, Cobden to Sale 4/7/1859.

51. Ibid. 226–9.

52. Parker, ii. 381–3, 7th and 16th May 1859.

53. Ibid. 388, Aberdeen to Graham 26/5/1859.

54. Morley's *Gladstone*, i. 627–8, to Sir W. Heathcote 16/6/1859. On 3/4/1859 Graham had noted that Gladstone was more implacable against Austria than Palmerston or Russell and he admitted his solidarity with them to Herbert, 29/5 (196–7 Stanmore, ii.). Though he could not bring himself to vote against the government on no confidence (Stanmore 185–97; Morley 623–4) it was known that he 'wished his former score rubbed off' (*G.* 327, early May) and by 3/6 Herbert had no doubt Gladstone would join a Liberal government.

55. *Gladstone to his Wife*, 124, 22/4/1859.

CHAPTER XXIV THE TRIUMVIRS, 1859–60

1. Beales, 92.

2. Ibid. 173. Cf. *G.* 355, 360, Granville to Canning 23/8 and 16/12/1859; Maxwell, ii. 205–6, Clarendon to Duchess of Manchester 7/1/1860.

3. *G.* 350–2, Granville to the Prince 13/7/1859. Granville's concert with the Palace was initiated by Albert's letter of 12/7 (ibid. 349–50) to which Granville responded that Palmerston and Russell 'would consider it as a want of confidence on the part of her Majesty, and an improper interference on the part of a colleague' but that he would comply provided 'no one should know' (Beales, 161).

4. *R. v. P.* 277, Albert memo. 31/12/1859 — '. . . a ready tool and convenient ally'; *G.* 348, 351, 355; *Arg.* ii. 144; Fortescue, 165.

5. Lorne, 191–2, June 1859; cf. Russell, quoted Beales, 100.

6. Ibid. 192–4; *R. v. P.* 261, P. to H.M. 4/7 and 6/7/1859; A. ii. 158–60, to Russell 6/7; *R. v. P.* 262–3, to H.M. 11/7; *V.L.* iii. 452–3 to Russell 13/7 (cf. 450–2). But see A. J. P. Taylor's 'European Mediation and the Agreement of Villafranca', *English Historical Review*, li. 1936.

7. A. ii. 161–3, P. to Persigny 13/7/1859; *G.* 351, Granville to Albert 13/7; *V.L.* iii. 461–6.

8. *R. v. P.* 266–7, P. to H.M. 13/8/1859 cites Britain, France, and

Belgium as instances of rulers belonging to the nation and not vice versa as, he implied, the Queen believed; A. ii. 174–80, P.'s memo. for cabinet 5/1/1860.

9. Beales, 103–5.

10. *V.L.* iii. 461–5, H.M. to Russell 21st, 23rd, and 24/8, Russell to H.M. 23/8, P. to H.M. 23/8/1859; ibid. 465–8 Granville to the Prince *re* P.'s anger at royal interference.

11. Ibid. 468–9; *G.* 356–8, Granville to Argyll 31/8/1859. '... Pam spoke for Johnny, and bitterly as regarded the Court. ... It has ended very well. Johnny has had a lesson that the Cabinet will support the Queen in preventing him and Pam acting on important occasions without the advice of their colleagues. ...': *Arg.* ii. 143–4, Gladstone to Argyll 31/8 — 'the conduct pursued has been hasty, inconsiderate and eminently juvenile'. The Duke replied: 'the decision of the Cabinet in respect to drafts is not given effect to, or ... what is said seems to leave the vaguest possible impression on Lord John's mind ...'.

12. *Arg.* ii. 144–5, Argyll to Gladstone 3/9/1859. But he saw no European objection to the annexations and hoped that 'our most timely protest' would have prevented France from employing force, or employing it successfully.

13. *V.L.* iii. 468–9, Granville to Albert 29/8/1859 and *G.* 356–8 Granville to Argyll 31/8.

14. Granville to Argyll 31/8, ibid; *V.L.* iii. 469–76, 5–11/9/1859 including H.M. to Russell 5/9 and P. to H.M. 9/9; *R. v. P.* 268–75; *G.* 361.

15. Beales, 114.

16. Ibid. 116–27; *R. v. P.* 275–7; *G.* 367–8; Maxwell, ii. 202–3.

17. *G.* 368, Granville to Palmerston 7/1/1860.

18. A. ii. 174–80, 5/1/1860.

19. *G.* 367–8, Albert to Granville 5/12/1859. P. (to Russell 4/11, A. ii. 187–9) contested this view but admitted that his reasoning might be wrong.

20. Maxwell, ii. 199, P. to Clarendon 4/1/1860; Beales, 121, P. to Russell 26/12/1859.

21. Morley's *Gladstone* memo. 656–70; Beales, 133, 134–7, 143–4; *V.L.* iii. 498–501.

22. A. ii. 166–7, 182–3, 186–90; *R. v. P.* 286–9; Lorne 198–202.

23. Lorne, ibid.: 'These reports may be incorrect, but they have their foundation in the general opinion of Europe that the Emperor has adopted a policy of aggrandisement'; Walpole, ii. 319, Russell to Hudson 31/1/1860: 'a beginning of natural frontiers'; Morley's *Gladstone*, 677, Herbert to Gladstone 23/11/1859; Barrington, ii. 197, Lewis to Wilson 19/11/1859; Fortescue, 172–3.

24. Maxwell, ii. 199–200, Clarendon to P. 8/1/1860. For Palmerston on French aims 'through Spain' at getting 'fortified points on each side of the Gut of Gibraltar' see A. ii. 166–7 to Russell 11/10/1859. Morley, *Cobden*, ii. 242 n. 4, describes this inference as 'a masterpiece of the perverse ingenuity of the Palmerston policy of alarm' but Flournoy (op.

cit., 200) indicates ground for believing that 'if Great Britain had become involved in war at that time with some other Power, Spain would almost certainly have joined the latter'.

25. T.–P. 211 ff.; Beales, 138; A. ii. 190–2, P.'s memo. on his talk with Flahault 27/3/1860; *R. v. P.* 281–3. Cf. *S.M.E.* 118, d'Azeglio to Cavour 1/4/1860.

26. The draft minute is in Lorne, 198–202. The cabinet did not adopt it — see Beales, 142–3.

27. T.–P. 291–2, Rechberg to Esterházy 30/6/1859.

28. Beales, 140.

29. But Cobden thought Persigny's warning finally decided the Emperor to approve the commercial treaty (Morley, ii. 256).

30. *Gladstone to his Wife*, 127, 5/12/1859; A. ii. 168–9, P. to Gladstone 15/12; *P.P.* 122–4, 6–7/2/1860.

31. *Gladstone to his Wife*, 128, 13/1/1860.

32. Cobden failed to see Russell when he wanted to in Nov. 59 (Morley, ii. 253). But Gladstone acknowledged Russell's help in cabinet after the treaty was signed — *Gladstone to his Wife*, 128, 11 and 13/1/1860.

33. *P.P.* 205–9, Palmerston to Gladstone 29/4/1862 — 'commercial interest is a link that snaps under the pressure of national passions'.

34. Cf. *Gladstone to his Wife*, 129, 28/1/1860 *re* cabinet — 'I could not have hoped for a better reception.'

35. Gladstone offered to go down on his knees to Russell if he would desist (Morley, 663–4). *Re* the compromise see Stanmore, ii. 186–7, 191, 21 and 24/5/59.

36. By Dec. 1859 P. thought any reduction of the borough test would mean an 'awful increase of voters' in all the large towns and reduction of the county test a 'leap in the dark' (Walpole, ii. 330). Lady P. spoke of 'that infernal Reform Bill' (Fortescue, 163–4, Apr. 1860). *Re* amendment and procedure see *P.P.* 133–4, P. to Gladstone 3/5/60, *R. v. P.* 285, P. to H.M. 24/5. Graham said the fear of dissolution was decisive (Stanmore, ii. 268).

37. The Reform Bill was withdrawn 11/6/1860. On 16/11 Russell admitted that no one wanted the only bill that could pass (Walpole, ii. 331–2).

On paper-duty decision, Maxwell, ii. 213 Lewis to Clarendon 12/4/1860. *Re* income-tax *P.P.* 124–6, 7–8/2/1860 and *Arg.* ii. 155. *Re* delays, *P.P.* 131, 133–4, 29/3 and 3/5/1860. *Re* dropping paper repeal, *P.P.* 132–3, 20–24/4/1860; Morley, 665 (Gladstone diary 5/5/1860).

38. *G.* 380, Granville to Canning 10/5/1860; *Arg.* ii. 159–62.

39. Derby Day was Wed., 23rd May; the Lords had defeated Paper Repeal on the night of 21st. The letter is not given in the *P.P.*

40. Morley's *Gladstone*, 666, memo. of 26/5/1860; *V.L.* iii. 510–11, P. to H.M. 22/5/1860.

41. Ibid. (both); Walpole, ii. 333 n. 2, Russell to P. 20/5; Morley, 671, Gladstone memo. 30/5.

42. M. 522, 1–2/6/1860.

43. Morley, 666 (memo. 26/5). For the resolutions & P.'s speech see Denison, 71/73, *P.P.* 138–40, *V.L.* iii. 512–14, *R. v. P.* 291, M. 524.

44. *V.L.* iii., P. to H.M. 2/7; *P.P.* 139–40, Gladstone to P. 4/7; Morley, 667–8, Phillimore, 6/7: 'A strange and memorable debate . . . Gladstone . . . loudly and tempestuously cheered by the radicals, and no one else. . . . Ought he to have spoken this as chancellor of the exchequer . . . after the first lord of the treasury had spoken in almost totally opposite sense? . . .'

45. *G.* 385–6. Granville to Canning 26/7/1860; *R. v. P.* 291–2, P. to H.M. 11/7: '. . . Viscount Palmerston is inclined to think that Mr. Gladstone means to resign on the fortification question', probably with Argyll.

46. *V.L.* iii. 395, H.M. to Derby 13/1/1859.

47. Morley, 679–80, Gladstone to Argyll 6/6/1860.

48. Ibid.; Morley, ii, Appendix, 812, Gladstone to Heathcoate 4/5/1861.

49. *P.P.* 214–16, P. to Gladstone 7/5/1862.

50. Bearce, 134, P. to Russell 5 and 7/2/1860.

51. Parker, ii. 398, Graham to Gladstone 2/6/1860; Gladstone saw Palmerston on 6/6 and was kindly and frankly warned of the danger to him (Gladstone) of resignation (Morley, 679–80, Gladstone to Argyll 6/6); *G.* 381–2, Granville to Canning 11/6: 'I thought two days ago that we were breaking up.' According to Clarendon (Maxwell, ii. 215, to Lewis 16/6) Aberdeen spoke very roughly to Gladstone when he admitted that he could not resign on China or the forts but would have opinion and Russell with him if he went on the Lords. Argyll told him he would damage himself if he went (see below, note 57).

52. Parker, ii. 393, Graham to Gladstone 18/1/1860; A. ii. 187–9, P. to Russell 4/11/1859.

53. *P.P.* 123, Gladstone to P. 7/2/1860.

54. Ibid. 131, P. to Gladstone 12/4/1860; Stanmore, ii. 248–56.

55. At the cabinet on 2/6 it had been decided that Palmerston should determine the date of the statement on Fortifications, Gladstone not committing himself to stay in (*P.P.* 135–7, Gladstone to P. 3/6). Argyll and Somerset sought a compromise; its acceptance is implicit in *P.P.* 140–1 (Gladstone to P. 5/7 and reply 9/7) but on 11th P. thought Gladstone would resign (*R. v. P.* 291–2). Palmerston's positive refusal of delay is in *P.P.* 142–3, 16/7/1860.

56. Ibid., cf. ibid. 115–18, P. to Gladstone 15/12/1859, 122–4, 6–7/2/1860.

57. *Arg.* ii. 164–5, Argyll to Gladstone 19/6/1860.

58. Maxwell, ii. 216, Lewis to Clarendon 19/7; Parker, ii. 399, Gladstone to Graham 22/7.

59. *R. v. P.* 292, P. to H.M. 22 and 24/7/1860.

60. H. of C. 23/7/1860: 'A very plucky speech' (M. 524). Cobden, still negotiating in Paris, was indignant (Morley, ii. 315–17). He had written to Palmerston on 10/7 against the armaments plan (ibid. 308–13) and got a reply *from Russell* on 31/7 saying 'I cannot consent to place my country at the mercy of France.'

For Gladstone's protest and P.'s reply see *P.P.* 146–8, 24/7. Granville wrote that Gladstone 'with great want of tact, having swallowed the last camel, could not get over the gnat of being in the House when Palmerston proposed the scheme. Palmerston . . . says that the only way to deal with him is to bully him a little'. (*G.* 386, to Canning 26/7.)

61. *G.* 386, ibid.; Fortescue, 166, 25/8/1860.

62. Bell, ii. 253–4; P.'s suspicion of Gladstone, e.g. *P.P.* 141, 13/7 on the paper import duty; using Whips' advice to bring pressure on Gladstone on paper imports also 145–8 (20–24/7) after 'the Cabinet, against my advice, came to the Decision to go on with your . . . Bill'. Lady P. (Fortescue, 166, 26/8) quoted with relish the Queen's letter of 22/8 (*R. v. P.* 294).

63. Fortescue, 164, 166.

64. Parker, ii. 401, 403, Graham to Aberdeen 29/9, Gladstone to Graham 27/11; Morley, ii. 669–70, Phillimore 12/8.

65. *G.* 388–9, Granville to Canning 24/8/1860.

66. *P.P.* 134–5, 18/5/1860.

67. *Gladstone to his Wife*, 130, 15–16/8/1860; *P.P.* 150, 16/8.

68. *G.* 388–9; Reid's *Milnes*, ii. 62–64.

CHAPTER XXV THE LORD WARDEN, 1861–3

1. Pemberton, *Lord Palmerston*, 279, 281.

2. Mack Smith, *Cavour and Garibaldi 1860*, 258 (P. to Russell 28/9/60); Maxwell, ii. 229, P. to Clarendon 10/10/1860.

3. (*a*) *R. v. P.* 279, Russell to H.M. 9/2/1860; *V.L.* iii. 494–5, H.M. to P. 10/5 et seq.; (*b*) Beales, 155–6; (*c*) ibid. 148, 6/6; (*d*) ibid. 149, 152, P. to Russell, 17/5 and 10/7/1860; Walpole, ii. 324, Russell to Cowley 23/7; (*e*) *V.L.* iii. 545–6, P. to H.M. 10/1/1861; (*f*) Mack Smith, 32–33, Russell to Corbett 25/8/1859; (*g*) Beales, 148; (*h*) ibid. 148, P. to Russell, 17/5; Mack Smith, 35, Russell to P. 18/5 and to H.M. 26/5; (*i*) Mack Smith, 102, Napoleon to Persigny, 25/7/1860; (*j*) ibid. 102.

4. (*a*) A. J. P. Taylor regards 'this . . . more revolutionary document than Lamartine's circular' as an 'unexpected' warning to the three Eastern monarchs then assembled at Warsaw (*S.M.E.* 123–4); Beales agrees (op. cit. 156) but says also that it was 'to make up for this misdemeanour' (the dispatch of 31/8, which Cavour had published), a verdict apparently based on Malmesbury's conclusion that this misdemeanour 'lost him his popularity with the Radicals, who were furious at his admitting the right of the Austrians to Venetia' (M. 528–9); (*b*) *V.L.* iii. 505–7, Russell to H.M. 30/4/1860 (twice).

5. For Clarendon's view (shared by Cowley) see Maxwell, ii. 199–201, 231–2. Albert let out, most indiscreetly, his German view, telling the Lord Chancellor, 'our only boundary is the Quadrilateral' (*Gladstone to his Wife*, 131, 15/12/1860). Palmerston suspected that Napoleon was staying in Rome to help in Venetia (A. ii. 216–19, to Russell 18/10/1861); *V.L.* iii. 524, Russell to H.M. 3/11/1860 and Beales, 157. The Queen objected to 'the expression of our hope, that Rome and Venetia, from their Italian nationality, will soon share in the freedom and good government of

the rest of Italy'. Palmerston had written to Russell on 21/9 that 'every liberal minded man will rejoice' when the day of the overthrow of Austrian occupation in Venetia arrived: 'Cavour and Victor Emmanuel may say and promise what they will, but. . . . They will be forced into a Quarrel with Austria about Venice. . . .' (T.–P. 229–30.)

6. *P.P.* 181–7, P. to Gladstone 21/7/1861; Morley's *Cobden*, ii. 319, 5/9/1860.

7. *P.P.* 181–7; *R. v. P.* 300–1, 19/2/1861; *P.P.* 160, 25/2/1861.

8. *P.P.* 157–60 and 161–2, 25–26/2/1861.

9. Morley's *Gladstone*, i. 673–4; *P.P.* 166–7, P. to Gladstone 14/4/1861.

10. Parker, ii. 409–10 gives Graham's well-merited snub to Gladstone on this (29/1/1861).

11. *P.P.* 167, Gladstone to P. 14/4; Fortescue, 180; A. ii. 215.

12. Fortescue, 180–1; *R. v. P.* 298–300, Albert to P. on Disraeli's talk 24/1/1861 and P. on Malmesbury's 27/1; for background see M. 533–5, Derby to Malmesbury 26/12/1860.

13. *P.P.* 162–4, P. to Gladstone 19/3/1861 and reply 20th, cf. *R. v. P.* 300–1.

14. *P.P.* 174–6, P. to Gladstone 19/7/1861 (6 p.m.) — for background see *R. v. P.* 295–6; *P.P.*, 172–4, P. to Gladstone 19/7/1861.

15. *P.P.* 157–60, Gladstone to P. 25/2/61 (cf. Disraeli H. of C. 3/6/1862); *P.P.* 160, P. to Gladstone 25/2/1861.

16. *P.P.* 172–4, 180, 181–7, P. to Gladstone 19 and 21/7, Gladstone to P. 20/7/1861.

17. *G.* 390, 407, Granville to Canning 24/1 and Aug. 1861.

18. *R. v. P.* 302–3, 307; A. ii. 206–7; *Milnes*, ii. 75; Fortescue, 188; *G.* 405–6; *Gladstone to his Wife*, 137; M. 551–2.

19. M., 539–40, on talk with Napoleon Apr. 1861: 'I think the party he would like to see governing England are the Radicals . . . who would diminish our army and navy, and so weaken our influence abroad.' He abused Palmerston. For Persigny's abuse of Palmerston, who, 'in a furious passion with the Emperor of the French for preventing the bombardment of Gaeta' (the last refuge of King Francis), procured his recall, see ibid. 531 (Nov.–Dec. 1860). For the Radical approaches to the Tories see note 12 above. For Cobden on P. and America see Morley's *Cobden*, ii. 388–9, letters of Dec. 1861–Jan. 1862.

20. *R. v. P.* 311, P. to H.M. 3/12/1861, 'that Government is not guided by reasonable men'; Walpole, ii. 343.

21. Morley's *Cobden*, ii. 392; Walpole, ii. 344, Russell to P. 17/10/1861; A. ii. 216–17, P. to Russell 18/10; A. ii. 210–11, P. to Milner Gibson 7/6/1861. On P.'s views see A. ii. 208 and Morley's *Gladstone*, i. 715–16, memo. 'Lord Palmerston desired the severance as the diminution of a dangerous power, but prudently held his tongue.' Cobden (Morley, ii. 405) reported to Sumner 11/7/1862 a unanimous feeling that the North could not subject the South and to Bright 6/12/1861 (ibid. 388) doubted whether another year's blockade would be borne by the world. For Gladstone's views see C. Collyer, 'Gladstone and the American Civil War', *Leeds Philosophical Society*, vi, viii, 583–94.

x

22. Cited Walpole, ii. 367.

23. Morley's *Cobden*, ii. 408, Cobden to Sumner 22/5/1863.

24. Walpole, ii. 343, Lyons to Russell 8/6/1861 on danger of sudden U.S. declaration of war on the U.K.; Morley's *Cobden*, ii. 390–2, Cobden to Sumner 29/11/1861; A. ii. 219–20, 226; *R. v. P.* 308, P. to H.M. 13/11/1861; Maxwell, ii. 250, Lewis to Clarendon 10/12/1861.

25. *Arg.* ii. 179–83; Morley's *Gladstone*, 707–8; Walpole, ii. 346–7; *R. v. P.* 309–10, 321–2; *V.L. 2*, i. 7–8, 10–11.

26. Morley's *Cobden*, ii. 392, Cobden to Sumner 12/12/1861, cf. *Arg.* ii. 179–80, Argyll to Gladstone 7/12/1861. Letters from Cobden and Bright were read at the American cabinet's meeting on Christmas Day (Morley's *Gladstone*, 709).

27. H. of C. 28/2/1861, 6/5/1861.

28. See K. Poolman, *The Alabama Incident*; Walpole, ii. 353–5, 359, 361 and notes ibid.; Russell, H. of L. 12/6/1871. Cobden opined 2/5/1863 that Russell had been 'tricked and angry at the escape' (Morley, ii. 407–8).

29. Walpole, ii. 356–9; Morley's *Cobden*, ii. 407–8.

30. Morley, 684, Gladstone's diary Jan.–Feb. 1862; *Gladstone to his Wife*, 139, 1/2/1862; H. of C. 7/4/1862; *P.P.*, 205–21, P. to Gladstone 29/4, 8/5, 25/5/1862, Gladstone to P. 2/5, 8/5; ibid. 232–6, 24–25/9/1862.

31. *R. v. P.* 325, P. to H.M. 4/4/1862.

32. Ibid. 325–6; cf. Bright H. of C. 27/8/1860 on building for obsolescence. P. was aware of the potentialities of improved gunnery — see e.g. *P.P.* 181 ff. 21/7/1861 — but had not thought of floating batteries as a substitute for land batteries. Morley's *Cobden*, ii. 380, Cobden to Lindsay 27/7/1861. Cobden's letter on limitation is given in A. ii. Appendix, and P.'s reply evading the argument ibid. 221, 8/1/1862.

33. H. of C. 3/6/1862.

34. *P.P.* 217–28, Gladstone to P. 9, 27 and 29/5 and P. to Gladstone 27–28/5; Denison, 117–20; Fortescue, 196–7; Lawson, 52–53.

35. Denison, 120–2. For Tory accounts see M. 556–7, Cranbrook, 156–7.

36. H. of C. 1/8/1862.

37. Maxwell, ii. 267, P. to Clarendon 20/10/1862; Morley's *Cobden*, 399–400, 7/8/62 to Hargreaves.

38. *R. v. P.* 298–9, Albert to Palmerston 24/1/1861.

39. *Gladstone to his Wife*, 142, 22/11/1862.

40. Morley, 709–10, *Gladstone to his Wife*, 29/7/1862 and to Argyll 3/8/1862.

41. *P.P.* 232–5, 24–25/9/1862; Walpole, ii. 349–51; *G.* 442–4, Granville to Russell 27/9/1862. Morley, 714, Russell to Gladstone from Walmer 20/10/1862; 717, Russell told Adams of his regret and P.'s and reaffirmed neutrality. But 717–18, Russell was still for intervention (13/10/1862) and Gladstone circulated a long reply to Lewis (*P.P.* 239–47, 25/10/1862).

42. Morley, 719, 11–13/11/1862. After the Proclamation against Slavery the Northern cause became more popular (Morley's *Cobden*, 405–6, Cobden to Sumner 13/3/1863).

43. Morley's *Cobden*, ii. 416–17, Cobden to Hargreaves 5/4/1863; A. ii. 233–4.

44. A. ii. 213–14; *G.* 395; A. ii. 236; Denison, 122–3.

45. Fortescue, 182–3; *G.* 390; *R.* v. *P.* 296–7, 304–7. Clarendon, after talking to Bedford, wrote to Lewis 10/10/1860 that if Lord John had carried his Reform Bill in 1860, he would have gone to the Lords then, as 'he feels that with Palmerston and Gladstone in the House of Commons . . . he is nobody and sinking fast' (Maxwell, ii. 227).

46. Morley's *Cobden*, ii. 403–4, Cobden to Chevalier 2/6/1863. Gladstone had complained to Aberdeen 10/9/1857 that liberty to the Principalities was stinted on ground of danger not to Europe but to Islam and used in H. of C. 4/5/1858 the famous phrase, 'There is no barrier like the breasts of freemen' (Morley's *Gladstone*, 637).

47. The Tory government had in 1858 appointed Gilbert Scott as architect for the Foreign Office but P. did not like the '*very foreign look*' of his design (see *Gentleman's Magazine*, 1859, N.S., 469) and demanded a Palladian instead of a Gothic plan. He rejected out of hand the next design ('Byzantine') and got his way (Bell, ii. 286–8). On 8/7/1861 he and Cowper, aided by Tite, the architect of the Royal Exchange, finally beat off a demand for Gothic, the associations of which were repugnant to P. ('Lord John Manners, swayed by erroneous views in religion and taste was enthusiastic for Gothic', P. to H.M. 8/7/1861, *V.L.* iii. 566).

P. always knew what he liked. Alone of the sponsoring committee, he opposed the siting of the Wellington statue at Hyde Park Corner on the ground that 'the statue spoils the arch and the arch spoils the statue' (*Tiverton Speech, 1847*, 18). He pleaded for the Albert Memorial to be 'something simple and concentrated . . . an open Grecian temple' (*R.* v. *P.* 335–6, 2/3/1863).

On Commons procedure, see Denison, 79–80 (Feb. 1861): Parker, ii. 408, Denison and ex-Speaker Lord Eversley to Graham Mar. 1861.

48. e.g. Fortescue, 135–6 (Oct. 1859); cf. 162, Lady Stanley of Alderley discusses Palmerston's 'technique' with the ladies; ibid. 58.

49. Trollope, 10 — 'The world has heard of no trouble into which he got about women.'

50. *Gladstone to his Wife*, 157–8, 10 and 11/11/1863 — 'It is said that he was extremely low and absent at Windsor — quite unlike himself. . . . I know that he has been much annoyed. . . . Lady P. very empressée. . . . He is seriously hit . . . in spirit, force and tone. The dart sticks.'

Chapter XXVI Faded Magic, 1863–4

1. P.'s classic attitude on bondholders was stated at Tiverton 1847 (*Speech*, 2nd ed., 35). Lewis said that the cabinet was committed to a most impolitic course on Mexico before it had met; the real reason for the operation, according to Clarendon, was 'to chastise them for years of ill-treatment of our subjects and violating every engagement but the occupation of insanitary ports would not reach the real culprits'

(Maxwell, ii. 240, 243, Clarendon to Lewis 4/10/1861, Lewis to Clarendon 27/10/1861). Lewis complained of 'another gratuitous scrape' — our semi-guarantee of the Moroccan loan, to be collected by British agents. Russell's acceptance of this without consulting Gladstone infuriated the chancellor (*Gladstone to his Wife*, 132–3, 18–19/1/1861) and threatened a cabinet crisis. Palmerston and Russell in October 1859 had wished to 'make a positive stand against these aggressions of Spain' in Morocco (P. to Russell 17/10/1859) but were overruled (or drew back because all the Powers sympathized with Spain). The Spanish-Moroccan War led to a treaty committing the Moroccans to pay an indemnity to Spain, and this in its turn to a request for a British Loan. P. saw that a government guarantee was impossible (Nov. 1860), but as the alternatives seemed to be renewal of war or a French loan Russell agreed to a joint guarantee with Spain; this Gladstone quashed in Jan. 1861, after a cabinet crisis threatened (*Gladstone to his Wife*, 132–3, 18–19/1/1861). But in Oct. 1861 Britain signed a treaty with Morocco providing that a British agent should receive one-half of the port customs duties, from which he would pay Spain an instalment of the indemnity and interest and sinking fund charges on a British-subscribed loan of £$\frac{1}{2}$ million (much smaller than the one originally proposed). This led to a reform of the Moroccan customs service and the loan, 'in contrast with many of the other (loans to 'backward states') . . . was disastrous neither to the lenders nor to the borrowers' (Fournoy, op. cit. 198–200, 204–6, 211–12, 218, 241, 255).

2. H. of C. 6/2/1862.

3. T.–P. 226–7.

4. See Eleutherios Prevelakis, *British Policy Towards the Change of Dynasty in Greece 1862–3*, quoted at pp. 27, 42–43; *V.L.2* i. 32–33, H.M. to Russell and reply 6–7/6/1862.

5. Ibid. 49, Russell to Scarlett 14/8/1862.

6. Ibid. 63–64, 4–6/11/1862.

7. Ibid. 67–68, P. and Trikoupes fils at Broadlands 4–5/11. P. had already in Feb. made this offer to Trikoupes *père* as a bribe for Otho taking no anti-Turkish action (ibid. 31–32).

8. Ibid. 73–75. The Alfred candidature was definitely abandoned after 25/11. See ibid. 80–81 for P.'s firmness to Brunnow about Leuchtenberg on 23/11/1862, and 84–85, 96–97 for the forging of the policy involving the cession of the Ionians.

9. Ibid. 133.

10. Ibid. 160–3, July and Sept.–Oct. 1863.

11. T.–P. 235. Mosse, 121, Buchanan to Russell 25/4/1863.

12. T.–P. 242–4, Apponyi report on P. 31/5/1863, cf. ibid. 240 Apponyi (22/4) complains that P. was 'more disposed to suffer, or even to second, to some degree, the projects of (Napoleon) . . . than resolutely to oppose them'.

13. Ibid. 244, 31/5. But Apponyi thought 'he will . . . end by being dragged into making common cause with (France)'.

14. Mosse, 112–18; T.–P. 239, P. to Russell 26/2/1863, 250, same to same, 3/3/1863.

15. Mosse, 119 (P. to Russell 7/4/1863). The note of 10/4 is quoted T.–P. 236.

16. T.–P. 237, on Russell 9/4 to Brunnow. In parliament on 25/3 Russell had said that one could not offer the Tsar advice on the mode of governing his own dominions!

17. Mosse, 123–5; T.–P. 241 and 244, P. to Russell 15/5/63, Apponyi's report on 31/5.

18. Mosse, 126–7, Cowley to Russell 20/6/1863, P. to Russell 30/7 and 3/8/1863.

19. *V.L.2*, i. 95–96, Russell to H.M. 27/6/1863. 'The Cabinet agreed with Lord Russell that it was impossible to say that in no case would we make war' because this would encourage Russian extremists (ibid.) but Cowley was instructed 3/7 to tell Drouyn that Britain would not go to war from sympathy with Poland (Mosse, 127).

20. Decision not to send identic note *V.L.2*, i. 102–3; T.–P. 238 and Walpole, ii. 371 on Russell's dispatch of 11/8/1863; T.–P. 244–7, P. to Russell 2/10 and 8/10/1863.

21. Mosse, 144–5, on Russell and Russia Sept.–Dec. 1863; ibid. 119, P. to Russell 7/4/1863.

22. A. ii. 236–44, P. to Leopold 15/11/1863 and to Russell 2/12/1863; T.–P. 254–8, P. to Russell 8/11/1863, 18/11/1856; on cabinet decision *V.L.2*, i. 117–18, P. to H.M. 19/11/1863; Russell to Cowley 25/11/1863 is summarized, Mosse, 141.

23. Mosse, 141–3; cf. *S.M.E.* 141: 'It was the end of Napoleon's Utopian dream of peaceful revision; the end of his hegemony in Europe; and the end, too, of the British alliance on which French security had been based.'

24. Mosse, 127, Russell to Cowley 3/7/1863.

25. On assumed French superiority T.–P. 250–1, P. to Russell 27/6/1863; Walpole, ii. 388 n. 1. P. to Russell 26/12/1863; cf. the Russian minister in Berlin, Oubril, 23/1/1864 (Mosse, 172). On proposal to intervene, Mosse, 176–7, Russell memo. 13/3/1864 and P.'s reply.

26. Mosse, 170 n. 2 — Brunnow to Gorchakov, undated.

27. *S.M.E.* 146–7; Russian determination not to fight was made clear to Denmark 9/12/1863, to Britain (in effect) 30/12, to Prussia 3/3/1864 — on the latter occasion *Russia* sought to deter Bismarck by the spectre of France, England and Sweden fighting (Mosse, 158, 165, 171–2). The French brush-off (3/1/1864) made pointed reference to Poland (ibid. 163) and, says Mosse, 'revealed that during 1863 the Anglo-French alliance . . . had been struck a mortal blow; . . . that the age of Palmerston and Louis Napoleon was ending and that of Bismarck had begun. . . . The French refusal also marked . . . the beginning of British isolation. . . .' (ibid. 164). The substance had been extracted from Russell's classic threat to Vienna of 29/7/1863 (ibid. 152–3).

On Napoleon's wish for a Great Scandinavia see Cowley to Russell 9/6/1864 (Mosse, 197); on Russell's appeal to Russia on this mid-April 1864 see ibid. 189–90; for Palmerston's view see *V.L.2*, i. 161–6, to H.M. 22/2/1864. On 9/1/1864 the Queen had *advocated* the succession of the

Danish Crown Prince at his father's death and that of the King of Sweden to 'the three Northern kingdoms . . . if *we* helped it, that large Northern kingdom would be friendly to us' and a good barrier against Russia (*G.* 456). This is an astonishing proposal from a monarch who complained of annexations to Piedmont; it shows how extraordinarily anxious she was to get the duchies away from Denmark. The King of Sweden was a pan-Scandinavian enthusiast, but it is not likely that the Swedes would have wished from 1872 to be ruled by the heir to Denmark, even if married (as he was in 1869) to their princess (she was twelve when Queen Victoria made the suggestion).

28. *V.L.2*, i. 117–19, Gen. Grey to P. 20/11/1863; *R.* v. *P.* 343–6, P. to H.M. 8/1/1864. For Palmerston's insistence that a treaty must be construed by its text see ibid. 127–9, 3/12/1863.

29. The Queen and Prince wanted partition — *V.L.2*, i. 23, H.M. to Russell 8/3/1862. On the 1850 convention and 1852 treaty see ibid. 116, 130, 153, H.M. to Leopold 19/11 and 3/12/1863 and to Crown Princess of Prussia 27/1/1864, and *R.* v. *P.* 340 to Russell 1/1/1864 and especially *G.* 458–9 to Granville 12/2/1864 — 'Lord Palmerston and the Emperor Nicholas are the cause of all the present trouble by framing that wretched Treaty of 1852.'

30. *V.L.2*, i. 140–1, P. to H.M. 4/1/1864.

31. Ibid. 138–40, H.M. to Russell 1/1/1864. For P.'s riposte see ibid. 140–1, 4/1/1864 (year stated wrongly T.–P. 272 n.), T.–P. 276, P. comment on Russell's memo. 6/6/1864. The argument that no plebiscite could be fair was stated by Gorchakov 5/4/1864 and Russell to Cowley 9/4/1864 (Mosse, 187, 189).

32. Mosse, 161, Russell to Malet after cab of 2/1/1864; cf. Apponyi's account of talk with Russell 19/12/1863 (T.–P. 262–4) when Russell said 'England might consider these acts as a *casus belli*, and lend Denmark the aid of her fleet'. Palmerston wrote to Russell 26/12 (Walpole, ii. 388) — 'Schleswig is no part of Germany, and its invasion . . . would be an act of war against Denmark, which would in my clear opinion entitle Denmark to our active military and naval support. But you and I could not announce such a determination without the concurrence of the Cabinet and the consent of the Queen.' There was confusion in the minds of ministers as to whether Russell proposed material assistance (alone if necessary) if Schleswig was invaded (see T.–P. 264 n. on Gladstone) or only if Augustenburg was installed there (ibid. 266, Wood 26/1/1864). On 26/12 Russell wrote to the Queen '. . . it will be impossible for your Majesty's Government to consent to a German occupation of Schleswig . . .' (*V.L.2*, i. 132).

33. Despite Russell to Malet (Mosse, 161) the decision of the cabinet was on 2/1/1864 'to seek the co-operation of France and other Powers before talking about the use in any event of force' (*Gladstone to his Wife*, 159). Phipps to H.M. 7/1/1864 records P.'s assurance to Granville at Broadlands and attributes his tone to gout (*V.L.2*, i. 142) but P. (*V.L.2*, i. 144–8, *R.* v. *P.* 343–6) on 8/1/1864 heartily concurred in Russell's opinion that 'England could not consistently with her own honour allow

Denmark to perish without aiding in her defence' and was sure that 'every impartial and right-minded man in your Majesty's dominions' would do so too. At the cabinet on 12th there was 'a great tussle' and Russell's opinion was struck out of the dispatch (ibid. 150, Granville to Phipps). 'It was a defeat for Palmerston and Russell', says Mosse, 163. Brunnow reported that to the inquiries to other Powers Russell expected 'a negative reply without practical result' (ibid. 170 n. 2). To the Palace Granville reported 'Lord John was a good deal annoyed, and once or twice alluded to not choosing to go on, if the Cabinet did not approve of his policy. Lord Palmerston supported Lord John strongly, but I got him to repeat before the Cabinet . . . that there was no question of our going to war single-handed' (*V.L.2*, i. 158, 14/1/1864).

H.M. to Granville 27/1/1864 (*G.* 456–7) — though Russell had said, 'There is Sweden, and she might join us', Russell was in her view 'very fair, but Lord Palmerston alarms him and overrules him'. Russell's own verdict was that he himself was 'somewhat reluctant' to admit that they could give material aid only if France would join, but 'Lord Palmerston was convinced that it would be inexcusable to rush into a war against the whole of Germany . . . without the security of a substantial alliance' (Walpole, ii. 389, Russell to Paget). And on 13/2 Palmerston was unwilling to pay France's price (see note 25 above). What he hoped for now was French *diplomatic* aid for 1852 and the integrity of Denmark (T.–P. 266, 26/1/1864).

34. H. of C. 4/2/1864. Bismarck on 31/1/1864 parried Russian request for a formal repetition in London of pledges made to Russia; the Austro-Prussian note of that date was an 'ambiguous document' (Mosse, 170–5).

35. Mosse 178 n. 2, 176, 180; A. ii. 249, P. to Somerset 20/2/1864; *V.L.2*, i., Somerset to H.M. 21/2.

36. Mosse, 181–4; *V.L.2*, i., H.M. to Russell 22/2 and message to P. via Gen. Grey (161–2); ibid. 166–7, Gen. Grey's memo, on cabinet of 24th.

37. *V.L. 2*, i. 157, Granville to Grey 13/2/1864 (cf. Grey to H.M. 16/2 on Wood, Mosse, 178). On cabinet views see Brunnow (cited Mosse 170 n. 2) and *V.L. 2*, i. 180–2, Granville to Russell 5/5/1864. T.–P. say that Derby was pacific because of royal influence; the Queen reported to P. 2/2/1864 her talk with the Leader of the Opposition (*R.* v. *P.* 347–8). Malmesbury says the country 'would like to fight for the Danes' (29/1) and *re* Derby that 'All his party are for the Danes, and he also sympathises with them; but the Court is against them' (M. 589, 592).

38. Mosse, 176–7 (Walpole, ii. 390 n.), P. to Russell 13/2/1864; *V.L. 2*, i. 161–6, P. to H.M. 22/2/1864.

39. Mosse, 205, Clarendon to H.M. 22/6/1864.

40. Derby, H. of L. 4/2/1864; *V.L.* iii, 462–3, P. to H.M. 23/8/1859.

41. H. of L. 13/7/1863, Argyll's speech in answer to Clanricarde.

42. A. ii. 257–8, P. to Russell 11/9/1864 – '. . . when . . . able men fill every department, such men will have opinions, and hold to them; but unfortunately they are often too busy . . . to follow up foreign questions so as to be fully masters of them, and their conclusions are generally on the timid side of what might be the best'.

43. There is an important difference between Russell's proposal as put to the Queen and, because of her objections, not put to the cabinet (*V.L. 2*, i. 173–4) and Palmerston's suggestion (Walpole, ii. 391, to Russell 18/4) to say what Russell proposed to say only 'if the French and Russians and Swedes would agree with us'.

44. T.–P. 268–72 gives Apponyi's account of 1/5/1864 interview; A. ii. 249–52, P. to Russell 1/5/1864 gives P.'s motive and account.

45. *V.L. 2*, i. 180–5 (5–10/5/1864); *G.* 463–5.

46. Ibid. 183–4, Gen. Grey to Granville 9/5/1864; *R.* v. *P.* 351–2, P. to H.M. 10/5 (*V.L. 2*, i. 186); *V.L. 2*, i. 187, Phipps to H.M. 11/5; *V.L. 2*, i. 187–8, H.M. to Leopold 12/5.

47. Ibid. 214–15, Gen. Grey to H.M. 6/6/1864.

48. *G.* 468–9, H.M. to Granville 5/6/1864. *Gladstone to his Wife*, 159–60, 23/7/1864 — 'For the first time she takes a just credit to herself for having influenced beneficially the course of policy and of affairs in the late controversy.' The Queen's defence was that 'the Queen and her *Cabinet* were always agreed' (*G.* 468 to Granville).

49. *V.L. 2*, i. 209–12, Coburg to H.M. 1/6 and reply 4/6; cf. ibid. 142–3, to Coburg 8/1/1864, 206–7 to Crown Princess of Prussia 31/5/1864, 241 for the praise of the King of Hanover (Victoria's cousin, George V) 'for having preserved the peace of the world'.

50. *V.L. 2*, i. 215–17; *G.* 469–70; Morley's *Gladstone*, 752, 'very stiff . . . but went well'.

51. *G.* 470; Mosse, 203 n. 4; *V.L. 2*, i. 220–1, Gladstone's account to Queen 16/6; ibid. 220, H.M. to Leopold 16/6/1864 — 'The others are all very angry, and indeed the whole Cabinet, including Pilgerstein, seems to be of the opinion that the responsibility and risk for this country to go to war single-handed would be *too* enormous. . . .'

52. *V.L. 2*, i. 223–4. This encouraged the Queen to explain to Russell (ibid. 226–7, 23/6) that Napoleon 'hopes to lead England so far in support of Denmark as to make it impossible for us to draw back with honour'.

53. Morley's *Gladstone*, 752 — 'a tolerable, not the best, conclusion' (Gladstone, 25/6). *V.L. 2*, i. 227–30; *G.* 472–3; T.–P. 276 gives the form of the final decision in Russell's hand. *S.M.E.* 153 cites Drouyn's comment: 'the British do nothing by halves; they are now retreating vigorously'.

54. Denison, 165–6; M. 598; *V.L. 2*, i. 233–4, Clarendon's comments; Russell's speech too had its grotesque side, for he said that no pledge of material assistance had ever been given, and that they could not make 'the duty, honour and interests of this country . . . subordinate to interests of any foreign power whatever' (H. of L. 27/6).

55. The debate on the vote of censure began on 4/7 and extended over four nights — see Denison, 166–9.

56. For Cobden's views see Morley, ii. 453, Cobden to Ashworth 1/7/1864 ascribing 'a revolution in our foreign policy' (ibid. 450 to Chevalier 5/11/1864) to the fact that exports at £160 million had trebled over twenty years, so that great material interests were at stake. Gladstone (Morley, 753) noted: 'This debate ought to be an epoch in foreign policy.' There is a good account of the debate in Mosse, 207–9.

57. Mosse, 206 n. 6. Palmerston, Russell, Westbury, Argyll, Somerset, de Grey, Stanley of Alderley, Geo. Grey v. Granville, Clarendon, Cardwell, Gibson, Gladstone, Villiers, Wood — cf. *V.L. 2*, i. Wood to Gen. Grey 24/6/1864.

58. On division prospects see Denison, 169–70; Walpole, ii. 396, Russell to Cowley 9/7: 'We have done better than could be expected in both Houses.' In the Lords the Opposition won by 177–168, in the Commons the Government won by 313–295. P. (*V.L. 2*, i. 240, 8/7) reported that 18 was 'a much larger majority than was expected; four was the calculation yesterday, and from six to eight to-day. Several Conservative members went or stayed away . . .'. In fact, though 18 Irish Liberals voted with the Opposition, five Tories voted with the Government and six more Tories did not vote than Liberals. This leaves more than a dozen Conservatives unaccounted for. See also T.–P. 278.

59. A. ii. 270–1, P. to Russell 13/9/1865. T.–P. comment 279. The occasion of this letter was the Convention of Gastein by which Prussia acquired Lauenburg and Schleswig and Austria the *damosa hereditas* of Holstein.

60. Mosse, 209, Cranborne to Torben Bille 4/7/1866.

CHAPTER XXVII 'REST AND BE THANKFUL'

1. *G.* 487, Clarendon to Granville 21/10/1865.

2. M. 291 (24/2/1864), Denison, 147, 149, 163, 165–6; Walford, 47; Cranbrook, 163–4.

3. Ashley, ii. 254.

4. Denison, 169 — the speech was 'temperate but not powerful'.

5. Ibid. 154–5, 160–3; Holland's *Devonshire*, i. 55, P. to Duke of Devonshire 7/2/1863; *V.L. 2*, i. 171.

6. Denison, 151–3, 156–7; *V.L. 2*, i. n. 5; M. 593; Maxwell, ii. 286.

7. *P.P.* 279; *V.L. 2*, i. 168–76; M. 593–5; Cranbrook, 165.

8. Bell, ii. 391–4.

9. Morley's *Cobden*, ii. 453–4, Cobden to Ashworth 26/7/1864; A. ii. 257–8, P. to Russell 11/9/1864.

10. A. ii. 258–60.

11. Morley's *Cobden*, ii. 453–4 (see n. 9).

12. A. ii. 322–3, conversation with Shaftesbury; cf. H.M. 19/11/1874, 'Lord Palmerston was not wrong . . .'.

13. *The Goschen Letters*, 58–60.

14. *P.P.* 279–80, P. to Gladstone and reply 11/5/1864; Lawson, 60.

15. *P.P.* 281–2, P. to Gladstone 12/5/1864.

16. Ibid. 282–3, 285–6, Gladstone to P. 13 and 21/5 (cf. ibid. 287, 23/5): ibid. 285, P. to Gladstone 21/5 (cf. ibid. 288, 16/6).

17. See Southgate, *The Passing of the Whigs*, 386–7.

18. *P.P.* 282–5, Gladstone to Palmerston 13 and 14/5, P. to Gladstone 12, 13 and 14/5/1864. *V.L. 2*, i. 189–90, H.M. to P. 15/5/1864; ibid. 187–8, H.M. to Leopold 12/5. The impertinent communications include ibid. 177–9, 29/4 on the See of Peterborough and ministerial responsibility,

taking 'a tone so different from that in which Lord Palmerston is in the habit of addressing her' (H.M. to P. ibid. 179, 2/5) and the letter of 10/5 (ibid. 186) on the leakage of her German prejudices.

19. *P.P.* 326–7, P. to Gladstone 27/3/1865; cf. Cranbrook, 168.

20. *Gladstone to his Wife*, 162, 7/10/1864; *P.P.* 292–6, Gladstone to P. 6/10/1864.

21. *Fortnightly Review* obituary.

22. *P.P.* 297–304, P. to Gladstone 19/10/1864 (cf. ibid. 270–1, 21/11/1863). *Gladstone to his Wife*, 168, said that he was all strung up at this 'very unfavourable letter'.

23. Ibid. 305–8, 310–13, Gladstone to Palmerston 22/10 and reply 7/11/1864 — *V.L. 2*, i. 243–4, H.M. returns the correspondence, relying on Palmerston.

24. Ibid. 314–15, Gladstone to P. 9/11/1864; *Gladstone to his Wife*, 165, 19 and 21/1/1865.

25. *P.P.* 320–22, Gladstone to P. 28/1/1865, P. to Gladstone 31/1/1865.

26. Ibid. 322–4, Gladstone to P. 2/2/1865.

27. Ibid. 327–37, P. to Gladstone 27/3, 18/4, 23/4/1865, Gladstone to P. 29/3, 19/4, 20/4. As to income-tax, Russell let down Palmerston, saying that 'abolition with a power of renewal would be a proof of power and confidence in our resources . . .' (Walpole, ii. 405, Russell to P. 6/4/1865).

28. Gladstone challenged the seamen 24/11/1863 and 22/10/1864 (to Palmerston, *P.P.* 271, 307) and on 20/1/1865 P. reported to the Queen (*V.L. 2*, i. 248–9) 'Mr. Gladstone . . . troublesome and wrongheaded as he often is . . .' on the same point. Hence *P.P.* 325–6, P. to Gladstone 12/3/1865 (and on Cobden).

29. *V.L. 2*, i. 262–3, P. to H.M. 13/3/1865; ibid. 250 for Wood's view 12/2/1865 that war was probable (and that it was not possible to hold Canada but they must try. Even Gladstone thought Cobden's view on Canada extreme. Cobden died after declining from Palmerston the chairmanship of the Audit Board; Palmerston advised (*R. v. P.* 355–6 to H.M. 7/2/1865) that 'no injury to the public interest would arise from his ceasing to be a member of the House of Commons'. The dying Cobden admitted that Palmerston 'was always a very generous enemy'.

30. *V.L. 2*, i. 252–3, H.M. to Russell 23/2/1865 and reply 24/2/1865.

31. Ibid. 248–9, P. to H.M. 20/1 and 262–3, 13/3/1865.

32. M. 604; Derby to Disraeli 15/10/1864 'the election . . . will decide the fate of parties at all events for my time' quoted Jones's *Derby*, 280.

33. Denison, 174. *Gladstone to his Wife*, 166, 31/1/1865 — 'The Queen . . . supposes this Govt will not be seriously assailed while Lord P. lasts, but expects him to have his usual winter attack after the session has begun.'

34. Denison, 177–8.

35. *R. v. P.* 354, Connell notes writing spidery from gout; *P.P.* 329; Denison, 179; A. ii. 271–2; M. 607; serious illness at end of session, *G.* 486–7, Russell to Granville 20/10/1865; A. ii. 322 Shaftesbury recalls 'a period of terrible toil and suffering'.

36. M. 607, 10/6/1865 — 'The general impression is that Lord Palmer-

ston is in a very bad state of health, and will not meet the new Parliament as Minister'; 20/6, 'Lord Palmerston's illness has been very severe'. Election prospects ibid. 608.

37. *R. v. P.* 356–7, 27/6 on the harvest. The last week of the parliament was marked by a government defeat over Lord Chancellor Westbury, whose resignation was accepted on 3/7 (see *G.* 483–4; Cranbrook, 173–4). For Tiverton see Snell, 98.

38. For the election in general see Southgate, *The Passing of the Whigs*, 296 and 3 ibid.; Though Malmesbury (M. 608) recorded, '. . . the Whigs have not gained. The increase is in the Radicals', Ward Hunt wrote that the new parliament, though not Derbyite, would not be more Radical than the last (Cranbrook, 181) and in 1868 Mill complained to Bouverie that it had a deplorable character because its 'so-called Liberal members' were rallied under the cry of supporting Lord Palmerston (*The Times* 21/10/1868). Palmerston himself thought the results 'highly satisfactory: not merely with reference to the greater strength we have acquired, but also with reference to the number of bores and troublesome men who have been thrown out' (A. ii. 267–8 to Wodehouse 28/7/1865).

For the last correspondence with Gladstone see *P.P.* 341–8, 23/8, 21/9, 3/10 and Gladstone to P. 19/8, 28/8, 29/9/1865.

39. A. ii. 264–6, P. to Fortescue 10/9/1864 and 12/9 on the theme that Irish Liberal members 'are ready to vote as Tories in obedience to foreign injunctions' and that the priesthood 'aim at nothing less than political domination, and strive to transfer the source and directing centre of that domination to a foreign authority'; *V.L. 2*, i. 250–1, on the Fenian danger and 255–7 on Tenant Right being 'Landlord's Wrong', on the priests wanting to check emigration out of regard for their fees and emoluments, and the design via land reform to destroy the Church of Ireland (P. to H.M. 17 and 24/2/1865).

40. A. ii. 275–6, P. to Sir G. Grey 3/10/1865 and to Earl de Grey and Ripon (S. of S. for War).

41. *V.L. 2*, i., P. to H.M. 4/9/1865; T.-P. 293–4, P. to Layard 8/1/1865; cf. to Cowley (A. ii. 268–70, 3/9/1865) — '. . . the French Government should not infer . . . that we shall be more likely to give way upon any matters in which the interests of England are concerned'.

42. *G.* 487, Clarendon to Granville 21/10/1865. Denison, 183–4, shows that he had consulted the Speaker on the date of a meeting of parliament; hence date fixed for cabinet on which he writes to Gladstone on 7/10 (*P.P.* 348). On 10/8 P., staying for the last time in his house at No. 94 Piccadilly, the scene of Lady P.'s famous Saturday evenings, assured the Queen that he deemed it a duty owed to H.M. 'to do his best to maintain that health which is essential for the performance of the duties of the post' of premier (*V.L. 2*, i. 272). The Queen then went to Germany for several weeks but was at Balmoral when Palmerston died. On 15th Oct. she heard that he was 'in extreme danger' and informed Leopold that she would 'call on Lord Russell to carry on the same Government' (ibid. 277–8), which she did on 19th (278–9). For the last weeks see A. ii. 272–3, J. E. Ritchie, *Life and Times of Lord Palmerston*, 721.

AND HIS WORKS DID FOLLOW HIM

1. *Memoirs and Letters of the Rt. Hon. Sir Thomas Acland*, ed. A. H. D. Acland, 255 — Gladstone to Acland 25/10/1865.

2. Horsman, H. of C. 12/3/1866; Maxwell, ii. 314, Brand to Wood 21/4/1866. For coalition projects see Southgate, *The Passing of the Whigs*, 312, 317–18 and M. 621.

3. For the general election of 1868 see Hanham, *Elections and Party Management*. For Gladstone's cabinet see Southgate, op. cit. 337–9, and for the drift of nobility and gentry, ibid. 353–4, 369–73, 376, 409, 412–14. For the predicted drift of moneyed men see Morley's *Cobden*, ii. 198, Cobden to Hargreaves 7/4/1857.

4. *The Times* 21/7/1863, quoted by Beales, 171–2.

5. T.–P. 268; *V.L. 2*, i. 233–4, Victoria's account of a conversation with Clarendon 2/7/1864 in which, a propos 'the deplorable tone of bullying' Clarendon is alleged to have said that this 'was certainly essentially Lord Palmerston's introducing, he was the father of that' and they 'both agreed in hoping this tone would die with him'.

6. R. W. Seton-Watson, *Disraeli Gladstone and the Eastern Question*, 3.

7. *V.L. 2*, i. 352–4, H.M. to Gen. Grey 30/6/1866 and Derby's defence of his son 1/7; T.–P. 306–7, Apponyi's report 3/7/1866 and Stanley to Bloomfield 21/7/1866.

8. The reasons for the Queen's objections in 1868 seem to have been personal rather than political but, on Belgium and Portugal, see *V.L. 2*, i. 589, 15/4/1869, where the Queen argues to Clarendon that if these countries can expect moral support only 'England would soon lose her position in Europe'.

9. T.–P. 279, Russell's 'dominion of Force' circular on the Convention of Gastein (14/9/1865); ibid. 305, 317–18, Apponyi's report 24/7/1866 and Gladstone to Gen. Grey 17/4/1869; ibid. 330 and *Gladstone to his Wife*, 181, 20/11/1870.

10. Disraeli, H. of C. 24/2/1871.

11. T.–P. 323, 324–7, including Gladstone to Granville 24/9/1870; Cardwell to Granville 29/4/1870 (*Granville Papers*, Gifts and Deposits, 53); Bright to Granville 29/5/1871 and cf. Bright's memo. against arms expenditure 26/1/1871 (ibid., box 52).

12. Seton-Watson, op. cit. 552, 570. On 30/9/1866 Disraeli wrote to Derby: 'Power and influence we should exercise in Asia; consequently in Eastern Europe, consequently also in Western Europe.'

13. See Beaconsfield, *Selected Speeches*; Morley's *Cobden*, ii. 194–5, Bright to Cobden 16/4/1857; Cobden, H. of C. 22/7/1864 motion to apply the principle of non-interference to the Empire of China. An interesting collection of articles published in 1850 by the Philosophical Radical William Lockey Harle under the title *A Career in the Commons* significantly departs from non-intervention when turning to the East. There must be wars with barbarous nations because of India, he says, and the statesmen are not sufficiently India-conscious (387 ff.).

14. This complaint by the Colonial Society in 1870 when it became the

headquarters of a 'United Empire' movement (quoted by Bodelsen, *Studies in Mid-Victorian Imperialism*) is not really a caricature.

15. Ibid. 43, Earl Grey to Elgin 18/5/1849.

16. Cornewall Lewis wrote *Essay on the Government of Dependencies* in 1841; cf. Barrington, ii. 110–11, Lewis to Wilson 24/12/1858: '. . . my belief is that we now starve all our domestic and internal institutions and establishments, for the sake of our colonial Empire. . . . The public, however, still think that Colonies are not dear at this price: in which I beg leave to differ from them.'

For Bright to Cobden 16/4/1857 see n. 13 above.

Goldwin Smith, *The Empire* (1863), 10.

17. For this letter of Disraeli's, and the other side of the coin, see n. 12 above. For Galt, see Bodelsen, op. cit. 44; for Granville H. of L. 13/2/1870 and Gladstone H. of C. 26/4/1870; for Jenkins, *Contemporary Review*, Jan. 1871. For the turn of the tide see Bodelsen, op. cit., and Schuyler, *The Fall of the Old Colonial System*.

18. Schuyler, op. cit., 116.

19. Morley's *Cobden*, ii, 6, 477. On distant wars and home panics, Cobden to Ashworth, ibid. 361–2, on Canada to Col. Cole 470–1.

20. Mill's views are summarized by Bodelsen, op. cit. *Career in the Commons* (see note 13 above) though non-interventionist and critical of colonial expenditure, insisted that great colonies were essential to national prosperity and, defending the retention of Malta, Gibraltar, St Helena, the Ionians, etc., declared, 'A great nation must incur no risks in such matters' (188–90).

BIBLIOGRAPHY

The principal sources used are prefixed by a dagger (†).
Works are referred to by their full name or the name of the author, except where capital letter symbols are given in the margin.

A. PUBLICATIONS DURING PALMERSTON'S LIFETIME

1. SPEECHES

Speech of Lord Viscount Palmerston to the Electors of Tiverton on 31st July 1847. 2nd ed., 1847.

G. H. Francis, *Opinions and Policy of Rt. Hon. Viscount Palmerston as Minister, Diplomatist and Statesman,* 1852.

An Account of the Tiverton Election (29th April 1859) with a revised Report of Lord Palmerston's Speech.

2. HOSTILE POLEMICS

Lord Grey and Lord Palmerston. A Letter Addressed to Rt. Hon. T. B. Macaulay on the occasion of his letter to M'Farlane, from a FREE TRADER, 1846.

Lord Palmerston and Prince Albert, by William Coningham, together with 'the Suppressed Pamphlet' entitled *Palmerston: What Has he Done* by 'One of the People', 1854.

Lord Palmerston and the Jesuits with a few Hints for the Next Ministry and the Next Election — 6 Letters to Lord Palmerston by a Protestant Whig of 1688 and an Administrative Reformer of 1855.

The Queen and the Premier, A Statement of their Struggle and Its Results, by David Urquhart, 1857.

3. OTHER

W. Wilks, *Palmerston in Three Epochs,* 1854.

T. Macknight, *Thirty Years of Foreign Policy,* 1855. Strives to do impartial justice to Aberdeen and Palmerston, but hostile to the Treaty of Vienna as violating great moral principles 'which no minister can ever be excused for sacrificing'.

James Ewing Ritchie, *Palmerston,* 1861. Radical and rather hostile.

The Two Great Statesmen, A Plutarchian Parallel between Earl Russell and Viscount Palmerston, M.P.

B. PUBLICATIONS AT THE TIME OF PALMERSTON'S DEATH

Obituaries in *The Times, Daily Telegraph, Morning Standard, Daily News, Fortnightly Review* and *Saturday Review.*

624

Edward Walford, *Memoir of Rt. Hon. Viscount Palmerston*, 1865.

John M'Gilchrist, *Lord Palmerston*. A Biography, 1865.

David Urquhart, *Materials for a True History of Lord Palmerston*, reprinted from the Free Press May–Nov. 1865. *Not* animated by the 'de mortuis nil nisi bonum' sentiment.

James Ewing Ritchie, *Life and Times of Lord Palmerston*, 2 vols., 1866–7.

†C. THE OFFICIAL LIFE

B. i — Rt. Hon. Sir Henry Lytton Bulwer, *The Life of Henry John Temple, Viscount Palmerston*, with selections from his Diaries and Correspondence: Volume i, 1870.

B. ii. — Volume ii, 1870.

B.–A. — Volume iii, 1874, edited by the Hon. Evelyn Ashley. In addition to connecting the 'eloquent tatters' left by Bulwer, Ashley added letters and speeches 1835–47.

A. i, A. ii — The Hon. Evelyn Ashley, *The Life of Henry John Temple Viscount Palmerston, 1846–65*, with Selections from His Speeches and Correspondence, 2 vols., 1876.

D. PUBLISHED PALMERSTON PAPERS

1. COLLECTIONS

Mabell, Countess of Airlie, *Lady Palmerston and Her Times*, 2 vols., 1922. Cited as Airlie.

†*P.P.* — Philip Guedalla, *The Palmerston Papers*, Gladstone and Palmerston, being the Correspondence of Lord Palmerston with Mr. Gladstone 1851–65 (1928).

Tresham Lever, *The Letters of Lady Palmerston*, 1957. Cited as Lever.

Brian Connell, *Portrait of a Whig Paper*. Compiled from the papers of the Second Viscount Palmerston 1739–1802 (1957).

†*R.* v. *P.* — Brian Connell, *Regina* v. *Palmerston*. The Correspondence between Queen Victoria and Her Foreign and Prime Minister 1837–1865 (1962).

2. LEARNED WORKS CONTAINING MUCH ORIGINAL MATERIAL

P. Guedalla, *Palmerston*, 1926. A work of art rather than biography.

†A.J.P.T. — A. J. P. Taylor, *The Italian Problem in European Diplomacy 1847–9*, 1934. A magnificent model of its genre.

H. C. F. Bell, *Lord Palmerston*, 2 vols., 1936. Though called by Gavin Henderson 'an admirable biography', this work seems to the present writer intensely irritating. It abounds in perversities such as 'Only long investigation would make it possible to say that he neglected his duties' and 'It would need much proof to establish that he tried to force on war while the cabinet . . . was attempting to preserve the peace' (ii, pp. 75, 91).

†T.–P. — H. W. V. Temperley and L. M. Penson, *Foundations of British Foreign Policy* from Pitt (1792) to Salisbury (1902), 1938.

†W. — Sir Charles F. Webster, *The Foreign Policy of Palmerston 1830–1841*, 2 vols., 1951. This is the prime secondary source for that period.

E. BIOGRAPHICAL STUDIES NOT BASED MAINLY ON UNPUBLISHED SOURCES

A. Trollope, *Lord Palmerston* (in the 'English Political Leaders' Series), 1882.

Marquess of Lorne, *Palmerston* (in the 'Prime Ministers of Queen Victoria' Series), 1892. Cited as Lorne.

F. J. Snell, *Palmerston's Borough*, 1894.

Lloyd C. Sanders, *The Life of Viscount Palmerston*, 1888.

E. F. Malcolm-Smith, *Palmerston* (in the 'Great Lives' Series), 1935.

W. Baring Pemberton, *Lord Palmerston*, 1954. Cited as Pemberton.

(The first three of these all benefit from contemporary information and, in Lorne's case, some access to documents.)

F. SHORT STUDIES IN OTHER WORKS

W. Bagehot, in *Biographical Studies*, 1856.

G. W. E. Russell, in *Prime Ministers and Some Others*, 1918.

A. Cecil, in *British Foreign Secretaries 1807–1916*, 1927.

F. J. C. Hearnshaw, in *British Prime Ministers of the Nineteenth Century*, 1930.

Gavin B. Henderson, in *Crimean War Diplomacy and Other Historical Essays*, 1947. Cited as Gavin Henderson.

The rest of this bibliography is merely a list of books cited. It is not meant to serve as a comprehensive bibliography; the author is, of course, indebted to many writers not listed.

G. MEMOIRS, DIARIES AND BIOGRAPHIES OF PALMERSTON'S CONTEMPORARIES

The Life of George, 4th Earl of Aberdeen, by Lady Frances Balfour, 2 vols., 1922. Cited as Balfour.

Memoirs and Letters of Rt. Hon. Sir Thomas Acland, A. H. D. Acland 1902.

The Prince Consort, by Roger Fulford, 1949.

The Journal of Mrs Arbuthnot, 1820–32, by Bamford and Duke of Wellington, 1950.

†*George Douglas 8th Duke of Argyll 1823–1900. Autobiography and Memoirs*, by the Dowager Duchess of Argyll (ed.), 2 vols., 1906. Cited as *Arg*.

Selected Speeches of the Late Right Honourable the Earl of Beaconsfield, by T. E. Kebbel, 2 vols., 1882.

The Foreign Policy of Canning, by H. W. Temperley, 1925.

George Canning, by P. J. V. Rolo, 1965.

Clemency Canning, Charles John, 1st Earl Canning, by Michael Maclagan, 1962.

The Life and Times of Sir Edwin Chadwick, by S. E. Finer, 1952.

The Life and Letters of the 4th Earl of Clarendon, by Sir Herbert Maxwell, 2 vols., 1913.

The Life of Richard Cobden, by John Morley, 2 vols., 1881. Cited as Morley's *Cobden*.

Gathorne Hardy, 1st Earl of Cranbrook. A Memoir with Extracts from his Diary and Correspondence, by Hon. A. E. Gathorne-Hardy (ed.), vol. i, 1910.

Notes from My Journal when Speaker of the House of Commons, by The Rt. Hon. John Evelyn Denison, Viscount Ossington, 1899. Cited as Denison.

The Life of Spencer Compton, 8th Duke of Devonshire, by Bernard Holland, vol. i, 1911.

'*. . . and Mr. Fortescue*'. A Selection from the Diaries from 1851 to 1862 of Chichester Fortescue, Lord Carlingford, K.P., by Osbert Wyndham Hewett (ed.), 1958. Cited as Fortescue.

The Life of William Ewart Gladstone, by John Morley, 2 vols., 1905. Cited as Morley's *Gladstone*.

Gladstone to his Wife, by A. Tilney Bassett (ed.), 1936.

Lord Goschen and His Friends (The Goschen Letters), by P. Colson (ed.), 1946.

Life and Letters of Sir James Graham, 2nd Baronet of Netherby, by Chas. Stuart Parker, 2 vols., 1907.

Random Recollections of the House of Commons, 1st Series, 1836, by James Grant.

†G. — *The Life of Granville George Leveson Gower, 2nd Earl Granville 1815–1891*, by Lord Edmond Fitzmaurice, vol. i, 1905.

The Greville Memoirs 1814–1860, by Lytton Strachey and Roger Fulford (eds.), 6 vols., 1938. Cited as Greville.

Lord Grey and the Reform Bill, by G. M. Trevelyan, 1920.

Sidney Herbert, Lord Herbert of Lea. A Memoir by Lord Stanmore, 2 vols., 1906.

Sir Wilfrid Lawson, by Rt. Hon. G. W. E. Russell (ed.), 1909. Cited as Lawson.

Layard of Nineveh, by Gordon Waterfield, 1963.

M. — *Memoirs of an ex-Minister*, by the Rt. Hon. the Earl of Malmesbury, new edition, 1885.

Papers of William Lamb, Viscount Melbourne, by L. C. Sanders (ed.), 1889. Cited as Melbourne Papers.

The Life, Letters and Friendships of Richard Monckton Milnes, 1st Lord Houghton, by T. Wemyss Reid, 2 vols., 1891.

Florence Nightingale, by Cecil Woodham-Smith, Penguin, 1955.

The Destruction of Lord Raglan, by Christopher Hibbert, 1961.
The Life of Lord John Russell, by Spencer Walpole, 2 vols., 1889. Cited as Walpole.
E.C.J.R. — *The Early Correspondence of Lord John Russell 1815–40*, by R. Russell (ed.), 1913.
L.C.J.R. — *The Later Correspondence of Lord John Russell 1840–78*, by G. P. Gooch (ed.), 1925.
Sir John Simon 1816–1904 and English Social Administration, by Royston Lambert, 1963.
V.L. i. — *The Letters of Queen Victoria, 1837–61*, by A. C. Benson and Viscount Esher (eds.), 3 vols., 1907: Volume i, 1837–43.
V.L. ii — Volume ii, 1843–53.
V.L. iii — Volume iii, 1853–61.
V.L. 2, i — *The Letters of Queen Victoria*, 2nd Series, vol. i (1862–69), G. E. Buckle (ed.).
The Servant of All. Papers from the Family, Social and Political Life of my Father, James Wilson, by Emilie I. Barrington, 2 vols., 1927.

H. OTHER WORKS CITED

W. C. Atkinson, *History of Spain and Portugal* (Penguin), 1960.
W. Bagehot, *The English Constitution* (Fontana), 1963.
C. J. Bartlett, *Great Britain and Sea Power 1815–1853*, 1963.
Derek Beales, *England and Italy 1859–60*, 1961. Cited as Beales.
G. D. Bearce, *British Attitudes Towards India 1784–1858*, 1961.
C. A. Bodelsen, *Studies in Mid-Victorian Imperialism*, 1924, reissued 1960.
Asa Briggs, *Victorian People 1851–1867*, 1954.
W. L. Burn, *The Age of Equipoise, A Study of the Mid-Victorian Generation*, 1964.
J. R. M. Butler, *The Passing of the Great Reform Bill*, 1914 (reissued 1964).
F. R. Flournoy, *British Policy Towards Morocco in the Age of Palmerston* (1830–65), 1935.
J. D. Hargreaves, *Prelude to the Partition of West Africa*, 1963.
W. L. Harle, *A Career in the Commons or Letters to a Young Member of Parliament*, 1850.
H. J. Hanham, *Elections and Party Management.* Politics in the Time of Disraeli and Gladstone, 1959.
Wm. Harris, *The History of the Radical Party in Parliament*, 1885.
N. Kaltchas, *Introduction to the Constitutional History of Modern Greece*, 1940.
Michael Lewis, *History of the British Navy* (Penguin), 1962.
S. Maccoby, *English Radicalism 1832–1852*, 1966.
S. Maccoby, *English Radicalism 1853–1886*, 1938.
J. P. Mackintosh, *The British Cabinet*, 1962.
T. E. Marston, *Britain's Imperial Role in the Red Sea Area 1800–1878*, 1961.

B. Kingsley Martin, *The Triumph of Lord Palmerston*, 1924, reissued 1963. Cited as Kingsley Martin.

R. B. Mowat, *The Victorian Age*, 1939.

W. E. Mosse, *The European Powers and the German Question 1848–71* with special reference to England and Russia, 1958.

W. E. Mosse, *The Rise and Fall of the Crimean System 1855–1871*, 1963.

K. Poolman, *The Alabama Incident* (1958).

E. Prevelakis, *British Policy Towards the Change of the Dynasty in Greece 1862–3*, Athens, 1953.

R. Robinson, J. Gallagher, and Alice Denny, *Africa and the Victorians*, 1961.

Admiral Sir Herbert Richmond, *Statesmen and Sea Power*, 1947.

R. L. Schuyler, *The Fall of the Old Colonial System*, 1945.

R. W. Seton-Watson, *Disraeli, Gladstone and the Eastern Question*, 1935, reissued 1962.

K. B. Smellie, *Great Britain since 1688*, 1962.

D. Mack Smith, *Cavour and Garibaldi, 1860, A Study in Political Conflict*, 1954.

Donald Southgate, *The Passing of the Whigs 1832–1886*, 1962.

C. Sproxton, *Palmerston and the Hungarian Revolution*, 1919.

S.M.E. — A. J. P. Taylor, *The Struggle for Mastery in Europe 1848–1918*, 1957 reprint.

H. W. V. Temperley, *The Victorian Age in Politics, War and Diplomacy*, 1928.

H. W. V. Temperley, *England and the Near East — L. The Crimea*, 1936.

J. T. Ward, *The Factory Movement 1830–1855*, 1963.

Cecil Woodham-Smith, *The Great Hunger*, 1962.

G. M. Young, *Victorian England — Portrait of an Age*, 2nd ed., 1953.

ARTICLES QUOTED

C. Collyer, 'Gladstone and the American Civil War', *Leeds Philosophical Society*, vi, pp. viii, 583–94.

M. Florescu, 'Stratford Canning, Palmerston and the Wallachian Revolution of 1848', *Journal of Modern History*, xxxv, no. 3, 1963.

G. F. Hickson, 'Palmerston and the Clayton–Bulwer Treaty', *Cambridge Historical Journal*, iii, 295–303.

Ann G. Imlah, 'Anglo-Swiss Relations 1845–60', *Bulletin of the Institute of Historical Research*, xxxvi, no. 94, Nov. 1963.

F. G. Weber, 'Palmerston and Prussian Liberalism 1848', *Journal of Modern History*, xxxv, n. 2, 1963.

INDEX

This is an index of persons. For topics and diplomatic relations with particular countries see the Table of Contents.

Note: All ministers who held office between 1807 and 1865 were at some time colleagues of Palmerston, unless their sole periods of office were May 1828–Nov. 1830, Nov. 1834–Apr. 1835, Aug. 1841–July 1846, Jan.–Dec. 1852, Feb. 1858–June 1859.

In the following entries, C = cabinet colleage of Palmerston; c = fellow-minister with Palmerston, but not in the cabinet; k.a. = known as; x = defeated in election.

Read Introduction and use table of Contents as index.

After Harrow, P. was at Edinburgh University 1801–3 and then at St John's, Cambridge. Contested Cambridge University Feb. 1806 (on the death of Pitt, being beaten by Lord Henry Petty, later his colleague Lansdowne), May 1807, May 1808 and sat for it Mar. 1811–Mar. 1831, when he was defeated. Unseated for Horsham early 1807, sat for Newport, Isle of Wight, mid-1808–11, for Bletchingley mid-1831–2, for South Hampshire Jan. 1833–Jan. 1835 (when he was defeated) and for Tiverton from April 1835 till his death.

Made a jr Lord of the Admiralty April 1807 and Sec. at War 28th Oct. 1809–May 1828 (under Perceval, Liverpool, Canning, Goderich and Wellington, being in the cabinet under the last three from 1827).

For. Sec. Nov. 1830–Nov. 1834, Apr. 1835–Aug. 1841, July 1846–Dec. 1851, and Home Sec. Dec. 1852–Jan. 1855.

Very briefly Leader of the House of Commons (under Aberdeen) in Jan. 1855, P.M. 4th Feb. 1855–Feb. 1858, Leader of the Opposition Feb. 1858–June 1859, and P.M. 12th June 1859 to his death.

P.'s letters to his only brother, Sir William Temple (1788–1856), a diplomat, were an important source for the Bulwer and Ashley volumes. His sister Frances (d. 1838) married Vice-Adm. Bowles, M.P., and his sister Elizabeth (d. 1837) married Lawrence Sulivan.

The titles of Visc. Palmerston and B. Temple of Mount Temple, in the peerage of Ireland, died with him. His wife's second son, William Cowper, succeeding to his estates on her death, assumed the name of Cowper-Temple and was cr. B. Mount Temple 1880. On his death in 1888 the estates passed to Evelyn Ashley, second son of William's eldest sister, the Countess of Shaftesbury. Evelyn's son Wilfrid was created B. Mount Temple in 1932 and was succeeded in the

PRINTED IN GREAT BRITAIN
BY ROBERT MACLEHOSE AND CO. LTD
THE UNIVERSITY PRESS, GLASGOW